THE BOOK ®

Vauxhall Corsa
Service and Repair Manual

Ian Barnes BSc

Models covered

(4087 - 272)

Corsa models with diesel engines, including special/limited editions;
Hatchback, Corsavan & Combo Van
1.5 litre (1488cc) & 1.7 litre (1686cc) diesel & turbo-diesel

Does NOT cover new Corsa range introduced October 2000
For coverage of petrol models, see manuals no.1985 ('93 to '97) and 3921 ('97 to '00)

© Haynes Publishing 2003

A book in the **Haynes Service and Repair Manual Series**

ISBN **1 84425 087 3**

British Library Cataloguing in Publication Data
A catalogue record for this book is available from the British Library.

ABCDE
FGHIJ
KLMNO
PQR

Printed in the USA

Haynes Publishing
Sparkford, Yeovil, Somerset BA22 7JJ, England

Haynes North America, Inc
861 Lawrence Drive, Newbury Park, California 91320, USA

Editions Haynes
4, Rue de l'Abreuvoir
92415 COURBEVOIE CEDEX, France

Haynes Publishing Nordiska AB
Box 1504, 751 45 UPPSALA, Sverige

Contents

LIVING WITH YOUR VAUXHALL CORSA

Roadside Repairs

Weekly Checks

Lubricants and fluids

Tyre pressures

MAINTENANCE

Routine maintenance and servicing

Contents

REPAIRS & OVERHAUL

Advanced driving

Many people see the words 'advanced driving' and believe that it won't interest them or that it is a style of driving beyond their own abilities. Nothing could be further from the truth. Advanced driving is straightforward safe, sensible driving - the sort of driving we should all do every time we get behind the wheel.

An average of 10 people are killed every day on UK roads and 870 more are injured, some seriously. Lives are ruined daily, usually because somebody did something stupid. Something like 95% of all accidents are due to human error, mostly driver failure. Sometimes we make genuine mistakes - everyone does. Sometimes we have lapses of concentration. Sometimes we deliberately take risks.

For many people, the process of 'learning to drive' doesn't go much further than learning how to pass the driving test because of a common belief that good drivers are made by 'experience'.

Learning to drive by 'experience' teaches three driving skills:

☐ Quick reactions. (Whoops, that was close!)
☐ Good handling skills. (Horn, swerve, brake, horn).
☐ Reliance on vehicle technology. (Great stuff this ABS, stop in no distance even in the wet...)

Drivers whose skills are 'experience based' generally have a lot of near misses and the odd accident. The results can be seen every day in our courts and our hospital casualty departments.

Advanced drivers have learnt to control the risks by controlling the position and speed of their vehicle. They avoid accidents and near misses, even if the drivers around them make mistakes.

The key skills of advanced driving are **concentration,** effective all-round **observation, anticipation** and **planning.** When **good vehicle handling** is added to these skills, all driving situations can be approached and negotiated in a safe, methodical way, leaving nothing to chance.

Concentration means applying your mind to safe driving, completely excluding anything that's not relevant. Driving is usually the most dangerous activity that most of us undertake in our daily routines. It deserves our full attention.

Observation means not just looking, but seeing and seeking out the information found in the driving environment.

Anticipation means asking yourself what is happening, what you can reasonably expect to happen and what could happen unexpectedly. (One of the commonest words used in compiling accident reports is 'suddenly'.)

Planning is the link between seeing something and taking the appropriate action. For many drivers, planning is the missing link.

If you want to become a safer and more skilful driver and you want to enjoy your driving more, contact the Institute of Advanced Motorists at www.iam.org.uk, phone 0208 996 9600, or write to IAM House, 510 Chiswick High Road, London W4 5RG for an information pack.

Working on your car can be dangerous. This page shows just some of the potential risks and hazards, with the aim of creating a safety-conscious attitude.

General hazards

Scalding

• Don't remove the radiator or expansion tank cap while the engine is hot.
• Engine oil, automatic transmission fluid or power steering fluid may also be dangerously hot if the engine has recently been running.

Burning

• Beware of burns from the exhaust system and from any part of the engine. Brake discs and drums can also be extremely hot immediately after use.

Crushing

• When working under or near a raised vehicle, always supplement the jack with axle stands, or use drive-on ramps. *Never venture under a car which is only supported by a jack.*

• Take care if loosening or tightening high-torque nuts when the vehicle is on stands. Initial loosening and final tightening should be done with the wheels on the ground.

Fire

• Fuel is highly flammable; fuel vapour is explosive.
• Don't let fuel spill onto a hot engine.
• Do not smoke or allow naked lights (including pilot lights) anywhere near a vehicle being worked on. Also beware of creating sparks (electrically or by use of tools).
• Fuel vapour is heavier than air, so don't work on the fuel system with the vehicle over an inspection pit.
• Another cause of fire is an electrical overload or short-circuit. Take care when repairing or modifying the vehicle wiring.
• Keep a fire extinguisher handy, of a type suitable for use on fuel and electrical fires.

Electric shock

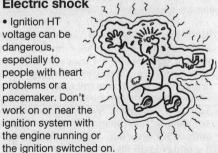

• Ignition HT voltage can be dangerous, especially to people with heart problems or a pacemaker. Don't work on or near the ignition system with the engine running or the ignition switched on.

• Mains voltage is also dangerous. Make sure that any mains-operated equipment is correctly earthed. Mains power points should be protected by a residual current device (RCD) circuit breaker.

Fume or gas intoxication

• Exhaust fumes are poisonous; they often contain carbon monoxide, which is rapidly fatal if inhaled. Never run the engine in a confined space such as a garage with the doors shut.

• Fuel vapour is also poisonous, as are the vapours from some cleaning solvents and paint thinners.

Poisonous or irritant substances

• Avoid skin contact with battery acid and with any fuel, fluid or lubricant, especially antifreeze, brake hydraulic fluid and Diesel fuel. Don't syphon them by mouth. If such a substance is swallowed or gets into the eyes, seek medical advice.
• Prolonged contact with used engine oil can cause skin cancer. Wear gloves or use a barrier cream if necessary. Change out of oil-soaked clothes and do not keep oily rags in your pocket.
• Air conditioning refrigerant forms a poisonous gas if exposed to a naked flame (including a cigarette). It can also cause skin burns on contact.

Asbestos

• Asbestos dust can cause cancer if inhaled or swallowed. Asbestos may be found in gaskets and in brake and clutch linings. When dealing with such components it is safest to assume that they contain asbestos.

Special hazards

Hydrofluoric acid

• This extremely corrosive acid is formed when certain types of synthetic rubber, found in some O-rings, oil seals, fuel hoses etc, are exposed to temperatures above 400°C. The rubber changes into a charred or sticky substance containing the acid. *Once formed, the acid remains dangerous for years. If it gets onto the skin, it may be necessary to amputate the limb concerned.*
• When dealing with a vehicle which has suffered a fire, or with components salvaged from such a vehicle, wear protective gloves and discard them after use.

The battery

• Batteries contain sulphuric acid, which attacks clothing, eyes and skin. Take care when topping-up or carrying the battery.
• The hydrogen gas given off by the battery is highly explosive. Never cause a spark or allow a naked light nearby. Be careful when connecting and disconnecting battery chargers or jump leads.

Air bags

• Air bags can cause injury if they go off accidentally. Take care when removing the steering wheel and/or facia. Special storage instructions may apply.

Diesel injection equipment

• Diesel injection pumps supply fuel at very high pressure. Take care when working on the fuel injectors and fuel pipes.

⚠️ *Warning: Never expose the hands, face or any other part of the body to injector spray; the fuel can penetrate the skin with potentially fatal results.*

Remember...

DO

• Do use eye protection when using power tools, and when working under the vehicle.

• Do wear gloves or use barrier cream to protect your hands when necessary.

• Do get someone to check periodically that all is well when working alone on the vehicle.

• Do keep loose clothing and long hair well out of the way of moving mechanical parts.

• Do remove rings, wristwatch etc, before working on the vehicle – especially the electrical system.

• Do ensure that any lifting or jacking equipment has a safe working load rating adequate for the job.

DON'T

• Don't attempt to lift a heavy component which may be beyond your capability – get assistance.

• Don't rush to finish a job, or take unverified short cuts.

• Don't use ill-fitting tools which may slip and cause injury.

• Don't leave tools or parts lying around where someone can trip over them. Mop up oil and fuel spills at once.

• Don't allow children or pets to play in or near a vehicle being worked on.

Introduction to the Vauxhall Corsa

The Corsa is available in 3- and 5-door Hatchback, Corsavan (3-door Van based on Hatchback), and Combo Van body styles, with a wide range of fittings and interior trim depending on the model specification.

This Manual covers the entire range of diesel-engined Corsas. A variety of petrol engines are available in the Corsa range; the petrol-engined ranges (1993 to 1997 and 1997 to 2000) are covered in SRMs 1985 and 3921.

Fully-independent front suspension is fitted; the rear suspension is semi-independent, with a torsion beam and trailing arms.

The manual gearbox is of the five-speed all synchromesh type.

A wide range of standard and optional equipment is available within the Corsa range to suit most tastes, including central locking, electric windows, electric sunroof, anti-lock braking system, electronic alarm system and supplemental restraint systems.

For the home mechanic, the Corsa is a relatively straightforward vehicle to maintain, and most of the items requiring frequent attention are easily accessible.

Your Vauxhall Corsa Manual

The aim of this manual is to help you get the best value from your vehicle. It can do so in several ways. It can help you decide what work must be done (even should you choose to get it done by a garage), provide information on routine maintenance and servicing, and give a logical course of action and diagnosis when random faults occur. However, it is hoped that you will use the manual by tackling the work yourself. On simpler jobs it may even be quicker than booking the car into a garage and going there twice, to leave and collect it. Perhaps most important, a lot of money can be saved by avoiding the costs a garage must charge to cover its labour and overheads.

The manual has drawings and descriptions to show the function of the various components so that their layout can be understood. Tasks are described and photographed in a clear step-by-step sequence.

References to the 'left' and 'right' of the vehicle are in the sense of a person sitting in the driver's seat facing forwards.

Acknowledgements

Certain illustrations are the copyright of Vauxhall Motors Limited, and are used with their permission. Thanks are due to Draper Tools Limited, who provided some of the workshop tools, and to all those people at Sparkford who helped in the production of this Manual.

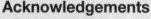

The following pages are intended to help in dealing with common roadside emergencies and breakdowns. You will find more detailed fault finding information at the back of the manual, and repair information in the main chapters.

If your car won't start and the starter motor doesn't turn

☐ Open the bonnet and make sure that the battery terminals are clean and tight.

☐ Switch on the headlights and try to start the engine. If the headlights go very dim when you're trying to start, the battery is probably flat. Try jump starting (see next page) using another car.

If your car won't start even though the starter motor turns as normal

☐ Is there fuel in the tank?

☐ Is there moisture on electrical components under the bonnet? Switch off the ignition, then wipe off any obvious dampness with a dry cloth. Spray a water-repellent aerosol product (WD-40 or equivalent) on fuel system electrical connectors (diesel engines don't normally suffer from damp).

A Check the security and condition of the battery connections.

B Check the connector plugs and wiring connections around the injection pump and fuel heater.

C Check that none of the engine compartment fuses have blown, and that the relays are operational.

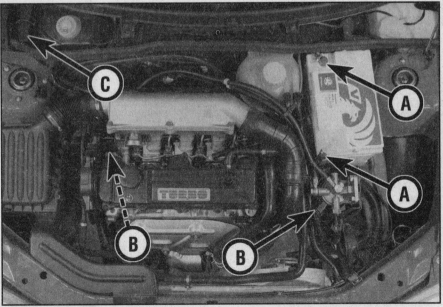

Check that all electrical connections are secure (with the ignition switched off). Spray the connector plugs with a water-dispersant spray like WD-40 if you suspect a problem due to damp. Diesel models do not usually suffer from damp starting problems, but check all visible connector plugs just in case.

Jump starting

When jump-starting a car using a booster battery, observe the following precautions:

✔ Before connecting the booster battery, make sure that the ignition is switched off.

✔ Ensure that all electrical equipment (lights, heater, wipers, etc) is switched off.

✔ Take note of any special precautions printed on the battery case.

✔ Make sure that the booster battery is the same voltage as the discharged one in the vehicle.

✔ If the battery is being jump-started from the battery in another vehicle, the two vehicles MUST NOT TOUCH each other.

✔ Make sure that the transmission is in neutral (or PARK, in the case of automatic transmission).

 HAYNES HINT

Jump starting will get you out of trouble, but you must correct whatever made the battery go flat in the first place. There are three possibilities:

1 *The battery has been drained by repeated attempts to start, or by leaving the lights on.*

2 *The charging system is not working properly (alternator drivebelt slack or broken, alternator wiring fault or alternator itself faulty).*

3 *The battery itself is at fault (electrolyte low, or battery worn out).*

1 Connect one end of the red jump lead to the positive (+) terminal of the flat battery

2 Connect the other end of the red lead to the positive (+) terminal of the booster battery.

3 Connect one end of the black jump lead to the negative (-) terminal of the booster battery

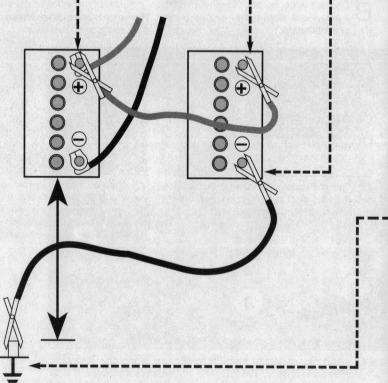

4 Connect the other end of the black jump lead to a bolt or bracket on the engine block, well away from the battery, on the vehicle to be started.

5 Make sure that the jump leads will not come into contact with the fan, drive-belts or other moving parts of the engine.

6 Start the engine using the booster battery and run it at idle speed. Switch on the lights, rear window demister and heater blower motor, then disconnect the jump leads in the reverse order of connection. Turn off the lights etc.

Wheel changing

Some of the details shown here will vary according to model.

 Warning: Do not change a wheel in a situation where you risk being hit by another vehicle. On busy roads, try to stop in a lay-by or a gateway. Be wary of passing traffic while changing the wheel - it is easy to become distracted by the job in hand.

Preparation

☐ When a puncture occurs, stop as soon as it is safe to do so.

☐ Park on firm level ground, if possible, and well out of the way of other traffic.

☐ Use hazard warning lights if necessary.

☐ If you have one, use a warning triangle to alert other drivers of your presence.

☐ Apply the handbrake and engage first or reverse gear.

☐ Chock the wheel diagonally opposite the one being removed – a couple of large stones will do for this.

☐ If the ground is soft, use a flat piece of wood to spread the load under the foot of the jack.

Changing the wheel

1 Remove the tool holder and unscrew the spare wheel clamp.

2 For safety, place the spare wheel under the car near the jacking point.

3 Remove the wheel trim (where fitted) and slacken each wheel bolt by half a turn.

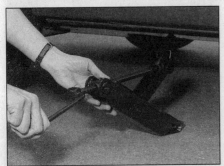

4 Raise the jack whilst locating below the jacking point (ensure that the jack is on firm ground and located on the car correctly).

5 Turn the handle clockwise until the wheel is raised clear of the ground. Remove the bolts and lift the wheel clear.

6 Position the spare wheel and fit the bolts. Hand tighten with the wheel brace and lower the car to the ground. Tighten the wheel bolts in the sequence shown, fit the wheel trim and secure the punctured wheel in the boot.

Finally...

☐ Remove the wheel chocks. Stow the jack and tools in the appropriate locations in the car.

☐ Check the tyre pressure on the wheel just fitted. If it is low, or if you don't have a pressure gauge with you, drive slowly to the next garage and inflate the tyre to the correct pressure.

☐ Have the damaged tyre or wheel repaired as soon as possible, or another puncture will leave you stranded.

Identifying leaks

Puddles on the garage floor or drive, or obvious wetness under the bonnet or underneath the car, suggest a leak that needs investigating. It can sometimes be difficult to decide where the leak is coming from, especially if the engine bay is very dirty already. Leaking oil or fluid can also be blown rearwards by the passage of air under the car, giving a false impression of where the problem lies.

 Warning: Most automotive oils and fluids are poisonous. Wash them off skin, and change out of contaminated clothing, without delay.

 The smell of a fluid leaking from the car may provide a clue to what's leaking. Some fluids are distinctively coloured. It may help to clean the car carefully and to park it over some clean paper overnight as an aid to locating the source of the leak.
Remember that some leaks may only occur while the engine is running.

Sump oil

Engine oil may leak from the drain plug...

Oil from filter

...or from the base of the oil filter.

Gearbox oil

Gearbox oil can leak from the seals at the inboard ends of the driveshafts.

Antifreeze

Leaking antifreeze often leaves a crystalline deposit like this.

Brake fluid

A leak occurring at a wheel is almost certainly brake fluid.

Power steering fluid

Power steering fluid may leak from the pipe connectors on the steering rack.

Towing

When all else fails, you may find yourself having to get a tow home – or of course you may be helping somebody else. Long-distance recovery should only be done by a garage or breakdown service. For shorter distances, DIY towing using another car is easy enough, but observe the following points:
☐ Use a proper tow-rope – they are not expensive. The vehicle being towed must display an ON TOW sign in its rear window.
☐ Always turn the ignition key to the 'on' position when the vehicle is being towed, so that the steering lock is released, and that the

direction indicator and brake lights work.
☐ Only attach the tow-rope to the towing eyes provided.
☐ Before being towed, release the handbrake and select neutral on the transmission.
☐ Note that greater-than-usual pedal pressure will be required to operate the brakes, since the vacuum servo unit is only operational with the engine running.
☐ On models with power steering, greater-than-usual steering effort will also be required.
☐ Make sure that both drivers know the route before setting off.

☐ The driver of the car being towed must keep the tow-rope taut at all times to avoid snatching.
☐ Only drive at moderate speeds and keep the distance towed to a minimum. Drive smoothly and allow plenty of time for slowing down at junctions.

⚠ *Warning: To prevent damage to the catalytic converter, a vehicle must not be push-started, or started by towing, when the engine is at operating temperature; use jump leads (see 'Jump starting').*

Introduction

There are some very simple checks which need only take a few minutes to carry out, but which could save you a lot of inconvenience and expense.

These *Weekly checks* require no great skill or special tools, and the small amount of time they take to perform could prove to be very well spent, for example;

☐ Keeping an eye on tyre condition and pressures, will not only help to stop them wearing out prematurely, but could also save your life.

☐ Many breakdowns are caused by electrical problems. Battery-related faults are particularly common, and a quick check on a regular basis will often prevent the majority of these.

☐ If your car develops a brake fluid leak, the first time you might know about it is when your brakes don't work properly. Checking the level regularly will give advance warning of this kind of problem.

☐ If the oil or coolant levels run low, the cost of repairing any engine damage will be far greater than fixing the leak, for example.

Underbonnet check points

◀ **1.5 litre engine**

A *Engine oil level dipstick*

B *Engine oil filler cap*

C *Coolant expansion tank*

D *Brake fluid reservoir*

E *Washer fluid reservoir*

F *Battery*

Engine oil level

Before you start

✔ Make sure that your car is on level ground.
✔ Check the oil level before the car is driven, or at least 5 minutes after the engine has been switched off.

 If the oil is checked immediately after driving the vehicle, some of the oil will remain in the upper engine components, resulting in an inaccurate reading on the dipstick.

The correct oil

Modern engines place great demands on their oil. It is very important that the correct oil for your car is used (See *Lubricants and fluids*).

Car Care

● If you have to add oil frequently, you should check whether you have any oil leaks. Place some clean paper under the car overnight, and check for stains in the morning. If there are no leaks, the engine may be burning oil, or the oil may only be leaking when the engine is running.

● Always maintain the level between the upper and lower dipstick marks (see photo 2). If the level is too low severe engine damage may occur. Oil seal failure may result if the engine is overfilled by adding too much oil.

1 The dipstick is often brightly coloured for easy identification (see *Underbonnet check points* on page 0•11 for exact location). Withdraw the dipstick.

2 Using a clean rag or paper towel remove all oil from the dipstick. Insert the clean dipstick into the tube as far as it will go, then withdraw it again. Note the level on the end of the dipstick, which should be between the upper (MAX) mark and lower (MIN) mark.

3 Oil is added through the filler cap. Unscrew the cap and top-up the level. A funnel may help to reduce spillage. Add the oil slowly, checking the level on the dipstick frequently. Avoid overfilling (see *Car Care*).

Coolant level

 Warning:
DO NOT attempt to remove the expansion tank pressure cap when the engine is hot, as there is a very great risk of scalding. Do not leave open containers of coolant about, as it is poisonous.

Car Care

● With a sealed-type cooling system, adding coolant should not be necessary on a regular basis. If frequent topping-up is required, it is likely there is a leak. Check the radiator, all hoses and joint faces for signs of staining or wetness, and rectify as necessary.

● It is important that antifreeze is used in the cooling system all year round, not just during the winter months. Don't top-up with water alone, as the antifreeze will become too diluted.

1 The coolant level varies with the temperature of the engine. When the engine is cold, the coolant level should be near the COLD (or KALT) mark.

2 If topping-up is necessary, **wait until the engine is cold**. Slowly unscrew the cap to release any pressure present in the cooling system and remove it.

3 Add a mixture of water and antifreeze to the expansion tank until the coolant level is up to the COLD/KALT mark.

Brake fluid level

Warning:
● Brake fluid can harm your eyes and damage painted surfaces, so use extreme caution when handling and pouring it.
● Do not use fluid that has been standing open for some time, as it absorbs moisture from the air, which can cause a dangerous loss of braking effectiveness.

 The fluid level in the reservoir will drop slightly as the brake pads wear down, but the fluid level must never be allowed to drop below the MIN mark.

Before you start

✔ Make sure that your car is on level ground.

Safety First!
● If the reservoir requires repeated topping-up this is an indication of a fluid leak somewhere in the system, which should be investigated immediately.

● If a leak is suspected, the car should not be driven until the braking system has been checked. Never take any risks where brakes are concerned.

1 The MIN and MAX marks are indicated on the reservoir. The fluid level must be kept between the marks at all times.

2 If topping-up is necessary, first wipe clean the area around the filler cap to prevent dirt entering the hydraulic system. Unscrew the reservoir cap.

3 Carefully add fluid, taking care not to spill it onto the surrounding components. Use only the specified fluid; mixing different types can cause damage to the system. Then securely refit the cap and wipe off any spilt fluid.

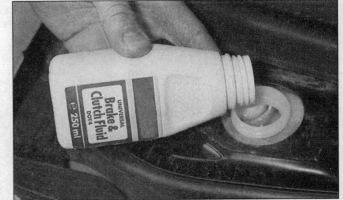

Power steering fluid level

Before you start

✔ Park the vehicle on level ground.
✔ Set the steering wheel straight-ahead.
✔ The engine should be turned off.

 For the check to be accurate, the steering must not be turned once the engine has been stopped.

Safety First!
● The need for frequent topping-up indicates a leak, which should be investigated immediately.

1 The reservoir is located at the front left-hand side of the engine compartment. The power steering fluid level is checked with a dipstick attached to the reservoir filler cap. Unscrew the filler cap from the top of the reservoir, and wipe all the fluid from the end with a clean rag or paper towel. Refit the reservoir filler cap, then remove it once more. Note the fluid level on the dipstick. When the engine is cold, the fluid level should be up to the lower mark on the dipstick. When the engine is at normal operating temperature, the fluid level should be up to the upper mark on the dipstick.

2 Top-up with the specified type of fluid if necessary and securely refit the reservoir filler cap on completion.

Tyre condition and pressure

It is very important that tyres are in good condition, and at the correct pressure - having a tyre failure at any speed is highly dangerous. Tyre wear is influenced by driving style - harsh braking and acceleration, or fast cornering, will all produce more rapid tyre wear. As a general rule, the front tyres wear out faster than the rears. Interchanging the tyres from front to rear ("rotating" the tyres) may result in more even wear. However, if this is completely effective, you may have the expense of replacing all four tyres at once! Remove any nails or stones embedded in the tread before they penetrate the tyre to cause deflation. If removal of a nail does reveal that the tyre has been punctured, refit the nail so that its point of penetration is marked. Then immediately change the wheel, and have the tyre repaired by a tyre dealer.

Regularly check the tyres for damage in the form of cuts or bulges, especially in the sidewalls. Periodically remove the wheels, and clean any dirt or mud from the inside and outside surfaces. Examine the wheel rims for signs of rusting, corrosion or other damage. Light alloy wheels are easily damaged by "kerbing" whilst parking; steel wheels may also become dented or buckled. A new wheel is very often the only way to overcome severe damage.

New tyres should be balanced when they are fitted, but it may become necessary to re-balance them as they wear, or if the balance weights fitted to the wheel rim should fall off. Unbalanced tyres will wear more quickly, as will the steering and suspension components. Wheel imbalance is normally signified by vibration, particularly at a certain speed (typically around 50 mph). If this vibration is felt only through the steering, then it is likely that just the front wheels need balancing. If, however, the vibration is felt through the whole car, the rear wheels could be out of balance. Wheel balancing should be carried out by a tyre dealer or garage.

1 *Tread Depth - visual check*
The original tyres have tread wear safety bands (B), which will appear when the tread depth reaches approximately 1.6 mm. The band positions are indicated by a triangular mark on the tyre sidewall (A).

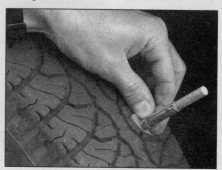

2 *Tread Depth - manual check*
Alternatively, tread wear can be monitored with a simple, inexpensive device known as a tread depth indicator gauge.

3 *Tyre Pressure Check*
Check the tyre pressures regularly with the tyres cold. Do not adjust the tyre pressures immediately after the vehicle has been used, or an inaccurate setting will result.

Tyre tread wear patterns

Shoulder Wear

Underinflation (wear on both sides)
Under-inflation will cause overheating of the tyre, because the tyre will flex too much, and the tread will not sit correctly on the road surface. This will cause a loss of grip and excessive wear, not to mention the danger of sudden tyre failure due to heat build-up.
Check and adjust pressures
Incorrect wheel camber (wear on one side)
Repair or renew suspension parts
Hard cornering
Reduce speed!

Centre Wear

Overinflation
Over-inflation will cause rapid wear of the centre part of the tyre tread, coupled with reduced grip, harsher ride, and the danger of shock damage occurring in the tyre casing.
Check and adjust pressures

If you sometimes have to inflate your car's tyres to the higher pressures specified for maximum load or sustained high speed, don't forget to reduce the pressures to normal afterwards.

Uneven Wear

Front tyres may wear unevenly as a result of wheel misalignment. Most tyre dealers and garages can check and adjust the wheel alignment (or "tracking") for a modest charge.
Incorrect camber or castor
Repair or renew suspension parts
Malfunctioning suspension
Repair or renew suspension parts
Unbalanced wheel
Balance tyres
Incorrect toe setting
Adjust front wheel alignment
Note: *The feathered edge of the tread which typifies toe wear is best checked by feel.*

Washer fluid level

● Screenwash additives not only keep the windscreen clean during foul weather, they also prevent the washer system freezing in cold weather - which is when you are likely to need it most. Don't top up using plain water as the screenwash will become too diluted, and will freeze during cold weather.

On no account use coolant antifreeze in the washer system - this could discolour or damage paintwork.

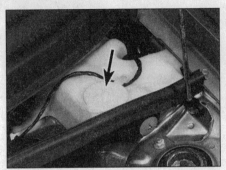

1 The screenwasher fluid reservoir is located at the rear left-hand corner of the engine compartment.

2 When topping-up the reservoir, a screen-wash additive should be added in the quantities recommended on the bottle.

Wiper blades

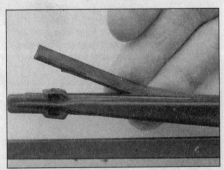

1 Check the condition of the wiper blades; if they are cracked or show any signs of deterioration, or if the glass swept area is smeared, renew them. Wiper blades should be renewed annually.

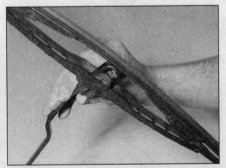

2 To remove a windscreen wiper blade, pull the arm fully away from the screen until it locks. Swivel the blade through 90°, press the locking tab with your fingers and slide the blade out of the arm's hooked end.

3 Don't forget to check the tailgate wiper blade as well. To remove the blade, depress the retaining tab and slide the blade out of the hooked end of the arm.

Battery

Caution: Before carrying out any work on the vehicle battery, read the precautions given in 'Safety first!' at the start of this manual.

✔ Make sure that the battery tray is in good condition, and that the clamp is tight. Corrosion on the tray, retaining clamp and the battery itself can be removed with a solution of water and baking soda. Thoroughly rinse all cleaned areas with water. Any metal parts damaged by corrosion should be covered with a zinc-based primer, then painted.

✔ Periodically (approximately every three months), check the charge condition of the battery, as described in Chapter 5A.

✔ If the battery is flat, and you need to jump start your vehicle, see *Roadside Repairs*.

1 The battery is located at the rear left-hand side of the engine compartment. The exterior of the battery should be inspected periodically for damage such as a cracked case or cover.

2 Check the tightness of the battery cable clamps to ensure good electrical connections. You should not be able to move them. Also check each cable for cracks and frayed conductors.

HAYNES HINT

Battery corrosion can be kept to a minimum by applying a layer of petroleum jelly to the clamps and terminals after they are reconnected.

3 If corrosion (white, fluffy deposits) is evident, remove the cables from the battery terminals, clean them with a small wire brush, then refit them. Automotive stores sell a tool for cleaning the battery post . . .

4 . . . as well as the battery cable clamps

Electrical systems

✔ Check all external lights and the horn. Refer to the appropriate Sections of Chapter 12 for details if any of the circuits are found to be inoperative.

✔ Visually check all accessible wiring connectors, harnesses and retaining clips for security, and for signs of chafing or damage.

HAYNES HINT

If you need to check your brake lights and indicators unaided, back up to a wall or garage door and operate the lights. The reflected light should show if they are working properly.

1 If a single indicator light, brake stop-light or headlight has failed, it is likely that a bulb has blown and will need to be replaced. Refer to Chapter 12 for details. If both brake lights have failed, it is possible that the stop-light switch operated by the brake pedal has failed. Refer to Chapter 9 for details.

2 If more than one indicator light or tail light has failed it is likely that either a fuse has blown or that there is a fault in the circuit (see Chapter 12). The main fuses are located in the fusebox situated behind the cover in the facia on the driver's side.

3 To renew a blown fuse, remove it, where applicable, using the plastic tool provided. Fit a new fuse of the same rating, available from car accessory shops. It is important that you find the reason that the fuse blew (see *Electrical fault finding* in Chapter 12).

Lubricants and fluids

Engine	Multigrade engine oil, viscosity SAE 5W/30 to 20W/50, to API CD, CCMC-PD2 and ACEA-B3.96
Manual gearbox	Vauxhall/Opel gear oil
Power steering fluid reservoir	Dexron type II automatic transmission fluid
Cooling system	Clean water and antifreeze to Vauxhall/Opel specification
Brake fluid reservoir	Hydraulic fluid to DOT 4

Choosing your engine oil

Engines need oil, not only to lubricate moving parts and minimise wear, but also to maximise power output and to improve fuel economy.

HOW ENGINE OIL WORKS

• Beating friction

Without oil, the moving surfaces inside your engine will rub together, heat up and melt, quickly causing the engine to seize. Engine oil creates a film which separates these moving parts, preventing wear and heat build-up.

• Cooling hot-spots

Temperatures inside the engine can exceed 1000° C. The engine oil circulates and acts as a coolant, transferring heat from the hot-spots to the sump.

• Cleaning the engine internally

Good quality engine oils clean the inside of your engine, collecting and dispersing combustion deposits and controlling them until they are trapped by the oil filter or flushed out at oil change.

OIL CARE - FOLLOW THE CODE

To handle and dispose of used engine oil safely, always:

OIL CARE · FOLLOW THE CODE
OIL BANK LINE
0800 66 33 66
www.oilbankline.org.uk

• *Avoid skin contact with used engine oil. Repeated or prolonged contact can be harmful.*
• *Dispose of used oil and empty packs in a responsible manner in an authorised disposal site. Call 0800 663366 to find the one nearest to you. Never tip oil down drains or onto the ground.*

Tyre pressures (cold)

Note: *Pressures are quoted for standard tyre fitments (see Chapter 10); consult a dealer or tyre specialist for alternative or revised recommendations.*

Corsa and Corsavan	Front	Rear
Normal load (up to 3 passengers):		
1.5 litre non-turbo models	2.2 bars (32 psi)	2.0 bars (29 psi)
1.5 litre turbo and 1.7 litre models	2.4 bars (35 psi)	2.2 bars (32 psi)
Fully laden:		
1.5 litre non-turbo models	2.3 bars (33 psi)	2.9 bars (42 psi)
1.5 litre turbo and 1.7 litre models	2.5 bars (36 psi)	2.9 bars (42 psi)
Combo Van		
Normal load (up to 3 passengers)	2.1 bars (30 psi)	2.1 bars (30 psi)
Fully laden	2.1 bars (30 psi)	3.5 bars (51 psi)

Notes

Chapter 1
Routine maintenance and servicing

Contents

Degrees of difficulty

Easy, suitable for novice with little experience	**Fairly easy,** suitable for beginner with some experience	**Fairly difficult,** suitable for competent DIY mechanic	**Difficult,** suitable for experienced DIY mechanic	**Very difficult,** suitable for expert DIY or professional

Lubricants and fluids

Refer to *Weekly checks* on page 0•17

Capacities

Engine oil

Including oil filter:

Up to 1996	3.75 litres
From 1996	4.25 litres
Difference between MIN and MAX on dipstick	1.0 litre

Cooling system

Non-turbo models	6.0 litres
Turbo models	6.3 litres

Transmission

Manual transmission	1.6 litres

Power steering fluid reservoir .... | 1.0 litres

Fuel tank

All models except Combo	46 litres
Combo	50 litres

Engine

Valve clearances (cold):

Inlet	0.15 mm
Exhaust	0.25 mm

Cooling system

Antifreeze mixtures (Vauxhall/Opel specification antifreeze):

	Antifreeze	Water
Protection to –10°C	20%	80%
Protection to –20°C	34%	66%
Protection to –30°C	44%	56%
Protection to –40°C	52%	48%

Note: *Refer to antifreeze manufacturer for latest recommendations.*

Fuel system

Idle speed	830 to 930 rpm

Maximum speed:

1.5 litre non-turbo models	5800 rpm
1.5 litre turbo models	5600 rpm
1.7 litre models	5300 rpm

Clutch

Clutch pedal travel	126.0 to 132.0 mm

Brakes

Friction material minimum thickness:

Front brake pads	7 mm
Rear brake shoes	0.5 mm above the rivet heads

Torque wrench settings

	Nm	lbf ft
Compressor drivebelt tensioner centre bolt	45	33
Engine oil filter	15	11
Fuel filter mounting plate nuts	25	18
Roadwheel bolts	110	81
Sump drain plug	78	58

1 The maintenance intervals in this manual are provided with the assumption that you, not the dealer, will be carrying out the work. These are the minimum maintenance intervals recommended by us for vehicles driven daily. If you wish to keep your vehicle in peak condition at all times, you may wish to perform some of these procedures more often. We encourage frequent maintenance, because it enhances the efficiency, performance and resale value of your vehicle.
2 If the vehicle is driven in dusty areas, used to tow a trailer, or driven frequently at slow speeds (idling in traffic) or on short journeys, more frequent maintenance intervals are recommended.
3 When the vehicle is new, it should be serviced by a factory-authorised dealer service department, in order to preserve the factory warranty.

Every 5000 miles (7500 km) or 6 months, whichever comes first

☐ Renew the engine oil and filter (Section 3)
Note: *Vauxhall recommend that the engine oil and filter are changed every 10 000 miles or 12 months. However, oil and filter changes are good for the engine and we recommend that the oil and filter are renewed more frequently, especially if the vehicle is used on a lot of short journeys.*

Every 10 000 miles (15 000 km) or 12 months, whichever comes first

☐ Check the condition and tension of the auxiliary drivebelts (Section 4)*
☐ Drain water from the fuel filter (Section 5)
☐ Idle speed and exhaust emission check (Section 6)
☐ Check the operation of all electrical systems (Section 7)*
☐ Check and if necessary adjust the headlight beam alignment (Section 8)
☐ Check the body and underbody for corrosion protection (Section 9)
☐ Check the front brake pads and discs for wear (Section 10)*
☐ Check the rear brake pads and discs (where applicable) for wear (Section 11)*
☐ Check all components, pipes and hoses for fluid leaks (Section 12)
☐ Check the roadwheel bolts are tightened to the specified torque (Section 13)*
☐ Check the rear brake pressure regulating valve (where applicable) (Section 14)*
☐ Renew the pollen filter (Section 15)* **Note:** *If the vehicle is used in dusty conditions, the pollen filter should be renewed more frequently.*
☐ Carry out a road test (Section 16)*
* *On vehicles covering a high mileage (more than 20 000 miles/ 30 000 km annually) carry out the items marked with an asterisk every 10 000 miles/15 000 km (regardless of time), then carry out the items not marked with an asterisk at the 12 month interval.*

Every 20 000 miles (30 000 km) or 2 years, whichever comes first

☐ Renew the air cleaner element (Section 17)
☐ Renew the fuel filter (Section 18)
☐ Check and, if necessary, adjust the valve clearances (Section 19)
☐ Check and if necessary top up the manual transmission oil level (Section 20)
☐ Lubricate all door locks and hinges, door stops, bonnet lock and release, and tailgate lock and hinges (Section 21)
☐ Check the rear brake shoes and drums for wear (Section 22)
☐ Check the steering and suspension components for condition and security (Section 23)
☐ Check the condition of the driveshaft gaiters (Section 24)
☐ Check the clutch cable adjustment (Section 25)

Every 2 years, regardless of mileage

☐ Renew the brake fluid (Section 26)
☐ Renew the coolant (Section 27)

Every 40 000 miles (60 000 km) or 4 years, whichever comes first

☐ Renew the timing belt (Section 28)
Note: *Although the normal interval for timing belt renewal is 80 000 miles/120 000 km or 8 years, it is strongly recommended that the interval is halved to 40 000 miles/60 000 km or 4 years on vehicles which are subjected to intensive use, ie, mainly short journeys or a lot of stop-start driving. The actual belt renewal interval is therefore up to the individual owner but, bearing in mind that severe engine damage will result should the belt break in use, we recommend you err on the side of caution.*

Underbonnet view of a 1.5 litre turbo

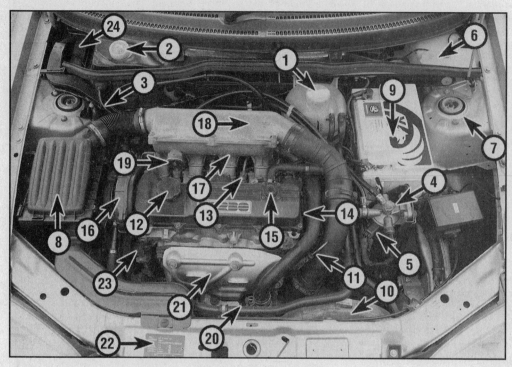

1 Cooling system filler/pressure cap
2 Brake fluid reservoir cap
3 Brake servo line
4 Fuel filter
5 Fuel heater
6 Screen washer reservoir
7 Suspension turret
8 Air cleaner housing
9 Battery
10 Radiator fan
11 Engine oil dipstick
12 Engine oil filler cap
13 Fuel injector
14 Thermostat housing (beneath hose)
15 Engine breather
16 Timing belt cover
17 Inlet manifold
18 Plenum chamber
19 Charge air safety valve
20 Turbocharger
21 Exhaust manifold heat shield
22 VIN plate
23 Coolant pump
24 Relay box

Underbonnet view of a 1.7 litre

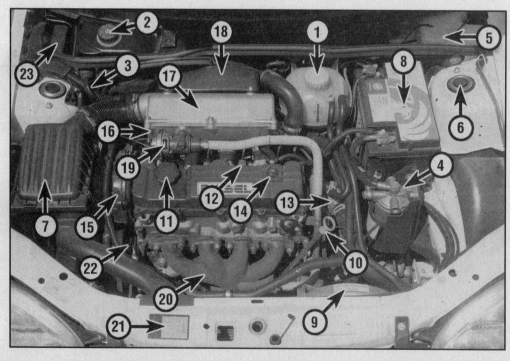

1 Cooling system filler/pressure cap
2 Brake fluid reservoir cap
3 Brake servo line
4 Fuel filter
5 Screen washer reservoir
6 Suspension turret
7 Air cleaner housing
8 Battery
9 Radiator fan
10 Engine oil dipstick
11 Engine oil filler cap
12 Fuel injector
13 Thermostat housing
14 Engine breather
15 Timing belt cover
16 Inlet manifold
17 Plenum chamber
18 Air resonator box
19 EGR valve
20 Exhaust manifold
21 VIN plate
22 Coolant pump
23 Relay box

Front underbody view of a 1.5 litre turbo

1 Fuel pipes
2 Lower suspension arm
3 Brake caliper
4 Alternator
5 Brake vacuum pump
6 Lower radiator hose
7 Turbocharger
8 Radiator fan
9 Left-hand engine
   mounting
10 Front suspension tie-bar
11 Brake hose
12 Left-hand driveshaft
13 Driveshaft gaiter
14 Brake pipes
15 Differential cover plate
16 Clutch cover plate
17 Rear engine mounting
18 Engine oil drain plug
19 Exhaust front section
20 Steering rack
21 Right-hand driveshaft

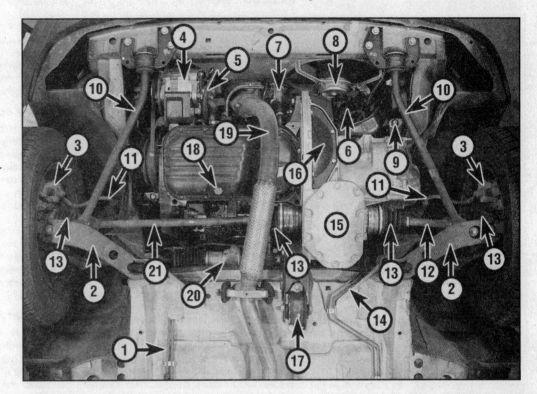

Rear underbody view

1 Brake pipes
2 Rear suspension training
   arm
3 Brake backplate
4 Coil spring
5 Silencer
6 Exhaust heat shield
7 Rear axle
8 Fuel filler and vent pipes
9 Fuel pipe
10 Fuel filter (not all models)
11 Fuel tank
12 Fuel tank securing strap
13 Exhaust rear section
14 Handbrake cable

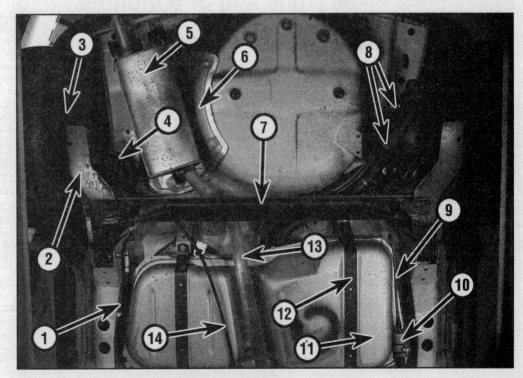

1 General information

1 This Chapter is designed to help the home mechanic maintain his/her vehicle for safety, economy, long life and peak performance.

2 The Chapter contains a master maintenance schedule, followed by Sections dealing specifically with each task in the schedule. Visual checks, adjustments, component renewal and other helpful items are included. Refer to the accompanying illustrations of the engine compartment and the underside of the vehicle for the locations of the various components.

3 Servicing your vehicle in accordance with the mileage/time maintenance schedule and the following Sections will provide a planned maintenance programme, which should result in a long and reliable service life. This is a comprehensive plan, so maintaining some items but not others at the specified service intervals, will not produce the same results.

4 As you service your vehicle, you will discover that many of the procedures can – and should – be grouped together, because of the particular procedure being performed, or because of the proximity of two otherwise-unrelated components to one another. For example, if the vehicle is raised for any reason, the exhaust can be inspected at the same time as the suspension and steering components.

5 The first step in this maintenance programme is to prepare yourself before the actual work begins. Read through all the Sections relevant to the work to be carried out, then make a list and gather all the parts and tools required. If a problem is encountered, seek advice from a parts specialist, or a dealer service department.

2 Regular maintenance

1 If, from the time the vehicle is new, the routine maintenance schedule is followed closely, and frequent checks are made of fluid levels and high-wear items, as suggested throughout this manual, the engine will be kept in relatively good running condition, and the need for additional work will be minimised.

2 It is possible that there will be times when the engine is running poorly due to the lack of regular maintenance. This is even more likely if a used vehicle, which has not received regular and frequent maintenance checks, is purchased. In such cases, additional work may need to be carried out, outside of the regular maintenance intervals.

3 If engine wear is suspected, a compression test or leakdown test (refer to Chapter 2A) will provide valuable information regarding the overall performance of the main internal components. Such a test can be used as a basis to decide on the extent of the work to be carried out. If, for example, a compression or leakdown test indicates serious internal engine wear, conventional maintenance as described in this Chapter will not greatly improve the performance of the engine, and may prove a waste of time and money, unless extensive overhaul work is carried out first.

4 The following series of operations are those most often required to improve the perform-ance of a generally poor-running engine:

Primary operations

a) Clean, inspect and test the battery (refer to 'Weekly checks').
b) Check all the engine-related fluids (refer to 'Weekly checks').
c) Check the condition and tension of the auxiliary drivebelt (Section 4).
d) Check the condition of the air filter, and renew if necessary (Section 17).
e) Renew the fuel filter (Section 18).
f) Check the condition of all hoses, and check for fluid leaks (Section 12).

5 If the above operations do not prove fully effective, carry out the following secondary operations:

Secondary operations

All items listed under Primary operations, plus the following:

a) Check the charging system (refer to Chapter 5A).
b) Check the pre-heating system (refer to Chapter 5)b.
c) Check the fuel system (refer to Chapter 4A).

Every 5000 miles (7500 km) or 6 months

3 Engine oil and filter renewal

1 Frequent oil and filter changes are the most important preventative maintenance procedures which can be undertaken by the DIY owner. As engine oil ages, it becomes diluted and contaminated, which leads to premature engine wear.

2 Before starting this procedure, gather together all the necessary tools and materials.

3.5 Sump drain plug

Also make sure that you have plenty of clean rags and newspapers handy, to mop up any spills. Ideally, the engine oil should be warm, as it will drain more easily, and more built-up sludge will be removed with it. Take care not to touch the exhaust or any other hot parts of the engine when working under the vehicle. To avoid any possibility of scalding, and to protect yourself from possible skin irritants

HAYNES HINT

As the drain plug threads release, move it sharply away so the stream of oil issuing from the sump runs into the container, not up your sleeve.

and other harmful contaminants in used engine oils, it is advisable to wear gloves when carrying out this work.

3 Firmly apply the handbrake then jack up the front of the vehicle and support it on axle stands (see Jacking and vehicle support).

4 Remove the oil filler cap.

5 Using a spanner, or preferably a suitable socket and bar, slacken the drain plug about half a turn (see illustration). Position the draining container under the drain plug, then remove the plug completely (see Haynes Hint).

6 Allow some time for the oil to drain, noting that it may be necessary to reposition the container as the oil flow slows to a trickle.

7 After all the oil has drained, wipe the drain plug and the sealing washer with a clean rag. Examine the condition of the sealing washer, and renew it if it shows signs of scoring or other damage which may prevent an oil-tight seal. Clean the area around the drain plug opening, and refit the plug complete with the washer and tighten it to the specified torque.

8 Move the container into position under the oil filter which is located on the rear of the cylinder block.

9 Use an oil filter removal tool to slacken the filter initially, then unscrew it by hand the rest

of the way **(see illustration)**. Empty the oil from the old filter into the container.

10 Use a clean rag to remove all oil, dirt and sludge from the filter sealing area on the engine.

11 Apply a light coating of clean engine oil to the sealing ring on the new filter, then screw the filter into position on the engine. Tighten the filter firmly by hand only – **do not** use any tools. If a genuine filter is being fitted and the special oil filter tool (a socket which fits over the end of the filter) is available, tighten the filter to the specified torque.

12 Remove the old oil and all tools from under the vehicle then lower the vehicle to the ground.

13 Fill the engine through the filler hole, using the correct grade and type of oil (refer to *Weekly Checks* for details of topping-up).

Pour in half the specified quantity of oil first, then wait a few minutes for the oil to drain into the sump. Continue to add oil, a small quantity at a time, until the level is up to the lower mark on the dipstick. Adding approximately a further 1.0 litre will bring the level up to the upper mark on the dipstick.

14 Start the engine and run it for a few minutes, while checking for leaks around the oil filter seal and the sump drain plug. Note that there may be a delay of a few seconds before the low oil pressure warning light goes out when the engine is first started, as the oil circulates through the new oil filter and the engine oil galleries before the pressure builds up.

15 Stop the engine, and wait a few minutes for the oil to settle in the sump once more. With the new oil circulated and the filter now

3.9 Remove the oil filter

completely full, recheck the level on the dipstick, and add more oil as necessary.

16 Dispose of the used engine oil safely with reference to *General repair procedures*.

Every 10 000 miles (15 000 km) or 12 months

4 Auxiliary drivebelt check and renewal

Checking

1 Drivebelts are prone to failure after a long period of time and should therefore be inspected regularly.

2 With the engine stopped, inspect the full length of the drivebelts for cracks and separation of the belt plies. It will be necessary to turn the engine (using a spanner or socket and bar on the crankshaft pulley bolt) in order to move the belt from the pulleys so that the belt can be inspected thoroughly. Twist the belt between the pulleys so that both sides can be viewed. Also check for fraying, and glazing which gives the belt a shiny appearance. Check the pulleys for nicks, cracks, distortion and corrosion.

3 If the belt shows signs of wear or damage, it must be renewed.

Renewal

4 Remove the air cleaner housing as described in Chapter 4A then proceed as described under the relevant sub-heading.

Air conditioning compressor drivebelt

5 Slacken the tensioner pulley centre bolt then release the belt tension by rotating the adjuster bolt. Slip the belt off from the pulleys and remove it from the engine.

6 Manoeuvre the new belt into position and seat it on the pulleys. Tension the belt, using the adjuster bolt, so that under firm thumb pressure there is about 10 mm of movement at the mid-point on the longest run of the belt.

7 Once the belt is correctly tensioned, tighten the tensioner pulley centre bolt to the

specified torque then refit the air cleaner housing (see Chapter 4A).

Power steering pump drivebelt

8 On models with air conditioning, remove the compressor drivebelt (see paragraph 5).

9 Slacken the pump mounting bolts to release the drivebelt tension and slip the belt off from the pulleys.

10 Manoeuvre the new belt into position and seat it on the pulleys. Tension the belt by positioning the pump so that under firm thumb pressure there is about 10 mm of movement at the mid-point on the longest run of the belt. Move the pump using an extension bar fitted to the square-section hole in the pump bracket and when its correctly positioned tighten its mounting bolts to the specified torque (see Chapter 10) **(see illustration)**.

11 Refit the air conditioning compressor drivebelt (where fitted) then refit the air cleaner housing (see Chapter 4A).

4.10 Tensioning the power steering pump drivebelt

A Socket drive in end of adjuster arm
B Adjuster strap bolt
C Pivot bolt

Alternator drivebelt

12 Firmly apply the handbrake then jack up the front of the vehicle and support it on axle stands (see *Jacking and vehicle support*). To improve access, remove the right-hand front roadwheel then undo the fasteners and remove the undercover from beneath the wing.

13 Remove the power steering pump drivebelt as described in this Section.

14 Slacken the alternator mounting bolts to release the drivebelt tension and slip the belt off the pulleys.

15 Manoeuvre the new belt into position and seat it on the pulleys. Tension the belt by positioning the alternator so that under firm thumb pressure there is about 10 mm of movement at the mid-point on the longest run of the belt. Move the alternator using an extension bar fitted to the square-section hole in the bracket and when its correctly positioned tighten its mounting bolts to the

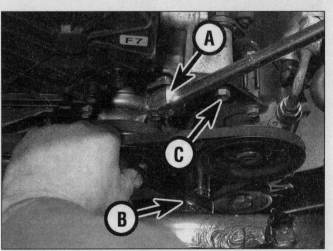
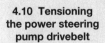

4.15 Tensioning the alternator drivebelt

A Socket drive in end of adjuster arm
B Adjuster strap bolt
C Pivot bolt

specified torque (see Chapter 5A) **(see illustration).**

16 Fit the power steering pump and (where necessary) the air conditioning compressor drivebelt as described in this Section.

17 Refit the undercover and lower the vehicle to the ground and tighten the wheel bolts to the specified torque.

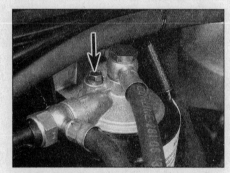

5.2a Fuel filter bleed screw (arrowed)

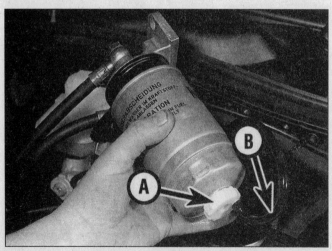

5.2b Drain screw (A) and tube (B)

---

5 Fuel filter water draining

Caution: Before starting any work on the fuel filter, wipe clean the filter assembly and the area around it; it is essential that no dirt or other foreign matter is allowed into the system. Obtain a suitable container into which the filter can be drained and place rags or similar material under the filter assembly to catch any spillages. Do not allow diesel fuel to contaminate components such as the alternator and starter motor, the coolant hoses and engine mountings, and any wiring.

1 In addition to taking the precautions noted above to catch any fuel spillages, connect a tube to the drain screw on the base of the fuel filter/filter housing. Place the other end of the tube in a clean jar or can.

2 Unscrew the drain screw and allow the filter to drain until clean fuel, free of dirt or water, emerges from the tube (approximately 100 cc is usually sufficient). Note that it maybe necessary to slacken the bleed screw to allow the fuel to drain **(see illustrations).**

3 Securely close the drain screw and remove the tube, containers and rag, mopping up any spilt fuel. Where necessary, securely tighten the bleed screw.

4 On completion, dispose safely of the drained fuel. Check carefully all disturbed components to ensure that there are no leaks (of air or fuel) when the engine is restarted.

5 Start the engine and bleed the fuel system as described in Chapter 4A.

---

6 Idle speed and exhaust emission check

Idle speed check

1 The usual type of tachometer (rev counter), which works from ignition system pulses, cannot be used on diesel engines. If it is not felt that adjusting the idle speed 'by ear' is satisfactory, it will be necessary to purchase or hire an appropriate tachometer, or else leave the task to a Vauxhall dealer or other suitably-equipped specialist.

2 Make sure that the accelerator cable is correctly adjusted (see Chapter 4A).

3 Warm the engine up to normal operating temperature and check that it idles at the specified speed (see Chapter 4A).

4 If adjustment is necessary, slacken the locknut and rotate the idle speed adjustment screw **(see illustration).** Once the engine is idling at the specified speed, securely tighten the locknut.

5 Where applicable, disconnect the tachometer on completion.

Exhaust emission check

6 Specialised equipment is needed to check the exhaust gas emission levels so this check

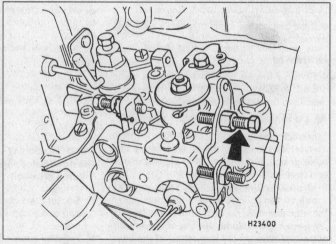

6.4 Engine idle speed adjustment screw (arrowed)

must be entrusted to a Vauxhall dealer or a suitably-equipped garage. In reality, if the vehicle is running correctly and no problems have been noticed then this check need not be carried out (if the vehicle is over 3 years old, the exhaust emissions will be checked as part of the MoT test anyway).

7 Electrical systems check

1 Check the operation of all electrical equipment, ie, lights, direction indicators, horn, wash/wipe system, etc. Refer to the appropriate Sections of Chapter 12 for details if any of the circuits are found to be inoperative.
2 Visually check all accessible wiring connectors, harnesses and retaining clips for security, and for signs of chafing or damage. Rectify any faults found.

8 Headlight beam alignment check

Refer to Chapter 12 for details

9 Body corrosion check

This work should be carried out by a Vauxhall/Opel dealer in order to validate the vehicle warranty. The work includes a thorough inspection of the vehicle paintwork and underbody for damage and corrosion

10 Front brake pad and disc check

1 Firmly apply the handbrake, then jack up the front of the vehicle and support it securely on axle stands (see *Jacking and vehicle support*). Remove the front roadwheels.
2 For a quick check, the pad thickness can be carried out via the inspection hole on the front of the caliper **(see Haynes Hint 1)**. Using a steel rule, measure the thickness of the pad lining including the backing plate. This must not be less than that indicated in the Specifications.
3 The view through the caliper inspection hole gives a rough indication of the state of the brake pads. For a comprehensive check, the brake pads should be removed and cleaned. The operation of the caliper can then also be checked, and the condition of the brake disc itself can be fully examined on both sides. Chapter 9 contains a detailed description of how the brake disc should be checked for wear and/or damage.

4 If any pad's friction material is worn to the specified thickness or less, *all four pads must be renewed as a set.* Refer to Chapter 9 for details.
5 On completion, refit the roadwheels and lower the vehicle to the ground.

11 Rear brake pad and disc check

1 Firmly apply the handbrake, then jack up the rear of the vehicle and support it securely on axle stands (see *Jacking and vehicle support*). Remove the rear roadwheels.
2 For a quick check, the pad thickness can be carried out via the inspection hole on the rear of the caliper. Using a steel rule, measure the thickness of the pad lining including the backing plate. This must not be less than that indicated in the Specifications.
3 The view through the caliper inspection hole gives a rough indication of the state of the brake pads. For a comprehensive check, the brake pads should be removed and cleaned. The operation of the caliper can then also be checked, and the condition of the brake disc itself can be fully examined on both sides. Chapter 9 contains a detailed description of how the brake disc should be checked for wear and/or damage.
4 If any pad's friction material is worn to the specified thickness or less, *all four pads must be renewed as a set.*
5 On completion, refit the roadwheels and lower the vehicle to the ground.

12 Hose and fluid leak check

1 Visually inspect the engine joint faces, gaskets and seals for any signs of water or oil leaks. Pay particular attention to the areas around the cylinder head cover, cylinder head, oil filter and sump joint faces. Bear in mind that, over a period of time, some very slight seepage from these areas is to be expected – what you are really looking for is any indication of a serious leak. Should a leak be found, renew the offending gasket or oil seal by referring to the appropriate Chapters in this manual.
2 Also check the security and condition of all the engine-related pipes and hoses, and all braking system pipes and hoses and fuel lines. Ensure that all cable ties or securing clips are in place, and in good condition. Clips which are broken or missing can lead to chafing of the hoses, pipes or wiring, which could cause more serious problems in the future.
3 Carefully check the radiator hoses and heater hoses along their entire length **(see Haynes Hint 2)**. Renew any hose which is

Haynes Hint 1; For a quick check, the thickness of friction material remaining on the inner brake pad can be measured through the aperture in the caliper body.

cracked, swollen or deteriorated. Cracks will show up better if the hose is squeezed. Pay close attention to the hose clips that secure the hoses to the cooling system components. Hose clips can pinch and puncture hoses, resulting in cooling system leaks. If the crimped-type hose clips are used, it may be a good idea to replace them with standard worm-drive clips.
4 Inspect all the cooling system components (hoses, joint faces, etc) for leaks.
5 Where any problems are found on system components, renew the component or gasket with reference to Chapter 3.
6 With the vehicle raised, inspect the fuel tank and filler neck for punctures, cracks and other damage. The connection between the filler neck and tank is especially critical. Sometimes a rubber filler neck or connecting hose will leak due to loose retaining clamps or deteriorated rubber.
7 Carefully check all rubber hoses and metal fuel lines leading away from the fuel tank. Check for loose connections, deteriorated hoses, crimped lines, and other damage. Pay particular attention to the vent pipes and hoses, which often loop up around the filler neck and can become blocked or crimped.

Haynes Hint 2; A leak in the cooling system will usually show up as white- or rust-coloured deposits on the area adjoining the leak.

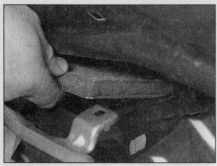

15.3 Pull up the rubber weatherseal, then open the cover and lift out the pollen filter

Follow the lines to the front of the vehicle, carefully inspecting them all the way. Renew damaged sections as necessary. Similarly, whilst the vehicle is raised, take the opportunity to inspect all underbody brake fluid pipes and hoses.

8 From within the engine compartment, check the security of all fuel, vacuum and brake hose attachments and pipe unions, and inspect all hoses for kinks, chafing and deterioration.

9 Check the condition of the power steering and, where applicable, the automatic transmission fluid pipes and hoses.

13 Wheel bolt tightness check

1 Remove the wheel trims and check the tightness of all the wheel bolts, using a torque wrench.

2 Refit the wheel trims on completion.

14 Rear brake pressure-regulating valve adjustment check

Check the operation of the valve and adjust it as described in Chapter 9.

15 Pollen filter renewal

1 Open the bonnet, and pull up the rubber weatherseal from the flange at the rear of the engine compartment.

2 Open the cover in the water deflector for access to the pollen filter.

3 Release the clips from each end, then lift out the filter **(see illustration)**.

4 Fit the new filter using a reversal of the removal procedure; make sure that the marking is visible on the right-hand end of the filter, as viewed through the cover.

16 Road test

Instruments and electrical equipment

1 Check the operation of all instruments and electrical equipment.

2 Make sure that all instruments read correctly, and switch on all electrical equipment in turn, to check that it functions properly.

Steering and suspension

3 Check for any abnormalities in the steering, suspension, handling or road 'feel'.

4 Drive the vehicle, and check that there are no unusual vibrations or noises.

5 Check that the steering feels positive, with no excessive 'sloppiness', or roughness, and check for any suspension noises when cornering and driving over bumps.

Drivetrain

6 Check the performance of the engine, clutch, transmission and driveshafts.

7 Listen for any unusual noises from the engine, clutch and transmission.

8 Make sure that the engine runs smoothly when idling, and that there is no hesitation when accelerating.

9 Check that, where applicable, the clutch action is smooth and progressive, that the drive is taken up smoothly, and that the pedal travel is not excessive. Also listen for any noises when the clutch pedal is depressed.

10 Check that all gears can be engaged smoothly without noise, and that the gear lever action is smooth and not abnormally vague or 'notchy'.

11 On automatic transmission models, make sure that all gearchanges occur smoothly, without snatching, and without an increase in engine speed between changes. Check that all of the gear positions can be selected with the vehicle at rest. If any problems are found, they should be referred to a Vauxhall/Opel dealer.

12 Listen for a metallic clicking sound from the front of the vehicle, as the vehicle is driven slowly in a circle with the steering on full-lock. Carry out this check in both directions. If a clicking noise is heard, this indicates wear in a driveshaft joint (see Chapter 8).

Braking system

13 Make sure that the vehicle does not pull to one side when braking, and that the wheels do not lock prematurely when braking hard.

14 Check that there is no vibration through the steering when braking.

15 Check that the handbrake operates correctly, without excessive movement of the lever, and that it holds the vehicle stationary on a slope.

16 Test the operation of the brake servo unit as follows. Depress the footbrake four or five times to exhaust the vacuum, then start the engine. As the engine starts, there should be a noticeable 'give' in the brake pedal as vacuum builds up. Allow the engine to run for at least two minutes, and then switch it off. If the brake pedal is now depressed again, it should be possible to detect a hiss from the servo as the pedal is depressed. After about four or five applications, no further hissing should be heard, and the pedal should feel considerably harder.

Every 20 000 miles (30 000 km) or 2 years

17.2 Release the clips then lift the air cleaner cover . . .

17.3 . . . and remove the filter element

17 Air cleaner element renewal

1 The air cleaner is located in the front right-hand corner of the engine compartment.

2 Release the securing clips, and lift the air cleaner cover sufficiently to enable removal of the filter element **(see illustration)**.

3 Lift out the filter element **(see illustration)**.

4 Wipe out the casing and the cover. Fit the new filter, noting that the rubber locating flange should be uppermost, and secure the cover with the clips.

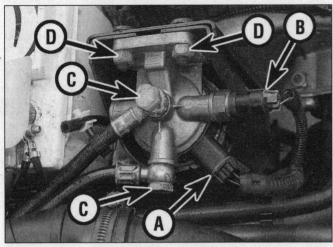

18.3 Fuel filter assembly

A Heating element connector　　*B Temperature sensor connector*
C Fuel pipe unions　　　　　　　*D Retaining nuts*

20.2 Transmission oil level plug location (arrowed)

18 Fuel filter renewal

Note: *On some models it may be possible to unscrew the filter with the mounting plate still in position.*

1 Drain the fuel filter as described in Section 5.
2 Disconnect the wiring connectors from the temperature switch and heating element which are fitted between the fuel filter and mounting plate.
3 Unscrew the union bolts and remove the fuel lines from the filter **(see illustration)**. Recover the sealing washers which are fitted on each side of the hose unions.
4 Unscrew the mounting nuts and remove the filter assembly from the bulkhead and separate the filter and its protective housing.
5 Retain the mounting plate and unscrew the filter. Remove the sealing rings from the filter head.
6 Ensure the mounting plate is clean then fit the new sealing rings to top of the new filter element.
7 Smear a little fuel on the new sealing rings and screw the new filter on the mounting plate, tightening securely by hand only.

20.4a Unscrew the breather valve . . .

8 Refit the filter assembly and protective housing to the bulkhead and tighten the mounting nuts to the specified torque.
9 Reconnect the fuel lines, positioning a new sealing washer on each side of the unions, and refit the union bolts. Securely tighten both union bolts then reconnect the wiring to the temperature switch and heating element.
10 Start the engine and bleed the fuel system as described in Chapter 4A.

19 Valve clearance check and adjustment

Refer to Chapter 2A.

20 Manual transmission oil level check

1 Position the vehicle over an inspection pit, on vehicle ramps, or jack it up, but make sure that it is level. The oil level must be checked before the car is driven, or at least 5 minutes after the engine has been switched off. If the oil is checked immediately after driving the car, some of the oil will remain distributed around the transmission components, resulting in an inaccurate level reading.
2 Wipe clean the area around the level plug which is located on the left-hand side of the transmission just behind the driveshaft inner joint. Unscrew the plug and clean it **(see illustration)**.
3 The oil level should reach the lower edge of the level plug hole.
4 If topping-up is necessary, unscrew the breather valve from the top of the transmission housing and add the specified type of oil through the valve hole until oil

begins to trickle out from the level plug hole **(see illustrations)**.
5 Allow the excess oil to drain out from the level plug hole then refit the level plug, tightening it to the specified torque (see Chapter 7).
6 Refit the breather valve to the top of the transmission unit, tightening it securely and wash off any spilt oil.

21 Hinge and lock lubrication

1 Work around the vehicle and lubricate the hinges of the bonnet, doors and tailgate with a light machine oil.
2 Lightly lubricate the bonnet release mechanism and exposed section of inner cable with a smear of grease.
3 Check carefully the security and operation of all hinges, latches and locks, adjusting them where required. Check the operation of the central locking system.
4 Check the condition and operation of the tailgate struts, renewing them both if either is leaking or no longer able to support the tailgate securely when raised.

20.4b . . . and top-up the transmission oil level via the breather valve hole

22 Rear brake shoe and drum check

Refer to the detailed description given in Chapter 9.

23 Suspension and steering check

Front suspension and steering

1 Raise the front of the vehicle, and securely support it on axle stands (see *Jacking and vehicle support*).

2 Visually inspect the balljoint dust covers and the steering rack-and-pinion gaiters for splits, chafing or deterioration. Any wear of these components will cause loss of lubricant, together with dirt and water entry, resulting in rapid deterioration of the balljoints or steering gear.

3 On vehicles with power steering, check the fluid hoses for chafing or deterioration, and the pipe and hose unions for fluid leaks. Also check for signs of fluid leakage under pressure from the steering gear rubber gaiters, which would indicate failed fluid seals within the steering gear.

4 Grasp the roadwheel at the 12 o'clock and 6 o'clock positions, and try to rock it **(see illustration)**. Very slight free play may be felt, but if the movement is appreciable, further investigation is necessary to determine the source. Continue rocking the wheel while an assistant depresses the footbrake. If the movement is now eliminated or significantly reduced, it is likely that the hub bearings are at fault. If the free play is still evident with the footbrake depressed, then there is wear in the suspension joints or mountings.

5 Now grasp the wheel at the 9 o'clock and 3 o'clock positions, and try to rock it as before. Any movement felt now may again be caused by wear in the hub bearings or the steering track-rod balljoints. If the outer balljoint is worn, the visual movement will be obvious. If the inner joint is suspect, it can be felt by placing a hand over the rack-and-pinion rubber gaiter and gripping the track-rod. If the wheel is now rocked, movement will be felt at the inner joint if wear has taken place.

6 Using a large screwdriver or flat bar, check for wear in the suspension mounting bushes by levering between the relevant suspension component and its attachment point. Some movement is to be expected, as the mountings are made of rubber, but excessive wear should be obvious. Also check the condition of any visible rubber bushes, looking for splits, cracks or contamination of the rubber.

7 With the car standing on its wheels, have an assistant turn the steering wheel back and forth, about an eighth of a turn each way. There should be very little, if any, lost movement between the steering wheel and roadwheels. If this is not the case, closely observe the joints and mountings previously described. In addition, check the steering column universal joints for wear, and also check the rack-and-pinion steering gear itself.

Rear suspension

8 Chock the front wheels, then jack up the rear of the vehicle and support securely on axle stands (see *Jacking and vehicle support*).

9 Working as described previously for the front suspension, check the rear hub bearings, the suspension bushes and the strut or shock absorber mountings (as applicable) for wear.

Shock absorbers

10 Check for any signs of fluid leakage around the shock absorber body, or from the rubber gaiter around the piston rod. Should any fluid be noticed, the shock absorber is defective internally, and should be renewed. **Note:** *Shock absorbers should always be renewed in pairs on the same axle.*

11 The efficiency of the shock absorber may be checked by bouncing the vehicle at each corner. Generally speaking, the body will return to its normal position and stop after being depressed. If it rises and returns on a rebound, the shock absorber is probably suspect. Also examine the shock absorber upper and lower mountings for any signs of wear.

24 Driveshaft gaiter check

1 With the vehicle raised and securely supported on stands, turn the steering onto full lock then slowly rotate the roadwheel. Inspect the condition of the outer constant velocity (CV) joint rubber gaiters while squeezing the gaiters to open out the folds **(see illustration)**. Check for signs of cracking, splits or deterioration of the rubber which may allow the grease to escape and lead to water and grit entry into the joint. Also check the security and condition of the retaining clips. Repeat these checks on the inner CV joints. If any damage or deterioration is found, the gaiters should be renewed as described in Chapter 8.

2 At the same time check the general condition of the CV joints themselves by first holding the driveshaft and attempting to rotate the wheel. Repeat this check by holding the inner joint and attempting to rotate the driveshaft. Any appreciable movement indicates wear in the joints, wear in the driveshaft splines or loose driveshaft retaining nut.

23.4 Check for wear in the hub bearings by grasping the wheel and trying to rock it

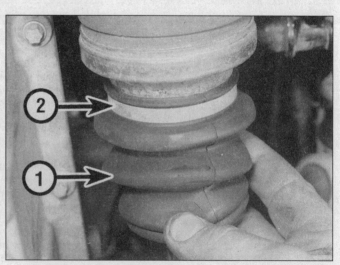

24.1 Check the condition of the driveshaft gaiters (1) and retaining clips (2)

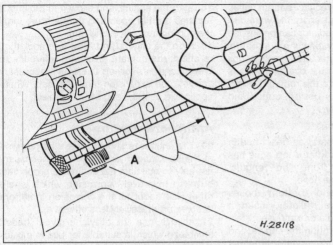

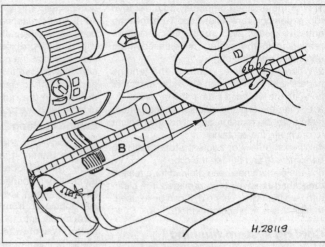

25.1a Measure the dimension (A) from the top edge of the pedal to the lowest point of the steering wheel . . .

25.1b . . . then fully depress the pedal and repeat the measurement (B)

25 Clutch cable adjustment check

1 Working inside the vehicle, ensure that the clutch pedal is in its normal rest position, then measure the distance from the centre of the top edge of the pedal to the lowest point of the steering wheel. Fully depress the pedal, and repeat the measurement **(see illustrations)**. The measurements can be taken using a suitable strip of wood or metal, as the important figure is the *difference* between the two measurements, ie the movement (stroke) of the pedal.

2 The difference between the two measurements must be as given in the Specifications – if not, adjust the clutch cable

as follows to achieve the specified pedal movement.

3 Working in the engine compartment, remove the clip from the threaded rod at the clutch release arm on the gearbox, then turn the threaded rod end fitting as required, using a spanner on the flats provided to hold the threaded rod as the end fitting is turned **(see illustration)**. Turn the end fitting clockwise to decrease pedal movement, or anti-clockwise to increase pedal movement. Recheck the pedal movement, and then refit the clip to the threaded rod on completion.

4 On a vehicle in which the clutch has covered a high mileage, it may no longer be possible to adjust the cable to achieve the specified pedal movement, and this indicates that the clutch friction disc requires renewal. Note that when correctly adjusted, the clutch

25.3 Removing the clip from the clutch pedal threaded rod. Threaded rod adjuster flats arrowed

pedal will rest slightly higher than the brake pedal – it is incorrect for the two pedals to be in alignment. If the pedals are aligned, the clutch cable requires adjustment.

Every 2 years, regardless of mileage

26 Brake fluid renewal

⚠️ *Warning: Brake hydraulic fluid can harm your eyes and damage painted surfaces, so use extreme caution when handling and pouring it. Do not use fluid that has been standing open for some time, as it absorbs moisture from the air. Excess moisture can cause a dangerous loss of braking effectiveness.*

1 The procedure is similar to that for the bleeding of the hydraulic system as described in Chapter 9.

2 Working as described in Chapter 9, open the first bleed screw in the sequence, and pump the brake pedal gently until nearly all the old fluid has been emptied from the master cylinder reservoir. Top-up to the MAX level with new fluid, and continue pumping

until only the new fluid remains in the reservoir, and new fluid can be seen emerging from the bleed screw. Tighten the screw, and top the reservoir level up to the MAX level line.

3 Work through all the remaining bleed screws in the sequence until new fluid can be seen at all of them. Be careful to keep the master cylinder reservoir topped-up to above the MIN level at all times, or air may enter the system and greatly increase the length of the task.

 HAYNES HiNT *Old hydraulic fluid is invariably much darker in colour than the new, making it easy to distinguish the two.*

4 When the operation is complete, check that all bleed screws are securely tightened, and that their dust caps are refitted. Wash off all traces of spilt fluid, and recheck the master cylinder reservoir fluid level.

5 Check the operation of the brakes before taking the car on the road.

27 Coolant renewal

Cooling system draining

⚠️ *Warning: Wait until the engine is cold before starting this procedure. Do not allow antifreeze to come in contact with your skin, or with the painted surfaces of the vehicle. Rinse off spills immediately with plenty of water. Never leave antifreeze lying around in an open container, or in a puddle in the driveway or on the garage floor. Children and pets are attracted by its sweet smell, but antifreeze can be fatal if ingested.*

1 With the engine completely cold, remove the expansion tank filler cap. Turn the cap anti-clockwise, wait until any pressure remaining in the system is released, then unscrew it and lift it off.

2 Where applicable, remove the engine undershield, then position a suitable container beneath the left-hand side of the radiator.

3 Loosen the clip and disconnect the bottom hose from the radiator, and allow the coolant to drain into the container.

4 When the flow of coolant stops, refit the bottom hose and tighten the clip.

5 If the coolant has been drained for a reason other than renewal, then provided it is clean and less than two years old, it can be re-used, though this is not recommended.

Cooling system flushing

6 If coolant renewal has been neglected, or if the antifreeze mixture has become diluted, then in time, the cooling system may gradually lose efficiency, as the coolant passages become restricted due to rust, scale deposits, and other sediment. The cooling system efficiency can be restored by flushing the system clean.

7 The radiator should be flushed independently of the engine, to avoid unnecessary contamination.

Radiator flushing

8 Disconnect the top and bottom hoses and any other relevant hoses from the radiator, with reference to Chapter 3.

9 Insert a garden hose into the radiator top inlet. Direct a flow of clean water through the radiator, and continue flushing until clean water emerges from the radiator bottom outlet.

10 If after a reasonable period, the water still does not run clear, the radiator can be flushed with a good proprietary cleaning agent. It is important that the manufacturer's instructions are followed carefully. If the contamination is particularly bad, remove the radiator, insert the hose in the radiator bottom outlet, and reverse-flush the radiator.

Engine flushing

11 Remove the thermostat as described in Chapter 3 then, if the radiator top hose has been disconnected from the engine, temporarily reconnect the hose.

12 With the top and bottom hoses disconnected from the radiator, insert a garden hose into the radiator top hose. Direct a clean flow of water through the engine, and continue flushing until clean water emerges from the radiator bottom hose.

13 On completion of flushing, refit the thermostat and reconnect the hoses with reference to Chapter 3.

Cooling system filling

14 Before attempting to fill the cooling system, make sure that all hoses and clips are in good condition, and that the clips are tight. Note that an antifreeze mixture must be used all year round, to prevent corrosion of the engine components.

15 Remove the expansion tank filler cap.

16 Slowly fill the system until the coolant level reaches the KALT/COLD mark on the side of the expansion tank.

17 Refit and tighten the expansion tank filler cap.

18 Start the engine, and allow it to run until it reaches normal operating temperature (until the cooling fan cuts in and out).

19 Stop the engine, and allow it to cool, then re-check the coolant level with reference to *Weekly checks*. Top-up the level if necessary and refit the expansion tank filler cap. Where applicable, refit the engine undershield.

Antifreeze mixture

20 The antifreeze should always be renewed at the specified intervals. This is necessary not only to maintain the antifreeze properties, but also to prevent corrosion which would otherwise occur as the corrosion inhibitors become progressively less effective.

21 Always use an ethylene-glycol based antifreeze which is suitable for use in mixed-metal cooling systems. The quantity of antifreeze and levels of protection are given in the Specifications.

22 Before adding antifreeze, the cooling system should be completely drained, preferably flushed, and all hoses checked for condition and security.

23 After filling with antifreeze, a label should be attached to the expansion tank, stating the type and concentration of antifreeze used, and the date installed. Any subsequent topping-up should be made with the same type and concentration of antifreeze.

24 Do not use engine antifreeze in the windscreen/tailgate washer system, as it will cause damage to the vehicle paintwork. A screenwash additive should be added to the washer system in the quantities stated on the bottle.

Every 40 000 miles (60 000 km) or 4 years

28 Timing belt renewal

1 Refer to Chapter 2A.

Chapter 2 Part A:
Engine in-car repair procedures

Contents

Degrees of difficulty

Easy, suitable for novice with little experience | **Fairly easy,** suitable for beginner with some experience | **Fairly difficult,** suitable for competent DIY mechanic | **Difficult,** suitable for experienced DIY mechanic | **Very difficult,** suitable for expert DIY or professional

Specifications

General

Engine type	Four-cylinder, in-line, water-cooled. Single overhead camshaft, belt-driven
Manufacturer's engine code:	
1.5 litre non-turbo	15 D (Isuzu code 4 EC1)
1.5 litre turbo	15 DT and X 15 DT (Isuzu code T4 EC1)
1.7 litre	17 D and X 17 D (Isuzu code 4 EE1)
Bore:	
1.5 litre	76.0 mm
1.7 litre	79.0 mm
Stroke:	
1.5 litre	82.0 mm
1.7 litre	86.0 mm
Capacity:	
1.5 litre	1488 cc
1.7 litre	1686 cc
Firing order	1-3-4-2 (No 1 cylinder at timing belt end)
Direction of crankshaft rotation	Clockwise (viewed from timing belt end of engine)
Compression ratio:	
15 DT, X 15 DT and 17 D	22:1
15 D and X 17 D	23:1
Maximum power:	
15 D	37 kW at 4800 rpm
15 DT and X 15 DT	49 kW at 4600 rpm
17 D	44 kW at 4500 rpm
X 17 D	44 kW at 4400 rpm
Maximum torque:	
15 D	90 Nm at 2400 rpm
15 DT	132 Nm at 2400 rpm
X 15 DT	132 Nm at 2600 rpm
17 D	108 Nm at 2600 rpm
X 17 D	112 Nm at 2650 rpm

Compression pressures

Standard	18.5 to 34.5 bar (268 to 500 psi)
Maximum difference between any two cylinders	1.5 bar (23 psi)

Cylinder head

Gasket thickness and identification:
  1.5 litre engines:
    Piston protrusion 0.58 to 0.64 mm .... 1.35 mm thick (one notch)
    Piston protrusion 0.65 to 0.70 mm .... 1.40 mm thick (two notches)
    Piston protrusion 0.71 to 0.78 mm .... 1.45 mm thick (three notches)
  1.7 litre engines:
    Piston protrusion 0.58 to 0.64 mm .... 1.40 mm thick (no holes)
    Piston protrusion 0.65 to 0.70 mm .... 1.45 mm thick (one hole)
    Piston protrusion 0.71 to 0.78 mm .... 1.50 mm thick (two holes)

Valve clearances

Engine cold:
  Inlet .... 0.15 mm
  Exhaust .... 0.25 mm

Camshaft

Endfloat .... 0.05 to 0.20 mm
Maximum permissible radial run-out .... 0.05 mm
Cam lift:
  Inlet valve .... 8.47 to 8.67 mm
  Exhaust valve .... 8.57 to 8.77 mm
Bearing running clearance:
  Standard .... 0.040 to 0.082 mm
  Service limit .... 0.110 mm

Lubrication system

Oil pump type .... Gear-type, driven by timing belt
Minimum permissible oil pressure at idle speed, with engine
  at operating temperature (oil temperature of at least 80°C) .... 2.0 bar (29 psi)

Oil pump clearances:	Standard	Service limit
Outer rotor-to-body clearance	0.24 to 0.36 mm	0.40 mm
Inner-to-outer rotor clearance	0.13 to 0.15 mm	0.20 mm
Rotor endfloat	0.035 to 0.100 mm	0.150 mm

Torque wrench settings	Nm	lbf ft
Baffle plate-to-cylinder block bolts	19	14
Camshaft bearing cap nuts	19	14
Coolant pump retaining bolts	20	15
Connecting rod big-end bearing cap nuts:		
Stage 1	25	18
Stage 2	Angle-tighten a further 100°	
Stage 3	Angle-tighten a further 15°	
Crankshaft pulley bolts	20	15
Crankshaft sprocket bolt	196	145
Cylinder head bolts:		
Stage 1	40	30
Stage 2	Angle-tighten a further 60 to 75°	
Stage 3	Angle-tighten a further 60 to 75°	
Engine/transmission mounting bolts:		
Right-hand mounting:		
Mounting-to-bracket/subframe nuts	45	33
Bracket-to-engine bolts	60	44
Upper bracket nuts	45	33
Left-hand mounting:		
Mounting-to-bracket/subframe nuts	45	33
Bracket-to-transmission bolts	60	44
Rear mounting:		
Mounting-to-bracket bolts	45	33
Mounting-to-subframe bolts	20	15
Bracket-to-transmission bolts	60	44
Engine-to-transmission unit bolts:		
M8 bolts	20	15
M10 bolts	40	30
M12 bolts	60	44
Flywheel bolts:		
Stage 1	30	22
Stage 2	Angle-tighten a further 45 to 60°	

Torque wrench settings (continued)

	Nm	lbf ft
Injection pump sprocket nut	69	51
Main bearing cap bolts	88	65
Oil cooler centre bolt	49	36
Oil pressure relief valve bolt	40	30
Oil pump pick-up/strainer bolts	19	14
Oil pump sprocket nut	44	32
Sump drain plug	78	58
Roadwheel bolts	110	81
Timing belt idler pulley bolt	76	56
Timing belt tensioner pulley bolts	19	14

1 General information

1 This Part of Chapter 2 describes those repair procedures that can reasonably be carried out on the engine while it remains in the car. If the engine has been removed from the car and is being dismantled as described in Part B, any preliminary dismantling procedures can be ignored.

2 Note that, while it may be possible physically to overhaul items such as the piston/connecting rod assemblies while the engine is in the car, such tasks are not normally carried out as separate operations. Usually, several additional procedures (not to mention the cleaning of components and of oilways) have to be carried out. For this reason, all such tasks are classed as major overhaul procedures, and are described in Part B of this Chapter.

3 Part B describes the removal of the engine/transmission unit from the vehicle, and the full overhaul procedures that can then be carried out.

Engine description

4 The engine is of the eight-valve, in-line four-cylinder, single overhead camshaft (SOHC) type, mounted transversely at the front of the car with the transmission attached to its left-hand end.

5 The crankshaft runs in five main bearings. Thrustwashers are fitted to No 2 main bearing (upper half) to control crankshaft endfloat.

6 The connecting rods rotate on horizontally-split bearing shells at their big-ends. The pistons are attached to the connecting rods by gudgeon pins, which are a sliding fit in the connecting rod small-end eyes and retained by circlips. The aluminium-alloy pistons are fitted with three piston rings – two compression rings and an oil control ring.

7 The cylinder block is made of cast iron and the cylinder bores are an integral part of the block. On this type of engine the cylinder bores are sometimes referred to as having dry liners.

8 The inlet and exhaust valves are each closed by coil springs, and operate in guides pressed into the cylinder head.

9 The camshaft is driven by the crankshaft by a timing belt and rotates directly in the head.

The camshaft operates the valves via followers which are situated directly below the camshaft. Valve clearances are adjusted using shims which are fitted between the camshaft and follower.

10 Lubrication is by means of an oil pump, which is driven off the timing belt. It draws oil through a strainer located in the sump, and then forces it through an externally-mounted filter into galleries in the cylinder block/crankcase. From there, the oil is distributed to the crankshaft (main bearings) and camshaft. The big-end bearings are supplied with oil via internal drillings in the crankshaft, while the camshaft bearings also receive a pressurised supply. The camshaft lobes and valves are lubricated by splash, as are all other engine components. An oil cooler is fitted to keep the oil temperature stable under arduous operating conditions.

Repair operations possible with the engine in the car

11 The following work can be carried out with the engine in the car:
a) Compression pressure – testing.
b) Camshaft cover – removal and refitting.
c) Timing belt cover – removal and refitting.
d) Timing belt – removal and refitting.
e) Timing belt tensioner and sprockets – removal and refitting.
f) Valve clearances – checking and adjustment.
g) Camshaft and followers – removal, inspection and refitting.
h) Cylinder head – removal and refitting.
i) Connecting rods and pistons – removal and refitting*.
j) Sump – removal and refitting.
k) Oil pump – removal, overhaul and refitting.
l) Oil cooler – removal and refitting.
m) Crankshaft oil seals – renewal.
n) Engine/transmission mountings – inspection and renewal.
o) Flywheel – removal, inspection and refitting.

* Although the operation marked with an asterisk can be carried out with the engine in the car after removal of the sump, it is better for the engine to be removed, in the interests of cleanliness and improved access. For this reason, the procedure is described in Chapter 2B.

2 Compression test – description and interpretation

Compression test

Note: *A compression tester specifically designed for diesel engines must be used for this test.*

1 When engine performance is down, or if misfiring occurs which cannot be attributed to the fuel system, a compression test can provide diagnostic clues as to the engine's condition. If the test is performed regularly, it can give warning of trouble before any other symptoms become apparent.

2 The tester is connected to an adapter which screws into the glow plug or injector hole. On these models, an adapter suitable for use in the glow plug holes will be required, due to the design of the injectors. It is unlikely to be worthwhile buying such a tester for occasional use, but it may be possible to borrow or hire one – if not, have the test performed by a garage.

3 Unless specific instructions to the contrary are supplied with the tester, observe the following points:
a) *The battery must be in a good state of charge, the air filter must be clean, and the engine should be at normal operating temperature.*
b) *All the glow plugs should be removed before starting the test (see Chapter 5B).*
c) *Release the retaining clip and disconnect the wiring connector from the fuel injection pump control unit (see Chapter 4A) to prevent the engine from running or fuel from being discharged.*

4 There is no need to hold the accelerator pedal down during the test, because the diesel engine air inlet is not throttled.

5 Crank the engine on the starter motor; after one or two revolutions, the compression pressure should build-up to a maximum figure, and then stabilise. Record the highest reading obtained.

6 Repeat the test on the remaining cylinders, recording the pressure in each.

7 All cylinders should produce very similar pressures; any difference greater than that specified indicates the existence of a fault. Note that the compression should build-up

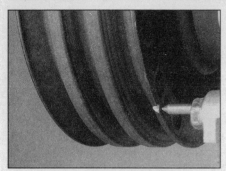

3.5 Align the crankshaft pulley notch with the pointer on the base of the oil pump cover

3.7a Lock the camshaft sprocket in position by screwing an M6 bolt (arrowed) into position . . .

3.7b . . . and lock the injection pump sprocket in position by screwing an M8 bolt (arrowed) into position

quickly in a healthy engine; low compression on the first stroke, followed by gradually-increasing pressure on successive strokes, indicates worn piston rings. A low compression reading on the first stroke, which does not build-up during successive strokes, indicates leaking valves or a blown head gasket (a cracked head could also be the cause). Deposits on the undersides of the valve heads can also cause low compression. **Note:** *The cause of poor compression is less easy to establish on a diesel engine than on a petrol one. The effect of introducing oil into the cylinders ('wet' testing) is not conclusive, because there is a risk that the oil will sit in the swirl chamber or in the recess on the piston crown instead of passing to the rings.*

8 On completion of the test, reconnect the injection pump wiring connector then refit the glow plugs as described in Chapter 5B.

Leakdown test

9 A leakdown test measures the rate at which compressed air fed into the cylinder is lost. It is an alternative to a compression test, and in many ways it is better, since the escaping air provides easy identification of where pressure loss is occurring (piston rings, valves or head gasket).

10 The equipment needed for leakdown testing is unlikely to be available to the home mechanic. If poor compression is suspected, have the test performed by a suitably-equipped garage.

3 Top dead centre (TDC) for No 1 piston – locating

Note: *If the engine is to be locked in position with No 1 piston at TDC on its compression stroke then a M6 and M8 bolt will be required.*

1 In its travel up-and-down its cylinder bore, Top Dead Centre (TDC) is the highest point that each piston reaches as the crankshaft rotates. While each piston reaches TDC both at the top of the compression stroke and again at the top of the exhaust stroke, for the purpose of timing the engine, TDC refers to the piston position (usually number 1) at the top of its compression stroke.

2 Number 1 piston (and cylinder) is at the right-hand (timing belt) end of the engine, and its TDC position is located as follows. Note that the crankshaft rotates clockwise when viewed from the right-hand side of the car.

3 Disconnect the battery negative terminal. To improve access to the crankshaft pulley, apply the handbrake, then jack up the front of the vehicle and support it on axle stands and remove the right-hand front wheel.

4 Remove the timing belt upper cover as described in Section 6.

5 Using a socket and extension bar on the crankshaft sprocket bolt, rotate the crankshaft until the notch on the crankshaft pulley rim is aligned with the pointer on the base of the oil pump cover **(see illustration)**. Once the mark is correctly aligned, No 1 and 4 pistons are at TDC.

6 To determine which piston is at TDC on its compression stroke, check the position of the timing holes in the camshaft and injection pump sprockets. When No 1 piston is at TDC on its compression stroke, both sprocket holes will be aligned with the threaded holes in the cylinder head/block. If the timing holes are 180° out of alignment then No 4 cylinder is at TDC on its compression stroke; rotate the crankshaft through a further complete turn (360°) to bring No 1 cylinder to TDC on its compression stroke.

7 With No 1 piston at TDC on its compression stroke, if necessary, the camshaft and fuel injection pump sprockets can be locked in position. Secure the camshaft sprocket in position by screwing a M6 bolt into the hole in

the cylinder head and lock the injection pump sprocket in position by screwing a M8 bolt into the cylinder block **(see illustrations)**.

4 Camshaft cover – removal and refitting

Removal

1 Release the retaining clip and disconnect the breather hose from the rear of the camshaft cover.

2 Slacken and remove the camshaft cover retaining bolts, along with their spacers, and lift the camshaft cover and seal away from the cylinder head. Remove the semi-circular rubber seal from the cut-out on the left-hand end of the cylinder head upper surface **(see illustration)**.

3 Examine the cover seal and semi-circular seal for signs of damage or deterioration and renew if necessary.

Refitting

4 Ensure the cover and cylinder head surfaces are clean and dry then fit the seal to the cover groove **(see illustration)**.

5 Apply a smear of sealant to the semi-circular cut-out on the left-hand end of the cylinder head then fit the seal to the cut-out.

6 Carefully lower the cover into position, ensuring the seal remains correctly seated. Refit the spacers and retaining bolts and tighten them securely.

4.2 Remove the semi-circular rubber seal from left-hand end of the cylinder head

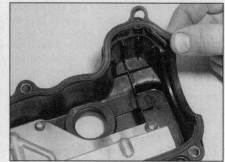

4.4 Ensure the seal is correctly located in the camshaft cover groove

5.4 Refit the crankshaft pulley, locating it on the sprocket pin (arrowed), and refit the retaining bolts

7 Reconnect the breather hose to the rear of the cover and secure in position with the retaining clip.

5 Crankshaft pulley – removal and refitting

Removal

1 Apply the handbrake, then jack up the front of the car and support it on axle stands. Remove the right-hand roadwheel.
2 Remove the auxiliary drivebelts as described in Chapter 1. Prior to removal, mark the direction of rotation on the belts to ensure each belt is refitted the same way around.
3 Slacken and remove the small retaining bolts securing the pulley to the crankshaft sprocket and remove the pulley from the engine. If necessary, prevent crankshaft rotation by holding the sprocket retaining bolt with a suitable socket.

Refitting

4 Refit the pulley to the crankshaft sprocket, aligning the pulley hole with the sprocket locating pin. Refit the pulley retaining bolts, tightening them to the specified torque **(see illustration)**.
5 Refit the auxiliary drivebelt as described in Chapter 1 using the mark made prior to removal to ensure the belt is fitted the correct way around.
6 Refit the roadwheel then lower the car to the ground and tighten the wheel bolts to the specified torque.

6 Timing belt covers – removal and refitting

Removal

Upper cover

1 Apply the handbrake, then jack up the front of the car and support it on axle stands. Remove the right-hand roadwheel.
2 Remove the air cleaner housing as described in Chapter 4A.

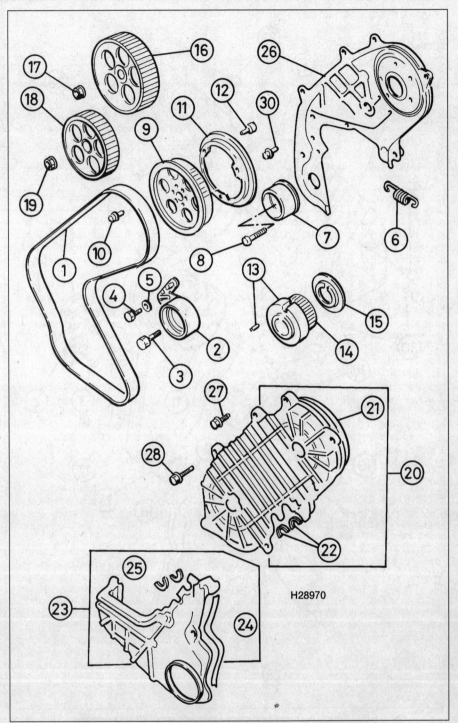

6.6a Timing belt and associated components (1.5 litre engine)

1 Timing belt	11 Camshaft sprocket flange	20 Upper cover
2 Tensioner pulley	12 Flange screw	21 Sealing strip
3 Tensioner bolt	13 Locating pin	22 Sealing strip
4 Tensioner bolt	14 Crankshaft sprocket	23 Lower cover
5 Tensioner washer	15 Flanged spacer	24 Sealing strip
6 Tensioner spring	16 Injection pump sprocket	25 Sealing strip
7 Idler pulley	17 Sprocket nut	26 Rear cover
8 Idler pulley bolt	18 Oil pump sprocket	27 Cover bolt
9 Camshaft sprocket	19 Sprocket nut	28 Cover bolt
10 Camshaft sprocket bolt		30 Cover bolt

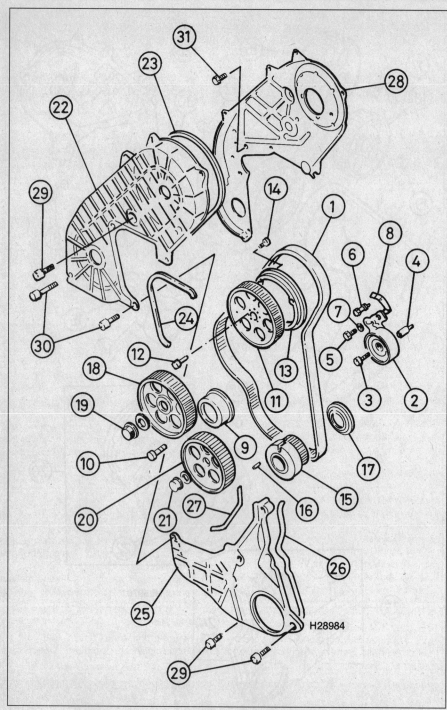

3 Remove the auxiliary drivebelts as described in Chapter 1. Prior to removal, mark the direction of rotation on each belt to ensure it is refitted the same way around.

4 On models equipped with air conditioning, unbolt the compressor drivebelt tensioner and remove it from the engine.

5 Referring to Section 19, support the engine/transmission unit then undo the retaining nuts and lift off the bracket from the right-hand mounting assembly. Unbolt the mounting bracket and remove it from the side of the cylinder block.

6 Slacken and remove the retaining bolts and remove the timing belt upper cover from the engine, along with its rubber sealing strips. Inspect the sealing strips for signs of damage or deterioration and renew if necessary **(see illustrations)**.

Lower cover

7 Remove the upper cover as described in paragraphs 1 to 6.

8 Remove the crankshaft pulley as described in Section 5.

9 Undo the retaining bolts and remove the lower cover from the engine unit, along with its rubber sealing strips. Inspect the sealing strips for signs of damage or deterioration and renew if necessary.

Inner cover

10 Remove the timing belt as described in Section 7.

11 Remove the camshaft sprocket, the fuel injection pump sprocket, the timing belt idler pulley and the tensioner assembly as described in Section 8

12 Unbolt the inner cover from the cylinder head/block and remove it from the engine unit.

Refitting

13 Refitting is the reverse of removal, ensuring the cover sealing strips are correctly fitted and all retaining bolts are tightened securely **(see illustration)**.

6.6b Timing belt and associated components (1.7 litre engine)

1 Timing belt	12 Camshaft sprocket bolt	21 Sprocket nut
2 Tensioner assembly	13 Camshaft sprocket	22 Upper cover
3 Tensioner bolt	flange	23 Sealing strip
4 Tensioner bolt	14 Flange screw	24 Sealing strip
5 Tensioner bolt	15 Crankshaft sprocket	25 Lower cover
6 Spring bolt	16 Locating pin	26 Sealing strip
7 Washer	17 Flanged spacer	27 Sealing strip
8 Tensioner spring	18 Injection pump	28 Rear cover
9 Idler pulley	sprocket	29 Cover bolts
10 Idler pulley bolt	19 Sprocket nut	30 Cover bolts
11 Camshaft sprocket	20 Oil pump sprocket	31 Cover bolts

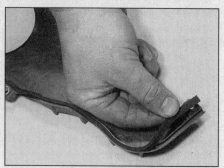

6.13 On refitting ensure the sealing strips are correctly seated in the cover grooves

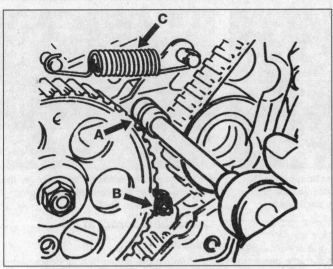

7.4 Release the timing belt tensioner pulley securing bolts (A and B) and remove the spring (C) (1.5 litre engine)

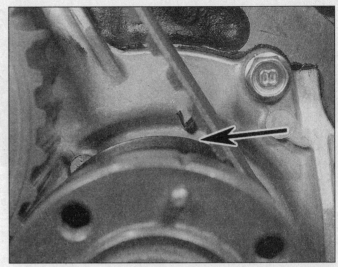

7.7 Check that the crankshaft sprocket cut-out is aligned with the mark on the oil pump cover (arrowed)

7 Timing belt – removal and refitting

Note: *The timing belt must be removed and refitted with the engine cold.*

Removal

1 Position No 1 cylinder at TDC on its compression stroke as described in Section 3. Lock the camshaft and injection pump sprockets in position by screwing the bolts into the threaded holes in the cylinder head/block.

2 Remove the crankshaft pulley as described in Section 5.

3 Unbolt the timing belt lower cover and remove it along with its rubber sealing strips.

4 Slacken the timing belt tensioner retaining bolts then carefully unhook the tensioner spring from its locating pins **(see illustration)**.

5 Slide the timing belt off from its sprockets and remove it from the engine. If the belt is to be re-used, use white paint or similar to mark the direction of rotation on the belt. **Do not** rotate the crankshaft until the timing belt has been refitted.

6 Check the timing belt carefully for any signs of uneven wear, splitting or oil contamination, and renew it if there is the slightest doubt about its condition. If the engine is undergoing an overhaul and is approaching the manufacturer's specified interval for belt renewal (see Chapter 1) renew the belt as a matter of course, regardless of its apparent condition. If signs of oil contamination are found, trace the source of the oil leak and rectify it, then wash down the engine timing belt area and all related components to remove all traces of oil.

Refitting

7 On reassembly, thoroughly clean the timing belt sprockets and ensure the camshaft and injection pump sprockets are locked correctly in position. Temporarily refit the crankshaft pulley to the sprocket and check that the pulley cut-out is still aligned with the pointer on the oil pump cover; the mark on the crankshaft sprocket should also be aligned with the mark on the oil pump cover **(see illustration)**.

8 Remove the pulley and fit the timing belt over the crankshaft, oil pump, injection pump and camshaft sprockets, ensuring that the belt rear run is taut (ie, all slack is on the tensioner pulley side of the belt). Do not twist the belt sharply while refitting it. Ensure that the belt teeth are correctly seated centrally in the sprockets, and that the timing marks remain in alignment. If a used belt is being refitted, ensure that the arrow mark made on removal points in the normal direction of rotation, as before.

9 Check that the tensioner moves freely and tension the belt by refitting the tensioner pulley spring, ensuring it is correctly located on its pins.

10 Check that the crankshaft sprocket timing mark is still correctly positioned then unscrew the locking bolts from the injection pump and camshaft sprockets.

1.7 litre engines

11 Slacken the tensioner pulley retaining bolts then rotate the crankshaft pulley approximately 60° **backwards** (anti-clockwise) to automatically adjust the timing belt tension. Hold the crankshaft pulley stationary and securely tighten the tensioner pulley retaining bolt **(see illustrations)**.

12 Rotate the crankshaft smoothly through two complete turns (720°) in the normal direction of rotation to settle the timing belt in position. Realign the crankshaft sprocket timing mark and check that the camshaft and injection pump sprocket locking bolts can be refitted.

13 Slacken the tensioner pulley retaining bolt then rotate the crankshaft pulley approximately 60° **backwards** (anti-clockwise) to automatically adjust the timing belt tension. Hold the crankshaft pulley stationary and tighten the tensioner pulley retaining bolts to the specified torque.

14 Return the crankshaft to TDC and make a final check that the sprocket timing mark/holes are correctly positioned.

All engines

15 Refit the timing belt covers then refit the crankshaft pulley as described in Sections 5 and 6.

7.11a Rotate the crankshaft 60° backwards to adjust the timing belt tension . . .

7.11b . . . then securely tighten the tensioner pulley bolts (1.7 litre engine)

8.3 Removing the camshaft sprocket (locating pin arrowed)

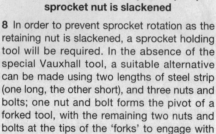

8.8 Using a sprocket holding tool to prevent rotation as the injection pump sprocket nut is slackened

8.10 Remove the sprocket and recover the Woodruff key from the injection pump shaft

8 Timing belt tensioner and sprockets – removal and refitting

Camshaft sprocket

Removal

1 Remove the timing belt as described in Section 7.

2 Screw the sprocket locking bolt fully into position then slacken and remove the sprocket retaining bolts, using the locking bolt to prevent rotation.

3 Unscrew the locking bolt and remove the sprocket from the end of the camshaft, noting which way around it is fitted **(see illustration)**. If the sprocket locating pin is a loose fit, remove it from the camshaft end and store it with the sprocket for safe-keeping.

Refitting

4 Ensure the locating pin is in position then refit the sprocket to the camshaft end aligning its locating hole with the pin.

5 Refit the sprocket retaining bolts then align the timing hole with the cylinder head hole and screw in the lock bolt. Use the locking bolt to retain the sprocket and tighten the sprocket bolts securely.

6 Refit the timing belt as described in Section 7.

Injection pump sprocket

Removal

7 Remove the timing belt as described in Section 7.

8 In order to prevent sprocket rotation as the retaining nut is slackened, a sprocket holding tool will be required. In the absence of the special Vauxhall tool, a suitable alternative can be made using two lengths of steel strip (one long, the other short), and three nuts and bolts; one nut and bolt forms the pivot of a forked tool, with the remaining two nuts and bolts at the tips of the 'forks' to engage with the sprocket spokes **(see illustration)**.

9 Unscrew the pulley locking bolt and slacken the sprocket retaining nut whilst using the tool to prevent rotation. **Do not** be tempted to use the locking bolt to prevent sprocket rotation.

10 Remove the sprocket from the injection pump shaft, noting which way around it is fitted. If the Woodruff key is a loose fit in the pump shaft, remove it and store it with the sprocket for safe-keeping **(see illustration)**. **Note:** *The sprocket is a tapered-fit on the injection pump shaft and in some cases a suitable puller may be needed to free it from the shaft.*

Refitting

11 Ensure the Woodruff key is correctly fitted to the pump shaft then refit the sprocket, aligning the sprocket groove with the key.

12 Refit the retaining nut and tighten it to the specified torque whilst using the holding tool to prevent rotation.

13 Align the sprocket timing hole with the threaded hole in the cylinder block and screw in the locking bolt.

14 Refit the timing belt as described in Section 7.

Crankshaft sprocket

Removal

15 Remove the timing belt as described in Section 7.

16 Slacken the crankshaft sprocket retaining bolt. To prevent crankshaft rotation, have an assistant select top gear and apply the brakes firmly. If the engine is removed from the vehicle it will be necessary to lock the flywheel (see Section 17).

17 Unscrew the retaining bolt and washer and remove the crankshaft sprocket from the end of the crankshaft. If the sprocket is a tight fit, draw it off of the crankshaft using a suitable puller **(see illustrations)**. If the Woodruff key is a loose fit in the crankshaft, remove it and store it with the sprocket for safe-keeping.

18 Slide the flanged spacer off of the crankshaft, noting which way around it is fitted **(see illustration)**.

Refitting

19 Refit the flanged spacer to the crankshaft with its convex surface facing away from the oil pump housing.

20 Ensure the Woodruff key is correctly fitted then slide on the crankshaft sprocket aligning its groove with the key.

21 Refit the retaining bolt and washer then lock the crankshaft by the method used on removal, and tighten the sprocket retaining bolt to the specified torque setting.

22 Refit the timing belt as described in Section 7.

8.17a Unscrew the retaining bolt and washer . . .

8.17b . . . and remove the crankshaft sprocket from the engine

8.18 Slide off the flanged spacer noting which way around it is fitted

8.24 Lock the oil pump sprocket in position using a socket and extension bar then unscrew the sprocket retaining nut

8.29 Unscrew the retaining bolts and remove the tensioner assembly (1.7 litre engine)

8.33 Removing the idler pulley

Oil pump sprocket

Removal

23 Remove the timing belt as described in Section 7.

24 Prevent the oil pump sprocket from rotating using a socket and extension bar fitted to one of the oil pump cover bolts then slacken and remove the sprocket retaining nut **(see illustration)**.

25 Remove the sprocket from the oil pump shaft, noting which way around it is fitted.

Refitting

26 Refit the sprocket, aligning it with the flat on the pump shaft, and fit the retaining nut. Tighten the sprocket retaining nut to the specified torque, using the socket and extension bar to prevent rotation.

27 Refit the timing belt as described in Section 7.

Tensioner assembly

Removal

28 Remove the timing belt as described in Section 7.

29 Unscrew the retaining bolts and remove the tensioner assembly from the engine **(see illustration)**.

Refitting

30 Fit the tensioner assembly to the engine tightening its retaining bolts by hand only.

31 Refit the timing belt as described in Section 7.

Idler pulley

Removal

32 Remove the timing belt as described in Section 7.

33 Slacken and remove the retaining bolt and remove the idler pulley from the engine **(see illustration)**.

Refitting

34 Refit the idler pulley and tighten the retaining bolt to the specified torque.

35 Refit the timing belt as described in Section 7.

9 Camshaft oil seal – renewal

1 Remove the camshaft sprocket as described in Section 8.

2 Slacken and remove the bolts securing the timing belt rear cover to the cylinder head and block and ease the cover away from the head to gain access to the oil seal **(see illustration)**. To gain full access to the seal, remove the rear cover as described in Section 6.

3 Carefully punch or drill two small holes opposite each other in the oil seal. Screw a self-tapping screw into each, and pull on the screws with pliers to extract the seal.

4 Clean the seal housing, and polish off any burrs or raised edges which may have caused the seal to fail in the first place.

5 Lubricate the lips of the new seal with clean engine oil, and press it into position using a suitable tubular drift (such as a socket) which bears only on the hard outer edge of the seal. Take care not to damage the seal lips during fitting; note that the seal lips should face inwards.

6 Refit the timing belt rear cover bolts, tightening them securely.

7 Refit the camshaft sprocket as described in Section 8.

10 Valve clearances – checking and adjustment

Checking

1 The importance of having the valve clearances correctly adjusted cannot be over-stressed, as they vitally affect the performance of the engine. Checking should not be regarded as a routine operation, however. It should only be necessary when the valve gear has become noisy, after engine overhaul, or when trying to trace the cause of power loss. The engine must be cold for the check to be accurate. The clearances are checked as follows.

2 Apply the handbrake, then jack up the front of the car and support it on axle stands.

Remove the right-hand front roadwheel to gain access to the crankshaft pulley.

3 Remove the camshaft cover as described in Section 4.

4 Using a socket and extension on the crankshaft sprocket bolt, rotate the crankshaft in the normal direction of rotation (clockwise when viewed from the right-hand end of the engine) until the notch on the crankshaft pulley is correctly aligned with the pointer on the base of the oil pump cover. **Note:** *The engine will be easier to turn if the fuel injectors or glow plugs are removed.*

5 Check that the camshaft lobes of No 1 cylinder (nearest the timing belt end of the engine) are pointing away from the followers indicating No 1 cylinder is at TDC on its compression stroke. If the lobes are pointing downwards, rotate the crankshaft through one more complete turn (360º) and realign the notch and pointer.

6 On a piece of paper, draw the outline of the engine with the cylinders numbered from the timing belt end. Show the position of each valve, together with the specified valve clearance. Since the clearance is different for inlet and exhaust valves – make sure that you are aware which valve you are dealing with. The valve sequence from the timing belt end of the engine is:

In – Ex – In – Ex – In – Ex – In – Ex

7 With No 1 cylinder at TDC on its compression stroke, using feeler blades, measure the clearance between the base of both No 1 cylinder cam lobes and their followers and record the clearances on the paper.

9.2 Timing belt rear cover-to-cylinder head bolts (arrowed)

10.14 With the camshaft lobe pointing upwards, depress the follower and carefully remove the shim

10.15 The thickness of each shim should be stamped on one of its surfaces

11 Camshaft and followers – removal, inspection and refitting

8 Rotate the crankshaft pulley through a half a turn (180°) to position No 3 cylinder at TDC on its compression stroke. Measure the clearance between the base of both No 3 cylinder cam lobes and their followers and record the clearances on the paper.

9 Rotate the crankshaft pulley through a half a turn (180°) and realign the pulley notch with the pointer so that No 4 cylinder is at TDC on its compression stroke. Measure the clearance between the base of both No 4 cylinder cam lobes and their followers and record the clearances on the paper.

10 Rotate the crankshaft pulley through a half a turn (180°) to position No 2 cylinder at TDC on its compression stroke. Measure the clearance between the base of both No 2 cylinder cam lobes and their followers and record the clearances on the paper.

11 If all the clearances are correct (or within 0.02 mm – the difference between shim sizes), refit the cylinder head cover (see Section 4), then refit the roadwheel and lower the vehicle to the ground and tighten the wheel bolts to the specified torque. If any clearance measured is not correct, adjustment must be carried out as described in the following paragraphs.

Adjustment

12 Rotate the crankshaft pulley until the lobe of the valve to be adjusted is pointing directly away from the follower.

13 Rotate the follower until the groove on its upper edge is facing towards the front of the engine.

14 In the absence of the special Vauxhall tool (KM-650), position a large flat-bladed screwdriver between the edge of the follower and the base of the camshaft. Use the screwdriver to carefully depress the follower until there is enough clearance to allow the shim to be slid out from between the follower and camshaft (a magnetic tool is particularly useful for this task) **(see illustration)**.

15 Clean the shim, and measure its thickness with a micrometer. The shims carry thickness markings, but wear may have reduced the original thickness, so be sure to check **(see illustration)**.

16 Add the measured clearance of the valve

to the thickness of the original shim then subtract the specified valve clearance from this figure. This will give you the thickness of the shim required. For example:

Clearance measured of valve	0.35 mm
Plus thickness of the original shim	2.70 mm
Equals	3.05 mm
Minus clearance required	0.25 mm
Thickness of shim required	2.80 mm

17 Obtain the correct thickness of shim required and lubricate it with clean engine oil. Carefully depress the follower and slide the shim into position, with the thickness number downwards, ensuring it is correctly located. Keep a note of all the shim thicknesses to assist valve clearance adjustment when they need to be done again.

> **HAYNES HINT** *It may be possible to correct the clearances by moving the shims around between the valves, but don't turn the engine with any shims missing.*

18 Repeat the procedure given in paragraphs 12 to 17 on the remaining valves which require adjustment.

19 Rotate the crankshaft a few times to settle all shims in position the recheck the valve clearances before refitting the camshaft cover (see Section 4).

20 Refit the roadwheel then lower the vehicle to the ground and tighten the wheel bolts to the specified torque.

11.5 Remove the camshaft bearing caps noting each caps identification marking (arrowed)

Removal

1 Remove the camshaft cover as described in Section 4.

2 Remove the camshaft sprocket as described in Section 8.

3 Slacken and remove the bolts securing the timing belt rear cover to the cylinder head.

4 Working in the **reverse** of the tightening sequence **(see illustration 11.16)**, slacken the camshaft bearing cap retaining nuts by one turn at a time, to relieve the pressure of the valve springs on the bearing caps gradually and evenly. Once the valve spring pressure has been relieved, the nuts can be fully unscrewed and removed.

Caution: If the bearing cap nuts are carelessly slackened, the bearing caps might break. If any bearing cap breaks then the complete cylinder head assembly must be renewed; the bearing caps are matched to the head and are not available separately.

5 Remove the bearing caps, noting each caps correct fitted location. The bearing caps are numbered 1 to 5 and the arrow on each cap points towards the timing belt end of the engine **(see illustration)**.

6 Lift the camshaft out of the cylinder head and slide off the oil seal.

7 Obtain eight small, clean plastic containers, and label them for identification. Alternatively, divide a larger container into compartments. Lift the followers and shims out from the top of the cylinder head and store each one in its respective fitted position. Make sure the followers and shims are not mixed to ensure the valve clearances remain correctly adjusted on refitting.

Inspection

8 Examine the camshaft bearing surfaces and cam lobes for signs of wear ridges and scoring. Renew the camshaft if any of these conditions are apparent. Examine the condition of the bearing surfaces both on the camshaft journals and in the cylinder head. If the head bearing surfaces are worn excessively, the cylinder head will need to be renewed.

9 Support the camshaft end journals on V-blocks, and measure the run-out at the centre journal using a dial gauge. If the run-out exceeds the specified limit, the camshaft should be renewed.

10 Examine the followers and their bores in the cylinder head for signs of wear or damage. If any follower is visibly worn it should be renewed.

Refitting

11 Where removed, lubricate the followers with clean engine oil and carefully insert each

11.11a Refit each follower to the cylinder head . . .

11.11b . . . and refit the shim, ensuring it is correctly seated

11.12 Lubricate the bearings with clean engine oil then lay the camshaft in position

one into its original location in the cylinder head. Ensure each shim is correctly located in the top of the its relevant follower (see illustrations).

12 Lubricate the camshaft followers with clean engine oil then lay the camshaft in position (see illustration). Ensure the crankshaft pulley notch is still correctly aligned with the pointer on the oil pump cover and the injection pump sprocket is locked in position. Position the camshaft so that the lobes of No 1 cylinder are pointing upwards and the sprocket locating pin is uppermost.

13 Ensure the mating surfaces of the bearing caps and cylinder head are clean and dry and lubricate the camshaft journals and lobes with clean engine oil.

14 Apply a smear of sealant to the areas of the cylinder head No 1 bearing cap mating surface, on each side of the camshaft end (see illustration).

15 Refit the camshaft bearing caps in their original locations on the cylinder head. The caps are numbered 1 to 5 (No 1 cap being at the timing belt end of the engine) and the arrow cast onto the top of each cap should point towards the timing belt end of the engine.

16 Refit the bearing cap nuts, tightening them by hand only. Working in the specified sequence, tighten the nuts by one turn at a time to gradually impose the pressure of the valve springs on the bearing caps (see

illustration). Repeat this sequence until all bearing caps are in contact with the cylinder head then go around in the specified sequence and tighten them to the specified torque.

Caution: If the bearing cap bolts are carelessly tightened, the bearing caps might break. If any bearing cap breaks then the complete cylinder head assembly must be renewed; the bearing caps are matched to the head and are not available separately.

17 Fit a new camshaft oil seal as described in Section 9.

18 Refit the timing belt rear cover retaining bolts and tighten them securely.

19 Refit the camshaft sprocket and timing belt as described in Sections 7 and 8.

20 Check the valve clearances as described in Section 10 then refit the camshaft cover as described in Section 4.

12 Cylinder head – removal and refitting

Caution: Be careful not to allow dirt into the fuel injection pump or injector pipes during this procedure.

Note: New cylinder head bolts will be required on refitting.

Removal

1 Drain the cooling system as described in Chapter 1.

2 Remove the inlet and exhaust manifolds as described in Chapter 4A.

3 Remove the camshaft sprocket as described in Section 8.

4 Slacken and remove the bolts securing the timing belt rear cover to the end of the cylinder head.

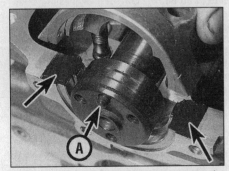

11.14 Apply sealant to the cylinder head mating surface of No 1 camshaft bearing cap (arrowed) then refit the caps ensuring the camshaft locating pin is correctly positioned (A)

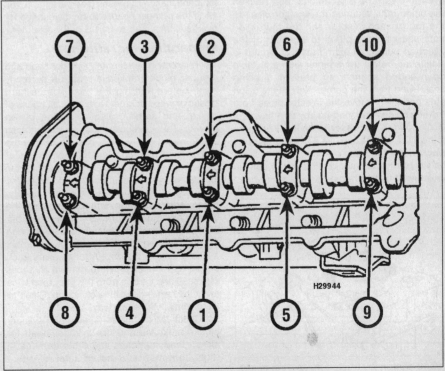

H29944

11.16 Camshaft bearing cap tightening sequence

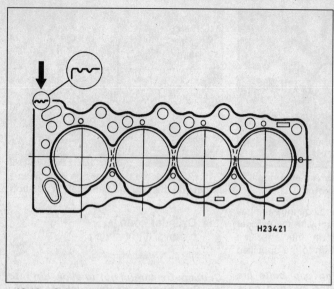

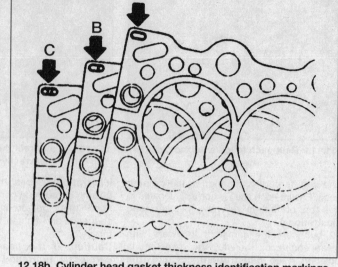

12.18a Cylinder head gasket thickness identification markings (1.5 litre engine)

One notch – 1.35 mm thickness
Two notches – 1.40 mm thickness
Three notches – 1.45 mm thickness

12.18b Cylinder head gasket thickness identification markings (1.7 litre engine)

A No hole – 1.40 mm thickness
B One hole – 1.45 mm thickness
C Two holes – 1.50 mm thickness

5 Release the retaining clips and disconnect the coolant hoses from thermostat housing and cylinder head.

6 Undo the retaining nut and disconnect the wiring connector from the glow plug.

7 Disconnect the wiring connectors from the coolant temperature sensors then free the wiring from its retaining clips and position it clear of the cylinder head.

8 Wipe clean the pipe unions then slacken the union nuts securing the injector pipes to the top of each injector and the four union nuts securing the pipes to the rear of the injection pump; as each pump union nut is slackened, retain the adapter with a suitable open-ended spanner to prevent it being unscrewed from the pump. With all the union nuts undone, remove the injector pipes from the engine unit and mop up any spilt fuel.

9 Working in the **reverse** of the sequence shown in illustration 12.27, progressively slacken the ten main cylinder head bolts by half a turn at a time, until all bolts can be unscrewed by hand.

12.19 Piston protrusion measuring points (arrowed)

10 Lift out the cylinder head bolts and recover the washers.

11 Lift the cylinder head away; seek assistance if possible, as it is a heavy assembly. Remove the gasket, noting the two locating dowels fitted to the top of the cylinder block. If they are a loose fit, remove the locating dowels and store them with the head for safe-keeping. Keep the head gasket for identification purposes (see paragraph 18).

12 If the cylinder head is to be dismantled for overhaul, then refer to Part B of this Chapter.

Preparation for refitting

13 The mating faces of the cylinder head and cylinder block/crankcase must be perfectly clean before refitting the head. Use a hard plastic or wood scraper to remove all traces of gasket and carbon; also clean the piston crowns. Take particular care, as the surfaces are damaged easily. Also, make sure that the carbon is not allowed to enter the oil and water passages – this is particularly important for the lubrication system, as carbon could block the oil supply to any of the engine's components. Using adhesive tape and paper, seal the water, oil and bolt holes in the cylinder block/crankcase. To prevent carbon entering the gap between the pistons and bores, smear a little grease in the gap. After cleaning each piston, use a small brush to remove all traces of grease and carbon from the gap, then wipe away the remainder with a clean rag. Clean all the pistons in the same way.

14 Check the mating surfaces of the cylinder block/crankcase and the cylinder head for nicks, deep scratches and other damage. If slight, they may be removed carefully with a file, but if excessive, machining may be the only alternative to renewal.

15 Ensure that the cylinder head bolt holes in the crankcase are clean and free of oil. Syringe or soak up any oil left in the bolt holes. This is most important in order that the correct bolt tightening torque can be applied and to prevent the possibility of the block being cracked by hydraulic pressure when the bolts are tightened.

16 The cylinder head bolts must be discarded and renewed, regardless of their apparent condition.

17 If warpage of the cylinder head gasket surface is suspected, use a straight-edge to check it for distortion. Refer to Part B of this Chapter if necessary.

18 On this engine, the cylinder head-to-piston clearance is controlled by fitting different thickness head gaskets. The gasket thickness can be determined by looking at the left-hand front corner of gasket and checking on the number of notches holes **(see illustrations)**. The correct thickness of gasket required is selected by measuring the piston protrusions as follows.

19 Ensure that the crankshaft is still correctly positioned in the TDC position. Mount a dial test indicator securely on the block so that its pointer can be easily pivoted between the piston crown and block mating surface. Zero the dial test indicator on the gasket surface of the cylinder block then carefully move the indicator over No 1 piston and measure its protrusion at the three points shown **(see illustration)**. Repeat this procedure on No 4 piston.

20 Rotate the crankshaft half a turn (180°) to bring No 2 and 3 pistons to TDC. Ensure the crankshaft is accurately positioned then measure the protrusions of No 2 and 3 pistons at the specified points. Once both pistons

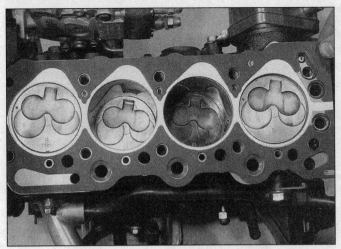

12.23 Fit a new gasket to the cylinder block

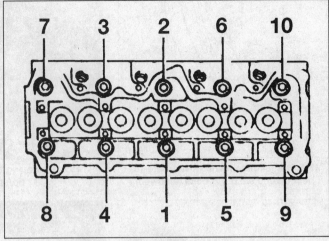

12.27 Cylinder head bolt tightening sequence

have been measured, rotate the crankshaft through a further one and a half turns (540°) to bring No 1 and 4 pistons back to TDC.

21 Find out the average piston protrusion by adding up the 12 different measurements taken (three for each piston) and dividing the total by 12. Using this average measurement, select the correct thickness of head gasket required using the information in the Specifications. **Note:** *If any one of the piston protrusion measurements taken exceeds the average protrusion by more than 0.05 mm, select the gasket from the next available thickness up from the average. For example, if the average protrusion is 0.59 mm but one of the protrusion measurements taken was 0.67 mm (a difference of 0.08 mm) then use a 1.45 mm thick gasket instead of a 1.40 mm thick gasket.*

Refitting

22 Wipe clean the mating surfaces of the cylinder head and cylinder block/crankcase.
23 Check that the two locating dowels are in position then fit a new gasket to the cylinder block **(see illustration)**.
24 Ensure the crankshaft pulley notch is still correctly aligned with the pointer on the oil pump cover with No 1 and 4 pistons at TDC

12.28 Use an angle-tightening gauge to ensure accuracy when tightening the cylinder head bolts

and the camshaft is correctly positioned with the lobes of No 1 cylinder pointing upwards and the camshaft sprocket locating pin uppermost.

25 With the aid of an assistant, carefully refit the cylinder head assembly to the block, aligning it with the locating dowels.
26 Apply a smear of oil to the threads and the underside of the heads of the new cylinder head bolts and carefully enter each bolt into its relevant hole (*do not drop them in*). Screw all bolts in, by hand only, until finger-tight.
27 Working progressively and in the sequence shown, tighten the cylinder head bolts to their Stage 1 torque setting, using a torque wrench and suitable socket **(see illustration)**.
28 Once all bolts have been tightened to the Stage 1 torque, working again in the specified sequence, go around and tighten all bolts through the specified Stage 2 angle. It is recommended that an angle-measuring gauge is used to ensure accuracy **(see illustration)**. If a gauge is not available, use white paint to make alignment marks prior to tightening; the marks can then be used to check that the bolt has been rotated through the correct angle.
29 Finally go around again in the specified sequence and angle tighten the bolts through the specified Stage 3 angle.
30 Refit the injector pipes to the engine unit and tighten the union nuts to the specified torque setting (see Chapter 4A).
31 Ensure the wiring is correctly routed and reconnect the connectors to the coolant temperature sensors. Reconnect the glow plug wiring and securely tighten its retaining nut.
32 Reconnect all coolant hoses to the cylinder head and thermostat housing, ensuring each one is securely held by its retaining clip.
33 Refit the bolts securing the timing belt cover to the cylinder head and tighten them securely.

34 Refit the camshaft sprocket and timing belt as described in Sections 7 and 8.
35 Refit the inlet and exhaust manifolds as described in Chapter 4A.
36 On completion refill the cooling system as described in Chapter 1.

13 Sump – removal and refitting

Removal

1 Disconnect the battery negative terminal.
2 Firmly apply the handbrake then jack up the front of the car and support it on axle stands. Where necessary, undo the retaining screws and remove the undercover from beneath the engine/transmission unit.
3 Drain the engine oil as described in Chapter 1, then fit a new sealing washer and refit the drain plug, tightening it to the specified torque.
4 Slacken and remove the bolts securing the sump lower pan to the main casting then remove the sump pan from underneath the vehicle **(see illustration)**.
5 To remove the main casting from the engine, remove the exhaust system front pipe as described in Chapter 4A.

13.4 If the lower pan is stuck to the main casting, carefully ease it away using a wide-bladed scraper

13.6 Remove the lower cover plate-to-bellhousing securing bolts (arrowed)

13.8 Removing the oil pump pick-up/strainer

13.10 On refitting fit a new sealing ring to the oil pump pick-up/strainer

13.12 Apply a coat of sealant to the main casting upper surface prior to refitting

6 Undo the retaining bolts and remove the flywheel lower cover plate from the base of the transmission unit **(see illustration)**.

7 Progressively slacken and remove the nuts and bolts securing the main casting to the base of the cylinder block/oil pump cover. Break the joint by striking the casting with the palm of the hand, then lower it away from the engine and withdraw it from underneath the vehicle.

8 While the sump main casting is removed, take the opportunity to check the oil pump pick-up/strainer for signs of clogging or splitting. If necessary, unbolt the pick-up/strainer and remove it from the engine along with its sealing ring **(see illustration)**. The strainer can then be cleaned easily in solvent or renewed.

Refitting

9 Remove all traces of dirt and oil from the

mating surfaces of the sump main casting and pan, the cylinder block and (where removed) the pick-up/strainer.

10 Where necessary, fit a new sealing ring to the oil pump pick-up/strainer and fit the strainer to the base of the cylinder block **(see illustration)**. Refit the strainer retaining bolt and tighten it to the specified torque.

11 Ensure the main casting and cylinder block mating surfaces are clean and dry and apply a coat of suitable sealant to the upper mating surface of the casting.

12 Offer up the main casting and loosely refit all the retaining nuts and bolts **(see illustration)**. Working out from the centre in a diagonal sequence, progressively tighten the main casting retaining bolts securely.

13 Refit the flywheel lower cover plate and tighten its retaining bolts securely.

14 Refit the exhaust front pipe as described in Chapter 4A.

15 Ensure the main casting and sump pan mating surfaces are clean and dry and apply a coat of suitable sealant to the upper mating surface of the pan. Refit the pan to the base of the main casting and tighten its retaining bolts securely.

16 Lower the vehicle to the ground then fill the engine with fresh oil, with reference to Chapter 1.

14 Oil pump – removal, inspection and refitting

Note: *The oil pressure relief valve is screwed into the cylinder block and can be removed without disturbing the pump (see paragraph 7).*

Removal

1 Remove the timing belt as described in Section 7.

2 Remove the oil pump and crankshaft timing belt sprockets as described in Section 8.

3 Remove the sump main casting as described in Section 13.

4 Slacken and remove the retaining bolts then slide the oil pump cover off of the end of the crankshaft, taking great care not to lose the locating dowels. Remove the sealing ring which is fitted around the oil pump housing section of the cover and discard it.

5 Using a suitable marker pen, mark the surface of the pump outer rotor; the mark can then be used to ensure the rotor is refitted the correct way around.

6 Remove the oil pump inner and outer rotors from the cylinder block **(see illustrations)**.

7 If necessary, unscrew the oil pressure relief valve assembly from the rear of the cylinder block, where it is located on the right-hand side of the injection pump lower mounting bracket **(see illustration)**. Remove the sealing ring.

Inspection

8 Clean the components, and carefully examine the rotors, pump housing and cover for any signs of scoring or wear. Renew any component which shows signs of wear or damage. If the pump housing in the cylinder block is marked then seek the advice of a Vauxhall dealer on the best course of action.

14.6a Remove the oil pump inner rotor . . .

14.6b . . . and outer rotor from the cylinder block

14.7 Removing the oil pressure relief valve from the cylinder block

9 If the components appear serviceable, fit the rotors into the housing and measure the clearance between the outer rotor and pump housing, and the inner rotor tip-to-outer rotor clearance using feeler blades (**see illustrations**). Also measure the rotor endfloat, and check the flatness of the end cover. If the clearances exceed the specified tolerances, renew the worn components.

10 If the relief valve has been removed, check that the valve piston is free to move easily and return smoothly under spring pressure (**see illustration**). If not renew the valve assembly.

Refitting

11 Where removed, fit a new sealing ring to the oil pressure relief valve then refit the valve assembly to the cylinder block and tighten it to the specified torque setting.

12 Lubricate the pump rotors with clean engine oil and refit them to the pump housing, using the mark made prior to removal to ensure the outer rotor is fitted the correct way around.

13 Prior to refitting, carefully lever out the crankshaft and oil pump oil seals using a flat-bladed screwdriver. Fit the new oil seals, ensuring that each seal's sealing lip is facing inwards, and press them squarely into the housing using a tubular drift which bears only on the hard outer edge of the seal. Press each seal into position so that it is flush with the housing then lubricate the oil seal lips with clean engine oil.

14 Ensure the mating surfaces of the oil pump and cylinder block are clean and dry and the locating dowels are in position. Remove all traces of sealant from the threads of the pump cover bolts.

15 Apply a smear of sealant to the oil pump cover mating surface. Coat the new oil pump sealing ring with the same sealant and seat the sealing ring in the cover groove (**see illustration**).

16 Carefully manoeuvre the oil pump cover

14.9a Using a feeler blade to measure inner rotor tip-to-outer rotor clearance

into position, taking great care not to damage the oil seal lips on the crankshaft and inner rotor shaft. Locate the cover on the dowels making sure the pump sealing ring remains correctly positioned.

17 Apply a smear of sealant to the threads of each cover retaining bolt then refit all bolts and tighten them securely.

18 Refit the timing belt sprockets and belt as described in Sections 7 and 8 then refit the sump as described in Section 13.

19 On completion refill the engine with clean oil as described in Chapter 1.

14.9b Checking outer rotor-to-pump housing clearance with a feeler blade

4 Lubricate the lips of the new seal with clean engine oil, and press it into position using a suitable tubular drift (such as a socket) which bears only on the hard outer edge of the seal. Take care not to damage the seal lips during fitting; note that the seal lips should face inwards.

5 Refit the oil pump sprocket as described in Section 8.

15 Oil pump seal – renewal

1 Remove the oil pump sprocket as described in Section 8.

2 Carefully punch or drill two small holes opposite each other in the oil seal. Screw a self-tapping screw into each, and pull on the screws with pliers to extract the seal.

Caution: Great care must be taken to avoid damage to the oil pump.

3 Clean the seal housing, and polish off any burrs or raised edges which may have caused the seal to fail in the first place.

16 Oil cooler – removal and refitting

Removal

1 Firmly apply the handbrake, then jack up the front of the vehicle and support it on axle stands. Where necessary, undo the retaining screws and remove the undercover to gain access to the oil cooler which is situated on the rear of the cylinder block.

2 Drain the cooling system as described in Chapter 1. Alternatively, clamp the oil cooler coolant hoses directly above the cooler, and be prepared for some coolant loss as the hoses are disconnected.

3 Position a suitable container beneath the oil filter. Unscrew the filter using an oil filter removal tool if necessary, and drain the oil

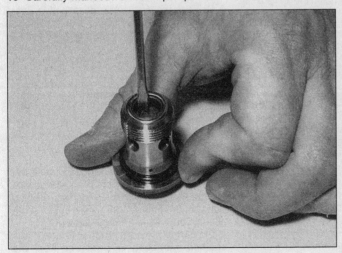

14.10 Checking the oil pressure relief valve

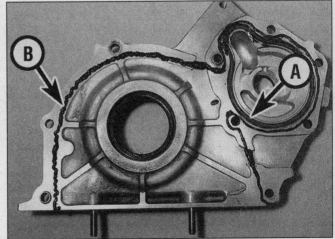

14.15 Coat the pump cover sealing ring (A) with sealant and apply a smear of sealant to the cover mating surface (B)

17.2 Fabricate a locking tool to retain the flywheel

17.3 Remove the retaining bolts and lift off the retaining plate

17.10 Use an angle-tighten gauge to ensure accuracy when tightening the flywheel bolts

into the container. If the oil filter is damaged or distorted during removal, it must be renewed. Given the low cost of a new oil filter relative to the cost of repairing the damage which could result if a re-used filter springs a leak, it is probably a good idea to renew the filter in any case.

4 Release the clips and disconnect the coolant hoses from the oil cooler.

5 Note the correct fitted location of the oil cooler unions then unscrew the centre bolt and remove the cooler from the cylinder block. Discard the oil cooler sealing ring; a new one must be used on refitting.

Refitting

6 Fit a new sealing ring to the recess in the rear of the cooler, then offer the cooler to the cylinder block.

7 Ensure that the oil cooler unions are correctly positioned, then refit the centre bolt and tighten it to the specified torque.

8 Reconnect the coolant hoses to the cooler and secure them in position with the retaining clips.

9 Fit the oil filter, then lower the vehicle to the ground. Top-up the engine oil level as described in *Weekly checks*.

10 Refill or top-up the cooling system as described in *Weekly checks* or Chapter 1 (as applicable). Start the engine, and check the oil cooler for signs of leakage.

17 Flywheel – removal, inspection and refitting

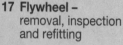

Note: *New flywheel retaining bolts will be required on refitting.*

Removal

1 Remove the transmission as described in Chapter 7 then remove the clutch assembly as described in Chapter 6.

2 Prevent the flywheel from turning by locking the ring gear teeth with a similar arrangement to that shown **(see illustration)**. Alternatively, bolt a strap between the flywheel and the cylinder block/crankcase. Make alignment marks between the flywheel and crankshaft using paint or a suitable marker pen.

3 Slacken and remove the retaining bolts and retaining plate then remove the flywheel **(see illustration)**. Do not drop it, as it is very heavy.

Inspection

4 Examine the flywheel for wear or chipping of the ring gear teeth. Renewal of the ring gear is possible but is not a task for the home mechanic; renewal requires the new ring gear to be heated (up to 180° to 230°C) to allow it to be fitted.

5 Examine the flywheel for scoring of the clutch face. If the clutch face is scored, the flywheel may be surface-ground, but renewal is preferable.

6 If there is any doubt about the condition of the flywheel, seek the advice of a Vauxhall dealer or engine reconditioning specialist. They will be able to advise if it is possible to recondition it or whether renewal is necessary.

Refitting

7 Clean the mating surfaces of the flywheel and crankshaft.

8 Apply a drop of locking compound to the threads of each of the new flywheel retaining bolts then refit the flywheel and retaining plate and install the new bolts. If the original is being refitted align the marks made prior to removal.

9 Lock the flywheel using the method employed on dismantling then, working in a diagonal sequence, evenly and progressively tighten the retaining bolts to the specified Stage 1 torque setting.

10 Once all bolts have been tightened to the Stage 1 torque, go around and tighten all bolts through the specified Stage 2 angle. It is recommended that an angle-measuring gauge is used during the final stages of the tightening, to ensure accuracy **(see illustration)**. If a gauge is not available, use white paint to make alignment marks prior to tightening; the marks can then be used to check that the bolt has been rotated through the correct angle.

11 Refit the clutch as described in Chapter 6 then remove the locking tool and refit the transmission as described in Chapter 7.

18 Crankshaft oil seals – renewal

Right-hand (timing belt end)

1 Remove the crankshaft sprocket as described in Section 8.

2 Carefully punch or drill two small holes opposite each other in the oil seal. Screw a self-tapping screw into each and pull on the screws with pliers to extract the seal.

3 Clean the seal housing and polish off any burrs or raised edges which may have caused the seal to fail in the first place.

4 Lubricate the lips of the new seal with clean engine oil and ease it into position on the end of the shaft. Press the seal squarely into position until it is flush with the housing. If necessary, a suitable tubular drift, such as a socket, which bears only on the hard outer edge of the seal can be used to tap the seal into position. Take great care not to damage the seal lips during fitting and ensure that the seal lips face inwards.

5 Wash off any traces of oil, then refit the crankshaft sprocket as described in Section 8.

Left-hand (flywheel end)

6 Remove the flywheel as described in Section 17.

7 Renew the seal as described in paragraphs 2 to 4.

8 Refit the flywheel as described in Section 17.

19 Engine/transmission mountings – inspection and renewal

Inspection

1 If improved access is required, raise the front of the car and support it securely on axle stands. Where necessary, undo the retaining bolts and remove the undercover from beneath the engine/transmission unit.

2 Check the mounting rubber to see if it is cracked, hardened or separated from the metal at any point; renew the mounting if any such damage or deterioration is evident.

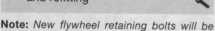
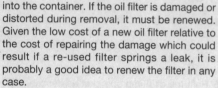

3 Check that all the mounting fasteners are securely tightened; use a torque wrench to check if possible **(see illustration)**.

4 Using a large screwdriver or a pry bar, check for wear in the mounting by carefully levering against it to check for free play; where this is not possible, enlist the aid of an assistant to move the engine/transmission unit back-and-forth, or from side-to-side, while you watch the mounting. While some free play is to be expected, even from new components, excessive wear should be obvious.

5 If excessive free play is found, check first that the fasteners are correctly secured, then renew any worn components as described below.

Renewal

Note: *Vauxhall recommend that both the right-hand and left-hand mountings should be renewed at the same time if either one is damaged.*

6 The flexible mountings can be renewed if they have deteriorated. To facilitate removal, take the weight of the engine/transmission on a hoist, or use a jack with a protective wooden block from below. Only remove and refit one mounting at a time.

7 With the mounting refitted, only nip up the retaining bolts at first, then tighten them to the specified torques.

8 Lower the hoist or jack and check that the mounting is not under strain. Slacken and retighten as necessary.

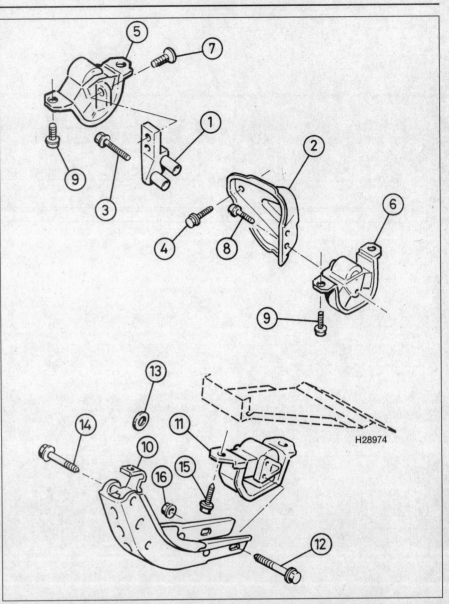

19.3 Engine/transmission mounting components (1.5 litre engine)

1 Right-hand mounting bracket
2 Left-hand mounting bracket
3 Bolt
4 Bolt
5 Flexible block – right-hand mounting
6 Flexible block – left-hand mounting
7 Bolt
8 Bolt
9 Bolt
10 Rear mounting bracket
11 Flexible block – rear mounting
12 Bolt
13 Washer
14 Bolt
15 Bolt
16 Nut

Chapter 2 Part B:
Engine removal and overhaul procedures

Contents

Degrees of difficulty

Easy, suitable for novice with little experience	Fairly easy, suitable for beginner with some experience	Fairly difficult, suitable for competent DIY mechanic	Difficult, suitable for experienced DIY mechanic	Very difficult, suitable for expert DIY or professional

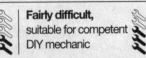

Specifications

1.5 litre diesel engine

Cylinder head

Maximum gasket face distortion	0.1 mm
Cylinder head height:	
Standard	131.45 to 131.55 mm
Service limit	131.25 mm
Valve seat width:	
Standard	1.2 to 1.5 mm
Service limit	2.0 mm
Swirl chamber protrusion	0.001 to 0.030 mm
Valve head depth below gasket face	0.5 to 1.0 mm

Valves and guides

Valve stem diameter:	
Inlet	6.880 to 7.000 mm
Exhaust	6.880 to 7.000 mm
Valve guide bore diameter	7.100 mm

Stem-to-guide clearance:	**Inlet**	**Exhaust**
Standard	0.02 to 0.20 mm	0.03 to 0.025 mm

Cylinder block

Cylinder bore diameter:	
Size group A	76.000 to 79.010 mm
Size group B	76.010 to 76.020 mm
Size group C	79.020 to 79.030 mm
Size group D	79.030 to 79.040 mm
Maximum cylinder bore ovality	0.015 mm
Maximum cylinder bore taper	0.015 mm

1.5 litre diesel engine (continued)

Pistons and rings

Piston-to-bore clearance	0.015 to 0.035 mm
Piston ring end gaps (fitted in bore):	
Top compression ring	0.25 to 0.80 mm
Second compression ring	0.20 to 0.80 mm
Oil control ring	0.20 to 0.80 mm
Piston ring-to-groove clearance:	
Top compression ring	0.09 to 0.15 mm
Second compression ring	0.04 to 0.10 mm
Oil control ring	0.025 to 0.100 mm
Piston ring thickness:	
Top and second compression ring	2.0 mm
Oil control ring	3.0 mm

Connecting rod

Big-end side clearance	0.20 to 0.40 mm

Crankshaft

Endfloat	0.06 to 0.30 mm
Run-out	Less than 0.06 mm

Torque wrench settings
Refer to Chapter 2A Specifications

1.7 litre diesel engine

Cylinder head

Maximum gasket face distortion	0.1 mm
Cylinder head height:	
Standard	131.45 to 131.55 mm
Service limit	131.25 mm
Valve seat width:	
Standard	1.2 to 1.5 mm
Service limit	2.0 mm
Swirl chamber protrusion	0.001 to 0.030 mm
Valve head depth below gasket face	0.5 to 1.0 mm

Valves and guides

	Inlet	Exhaust
Valve stem diameter:		
Inlet	6.959 to 6.977 mm	
Exhaust	6.960 to 6.978 mm	
Valve guide bore diameter	7.000 to 7.015 mm	
Stem-to-guide clearance:		
Standard	0.02 to 0.20 mm	0.03 to 0.025 mm

Cylinder block

Cylinder bore diameter:	
Size group A	79.000 to 79.009 mm
Size group B	79.010 to 79.019 mm
Size group C	79.020 to 79.029 mm
Maximum cylinder bore ovality	0.015 mm
Maximum cylinder bore taper	0.015 mm

Pistons and rings

Piston-to-bore clearance	0.016 to 0.034 mm
Piston ring end gaps (fitted in bore):	
Top compression ring	0.25 to 0.80 mm
Second compression ring	0.20 to 0.80 mm
Oil control ring	0.20 to 0.80 mm
Piston ring-to-groove clearance:	
Top compression ring	0.12 to 0.18 mm
Second compression ring	0.05 to 0.15 mm
Oil control ring	0.02 to 0.15 mm
Piston ring thickness:	
Top and second compression ring	2.0 mm
Oil control ring	3.0 mm

Connecting rod

Big-end side clearance	0.20 to 0.40 mm
Maximum permissible weight difference between connecting rods	4 grams

1.7 litre diesel engine (continued)

Crankshaft
Endfloat . . . . 0.06 to 0.30 mm
Run-out . . . . Less than 0.06 mm

Torque wrench settings
Refer to Chapter 2A Specifications

1 General information

1 Included in this Part of Chapter 2 are details of removing the engine/transmission from the car and general overhaul procedures for the cylinder head, cylinder block and all other engine internal components.

2 The information given ranges from advice concerning preparation for an overhaul and the purchase of new parts, to detailed step-by-step procedures covering removal, inspection, renovation and refitting of engine internal components.

3 After Section 5, all instructions are based on the assumption that the engine has been removed from the car. For information concerning in-car engine repair, as well as the removal and refitting of those external components necessary for full overhaul, refer to the in-car repair procedure section of this Chapter and to Section 6. Ignore any preliminary dismantling operations described in the relevant in-car repair sections that are no longer relevant once the engine has been removed from the car.

4 Apart from torque wrench settings, which are given at the beginning of the in-car repair procedure Chapter, all specifications relating to engine overhaul are at the beginning of this Part of Chapter 2.

2 Engine overhaul –
general information

1 It is not always easy to determine when, or if, an engine should be completely overhauled, as a number of factors must be considered.

2 High mileage is not necessarily an indication that an overhaul is needed, while low mileage does not preclude the need for an overhaul. Frequency of servicing is probably the most important consideration. An engine which has had regular and frequent oil and filter changes, as well as other required maintenance, should give many thousands of miles of reliable service. Conversely, a neglected engine may require an overhaul very early in its life.

3 Excessive oil consumption is an indication that piston rings, valve seals and/or valve guides are in need of attention. Make sure that oil leaks are not responsible before

deciding that the rings and/or guides are worn. Perform a compression test, as described in the Part A of this Chapter, to determine the likely cause of the problem.

4 Check the oil pressure with a gauge fitted in place of the oil pressure switch, and compare it with that specified. If it is extremely low, the main and big-end bearings, and/or the oil pump, are probably worn out.

5 Loss of power, rough running, knocking or metallic engine noises, excessive valve gear noise, and high fuel consumption may also point to the need for an overhaul, especially if they are all present at the same time. If a complete service does not remedy the situation, major mechanical work is the only solution.

6 An engine overhaul involves restoring all internal parts to the specification of a new engine. During an overhaul, the pistons and the piston rings are renewed. New main and big-end bearings are generally fitted; if necessary, the crankshaft may be renewed, to restore the journals. The valves are also serviced as well, since they are usually in less-than-perfect condition at this point. While the engine is being overhauled, other components, such as the starter and alternator, can be overhauled as well. The end result should be an as-new engine that will give many trouble-free miles. **Note:** *Critical cooling system components such as the hoses, thermostat and coolant pump should be renewed when an engine is overhauled. The radiator should be checked carefully, to ensure that it is not clogged or leaking. Also, it is a good idea to renew the oil pump whenever the engine is overhauled.*

7 Before beginning the engine overhaul, read through the entire procedure, to familiarise yourself with the scope and requirements of the job. Overhauling an engine is not difficult if you follow carefully all of the instructions, have the necessary tools and equipment, and pay close attention to all specifications. It can, however, be time-consuming. Plan on the car being off the road for a minimum of two weeks, especially if parts must be taken to an engineering works for repair or reconditioning. Check on the availability of parts and make sure that any necessary special tools and equipment are obtained in advance. Most work can be done with typical hand tools, although a number of precision measuring tools are required for inspecting parts to determine if they must be renewed. Often the engineering works will handle the inspection of parts and offer advice concerning reconditioning and renewal. **Note:** *Always*

wait until the engine has been completely dismantled, and until all components (especially the cylinder block and the crankshaft) have been inspected, before deciding what service and repair operations must be performed by an engineering works. The condition of these components will be the major factor to consider when determining whether to overhaul the original engine, or to buy a reconditioned unit. Do not, therefore, purchase parts or have overhaul work done on other components until they have been thoroughly inspected. As a general rule, time is the primary cost of an overhaul, so it does not pay to fit worn or sub-standard parts.

8 As a final note, to ensure maximum life and minimum trouble from a reconditioned engine, everything must be assembled with care, in a spotlessly-clean environment.

3 Engine removal –
methods and precautions

1 If you have decided that the engine must be removed for overhaul or major repair work, several preliminary steps should be taken.

2 Locating a suitable place to work is extremely important. Adequate work space, along with storage space for the car, will be needed. If a workshop or garage is not available, at the very least, a flat, level, clean work surface is required.

3 Cleaning the engine compartment and engine/transmission before beginning the removal procedure will help keep tools clean and organised.

4 An engine hoist or A-frame will also be necessary. Make sure the equipment is rated in excess of the combined weight of the engine and transmission. Safety is of primary importance, considering the potential hazards involved in lifting the engine/transmission out of the car.

5 If this is the first time you have removed an engine, an assistant should ideally be available. Advice and aid from someone more experienced would also be helpful. There are many instances when one person cannot simultaneously perform all of the operations required when lifting the engine out of the vehicle.

6 Plan the operation ahead of time. Before starting work, arrange for the hire of or obtain all of the tools and equipment you will need. Some of the equipment necessary to perform engine/transmission removal and installation safely and with relative ease (in addition to an

engine hoist) is as follows: a heavy duty trolley jack, complete sets of spanners and sockets as described in the back of this manual, wooden blocks, and plenty of rags and cleaning solvent for mopping-up spilled oil, coolant and fuel. If the hoist must be hired, make sure that you arrange for it in advance, and perform all of the operations possible without it beforehand. This will save you money and time.

7 Plan for the car to be out of use for quite a while. An engineering works will be required to perform some of the work which the do-it-yourselfer cannot accomplish without special equipment. These places often have a busy schedule, so it would be a good idea to consult them before removing the engine, in order to accurately estimate the amount of time required to rebuild or repair components that may need work.

8 Always be extremely careful when removing and refitting the engine/transmission. Serious injury can result from careless actions. Plan ahead and take your time, and a job of this nature, although major, can be accomplished successfully.

4 Engine and transmission unit – removal, separation and refitting

Removal

Note: *The engine can be removed from the car only as a complete unit with the transmission; the two are then separated for overhaul. The engine/transmission unit is lowered out of position, and withdrawn from under the vehicle. Bearing this in mind, ensure the vehicle is raised sufficiently so that there is enough clearance between the front of the vehicle and the floor to allow the engine/transmission unit to be slid out once it has been lowered out of position.*

1 Park the vehicle on firm, level ground then remove the bonnet as described in Chapter 11.
2 Remove the battery and mounting plate as described in Chapter 5A.
3 Chock the rear wheels, firmly apply the handbrake, then jack up the front of the vehicle. Securely support it on axle stands, bearing in mind the note at the start of this Section. Where necessary, undo the retaining screws and remove the undercover from beneath the engine/transmission unit.
4 If the engine is to be dismantled, working as described in Chapter 1, first drain the engine oil and remove the oil filter. Also drain the cooling system.
5 Referring to Chapter 4A, carry out the following procedures.
  a) *Remove the air cleaner housing and associated components.*
  b) *Remove the exhaust front pipe.*
  c) *Disconnect the fuel feed and return hoses from the injection pump.*
  d) *Disconnect the brake servo hose and*

various vacuum hoses and from the inlet manifold and exhaust manifolds, noting each hoses correct fitted location.
  e) *Disconnect the wiring connectors from the inlet manifold electrical components and free the wiring so it can be positioned clear of the engine unit.*
  f) *Disconnect the accelerator cable and position it clear of the engine.*
6 Referring to Chapter 3, carry out the following procedures.
  a) *Release the retaining clips and disconnect the various coolant hoses from the cylinder head and the block.*
  b) *On models with air conditioning, unbolt the compressor and position it clear of the engine.* **Do not** *open the refrigerant circuit.*
  c) *Release the coolant/air-conditioning hoses/pipes (as applicable) from any relevant clips and ties and position them clear of the engine unit.*
7 Referring to Chapter 5A, disconnect the wiring from the starter motor, alternator, oil pressure warning light switch and (where fitted) the oil level/oil temperature sensor. Unbolt any relevant earth leads from the cylinder block/transmission then unbolt/unclip the wiring from the engine unit and position it clear.
8 Referring to Chapter 10, unbolt the power steering pump and position it clear of the engine unit with its hoses still attached.
9 Referring to Chapter 7, carry out the following procedures.
  a) *Drain the transmission oil or be prepared for oil spillage as the engine/transmission unit is removed.*
  b) *Disconnect the wiring connector from the reversing light switch.*
  c) *Remove the gearchange linkage assembly from the top of the transmission unit.*
  d) *Slide out the retaining clip and disconnect the clutch hose end fitting from the top of the transmission bellhousing. Do not depress the clutch pedal whilst the hose is disconnected.*
10 Manoeuvre the engine hoist into position, and attach it to the lifting brackets bolted onto the engine/transmission. Raise the hoist until it is supporting the weight of the engine.
11 With the engine securely supported, remove the front suspension subframe assembly as described in Chapter 10.
12 Referring to Chapter 8, free the driveshaft inner constant velocity joints from the transmission unit and position them clear. Note that it is not necessary to remove the driveshafts, they can be left attached to the hub assemblies. **Note:** *Do not allow the shafts to hang down under their own weight as this could damage the constant velocity joints/gaiters.*
13 Make a final check that any components which would prevent the removal of the engine/transmission from the car have been removed or disconnected. Ensure that components such as the driveshafts are

secured so that they cannot be damaged on removal.
14 Undo the retaining nuts and remove the bracket securing the right-hand engine mounting to the cylinder head.
15 If available, a low trolley should be placed under the engine/transmission assembly, to facilitate its easy removal from under the vehicle. Lower the engine/transmission assembly, making sure that nothing is trapped, taking great care not to damage the radiator/cooling fan assembly. Enlist the help of an assistant during this procedure, as it may be necessary to tilt the assembly slightly to clear the body panels. Great care must be taken to ensure that no components are trapped and damaged during the removal procedure.
16 Detach the hoist and withdraw the engine/transmission unit from under the vehicle.

Separation

17 With the engine/transmission assembly removed, support the assembly on suitable blocks of wood, on a workbench (or failing that, on a clean area of the workshop floor).
18 On models with a pressed steel sump, undo the retaining bolts and remove the flywheel lower cover plate from the transmission.
19 Undo the retaining bolts and remove the starter motor from the transmission (see Chapter 5A).
20 Ensure that both engine and transmission are adequately supported, then slacken and remove the remaining bolts securing the transmission housing to the engine. Note the correct fitted positions of each bolt (and the relevant brackets) as they are removed, to use as a reference on refitting.
21 Carefully withdraw the transmission from the engine, ensuring that the weight of the transmission is not allowed to hang on the input shaft while it is engaged with the clutch friction disc.
22 If they are loose, remove the locating dowels from the engine or transmission, and keep them in a safe place.

Refitting

23 If the engine and transmission have been separated, perform the operations described below in paragraphs 24 to 26. If not, proceed as described from paragraph 27 onwards.
24 Ensure the locating dowels are correctly positioned then carefully offer the transmission to the engine, until the locating dowels are engaged. Ensure that the weight of the transmission is not allowed to hang on the input shaft as it is engaged with the clutch friction disc.
25 Refit the transmission housing-to-engine bolts, ensuring that all the necessary brackets are correctly positioned, and tighten them to the specified torque setting.
26 Refit the starter motor and tighten its mounting bolts to the specified torque (see Chapter 5A).

27 Slide the engine/transmission unit into position and reconnect the hoist and lifting tackle to the engine lifting brackets.

28 With the aid of an assistant, carefully lift the assembly into position the engine compartment, manipulating the hoist and lifting tackle as necessary, taking great care not to trap any components.

29 Align the engine with the right-hand mounting then refit the mounting bracket, tightening its nuts by hand only at this stage.

30 Renew the driveshaft oil seals (see Chapter 7) then carefully engage the driveshaft inner constant velocity joints with the transmission (see Chapter 8).

31 Refit the front suspension subframe as described in Chapter 10.

32 With the subframe assembly correctly installed, tighten the right-hand mounting bracket nuts to the specified torque.

33 The remainder of the refitting procedure is a direct reversal of the removal sequence, noting the following points:

a) *Ensure that all wiring is correctly routed and retained by all the relevant retaining clips and that all connectors are correctly and securely reconnected.*

b) *Ensure that all disturbed hoses are correctly reconnected, and securely retained by their retaining clips.*

c) *Fit new sealing washers to the injection pump fuel hose unions and tighten the union bolts to the specified torque (see Chapter 4A).*

d) *Fit a new sealing ring to the clutch fitting on the transmission unit and reconnect the end fitting, ensuring it is securely retained by the clip. On completion, check the bleed the hydraulic system as described in Chapter 6.*

e) *Refit the gearchange linkage to the transmission and adjust as described in Chapter 7.*

f) *Adjust the accelerator cable as described in the Chapter 4A.*

g) *Refill the transmission with correct quantity and type of oil, as described in Chapter 7. If the oil was not drained, top-up the level as described in Chapter 1.*

h) *Refill the engine with oil as described in Chapter 1 and also refill the cooling system.*

5 Engine overhaul – dismantling sequence

1 It is much easier to dismantle and work on the engine if it is mounted on a portable engine stand. These stands can often be hired from a tool hire shop. Before the engine is mounted on a stand, the flywheel should be removed, so that the stand bolts can be tightened into the end of the cylinder block.

2 If a stand is not available, it is possible to dismantle the engine with it blocked up on a sturdy workbench, or on the floor. Be extra-careful not to tip or drop the engine when working without a stand.

3 If you are going to obtain a reconditioned engine, all the external components must be removed first, to be transferred to the new engine (just as they will if you are doing a complete engine overhaul yourself). These components include the following:

a) *Inlet and exhaust manifolds (Chapter 4A).*
b) *Alternator/power steering pump/air conditioning compressor bracket(s) (as applicable).*
c) *Coolant pump (Chapter 3).*
d) *Fuel system components (Chapter 4A).*
e) *Wiring harness and all electrical switches and sensors.*
f) *Oil filter (Chapter 1).*
g) *Flywheel (Chapter 2A).*

Note: *When removing the external components from the engine, pay close attention to details that may be helpful or important during refitting. Note the fitted position of gaskets, seals, spacers, pins, washers, bolts, and other small items.*

4 If you are obtaining a 'short' engine (which consists of the engine cylinder block, crankshaft, pistons and connecting rods all assembled), then the cylinder head, sump, oil pump, and timing belt will have to be removed also.

5 If you are planning a complete overhaul, the engine can be dismantled, and the internal components removed, in the order given below, referring to the relevant Part of this Chapter unless otherwise stated.

a) *Inlet and exhaust manifolds (Chapter 4A).*

b) *Timing belt, sprockets and tensioner*
c) *Cylinder head.*
d) *Flywheel.*
e) *Sump.*
f) *Oil pump.*
h) *Piston/connecting rod assemblies.*
i) *Crankshaft.*

6 Before beginning the dismantling and overhaul procedures, make sure that you have all of the correct tools necessary. Refer to the *Tools and working facilities* Section of this manual for further information.

6 Cylinder head – dismantling

Note: *New and reconditioned cylinder heads are available from the manufacturer, and from engine overhaul specialists. Be aware that some specialist tools are required for the dismantling and inspection procedures, and new components may not be readily available. It may therefore be more practical and economical for the home mechanic to purchase a reconditioned head, rather than dismantle, inspect and recondition the original head.*

1 Working as described in Part A of this Chapter, remove the camshaft, followers and shims. Unscrew the glow plugs (Chapter 5B) and injectors (Chapter 4A) from the cylinder head then remove the cylinder head from the engine.

2 On all models, using a valve spring compressor, compress each valve spring in turn until the split collets can be removed. Release the compressor, and lift off the spring retainer and spring. Using a pair of pliers, carefully extract the valve stem seal from the top of the guide then slide off the spring seat **(see illustrations and Haynes hint)**.

3 If, when the valve spring compressor is screwed down, the spring retainer refuses to free and expose the split collets, gently tap the top of the tool, directly over the retainer, with a light hammer. This will free the retainer.

4 Withdraw the valve through the combustion chamber. It is essential that each valve is stored together with its collets, retainer, spring, and spring seat. The valves should

6.2a Using a valve spring compressor . . .

6.2b . . . compress the valve spring until the collets can be removed from the valve

6.2c Remove the compressor then lift off the spring retainer . . .

6.2d . . . and remove the valve spring

6.2e Pull the seal off the top of the valve guide . . .

6.2f . . . then remove the spring seat

also be kept in their correct sequence, unless they are so badly worn that they are to be renewed.

---

7 Cylinder head and valves – cleaning and inspection

1 Thorough cleaning of the cylinder head and valve components, followed by a detailed inspection, will enable you to decide how much valve service work must be carried out during the engine overhaul. **Note:** *If the engine has been severely overheated, it is best to assume that the cylinder head is warped – check carefully for signs of this.*

Cleaning

2 Scrape away all traces of old gasket material from the cylinder head.
3 Scrape away the carbon from the

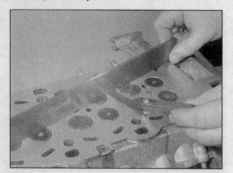

7.6 Using a straight-edge and feeler gauge to check cylinder head surface distortion

If the components are to be refitted, place each valve and its associated components in a labelled polythene bag or similar small container, and mark the bag/container with the relevant valve number to ensure that it is refitted in its original location.

combustion chambers and ports, then wash the cylinder head thoroughly with paraffin or a suitable solvent.
4 Scrape off any heavy carbon deposits that may have formed on the valves, then use a power-operated wire brush to remove deposits from the valve heads and stems.

Inspection

Note: *Be sure to perform all the following inspection procedures before concluding that the services of a machine shop or engine overhaul specialist are required. Make a list of all items that require attention.*

Cylinder head

5 Inspect the head very carefully for cracks,

7.11 Using a dial gauge to check swirl chamber protrusion

evidence of coolant leakage, and other damage. If cracks are found, a new cylinder head should be obtained.
6 Use a straight-edge and feeler gauge blade to check that the cylinder head surface is not distorted **(see illustration)**. If it is, it may be possible to resurface it, provided that the cylinder head is not reduced to less than the minimum specified height.
7 Examine the valve seats in each of the combustion chambers. If they are severely pitted, cracked or burned, then they will need to be renewed or recut by an engine overhaul specialist. If they are only slightly pitted, this can be removed by grinding-in the valve heads and seats with fine valve-grinding compound, as described below.
8 If the valve guides are worn (indicated by a side-to-side motion of the valve, and accompanied by excessive blue smoke in the exhaust when running) new guides must be fitted. Measure the diameter of the existing valve stems (see below) and the bore of the guides, then calculate the clearance and compare the result with the specified value. If the clearance is not within the specified limits, renew the valves and/or guides as necessary.
9 The renewal of valve guides is best carried out by an engine overhaul specialist.
10 If the valve seats are to be recut this must be done after the guides have been renewed.
11 Inspect the swirl chambers for burning or damage such as cracking. Small cracks in the chambers are acceptable; renewal of the chambers will only be required if chamber tracts are badly burned and disfigured, or if they are no longer a tight fit in the cylinder head. If there is any doubt as to the swirl chamber condition, seek the advice of a Vauxhall dealer or a suitable repairer who specialises in diesel engines. Swirl chamber renewal should be entrusted to a specialist. Using a dial test indicator, check that the swirl chamber protrusion is within the limits given in the Specifications. Zero the dial test indicator on the gasket surface of the cylinder head, then measure the protrusion of the swirl chamber **(see illustration)**. If the protrusion is not within the specified limits, the advice of a Vauxhall dealer or suitable repairer who specialises in diesel engines should be sought.

Valves

12 Examine the head of each valve for pitting, burning, cracks and general wear, and check the valve stem for scoring and wear ridges. Rotate the valve, and check for any obvious indication that it is bent. Look for pitting and excessive wear on the tip of each valve stem. Renew any valve that shows any such signs of wear or damage.
13 If the valve appears satisfactory at this stage, measure the valve stem diameter at several points using a micrometer **(see illustration)**. Any significant difference in the readings obtained indicates wear of the valve stem. Should any of these conditions be apparent, the valve(s) must be renewed.

7.13 Using a micrometer to measure valve stem diameter

7.16 Grinding-in a valve

14 If the valves are in satisfactory condition, they should be ground (lapped) into their respective seats, to ensure a smooth gas-tight seal. If the seat is only lightly pitted, or if it has been recut, fine grinding compound **only** should be used to produce the required finish. Coarse valve-grinding compound should **not** be used unless a seat is badly burned or deeply pitted; if this is the case, the cylinder head and valves should be inspected by an expert to decide whether seat recutting, or even the renewal of the valve or seat insert, is required.

15 Valve grinding is carried out as follows. Place the cylinder head upside-down on a bench.

16 Smear a trace of the appropriate grade of valve-grinding compound on the seat face, and press a suction grinding tool onto the valve head. With a semi-rotary action, grind the valve head to its seat, lifting the valve

occasionally to redistribute the grinding compound **(see illustration)**.

> **HAYNES HiNT**
> *A light spring placed under the valve head will greatly ease the valve grinding operation.*

17 If coarse grinding compound is being used, work only until a dull, matt even surface is produced on both the valve seat and the valve, then wipe off the used compound and repeat the process with fine compound. When a smooth unbroken ring of light grey matt finish is produced on both the valve and seat, the grinding operation is complete. **Do not** grind in the valves any further than absolutely necessary, or the seat will be prematurely sunk into the cylinder head.

18 When all the valves have been ground-in, carefully wash off all traces of grinding

compound using paraffin or a suitable solvent before reassembly of the cylinder head.

Valve components

19 Examine the valve springs for signs of damage and discoloration; if possible; also compare the existing spring free length with new components.

20 Stand each spring on a flat surface, and check it for squareness. If any of the springs are damaged, distorted or have lost their tension, obtain a complete new set of springs.

8 Cylinder head – reassembly

1 Lubricate the stems of the valves, and insert them into their original locations **(see illustration)**. If new valves are being fitted, insert them into the locations to which they have been ground.

2 Working on the first valve, refit the spring seat. Dip the new valve stem seal in fresh engine oil, then carefully locate it over the valve and onto the guide. Take care not to damage the seal as it is passed over the valve stem. Use a suitable socket or metal tube to press the seal firmly onto the guide. **Note:** *If genuine seals are being fitted, use the oil seal protector which is supplied with the seals; the protector fits over the valve stem and prevents the oil seal lip being damaged on the valve* **(see illustrations)**.

3 Locate the spring on the seat and fit the spring retainer **(see illustration)**.

8.1 Lubricate the valve stem with engine oil and insert the valve into the correct guide

8.2a Fit the spring seat . . .

8.2b . . . then fit the seal protector (where supplied) to the valve . . .

8.2c . . . and install the new valve guide oil seal . . .

8.2d . . . pressing it onto the valve guide with a suitable socket

8.3 Refit the valve spring and fit the spring retainer

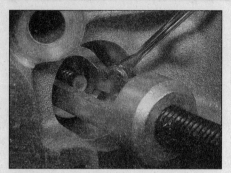

8.4 Compress the valve and locate the collets in the recess on the valve stem

4 Compress the valve spring, and locate the split collets in the recess in the valve stem **(see illustration and Haynes hint)**. Release the compressor, then repeat the procedure on the remaining valves.

5 With all the valves installed, place the cylinder head flat on the bench and, using a hammer and interposed block of wood, tap the end of each valve stem to settle the components.

6 Working as described in Part A, refit the cylinder head to the engine and install the followers, shims and camshaft. Refit the injectors and glow plugs as described in Chapters 4A and 5B.

9.3 Checking connecting rod big-end side clearance

9.4 Prior to removal, make identification markings on the connecting rods and bearing caps (circled)

Note that lug on the bearing cap faces towards the flywheel end of the engine

Use a little dab of grease to hold the collets in position on the valve stem while the spring compressor is released.

9 Piston/connecting rod assembly – removal

Note: *New connecting rod big-end cap bolts and nuts will be needed on refitting*

1 Referring to Part A of this Chapter, remove the cylinder head and sump then remove the pick-up/strainer from the base of the oil pump. Undo the retaining bolts and remove the baffle plate from the base of the cylinder block **(see illustration)**.

2 If there is a pronounced wear ridge at the top of any bore, it may be necessary to remove it with a scraper or ridge reamer, to avoid piston damage during removal. Such a ridge indicates excessive wear of the cylinder bore.

3 Prior to removal, using feeler blades, measuring the connecting rod big-end side clearance of each rod **(see illustration)**. If any rod exceeds the specified clearance, it must be renewed.

4 Using a hammer and centre-punch, paint or similar, mark each connecting rod and its bearing cap with its respective cylinder number on the flat machined surface provided; if the engine has been dismantled before, note carefully any identifying marks made previously **(see illustration)**. Note that No 1 cylinder is at the timing belt end of the engine.

5 Turn the crankshaft to bring pistons 1 and 4 to BDC (bottom dead centre).

6 Unscrew the nuts/bolts from No 1 piston big-end bearing cap. Take off the cap and recover the bottom half bearing shell. If the bearing shells are to be re-used, tape the cap and the shell together.

Caution: On some engines, the connecting rod/bearing cap mating surfaces are not machined flat; the big-end bearing caps are 'cracked' off from the rod during production and left untouched to ensure the cap and rod mate perfectly. Where this type of connecting rod is fitted, great care must be taken to ensure the mating surfaces of the cap and rod are not marked

9.1 Unbolt the baffle plate from the base of the cylinder block

or damaged in anyway. Any damage to the mating surfaces will adversely affect the strength of the connecting rod and could lead to premature failure.

7 Using a hammer handle, push the piston up through the bore, and remove it from the top of the cylinder block. Recover the bearing shell, and tape it to the connecting rod for safe-keeping.

8 Loosely refit the big-end cap to the connecting rod, and secure with the nuts/bolts – this will help to keep the components in their correct order.

9 Remove No 4 piston assembly in the same way.

10 Turn the crankshaft through 180° to bring pistons 2 and 3 to BDC (bottom dead centre), and remove them in the same way.

10 Crankshaft – removal

Note: *New main bearing cap bolts will be required on refitting.*

1 Working as described in Part A of this Chapter, remove the flywheel and unbolt the oil pump cover from the right-hand end of the cylinder block.

2 Unbolt the crankshaft oil seal housing and remove it from the cylinder block **(see illustration)**. If the housing locating dowels are a loose fit, remove them and store them with the housing for safe-keeping.

10.2 Unbolt the oil seal housing and remove it from the engine

3 Remove the piston and connecting rod assemblies as described in Section 9. If no work is to be done on the pistons and connecting rods, unbolt the caps and push the pistons far enough up the bores that the connecting rods are positioned clear of the crankshaft journals.

4 Check the crankshaft endfloat as described in Section 13, then proceed as follows.

5 The main bearing caps should be numbered 1 to 5 from the timing belt end of the engine, and the arrow on each cap should point towards the timing belt end of the engine. **Note:** *On some engines the flywheel end (number 5) bearing cap may not be numbered but is easily identified anyway.* If the bearing caps are not marked, using a hammer and punch or a suitable marker pen, number the caps from 1 to 5 from the timing belt end of the engine and mark each cap to indicate its correct fitted direction to avoid confusion on refitting.

6 Working in a diagonal sequence, evenly and progressively slacken the ten main bearing cap retaining bolts by half a turn at a time until all bolts are loose. Remove all bolts.

7 Carefully remove each cap from the cylinder block, ensuring that the lower main bearing shell remains in position in the cap.

8 Carefully lift out the crankshaft, taking care not to displace the upper main bearing shells **(see illustration)**. Remove the rear oil seal and discard it.

9 Recover the upper bearing shells from the cylinder block, and tape them to their respective caps for safe-keeping.

10 With the crankshaft removed, remove the thrustwasher halves from the sides of number 2 main bearing.

11 Cylinder block – cleaning and inspection

Cleaning

1 Remove all external components and electrical switches/sensors from the block. For complete cleaning, the core plugs should ideally be removed. Drill a small hole in the plugs, then insert a self-tapping screw into the hole. Pull out the plugs by pulling on the screw with a pair of grips, or by using a slide hammer.

2 Remove the piston oil spray nozzles from inside the cylinder block. The nozzles are a push-fit in the block.

3 Scrape all traces of gasket from the cylinder block, and from the main bearing casting (where fitted), taking care not to damage the gasket/sealing surfaces.

4 Remove all oil gallery plugs (where fitted). The plugs are usually very tight – they may have to be drilled out, and the holes re-tapped. Use new plugs when the engine is reassembled.

5 If any of the castings are extremely dirty, all should be steam-cleaned.

10.8 Removing the crankshaft

6 After the castings are returned, clean all oil holes and oil galleries one more time. Flush all internal passages with warm water until the water runs clear. Dry thoroughly, and apply a light film of oil to all mating surfaces, to prevent rusting. Also oil the cylinder bores. If you have access to compressed air, use it to speed up the drying process, and to blow out all the oil holes and galleries.

 Warning: Wear eye protection when using compressed air.

7 If the castings are not very dirty, you can do an adequate cleaning job with hot (as hot as you can stand), soapy water and a stiff brush. Take plenty of time, and do a thorough job. Regardless of the cleaning method used, be sure to clean all oil holes and galleries very thoroughly, and to dry all components well. Protect the cylinder bores as described above, to prevent rusting.

8 All threaded holes must be clean, to ensure accurate torque readings during reassembly. To clean the threads, run the correct-size tap into each of the holes to remove rust, corrosion, thread sealant or sludge, and to restore damaged threads. If possible, use compressed air to clear the holes of debris produced by this operation. A good alternative is to inject aerosol-applied water-dispersant lubricant into each hole, using the long spout usually supplied.

 Warning: Wear eye protection when cleaning out these holes in this way.

9 Apply suitable sealant to the new oil gallery plugs, and insert them into the holes in the block. Tighten them securely. Similarly, apply sealant to the core plugs and push them into the block using a close-fitting tube or socket.

10 Refit the piston oil spray nozzles to the cylinder block. Press the nozzles securely into position ensuring that each one is positioned exactly at a right-angle to the crankshaft axis.

11 If the engine is not going to be reassembled right away, cover it with a large plastic bag to keep it clean; protect all mating surfaces and the cylinder bores as described above, to prevent rusting.

Inspection

12 Visually check the castings for cracks and corrosion. Look for stripped threads in the

threaded holes. If there has been any history of internal water leakage, it may be worthwhile having an engine overhaul specialist check the cylinder block/crankcase with special equipment. If defects are found, have them repaired if possible, or renew the assembly.

13 Check the bore of each cylinder for scuffing and scoring.

14 Measure the diameter of each cylinder bore at the top (just below the wear ridge), centre and bottom of the bore, both parallel to the crankshaft axis and at right angles to it, so that a total of six measurements are taken. Note that there are various size groups of standard bore diameter to allow for manufacturing tolerances; the size group markings are stamped on the cylinder block.

15 Compare the results with the Specifications at the beginning of this Chapter; if any measurement exceeds the service limit specified, the cylinder block must be rebored if possible, or renewed and new piston assemblies fitted.

16 If the cylinder bores are badly scuffed or scored, or if they are excessively worn, out-of-round or tapered, or if the piston-to-bore clearance is excessive (see Section 12), the cylinder block must be rebored (if possible) or renewed and new pistons fitted.

17 If the bores are in reasonably good condition and not worn to the specified limits, then the piston rings should be renewed. If this is the case, the bores should be honed to allow the new rings to bed in correctly and provide the best possible seal. The conventional type of hone has spring-loaded stones, and is used with a power drill. You will also need some paraffin (or honing oil) and rags. The hone should be moved up-and-down the bore to produce a crosshatch pattern, and plenty of honing oil should be used. Ideally, the crosshatch lines should intersect at approximately a 60° angle. Do not take off more material than is necessary to produce the required finish. If new pistons are being fitted, the piston manufacturers may specify a finish with a different angle, so their instructions should be followed. Do not withdraw the hone from the bore while it is still being turned – stop it first. After honing a bore, wipe out all traces of the honing oil. If equipment of this type is not available, or if you are not sure whether you are competent to undertake the task yourself, an engine overhaul specialist will carry out the work at moderate cost.

12 Piston/connecting rod assembly – inspection

1 Before the inspection process can begin, the piston/connecting rod assemblies must be cleaned, and the original piston rings removed from the pistons.

2 Carefully expand the old rings over the top of the pistons. The use of two or three old

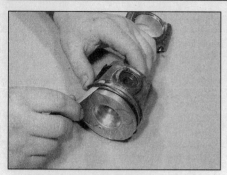

12.2 Using a feeler blade to remove a piston ring

feeler blades will be helpful in preventing the rings dropping into empty grooves **(see illustration)**. Be careful not to scratch the piston with the ends of the ring. The rings are brittle, and will snap if they are spread too far. They're also very sharp – protect your hands and fingers. Note that the third (oil control) ring consists of a spacer and two side rails. Always remove the rings from the top of the piston. Keep each set of rings with its piston if the old rings are to be re-used.

3 Scrape away all traces of carbon from the top of the piston. A hand-held wire brush (or a piece of fine emery cloth) can be used, once the majority of the deposits have been scraped away. The piston identification markings should now be visible.

4 Remove the carbon from the ring grooves in the piston, using an old ring. Break the ring in half to do this (be careful not to cut your fingers). Be careful to remove only the carbon deposits – do not remove any metal, and do not nick or scratch the sides of the ring grooves.

5 Once the deposits have been removed, clean the piston/connecting rod assembly with paraffin or a suitable solvent, and dry thoroughly. Make sure that the oil return holes in the ring grooves are clear.

6 If the cylinder bores are not damaged or worn excessively, and if the cylinder block does not need to be rebored (see Section 12), check the pistons as follows.

7 Carefully inspect each piston for cracks around the skirt, around the gudgeon pin holes, and at the piston ring 'lands' (between the ring grooves).

8 Look for scoring and scuffing on the piston

12.15 Prise out the circlips then remove the gudgeon pin and separate the piston and connecting rod

skirt, holes in the piston crown, and burned areas at the edge of the crown. If the skirt is scored or scuffed, the engine may have been suffering from overheating, and/or abnormal combustion which caused excessively high operating temperatures. The cooling and lubrication systems should be checked thoroughly. Scorch marks on the sides of the pistons show that blow-by has occurred. A hole in the piston crown, or burned areas at the edge of the piston crown, indicates that abnormal combustion (pre-ignition, knocking, or detonation) has been occurring. If any of the above problems exist, the causes must be investigated and corrected, or the damage will occur again. The causes may include incorrect injection pump timing, or a faulty injector.

9 Corrosion of the piston, in the form of pitting, indicates that coolant has been leaking into the combustion chamber and/or the crankcase. Again, the cause must be corrected, or the problem may persist in the rebuilt engine.

10 Measure the piston diameter at right angles to the gudgeon pin axis. Note that there are various size groups of standard piston diameter to allow for manufacturing tolerances; the size group markings are stamped on the piston crown.

11 To measure the piston-to-bore clearance, either measure the bore (see Section 11) and piston skirt as described and subtract the skirt diameter from the bore measurement, or insert each piston into its original bore, then select a feeler gauge blade and slip it into the bore along with the piston. The piston must be aligned exactly in its normal attitude, and the feeler gauge blade must be between the

piston and bore, on one of the thrust faces, just up from the bottom of the bore. Divide the measured clearance by two, to provide the clearance when the piston is central in the bore. If the clearance is excessive, a new piston will be required. If the piston binds at the lower end of the bore and is loose towards the top, the bore is tapered. If tight spots are encountered as the piston/feeler gauge blade is rotated in the bore, the bore is out-of-round.

12 Repeat this procedure for the remaining pistons and cylinder bores. Any piston which is worn beyond the specified limits must be renewed.

13 Examine each connecting rod carefully for signs of damage, such as cracks around the big-end and small-end bearings. Check that the rod is not bent or distorted. Damage is highly unlikely, unless the engine has been seized or badly overheated. Detailed checking of the connecting rod assembly can only be carried out by a Vauxhall dealer or engine repair specialist with the necessary equipment.

14 The gudgeon pins are of the floating type, secured in position by two circlips. The pistons and connecting rods can be separated as follows.

15 Using a small flat-bladed screwdriver, prise out the circlips, and push out the gudgeon pin **(see illustration)**. Hand pressure should be sufficient to remove the pin. Identify the piston and rod to ensure correct reassembly. Discard the circlips – new ones *must* be used on refitting.

16 Examine the gudgeon pin and connecting rod small-end bearing for signs of wear or damage **(see illustration)**. Wear will require the renewal of both the pin and connecting rod. The small-end bush is available separately, but bush renewal is a specialist job – press facilities are required, and the new bush must be reamed accurately.

17 Examine all components, and obtain any new parts from your Vauxhall dealer. If new pistons are purchased, they will be supplied complete with gudgeon pins and circlips. Circlips can also be purchased individually.

18 Assemble the piston and connecting rod so that the timing mark (dot) on the piston crown is on the same side as the raised mark which is cast onto the side of the connecting rod **(see illustrations)**.

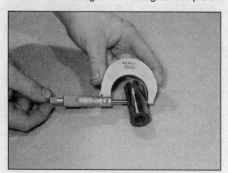

12.16 Measuring gudgeon pin diameter with a micrometer

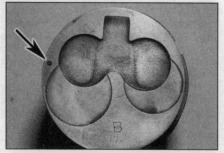

12.18a Assemble the piston and connecting rod so that the piston timing mark (arrowed) . . .

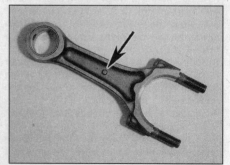

12.18b . . . is on the opposite side to the connecting rod raised mark (arrowed)

19 Apply a smear of clean engine oil to the gudgeon pin. Slide it into the piston and through the connecting rod small-end. Check that the piston pivots freely on the rod, then secure the gudgeon pin in position with two new circlips, ensuring that each circlip is correctly located in its groove in the piston **(see illustrations)**.

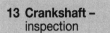

13 Crankshaft – inspection

Checking endfloat

1 If the crankshaft endfloat is to be checked, this must be done when the crankshaft is still installed in the cylinder block, but is free to move (see Section 10).
2 Check the endfloat using a dial gauge in contact with the end of the crankshaft. Push the crankshaft fully one way, and then zero the gauge. Push the crankshaft fully the other way, and check the endfloat **(see illustration)**. The result can be compared with the specified amount, and will give an indication as to whether new thrustwasher halves are required.
3 If a dial gauge is not available, feeler gauges can be used. First push the crankshaft fully towards the flywheel end of the engine, then use feeler gauges to measure the gap between the web of the crankpin and the side of thrustwasher **(see illustration)**. Separate thrustwashers are fitted to the sides of number 2 main bearing upper shell.

Inspection

4 Clean the crankshaft using paraffin or a suitable solvent, and dry it, preferably with compressed air if available. Be sure to clean the oil holes with a pipe cleaner or similar probe, to ensure that they are not obstructed.

 Warning: Wear eye protection when using compressed air.

5 Check the main and big-end bearing journals for uneven wear, scoring, pitting and cracking.
6 Big-end bearing wear is accompanied by distinct metallic knocking when the engine is running (particularly noticeable when the engine is pulling from low speed) and some loss of oil pressure.
7 Main bearing wear is accompanied by severe engine vibration and rumble – getting progressively worse as engine speed increases – and again by loss of oil pressure.
8 Check the main and crankpin (big-end) bearing journals carefully. If uneven wear, scoring, pitting and cracking are evident then the crankshaft should be reground (where possible) by an engineering workshop, and refitted to the engine with new undersize bearings.
9 Rather than attempt to determine the crankshaft journal sizes, and the bearing clearances, take the crankshaft to an

12.19a Ensure the piston and connecting rod are correctly assembled then insert the gudgeon pin . . .

12.19b . . . and secure it with new circlips

13.2 Check the crankshaft endfloat using a dial gauge . . .

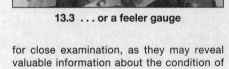
13.3 . . . or a feeler gauge

automotive engineering workshop. Have them perform the necessary measurements, grind the journals if necessary, and supply the appropriate new shell bearings.
10 Check the oil seal journals at each end of the crankshaft for wear and damage. If either seal has worn an excessive groove in its journal, it may cause the new seals to leak when the engine is reassembled. Consult an engine overhaul specialist, who will be able to advise whether a repair is possible, or whether a new crankshaft is necessary.

14 Main and big-end bearings – inspection

1 Even though the main and big-end bearings should be renewed during the engine overhaul, the old bearings should be retained

for close examination, as they may reveal valuable information about the condition of the engine **(see illustration)**.
2 Bearing failure can occur due to lack of lubrication, the presence of dirt or other foreign particles, overloading the engine, or corrosion **(see illustration)**. Regardless of the cause of bearing failure, the cause must be corrected (where applicable) before the engine is reassembled, to prevent it from happening again.

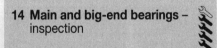

14.1 Typical main bearing shell identification markings

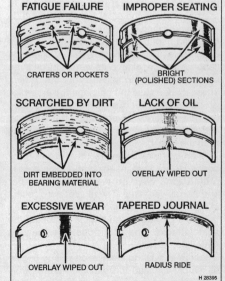
14.2 Typical bearing failures

3 When examining the bearing shells, remove them from the cylinder block, the main bearing caps, the connecting rods and the connecting rod big-end bearing caps. Lay them out on a clean surface in the same general position as their location in the engine. This will enable you to match any bearing problems with the corresponding crankshaft journal.

4 Dirt and other foreign matter gets into the engine in a variety of ways. It may be left in the engine during assembly, or it may pass through filters or the crankcase ventilation system. It may get into the oil, and from there into the bearings. Metal chips from machining operations and normal engine wear are often present. Abrasives are sometimes left in engine components after reconditioning, especially when parts are not thoroughly cleaned using the proper cleaning methods. Whatever the source, these foreign objects often end up embedded in the soft bearing material, and are easily recognised. Large particles will not embed in the bearing, and will score or gouge the bearing and journal. The best prevention for this cause of bearing failure is to clean all parts thoroughly, and keep everything spotlessly-clean during engine assembly. Frequent and regular engine oil and filter changes are also recommended.

5 Lack of lubrication (or lubrication breakdown) has a number of interrelated causes. Excessive heat (which thins the oil), overloading (which squeezes the oil from the bearing face) and oil leakage (from excessive bearing clearances, worn oil pump or high engine speeds) all contribute to lubrication breakdown. Blocked oil passages, which usually are the result of misaligned oil holes in a bearing shell, will also oil-starve a bearing, and destroy it. When lack of lubrication is the cause of bearing failure, the bearing material is wiped or extruded from the steel backing of the bearing. Temperatures may increase to the point where the steel backing turns blue from overheating.

6 Driving habits can have a definite effect on bearing life. Full-throttle, low-speed operation (labouring the engine) puts very high loads on bearings, tending to squeeze out the oil film. These loads cause the bearings to flex, which produces fine cracks in the bearing face (fatigue failure). Eventually, the bearing material will loosen in pieces, and tear away from the steel backing.

7 Short-distance driving leads to corrosion of bearings, because insufficient engine heat is produced to drive off the condensed water and corrosive gases. These products collect in the engine oil, forming acid and sludge. As the oil is carried to the engine bearings, the acid attacks and corrodes the bearing material.

8 Incorrect bearing installation during engine assembly will lead to bearing failure as well. Tight-fitting bearings leave insufficient bearing running clearance, and will result in oil starvation. Dirt or foreign particles trapped

behind a bearing shell result in high spots on the bearing, which lead to failure.

9 As mentioned at the beginning of this Section, the bearing shells should be renewed as a matter of course during engine overhaul; to do otherwise is false economy.

15 Engine overhaul – reassembly sequence

1 Before reassembly begins, ensure that all new parts have been obtained, and that all necessary tools are available. Read through the entire procedure to familiarise yourself with the work involved, and to ensure that all items necessary for reassembly of the engine are at hand. In addition to all normal tools and materials, thread-locking compound will be needed. A good quality tube of liquid sealant will also be required for the joint faces that are fitted without gaskets.

2 In order to save time and avoid problems, engine reassembly can be carried out in the following order:
  a) Crankshaft.
  b) Piston/connecting rod assemblies.
  c) Oil pump.
  d) Sump.
  e) Flywheel/driveplate.
  f) Cylinder head.
  g) Timing belt tensioner and sprockets, and belts.
  h) Inlet and exhaust manifolds (Chapter 4A).
  i) Engine external components.

3 At this stage, all engine components should be absolutely clean and dry, with all faults repaired. The components should be laid out (or in individual containers) on a completely clean work surface.

16 Piston rings – refitting

1 Before fitting new piston rings, the ring end gaps must be checked as follows.

2 Lay out the piston/connecting rod

16.4 Measuring a piston ring end gap using a feeler gauge

assemblies and the new piston ring sets, so that the ring sets will be matched with the same piston and cylinder during the end gap measurement and subsequent engine reassembly.

3 Insert the top ring into the first cylinder, and push it down the bore using the top of the piston. This will ensure that the ring remains square with the cylinder walls. Push the ring down into the bore until it is positioned 15 to 20 mm down from the top edge of the bore, then withdraw the piston.

4 Measure the end gap using feeler gauges, and compare the measurements with the figures given in the Specifications (see illustration).

5 If the gap is too small (unlikely if genuine Vauxhall parts are used), it must be enlarged, or the ring ends may contact each other during engine operation, causing serious damage. Ideally, new piston rings providing the correct end gap should be fitted. As a last resort, the end gap can be increased by filing the ring ends very carefully with a fine file. Mount the file in a vice with soft jaws, slip the ring over the file with the ends contacting the file face, and slowly move the ring to remove material from the ends. Take care, as piston rings are sharp, and are easily broken.

6 With new piston rings, it is unlikely that the end gap will be too large. If the gaps are too large, check that you have the correct rings for your engine and for the particular cylinder bore size group.

7 Repeat the checking procedure for each ring in the first cylinder, and then for the rings in the remaining cylinders. Remember to keep rings, pistons and cylinders matched up.

8 Once the ring end gaps have been checked and if necessary corrected, the rings can be fitted to the pistons.

9 Fit the piston rings using the same technique as for removal. Fit the bottom (oil control) spacer first then install both the side rails, noting that both the spacer and side rails can be installed either way up.

10 The second and top rings are different and can be identified by the marks on the ring top surface; the top ring has a square cross-section and is marked T whilst the second ring has a stepped cross-section and is marked 2T. Fit the second and top compression rings ensuring that each ring is fitted the correct way up with its identification mark uppermost (see illustration opposite). Note: Always follow any instructions supplied with the new piston ring sets – different manufacturers may specify different procedures. Do not mix up the top and second compression rings.

11 With the piston rings correctly installed, check that each ring is free to rotate easily in its groove. Check the ring-to-groove clearance of each ring using feeler gauges and check that the clearance is within the specified range then position the ring end gaps as shown (see illustration 16.10).

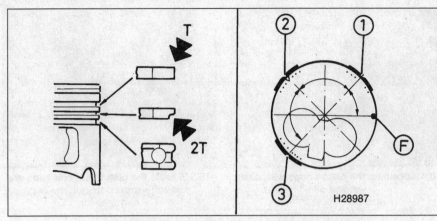

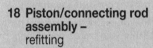

16.10 Piston ring identification and end gap locations

1 Top compression ring
2 Second compression ring
3 Oil scraper ring
F Timing mark (dot) on piston crown

17 Crankshaft – refitting

Note: *It is recommended that new main bearing shells are fitted regardless of the condition of the original ones.*

1 Place the bearing shells in their locations. If new shells are being fitted, ensure that all traces of the protective grease are cleaned off using paraffin. Wipe dry the shells and caps with a lint-free cloth.

2 Using a little grease, stick the thrust washers to each side of the number 2 main bearing upper location; ensure that the oilway grooves on each thrustwasher face outwards **(see illustration)**.

3 Lubricate the upper shells with clean engine oil then lower the crankshaft into position.

4 Ensure the crankshaft is correctly seated then check the endfloat as described in Section 13.

5 Ensure the bearing shells are correctly located in the caps and refit the caps to the cylinder block **(see illustration)**. Ensure the caps are fitted in their correct locations, with number 1 cap at the timing belt end, and are fitted the correct way around so that the arrows all point towards the timing belt end of the engine. Prior to refitting number 1 cap, apply a smear of sealant to its mating surface.

6 Apply a smear of clean engine to oil to the threads and underneath the heads of the new main bearing cap bolts. Fit the bolts tightening them all by hand then working in a diagonal sequence from the centre outwards, evenly and progressively tighten them to the specified torque setting **(see illustration)**.

7 Check that the crankshaft is free to rotate smoothly; if excessive pressure is required to turn the crankshaft, investigate the cause before proceeding further.

8 Ensure that the mating surfaces of oil seal housing and cylinder block are clean and dry. Note the correct fitted depth of the oil seal then tap/lever the seal out of the housing **(see illustration)**.

9 Apply a smear of sealant to the oil seal housing mating surface, and make sure that the locating dowels are in position **(see illustration)**. Slide the housing over the end of the crankshaft, and into position on the cylinder block, then tighten the retaining bolts securely.

10 Refit/reconnect the piston connecting rod assemblies to the crankshaft as described in Section 18. Referring to Part A of this Chapter fit a new crankshaft oil seal, then refit the flywheel, oil pump cover, cylinder head, timing belt sprocket(s) and fit a new timing belt.

18 Piston/connecting rod assembly – refitting

Note: *It is recommended that new piston rings and big-end bearing shells are fitted regardless of the condition of the original ones.*

1 Clean the backs of the bearing shells and the bearing locations in both the connecting rod and bearing cap.

2 Press the bearing shells into their locations, ensuring that the tab on each shell engages in the notch in the connecting rod and cap **(see illustration)**.

3 If new shells are being fitted, ensure that all traces of the protective grease are cleaned off using paraffin. Wipe dry the shells and connecting rods with a lint-free cloth.

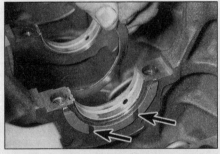

17.2 Fit the thrustwasher to each side of number 2 main bearing ensuring the oilway grooves (arrowed) are facing outwards

17.5 Refit the main bearing caps . . .

17.6 . . . then fit the new retaining bolts and tighten them evenly and progressively to the specified torque

17.8 Remove the oil seal from the housing prior to refitting

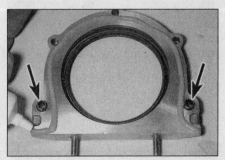

17.9 Apply a bead of sealant to the oil seal housing mating surface and refit the housing to the engine (locating dowels arrowed)

18.2 Fit the bearing shells making sure their tabs are correctly located in the connecting rod/cap groove (arrowed)

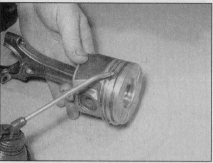

18.4 Lubricate the piston rings with clean engine oil

18.5 Ensure the piston ring end gaps are correctly spaced then fit the ring compressor

18.6 Renew the connecting rod bearing cap bolts before refitting the piston/connecting rod assemblies

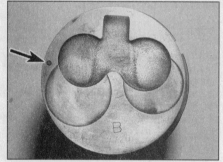

18.7a Insert the piston connecting rod into the correct bore ensuring the timing mark (arrowed) on the piston crown is pointing towards the timing belt end of the engine

18.7b Tap the piston gently into the bore using handle of a hammer

4 Lubricate the bores, the pistons and piston rings then lay out each piston/connecting rod assembly in its respective position **(see illustration)**.

5 Starting with assembly number 1, make sure that the piston rings are still spaced as described in Section 16, then clamp them in position with a piston ring compressor **(see illustration)**.

6 Prior to refitting, carefully tap the original bolts out from the connecting rod and install the new bolts **(see illustration)**.

7 Insert the piston/connecting rod assembly into the top of cylinder No 1, ensuring that the timing mark (dot) on the piston crown is pointing towards the timing belt end of the engine. Using a block of wood or hammer handle against the piston crown, tap the assembly into the cylinder until the piston crown is flush with the top of the cylinder **(see illustrations)**.

8 Taking care not to mark the cylinder bore, liberally lubricate the crankpin and both bearing

shells, then pull the piston/connecting rod assembly down the bore and onto the crankpin and refit the big-end bearing cap, using the markings to ensure it is fitted the correct way around (the lug on the bearing cap base should be facing the flywheel end of the engine) and fit the new retaining nuts **(see illustration)**.

9 Tighten both bearing cap nuts to the specified Stage 1 torque setting then tighten them through the specified Stage 2 angle, and finally through the specified Stage 3 angle **(see illustration)**. It is recommended that an angle-measuring gauge is used during the

18.8 Refit the bearing cap to the connecting rod making sure its lug (arrowed) is facing the flywheel end of the engine

18.9 Tighten the connecting rod nuts to the specified Stage 1 torque and then through the specified Stages 2 and 3 angles

final stages of the tightening, to ensure accuracy. If a gauge is not available, use white paint to make alignment marks between the nut and cap prior to tightening; the marks can then be used to check that the bolt has been rotated through the correct angle.

10 Refit the remaining three piston and connecting rod assemblies in the same way.

11 Rotate the crankshaft, and check that it turns freely, with no signs of binding or tight spots.

12 Refit the baffle plate to the base of the cylinder block and tighten its retaining bolts securely.

13 Refit the oil pump strainer, sump and the cylinder head as described in Part A of this Chapter.

19 Engine –
initial start up after overhaul

1 With the engine refitted in the vehicle, double-check the engine oil and coolant levels. Make a final check that everything has been reconnected, and that there are no tools or rags left in the engine compartment.

2 Switch on the ignition and immediately turn the engine on the starter (without allowing the glow plugs to heat up) until the oil pressure warning light goes out.

3 Start the engine as normal noting that this may take a little longer than usual, due to the fuel system components having been disturbed.

4 While the engine is idling, check for fuel, water and oil leaks. Don't be alarmed if there are some odd smells and smoke from parts getting hot and burning off oil deposits.

5 Assuming all is well, keep the engine idling until hot water is felt circulating through the top hose, then switch off the engine.

6 Allow the engine to cool then recheck the oil and coolant levels as described in *Weekly Checks*, and top-up as necessary.

7 If new pistons, rings or crankshaft bearings have been fitted, the engine must be treated as new, and run-in for the first 500 miles (800 km). *Do not* operate the engine at full-throttle, or allow it to labour at low engine speeds in any gear. It is recommended that the oil and filter be changed at the end of this period.

Chapter 3
Cooling, heating and ventilation systems

Contents

Degrees of difficulty

Easy, suitable for novice with little experience	**Fairly easy,** suitable for beginner with some experience	**Fairly difficult,** suitable for competent DIY mechanic	**Difficult,** suitable for experienced DIY mechanic	**Very difficult,** suitable for expert DIY or professional 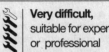

Specifications

System type . . . . Pressurised, with remote expansion tank

Thermostat
Opening temperatures:
    Starts to open . . . . 92°C
    Fully open . . . . 107°C

Electric cooling fan operating temperature
Cooling fan on . . . . 100°C
Cooling fan off . . . . 95°C

Expansion tank cap
Opening pressure . . . . 1.2 to 1.35 bars

Torque wrench settings	**Nm**	**lbf ft**
Air conditioning compressor mounting bolt	35	26
Air conditioning refrigerant line	27	20
Coolant pump	20	15
Coolant pump pulley securing nuts	20	15
Right-hand engine mounting nut	45	33
Thermostat cover	30	22
Thermostat housing	30	22

1 General information and precautions

General information

The cooling system is of pressurised type, comprising a pump driven by the timing belt on petrol engines or the auxiliary drivebelt on diesel engines, a crossflow radiator, electric cooling fan(s), and thermostat(s). The system functions as follows. Cold coolant from the radiator passes through the bottom hose to the coolant pump, where it is pumped around the cylinder block, head passages and heater matrix. After cooling the cylinder bores, combustion surfaces and valve seats, the coolant reaches the underside of the thermostat, which is initially closed. The coolant passes through the heater, and is returned to the coolant pump.

When the engine is cold, the coolant circulates only through the cylinder block, cylinder head and heater. When the coolant reaches a predetermined temperature, the thermostat opens and the coolant passes through to the radiator. As the coolant circulates through the radiator, it is cooled by the inrush of air when the car is in forward motion. Airflow is supplemented by the action of the electric cooling fan when necessary. Once the coolant has passed through the radiator, and has cooled, the cycle is repeated.

The electric cooling fan, mounted on the rear of the radiator, is controlled by a thermostatic switch. At a predetermined coolant temperature, the switch actuates the fan.

An expansion tank is fitted to the left-hand side of the engine compartment to accommodate expansion of the coolant when hot. The expansion tank is connected to the top of the radiator.

Refer to Section 11 for information on the air conditioning system.

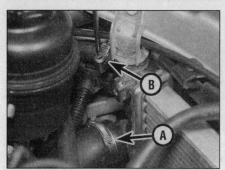

3.9a Slacken the retaining clips, and disconnect the coolant hose (A) and expansion tank hose (B) from the left-hand end of the radiator . . .

3.9b . . . and the coolant hose from the right-hand end of the radiator

Precautions

⚠️ **Warning:** *Do not attempt to remove the expansion tank filler cap, or disturb any part of the cooling system, while the engine is hot; there is a high risk of scalding. If the expansion tank filler cap must be removed before the engine and radiator have fully cooled (even though this is not recommended) the pressure in the cooling system must first be relieved. Cover the cap with a thick layer of cloth, to avoid scalding, and slowly unscrew the filler cap until a hissing sound can be heard. When the hissing has stopped, indicating that the pressure has reduced, slowly unscrew the filler cap until it can be removed; if more hissing sounds are heard, wait until they have stopped before unscrewing the cap completely. At all times, keep well away from the filler cap opening.*

⚠️ **Warning:** *Do not allow antifreeze to come into contact with skin, or with the painted surfaces of the vehicle. Rinse off spills immediately, with plenty of water. Never leave antifreeze lying around in an open container, or in a puddle on the driveway or garage floor. Children and pets are attracted by its sweet smell, but antifreeze can be fatal if ingested.*

⚠️ **Warning:** *If the engine is hot, the electric cooling fan may start rotating even if the engine is not running; be careful to keep hands, hair and*

loose clothing well clear when working in the engine compartment.

⚠️ **Warning:** *Refer to Section 11 for precautions to be observed when working on models equipped with air conditioning.*

2 Cooling system hoses – disconnection and renewal

Note: *Refer to the warnings given in Section 1 of this Chapter before proceeding. Do not attempt to disconnect any hose while the system is still hot.*

1 If the checks described in Chapter 1 reveal a faulty hose, it must be renewed as follows.

2 First drain the cooling system (see Chapter 1). If the coolant is not due for renewal, it may be re-used if it is collected in a clean container.

3 Before disconnecting a hose, first note its routing in the engine compartment, and whether it is secured by any additional retaining clips or cable ties. Use a pair of pliers to release the clamp-type clips, or a screwdriver to slacken the screw-type clips, then move the clips along the hose, clear of the relevant inlet/outlet union. Carefully work the hose free.

4 Note that the radiator inlet and outlet unions are fragile; do not use excessive force when attempting to remove the hoses. If a hose proves to be difficult to remove, try to release it by rotating the hose ends before attempting to free it.

3.10a Unscrew the retaining bolt . . .

3.10b . . . and remove each radiator upper mounting bracket and rubber

HAYNES HiNT *If all else fails, cut the coolant hose with a sharp knife, then slit it so that it can be peeled off in two pieces. Although this may prove expensive if the hose is otherwise undamaged, it is preferable to buying a new radiator.*

5 When fitting a hose, first slide the clips onto the hose, then work the hose into position. If clamp-type clips were originally fitted, it is a good idea to replace them with screw-type clips when refitting the hose. If the hose is stiff, use a little soapy water (washing-up liquid is ideal) as a lubricant, or soften the hose by soaking it in hot water.

6 Work the hose into position, checking that it is correctly routed and secured. Slide each clip along the hose until it passes over the flared end of the relevant inlet/outlet union, before tightening the clips securely.

7 Refill the cooling system with reference to Chapter 1.

8 Check thoroughly for leaks as soon as possible after disturbing any part of the cooling system.

3 Radiator – removal, inspection and refitting

HAYNES HiNT *If leakage is the reason for wanting to remove the radiator, bear in mind that minor leaks can often be cured using a radiator sealant without removing the radiator.*

Removal

1 Disconnect the battery negative terminal (refer to *Disconnecting the battery* in the Reference Chapter).

2 Drain the cooling system as described in Chapter 1.

3 Undo the plastic stud securing the air cleaner air intake trunking to the engine compartment front crossmember.

4 Disconnect the wiring connector(s) from the cooling fan switch(es) on the right-hand end of the radiator.

5 Remove the engine oil dipstick and, where applicable, the automatic transmission fluid dipstick.

6 On engines with air conditioning, free the refrigerant pipe from the support bracket, then unbolt the support bracket from the exhaust manifold or cylinder head, as applicable.

7 Remove the cooling fan assembly as described in Section 5.

8 To improve clearance on models with power steering, unbolt the power steering fluid reservoir, and place it clear of the radiator.

3.11 Free the radiator from its lower mounting rubbers, and lift it out of the engine compartment

3.17 Inspect the mounting rubbers for signs of damage, and renew if necessary

3.18 On refitting, ensure that the radiator pegs engage with lower mounting rubbers (arrowed)

9 Slacken the retaining clips, and disconnect the coolant and expansion tank hoses from the left-hand end of the radiator. Also disconnect the coolant hose from the radiator right-hand end **(see illustrations)**.

10 Undo the retaining bolts, and remove the left- and right-hand mounting brackets from the top of the radiator **(see illustrations)**.

11 Free the radiator from its lower mounting rubbers, and lift it out of the engine compartment **(see illustration)**.

Inspection

12 If the radiator has been removed due to suspected blockage, reverse-flush it as described in Chapter 1, Section 27. Clean dirt and debris from the radiator fins, using an air line (in which case, wear eye protection) or a soft brush. Be careful, as the fins are easily damaged, and are sharp.

13 If necessary, a radiator specialist can perform a 'flow test' on the radiator, to establish whether an internal blockage exists.

14 A leaking radiator must be referred to a specialist for permanent repair. Do not attempt DIY repairs to a leaking radiator, as damage may result.

15 In an emergency, minor leaks from the radiator can be cured by using a suitable radiator sealant (in accordance with its manufacturer's instructions) with the radiator *in situ*.

16 If the radiator is to be sent for repair, or is to be renewed, remove the cooling fan switch(es).

17 Inspect the radiator mounting rubbers, and renew them if necessary **(see illustration)**.

Refitting

18 Refitting is a reversal of removal, bearing in mind the following points:
- a) *Ensure that the lower lugs on the radiator are correctly engaged with the mounting rubbers in the body panel* **(see illustration)**.
- b) *Ensure that all hoses are correctly reconnected, and their retaining clips securely tightened.*
- c) *On completion, refill the cooling system as described in Chapter 1.*

---

4 Thermostat – removal, testing and refitting

Removal

1 Disconnect the battery negative (earth) lead (refer to *Disconnecting the battery* in the Reference Chapter).

2 Drain the cooling system as described in Chapter 1.

3 Remove the battery and support bracket as described in Chapter 5A.

4 Loosen the clip and disconnect the top hose from the thermostat cover located on the left-hand side of the cylinder head.

5 Unscrew the bolts and remove the thermostat cover noting the location of the wiring support bracket on the top bolt. Recover the gasket.

Testing

6 A rough test of the thermostat's operation may be made by suspending it with a piece of string in a container full of water. Heat the water to bring it to the boil - the thermostat must open by the time the water boils. If not, renew it **(see illustration)**.

7 The opening temperature is usually marked on the thermostat. If a thermometer is available, the precise opening temperature of the thermostat may be determined, and compared with the value marked on the thermostat.

4.6 Testing the thermometer opening temperature

---

8 A thermostat which fails to close as the water cools must also be renewed.

Refitting

9 Thoroughly clean the mating faces of the thermostat cover and housing.

10 Locate the thermostat in the housing with the vent hole at the top.

11 Refit the cover together with a new gasket and tighten the bolts to the specified torque.

12 Refit the top hose and tighten the clip.

13 Refit the battery support bracket and battery with reference to Chapter 5A.

14 Refill and bleed the cooling system as described in Chapter 1.

15 Reconnect the battery negative (earth) lead.

---

5 Electric cooling fan – testing, removal and refitting

Testing

1 The cooling fan is supplied with current via the ignition switch, relay(s) and a fuse (see Chapter 12). The circuit is completed by the cooling fan thermostatic switch, which is mounted in the right-hand end of the radiator. **Note:** *On models with air conditioning, there are two switches fitted to the radiator; both switches operate the cooling fan and the air conditioning auxiliary cooling fan simultaneously. The lower switch operates at 100ºC, switching the fans on at a slow speed. If the coolant temperature reaches 105ºC, the upper switch operates both fans at full speed.*

2 If a fan does not appear to work, run the engine until normal operating temperature is reached, then allow it to idle. If the fan does not cut in within a few minutes (or before the temperature gauge indicates overheating), switch off the ignition and disconnect the wiring plug from the cooling fan switch. Bridge the two contacts in the wiring plug using a length of spare wire, and switch on the ignition. If the fan now operates, the switch is probably faulty, and should be renewed.

3 If the fan still fails to operate, check that full

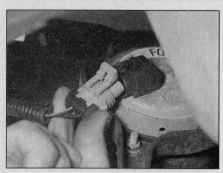

5.7 Disconnecting the wiring connector from the cooling fan motor (viewed from underneath)

battery voltage is available at the feed wire to the switch; if not, then there is a fault in the feed wire (possibly due to a fault in the fan motor, or a blown fuse). If there is no problem with the feed, check that there is continuity between the switch earth terminal and a good earth point on the body. If not, then the earth connection is faulty, and must be re-made.

4 If the switch and the wiring are in good condition, the fault must lie in the motor itself. The motor can be checked by disconnecting the motor wiring connector and connecting a 12 volt supply directly to the motor terminals. If the motor fails this test, it is proved faulty, and must be renewed complete.

Removal

Models without air conditioning

5 Disconnect the battery negative terminal (refer to *Disconnecting the battery* in the Reference Chapter).
6 Undo the plastic stud securing the air cleaner air intake trunking to the engine compartment front crossmember.
7 Disconnect the wiring connector from the cooling fan **(see illustration)**.
8 Unscrew the fan shroud retaining bolts, then tilt the assembly back slightly towards the engine, and withdraw it upwards away from the radiator **(see illustration)**. Where necessary, push the coolant hoses aside to provide sufficient clearance for removal.
9 To separate the fan motor from the shroud, unscrew the three retaining nuts, and remove the fan motor from the shroud.

5.8 Undo the retaining bolts, and lift the cooling fan assembly out from the engine compartment

10 No spare parts are available for the motor, and if the unit is faulty, it must be renewed complete.

Models with air conditioning

11 Disconnect the battery negative terminal (refer to *Disconnecting the battery* in the Reference Chapter).
12 Undo the plastic stud securing the air cleaner air intake trunking to the engine compartment front crossmember.
13 Undo the retaining bolts, and remove the left- and right-hand mounting brackets from the top of the radiator.
14 Unbolt the refrigerant pipe support bracket from the engine lifting bracket, then remove the engine lifting bracket from the cylinder head.
15 Remove the engine oil dipstick.
16 Unbolt the condenser left-hand mounting bracket from the front crossmember.
17 Unscrew the fan shroud retaining bolts, carefully push the top of the radiator towards the front of the car and withdraw the fan and shroud upwards from the radiator.
18 To separate the fan motor from the shroud, unscrew the three retaining nuts, and remove the fan motor from the shroud.
19 No spare parts are available for the motor, and if the unit is faulty, it must be renewed complete.

Refitting

20 Refitting is a reversal of removal, ensuring that the shroud is correctly located in the radiator clips.
21 On completion, start the engine and run it until it reaches normal operating temperature; continue to run the engine, and check that the cooling fan cuts in and functions correctly.

6 Cooling system electrical switches – testing, removal and refitting

Electric cooling fan thermostatic switch(es)

Testing

1 Testing of the switch(es) is described in Section 5, as part of the electric cooling fan test procedure.

Removal

2 The switch(es) is/are located in the left-hand side of the radiator. The engine and radiator should be cold before removing the switch.
3 Disconnect the battery negative terminal (refer to *Disconnecting the battery* in Reference). Firmly apply the handbrake, then jack up the front of the car and support it securely on axle stands (see *Jacking and vehicle support*). Access to the switch can then be gained from underneath the vehicle.
4 Either drain the cooling system to below the level of the switch (as described in Chapter 1), or have a suitable plug ready which can be

used to block the switch aperture in the radiator whilst the switch is removed. If a plug is used, take great care not to damage the radiator, and do not use anything which will allow foreign matter to enter the radiator.
5 Disconnect the wiring plug from the switch.
6 Carefully unscrew the switch from the radiator, and recover the sealing ring/washer

Refitting

7 Refitting is a reversal of removal, using a new sealing ring/washer. Securely tighten the switch, and top-up/refill the cooling system as described in Chapter 1.
8 On completion, start the engine and run it until it reaches normal operating temperature; continue to run the engine, and check that the cooling fan cuts in and functions correctly.

Coolant temperature sender

Testing

9 Testing of the coolant temperature sensor circuit must be entrusted to a Vauxhall/Opel dealer, who will have the necessary specialist diagnostic equipment.

Removal

10 Drain the cooling system as described in Chapter 1.
11 The temperature sensor is located on the thermostat housing on the left-hand end of the cylinder head.
12 Drain the cooling system as described in Chapter 1.
13 Disconnect the wiring, then unscrew the sensor from the thermostat housing.

Refitting

14 Refitting is a reversal of removal, but tighten the sensor to the specified torque and refill the cooling system with reference to Chapter 1.

7 Coolant pump – removal and refitting

Removal

1 Disconnect the battery negative (earth) lead (refer to *Disconnecting the battery* in the Reference Chapter).
2 Drain the cooling system as described in Chapter 1.
3 Remove the auxiliary drivebelt as described in Chapter 1.
4 Hold the coolant pump pulley stationary using an old auxiliary drivebelt or an oil filter strap wrench, then unscrew and remove the nuts and remove the pulley from the drive flange on the coolant pump.
5 Unscrew and remove the coolant pump securing bolts.
6 Withdraw the coolant pump from the cylinder block, noting that it may be necessary to tap the pump lightly with a soft-faced mallet to free it from the cylinder block. Remove the coolant duct-to-cylinder block guide.

7 Recover the gasket and discard it; a new one must be used on refitting.

8 Note that it is possible to obtain overhaul parts for the coolant pump, however a press is required to fit the bearing. If the pump is worn excessively, it will probably be more economical to obtain a replacement pump rather than overhaul the old one.

Refitting

9 Ensure that the pump and cylinder block mating surfaces are clean and dry.

10 Refit the coolant duct then install the coolant pump to the cylinder block together with a new gasket.

11 Insert the securing bolts and tighten progressively to the specified torque.

12 Refit the pulley and tighten the securing nuts to the specified torque while holding the pulley stationary using the method used on removal.

13 Refit and tension the auxiliary drivebelt as described in Chapter 1.

14 Reconnect the battery negative lead.

15 Refill and bleed the cooling system with reference to Chapter 1.

---

8 Heater/ventilation system – general information

The heater/ventilation system consists of a four-speed blower motor (housed in the engine compartment), face-level vents in the centre and at each end of the facia, and air ducts to the front footwells.

The control unit is located in the facia, and the controls operate flap valves to deflect and mix the air flowing through the various parts of the heater/ventilation system. The flap valves are contained in the air distribution housing, which acts as a central distribution unit, passing air to the various ducts and vents.

Cold air enters the system through the grille at the rear of the engine compartment. On most models (depending on specification) a pollen filter is fitted to the ventilation intake, to filter out dust, soot, pollen and spores from the air entering the vehicle.

The air (boosted by the blower fan if required) then flows through the various ducts, according to the settings of the controls. Stale air is expelled through ducts behind the doors. If warm air is required, the cold air is passed through the heater matrix, which is heated by the engine coolant.

A recirculation lever enables the outside air supply to be closed off, while the air inside the vehicle is recirculated. This can be useful to prevent unpleasant odours entering from outside the vehicle, but should only be used briefly, as the recirculated air inside the vehicle will soon deteriorate.

Certain models may be fitted with heated front seats. The heat is produced by electrically-heated mats in the seat and backrest cushions (see Chapter 12). The

9.4a Lever off the knob from the air recirculation lever . . .

9.5a Undo the four retaining screws (arrowed) . . .

temperature is regulated automatically by a thermostat, and cannot be adjusted.

---

9 Heater/ventilation system components – removal and refitting

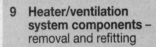

Control unit

Removal

1 Disconnect the battery negative terminal (refer to *Disconnecting the battery* in the Reference Chapter).

2 Remove the two centre vents from the facia panel as described in Section 10.

3 Remove the hazard warning light and heated rear window switches as described in Chapter 12. On models with heated front seats, also remove the seat heating switches.

4 Carefully lever the knob off the air recirculation lever, then prise the lever surround out of the centre facia panel, taking great care not to mark the panel **(see illustrations)**.

5 Undo the four retaining centre facia panel retaining screws, then withdraw the panel from the facia until access can be gained to the rear of the control panel **(see illustrations)**.

6 Unclip the four control cables, and release each cable from the control unit, noting each cable's correct fitted location and routing. **Note:** *The control cable end fittings are*

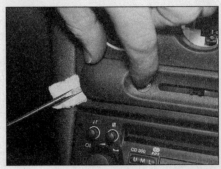

9.4b . . . then carefully prise out the lever surround. Note the use of a piece of card to avoid marking the facia panel

9.5b . . . then withdraw the centre facia panel from the facia

colour-coded for identification purposes. The outer cables are released by simply lifting the retaining clips.

7 Disconnect the wiring connectors from the control panel, and unclip the switch wiring connectors from the rear of the centre facia panel **(see illustration)**. Remove the centre facia panel from the vehicle.

8 If necessary, carefully prise off the remaining control knobs, then undo the two retaining screws, and unclip the heater control unit and vent from the centre facia panel **(see illustrations)**.

Refitting

9 Refitting is reversal of removal. Ensure that the control cables are correctly routed and reconnected to the control panel, as noted before removal. Clip the outer cables in

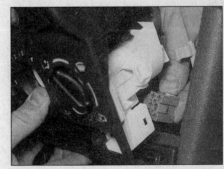

9.7 Free the wiring connectors from the rear of the centre facia panel and control unit, and remove the assembly from the facia

9.8a Unclip the remaining control knobs . . .

9.8b . . . then undo the two retaining screws (arrowed) . . .

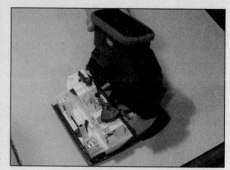

9.8c . . . and separate the vent and control unit from the facia panel

position, and check the operation of each knob/lever before refitting the centre facia panel.

Control cables renewal

Lower air distribution control

10 Remove the heater/ventilation control unit from the facia, as described above in paragraphs 1 to 5.

11 Unclip the lower air distribution cable (with the grey end fitting) and free the cable from the right-hand side of the control unit. The outer cable is released by simply lifting the retaining clip **(see illustration).**

12 Follow the run of the cable behind the facia, taking note of its routing, and disconnect the cable from the lever on the air distribution housing. Note that the method of fastening is the same as that used at the control unit. On right-hand drive models, if necessary, undo the two screws and remove the trim panel from the right-hand side of the facia centre panel to improve access to the cable.

13 Fit the new cable, ensuring that it is correctly routed, and free from kinks and obstructions.

14 Connect the cable to the control unit and air distribution housing, making sure the outer cable is clipped securely in position.

15 Check the operation of the control knob, then refit the control unit as described previously in this Section.

Upper air distribution control

16 Remove the heater/ventilation control unit

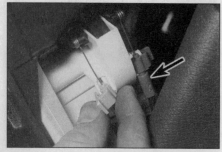

9.11 Unclipping the lower air distribution cable from the heater control unit. The rear cable (arrowed) is the upper air distribution cable

from the facia, as described above in paragraphs 1 to 5.

17 Unclip the upper air distribution cable (with the brown end fitting) and free the cable from the right-hand side of the control unit **(see illustration 9.11)**. The outer cable is released by simply lifting the retaining clip.

18 On left-hand drive models, remove the storage compartment (where fitted) from underneath the passenger side of the facia. The compartment is secured in position by a retaining screw and clip.

19 On all models, follow the run of the cable behind the facia, taking note of its routing, and disconnect the cable from the lever on the air distribution housing. Note that the method of fastening is the same as that used at the control unit. Release the cable from its retaining clip on the air distribution housing, and remove it from behind the facia.

20 Fit the new cable as described in paragraphs 13 to 15.

Air temperature control

21 Remove the heater/ventilation control unit from the facia, as described above in paragraphs 1 to 5.

22 Unclip and detach the upper and lower air distribution cables from the control unit (see paragraphs 11 and 17), noting the correct fitted location of each cable. Swing the control panel away from the facia, and disconnect the air temperature cable (with the black end fitting) from the left-hand side of the control unit.

23 On right-hand drive models, remove the storage compartment (where fitted) from underneath the passenger side of the facia. The compartment is secured in position by a retaining screw and clip.

24 On all models, follow the run of the cable behind the facia, taking note of its routing, and disconnect the cable from the lever on the air distribution housing. Note that the method of fastening is the same as that used at the control unit. Release the cable from its retaining clip on the air distribution housing, and remove it from behind the facia.

25 Fit the new cable, ensuring that it is correctly routed, and free from kinks and obstructions.

26 Connect the cable to the control unit and air distribution housing, making sure the outer

cable is clipped securely in position. Also clip the air distribution cables into their correct positions.

27 Check the operation of the control knobs, then refit the control unit as described previously in this Section.

Air recirculation control

28 Remove the heater/ventilation control unit from the facia, as described above in paragraphs 1 to 5.

29 Unclip and detach the upper and lower air distribution cables from the control unit (see paragraphs 11 and 17), noting the correct fitted location of each cable.

30 Swing the control panel away from the facia, and disconnect the air recirculation cable (with the blue or yellow end fitting) from the rear of the control unit **(see illustration)**.

31 On left-hand drive models, remove the storage compartment (where fitted) from underneath the passenger side of the facia. The compartment is secured in position by a retaining screw and clip.

32 On all models, remove the cable and install the new one as described in paragraphs 24 to 27. Note that, on models with air conditioning, it will also be necessary to remove the glovebox (see Chapter 11, Section 26) and detach the cable from the evaporator housing.

Heater matrix

Removal

33 With the engine cold, unscrew the expansion tank cap (referring to the warning

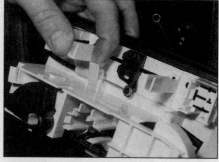

9.30 Disconnecting the air recirculation cable from the rear of the control unit

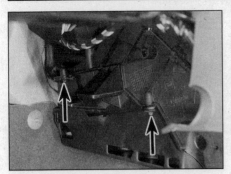

9.40a Undo the two left-hand retaining screws (arrowed) . . .

9.40b . . . and the three right-hand screws (arrowed) . . .

9.40c . . . then detach the air distribution housing base and remove it from the left-hand side

note in Section 1) to release any pressure present in the cooling system, then securely refit the cap.

34 On right-hand drive vehicles, remove the battery as described in Chapter 5A.

35 Undo the expansion tank retaining nuts, and free the tank from the engine compartment bulkhead. Place the tank clear of the bulkhead to gain access to the heater matrix hose unions.

36 Clamp both heater hoses as close to the bulkhead as possible, to minimise coolant loss. Alternatively, drain the cooling system as described in Chapter 1.

37 Slacken the retaining clips, and disconnect both hoses from the heater matrix unions. Unscrew the retaining screw which is situated between the unions.

38 Working inside the vehicle, remove the storage compartment (where fitted) from underneath the passenger side of the facia. The compartment is secured in position by a retaining screw and clip.

39 On left-hand drive models, undo the two screws and remove the trim panel from the centre of the facia, on the driver's side. Unbolt the support strut (where fitted, this is situated on the driver's side of the air distribution housing) from the floor, and swing the strut away from the housing.

40 Undo the five retaining screws (two on the left-hand side, and three on the right-hand side) securing the lower cover to the base of the air distribution housing. Unclip the cover and remove it from the vehicle (**see illustrations**).

41 Detach the intermediate housing from bottom of the distribution housing, and remove it towards the left-hand side of the vehicle (**see illustration**). On left-hand drive models, it may be necessary to depress the brake and clutch pedals to allow the housing to be removed.

42 Cover the carpet directly underneath the air distribution housing, to catch any coolant which may be spilt from the matrix as it is removed. Alternatively, release the carpet fasteners, and fold the carpet back from the bulkhead so that any spilt coolant will go behind the carpet.

43 Lower the heater matrix out from the air distribution housing, swing it to the left, then disengage the matrix unions from the bulkhead and remove the matrix from the vehicle (**see illustration**). **Note:** *Keep the matrix unions uppermost as the matrix is removed, to prevent coolant spillage.* Mop up any spilt coolant immediately, and wipe the affected area with a damp cloth to prevent staining.

44 Where necessary, recover the sealing grommets from the matrix unions, and refit them to the bulkhead.

Refitting

45 Refitting is a reversal of the removal procedure, bearing in mind the following points:

a) Apply a smear of oil to the matrix sealing grommets, to ease installation.

b) Ensure that the heater hose retaining clips are securely tightened.

c) On completion, top-up/refill the cooling system as described in Chapter 1.

Heater blower motor renewal

Models without air conditioning

46 Disconnect the battery negative terminal (refer to *Disconnecting the battery* in the Reference Chapter).

47 Remove both windscreen wiper arms as described in Chapter 12.

48 Carefully prise out the wiper spindle sealing grommets from the windscreen cowl panel.

49 Undo the retaining screws, and remove both halves of the windscreen cowl panel from the vehicle.

50 Peel the bonnet seal off the engine compartment bulkhead, and remove it from the vehicle.

51 Unscrew the large plastic nut from each wiper spindle.

52 Prise out the two clips from the centre of the water deflector shield. Release the deflector from the engine compartment bulkhead and wiper spindles, and remove it from the vehicle.

53 Where necessary, release the retaining clips and lift out the pollen filter (**see illustration**).

54 Undo the screws, and remove the frame from the top of the heater/ventilation intake duct (**see illustrations**).

55 Set the air recirculation control to the 'fresh air' position.

9.41 Unclip the air distribution intermediate housing, and remove it from the left-hand side

9.43 Lower the heater matrix out of position, and swing it to the left to disengage its unions from the bulkhead

9.53 Where necessary, remove the pollen filter from the heater/ventilation intake

9.54a Undo the four retaining screws (arrowed) . . .

9.54b . . . and lift out the frame

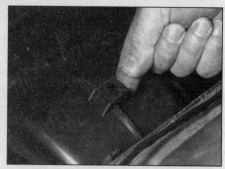

9.56a Release the retaining clips . . .

9.56b . . . and remove the right-hand . . .

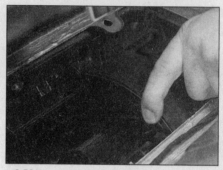

9.56c . . . and left-hand covers from the blower motor

9.57 Unhook the retaining clip (arrowed) . . .

56 Release the retaining clips, and remove the blower motor right-hand, then left-hand covers from inside the intake duct **(see illustrations)**.

57 Unhook the blower motor retaining clip, noting how the wiring is routed through the clip **(see illustration)**.

58 Disconnect the motor wiring connectors from the resistor, noting the correct routing of the wiring, and manoeuvre the blower motor out from its housing **(see illustration)**.

59 Refitting is a reversal of the removal procedure, noting the following points:
  a) Make sure that the motor wiring is correctly routed underneath the blower motor retaining clip **(see illustration)** so that there is no danger of the wiring contacting the fan blades.
  b) Make sure that the blower motor covers are correctly engaged with each other, and clipped securely in position.

Models with air conditioning

60 Remove the windscreen wiper motor as described in Chapter 12.

61 Where necessary, release the retaining clips and remove the pollen filter.

62 Undo the screws, and remove the frame from the top of the heating/ventilation intake duct. Where necessary, also cut the intake mesh to allow access to the motor assembly.

63 Set the air recirculation control to the 'fresh air' position.

64 Undo the retaining screws, and remove both halves of the blower motor cover.

65 Disconnect the wiring connectors from the resistor, then undo the two screws and remove the blower motor retaining clamp.

66 Lift the blower motor assembly out of position.

67 Refitting is a reverse of the removal procedure, noting the following points:

  a) Make sure that the motor wiring is correctly routed underneath the blower motor retaining clamp, so that there is no danger of the wiring contacting the fan blades.
  b) Make sure that the blower motor covers are correctly engaged with each other, and clipped securely in position.

Heater blower motor resistor

Removal

68 On models without air conditioning, carry out the operations described above in paragraphs 46 to 56. On models with air conditioning, carry out the operations described in paragraphs 60 to 64.

69 From inside the vehicle, reach up behind the facia, and disconnect the wiring connector from the underside of the blower motor resistor, which is on the left-hand side of the air distribution housing **(see illustration)**.

9.58 . . . and lift the blower motor out from its housing

9.59 Secure the blower motor in position with the retaining clip, making sure its wiring is correctly routed (arrowed)

9.69 Disconnecting the wiring connector from the blower motor resistor (viewed through glovebox aperture)

70 Return to the engine compartment, then undo the retaining screw and disconnect the blower motor wiring connectors from the resistor. Remove the resistor from the vehicle **(see illustrations)**.

Refitting

71 Refitting is the reverse of removal.

Air distribution housing renewal

Models without air conditioning

72 Remove the facia assembly as described in Chapter 11.

73 Carry out the operations described in paragraphs 33 to 37.

74 Where necessary, release the retaining clips and remove the pollen filter.

75 Undo the screws, and remove the frame from the top of the heating/ventilation intake duct.

76 Cover the carpet directly underneath the air distribution housing, to catch any coolant which may be spilt from the matrix as the housing assembly is removed.

77 Disconnect the wiring connector from the blower motor resistor on the left-hand side of the housing.

78 Disconnect the duct from the driver's side of the housing, and remove the housing from the vehicle **(see illustration)**. **Note:** *Keep the matrix unions uppermost as the housing is removed, to prevent coolant spillage.* Mop up any spilt coolant immediately, and wipe the affected area with a damp cloth to prevent staining. Recover the foam spacers from behind the housing.

79 Refitting is the reverse of removal. On completion, top-up the cooling system as described in Chapter 1.

Models with air conditioning

80 On models with air conditioning, it is not possible to remove the air distribution housing without opening the refrigerant circuit (see Section 11). Therefore, this task must be entrusted to a Vauxhall/Opel dealer.

10	Heater/ventilation vents and ducts – removal and refitting

Vents

1 Point the vent fully downwards then, using a suitable screwdriver, carefully lever between the top of the vent and the vent housing until a gap of approximately 2 mm appears. Position a piece of card behind screwdriver blade, to avoid damaging the housing.

2 Insert a small, flat-bladed screwdriver in through the gap, and carefully lever between the sides of the vent and the housing to release the vent from its locating pegs **(see illustration)**.

3 Once the vent is free from both its locating pegs, it can be withdrawn from the facia **(see illustration)**.

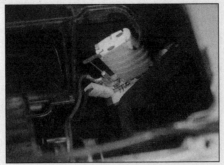

9.70a Disconnect the wiring connectors . . .

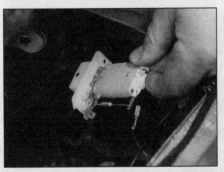

9.70c . . . and lift the blower motor resistor out of position

4 On refitting, carefully manoeuvre the vent back into the facia, ensuring it is correctly engaged with the locating pegs.

Driver's side heater/ventilation housing

5 Disconnect the battery negative terminal (refer to *Disconnecting the battery* in the Reference Chapter).

6 Remove the cover from the fusebox.

7 Remove the driver's side vent as described in paragraphs 1 to 3.

8 Remove the lighting switch as described in Chapter 12.

9 Undo the four retaining screws, and withdraw the vent housing/switch assembly from the facia, disconnecting its wiring connectors as they become accessible **(see illustrations)**.

10 Refitting is a reversal of the removal procedure, ensuring that the housing is

10.3 . . . to release them from their locating pegs(arrowed)

9.70b . . . then undo the retaining screw (arrowed) . . .

9.78 Removing the air distribution housing

correctly located with the duct.

Passenger side duct

11 Remove the glovebox as described in Chapter 11, Section 26.

10.2 Remove the heater/ventilation ducts as described in text . . .

10.9a Undo the four retaining screws (arrowed) . . .

10.9b . . . then withdraw the vent housing/ switch assembly from the facia . . .

10.9c . . . and free the wiring connectors from the rear of the housing

10.12a Undo the three retaining screws (arrowed) . . .

10.12b . . . and remove the vent housing from the facia

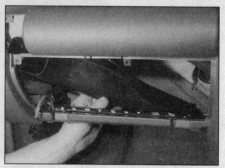

10.13 Disconnect the duct from the air distribution housing, and remove it from underneath the facia

12 Undo the three retaining screws, and remove the vent housing from the facia **(see illustrations)**.

13 Disconnect the duct from the air distribution housing, and manoeuvre the duct out through the glovebox aperture, or from underneath the facia **(see illustration)**.

14 Refitting is a reversal of the removal procedure, ensuring that the duct is securely reconnected to the air distribution housing.

11 Air conditioning system – general information and precautions

General information

1 Air conditioning is available on certain models **(see illustration)**. It enables the temperature of incoming air to be lowered, and also dehumidifies the air, which makes for rapid demisting and increased comfort.

2 The cooling side of the system works in the same way as a domestic refrigerator. Refrigerant gas is drawn into a belt-driven compressor, and passes into a condenser mounted in front of the radiator, where it loses heat and becomes liquid. The liquid passes through an expansion valve to an evaporator, where it changes from liquid under high pressure to gas under low pressure. This change is accompanied by a drop in

temperature, which cools the evaporator. The refrigerant returns to the compressor, and the cycle begins again.

3 Air blown through the evaporator passes to the air distribution unit, where it is mixed with hot air blown through the heater matrix, to achieve the desired temperature in the passenger compartment.

4 The heating side of the system works in the same way as on models without air conditioning (see Section 8).

5 The operation of the system is controlled electronically by the coolant temperature switches (see Section 5), which are screwed into the right-hand end of the radiator, and pressure switches which are screwed into the compressor high-pressure line. Any problems with the system should be referred to a Vauxhall/Opel dealer.

Precautions

6 It is necessary to observe special precautions whenever dealing with any part of the system, its associated components, and any items which necessitate disconnection of the system.

⚠️ *Warning: The refrigeration circuit contains a liquid refrigerant. This refrigerant is potentially danger-ous, and should only be handled by qualified persons. If it is splashed onto the skin, it can cause frostbite. It is not itself poisonous, but in the presence of a naked*

flame it forms a poisonous gas; inhalation of the vapour through a lighted cigarette could prove fatal. Uncontrolled discharging of the refrigerant is dangerous, and potentially damaging to the environment. It is therefore dangerous to disconnect any part of the system without specialised knowledge and equipment. If for any reason the system must be disconnected, entrust this task to your Vauxhall/Opel dealer or a refrigeration engineer.

7 Do not operate the air conditioning system if it is known to be short of refrigerant, as this may damage the compressor.

12 Air conditioning system components – removal and refitting

⚠️ *Warning: Do not attempt to open the refrigerant circuit. Refer to the precautions given in Section 11.*

1 The only operation which can be carried out easily, without discharging the refrigerant, is renewal of the compressor drivebelt, which is covered in Chapter 1. All other operations must be referred to a Vauxhall/Opel dealer or an air conditioning specialist.

2 Where required for improved access, the compressor can be unbolted and moved aside, **without disconnecting its flexible hoses**, after removing the drivebelt.

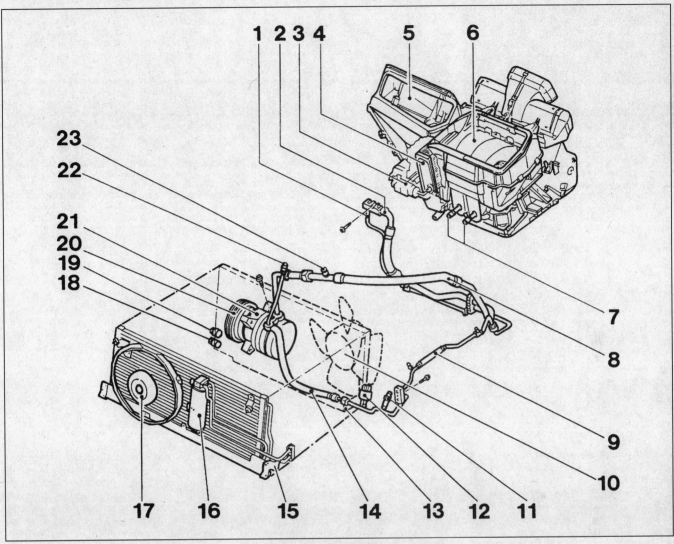

11.1 Air conditioning system components

1 High-pressure refrigerant pipe
2 Low-pressure refrigerant hose
3 Thermostatically-controlled expansion valve
4 Evaporator
5 Recirculation air duct
6 Blower motor
7 Heater matrix unions
8 Low-pressure refrigerant hose

9 High pressure refrigerant hose
10 Cooling fan
11 Idle-up switch
12 Auxiliary cooling fan switch
13 Radiator
14 High-pressure refrigerant hose
15 Condenser

16 Accumulator
17 Auxiliary cooling fan
18 Coolant temperature switch
19 Coolant temperature switch
20 Compressor drive pulley with integral clutch
21 Compressor
22 Low-pressure service connection
23 High-pressure service connection

Notes

Chapter 4 Part A:
Fuel and exhaust systems

Contents

Degrees of difficulty

Easy, suitable for novice with little experience 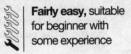	Fairly easy, suitable for beginner with some experience	Fairly difficult, suitable for competent DIY mechanic	Difficult, suitable for experienced DIY mechanic	Very difficult, suitable for expert DIY or professional

Specifications

Adjustment data

Idle speed . . . . 830 to 930 rpm

Maximum speed:
  1.5 litre non-turbo models . . . . 5800 rpm
  1.5 litre turbo models . . . . 5600 rpm
  1.7 litre models . . . . 5300 rpm

Injection pump

Direction of rotation . . . . Clockwise, viewed from sprocket end

Pump timing measurement (static):
  1.5 litre non-turbo models . . . . 0.90 ± 0.05 mm
  1.5 litre turbo models . . . . 0.68 ± 0.05 mm
  1.7 litre models . . . . 0.65 ± 0.05 mm

Injectors

Opening pressure . . . . 142 to 162 bar

Torque wrench settings

	Nm	lbf ft
Accelerator pedal nuts	20	15
Charge air safety valve to inlet manifold	50	38
Exhaust front pipe-to-turbocharger nuts	65	48
Exhaust manifold:		
Retaining nuts and bolts	24	18
Support bracket bolts	51	38
Fuel injector return pipe nuts	29	21
Fuel injectors	50	37
Fuel pipe union nuts	25	18
Fuel tank retaining strap bolts	20	15
Inlet manifold nuts and bolts:		
Non-turbo models	24	18
Turbo models	30	22

Torque wrench settings (continued)

	Nm	lbf ft
Injection pump:		
Front mounting nuts	23	17
Rear mounting bracket bolts:		
M8 bolts	25	18
M10 bolts	40	30
Timing access hole plug	20	15
Timing belt sprocket nut	69	51
Turbocharger:		
Exhaust flange nuts	27	20
Turbocharger-to-manifold nuts	27	20

1 General information and precautions

General information

The fuel and exhaust systems fitted follow normal practice for modern passenger diesel vehicles. A combined lift and injection pump, driven from the camshaft drivebelt, draws fuel from the tank and distributes it to each cylinder in turn. The injectors deliver a high pressure spray of fuel into the swirl chambers, where combustion starts. On the turbocharged engine, this fuel spray is accompanied by pressurised air supplied by a turbocharger. Excess fuel from the pump and the injectors is returned to the tank. A filter, which also acts as a water trap, protects the pump from contaminated fuel.

Cold starting is assisted by pre-heating the combustion chambers electrically. This system is automatically controlled. A thermo-statically-controlled cold start accelerator device attached to the side of the injection pump and interconnected to the engine cooling system, causes the pump to deliver extra fuel and alters the injection timing slightly to improve cold start performance.

Manual bleeding or venting of the fuel system is not necessary, even if the fuel tank is run dry. Provided that the battery is in good condition, simply cranking the engine on the starter motor will eventually bleed the system. Note that the starter motor should not be operated for more than ten seconds at a time whilst allowing five seconds between periods of operation.

The fuel injection system is inherently robust and reliable. If the specified maintenance is carried out conscientiously it should give little trouble. Some components can only be overhauled or repaired by specialists and the home mechanic is warned against attempting operations beyond those described in this Chapter, unless qualified to do so.

Turbocharger

The turbocharger enables the engine to produce appreciably greater power and torque than the normally-aspirated unit.

Mounted between the exhaust manifold and front exhaust pipe, and driven by the exhaust gases, the turbocharger takes its air supply from the filter housing, through a plenum chamber and passes air under pressure to the inlet manifold.

Lubrication for the turbocharger is provided by a dedicated oil supply. The turbocharger has an integral wastegate valve and vacuum actuator diaphragm, which is used to control the boost pressure applied to the inlet manifold.

Precautions

⚠️ *Warning: It is necessary to take certain precautions when working on the fuel system components, particularly the fuel injectors. Before carrying out any operations on the fuel system, refer to the precautions given in 'Safety first!' at the beginning of this manual, and to any additional warning notes at the start of the relevant Sections. Caution: Do not operate the engine if any*

of air intake ducts are disconnected or the filter element is removed. Any debris entering the engine will cause severe damage.
Caution: To prevent damage to the turbocharger, do not race the engine immediately after start-up, especially if it is cold. Allow it to idle smoothly to give the oil a few seconds to circulate around the turbocharger bearings. Always allow the engine to return to idle speed before switching it off – do not blip the throttle and switch off, as this will leave the turbo spinning without lubrication.
Caution: Observe the recommended intervals for oil and filter changing, and use a reputable oil of the specified quality. Neglect of oil changing, or use of inferior oil, can cause carbon formation on the turbo shaft, leading to subsequent failure.

2 Air cleaner assembly and intake ducts – removal and refitting

Removal

1 Slacken the retaining clip and detach the intake duct from the air cleaner housing (**see illustrations**). If necessary, slacken the other retaining clip then detach the duct from the manifold and remove it from the engine compartment (**see illustrations**).
2 Undo the nuts securing the air cleaner mountings to the body then free the housing from its air intake and remove the assembly from the engine compartment.

2.1a Slacken the retaining clip . . .

2.1b . . . and detach the intake duct from the air cleaner housing

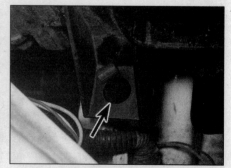

2.2a Pull the air cleaner housing free at the front . . .

3 On turbo models, the remaining ducts linking the turbocharger, intercooler and inlet manifold can be removed once their retaining clips and (where necessary) bolts have been slackened.

Refitting

4 Refitting is the reverse of removal, ensuring that all intake ducts are properly reconnected and their retaining clips securely tightened.

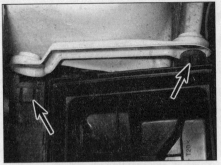

2.2b . . . and at the rear . . .   2.2c . . . and remove the assembly

3 Accelerator cable – removal, refitting and adjustment

Note: *Access to the injection pump is very poor and can only be significantly improved by removing the inlet manifold (see Section 17).*

Removal

1 Working in the engine compartment, release the inner cable retaining clip then slide the clip out of the end fitting and release the cable from the injection pump accelerator lever **(see illustration)**.

2 Free the accelerator outer cable from its mounting bracket, taking care not to lose the adjusting clip **(see illustration)**. Work back along the length of the cable, free it from any retaining clips or ties, noting its correct routing.

3 From inside the vehicle, unscrew the fasteners and remove the lower trim panel from underneath the driver's side of the facia to gain access to the accelerator pedal.

4 Reaching up behind the facia, unclip the accelerator inner cable from the top of the accelerator pedal **(see illustration)**.

5 Return to the engine compartment then free the cable sealing grommet from the bulkhead and remove the cable and grommet from the vehicle.

6 Examine the cable for signs of wear or damage and renew if necessary. Check the rubber grommet for signs of damage or deterioration and renew it if necessary.

Refitting

7 Feed the cable into position from the engine compartment and seat the outer cable grommet in the bulkhead.

8 From inside the vehicle, clip the inner cable into position in the pedal end and check to make sure the grommet is correctly located in the bulkhead. Check that the cable is securely retained, then refit the trim panel to the facia.

9 From within the engine compartment, ensure the outer cable is correctly seated in the bulkhead, then work along the cable, securing it in position with the retaining clips and ties, ensuring that the cable is correctly routed.

10 Connect the inner cable to the injection pump accelerator lever and secure it in position with the retaining clip. Clip the outer cable into its mounting bracket and adjust the cable as described below.

Adjustment

11 Working in the engine compartment, slide the adjustment clip from accelerator outer cable.

12 With the clip removed, ensure that the injection pump accelerator lever is fully against its stop. Gently pull the cable out of its grommet until all free play is removed from the inner cable.

13 With the cable held in this position, refit the spring clip to the last exposed outer cable groove in front of the rubber grommet. When the clip is refitted and the outer cable is released, there should be only a small amount of free play in the inner cable.

14 Have an assistant depress the accelerator pedal, and check that the injection pump accelerator lever opens fully and returns smoothly to its stop.

4 Accelerator pedal – removal and refitting

1 From inside the vehicle, unscrew the fasteners and remove the lower trim panel from underneath the driver's side of the facia to gain access to the accelerator pedal.

2 Reaching up behind the facia, unclip the accelerator inner cable from the top of the accelerator pedal.

3 Unscrew the retaining nuts and remove the pedal assembly from the bulkhead.

4 Inspect the pedal assembly for signs of wear, paying particular attention to the pedal bushes, and renew as necessary. To dismantle the assembly, unhook the return spring then slide off the retaining clip and separate the pedal, mounting bracket, return spring and pivot bushes.

5 If the assembly has been dismantled, apply a smear of multi-purpose grease to the pedal pivot shaft and bushes. Fit the bushes and return spring to the mounting bracket and insert the pedal, making sure it passes through the return spring bore. Secure the pedal in position with the retaining clip and hook the return spring back behind the pedal.

6 Refit the pedal assembly and tighten its retaining nuts to the specified torque setting.

7 Clip the accelerator cable into position on the pedal then refit the trim panel to the facia.

8 On completion, adjust the accelerator cable as described in Section 3.

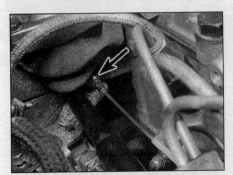

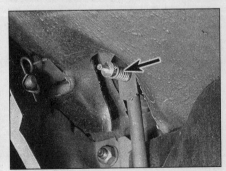

3.1 Remove the retaining clip then free the inner cable end fitting from its balljoint . . .   **3.2 . . . and detach the outer cable from its bracket**   **3.4 Accelerator cable fitting at pedal end**

6.2 Prise out the access cover to expose the fuel pick-up

5 Fuel system – priming and bleeding

1 It is not necessary to manually prime and bleed the fuel system after any operation on the system components. Start the engine (this may take longer than usual, especially if the fuel system has been allowed to run dry – operate the starter in ten second bursts with 5 seconds' rest in between each operation) and run it a fast idle speed for a minute or so to purge any trapped air from the fuel lines. After this time the engine should idle smoothly at a constant speed.

2 If the engine idles roughly, then there is still some air trapped in the fuel system. Increase the engine speed again for another minute or so then recheck the idle speed. Repeat this procedure as necessary until the engine is idling smoothly.

6 Fuel gauge sender unit – removal and refitting

⚠ **Warning: Refer to the warning note in Section 1 before proceeding.**
Note: *A new fuel pick-up cover sealing ring will be required on refitting.*

Removal

1 Disconnect the battery negative lead.
2 Fold the rear seat cushion forwards and lift

up the flap in the carpet to reveal the fuel pick-up access cover **(see illustration)**.

3 Using a screwdriver, carefully prise the plastic access cover from the floor to expose the fuel pick-up.

4 Mark the fuel hoses for identification purposes. The hoses are equipped with quick-release fittings to ease removal. To disconnect each hose, compress the clips located on each side of the fitting and ease the fitting off of its union. Disconnect both hoses from the top of the pick-up, noting the correct fitted position of the sealing rings and plug the hose ends to minimise fuel loss.

5 Unscrew the locking ring and remove it from the tank. This is best accomplished by using a screwdriver on the raised ribs of the locking ring. Carefully tap the screwdriver to turn the ring anti-clockwise until it can be unscrewed by hand.

6 Carefully lift the fuel pick-up cover away from tank. Make alignment marks between the cover and hoses then release the retaining clips and remove the cover from the vehicle along with its sealing ring. Discard the sealing ring; a new one must be used on refitting.

7 The fuel gauge sender unit is clipped to the side of the fuel reservoir. Carefully release the retaining clip then slide the sender unit upwards to release it from its mounting.

8 Manoeuvre the sender unit through the fuel tank aperture, taking great care not damage the float arm.

Refitting

9 Manoeuvre the sender unit carefully in through the tank aperture and slide it into position on the side of the fuel reservoir.

10 Ensure the sender unit is clipped securely in position.

11 Fit a new sealing ring to the tank.

12 Reconnect the fuel hoses to the fuel pick-up cover, using the marks made on removal, and securely tighten their retaining clips. Seat the cover on the tank.

13 Refit the locking ring to the fuel tank and tighten it securely.

14 Reconnect the fuel hoses to the fuel pick-up cover, ensuring each fitting clicks securely into position.

15 Reconnect the battery then start the engine and check for fuel leaks. If all is well,

refit the access cover and fold the seat back into position.

7 Fuel tank – removal and refitting

⚠ **Warning: Refer to the warning note in Section 1 before proceeding.**

Removal

1 Disconnect the battery negative terminal.

2 Before removing the fuel tank, all fuel must be drained from the tank. Since a fuel tank drain plug is not provided, it is therefore preferable to carry out the removal operation when the tank is nearly empty. The remaining fuel can then be syphoned or hand-pumped from the tank.

3 Remove the exhaust system and relevant heat shield(s) as described in Section 18.

4 Open up the fuel filler flap and remove the rubber cover from around the filler neck aperture. Slacken and remove the retaining bolt which secures the filler neck to the body **(see illustrations)**.

5 Remove the right-hand rear wheel then remove the retaining screws and clips and remove the plastic wheel arch liner.

6 Make alignment marks between the small hoses and the top of the filler neck assembly then release the retaining clips and disconnect both hoses.

7 Slacken the retaining clips and disconnect the main hoses from the base of the filler neck. Unscrew the filler neck lower retaining bolt and manoeuvre the assembly out from underneath the vehicle.

8 Trace the fuel feed and return hoses from the tank to their unions in front of the tank **(see illustration)**. Make alignment marks between the hoses then release the retaining clips and disconnect both hoses. If the hoses are equipped with quick-release fittings, disconnect each hose by depressing the clips on each side of the fitting and easing the fitting of the pipe.

9 Plug the fuel hose ends to prevent the fuel draining from the system; this will enable the engine to be started more easily once the fuel tank has been refitted (see Section 5).

7.4a Remove the rubber cover from the fuel tank filler neck . . .

7.4b . . . then undo the retaining screw (arrowed)

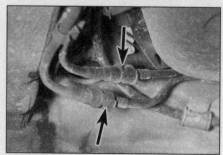

7.8 Disconnect the fuel feed and return hoses (arrowed) at the unions at the front of the tank

7.11 Fuel tank retaining strap bolt (arrowed)

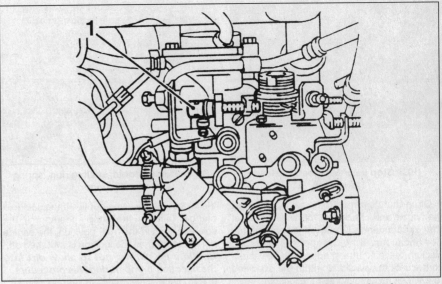

8.3 The maximum speed adjusting screw (1) is sealed with a lead seal

10 Place a trolley jack with an interposed block of wood beneath the tank, then raise the jack until it is supporting the weight of the tank.

11 Slacken and remove the retaining bolts and remove the two retaining straps from underneath the fuel tank (see illustration).

12 Slowly lower the fuel tank out of position, disconnecting any other relevant vent pipes as they become accessible (where necessary), and remove the tank from underneath the vehicle.

13 If the tank is contaminated with sediment or water, remove the fuel gauge sender cover (Section 6), and swill the tank out with clean fuel. The tank is injection-moulded from a synthetic material - if seriously damaged, it should be renewed. However, in certain cases, it may be possible to have small leaks or minor damage repaired. Seek the advice of a specialist before attempting to repair the fuel tank.

Refitting

14 Refitting is the reverse of the removal procedure, noting the following points:

a) When lifting the tank back into position, take care to ensure that none of the hoses become trapped between the tank and vehicle body. Refit the retaining straps and tighten the bolts to the specified torque.

b) Ensure all pipes and hoses are correctly routed and all hoses unions are securely joined.

c) On completion, refill the tank with a small amount of fuel, and check for signs of leakage prior to taking the vehicle out on the road.

8 Maximum speed – checking and adjustment

Caution: The maximum speed adjustment screw is sealed by the manufacturers at the factory, using paint or a locking wire and a lead seal. There is no reason why it should require adjustment. Do not disturb the screw if the vehicle is still within the warranty period, otherwise the warranty will be invalidated. This adjustment

requires the use of a tachometer – refer to Chapter 1 for alternative methods.

1 Run the engine to normal operating temperature.

2 Have an assistant fully depress the accelerator pedal, and check that the maximum engine speed is as given in the Specifications. Do not keep the engine at maximum speed for more than two or three seconds.

3 If adjustment is necessary, stop the engine, then loosen the locknut, turn the maximum speed adjustment screw as necessary, and retighten the locknut (see illustration).

4 Repeat the procedure in paragraph 2 to check the adjustment.

5 Stop the engine and disconnect the tachometer.

9 Cold start advance (CSA) system – general information and adjustment

General information

1 A cold start advance (CSA) capsule is fitted to the injection pump to improve the running and lessen exhaust emissions when the

engine is cold. The coolant circulates around the thermostatic capsule which contains an expandable element. When the engine is cold, the element advances the injection timing and raises the engine idle speed approximately 150 rpm. This prevents the engine stalling and also lessens exhaust smoke.

Adjustment

2 Check and, if necessary, adjust the idle speed as described in Chapter 1 then allow the engine to cool fully.

3 With the engine cool, measure the clearance between the cold start advance lever adjustment screw and the injection pump accelerator lever. At a coolant temperature of 20°C (68°F) the clearance should be 0.8 to 1.1 mm. **Note:** *If the coolant temperature is hotter or colder than 20°C (68°F) then this should be taken into consideration when making the measurement; the cooler the temperature the larger the clearance and the warmer the temperature the smaller the clearance. If necessary, slacken the locknut and adjust the clearance by rotating the cold start lever adjustment screw* **(see illustrations)**. Once the clearance is correctly set, hold the screw and securely tighten the locknut.

9.3a Measure the clearance between cold start advance lever screw and the accelerator lever . . .

9.3b . . . and, if necessary, adjust by slackening the locknut and rotating the adjustment screw

10.3 Stop solenoid electrical lead (arrowed)

10.4 Stop solenoid, sealing ring, spring and plunger

4 Once the clearance is correctly set, start the engine and check that the engine idles at the recommended speed given in the Specifications. If adjustment is necessary, slacken the locknut and adjust the idle speed screw until the speed is within the specified range then securely tighten the locknut.

5 Warm the engine up to normal operating temperature and recheck the idle speed. As the engine warms, the gap between the cold start advance lever and the accelerator lever should steadily decrease until the two are in contact. If this is not the case, there is a fault in the cold start advance system and the vehicle should be taken to a Vauxhall dealer for testing.

6 Where applicable, disconnect the tachometer on completion.

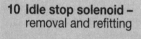

10 Idle stop solenoid – removal and refitting

1 The only electrical component in the injection system is the stop solenoid. The solenoid is located on the top of the fuel injection pump, at the rear, its purpose being to cut the fuel supply when the ignition is switched off. If an open-circuit occurs in the solenoid or supply wiring, it will be impossible to start the engine, as the fuel will not reach

the injectors. The same applies if the solenoid plunger jams in the 'stop' position. If the solenoid jams in the 'run' position, the engine will not stop when the ignition is switched off.

Caution: Be careful not to allow dirt into the injection pump during this procedure.

2 Remove the inlet manifold (see Section 17).

3 Remove the rubber cover from the top of the solenoid then slacken and remove the nut and washer and disconnect the feed wire **(see illustration)**.

4 Carefully clean around the solenoid, then unscrew and withdraw the solenoid, and recover the sealing washer/ring (as applicable). Recover the solenoid plunger and spring if they remain in the pump **(see illustration)**. If the solenoid is to be removed for any length of time, cover the injection pump to prevent the entry of dirt.

5 Refitting is a reversal of removal, using a new sealing washer/ring and tightening the solenoid securely.

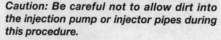

11 Fuel injection pump – removal and refitting

Caution: Be careful not to allow dirt into the injection pump or injector pipes during this procedure.

Removal

1 Disconnect the battery negative lead then remove the inlet manifold as described in Section 17.

2 Remove the injection pump timing belt sprocket as described in Chapter 2A.

3 Remove the engine oil filter as described in Chapter 1. If the oil filter is damaged on removal (which is likely), drain the engine oil then fit a new filter on refitting and refill the engine with fresh oil.

4 Remove the retaining clip and free the accelerator cable from the injection pump.

5 Clamp the coolant hoses to minimise coolant loss then release the retaining clips and disconnect both hoses from the injection pump cold start advance capsule **(see illustration)**. Mop up any spilt coolant.

6 Remove all traces of dirt and make identification marks between the fuel feed and return hoses and their pump unions. Release the retaining clips and disconnect both hoses from the pump. Plug the hose ends to minimise fuel loss and prevent the entry of dirt.

7 Wipe clean the pipe unions then slacken the union nuts securing the injector pipes to the top of each injector and the four union nuts securing the pipes to the rear of the injection pump; as each pump union nut is slackened, retain the adapter with a suitable open-ended spanner to prevent it being unscrewed from the pump. With all the union nuts undone, remove the injector pipes from the engine unit and mop up any spilt fuel.

8 Disconnect the wiring connector from the injection pump solenoid/solenoid control unit (as applicable).

9 Mark the fuel injection pump front flange in relation to the mounting bracket, using a scriber or felt tip pen. This will ensure the correct pump timing is retained when refitting.

10 Slacken and remove the retaining bolts securing the pump rear mounting bracket to the cylinder block bracket **(see illustration)**.

11 Slacken and remove the pump front

11.5 The fuel injection pump cold start advance capsule (arrowed)

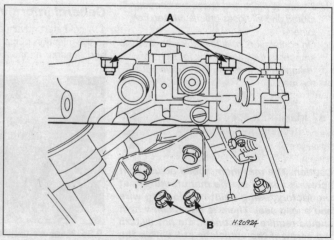

11.10 Fuel injection pump front mounting nuts (A) and rear mounting bracket bolts (B)

mounting nuts and remove the pump assembly from the engine.

Caution: Never attempt to dismantle the pump assembly. If there is a problem, take the pump to a Vauxhall dealer/diesel injection specialist for testing/repair.

Refitting

12 Manoeuvre the pump into position and loosely refit its front mounting nuts and rear mounting bolts.

13 Align the marks made on the pump and mounting bracket before removal and lightly tighten the mounting nuts and bolts. If a new pump is being fitted, transfer the mark from the old pump to give an approximate setting.

14 Refit the injection pump sprocket and timing belt as described in Chapter 2A.

15 Adjust the injection timing, as described in Section 13 then tighten the pump mounting nuts and bolts to the specified torque.

16 Ensure the unions are clean and dry then refit the injector pipes, tightening their union nuts to the specified torque.

17 Reconnect the wiring to the injection pump solenoid/solenoid control unit (as applicable).

18 Reconnect the feed and return hoses to the injection pump, securing them in position with the retaining clips.

19 Reconnect the coolant hoses to the cold start advance capsule and secure in position with the retaining clips.

20 Reconnect the accelerator cable to the pump and secure it position with the retaining clip.

21 Refit the inlet manifold as described in Section 17.

22 Fit the oil filter and top-up/refill the engine with oil (see Chapter 1 and *Weekly checks*).

23 Reconnect the battery negative lead then start the engine and bleed the fuel system as described in Section 5.

24 Warm the engine up to normal operating temperature then check and, if necessary, adjust the idle speed as described in Chapter 1.

12 Injection timing – checking methods

1 Checking the injection timing is not a routine operation. It is only necessary after the injection pump has been disturbed.

2 Dynamic timing equipment does exist, but it is unlikely to be available to the home mechanic. The equipment works by converting pressure pulses in an injector pipe into electrical signals. If such equipment is available, use it in accordance with its maker's instructions.

3 Static timing as described in this Chapter gives good results if carried out carefully. A dial gauge will be needed, with probes and adapters appropriate to the type of injection pump **(see illustration)**. Read through the procedures before starting work, to find out what is involved.

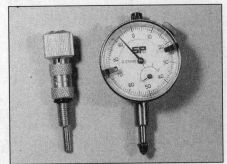

12.3 Dial gauge and adapter needed to check the injection timing

13 Injection timing – checking and adjustment

Caution: Be careful not to allow dirt into the injection pump or injector pipes during this procedure.

Caution: Some of the injection pump settings and access plugs may be sealed by the manufacturers at the factory, using paint or locking wire and lead seals. Do not disturb the seals if the vehicle is still within the warranty period, otherwise the warranty will be invalidated. Also do not attempt the timing procedure unless accurate instrumentation is available.

1 If the injection timing is being checked with the pump in position on the engine unit, rather than as part of the pump refitting procedure, disconnect the battery negative lead. Firmly apply the handbrake then jack up the front of the vehicle and support it on axle stands, where necessary, undo the retaining screws and remove the undercover. Remove all traces of dirt from the unions of cylinder No 1 and 2 injector pipes then slacken the union nuts and remove the pipes from the engine; as each pump union nut is slackened, retain the adapter with a suitable open-ended spanner to prevent it being unscrewed from the pump. With all the union nuts undone, remove the injector pipe assembly from the engine unit and mop up any spilt fuel.

2 Unscrew the access screw, situated in the centre of the four injector pipe unions, from

13.3 Release the cold start advance mechanism by passing a screwdriver up through the levers as shown

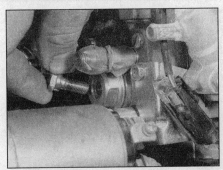

13.2 Remove the access screw from the rear of the pump

the rear of the injection pump **(see illustration)**. As the screw is removed, position a suitable container beneath the pump to catch any escaping fuel. Mop up any split fuel with a clean cloth.

3 Release the cold start advance mechanism by passing a screwdriver through the two holes on the side of the advance lever mechanism **(see illustration)**.

4 Referring to Chapter 2A, Section 3, position No 1 cylinder at TDC on its compression stroke then from that position turn the crankshaft **backwards** (anti-clockwise) approximately a quarter of a turn.

5 Screw the adapter into the rear of the pump and mount the dial gauge in the adapter **(see illustration)**. If access to the special adapter and dial gauge cannot be gained (Vauxhall tool No. KM-798), they can be purchased from most good motor factors. Position the dial gauge so that its plunger is at the mid-point of its travel and securely tighten the adapter locknut.

6 Slowly rotate the crankshaft back-and-forth whilst observing the dial gauge, to determine when the injection pump piston is at the bottom of its travel (BDC). When the piston is correctly positioned, zero the dial gauge.

7 Rotate the crankshaft slowly in the correct direction until the crankshaft pulley mark is correctly realigned with the pointer (No 1 cylinder at TDC on its compression stroke).

8 The reading obtained on the dial gauge should be equal to the specified pump timing measurement given in the Specifications at the start of this Chapter. If adjustment is necessary, slacken the pump front mounting

13.5 Screw the adapter into the rear of the pump and fit the dial gauge

14.7a Fit the heat sleeve to the cylinder head . . .

14.7b . . . followed by the fire seal washer . . .

14.7c . . . and sealing ring, ensuring each component is fitted the correct way up

nuts and rear mounting bolts and slowly rotate the pump body until the point is found where the specified reading is obtained. When the pump is correctly positioned, tighten both its front and rear mounting nuts and bolts to the specified torque.

9 Rotate the crankshaft through one and three quarter rotations in the normal direction of rotation. Find the injection pump piston BDC as described in paragraph 6 and zero the dial gauge.

10 Rotate the crankshaft slowly in the correct direction of rotation until the crankshaft pulley mark is realigned with the pointer (bringing the engine back to TDC). Recheck the timing measurement.

11 If adjustment is necessary, slacken the pump sprocket bolts and repeat the operations in paragraphs 8 to 10.

12 When the pump timing is correctly set unscrew the adapter and remove the dial gauge. Also remove the screwdriver from the cold start advance mechanism.

13 Refit the screw and sealing washer to the pump and tighten it to the specified torque.

14 If the procedure is being carried out as part of the pump refitting sequence, proceed as described in Section 11.

15 If the procedure is being carried out with the pump fitted to the engine, refit the fuel pipes to the pump and injectors and tighten the union nuts to the specified torque. Lower

the vehicle to the ground then reconnect the battery. Start the engine and bleed the fuel system as described in Section 5. On completion check and, if necessary, adjust the idle speed as described in Chapter 1.

14 Fuel injectors – removal and refitting

⚠️ *Warning: Exercise extreme caution when working on the fuel injectors. Never expose the hands or any part of the body to injector spray, as the high working pressure can cause the fuel to penetrate the skin, with possibly fatal results. You are strongly advised to have any work which involves testing the injectors under pressure carried out by a dealer or fuel injection specialist.*
Caution: Be careful not to allow dirt into the injection pump, injectors or pipes during this procedure.
Caution: Take care not to drop the injectors, or allow the needles at their tips to become damaged. The injectors are precision-made to fine limits, and must not be handled roughly. In particular, never mount them in a bench vice.

Removal

1 To gain access to the injectors, remove the inlet manifold as described in Section 17.

2 Wipe clean the pipe unions then slacken the union nuts securing the injector pipes to the top of each injector and the four union nuts securing the pipes to the rear of the injection pump; as each pump union nut is slackened, retain the adapter with a suitable open-ended spanner to prevent it being unscrewed from the pump. With all the union nuts undone, remove the injector pipes from the engine unit and mop up any spilt fuel.

3 Unscrew the nut from the top of each injector then lift off the fuel return pipe assembly. Recover the sealing washer from the top of each injector and discard them; new ones must be used on refitting.

4 Clean around the base of the injector(s) to be removed then unscrew the injector(s) and remove them from the cylinder head.

Caution: Ensure you unscrew each injector holder from the cylinder head and remove the complete injector assembly rather than unscrewing the injector body from the holder. If the body is unscrewed from the holder, the small internal components of the injector will be disturbed and it will be necessary to take them to a specialist to have them reassembled and tested prior to refitting.

5 Remove the sealing ring, fire seal washer and heat sleeve from the injector/cylinder head and discard; new ones must be used on refitting. **Do not** attempt to dismantle the injectors any further.

6 Testing of the injectors requires the use of special equipment. If any injector is thought to be faulty have it tested and, if necessary, reconditioned by a diesel engine specialist or Vauxhall dealer.

Refitting

7 Commence refitting by inserting the heat sleeves, fire seal washers and sealing rings into the cylinder head, ensuring that each component is fitted the correct way up (see illustrations).

8 Carefully fit the injector(s) and tighten to the specified torque. When each injector is correctly tightened, the mark (either a punch mark or a coloured dot) on the injector body should align with the projection on the cylinder head (see illustration).

9 Fit a new sealing washer to the top of each injector then refit the return pipe assembly, tightening its retaining nuts to the specified torque.

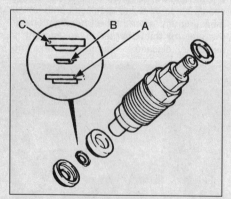

14.7d Correct fitted locations of injector components

A Heat sleeve | *C Sealing ring*
B Fire seal washer

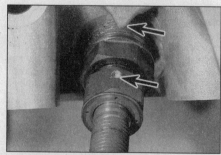

14.8 When the injector is tightened to the specified torque, its mark should align with the cylinder head projection (arrowed)

10 Refit the injector pipes to the engine and tighten the union nuts to the specified torque.

11 Refit the inlet manifold as described in Section 17.

12 On completion start the engine and bleed the fuel system as described in Section 5.

15 Charge air safety valve –
removal and refitting

1 The charge air safety valve is located in the front of the inlet manifold **(see illustration)**.

2 To remove the valve, unscrew it from the manifold casing.

3 When fitting the valve, coat its threads with locking compound to GM spec 15 10 177 and tighten it to the specified torque setting.

16 Turbocharger –
removal and refitting

Caution: Never run the engine with the turbocharger air inlet hose disconnected. Depression at the inlet can build up very suddenly if the engine speed is raised, increasing the risk of foreign objects being sucked in and ejected at very high speed.

Note: *Before removing the turbocharger, prevent the ingress of dirt by cleaning the area around all unions before disconnection. Store dismantled components in a sealed container to prevent contamination. Cover the turbocharger air inlet ducts to prevent debris entering and clean with lint-free cloth only.*

Note: *If the wastegate vacuum unit is damaged, then the complete turbocharger unit must be replaced.*

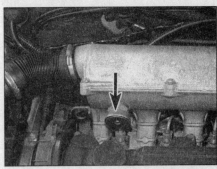

15.1 The charge air safety valve

Removal

1 With the engine in the vehicle, it is recommended that the turbocharger and exhaust manifold are removed as one assembly **(see illustration)**.

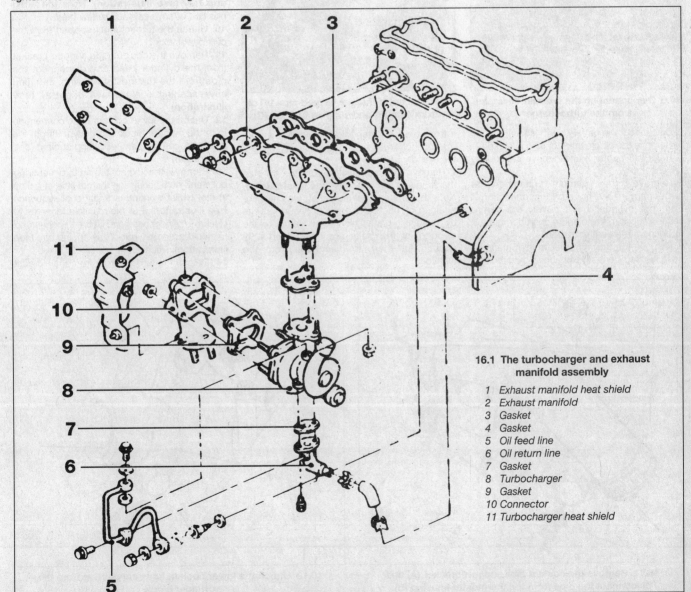

16.1 The turbocharger and exhaust manifold assembly

1 Exhaust manifold heat shield
2 Exhaust manifold
3 Gasket
4 Gasket
5 Oil feed line
6 Oil return line
7 Gasket
8 Turbocharger
9 Gasket
10 Connector
11 Turbocharger heat shield

16.5 Remove the air filter to turbocharger feed hose

16.7a Removing the heat shield from the exhaust manifold . . .

16.7b . . . and the heat shield from the turbocharger

16.8 Disconnecting the exhaust downpipe from the turbocharger

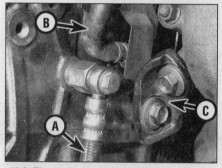

16.9 The turbocharger oil feed pipe (A) oil return pipe (B) and support bracket (C)

2 Disconnect the battery earth lead.

3 Remove the air cleaner housing inlet pipe.

4 Refer to Chapter 3 and remove the cooling fan assembly.

5 Remove the plenum chamber to turbocharger feed hose by disconnecting it from the cylinder head cover, the centre section support, the plenum chamber and the turbocharger **(see illustration)**.

6 Remove the turbocharger to inlet manifold hose located beneath the above by unbolting

it from the inlet manifold, unclipping it from the turbocharger and then releasing it from the cylinder head.

7 Remove the heat shields from the exhaust manifold and turbocharger **(see illustrations)**. Note that the special insulating washers are retained on each of the shield securing bolts by a retaining plate which should stay in place as long as the bolts are unscrewed only enough for them to disengage from the manifold.

8 Disconnect the exhaust downpipe from the turbocharger and recover the flange gasket **(see illustration)**.

9 Disconnect the turbocharger oil feed and return pipelines, catching any escaping oil in a drip tray **(see illustration)**. Note the fitted position of any seals and renew them.

10 Unbolt the turbocharger support from the cylinder block.

11 Remove the coolant pipe support bracket from the cylinder head and disconnect the pipe from the thermostat housing, catching any escaping coolant in a drip tray **(see illustration)**.

12 Unbolt the lower coolant hose connection from the cylinder block and detach it from the pipe end, catching any escaping coolant **(see illustration)**.

13 Remove the exhaust manifold securing bolts and nuts, loosening them a little at a time at first whilst working in a diagonal sequence **(see illustration)**. Pull the manifold forwards to clear the cylinder head and lift the turbocharger/ manifold assembly out of the engine bay **(see illustration)**. Recover the manifold gasket.

14 Detach the turbocharger from the exhaust

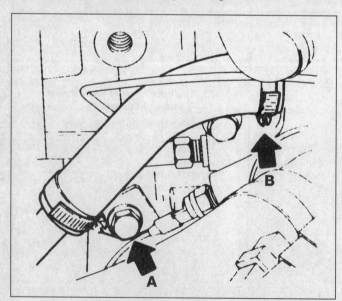

16.11 Remove the coolant pipe support bracket (A) and disconnect the pipe from the thermostat housing (B)

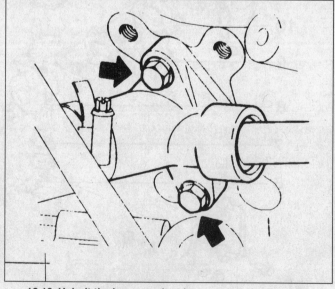

16.12 Unbolt the lower coolant hose connection from the cylinder block

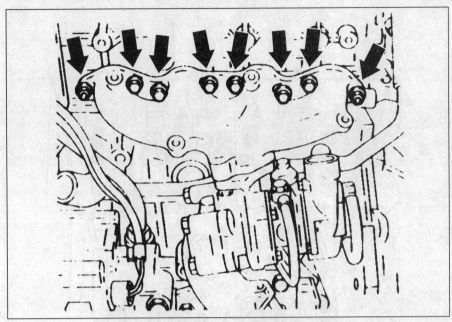

16.13a Exhaust manifold securing bolts and nuts

16.13b Turbocharger/manifold assembly

16.17 Placing a new exhaust manifold gasket on the cylinder head

manifold, having released its securing bolts. Recover the flange gasket.

15 Clean the manifold, cylinder head and turbocharger mating surfaces.

Refitting

16 Reattach the turbocharger to the exhaust manifold, fitting a new flange gasket and tightening its securing bolts in a diagonal sequence to the specified torque setting.

17 Place a new manifold gasket on the cylinder head and refit the turbocharger/ manifold assembly **(see illustration)**. Take care to avoid damaging any oil and coolant pipelines when lowering the assembly into position. Tighten the manifold retaining bolts and nuts evenly, in a diagonal sequence, to the specified torque.

18 Reconnect the coolant hoses, renewing all sealing rings and gaskets.

19 Reattach the turbocharger support to the cylinder block, tightening its retaining bolts to the specified torque setting.

20 Reconnect the turbocharger oil feed and return pipelines, using new seals and tightening the connections to the specified torque settings.

21 Refit the exhaust downpipe to the turbocharger, fitting a new flange gasket and tightening its securing bolts to the specified torque setting.

22 Refit both heat shields, tightening their securing bolts to the specified torque setting.

23 Refit the turbocharger to inlet manifold hose and the plenum chamber to turbocharger hose.

24 Refer to Chapter 6 and refit the cooling fan assembly.

25 Refit the air cleaner housing inlet pipe.

26 Replenish the engine oil and coolant.

27 Reconnect the battery and start the engine.

28 Check all disturbed connections for leaks.

17 Manifolds – removal and refitting

Inlet manifold

Normally aspirated engine

1 Disconnect the battery earth lead.

2 Detach the air resonator box from the plenum chamber by removing the lower hose clamp and the box securing bolts **(see illustration)**.

3 Where an EGR system is fitted, remove the valve and pipe assembly from the inlet and exhaust manifolds by removing the pipe flange to exhaust manifold bolts, the pipe to cylinder head support, the vacuum pipe from the valve and the valve to inlet manifold bolts **(see illustrations)**.

4 Detach the air cleaner housing outlet tube from the manifold by releasing its retaining clamp.

5 Detach the cylinder head cover to manifold vent hose **(see illustration)**.

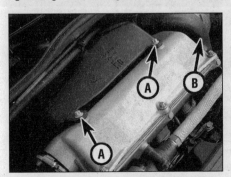

17.2 The air resonator box securing bolts (A) and lower hose clamp (B)

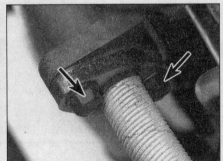

17.3a Remove the EGR pipe flange to exhaust manifold bolts (arrowed) . . .

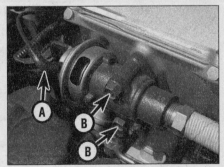

17.3b . . . the EGR valve vacuum pipe (A) and the valve to inlet manifold bolts (B)

17.5 Detach the cylinder head cover to manifold vent hose (arrowed)

6 Release all cable-ties from the manifold.
7 If fitted, disconnect the manifold heater.
8 Disconnect all remaining hoses from beneath the manifold.
9 Remove the manifold to cylinder head securing bolts and nuts, working in a diagonal sequence (see illustration). Withdraw the manifold and recover the gasket.
10 Clean the manifold and cylinder head mating surfaces.
11 Refitting of the manifold is a reversal of removal.
12 Place a new gasket on the cylinder head and refit the manifold. Tighten the manifold retaining bolts evenly, in a diagonal sequence, to the specified torque setting.
13 Reconnect all disturbed hoses, cable-ties and electrical connections.
14 Reconnect the battery.

Turbocharged engine

15 Disconnect the battery earth lead.
16 Remove the hose from between the air cleaner housing and plenum chamber (see illustration).
17 Remove the section of plenum chamber to turbocharger feed hose nearest to the manifold by disconnecting the hose to

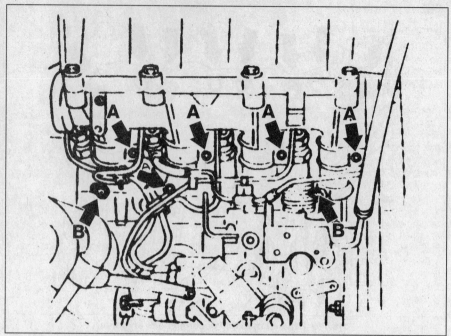

17.9 Remove the inlet manifold securing bolts (A) followed by the outer nuts (B)

cylinder head cover breather pipe, the hose to plenum chamber securing clamp and the hose to pipe securing clamp.
18 Unbolt the turbocharger to inlet manifold pipe (located beneath the turbo) from the inlet manifold. Detach the pipe from the side of the cylinder head and ease it clear of the manifold.
19 Release all cable-ties from the manifold.
20 Disconnect the manifold to fuel injection pump air hose (see illustration).
21 If fitted, disconnect the manifold heater.
22 Remove the manifold to cylinder head securing bolts working in a diagonal

sequence. Withdraw the manifold and recover the gasket.
23 Clean the manifold and cylinder head mating surfaces.
24 Refitting of the manifold is a reversal of removal.
25 Place a new gasket on the cylinder head and refit the manifold. Tighten the manifold retaining bolts evenly, in a diagonal sequence, to the specified torque setting.
26 Reconnect all disturbed hoses, cable-ties and electrical connections, renewing all seals and gaskets.
27 Reconnect the battery.

17.16 Inlet manifold hose connections

A Air cleaner housing-to-plenum chamber hose
B Plenum chamber-to-turbocharger feed hose
C Turbocharger-to-inlet manifold pipe

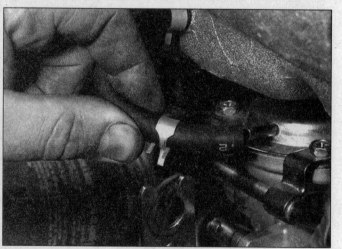

17.20 Disconnecting the inlet manifold to fuel injection pump hose

Exhaust manifold

Normally aspirated engine

28 From beneath the vehicle, disconnect the exhaust pipe from the manifold and mounting bracket. Recover the manifold flange gasket.

29 Remove the EGR pipe flange to exhaust manifold retaining bolts. Detach the pipe from the cylinder head and ease it free of the manifold **(see illustration)**.

30 Remove the exhaust manifold securing bolts and nuts, working in a diagonal sequence. Pull the manifold forwards to detach it from the cylinder head and lift it clear of the engine. Recover the gasket.

31 Clean the manifold and cylinder head mating surfaces.

32 Refitting is a reversal of removal.

33 Place a new gasket on the cylinder head and refit the manifold. Tighten the manifold retaining nuts and bolts evenly, a little at a time, in a diagonal sequence, to the specified torque setting.

34 Refit the EGR pipe assembly to the manifold and cylinder head, with a new flange gasket. Tighten its bolts to the specified torque.

35 Reconnect the exhaust pipe to the manifold, using a new gasket and tightening its bolts to the specified torque. Reconnect the exhaust pipe to its mounting bracket.

Turbocharged engine

36 With the engine in the vehicle, it is recommended that the exhaust manifold and turbocharger are removed as one assembly. Refer to Section 16 of this Chapter.

---

18 Exhaust system –
general information, removal and refitting

General information

1 The exhaust system consists of three sections: the front pipe (which incorporates the catalytic converter), the intermediate pipe and the tailpipe. The front pipe is fitted with a flexible section to allow for movement in the exhaust system.

2 The system is suspended throughout its entire length by rubber mountings.

Removal

3 Each exhaust section can be removed individually, or the complete system can be removed as a unit. Even if only one part of the system needs attention, in some case it can be easier to remove the whole system and separate the sections on the bench.

4 To remove the system or part of the system, first jack up the front or rear of the car, and support it on axle stands. Alternatively, position the car over an inspection pit, or on car ramps. Where necessary, undo the retaining bolts and remove the undercover from beneath the engine/transmission unit.

Front pipe (with catalytic converter)

5 Undo the nuts securing the front pipe to the turbocharger/manifold. Slacken and remove the bolts securing the front pipe to the intermediate pipe.

6 Free the front pipe, recovering the gasket, and intermediate pipe then remove it from underneath the vehicle.

Intermediate pipe

Note: *If the intermediate pipe is corroded into the tailpipe, remove the intermediate pipe and tailpipe as an assembly and separate them on the bench.*

7 Slacken and remove the bolts securing the intermediate pipe to the front pipe and the clamp securing it to the tailpipe.

8 Remove the securing clips and release the intermediate pipe from its mounting rubbers. Disengage the intermediate pipe from the front pipe and tailpipe and remove it from underneath the vehicle.

Tailpipe

9 Slacken the clamp securing the tailpipe to the intermediate pipe and disengage the clamp from the joint.

10 Remove the securing clips then unhook the tailpipe from its mounting rubbers, and free it from the intermediate pipe.

Complete system

11 Slacken and remove the nuts securing the front pipe flange joint to the turbocharger/manifold.

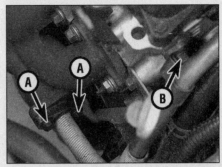

17.29 Remove the EGR pipe to exhaust manifold retaining bolts (A) and pipe to cylinder head bolt (B)

12 Remove the securing clips then free the system from its mounting rubbers and remove it from underneath the vehicle. Recover the gasket from the front pipe joint.

Heat shield(s)

13 The heat shields are secured to the underside of the body by various nuts and bolts. Each shield can be removed once the relevant exhaust section has been removed. If a shield is being removed to gain access to a component located behind it, it may prove sufficient in some cases to remove the retaining nuts and/or bolts, and simply lower the shield, without disturbing the exhaust system.

Refitting

14 Each section is refitted by reversing the removal sequence, noting the following points:

a) *Ensure that all traces of corrosion have been removed from the flanges, and renew all necessary gaskets. Where no gasket is fitted, apply a smear of exhaust system jointing paste to the joint to ensure a gas-tight seal.*

b) *Inspect the rubber mountings for signs of damage or deterioration, and renew as necessary.*

c) *Prior to tightening the exhaust system fasteners, ensure that all rubber mountings are correctly located, and that there is adequate clearance between the exhaust system and vehicle underbody.*

Chapter 4 Part B:
Emission control systems

Contents

Degrees of difficulty

Easy, suitable for novice with little experience	Fairly easy, suitable for beginner with some experience	Fairly difficult, suitable for competent DIY mechanic	Difficult, suitable for experienced DIY mechanic	Very difficult, suitable for expert DIY or professional

Specifications

Torque wrench setting	Nm	lbf ft
Exhaust gas recirculation valve bolts	24	18

1 General information

1 All models are also designed to meet strict emission requirements. All models are fitted with a crankcase emission control system and a catalytic converter to keep exhaust emissions down to a minimum. All models are also fitted with an exhaust gas recirculation (EGR) system to further decrease exhaust emissions.
2 The emission control systems function as follows.

Crankcase emission control

3 To reduce the emission of unburned hydrocarbons from the crankcase into the atmosphere, the engine is sealed and the blow-by gases and oil vapour are drawn from inside the crankcase, through a wire mesh oil separator, into the inlet tract to be burned by the engine during normal combustion.

Exhaust emission control

4 To minimise the level of exhaust pollutants released into the atmosphere, a catalytic converter is fitted in the exhaust system.
5 The catalytic converter consists of a canister containing a fine mesh impregnated with a catalyst material, over which the hot exhaust gases pass. The catalyst speeds up the oxidation of harmful carbon monoxide, unburned hydrocarbons and soot, effectively reducing the quantity of harmful products released into the atmosphere via the exhaust gases.

Exhaust gas recirculation (EGR)

6 This system is designed to recirculate small quantities of exhaust gas into the inlet tract, and therefore into the combustion process. This process reduces the level of unburnt hydrocarbons present in the exhaust gas before it reaches the catalytic converter.
7 The EGR system comprises the following components:

a) *The EGR valve – mounted on the inlet manifold and connected by a supply pipe to the exhaust manifold* **(see illustration)**.
b) *The Thermal-Operated Vacuum Switch – fitted to the thermostat housing* **(see illustration)**.
c) *The Vacuum Regulator Valve – mounted on the top of the fuel injection pump.*
d) *The Vacuum Delay Valve – fitted in the vacuum line* **(see illustration)**.

2 Emission control systems – testing and component renewal

Crankcase emission control

1 The components of this system require no attention other than to check that the hose(s) are clear and undamaged at regular intervals.

Exhaust emission control

2 The performance of the catalytic converter

1.7a The EGR valve

1.7b The thermal-operated vacuum switch (arrowed)

1.7c The vacuum delay valve

can be checked only by measuring the exhaust gases using a good-quality, carefully-calibrated exhaust gas analyser.

3 If the catalytic converter is thought to be faulty, before assuming the catalytic converter is faulty, it is worth checking the problem is not due to a faulty injector(s). Refer to your Vauxhall dealer for further information.

Catalytic converter renewal

4 The catalytic converter is an integral part of the exhaust system front pipe. Refer to Chapter 4A for removal and refitting details.

Exhaust gas recirculation system

Testing

5 The system is virtually maintenance-free, the only routine operations necessary are checks for condition and security of the component parts.

6 Whenever the fuel injection pump is removed the vacuum regulator valve setting must be checked and, if necessary, adjusted. Checking and adjustment of the valve is only possible if a hand-operated vacuum pump/gauge is available. At the time of writing, no information was available for valve adjustment. It is therefore recommended that before carrying out any work on the fuel injection pump, advice is sought from a Vauxhall/Opel dealer.

7 To check the system operation, warm the engine up to normal operating temperature and allow it to idle. Disconnect and reconnect the vacuum pipe from the top of the EGR valve several times. The valve should be heard to operate each time.

8 If the EGR valve does not operate and vacuum can be felt at the pipe end, first check the setting of the vacuum regulator valve.

9 If the vacuum regulator valve is functioning correctly, the fault must be in the EGR valve, which must then be renewed. If the valve is to

be renewed, it is always worth first trying the effect of cleaning any carbon build-up from its passages to check whether this is the reason for the failure. If the valve diaphragm has failed, on the other hand, there is no alternative to the renewal of the complete valve unit.

10 If no vacuum can be felt, check back through the system until the leak or blockage is found and rectified.

EGR valve renewal

11 Release the retaining clips and retaining bracket bolts, and (where necessary) remove the charge air pipe from the intercooler to the turbocharger.

12 Disconnect the vacuum hose from the EGR valve, pull out the retaining clip, and remove the EGR valve from the left-hand end of the inlet manifold.

13 Refitting is a reversal of removal.

Thermal vacuum switch renewal

14 Drain the cooling system, either completely or down as far as the thermostat.

15 Disconnect the vacuum pipes from the switch, having noted their fitted positions.

16 Unscrew the vacuum switch.

17 On fitting the new switch, ensure that a new sealing washer is used. Tighten the switch securely.

18 Refill the cooling system.

Vacuum regulator valve renewal

19 Note the fitted position of each valve pipe for reference when refitting.

20 Disconnect each pipe.

21 Unbolt and remove the regulator valve.

22 Refitting is a reversal of removal but if a new valve is being fitted then it must be adjusted.

23 Checking and adjustment of the vacuum regulator valve is only possible if a hand-operated vacuum pump/gauge is available. At the time of writing, no information was

available for valve adjustment. It is therefore recommended that advice is sought from a Vauxhall/Opel dealer.

Vacuum delay valve renewal

24 At the time of writing, no information was available concerning this unit is available separately from the vacuum pipes. Consult your local Vauxhall/Opel dealer for details.

25 Note that valves of this type are usually clearly marked to show which way round they are to be fitted. Note any such markings before removing the valve.

26 Refitting is a reversal of removal. Check that all pipe connections are secure.

3 Catalytic converter – general information and precautions

1 The catalytic converter is a reliable and simple device which needs no maintenance in itself, but there are some facts of which an owner should be aware if the converter is to function properly for its full service life.

a) DO NOT use fuel or engine oil additives – these may contain substances harmful to the catalytic converter.

b) DO NOT continue to use the car if the engine burns oil to the extent of leaving a visible trail of blue smoke.

c) Remember that the catalytic converter operates at very high temperatures. DO NOT, therefore, park the car in dry undergrowth, over long grass or piles of dead leaves after a long run.

d) Remember that the catalytic converter is FRAGILE – do not strike it with tools during servicing work.

e) The catalytic converter, used on a well-maintained and well-driven car, should last for between 50 000 and 100 000 miles – if the converter is no longer effective it must be renewed.

Chapter 5 Part A:
Starting and charging systems

Contents

Degrees of difficulty

Easy, suitable for novice with little experience	**Fairly easy,** suitable for beginner with some experience	**Fairly difficult,** suitable for competent DIY mechanic	**Difficult,** suitable for experienced DIY mechanic	**Very difficult,** suitable for expert DIY or professional

Specifications

General
Electrical system type .... 12 volt negative earth

Battery
Type .... Lead-acid, 'maintenance-free' (sealed for life)
Battery capacity .... 36, 44, 55, 60 or 66 Ah (depending on model)

Alternator
Type .... Bosch, Hitachi or Delco-Remy
Maximum output .... 55, 70 or 100 amps (depending on model)
Regulated voltage .... 13.7 to 14.7 volts (approximately)
Brush minimum length:
  Bosch .... 5.0 mm
  Hitachi .... 14.0 mm
  Delco-Remy:
    55 amp .... 12.0 mm
    70 and 100 amp .... 20.0 mm

Starter motor
Type .... Pre-engaged, Delco-Remy, Hitachi or Valeo
Brush minimum length:
  Delco-Remy:
    Except code number 09 000 756 .... 4.0 mm
    Code number 09 000 756 .... 8.5 mm
  Valeo .... 13.0 mm
  Hitachi .... 10.0 mm

Torque wrench settings	Nm	lbf ft
Alternator fixings:		
M8 bolts	24	18
M10 bolts	48	35
Oil pressure switch	20	15
Starter motor bolts	38	28

1 General information and precautions

General information

The engine electrical system consists mainly of the charging and starting systems (covered in this Part of Chapter 5) and the pre-heating system (covered in Part B of this Chapter). Because of their engine-related functions, these components are covered separately from the body electrical devices such as the lights, instruments, etc (which are covered in Chapter 12).

The electrical system is of the 12 volt negative earth type.

The battery is of the 'maintenance-free' (sealed for life) type, and is charged by the alternator, which is belt-driven from a crankshaft-mounted pulley.

The starter motor is of the pre-engaged type, incorporating an integral solenoid. On starting, the solenoid moves the drive pinion into engagement with the flywheel ring gear before the starter motor is energised. Once the engine has started, a one-way clutch prevents the motor armature being driven by the engine while the pinion disengages from the flywheel.

Further details of the various systems are given in the relevant Sections of this Chapter. While some repair procedures are given, the usual course of action is to renew the component concerned. The owner whose interest extends beyond mere component renewal should obtain a copy of the *Automotive Electrical & Electronic Systems Manual*, available from the publishers of this manual.

Precautions

It is necessary to take extra care when working on the electrical system, to avoid damage to semi-conductor devices (diodes and transistors), and to avoid the risk of personal injury. In addition to the precautions given in 'Safety first!' at the beginning of this manual, observe the following when working on the system:

• *Always remove rings, watches, etc, before working on the electrical system. Even with the battery disconnected, capacitive discharge could occur if a component's live terminal is earthed through a metal object. This could cause a shock or nasty burn.*
• *Do not reverse the battery connections. Components such as the alternator, ignition system components, or any other components having semi-conductor circuitry, could be irreparably damaged.*
• *If the engine is being started using jump leads and a slave battery, connect the batteries as shown in the preliminary section of this manual (see 'Jump starting'). This also applies when connecting a battery charger.*
• *Never disconnect the battery terminals,*

3.2 Battery condition indicator (arrowed)

the alternator, any electrical wiring, or any test instruments, when the engine is running.
• *Do not allow the engine to turn the alternator when the alternator is not connected.*
• *Never 'test' for alternator output by 'flashing' the output lead to earth.*
• *Never use an ohmmeter of the type incorporating a hand-cranked generator for circuit or continuity testing.*
• *Always ensure that the battery negative lead is disconnected when working on the electrical system.*
• *Before using electric-arc welding equipment on the car, disconnect the battery, alternator and components such as the engine management and the ABS electronic control units to protect them from the risk of damage.*
• *Several systems fitted to the vehicle require battery power to be available at all times, either to ensure their continued operation (such as the clock) or to maintain control unit memories or security codes which would be wiped if the battery were to be disconnected. To ensure that there are no unforeseen consequences of this action, Refer to 'Disconnecting the battery' in the Reference Chapter for further information.*

2 Electrical fault finding – general information

Refer to Chapter 12.

4.4 Unscrewing the battery clamp bolt

3 Battery – testing and charging

Note: *The following information refers only to the maintenance-free type battery fitted as original equipment.*

1 Topping-up and testing of the electrolyte in each battery cell is not possible. The condition of the battery can therefore only be tested by observing the battery condition indicator.

2 The battery condition indicator is located in the top of the battery casing, and indicates the condition of the battery by its colour **(see illustration)**. If the indicator shows green, then the battery is in a good state of charge. If the indicator turns darker, eventually to black, then the battery requires charging, as described later in this Section. If the indicator shows clear/yellow, then the electrolyte level in the battery is too low to allow further use, and the battery should be renewed. **Do not** attempt to charge, load or jump start a battery when the indicator shows clear/yellow.

3 If the battery is to be charged, remove it from the vehicle, as described in Section 4, and charge it as follows.

4 The maintenance-free type battery takes considerably longer to fully recharge than the standard type, the time taken being dependent on the extent of discharge.

5 A constant-voltage type charger is required; connect it up and set it to 13.9 to 14.9 volts, with a charge current below 25 amps.

6 If the battery is to be charged from a fully-discharged state (less than 12.2 volts output), have it recharged by a Vauxhall/Opel dealer or a competent automotive electrician, as the charge rate is high, and constant supervision during charging is necessary.

4 Battery – removal and refitting

Note: *Refer to 'Disconnecting the battery' in Reference before proceeding.*

Removal

1 On right-hand drive models, the battery is located on the left-hand side of the engine compartment, towards the rear. On left-hand drive models the battery is located under the windscreen cowl panel on the right-hand side. To remove the cowl panel, undo the five screws, lift the panel up in the centre and remove the right-hand half forwards from the plenum chamber.

2 Disconnect the lead(s) at the negative (earth) terminal by unscrewing the retaining nut and removing the terminal clamp.

3 Disconnect the positive terminal lead(s) in the same way.

4 Unscrew the clamp bolt sufficiently to enable the battery to be lifted from its location **(see illustration)**. Keep the battery upright.

5 If necessary the battery tray can be removed after undoing the four retaining bolts. Release any wiring or hose clips from the tray and lift the tray from the engine compartment.

Refitting

6 Refitting is a reversal of removal, but smear petroleum jelly on the terminals when reconnecting the leads, and always reconnect the positive lead first, and the negative lead last.

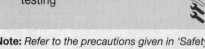

5 Charging system – testing

Note: *Refer to the precautions given in 'Safety first!' and in Section 1 of this Chapter before starting work.*

1 If the ignition/no-charge warning light fails to illuminate when the ignition is switched on, first check the alternator wiring connections for security. If satisfactory, check that the warning light bulb has not blown, and that the bulbholder is secure in its location in the instrument panel. If the light still fails to illuminate, check the continuity of the warning light feed wire from the alternator to the bulbholder. If all is satisfactory, the alternator is at fault, and should be renewed, or taken to an auto-electrician for testing and repair.

2 If the ignition warning light illuminates when the engine is running, stop the engine and check that the drivebelt is correctly tensioned (see Chapter 1) and that the alternator connections are secure. If all is so far satisfactory, check the alternator brushes and slip rings (see Section 7). If the fault persists, the alternator should be renewed, or taken to an auto-electrician for testing and repair.

3 If the alternator output is suspect even though the warning light functions correctly, the regulated voltage may be checked as follows.

4 Connect a voltmeter across the battery terminals, and start the engine.

5 Increase the engine speed until the voltmeter reading remains steady; the reading should be approximately 12 to 13 volts, and no more than 14 volts.

6 Switch on as many electrical accessories (eg, the headlights, heated rear window and heater blower) as possible, and check that the alternator maintains the regulated voltage at around 13.5 to 14.5 volts.

7 If the regulated voltage is not as stated, the fault may be due to worn brushes, weak brush springs, a faulty voltage regulator, a faulty diode, a severed phase winding, or worn or damaged slip rings. The brushes and slip rings may be checked (see Section 7), but if the fault persists, the alternator should be renewed, or taken to an auto-electrician for testing and repair.

6 Alternator – removal and refitting

Removal

1 Firmly apply the handbrake then jack up the front of the vehicle and support it securely on axle stands. Where necessary, undo the retaining bolts and remove the undercover from beneath the engine/transmission unit. Disconnect the battery negative lead and proceed as described under the relevant sub-heading.

2 Release the auxiliary drivebelt as described in Chapter 1 and disengage it from the alternator pulley.

3 Referring to Chapter 9, remove the braking system vacuum pump (which is mounted onto the rear of the alternator). **Note:** *If the alternator is not to be renewed, the pump can be left attached to the alternator and the vacuum pipe and oil lines disconnected.*

4 Trace the wiring back from the alternator and disconnect it at the connector.

5 Slacken and remove the alternator mounting bolts and manoeuvre it out from underneath the vehicle.

Refitting

6 Refitting is the reverse of removal tightening all mounting bolts to their specified torque settings (where given). Ensure the drivebelt is correctly refitted and tensioned as described in Chapter 1.

7 Alternator – testing and overhaul

1 If the alternator is thought to be suspect, it should be removed from the vehicle and taken to an auto-electrician for testing. Most auto-electricians will be able to supply and fit brushes at a reasonable cost. However, check on the cost of repairs before proceeding as it may prove more economical to obtain a new or exchange alternator.

8 Starting system – testing

Note: *Refer to the precautions given in 'Safety first!' and in Section 1 of this Chapter before starting work.*

1 If the starter motor fails to operate when the ignition key is turned to the appropriate position, the possible causes are as follows:

 a) *The battery is faulty.*
 b) *The electrical connections between the switch, solenoid, battery and starter motor are somewhere failing to pass the necessary current from the battery through the starter to earth.*
 c) *The solenoid is faulty.*
 d) *The starter motor is mechanically or electrically defective.*

2 To check the battery, switch on the headlights. If they dim after a few seconds, this indicates that the battery is discharged – recharge (see Section 3) or renew the battery. If the headlights glow brightly, operate the starter switch while watching the headlights. If they dim, then this indicates that current is reaching the starter motor, therefore the fault must lie in the starter motor. If the lights continue to glow brightly (and no clicking sound can be heard from the starter motor solenoid), this indicates that there is a fault in the circuit or solenoid – see the following paragraphs. If the starter motor turns slowly when operated, but the battery is in good condition, then this indicates either that the starter motor is faulty, or there is considerable resistance somewhere in the circuit.

3 If a fault in the circuit is suspected, disconnect the battery leads (including the earth connection to the body), the starter/ solenoid wiring and the engine/ transmission earth strap. Thoroughly clean the connections, and reconnect the leads and wiring. Use a voltmeter or test light to check that full battery voltage is available at the battery positive lead connection to the solenoid. Smear petroleum jelly around the battery terminals to prevent corrosion – corroded connections are among the most frequent causes of electrical system faults.

4 If the battery and all connections are in good condition, check the circuit by disconnecting the switched feed wire from the solenoid (the thinner wire). Connect a voltmeter or test light between the wire end and a good earth (such as the battery negative terminal), and check that the wire is live when the ignition switch is turned to the 'start' position. If it is, then the circuit is sound – if not, there is a fault in the ignition/starter switch or wiring.

5 The solenoid contacts can be checked by connecting a voltmeter or test light between the battery positive feed connection on the starter side of the solenoid, and earth. When the ignition switch is turned to the 'start' position, there should be a reading or lighted bulb, as applicable. If there is no reading or lighted bulb, the solenoid is faulty and should be renewed.

6 If the circuit and solenoid are proved sound, the fault must lie in the starter motor. Begin checking the starter motor by removing it (see Section 9), and checking the brushes (see Section 10). If the fault does not lie in the brushes, the motor windings must be faulty. In this event, the starter motor must be renewed, unless an auto-electrical specialist can be found who will overhaul the unit at a cost significantly less than that of a new or exchange starter motor.

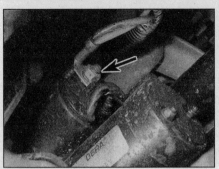

9.3 Starter motor wiring securing nut (arrowed) – viewed from underneath vehicle

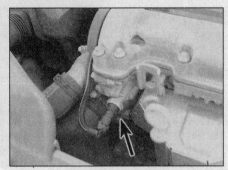

12.1 Oil pressure warning light switch location (arrowed)

9 Starter motor – removal and refitting

Removal

1 Disconnect the battery negative lead then firmly apply the handbrake then jack up the front of the vehicle and support it on axle stands. Where necessary, undo the retaining bolts and remove the undercover from beneath the engine/transmission unit.

2 Slacken and remove the two retaining nuts and disconnect the wiring from the starter motor solenoid. Recover the washers under the nuts.

3 Slacken and remove the retaining bolts then manoeuvre the starter motor out from underneath the engine **(see illustration)**.

Refitting

4 Refitting is a reversal of removal tightening the retaining bolts to the specified torque. Ensure all wiring is correctly routed and its retaining nuts are securely tightened.

10 Starter motor – testing and overhaul

1 If the starter motor is thought to be suspect, it should be removed from the vehicle and taken to an auto-electrician for testing. Most auto-electricians will be able to supply and fit brushes at a reasonable cost. However, check on the cost of repairs before proceeding as it may prove more economical to obtain a new or exchange motor.

11 Ignition switch – removal and refitting

The switch is integral with the steering column lock, and removal and refitting is described in Chapter 10.

12 Oil pressure warning light switch – removal and refitting

Removal

1 The oil pressure switch is screwed into the left-hand end of the cylinder block and can be reached from above **(see illustration)**.

2 Disconnect the wiring connector then unscrew the switch and recover the sealing washer. Be prepared for oil spillage, and if the switch is to be left removed from the engine for any length of time, plug the switch aperture.

Refitting

3 Examine the sealing washer for signs of damage or deterioration and if necessary renew.

4 Refit the switch and washer, tightening it to the specified torque, and reconnect the wiring connector.

5 Lower the vehicle to the ground (where necessary) then check and, if necessary, top up the engine oil as described in *Weekly checks*.

Chapter 5 Part B:
Preheating system

Contents

Degrees of difficulty

Easy, suitable for novice with little experience	**Fairly easy,** suitable for beginner with some experience	**Fairly difficult,** suitable for competent DIY mechanic	**Difficult,** suitable for experienced DIY mechanic	**Very difficult,** suitable for expert DIY or professional

Specifications

Glow plugs

Type . . . .   Bosch 0 250 312 003

Torque wrench setting	**Nm**	**lbf ft**
Glow plugs	20	15

1 Preheating system – description and testing

Description

1 Each cylinder of the engine is fitted with a heater plug (commonly called a glow plug) screwed into it. The plugs are electrically-operated before and during start-up when the engine is cold. Electrical feed to the glow plugs is controlled via a relay and the preheating system control unit.

2 A warning light in the instrument panel tells the driver that preheating is taking place. When the light goes out, the engine is ready to be started. The voltage supply to the glow plugs continues for several seconds after the light goes out. If no attempt is made to start, the timer then cuts off the supply, in order to avoid draining the battery and overheating the glow plugs.

3 The glow plugs also provide a 'post-heating' function, whereby the glow plugs remain switched on for a period after the engine has started. The length of time 'post-heating' takes place for is also determined by the control unit but it can be anything up to 6 minutes, depending on engine temperature.

4 The fuel filter is also fitted with a heating element to prevent the fuel 'waxing' in extreme conditions and to improve combustion. The heating element is fitted between the filter and its housing and is controlled by the preheating system control unit via the temperature switch on the filter housing. The heating element is switched on if the temperature of the fuel passing through the filter is less than 5°C (41°F) and switches off when the fuel temperature reaches 16°C (61°F).

Testing

5 If the system malfunctions, testing is ultimately by substitution of known good units, but some preliminary checks may be made as follows.

6 Connect a voltmeter or 12 volt test lamp between the glow plug supply cable and earth (engine or vehicle metal). Make sure that the live connection is kept clear of the engine and bodywork.

7 Have an assistant switch on the ignition, and check that voltage is applied to the glow plugs. Note the time for which the warning light is lit, and the total time for which voltage is applied before the system cuts out. Switch off the ignition.

8 At an under-bonnet temperature of 20°C (68°F), typical times noted should be approximately 3 seconds for warning light operation. Warning light time will increase with lower temperatures and decrease with higher temperatures.

9 If there is no supply at all, the control unit, relay or associated wiring is at fault.

10 To locate a defective glow plug, slacken and remove the nuts and washers (where fitted) then disconnect the main supply lead(s) and the electrical supply rail from the plugs. On later models simply pull off the wiring connector from each plug

11 Use a continuity tester, or a 12 volt test lamp connected to the battery positive terminal, to check for continuity between each glow plug terminal and earth. The resistance of a glow plug in good condition is very low (less than 1 ohm), so if the test lamp does not light or the continuity tester shows a high resistance, the glow plug is certainly defective.

12 If an ammeter is available, the current draw of each glow plug can be checked. After an initial surge of 15 to 20 amps, each plug should draw 12 amps. Any plug which draws much more or less than this is probably defective.

13 As a final check, the glow plugs can be removed and inspected as described in the following Section.

2 Glow plugs – removal, inspection and refitting

Caution: If the preheating system has just been energised, or if the engine has been running, the glow plugs will be very hot.

Removal

1 Disconnect the battery negative lead. To improve access, disconnect the breather hose from the rear of the cylinder head cover.

2 Slacken the nut securing the electrical supply rail to each glow plug **(see illustration)**.

2.2 Slacken the nut securing the electrical supply rail to each glow plug

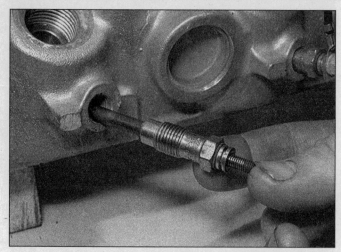

2.3 Remove the glow plug(s) from the cylinder head

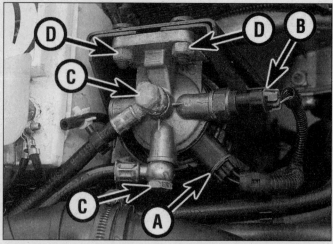

3.3a The wiring connector for the fuel heater on 1.5 litre models . . .

A Heating element connector   C Fuel pipe unions
B Temperature sensor   D Retaining nuts
   connector

3 Unscrew the glow plug(s) and remove from the cylinder head **(see illustration)**.

Inspection

4 Inspect each glow plug for physical damage. Burnt or eroded glow plug tips can be caused by a bad injector spray pattern. Have the injectors checked if this sort of damage is found.

5 If the glow plugs are in good physical condition, check them electrically using a 12 volt test lamp or continuity tester as described in the previous Section.

6 The glow plugs can be energised by applying 12 volts to them to verify that they heat up evenly and in the required time. Observe the following precautions.

  a) Support the glow plug by clamping it carefully in a vice or self-locking pliers. Remember it will become red-hot.

  b) Make sure that the power supply or test lead incorporates a fuse or overload trip to protect against damage from a short-circuit.

  c) After testing, allow the glow plug to cool for several minutes before attempting to handle it.

7 A glow plug in good condition will start to glow red at the tip after drawing current for 5 seconds or so. Any plug which takes much longer to start glowing, or which starts glowing in the middle instead of at the tip, is defective.

Refitting

8 Carefully refit the plug(s) and tighten to the specified torque. Do not overtighten, as this can damage the glow plug element.

9 Ease the electrical supply rail into position, ensuring it is correctly engaged with each of the four glow plugs, and securely tighten the glow plug nuts.

10 Reconnect the breather hose then connect the battery and check the operation of the glow plugs.

---

3 Preheating system components – removal and refitting

Coolant temperature switch

1 The coolant temperature switch is screwed

into the thermostat housing. Refer to Chapter 3 for removal and refitting details.

Fuel filter heater

2 Remove the fuel filter as described in Chapter 1. If the filter is damaged on removal (which is likely), a new one should be used on refitting.

3 Disconnect the battery negative terminal then disconnect the wiring connector from the heating element **(see illustrations)**.

4 Unscrew the bolt and remove the heating element from the filter housing. Recover the sealing ring and discard, a new one should be used on refitting.

5 Fit a new sealing ring the heating element recess then refit the element to the filter housing and securely tighten the bolt.

6 Reconnect the battery then fit the fuel filter as described in Chapter 1.

Fuel filter heater switch

7 Disconnect the battery negative terminal then disconnect the wiring connector from the temperature switch which is screwed into the fuel filter housing **(see illustration and illustration 3.3a)**.

8 Position a wad of rag beneath the filter housing to catch any spilt fuel then unscrew the switch and remove it from the housing. Plug the housing aperture to prevent the entry of dirt and minimise fuel loss. Remove the sealing rings from the switch and renew them.

9 Fit new sealing rings to the switch recesses then refit the switch to the filter housing and tighten securely. Reconnect the wiring connector to the switch then reconnect the battery.

Relays and fuses

10 The glow plug and fuel heating element relays and fuses are located in the box in the engine compartment.

3.3b . . . and on 1.7 litre models

3.7 On some models, the fuel temperature sensor is combined with the hose union banjo bolt

Chapter 6
Clutch

Contents

Degrees of difficulty

Easy, suitable for novice with little experience	**Fairly easy,** suitable for beginner with some experience	**Fairly difficult,** suitable for competent DIY mechanic	**Difficult,** suitable for experienced DIY mechanic	**Very difficult,** suitable for expert DIY or professional

Specifications

General
Type . . . . Single dry plate, cable-operated

Clutch disc
Diameter . . . . 190.0 mm
Lining thickness (new) . . . . 3.5 mm

Torque wrench settings	Nm	lbf ft
Clutch pressure plate-to-flywheel bolts	15	11
Clutch release fork-to-pivot shaft bolt	35	26
Gearbox endplate bolts:		
M7 bolts	15	11
M8 bolts	20	15
Input shaft socket-headed screw	15	11

1 General information

All models are fitted with a single dry plate clutch, which consists of five main components; friction disc, pressure plate, diaphragm spring, cover and release bearing.

The friction disc is free to slide along the splines of the gearbox input shaft, and is held in position between the flywheel and the pressure plate by the pressure exerted on the pressure plate by the diaphragm spring. Friction lining material is riveted to both sides of the friction disc, and spring cushioning between the friction linings and the hub absorbs transmission shocks, and helps to ensure a smooth take-up of power as the clutch is engaged.

The diaphragm spring is mounted on pins, and is held in place in the cover by annular fulcrum rings.

The release bearing is located on a guide sleeve at the front of the gearbox. The bearing is free to slide on the sleeve, under the action of the release arm, which pivots inside the clutch bellhousing.

The release arm is operated by the clutch pedal, via a cable. As wear takes place on the friction disc over a period of time, the clutch pedal will rise progressively, relative to its original position. Cable adjustment should be periodically checked as described in Chapter 1.

When the clutch pedal is depressed, the release arm is actuated by means of the cable. The release arm pushes the release bearing to bear against the centre of the diaphragm spring, thus pushing the centre of the diaphragm spring inwards. The diaphragm spring acts against the fulcrum rings in the cover. As the centre of the spring is pushed in, the outside of the spring is pushed out, so allowing the pressure plate to move backwards away from the friction disc.

When the clutch pedal is released, the diaphragm spring forces the pressure plate into contact with the friction linings on the friction disc, and simultaneously pushes the friction disc forwards on its splines, forcing it against the flywheel. The friction disc is now firmly sandwiched between the pressure plate and the flywheel, and drive is taken up.

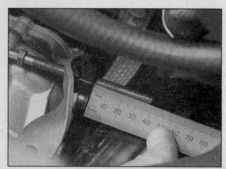

2.2a Measuring the length of threaded rod protruding through the plastic block at the end of the clutch cable . . .

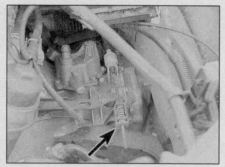

2.2b . . . or protruding through the end of the damper block (arrowed) on certain later models

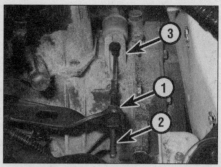

2.3 Remove the clip (1) from the threaded rod, slide the threaded rod (2) from the release arm, and pull the assembly from the lug (3)

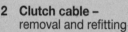

2 Clutch cable – removal and refitting

Removal

1 Depending on model, to improve access to the clutch cable at the gearbox end, it may be beneficial to release the power steering fluid reservoir from its clamp and move it to one side.

2 Working in the engine compartment, measure the length of the threaded rod protruding through the plastic block at the release arm end of the cable **(see illustration)**. This will enable approximate pre-setting of the cable when refitting. On certain later models a damper block is fitted to the end of the cable **(see illustration)**. On these models, measure the length of threaded rod protruding through the end of the damper block.

3 Remove the clip from the threaded rod at the release arm, then slide the rod from the release arm **(see illustration)**. Push the release arm towards the engine; if necessary, slacken the cable adjuster to aid removal.

4 Pull the cable assembly from the lug on the clutch bellhousing.

5 From inside the car, disconnect the cable end from the plastic segment at the top of the pedal. Access is limited, and it may prove easier to remove the clutch pedal, as described in Section 3, before disconnecting the cable.

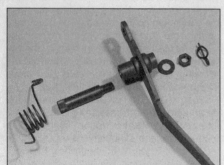

3.3 Clutch pedal pivot components

6 The cable assembly can now be withdrawn into the engine compartment, by pulling it through the bulkhead. Take care not to damage the bulkhead grommet as the cable is withdrawn. Unclip the cable from any support brackets, and take note of the cable routing to aid refitting.

Refitting

7 Refitting is a reversal of removal, bearing in mind the following points:
  a) Ensure that the cable is routed as noted before removal.
  b) Position the threaded rod so that the length of thread protruding through the plastic block, or damper block is as noted before removal, then adjust the cable as described in Chapter 1.
  c) Ensure that the bulkhead grommet is correctly seated.
  d) Refit any components removed for access.

3 Clutch pedal – removal and refitting

Removal

1 Proceed as described in paragraphs 1 to 4 in the previous Section. Then, working in the driver's footwell, remove the locking clip from the right-hand end of the clutch pedal pivot shaft, then unscrew the pedal retaining nut and recover the washer(s).

2 Push the pivot shaft out of the pedal bracket (to the left), then lower the pedal and return spring. Note the position of any washers and/or spacers on the pivot shaft, so that they can be refitted in their original positions.

3 Disconnect the cable end from the pedal, and withdraw the pedal and return spring from the vehicle **(see illustration)**.

Refitting

4 Refitting is a reversal of removal, but before inserting the pedal pivot shaft, smear the surface with a little molybdenum disulphide grease.

5 On completion, adjust the clutch cable if necessary, as described in Chapter 1.

4 Clutch assembly – removal, inspection and refitting

 Warning: Dust created by clutch wear (which gets deposited on the clutch components) may contain asbestos, which is a health hazard. DO NOT blow it out with compressed air, or inhale any of it. DO NOT use petrol (or petroleum-based solvents) to clean off the dust. Brake system cleaner or methylated spirit should be used to flush the dust into a suitable receptacle. After the clutch components are wiped clean with rags, dispose of the contaminated rags and cleaner in a sealed, marked container.

Note: On early models fitted with a 'standard' flywheel, the clutch can be removed and refitted without removing the engine or the gearbox, provided certain special tools can be obtained or improvised. Later engines are fitted with a 'pot' flywheel during production. The 'pot' flywheel is significantly thicker than the 'standard' item, and the clutch assembly is recessed into the flywheel. Consequently there is insufficient clearance between the flywheel and the clutch bellhousing to enable the clutch to be removed with the engine and gearbox in the vehicle. Before attempting to remove the clutch, remove the clutch bellhousing cover plate and examine the flywheel to ascertain which type is fitted, then proceed as follows, according to flywheel type.

Models with 'standard' flywheel

Note: The manufacturers recommend the use of special tools for this procedure, although suitable alternatives can be improvised as described in the text. It is suggested that this Section is read thoroughly before work commences, in order that suitable tools can be made available as required. The circlip in the end of the input shaft, and the gearbox endplate gasket, should be renewed on reassembly. If the special tools required cannot be obtained or improvised, the clutch can be removed as described later in this Section for models with a 'pot' flywheel, after removing the gearbox.

4.5 Removing the gearbox endplate

4.7 Extract the circlip (arrowed) from the end of the gearbox input shaft

4.8 Unscrew the screw from the end of the input shaft

4.9a Improvised tool for disengaging gearbox input shaft from clutch

4.9b Disengaging the input shaft from the clutch using the improvised tool

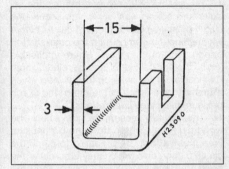

4.12 Clutch pressure plate retaining clamp dimensions – in mm

Removal

1 Where applicable, remove the left-hand front wheel trim, then loosen the roadwheel bolts. Apply the handbrake, jack up the front of the vehicle, and support securely on axle stands (see *Jacking and vehicle support*). Remove the roadwheel for improved access.

2 Unscrew the securing bolts, and remove the cover plate from the base of the clutch bellhousing.

3 For improved access, remove the wheel arch liner, as described in Chapter 11, Section 22.

4 Where applicable, unscrew the retaining nut, and disconnect the earth strap from the gearbox endplate.

5 Place a suitable container beneath the gearbox endplate, to catch the oil which will be released, then unscrew the securing bolts and remove the endplate **(see illustration)**. Note the location of the bolts (including the stud for the earth strap, where applicable), as two different lengths are used.

6 Recover the gasket.

7 Extract the circlip from inside the end of the gearbox input shaft, using a pair of circlip pliers **(see illustration)**.

8 Using a twelve-point splined key, unscrew the screw from the end of the input shaft **(see illustration)**.

9 The input shaft can now be pulled out of engagement with the splined hub of the clutch friction disc. The manufacturers specify the use of special tools for this operation (GM Nos KM-556-A and KM-556-4), but an

alternative can be improvised **(see illustrations)**. The tool bolts into place on the end of the gearbox, using the endplate securing bolts. Tool dimensions will vary according to gearbox type.

10 Alternatively, screw an M7 bolt into the end of the input shaft, and use the bolt to pull the shaft out to its stop. It is likely that the input shaft will be a very tight fit, in which case it may prove difficult to withdraw, without using the special tool previously described. In extreme cases, a slide hammer can be attached to the end of the shaft to enable it to be withdrawn - although this is not recommended, as damage to the gearbox components may result.

11 Before the clutch assembly can be removed, the pressure plate must be compressed against the tension of the diaphragm spring, otherwise the assembly will be too thick to be withdrawn through the

space between the flywheel and the edge of the bellhousing.

12 Three special clamps are available from the manufacturers for this purpose (GM No KM-526-A), but suitable alternatives can be made up from strips of metal 3 mm thick. The clamps should be U-shaped, and made to the dimensions shown **(see illustration)**. Bevel the edges of the clamps to ease fitting, and cut a slot in one of the U-legs to clear the pressure plate rivets.

13 Have an assistant depress the clutch pedal fully, then fit each clamp securely over the edge of the pressure plate, engaging the clamps in the apertures around the rim of the pressure plate **(see illustrations)**. Turn the crankshaft using a suitable socket or spanner on the crankshaft pulley/sprocket bolt, to bring each clamp location into view.

14 Once the clamps have been fitted, have the assistant release the clutch pedal.

4.13a Fitting a suitable clamp . . .

4.13b . . . to compress the clutch pressure plate prior to removal

4.15a Loosening a clutch cover-to-flywheel bolt

4.15b Stamped mark on flywheel (arrowed) aligned with notch in clutch cover

15 Progressively loosen and remove the six bolts and spring washers which secure the clutch pressure plate to the flywheel. As before when fitting the clamps, turn the crankshaft to bring each bolt into view. Where applicable (and if the original clutch is to be refitted), note the position of the mark on the flywheel which aligns with the notch in the rim of the clutch pressure plate **(see illustrations)**.

16 The clutch assembly can now be withdrawn downwards from the bellhousing **(see illustration)**. Be prepared to catch the clutch friction disc, which may drop out of the pressure plate as it is withdrawn, and note which way round the friction disc is fitted. The greater-projecting side of the hub faces away from the flywheel.

17 In order to remove the clamps, the pressure plate can be compressed against the tension of the diaphragm spring in a vice fitted with soft jaw protectors.

Inspection

18 With the clutch assembly removed, clean off all traces of dust using a dry cloth. Although most friction discs now have asbestos-free linings, some do not, and it is wise to take suitable precautions; *asbestos dust is harmful, and must not be inhaled.*

19 Examine the linings of the clutch disc for wear and loose rivets, and the disc for distortion, cracks, broken torsion springs and worn splines. The surface of the friction linings may be highly glazed, but, as long as the friction material pattern can be clearly seen, this is satisfactory. If there is any sign of oil contamination, indicated by a continuous, or

patchy, shiny black discolouration, the disc must be renewed. The source of the contamination must be traced and rectified before fitting new clutch components; typically, a leaking crankshaft oil seal or gearbox input shaft oil seal – or both – will be to blame (renewal procedures are given in Chapters 2A and 7 respectively). The disc must also be renewed if the lining thickness has worn down to, or just above, the level of the rivet heads.

20 Check the machined faces of the flywheel and pressure plate. If either is grooved, or heavily scored, renewal is necessary. The pressure plate must also be renewed if any cracks are apparent, or if the diaphragm spring is damaged, or its pressure suspect.

21 With the clutch removed, it is advisable to check the condition of the release bearing, as described in Section 5.

Refitting

22 Some replacement clutch assemblies are supplied with the pressure plate already compressed using the three clamps described in paragraph 12. If this is not the case, the pressure plate should first be compressed against the tension of the diaphragm spring. Use a vice fitted with soft jaw protectors, and fit the clamps used during removal.

23 It is important to ensure that no oil or grease gets onto the friction disc linings, or the pressure plate and flywheel faces. It is advisable to refit the clutch assembly with clean hands, and to wipe down the pressure plate and flywheel faces with a clean rag before assembly begins.

24 Apply a smear of molybdenum disulphide grease to the splines of the friction disc hub, then offer the disc to the flywheel, with the greater-projecting side of the hub facing away from the flywheel. Hold the friction disc against the flywheel while the pressure plate assembly is offered into position.

25 The input shaft must now be pushed through the hub of the friction disc, until its end engages in the end of the crankshaft. Under no circumstances must the shaft be hammered home, as gearbox damage may result. If the input shaft cannot be pushed home by hand, steady pressure should be exerted on the end of the shaft. The manufacturers specify the use of a special tool for this operation (GM No KM-564), but the improvised tool used to withdraw the shaft during the removal procedure can be used by repositioning the nut as shown **(see illustration)**.

26 With the input shaft pushed fully home, position the pressure plate assembly so that the mark on the flywheel is in alignment with the notch on the rim of the clutch pressure plate, then refit and progressively tighten the six clutch pressure plate-to-flywheel bolts (ensuring that the spring washers are fitted) in a diagonal sequence. Turn the crankshaft, using a suitable socket or spanner on the crankshaft pulley/sprocket bolt, to gain access to each bolt in turn, and finally tighten all the bolts to the specified torque.

27 Have an assistant depress the clutch pedal, then remove the three clamps from the edge of the pressure plate, again turning the crankshaft for access to each clamp.

28 Once the clamps have been removed, have the assistant release the clutch pedal.

29 Refit and tighten the gearbox input shaft screw to the specified torque, then fit a new circlip.

30 Using a new gasket, refit the gearbox endplate, and tighten the securing bolts to the specified torque. Where applicable, ensure that the studded bolt which retains the earth strap is fitted to its correct location, as noted during removal.

31 Where applicable, reconnect the gearbox earth strap, and fit the retaining nut.

32 Refit the cover plate to the base of the clutch bellhousing, and tighten the securing bolts. Where applicable, refit the wheel arch liner.

33 Refit the roadwheel, then lower the vehicle to the ground and finally tighten the roadwheel bolts. Refit the wheel trim, where applicable.

34 Check the clutch cable adjustment, as described in Chapter 1.

35 Check and if necessary top-up the gearbox oil level, as described in Chapter 1.

Models with 'pot' flywheel

Removal

36 Due to the size of the 'pot' flywheel, there is insufficient space for the clutch to be

4.16 Withdrawing the clutch assembly from the bellhousing

4.25 Using the improvised tool to engage the input shaft with the clutch friction disc

4.39 Unscrew the clutch cover securing bolts – note alignment marks (arrowed) . . .

4.40 . . . and withdraw the clutch assembly – model with 'pot' flywheel

4.45 Centralising the clutch friction disc using a socket and extension bar

withdrawn through the aperture in the clutch bellhousing, as described previously for models with a 'standard' flywheel.

37 Unless the complete engine/gearbox assembly is to be removed from the vehicle and separated for major overhaul (see Chapter 2B), access to the clutch can be obtained by removing the gearbox (Chapter 7).

38 With the engine and gearbox separated, proceed as follows.

39 Where applicable (and if the original clutch is to be refitted), note the position of the mark on the flywheel which aligns with the notch in the rim of the clutch pressure plate, then progressively unscrew the six bolts and spring washers which secure the clutch pressure plate to the flywheel **(see illustration).**

40 With all the bolts removed, lift off the clutch assembly **(see illustration)**. Be prepared to catch the friction disc as the pressure plate assembly is lifted from the flywheel, and note which way round the friction disc is fitted. The greater-projecting side of the hub should face away from the flywheel.

Inspection

41 Proceed as described in paragraphs 18 to 21 inclusive for models with a 'standard' flywheel.

Refitting

42 Proceed as described in paragraphs 23 and 24.

43 Fit the clutch pressure plate assembly, where applicable aligning the mark on the flywheel with the notch in the rim of the clutch pressure plate. Insert the six bolts and spring washers, and tighten them finger-tight, so that the friction disc is gripped, but can still be moved.

44 The friction disc must now be centralised, so that when the engine and gearbox are mated, the gearbox input shaft splines will pass through the splines in the friction disc hub.

45 Centralisation can be carried out by inserting a round bar or a long screwdriver through the hole in the centre of the friction disc, so that the end of the bar rests in the spigot bearing in the centre of the crankshaft **(see illustration)**. Where possible, use a blunt instrument – if a screwdriver or similar is used, wrap tape around the blade to prevent damage to the bearing surface. Moving the bar/screwdriver sideways or up-and-down as necessary, move the friction disc as necessary to achieve centralisation. With the bar removed, view the friction disc hub in relation to the hole in the centre of the crankshaft and the circle created by the ends of the diaphragm spring fingers. When the hub appears exactly in the centre, all is correct. Alternatively, if a suitable clutch alignment tool can be obtained, this will eliminate all the guesswork, and obviate the need for visual alignment.

46 Tighten the pressure plate retaining bolts gradually in a diagonal sequence, to the specified torque. Remove the alignment tool.

47 Refit the engine or the gearbox, as described in the relevant Chapter.

48 On completion, check the clutch cable adjustment, as described in Chapter 1.

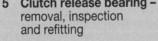

5 Clutch release bearing – removal, inspection and refitting

Note: *Refer to the note and warning at the beginning of Section 4 before proceeding.*

Removal

1 The gearbox must be removed for access to the release bearing. Unless the complete engine/gearbox assembly is to be removed from the vehicle and separated for major overhaul (see Chapter 2B), access to the clutch is most easily obtained by removing the gearbox, as described in Chapter 7.

2 Unscrew the clamp bolt securing the release fork to the release arm pivot shaft.

3 Pull the release arm pivot shaft up and out of the bellhousing, then withdraw the release fork and the bearing. Where necessary, slide the bearing from the release fork, and where applicable, pull the bearing from the plastic collar.

4 If desired, the gearbox input shaft oil seal can be renewed after removing the release bearing guide sleeve, as described in Chapter 7.

Inspection

5 Spin the release bearing, and check it for excessive roughness. Hold the outer race, and attempt to move it laterally against the inner race. If any excessive movement or roughness is evident, renew the bearing. If a new clutch has been fitted, it is wise to renew the release bearing as a matter of course.

6 The nylon bushes supporting the release arm pivot shaft can be renewed if necessary, by tapping them from their lugs in the bellhousing using a suitable drift. Drive the new bushes into position, ensuring that their locating tabs engage with the slots in the bellhousing lugs.

Refitting

7 Refitting of the release bearing and arm is a reversal of the removal procedure, bearing in mind the following points:

a) *Lightly smear the inner surfaces of the release arm pivot bushes, and the outer surfaces of the release bearing guide sleeve, with molybdenum disulphide grease.*

b) *Where applicable, fit the release bearing to the plastic collar, then fit the release bearing and fork together, and tighten the release fork clamp bolt to the specified torque.*

c) *Refit the gearbox as described in Chapter 7, or the engine/gearbox assembly as described in Chapter 2B, as applicable.*

d) *On completion, check the clutch cable adjustment as described in Chapter 1.*

Chapter 7
Manual gearbox

Contents

Degrees of difficulty

Easy, suitable for novice with little experience 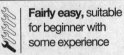	**Fairly easy,** suitable for beginner with some experience	**Fairly difficult,** suitable for competent DIY mechanic 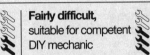	**Difficult,** suitable for experienced DIY mechanic	**Very difficult,** suitable for expert DIY or professional

Specifications

General

Type .... Five forward speeds and one reverse, synchromesh on all forward gears. Integral differential

Manufacturer's designation .... F 13/5 WR

Gear ratios

1st .... 3.55 or 3.73:1
2nd 1.96:1
3rd .... 1.30 or 1.31:1
4th .... 0.89 or 0.95:1
5th .... 0.71 or 0.76:1
Reverse 3.31:1
Final drive ratio .... 3.55, 3.74:1 or 4.18:1

Torque wrench settings	Nm	lbf ft
Clutch bellhousing cover plate bolts	7	5
Clutch release bearing guide sleeve bolts	5	4
Differential housing cover plate bolts:		
Steel plate	30	22
Alloy plate	18	13
Engine/gearbox mountings:		
Left-hand:		
Gearbox bracket-to-gearbox bolts	60	44
Gearbox bracket-to-mounting block bolts	60	44
Mounting block-to-body bolts*	65	48
Rear:		
Gearbox bracket-to-gearbox bolts	70	52
Gearbox bracket-to-mounting block bolts	65	48
Mounting block-to-body bolts	65	48
Engine-to-gearbox bolts	60	44
Gearchange lever housing-to-floorpan bolts	6	4
Speedometer drivegear retaining plate bolt	4	3
Reversing light switch	20	15

*Use thread-locking compound.

2.1 Differential cover plate securing bolts (arrowed)

1 General information

Drive from the clutch is transmitted to the input shaft, which runs in parallel with the mainshaft. The input shaft and mainshaft gears are in constant mesh, and selection of gears is by sliding synchromesh hubs, which lock the appropriate mainshaft gear to the mainshaft.

The 5th speed gear components are located in an extension housing at the end of the gearbox.

Reverse gear is obtained by sliding an idler gear into mesh with two straight-cut gears on the input shaft and mainshaft.

The differential is mounted in the main gearbox casing, and drive is transmitted to the differential by a pinion gear on the end of

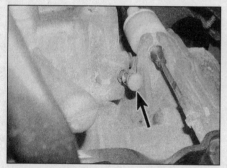

3.1 Spring-loaded type gearchange linkage adjustment plunger (arrowed)

3.4 Gear selector rod-to-clamp sleeve clamp nut (arrowed)

the mainshaft. The inboard ends of the driveshafts locate directly into the differential. The gearbox and differential unit share the same lubricating oil.

Gear selection is by a floor-mounted gear-change lever, via a remote control linkage.

2 Gearbox oil – draining and refilling

Draining

1 Place a suitable container under the differential cover plate. Unscrew the securing bolts and withdraw the cover plate, allowing the gearbox oil to drain into the container **(see illustration)**.
2 Refit the differential cover plate, and tighten the securing bolts when the oil has drained.

Refilling

3 Proceed as described for the gearbox oil level check in Chapter 1.

3 Gearchange linkage/mechanism – adjustment

Note: *According to gearbox type (see text), a new plug should be fitted to the gear linkage adjuster hole in the gear selector housing on completion of adjustment.*

1 Observe the gear selector housing on the top of the gearbox, adjacent to the clutch

3.2 Extract the plastic plug (where fitted) from the adjuster hole

3.5 Insert a twist drill to engage with the selector lever – viewed with gearbox removed for clarity

cable. On the front or rear of the housing there should be a spring-loaded adjustment plunger (usually coloured orange) protruding from the edge of the housing **(see illustration)**.
2 If an adjustment plunger is not present, observe the rear of the housing where there will be a plastic plug. Extract this plug, if present, from the adjuster hole **(see illustration)**. If necessary, for improved access to the gear selector housing, remove the battery with reference to Chapter 5A.
3 Jack up the front of the vehicle and support securely on axle stands (see *Jacking and vehicle support*).
4 Working underneath the vehicle, loosen the clamp nut and bolt securing the gear selector rod to the clamp sleeve **(see illustration)**.
5 Looking towards the engine compartment bulkhead, with the selector rod in the neutral plane, grip the gear selector rod, and twist it clockwise. If the housing has an adjustment plunger, move the selector rod back-and-forth slightly until the plunger can be pushed fully into the housing to engage with a corresponding hole in the selector rod. Release the selector rod and the plunger should remain in engagement. Alternatively, insert a 4.5 mm diameter twist drill through the adjuster hole at the rear of the gear selector housing, to engage with the hole in the selector lever **(see illustration)**.
6 Working inside the vehicle, pull back on the front edge of the gearchange lever gaiter, and free its lower end from the centre console, to allow access to the base of the gearchange lever.
7 Move the gearchange lever to the neutral position in the 1st/2nd gear plane. Adjust the position of the lever until a suitable tool can be inserted through the holes in the base of the lever assembly and the lever housing to lock the lever in position **(see illustration)**.
8 Without moving the gearchange lever, tighten the clamp bolt and nut securing the gear selector rod to the clamp sleeve in the engine compartment.
9 Pull out the adjustment plunger, or remove the twist drill from the adjuster hole in the gear selector housing. Seal the hole with a new plug.
10 Refit the gearchange lever gaiter to the centre console.

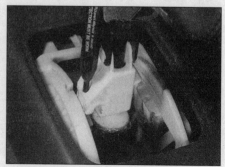

3.7 Using a pin punch to lock the gearchange lever in position

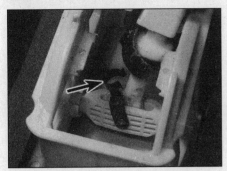

4.3a Release the gearchange lever securing clip (arrowed) . . .

4.3b . . . then withdraw the pivot pin . . .

4.3c . . . and lift out the lever (viewed with centre console removed)

11 Refit the battery (if removed), and reconnect the battery leads.

12 Finally check that all gears can be engaged easily, first with the engine off, then with the engine running.

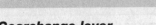

4 Gearchange linkage/mechanism – removal, overhaul and refitting

Gearchange lever

Removal

1 Ensure that the lever is in neutral.

2 Pull back on the front edge of the gearchange lever gaiter, and free its lower end from the centre console to allow access to the base of the lever.

3 Release the clip from the base of the lever shaft, then withdraw the pivot pin, and lift out the lever **(see illustrations)**.

Overhaul

4 To renew the gearchange lever gaiter and/or the knob, proceed as follows. **Note:** *There is a strong possibility that the knob will be destroyed during the removal process.*

5 On models with a plastic lever knob, immerse the knob in hot water (approximately 80ºC) for a few minutes, then twist the knob and tap it from the lever. On models with a leather-covered lever knob, clamp the lever in a vice fitted with soft jaw protectors, and place an open-ended spanner under the metal insert at the bottom of the knob; tap the knob from the lever, using the spanner as an insulator to protect the knob.

6 If renewing the gaiter, slide the old gaiter from the lever, and fit the new one. Use a little liquid detergent (eg, washing-up liquid) to aid fitting if necessary.

7 Refit the knob (or fit the new knob, as applicable). When fitting a plastic knob, preheat it in hot water, as during removal. When fitting a leather-covered knob, preheat the metal insert at the base of the knob using a hair drier or hot-air gun. Ensure that the knob is fitted the correct way round.

Refitting

8 Refitting the lever is a reversal of removal.

Gearchange lever housing assembly

Removal

9 Working in the engine compartment, loosen the clamp bolt securing the gear selector rod to the clamp sleeve.

10 Remove the gearchange lever, as described previously in this Section.

11 Remove the centre console, as described in Chapter 11.

12 Unscrew the four bolts securing the gearchange lever housing to the floorpan **(see illustration)**.

13 The housing and clamp sleeve can now be withdrawn. Pull the assembly towards the rear of the vehicle, to feed the clamp sleeve through the bulkhead. As the clamp sleeve is fed through the bulkhead, have an assistant remove the clamp from the end of the clamp sleeve in the engine compartment, to avoid damage to the rubber boot on the bulkhead.

Overhaul

14 If desired, the rubber boot can be renewed by pulling the old boot from the bulkhead, and pushing the new boot into position, ensuring that it is correctly seated.

15 The clamp sleeve bush in the gearchange lever housing can be renewed after sliding the clamp sleeve from the housing. Prise the bush insert from the front of the housing, then prise the bush from the insert. Fit the new bush using a reversal of the removal procedure, but lubricate the inside of the bush with a little silicone grease.

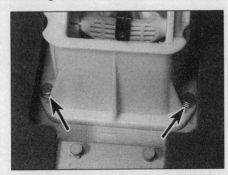

4.12 Two of the gearchange lever housing securing bolts (arrowed)

Refitting

16 Refitting of the assembly is a reversal of removal, but before tightening the clamp bolt, adjust the gear selector linkage as described in Section 3.

Gear selector linkage

Removal

17 Ensure that the gearchange lever is in neutral.

18 Remove the securing pin (squeeze the two retaining lugs to release the pin), and separate the two sections of the linkage universal joint **(see illustration)**.

19 Loosen the clamp bolt securing the clamp sleeve to the linkage, and pull the clamp sleeve from the selector rod.

20 Release the spring clip, then pull the bellcrank pivot pin from the bracket on the rear engine/gearbox mounting.

21 Withdraw the linkage from the vehicle.

Overhaul

22 Check the linkage components for wear, and renew as necessary. The pivot bushes can be renewed by prising out the old bushes and pressing in the new, and the link can be renewed by pulling it from the balljoints. Further dismantling is not recommended.

Refitting

23 Refitting is a reversal of removal, but lubricate all moving components with a little grease and, before tightening the clamp bolt, adjust the gear selector linkage as described in Section 3.

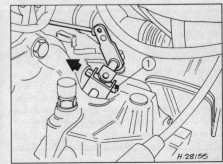

4.18 Gear linkage universal joint pin retaining lug (1)

5 Speedometer drive – removal and refitting

Removal

Note: *On later models the speedometer drive is replaced by an electronic vehicle speed sensor. The removal and refitting procedures are basically the same except that there is no speedometer cable or speedometer driven gear on the vehicle speed sensor.*

1 Unscrew the securing sleeve, and disconnect the speedometer cable from the top of the gearbox **(see illustration)**. If a vehicle speed sensor is fitted, disconnect the wiring connector from the sensor.

2 Unbolt the retaining plate, and withdraw the speedometer drive/vehicle speed sensor assembly **(see illustrations)**.

3 Where applicable, the speedometer driven gear can be withdrawn from its sleeve, in which case note the thrustwasher under the gear **(see illustration)**.

Refitting

4 If the driven gear has been removed from the sleeve, lubricate the gear shaft with a little silicone grease, then slide the gear into the sleeve, ensuring that the thrustwasher is in place on the gear shaft.

5 Inspect the O-ring seal on the sleeve, and renew if worn or damaged.

6 Further refitting is a reversal of removal.

6 Oil seals – renewal

Differential side (driveshaft) oil seals

1 Apply the handbrake, then jack up the front of the vehicle and support securely on axle stands (see *Jacking and vehicle support*). Remove the relevant front roadwheel.

2 Disconnect the inner end of the relevant driveshaft from the differential as described in Chapter 8. There is no need to disconnect the driveshaft from the swivel hub. Support the driveshaft by suspending it with wire or string – do not allow the driveshaft to hang down under its own weight, or the joints may be damaged.

3 Prise the now-exposed oil seal from the differential housing, using a screwdriver or similar instrument **(see illustration)**.

4 Smear the sealing lip of the new oil seal with a little gearbox oil, then using a metal tube or socket of suitable diameter, drive the new seal into the differential casing until the outer surface of the seal is flush with the outer surface of the differential casing **(see illustration)**.

5 Reconnect the driveshaft to the differential as described in Chapter 8.

5.1 Disconnecting the speedometer cable from the gearbox

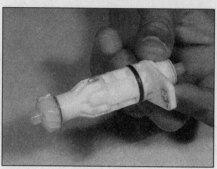

5.2b . . . and withdraw the speedometer drive assembly

6 Refit the roadwheel, then lower the vehicle to the ground.

Input shaft (clutch) oil seal

7 Remove the gearbox (see Section 8).

6.3 Prising out a differential side oil seal

6.8a Withdraw the clutch release bearing guide sleeve . . .

5.2a Unbolt the retaining plate . . .

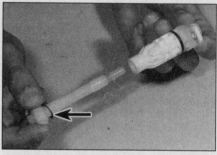

5.3 Withdrawing the speedometer driven gear from its sleeve. Note thrustwasher (arrowed)

8 Unscrew the securing bolts, and withdraw the clutch release bearing guide sleeve from the bellhousing. Recover the O-ring which fits between the guide sleeve and the bellhousing **(see illustrations)**.

6.4 Driving a new differential side oil seal into position

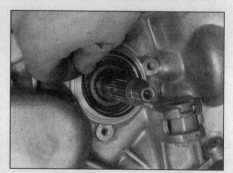

6.8b . . . and recover the O-ring

9 Drive the old seal from the guide sleeve (**see illustration**), and fit a new seal using a suitable tube or socket. Press the new seal into position – do not drive it in, as the seal is easily damaged.

10 Fill the space between the lips of the new seal with lithium-based grease, then refit the guide sleeve using a new O-ring. The O-ring should be fitted dry.

11 Refit the guide sleeve to the bellhousing, and tighten the securing bolts.

12 Refit the gearbox as described in Section 8.

6.9 Driving the oil seal from the clutch release bearing guide sleeve

7.5 Disconnect the wiring from the reversing light switch (arrowed)

7 Reversing light switch – testing, removal and refitting

Testing

1 The reversing light circuit is operated by a plunger-type switch, mounted in the front of the gearbox casing.

2 To test the switch, disconnect the wiring, and use a suitable meter or a battery-and-bulb test circuit to check for continuity between the switch terminals. Continuity should only exist when reverse gear is selected. If this is not the case, and there are no obvious breaks or other damage to the wires, the switch is faulty and must be renewed.

Removal

3 The reversing light switch is located in the front of the gearbox casing, and is accessible from the engine compartment.

4 Disconnect the battery negative terminal (refer to *Disconnecting the battery* in the Reference Chapter).

5 Disconnect the wiring from the switch, then unscrew the switch from the gearbox (**see illustration**).

Refitting

6 Refitting is a reversal of removal.

8 Manual gearbox – removal and refitting

Note: *This is an involved procedure, and it may prove easier in many cases to remove the gearbox complete with the engine as an assembly, as described in Chapter 2B. If removing the gearbox on its own, it is suggested that this Section is read through thoroughly before commencing work. Suitable equipment will be required to support the engine and gearbox, and the help of an assistant will be required.*

Removal

1 Disconnect the battery negative terminal (refer to *Disconnecting the battery* in the Reference Chapter).

2 Remove the retaining clip (where applicable), then slide the clutch cable from the release lever, pushing the release lever back towards the bulkhead, if necessary, to allow the cable to be disconnected (**see illustration**).

3 Pull the cable support from the bracket on the gearbox casing, then move the cable to one side out of the way, taking note of its routing (**see illustration**).

4 Disconnect the wiring from the reversing light switch, located at the front of the gearbox, above the mounting bracket (see Section 7).

5 Disconnect the wiring from the vehicle speed sensor or, alternatively, unscrew the securing sleeve, and disconnect the speedometer cable from the top of the gearbox. Note that on certain models, the cable is in two sections, joined by a connector near the engine compartment bulkhead – in

this case, it may be easier to separate the two cable sections at the connector, rather than to disconnect the cable from the gearbox (**see illustration**).

6 Unscrew and remove the three upper engine-to-gearbox bolts, noting the locations of any brackets secured by the bolts. On certain models, the plastic coolant gallery may prevent access to the centre upper bolt (**see illustrations**) in which case, proceed as follows:

a) Drain the cooling system as described in Chapter 1 (if not already done), then disconnect the radiator hose from the front of the coolant gallery.

b) Remove the rear upper engine-to-gearbox bolt, which also secures the coolant gallery and a clutch cable bracket.

c) Move the coolant gallery as necessary to enable access to the centre upper engine-to-gearbox bolt.

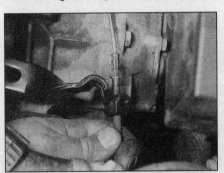
8.2 Slide the clutch cable from the release lever . . .

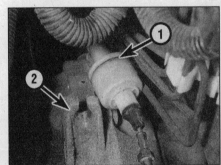
8.3 . . . and pull the cable support (1) from the bracket (2) on the gearbox casing

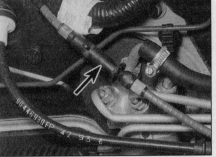
8.5 Speedometer cable connector (arrowed) – viewed with engine removed

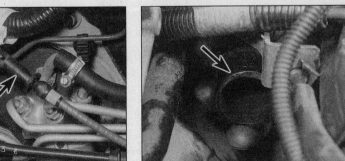
8.6a It may be necessary to move the coolant gallery (arrowed) . . .

8.6b . . . to allow access to one of the engine-to-gearbox bolts

8.6c Coolant gallery and clutch cable brackets located on upper engine-to-gearbox bolts

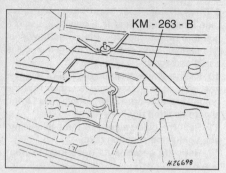

8.9 Vauxhall/Opel tool No KM-263-B used to support engine

7 Apply the handbrake, then jack up the front of the vehicle, and support securely on axle stands (see *Jacking and vehicle support*). Note that the vehicle must be raised sufficiently high to enable the gearbox be withdrawn from under the front of the vehicle.

8 Remove the roadwheels.

9 The engine must now be supported. Ideally, the engine should be supported using chains suspended from a strong wooden or metal beam resting on blocks positioned securely in the channels at the sides of the engine compartment. A Vauxhall/Opel special tool is available for this purpose **(see illustration)**. Alternatively, the engine can be supported using a suitable hoist and lifting tackle, but the hoist must be capable of supporting the engine with the front of the vehicle raised off the ground, leaving sufficient clearance to withdraw the gearbox from under the front of

the vehicle (see previous paragraph). As a further alternative, the engine can be supported using a jack and interposed block of wood under the sump, but great care must be taken when removing the gearbox, not to move the engine off the jack – it is strongly recommended that the engine is additionally supported using a hoist or bar as described previously, to avoid any possibility of injury. Note that if a hoist is used to support the engine, a further hoist will be required to carry out removal of the gearbox safely. (The alternative to all this is to remove the engine and gearbox as an assembly, as described in Chapter 2B.)

10 With the engine supported, proceed as follows.

11 Where applicable, unbolt the earth strap from the end of the gearbox.

12 On engines with a steel sump, unscrew the securing bolts, and remove the engine-to-

gearbox blanking plate from the bellhousing **(see illustration)**.

13 Loosen the clamp nut and bolt securing the gear selector rod to the linkage, then pull the selector tube towards the engine compartment bulkhead to separate it from the linkage **(see illustration)**.

14 Disconnect the exhaust front section from the manifold as described in Chapter 4A, and release the system from the forward rubber mountings – this will allow the engine to be lowered later in the procedure.

15 Place a suitable container under the differential cover plate, then remove the securing bolts, and withdraw the cover plate to drain the gearbox oil.

16 Refit the differential cover plate on completion of draining.

17 Remove the front anti-roll bar as described in Chapter 10.

18 Remove the left-hand front suspension lower arm and tie-bar as described in Chapter 10.

19 Disconnect the inner ends of the driveshafts from the gearbox as described in Chapter 8. There is no need to disconnect the driveshafts from the swivel hubs. Be prepared for oil spillage, and plug the openings in the gearbox, to prevent dirt ingress and further oil loss. Do not allow the driveshafts to hang down under their own weight, or the joints may be damaged – support the driveshafts with wire or string.

20 Support the gearbox with a trolley jack, with an interposed block of wood to spread the load. Ensure that the engine is adequately supported as described in paragraph 9.

21 Additionally, the gearbox should be supported from above, using a hoist. Fit a suitable strap around the gearbox casing, passing it through the hole in the battery tray (remove the battery as described in Chapter 5A, if not already done), and suspend the strap from the hoist **(see illustration)**. This will enable the gearbox to be lowered safely during removal.

22 Remove the left-hand engine/gearbox mounting bracket completely, by unscrewing the two bolts securing the bracket to the rubber mounting, and the three bolts securing the mounting bracket to the gearbox **(see illustration)**.

8.12 Removing the engine-to-gearbox blanking plate

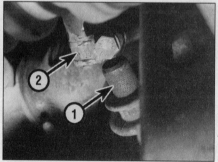

8.13 Pull the selector tube (1) from the gear linkage (2)

8.21 Strap passed through battery tray and around gearbox casing to support gearbox

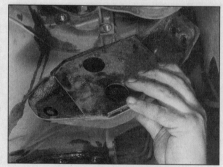

8.22 Removing the left-hand engine/gearbox mounting bracket

23 Remove the nut and through-bolt securing the rear engine/gearbox mounting bracket to the mounting on the body **(see illustration)**.

24 Release the spring clip, then pull the gear linkage pivot pin from the bracket on the rear engine/gearbox mounting.

25 Remove the two bolts securing the rear engine/gearbox mounting bracket to the gearbox, and withdraw the mounting bracket.

26 Make a final check to ensure that all relevant wiring, hoses, etc, have been disconnected to facilitate gearbox removal. Note that on certain models, the wiring for the oxygen sensor may be secured to the lug on the gearbox with a cable-tie.

27 Using the lifting tackle, and the jack(s), lower the engine and gearbox slightly.

28 Unscrew and remove the remaining engine-to-gearbox bolts **(see illustration)**, noting the locations of any brackets secured by the bolts.

29 With the aid of an assistant, carefully separate the gearbox from the engine (use the hoist to take the weight of the gearbox). It may be necessary to rock the gearbox a little to release it from the engine. Take care not to allow the weight of the gearbox to hang on the input shaft as the gearbox is separated from the engine.

30 Lower the gearbox from the engine compartment, taking care not to damage surrounding components.

Refitting

31 Before refitting, check that the left-hand engine/gearbox mounting-to-body bolts rotate freely in their threaded holes in the body. If necessary, re-cut the threaded holes in the body using a suitable tap.

32 Commence refitting by positioning the gearbox under the front of the vehicle, supporting with the hoist and strap, and the trolley jack and interposed block of wood, as during removal.

33 Raise the gearbox sufficiently to enable the engine and gearbox to be mated together. Ensure that the gearbox input shaft engages correctly with the clutch friction disc as the gearbox is joined to the engine.

34 Refit the lower engine-to-gearbox bolts, but do not fully tighten them at this stage. Ensure that any brackets or clips noted during removal are in place on the bolts.

35 Coat the threads of the left-hand engine/gearbox mounting-to-body bolts with thread-locking compound, then raise the engine and gearbox sufficiently to enable the mounting bracket to be refitted.

36 Refit the left-hand engine/gearbox mounting, and tighten the mounting bolts to the specified torque.

37 Refit the rear engine/gearbox mounting bracket to the gearbox, and tighten the bolts to the specified torque.

38 Refit the through-bolt and nut securing the rear engine/gearbox mounting to the mounting on the body.

8.23 Remove the nut and through-bolt securing the rear engine/gearbox mounting

39 Refit the gear linkage to the bracket on the rear engine/gearbox mounting, and secure with the pivot pin.

40 The hoist and jack used to support the gearbox can now be withdrawn.

41 Tighten the lower engine-to-gearbox bolts to the specified torque.

42 Refit the left-hand front suspension lower arm and tie-bar as described in Chapter 10.

43 Refit the front anti-roll bar as described in Chapter 10.

44 Reconnect the inner ends of the driveshafts to the gearbox as described in Chapter 8.

45 Refit or reconnect the exhaust front section as described in Chapter 4A.

46 Reconnect the gear selector rod to the gear linkage, and adjust the linkage as described in Section 3.

47 On engines with a steel sump, refit the engine-to-gearbox blanking plate to the bellhousing.

48 Where applicable, reconnect the earth strap to the end of the gearbox.

49 Remove or disconnect the equipment used to support the engine, and lower the vehicle to the ground.

50 Refit and tighten the three upper engine-to-gearbox bolts (where necessary, gaining access as described during removal); ensure that the coolant gallery (where applicable) and any brackets noted during removal are in place on the bolts. Where applicable, reconnect the radiator hose to the coolant gallery.

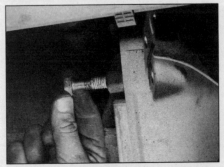

8.28 Removing one of the lower engine-to-gearbox bolts

51 Where fitted, reconnect the speedometer cable to the gearbox, or reconnect the two sections of the cable, as applicable, with reference to Chapter 12. Alternatively, reconnect the wiring to the vehicle speed sensor.

52 Reconnect the reversing light switch wiring.

53 Reconnect the clutch cable to the release lever, and check the clutch cable adjustment as described in Chapter 1. Ensure that the cable is routed as noted during removal.

54 Where applicable, refill the cooling system as described in Chapter 1.

55 Refill the gearbox with oil as described in Section 2.

56 Refit the battery (if removed), then reconnect the battery terminals.

9 Manual gearbox overhaul – general information

1 The complete overhaul of a manual gearbox is a complicated task, requiring a number of special tools, and previous experience is a great help. It is therefore recommended that owners remove the gearbox themselves, if wished, but then either fit a new or reconditioned unit, or have the existing unit overhauled by a Vauxhall/Opel dealer or gearbox specialist.

2 The dismantling of the gearbox into its major assemblies is a reasonably straightforward operation, and can be carried out to enable an assessment of wear or damage to be made (suitable exploded views of the gearboxes are provided to assist owners who wish to do this). From this assessment, a decision can be taken on whether or not to proceed with a full overhaul. Note, however, that any overhaul work will require the dismantling and reassembly of many small and intricate assemblies, as well as taking several precise measurements to assess wear. This will require a number of special tools, and previous experience will prove invaluable. As a minimum, the following tools will be required:

a) *Internal and external circlip pliers.*
b) *A selection of pin punches.*
c) *A selection of Torx and splined bits.*
d) *A bearing puller.*
e) *A hydraulic press.*
f) *A slide hammer.*
g) *A selection of heat-sensitive marker pencils.*

3 While the *Fault finding* Section at the end of this manual should help to isolate most gearbox faults to enable a decision to be taken on what course of action to follow, remember that economic considerations may rule out an apparently-simple repair. For example, a common reason for gearbox dismantling is to renew the synchromesh units, wear or faults in these assemblies being indicated by noise when changing gear. Jumping out of gear or similar gear selection faults may be due to worn selector forks, or synchro-sleeves. General noise during operation may be due to worn bearings, shafts or gears. The cumulative cost of renewing all worn components may make it more economical to renew the gearbox complete.

4 To establish whether gearbox overhaul is economically viable, first establish the cost of a complete replacement gearbox, comparing the cost of a new unit with that of an exchange reconditioned unit (if available), or even a good secondhand unit (with a guarantee) from a vehicle breaker. Compare these costs with the likely cost of the replacement parts which will be required if the existing gearbox is overhauled; do not forget to include all items which must be renewed when they are disturbed, such as oil seals, O-rings, roll pins, circlips, snap-rings, etc.

Chapter 8
Driveshafts

Contents

Degrees of difficulty

Easy, suitable for novice with little experience	**Fairly easy,** suitable for beginner with some experience	**Fairly difficult,** suitable for competent DIY mechanic	**Difficult,** suitable for experienced DIY mechanic	**Very difficult,** suitable for expert DIY or professional

Specifications

Type
All models ....   Unequal length shafts with ball-and-cage type constant velocity joint at each end

Lubrication (overhaul only – see text)
Lubricant type/specification ....   Use only special grease supplied in sachets with gaiter kits – joints are otherwise pre-packed with grease and sealed

Torque wrench settings

	Nm	lbf ft
Driveshaft retaining nut:*		
Stage 1	130	96
Stage 2	Slacken the nut completely	
Stage 3	20	15
Stage 4	Angle-tighten through a further 90º	
Lower arm balljoint clamp bolt nut*	30	22
Roadwheel bolts	110	81

*Use new nuts/bolts.

1   General information

Drive is transmitted from the differential to the front wheels by means of two solid steel driveshafts of unequal length. The right-hand driveshaft is longer than the left-hand one, due to the position of the transmission unit.

Both driveshafts are splined at their outer ends to accept the wheel hubs, and are threaded so that each hub can be fastened by a large nut. The inner end of each driveshaft is splined to accept the differential sun gear.

Constant velocity (CV) joints are fitted to each end of the driveshafts, to ensure the smooth and efficient transmission of drive at all the angles possible as the roadwheels move up-and-down with the suspension, and as they turn from side-to-side under steering. Both inner and outer constant velocity joints are of the ball-and-cage type.

2   Driveshafts – removal and refitting

Note: *A new driveshaft retaining nut and balljoint clamp bolt nut will be needed on refitting.*

2.2 Extract the split pin from the driveshaft retaining nut

Removal

> **HAYNES HiNT** *If work is being carried out without the aid of an assistant, remove the wheel trim/hub cap (as applicable) then withdraw the split pin and slacken the driveshaft retaining nut with the vehicle resting on its wheels.*

1 Firmly apply the handbrake, then jack up the front of the car and support it securely on axle stands (see *Jacking and vehicle support*). Remove the relevant front roadwheel.

2 Extract the split pin from the driveshaft retaining nut and discard it; a new one must be used on refitting **(see illustration)**.

3 Refit at least two roadwheel bolts to the front hub, and tighten them securely. Have an assistant firmly depress the brake pedal to prevent the front hub from rotating, then using a socket and extension bar, slacken and remove the driveshaft retaining nut. Alternatively, a tool can be fabricated from

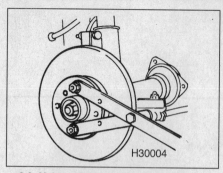

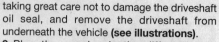

2.3 Using a fabricated tool to hold the front hub stationary whilst the driveshaft retaining nut is slackened

2.5 Withdraw the clamp bolt, and free the lower arm balljoint from the swivel hub

taking great care not to damage the driveshaft oil seal, and remove the driveshaft from underneath the vehicle (see illustrations).

9 Plug the opening in the differential, to prevent further oil loss and dirt ingress.

10 **Do not** *allow the vehicle to rest on its wheels with one or both driveshaft(s) removed, as damage to the wheel bearing(s) may result.* If moving the vehicle is unavoidable, temporarily insert the outer end of the driveshaft(s) in the hub(s), and tighten the hub nut(s): in this case, the inner end(s) of the driveshaft(s) must be supported, for example by suspending with string from the vehicle underbody. **Do not** *allow the driveshaft to hang down under its own weight, or the joints may be damaged.*

Refitting

11 Before installing the driveshaft, examine the driveshaft oil seal in the transmission for signs of damage or deterioration. Renew if necessary, referring to the relevant part of Chapter 7 for further information.

12 Check the circlip fitted to the inner constant velocity joint splines for signs of damage, and renew if necessary. Ensure that the circlip is correctly seated in its groove (see illustration).

13 Thoroughly clean the driveshaft splines, and the apertures in the transmission unit and hub assembly. Apply a thin film of grease to the oil seal lips, and to the driveshaft splines and shoulders. Check that all gaiter clips are securely fastened.

14 Remove the plug from the transmission (see paragraph 9) and offer up the driveshaft. Locate the joint splines with those of the differential sun gear, taking great care not to damage the oil seal.

15 Place a screwdriver or similar tool on the weld bead of the inner driveshaft joint, not the metal cover, and drive the shaft into the differential until the retaining snap-ring engages positively (see illustration). Pull on the joint, not the shaft, to make sure that the joint is securely retained by the circlip.

16 Locate the outer constant velocity joint splines with those of the swivel hub, and slide the joint back into position in the hub. Fit the washer and new driveshaft retaining nut, tightening it by hand only at this stage.

17 Locate the lower arm balljoint in the swivel hub, and insert the clamp bolt from the rear of the swivel hub, so that its threads are facing forwards. Fit a new nut to the clamp bolt, and tighten it to the specified torque setting.

18 Using the method employed on removal to prevent rotation, tighten the driveshaft retaining nut through the stages given in the Specifications at the start of this Chapter (see illustrations).

19 With the nut correctly tightened, secure it in position with a new split pin (see illustrations). If the holes in the driveshaft are not aligned with any of the slots in the nut, loosen (do not tighten) the nut by the smallest possible amount until the split pin can be inserted.

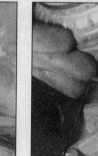

2.8a Lever the driveshaft CV joint out from the transmission to release its circlip from the differential . . .

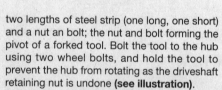

2.8b . . . then withdraw the shaft, taking great care not to damage the oil seal in the transmission

two lengths of steel strip (one long, one short) and a nut an bolt; the nut and bolt forming the pivot of a forked tool. Bolt the tool to the hub using two wheel bolts, and hold the tool to prevent the hub from rotating as the driveshaft retaining nut is undone (see illustration).

4 Unscrew the driveshaft retaining nut, and remove the washer. Discard the nut; a new one must be used on refitting.

5 Slacken and remove the lower arm balljoint clamp nut and bolt, and free the lower arm from the swivel hub (see illustration). Discard the clamp bolt nut; a new one must be used on refitting.

6 Carefully pull the swivel hub assembly outwards, and withdraw the driveshaft outer constant velocity joint from the hub assembly.

If necessary, the shaft can be tapped out of the hub using a soft-faced mallet. Support the driveshaft by suspending it with wire or string; do not allow it to hang under its own weight, or the joints may be damaged.

7 A suitable tool will now be required to release the inner end of the driveshaft from the differential. To release the right-hand driveshaft, a flat steel bar with a good chamfer on one end can be used. The left-hand driveshaft may prove more difficult to release, and a suitable square- or rectangular-section bar may be required.

8 Lever between the driveshaft and the differential housing to release the driveshaft circlip from the differential. Carefully withdraw the driveshaft from the transmission unit,

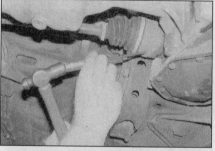

2.12 Prior to refitting, ensure that the circlip (arrowed) is correctly located in the inner CV joint groove

2.15 Using a screwdriver on the CV joint weld bead to drive the joint into the differential until the snap-ring engages positively

20 Refit the roadwheel, then lower the vehicle to the ground and tighten the roadwheel bolts to the specified torque.
21 Top-up the transmission with the specified type of oil/fluid using the information given in Chapter 1.

3 Driveshaft rubber gaiters – renewal

Note: *If both driveshaft gaiters are to renewed at the same time, it is only necessary to remove one of the constant velocity joints. The second gaiter can then be slid along and removed from the exposed end of the driveshaft. The inner and outer CV joints are identical and the following procedure can be used for either joint.*

1 Remove the driveshaft from the car as described in Section 2.
2 Secure the driveshaft in a vice equipped with soft jaws, and release the two retaining clips on the gaiter which is to be renewed. If necessary, the retaining clips can be cut to release them.
3 Slide the rubber gaiter down the shaft to expose the constant velocity joint. Scoop out any excess grease.
4 Using circlip pliers, expand the circlip which secures the joint to the driveshaft (see illustration).
5 Using a soft-faced mallet, tap the joint off the end of the driveshaft.
6 Slide the rubber gaiter off the driveshaft, and discard it.
7 If both gaiters are to be renewed, release the retaining clips, then slide the second gaiter along the driveshaft and remove it. If the driveshaft is fitted with a vibration damper, mark the damper fitted position, then unbolt and remove it from the driveshaft.
8 Thoroughly clean the constant velocity joint(s) using paraffin, or a suitable solvent, and dry thoroughly. Carry out a visual inspection as follows.
9 Move the inner splined driving member from side-to-side, to expose each ball in turn at the top of its track. Examine the balls for cracks, flat spots, or signs of surface pitting (see illustration).
10 Inspect the ball tracks on the inner and outer members. If the tracks have widened, the balls will no longer be a tight fit. At the same time, check the ball cage windows for wear or cracking between the windows.
11 If on inspection any of the constant velocity joint components are found to be worn or damaged, it will be necessary to renew the complete joint assembly (refer to the Note at the end of Section 4). If the joint is in satisfactory condition, obtain a repair kit consisting of a new gaiter and retaining clips, a constant velocity joint circlip, and the correct type and quantity of grease (see illustration).
12 Wind tape around the splines on the end

of the driveshaft, to protect the gaiter as it is slid into place.
13 Where both gaiters have been removed, slide on the first gaiter and proceed as

described in paragraphs 15 to 18.
14 Slide the (second) gaiter onto the end of the driveshaft (see illustration), then remove the tape from the driveshaft splines.

2.18a Working in the stages given in the Specifications, tighten the driveshaft retaining nut to the specified torque setting . . .

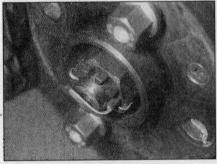
2.18b . . . and then through the specified angle (note the use of an angle gauge)

2.19a Insert a new split pin . . .

2.19b . . . and secure in position by bending over the split pin ends

3.4 Expand the CV joint circlip, and tap the joint off the end of the driveshaft

3.9 Examine the constant velocity joint balls and cage for signs of wear or damage

3.11 Components required for driveshaft gaiter renewal

3.14 Slide the gaiter onto the end of the driveshaft

3.15a Fit a new circlip . . .

3.15b . . . ensuring it is correctly located in the joint inner member

3.15c Slide the joint onto the driveshaft until the circlip is correctly located in the driveshaft groove

3.16 Pack the CV joint and gaiter with the grease supplied

3.18a Hook the large outer retaining clip ends together . . .

3.18b . . . then secure the clip in position by compressing the raised section of the clip

15 Fit a new circlip to the constant velocity joint, then tap the joint onto the driveshaft until the circlip engages in its groove **(see illustrations)**. Make sure that the joint is securely retained by the circlip, by pulling on the joint, not the shaft.

16 Pack the joint with the specified type of grease **(see illustration)**. Work the grease well into the bearing tracks whilst twisting the joint, and fill the rubber gaiter with any excess.

17 Ease the gaiter over the joint, and ensure that the gaiter lips are correctly located in the grooves on both the driveshaft and constant velocity joint. Lift the outer sealing lip of the gaiter, to equalise air pressure within the gaiter.

18 Fit the large metal retaining clip to the gaiter. Pull the clip as tight as possible, and locate the hooks on the clip in their slots. Remove any slack in the gaiter retaining clip by carefully compressing the raised section of the clip. In the absence of the special tool, a pair of side cutters may be used. Secure the small retaining clip using the same procedure **(see illustrations)**.

19 Check that both constant velocity joints move freely in all directions then, where applicable, refit the vibration damper its

original position on the driveshaft. On completion, refit the driveshaft to the car as described in Section 2.

4 Driveshaft overhaul – general information

1 If any of the checks described in Chapter 1 reveal wear in a driveshaft joint, first remove the roadwheel trim or centre cap (as appropriate).

2 If the split pin is in position, the driveshaft nut should be correctly tightened. If in doubt, the only alternative is to obtain a new nut and split pin, then fit and tighten the nut using the procedures described in Section 2. Once tightened, secure the nut in position with the new split pin, and refit the centre cap or trim. Repeat this check on the other driveshaft nut.

3 Road test the vehicle, and listen for a metallic clicking from the front as the vehicle, is driven slowly in a circle on full-lock. If a clicking noise is heard, this indicates wear in the outer constant velocity joint. This means that the joint must be renewed; as reconditioning is not possible.

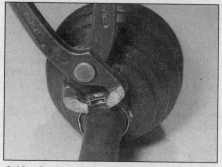

3.18c Small inner retaining clip is secured in position in the same way

4 If vibration, consistent with road speed, is felt through the car when accelerating, there is a possibility of wear in the inner constant velocity joints.

5 To check the joints for wear, remove the driveshafts, then dismantle them as described in Section 3; if any wear or free play is found, the affected joint must be renewed. **Note:** *If driveshaft joint wear is apparent on a vehicle which has covered in excess of 50 000 miles (80 000 km), the manufacturer recommends that the complete driveshaft is renewed.*

Chapter 9
Braking system

Contents

Degrees of difficulty

Easy, suitable for novice with little experience

Fairly easy, suitable for beginner with some experience

Fairly difficult, suitable for competent DIY mechanic

Difficult, suitable for experienced DIY mechanic

Very difficult, suitable for expert DIY or professional

Specifications

Front brakes

Type	Disc, with single-piston sliding caliper
Disc thickness:	
New:	
Solid disc	12.7 mm
Ventilated disc	20.0 mm
Minimum thickness:	
Solid disc	9.7 mm
Ventilated disc	17.0 mm
Maximum disc run-out	0.1 mm
Brake pad minimum thickness (including backing plate)	7.0 mm

Rear brakes

Type	Single leading shoe drum
Drum diameter:	
New:	
Corsa and Corsavan models	200 mm
Combo Van models	230 mm
Maximum diameter:	
Corsa and Corsavan models	201 mm
Combo Van models	231 mm
Maximum drum out-of-round	0.1 mm
Minimum friction material thickness	2.5 mm
Minimum friction material-to-rivet depth	0.5 mm

Torque wrench settings

	Nm	lbf ft
ABS components:		
ECU-to-modulator retaining screws*	3	2
Front wheel sensor bolt	8	6
Modulator block retaining nuts	8	6
Rear wheel sensor screw	4	3
Brake hose union bolt	40	30
Brake pedal pivot shaft nut	18	13
Brake pipe union nut	16	12
Front brake caliper:		
Guide bolts	30	22
Mounting bracket-to-swivel hub bolts*	95	70
Master cylinder mounting nuts*	22	16
Master cylinder reservoir support bracket:		
Bracket-to-bulkhead nut*	20	15
Bracket-to-reservoir bolt	12	9
Pressure-regulating valve:*		
Mounting bolts	20	15
Spring bolt (Corsa and Corsavan)	20	15
Spring clamp nuts (Combo Van)	20	15
Rear hub nut (pre-load)	25	18
Roadwheel bolts	110	81
Servo unit mounting nuts	22	16
Vacuum hose to vacuum pump	18	13

*Use new nuts/bolts

1 General information

The braking system is of the servo-assisted, dual-circuit hydraulic type. The arrangement of the hydraulic system is such that each circuit operates one front and one rear brake from a tandem master cylinder. Under normal circumstances, both circuits operate in unison. However, in the event of hydraulic failure in one circuit, full braking force will still be available at two wheels.

All models have front disc brakes and rear drum brakes. An Anti-lock Braking System (ABS) is fitted as standard or optional equipment, according to model (refer to Section 19 for further information on ABS operation).

The front disc brakes are actuated by single-piston sliding type calipers, which ensure that equal pressure is applied to each disc pad.

The rear drum brakes incorporate leading and trailing shoes, which are actuated by twin-piston wheel cylinders. A self-adjust mechanism is incorporated to automatically compensate for brake shoe wear. As the brake shoe linings wear, the footbrake operation automatically operates the adjuster mechanism, which effectively lengthens the shoe strut, and repositions the brake shoes to maintain the lining-to-drum clearance.

Pressure-regulating valves are situated in the hydraulic lines to control the pressure applied to the rear brakes. The regulating valves help to prevent rear wheel lock-up during emergency braking. On all models,

they are of the load-dependent type, which actually alter the pressure to suit the load being carried by the vehicle.

The cable-operated handbrake provides an independent mechanical means of rear brake application.

Note: *When servicing any part of the system, work carefully and methodically; also observe scrupulous cleanliness when overhauling any part of the hydraulic system. Always renew components (in axle sets, where applicable) if in doubt about their condition, and use only genuine Vauxhall/Opel replacement parts, or at least those of known good quality. Note the warnings given in 'Safety first!' and at relevant points in this Chapter concerning the dangers of asbestos dust and hydraulic fluid.*

2 Hydraulic system – bleeding

Note: *Hydraulic fluid is poisonous; wash off immediately and thoroughly in the case of skin contact, and seek immediate medical advice if any fluid is swallowed or gets into the eyes. Certain types of hydraulic fluid are inflammable, and may ignite when allowed into contact with hot components. When servicing any hydraulic system, it is safest to assume that the fluid IS inflammable, and to take precautions against the risk of fire as though it is petrol that is being handled. Finally, it is hygroscopic (it absorbs moisture from the air) – old fluid may be contaminated, and unfit for further use. When topping-up or renewing the fluid, always use the recommended type, and ensure that it comes from a freshly-opened sealed container.*

> **HAYNES HINT** *Hydraulic fluid is also an effective paint stripper, and will attack plastics; if any is spilt, it should be washed off immediately using copious quantities of water.*

General

1 Any hydraulic system will only function correctly once all the air has been removed from the components and circuit; this is achieved by bleeding the system.

2 During the bleeding procedure, add only clean, fresh hydraulic fluid of the recommended type; never use old fluid, nor re-use any which has already been bled from the system. Ensure that sufficient fresh fluid is available before starting work.

3 If there is any possibility of the wrong fluid being in the system, the brake components and circuit must be flushed completely with uncontaminated, correct fluid, and new seals should be fitted to the various components.

4 If hydraulic fluid has been lost from the system (or if air has entered) because of a leak, ensure that the fault is cured before proceeding further.

5 Park the vehicle on level ground, switch off the engine and select first or reverse gear, then chock the wheels and release the handbrake.

6 Check that all pipes and hoses are secure, that the pipe unions are tight, and that the bleed screws are closed. Clean any dirt from around the bleed screws.

7 Unscrew the master cylinder reservoir cap, and top the master cylinder reservoir up to the MAX level line; refit the cap loosely, and remember to maintain the fluid level at least above the MIN level line throughout the procedure, to avoid the risk of further air entering the system.

8 There are a number of one-man, do-it-yourself brake bleeding kits currently available from motor accessory shops. It is recommended that one of these kits is used whenever possible, as they greatly simplify the bleeding operation, and also reduce the risk of expelled air and fluid being drawn back into the system. If such a kit is not available, the basic (two-man) method must be used, which is described in detail below.
Caution: Vauxhall/Opel recommend using a pressure bleeding kit for this operation (see paragraphs 24 to 27).

9 If a kit is to be used, prepare the vehicle as described previously, and follow the kit manufacturer's instructions, as the procedures may vary slightly according to the type being used; generally, they will be as outlined below in the relevant sub-section.

10 Whichever method is used, the same sequence must be followed (paragraphs 11 and 12) to ensure the removal of all air from the system.

Bleeding

11 If the system has been only partially disconnected, and suitable precautions were taken to minimise fluid loss, it should only be necessary to bleed that part of the system (ie, the primary or secondary circuit).

12 If the complete system is to be bled, then it should be done working in the following sequence:
 a) *Right-hand rear brake.*
 b) *Left-hand rear brake.*
 c) *Right-hand front brake.*
 d) *Left-hand front brake.*

Basic (two-man) method

13 Collect a clean glass jar, a suitable length of plastic or rubber tubing which is a tight fit over the bleed screw, and a ring spanner to fit the bleed screw. The help of an assistant will also be required.

14 Remove the dust cap from the first screw in the sequence. Fit the spanner and tube to the screw, place the other end of the tube in the jar, and pour in sufficient fluid to cover the end of the tube.

15 Ensure that the master cylinder reservoir fluid level is maintained at least above the MIN level line throughout the procedure.

16 Have the assistant fully depress the brake pedal several times to build up pressure, then maintain it on the final stroke.

17 While pedal pressure is maintained, unscrew the bleed screw (approximately one turn) and allow the compressed fluid and air to flow into the jar. The assistant should maintain pedal pressure, following it down to the floor if necessary, and should not release it until instructed to do so. When the flow stops, tighten the bleed screw again; the pedal should then be released slowly, and the

reservoir fluid level checked and topped-up.

18 Repeat the steps given in paragraphs 16 and 17 until the fluid emerging from the bleed screw is free from air bubbles. If the master cylinder has been drained and refilled, and air is being bled from the first screw in the sequence, allow approximately five seconds between cycles for the master cylinder passages to refill.

19 When no more air bubbles appear, tighten the bleed screw securely, remove the tube and spanner, and refit the dust cap. Do not overtighten the bleed screw.

20 Repeat the procedure on the remaining screws in the sequence, until all air is removed from the system and the brake pedal feels firm again.

Using a one-way valve kit

21 As their name implies, these kits consist of a length of tubing with a one-way valve fitted, to prevent expelled air and fluid being drawn back into the system; some kits include a translucent container, which can be positioned so that the air bubbles can be more easily seen flowing from the end of the tube.

22 The kit is connected to the bleed screw, which is then opened **(see illustration)**. The user returns to the driver's seat, depresses the brake pedal with a smooth, steady stroke, then slowly releases it; this is repeated until the expelled fluid is clear of air bubbles.

23 These kits simplify work so much that it is easy to forget the master cylinder reservoir fluid level; ensure that this is maintained at least above the MIN level line at all times, or air will be drawn into the system.

Using a pressure bleeding kit

24 These kits are usually operated by the reservoir of pressurised air contained in the spare tyre, noting that it will probably be necessary to reduce the pressure to less than normal; refer to the instructions supplied with the kit.

25 By connecting a pressurised, fluid-filled container to the master cylinder reservoir, bleeding can be carried out simply by opening each screw in turn (in the specified sequence) and allowing the fluid to flow out until no more air bubbles can be seen in the expelled fluid.

26 This method has the advantage that the

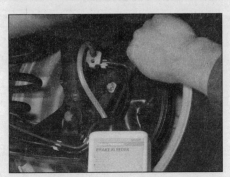

2.22 Using a one-way valve kit to bleed the rear brake

large reservoir of fluid provides an additional safeguard against air being drawn into the system during bleeding.

27 Pressure bleeding is particularly effective when bleeding 'difficult' systems, or when bleeding the complete system at the time of routine fluid renewal.

All methods

28 When bleeding is complete and firm pedal feel is restored, wash off any spilt fluid, tighten the bleed screws securely, and refit their dust caps.

29 Check the hydraulic fluid level, and top-up if necessary (see *Weekly checks*).

30 Discard any hydraulic fluid that has been bled from the system; it will not be fit for re-use. Bear in mind that this fluid may be inflammable.

31 Check the feel of the brake pedal. If it feels at all spongy, air must still be present in the system, and further bleeding is required. Failure to bleed satisfactorily after a reasonable repetition of the bleeding procedure may be due to worn master cylinder seals.

| 3 | Hydraulic pipes and hoses – renewal | |

Note: *Before starting work, refer to the note at the beginning of Section 2 concerning the dangers of hydraulic fluid.*

1 If any pipe or hose is to be renewed, minimise fluid loss by first removing the master cylinder reservoir cap and screwing it down onto a piece of polythene. Alternatively, flexible hoses can be sealed, if required, using a proprietary brake hose clamp. Metal brake pipe unions can be plugged (if care is taken not to allow dirt into the system) or capped immediately they are disconnected. Place a wad of rag under any union that is to be disconnected, to catch any spilt fluid.

2 If a flexible hose is to be disconnected, unscrew the brake pipe union nut before removing the spring clip which secures the hose to its mounting bracket.

3 To unscrew the union nuts, it is preferable to obtain a brake pipe spanner of the correct size; these are available from most large motor accessory shops. Failing this, a close-fitting open-ended spanner will be required, though if the nuts are tight or corroded, their flats may be rounded-off if the spanner slips. In such a case, a self-locking wrench is often the only way to unscrew a stubborn union, but it follows that the pipe and the damaged nuts must be renewed on reassembly. Always clean a union and surrounding area before disconnecting it. If disconnecting a component with more than one union, make a careful note of the connections before disturbing any of them.

4 If a brake pipe is to be renewed it can be obtained, cut to length and with the union

4.2 Using a screwdriver, carefully prise out the pad retaining spring from the caliper

4.3 Remove the guide bolt dust caps . . .

nuts and end flares in place, from Vauxhall/Opel dealers. All that is then necessary is to bend it to shape, following the line of the original, before fitting it to the car. Alternatively, most motor accessory shops can make up brake pipes from kits, but this requires very careful measurement of the original to ensure that the replacement is of the correct length. The safest answer is usually to take the original to the shop as a pattern.

5 On refitting, do not overtighten the union nuts. It is not necessary to exercise brute force to obtain a sound joint.

6 Ensure that the pipes and hoses are correctly routed, with no kinks, and that they are secured in the clips or brackets provided. After fitting, remove the polythene from the reservoir, and bleed the hydraulic system as described in Section 2. Wash off any spilt fluid, and check carefully for fluid leaks.

4.4a . . . then unscrew the guide bolts . . .

4.4c Tie the caliper to the suspension strut, to avoid placing any strain on the hydraulic brake hose

4 Front brake pads – renewal

> **Warning: Renew BOTH sets of front brake pads at the same time – NEVER renew the pads on only one wheel, as uneven braking may result. Note that the dust created by wear of the pads may contain asbestos, which is a health hazard. Never blow it out with compressed air, and don't inhale any of it. An approved filtering mask should be worn when working on the brakes. DO NOT use petroleum-based solvents to clean brake parts – use brake cleaner or methylated spirit only.**

1 Firmly apply the handbrake, then jack up the front of the car and support it securely on axle stands (see *Jacking and vehicle support*). Remove the front roadwheels.

4.4b . . . and slide off the caliper and inner pad assembly

4.7 Measuring brake pad thickness

2 Using a screwdriver, prise the pad retaining spring from the outer edge of the caliper, noting its correct fitted position **(see illustration)**.

3 Prise out the two guide bolt dust caps from the inner edge of the caliper **(see illustration)**.

4 Unscrew the guide bolts from the caliper, and lift the caliper and inner pad away from the mounting bracket. Tie the caliper to the suspension strut using a suitable piece of wire **(see illustrations)**. Do not allow the caliper to hang unsupported on the flexible brake hose.

5 Remove the inner pad from the caliper piston, noting that it is retained by a clip attached to the pad backing plate, and recover the outer pad from the mounting bracket.

6 Brush the dirt and dust from the caliper mounting bracket, but take care not to inhale it. Carefully remove any rust from the edge of the brake disc.

7 First measure the thickness of each brake pad (friction material and backing plate) **(see illustration)**. If either pad is worn at any point to the specified minimum thickness or less, all four pads must be renewed. The pads should also be renewed if any are fouled with oil or grease; there is no satisfactory way of degreasing friction material, once contaminated. If any of the brake pads are worn unevenly, or fouled with oil or grease, trace and rectify the cause before reassembly. The pad retaining spring should also be renewed if new pads are to be fitted. New brake pads and retaining springs are available from Vauxhall/Opel dealers.

8 If the brake pads are still serviceable, carefully clean them using a clean, fine wire brush or similar, paying particular attention to the sides and back of the metal backing. Clean out the grooves in the friction material, and pick out any large embedded particles of dirt or debris. Carefully clean the pad locations in the caliper body/mounting bracket.

9 Prior to fitting the pads, check that the guide bolts are a snug fit in the caliper bushes. Brush the dust and dirt from the caliper and piston, but do not inhale it, as it is injurious to health. Inspect the dust seal around the piston for damage, and the piston for evidence of fluid leaks, corrosion or damage. If attention to any of these components is necessary, refer to Section 8.

10 If new brake pads are to be fitted, the caliper piston must be pushed back into the cylinder to make room for them. We recommend that the caliper bleed screw is loosened and the excess fluid drained into a container, rather than forcing the fluid through the circuit into the reservoir. *It is imperative that the caliper piston is pushed back as slowly as possible, using minimal force.* Either use a G-clamp or similar tool, or use suitable pieces of wood as levers to move the piston fully into the caliper bore. Tighten the bleed screw. **Note:** *Pushing the piston into the cylinder without undoing the bleed screw may cause the system seals to fail.*

11 Fit the inner pad to the caliper, ensuring

that its clip is correctly located in the caliper piston **(see illustration)**.

12 Fit the outer pad to the caliper mounting bracket, ensuring that its friction material is facing the brake disc **(see illustration)**.

13 Slide the caliper and inner pad into position over the outer pad, and locate it in the mounting bracket.

14 Install the caliper guide bolts, and tighten them to the specified torque setting **(see illustration)**.

15 Refit the guide bolt dust caps to the caliper.

16 Refit the pad retaining spring to the caliper, ensuring that its ends are correctly located in the caliper holes **(see illustration)**.

17 Depress the brake pedal repeatedly, until normal (non-assisted) pedal pressure is restored, and the pads are pressed into firm contact with the brake disc. **Note:** *It might be necessary to bleed air from the system (see Section 2) which could have entered when opening the bleed screw.*

18 Repeat the above procedure on the remaining front brake caliper.

19 Refit the roadwheels, aligning the marks made on removal, then lower the vehicle to the ground and tighten the roadwheel bolts to the specified torque setting.

20 Check the hydraulic fluid level as described in *Weekly checks*.

4.11 Clip the inner pad securely into the caliper piston . . .

4.12 . . . and fit the outer pad to the caliper mounting bracket

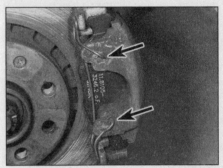

4.14 Slide the caliper into position and install the guide bolts, tightening them to the specified torque setting

4.16 When refitting, ensure that the pad retaining spring ends are correctly located in the caliper holes (arrowed)

5 Rear brake shoes – renewal
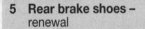
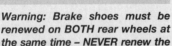

![Warning triangle] **Warning: Brake shoes must be renewed on BOTH rear wheels at the same time – NEVER renew the shoes on only one wheel, as uneven braking may result. The dust created as the shoes wear may contain asbestos, which is a health hazard. Never blow it out with compressed air, and don't inhale any of it. An approved filtering mask should be worn when working on the brakes. DO NOT use petroleum-based solvents to clean brake parts – use brake cleaner or methylated spirit only.**

1 Remove the brake drum as described in Section 7.

2 Working carefully and taking the necessary precautions, remove all traces of brake dust from the brake drum, backplate and shoes.

3 Measure the thickness of the friction material of each brake shoe, at several points. If the friction material thickness or the depth from the friction material surface to any of the of rivet heads is equal to or less than the specified minimum, all four shoes must be renewed as a set **(see illustrations)**. Also, the shoes should be renewed if any are fouled with oil or grease; there is no satisfactory way of degreasing friction material, once contaminated.

4 If any of the brake shoes are worn unevenly, or fouled with oil or grease, trace and rectify the cause before reassembly. If the shoes are to be renewed proceed as described below. If

all is well refit the drums as described in Section 7.

5 Note the location and orientation of all components before dismantling, as an aid to reassembly **(see illustration)**.

6 Using a pair of pliers, carefully unhook the upper shoe return spring, and remove it from the brake shoes **(see illustration)**.

5.3a Brake shoe wear can be assessed by measuring the thickness of the friction material . . .

5.3b . . . or by measuring the depth from the friction material surface to the rivet heads (a tyre tread depth indicator may be used)

5.5 Note the correct fitted locations of all components, paying particular attention to the adjuster strut components

5.6 Unhook the upper return spring, and remove it from the brake shoes

5.7 Remove the retaining spring, followed by the lever and return spring (arrowed)

5.9a Using pliers, remove the spring cup . . .

5.9b . . . then lift off the spring and retainer pin

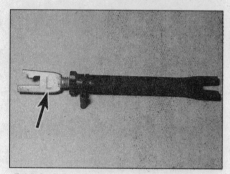

5.14 Left-hand adjuster strut assembly is marked L (arrowed)

5.15 Dismantling the adjuster strut for cleaning

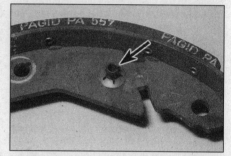

5.17 It may be necessary to transfer the adjusting lever pivot pin and clip (arrowed) from the original shoes to the new ones

7 Prise the adjusting lever retaining spring out of the front shoe, and remove the retaining spring, lever and return spring from the brake shoe, noting each component's correct fitted position **(see illustration)**.

8 Prise the upper ends of the brake shoes apart, and withdraw the adjuster strut from between the shoes.

9 Using a pair of pliers, remove the front shoe retainer spring cup by depressing and turning it through 90°. With the cup removed, lift off the spring and withdraw the retainer pin **(see illustrations)**.

10 Detach the front shoe from the lower return spring, and remove both the shoe and return spring.

11 Remove the rear shoe retainer spring cup, spring and retainer pin as described in

paragraph 9, then remove the shoe, detaching it from the handbrake cable.

12 Do not depress the brake pedal until the brakes are reassembled. As a precaution, wrap a strong elastic band around the wheel cylinder pistons to retain them.

13 Although linings are available separately (without shoes), renewal of the shoes complete with linings is to be preferred, unless the necessary skills and equipment are available to fit new linings to the old shoes.

14 If both brake assemblies are dismantled at the same time, take care not to mix up the components. Note that the left-hand and right-hand adjuster components are marked as such; the threaded rod is marked L or R, and the other 'handed' components are colour-coded black for the left-hand side, and

silver for the right-hand side **(see illustration)**.

15 Dismantle and clean the adjuster strut. Apply a smear of silicone-based grease to the adjuster threads **(see illustration)**.

16 Examine the return springs. If they are distorted, or if they have seen extensive service, renewal is advisable. Weak springs may cause the brakes to bind.

17 If a new handbrake operating lever was not supplied with the new shoes (where applicable), transfer the lever from the old shoes. The lever may be secured with a pin and circlip, or by a rivet, which will have to be drilled out. It may also be necessary to transfer the adjusting lever pivot pin and clip from the original front shoe to the new shoe **(see illustration)**.

18 Peel back the rubber protective caps, and check the wheel cylinder for fluid leaks or other damage. Ensure that both cylinder pistons are free to move easily. Refer to Section 9, if necessary, for information on wheel cylinder overhaul.

19 Prior to installation, clean the backplate thoroughly. Apply a thin smear of high-temperature copper-based brake grease or anti-seize compound to all those surfaces of the backplate which bear on the shoes, particularly the wheel cylinder pistons and lower pivot point **(see illustration)**. Do not allow the lubricant to foul the friction material.

20 Ensure that the handbrake cable is correctly retained by the clip on the lower brake shoe pivot point, then engage the rear shoe with the cable. Locate the shoe on the backplate **(see illustration)**.

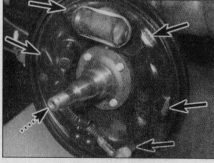

5.19 Apply a smear of anti-seize compound to the contact surfaces of the backplate (arrowed). Note the elastic band wrapped around the wheel cylinder

5.20 Engage the rear brake shoe with the handbrake cable, and locate the shoe on the backplate

5.22a Install the front shoe and lower return spring . . .

5.22b . . . and secure it in position with the retainer pin, spring and spring cup

5.24 Refit the adjuster strut, noting that the longer, straight part of the fork (arrowed) must be behind the shoe

21 Install the rear shoe retainer pin and spring, and secure it in position with the spring cup.

22 Hook the lower return spring onto the rear shoe, then engage the front shoe with the return spring. Locate the front shoe on the backplate, and secure it in position with its retainer pin, spring and spring cup **(see illustrations)**.

23 Screw the adjuster strut wheel fully onto the forked end of the adjuster, so that the adjuster strut is set to its shortest possible length. Back the wheel off a half a turn, and check that it is free to rotate easily.

24 Manoeuvre the adjuster strut assembly into position between the brake shoes. Make sure that both ends of the strut are correctly engaged with the shoes, noting that the forked end of the strut must be positioned so that its longer, straight fork is to the back of the shoe **(see illustration)**.

25 Engage the adjusting lever return spring with the front shoe and adjusting lever, and locate the lever on its pivot pin **(see illustration)**. Check that the lever and spring are correctly located, and secure the lever in position with the retaining spring, making sure the spring ends are securely located in the retaining pin and shoe **(see illustration 5.5)**.

26 Remove the rubber band from the wheel cylinder. Make sure that both shoes are correctly positioned on the wheel cylinder pistons, then fit the upper return spring **(see illustration)**.

27 Ensure that the handbrake operating lever stop peg is correctly positioned against the edge of the shoe web, then refit the brake drum as described in Section 7.

28 Repeat the operation on the remaining brake.

29 Once both sets of rear shoes have been renewed, with the handbrake fully released, adjust the lining-to-drum clearance by repeatedly depressing the brake pedal 20 to 25 times. Whilst depressing the pedal, have an assistant listen to the rear drums, to check that the adjuster strut is functioning correctly; if so, a clicking sound will be emitted by the strut as the pedal is depressed.

30 Check and, if necessary, adjust the handbrake as described in Section 14.

31 On completion, check the hydraulic fluid level as described in *Weekly checks*.

---

6 Front brake disc – inspection, removal and refitting

Note: *Before starting work, refer to the note at the beginning of Section 4 concerning the dangers of asbestos dust.*

Inspection

Note: *If either disc requires renewal, BOTH should be renewed at the same time, to ensure even and consistent braking.*

1 Chock the rear wheels, firmly apply the handbrake, then jack up the front of the car and support it on axle stands. Remove the appropriate front roadwheel.

2 Slowly rotate the brake disc so that the full area of both sides can be checked; remove the brake pads if better access is required to the inner surface. Light scoring is normal in the area swept by the brake pads, but if heavy scoring is found, the disc must be renewed.

3 It is normal to find a lip of rust and brake dust around the disc's perimeter; this can be scraped off if required. If, however, a lip has formed due to excessive wear of the brake pad swept area, then the disc's thickness must be measured using a micrometer. Take measurements at several places around the disc, at the inside and outside of the pad

swept area; if the disc has worn at any point to the specified minimum thickness or less, the disc must be renewed.

4 If the disc is thought to be warped, it can be checked for run-out either using a dial gauge mounted on any convenient fixed point, while the disc is slowly rotated, or by using feeler gauges to measure (at several points all around the disc) the clearance between the disc and a fixed point such as the caliper mounting bracket. To ensure that the disc is squarely seated on the hub, fit two wheel bolts, complete with spacers approximately 10 mm thick, and tighten them securely. If the measurements obtained are at the specified maximum or beyond, the disc is excessively warped and must be renewed; however, it is worth checking first that the hub bearing is in good condition (Chapters 1 and/or 10).

5 Check the disc for cracks, especially around the wheel bolt holes, and for any other wear or damage, and renew if necessary.

Removal

Note: *New brake caliper mounting bracket-to-swivel hub bolts will be required when refitting.*

6 Unscrew the two bolts securing the brake caliper assembly to the swivel hub, and slide the caliper assembly off the disc **(see illustrations)**. Using a piece of wire or string, tie the caliper to the front suspension coil spring, to avoid placing any strain on the hydraulic brake hose. Discard the caliper

5.25 Refit the adjusting lever and spring, making sure that the spring is correctly engaged in the front brake shoe hole (arrowed)

5.26 Make sure that both shoes are correctly aligned with the wheel cylinder, then install the upper return spring

6.6a Slacken and remove the two bolts (arrowed) securing the brake caliper mounting bracket to the hub . . .

6.6b . . . then slide the caliper assembly off the brake disc

6.7a Undo the retaining screw . . .

6.7b . . . and remove the brake disc from the hub

6.8a Apply thread-locking compound to the threads of the brake caliper mounting bracket bolts . . .

6.8b . . . and tighten them to the specified torque setting

mounting bolts; they must be renewed whenever they are disturbed.

7 Remove the screw securing the brake disc to the hub, and remove the disc. If it is tight,

lightly tap its rear face with a hide or plastic mallet **(see illustrations)**.

Refitting

8 Refitting is the reverse of the removal procedure, noting the following points:

a) *Ensure that the mating surfaces of the disc and hub are clean and flat.*
b) *Tighten the disc retaining screw securely.*
c) *If a new disc has been fitted, use a suitable solvent to wipe any preservative coating from the disc before refitting the caliper.*
d) *Remove all traces of old thread-locking compound from the brake caliper holes in the swivel hub, ideally by running a tap of the correct size and pitch through them. If the threads of the new caliper mounting bracket bolts are not already pre-coated with compound, apply a suitable thread-locking compound to them. Slide the caliper assembly into position over the*

disc, then fit the mounting bolts and tighten them to the specified torque setting **(see illustrations)**.
e) *Refit the roadwheel, aligning the marks made on removal, then lower the vehicle to the ground and tighten the roadwheel bolts to the specified torque. On completion, repeatedly depress the brake pedal until normal (non-assisted) pedal pressure returns.*

7 Rear brake drum – removal, inspection and refitting

Note: *Before starting work, refer to the note at the beginning of Section 5 concerning the dangers of asbestos dust.*

Removal

1 Chock the front wheels, then jack up the rear of the vehicle and support it on axle stands. Remove the appropriate rear wheel and release the handbrake. Proceed as described under the relevant sub-heading.

Corsa and Corsavan

2 Prise out the cap from the centre of the drum **(see illustration)**.
3 Extract the split pin from the hub nut and discard it; a new one must be used on refitting.
4 Slacken and remove the rear hub nut, then slide off the toothed washer and remove the outer bearing from the centre of the drum **(see illustrations)**.

7.2 Remove the cap from the centre of the drum to gain access to the hub nut

7.4a Slacken and remove the hub nut and washer . . .

7.4b . . . followed by the outer bearing

5 It should now be possible to withdraw the brake drum assembly from the stub axle by hand. It may be difficult to remove the drum, due to the brake shoes binding on the inner circumference of the drum. If the brake shoes are binding, first check that the handbrake is fully released, then proceed as follows.

6 Referring to Section 14 for further information, fully slacken the handbrake cable adjuster nut to obtain maximum free play in the cable.

7 Remove the plug from the inspection hole in the brake backplate, and push the handbrake operating lever outwards away from the brake shoe. This will release the handbrake lever stop-peg from the edge of the brake shoe, and further collapse the shoes **(see illustrations)**. The brake drum can then be withdrawn from the stub axle.

Combo Van

8 Slacken and remove the drum retaining screw, and remove the drum from the vehicle. It may be difficult to remove the drum due to the brake shoes binding on the inner circumference of the drum. If the brake shoes are binding, first check that the handbrake is fully released, then proceed as described above in paragraphs 6 and 7.

Inspection

Note: *If either drum requires renewal, BOTH should be renewed at the same time, to ensure even and consistent braking.*

9 Working carefully, remove all traces of brake dust from the drum, but *avoid inhaling the dust, as it is a health-hazard.*

10 Scrub clean the outside of the drum, and check it for obvious signs of wear or damage (such as cracks around the roadwheel bolt holes); renew the drum if necessary.

11 Examine the inside of the drum carefully. Light scoring of the friction surface is normal, but if heavy scoring is found, the drum must be renewed. It is usual to find a lip on the drum's inboard edge which consists of a mixture of rust and brake dust; this should be scraped away, to leave a smooth surface which can be polished with fine (120- to 150-grade) emery paper. If, however, the lip is due to the friction surface being recessed by excessive wear, then the drum must be renewed.

12 If the drum is thought to be excessively worn, or oval, its internal diameter must be measured at several points using an internal micrometer. Take measurements in pairs, the second at right-angles to the first, and compare the two to check for signs of ovality. Provided that it does not enlarge the drum to beyond the specified maximum diameter, it may be possible to have the drum refinished by skimming or grinding; if this is not possible, the drums on both sides must be renewed. Note that if the drum is to be skimmed, both drums must be refinished, to maintain a consistent internal diameter on both sides.

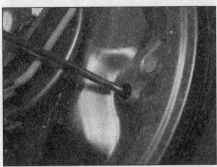

7.7a If necessary, release the handbrake lever stop-peg by inserting a screwdriver in through the hole in the rear of the backplate . . .

Refitting

13 If a new brake drum is to be installed, use a suitable solvent to remove any preservative coating that may have been applied to its interior. Note that it may also be necessary to shorten the adjuster strut length by rotating the strut wheel, to allow the new drum to pass over the brake shoes.

Corsa and Corsavan

14 Ensure that the handbrake lever stop-peg is correctly repositioned against the edge of the brake shoe web **(see illustration)**, and apply a smear of grease to the drum oil seal.

15 Slide the drum into position, then refit the outer bearing and toothed thrustwasher, ensuring that its tooth is correctly engaged in the axle slot **(see illustration)**.

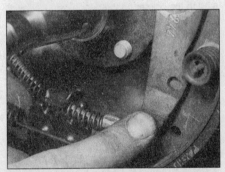

7.14 Prior to refitting the drum, check that the handbrake lever is correctly positioned on the shoe

7.16a Tighten the hub nut to the specified torque setting while rotating the drum

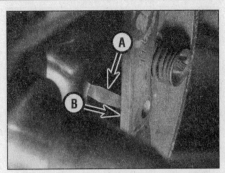

7.7b . . . and use screwdriver (A) to push handbrake lever away from the brake shoe in the direction of arrow (B) – shown with drum removed

16 Refit the hub nut, and tighten it to the specified pre-load torque setting, while rotating the brake drum to settle the hub bearings in position. Gradually slacken the hub nut until the position is found where it is just possible to move the toothed washer from side-to-side using a screwdriver **(see illustrations)**. **Note:** *Only a small amount of force should be needed to move the washer; do not use the screwdriver as a lever to move the washer.* When the hub nut is correctly positioned, secure it in position with a new split pin.

17 If the stub axle holes are not aligned with any of the slots in the hub nut, tighten the nut by the *smallest amount possible* until the split pin can be inserted. With the nut in this position, check that it is still possible to move the toothed washer. If it is, insert the split pin

7.15 Fit the toothed washer, making sure its tooth is correctly engaged with the stub axle slot

7.16b Gradually slacken the hub nut until the position is found where it is just possible to move the toothed washer

7.17 When the hub bearing is correctly adjusted, secure the nut in position with a new split pin

and secure it in position. If it is not possible to move the washer, slacken the nut slightly until the next hub nut slot/axle hole aligns. Check that it is possible to move the toothed washer, then secure the hub nut in position with the new split pin **(see illustration)**.

18 Fit the cap to the centre of the brake drum.

19 With the handbrake fully released, adjust the lining-to-drum clearance by repeatedly depressing the brake pedal 20 to 25 times. Whilst depressing the pedal, have an assistant listen to the rear drums, to check that the adjuster strut is functioning correctly; if so, a clicking sound will be emitted by the strut as the pedal is depressed.

20 With the lining-to-drum clearance set, check and, if necessary, adjust the handbrake as described in Section 14.

21 Refit the roadwheel, aligning the marks made on removal, then lower the vehicle to the ground and tighten the roadwheel bolts to the specified torque setting.

Combo Van

22 Ensure that the drum and hub flange mating surfaces are clean and dry, and remove all traces of corrosion.

23 Ensure that the handbrake lever stop-peg is correctly repositioned against the edge of the brake shoe web, and locate the drum on the hub. Refit the drum retaining screw, and tighten it securely.

24 Carry out the operations described in paragraphs 19 to 21.

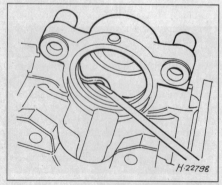

8.7 Removing the piston seal from the caliper body

8 Front brake caliper – 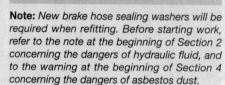 removal, overhaul and refitting

Note: *New brake hose sealing washers will be required when refitting. Before starting work, refer to the note at the beginning of Section 2 concerning the dangers of hydraulic fluid, and to the warning at the beginning of Section 4 concerning the dangers of asbestos dust.*

Removal

1 Chock the rear wheels, apply the handbrake, then jack up the front of the vehicle and support it on axle stands. Remove the appropriate roadwheel.

2 Minimise fluid loss by first removing the master cylinder reservoir cap, then tightening it down onto a piece of polythene to obtain an airtight seal. Alternatively, use a brake hose clamp, a G-clamp or a similar tool to clamp the flexible hose.

3 Clean the area around the caliper brake hose union. Slacken and remove the union bolt, and recover the sealing washer from either side of the hose union. Discard the washers; new ones must be used on refitting. Plug the hose end and caliper hole, to minimise fluid loss and prevent the ingress of dirt into the hydraulic system.

4 Remove the brake pads as described in paragraphs 2 to 5 of Section 4, and remove the caliper from the vehicle.

Overhaul

5 With the caliper on the bench, wipe away all traces of dust and dirt, but *avoid inhaling the dust, as it is a health hazard.*

6 Withdraw the partially-ejected piston from the caliper body, and remove the dust seal. The piston can be withdrawn by hand, or if necessary pushed out by applying compressed air to the brake hose union hole. Only low pressure should be required, such as is generated by a foot pump.

7 Using a small screwdriver, carefully remove the piston seal from the caliper, taking great care not mark the bore **(see illustration)**.

8 Carefully press the guide bushes out of the caliper body.

9 Thoroughly clean all components, using only methylated spirit, isopropyl alcohol or clean hydraulic fluid as a cleaning medium. Never use mineral-based solvents such as petrol or paraffin, which will attack the hydraulic system's rubber components. Dry the components immediately, using compressed air or a clean, lint-free cloth. Use compressed air to blow clear the fluid passages, if available (wear eye protection).

10 Check all components, and renew any that are worn or damaged. Check particularly the cylinder bore and piston; these should be renewed (note that this means the renewal of the complete body assembly) if they are scratched, worn or corroded in any way. Similarly check the condition of the guide

bushes and bolts; both bushes and bolts should be undamaged and (when cleaned) a reasonably tight sliding fit in each other. If there is any doubt about the condition of any component, renew it.

11 If the assembly is fit for further use, obtain the necessary components from your Vauxhall/Opel dealer. Renew the caliper seals as a matter of course; these should never be re-used.

12 On reassembly, ensure that all components are absolutely clean and dry.

13 Soak the piston and the new piston (fluid) seal in clean hydraulic fluid. Smear clean fluid on the cylinder bore surface.

14 Fit the new piston (fluid) seal, using only the fingers to manipulate it into the cylinder bore groove.

15 Fit the new dust seal to the piston, refit it to the cylinder bore using a twisting motion, and ensure that the piston enters squarely into the bore. Press the dust seal fully into the caliper body, and push the piston fully into the caliper bore.

16 Ease the guide bushes into position in the caliper body.

Refitting

17 Refit the caliper and brake pads as described in paragraphs 11 to 16 of Section 4.

18 Position a new sealing washer on each side of the hose union, and connect the brake hose to the caliper. Ensure that the hose is correctly positioned against the caliper body lug, then install the union bolt and tighten it to the specified torque setting.

19 Remove the brake hose clamp or the polythene, where fitted, and bleed the hydraulic system as described in Section 2. Note that, providing the precautions described were taken to minimise brake fluid loss, it should only be necessary to bleed the relevant front brake.

20 Refit the roadwheel, aligning the marks made on removal, then lower the vehicle to the ground and tighten the roadwheel bolts to the specified torque.

9 Rear wheel cylinder – removal, overhaul and refitting

Note: *Before starting work, refer to the note at the beginning of Section 2 concerning the dangers of hydraulic fluid, and to the warning at the beginning of Section 5 concerning the dangers of asbestos dust.*

Removal

1 Remove the brake drum as described in Section 7.

2 Using pliers, carefully unhook the upper brake shoe return spring, and remove it from both brake shoes. Pull the upper ends of the shoes away from the wheel cylinder to disengage them from the pistons.

3 Minimise fluid loss by first removing the master cylinder reservoir cap, then tightening

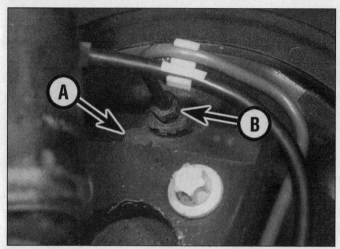

9.4 Rear wheel cylinder retaining bolt (A) and brake pipe union nut (B)

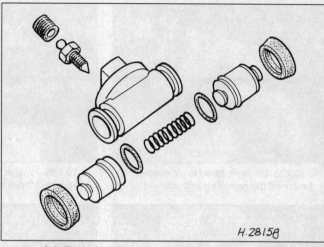

9.6 Exploded view of a rear brake wheel cylinder

it down onto a piece of polythene to obtain an airtight seal. Alternatively, use a brake hose clamp, a G-clamp or a similar tool to clamp the flexible hose at the nearest convenient point to the wheel cylinder.

4 Wipe away all traces of dirt around the brake pipe union at the rear of the wheel cylinder, and unscrew the union nut. Carefully ease the pipe out of the wheel cylinder, and plug or tape over its end to prevent dirt entry. Wipe off any spilt fluid immediately **(see illustration)**.

5 Unscrew the two wheel cylinder retaining bolts from the rear of the backplate, and remove the cylinder, taking great care not to allow surplus hydraulic fluid to contaminate the brake shoe linings.

Overhaul

6 Brush the dirt and dust from the wheel cylinder, but take care not to inhale it **(see illustration)**.

7 Pull the rubber dust seals from the ends of the cylinder body.

8 The pistons will normally be ejected by the pressure of the coil spring, but if they are not, tap the end of the cylinder body on a piece of wood, or apply low air pressure (eg, from a foot pump) to the hydraulic fluid union hole to eject the pistons from their bores.

9 Inspect the surfaces of the pistons and their bores in the cylinder body for scoring, or evidence of metal-to-metal contact. If evident, renew the complete wheel cylinder assembly.

10 If the pistons and bores are in good condition, discard the seals and obtain a repair kit, which will contain all the necessary renewable items.

11 Lubricate the piston seals with clean brake fluid, and insert them into the cylinder bores, with the spring between them, using finger pressure only.

12 Dip the pistons in clean brake fluid, and insert them into the cylinder bores.

13 Fit the dust seals, and check that the pistons can move freely in their bores.

Refitting

14 Ensure that the backplate and wheel cylinder mating surfaces are clean, then spread the brake shoes and manoeuvre the wheel cylinder into position.

15 Engage the brake pipe, and screw in the union nut two or three turns to ensure that the thread has started.

16 Insert the two wheel cylinder retaining bolts, and tighten them securely. Now tighten the brake pipe union nut to the specified torque.

17 Remove the clamp from the flexible brake hose, or the polythene from the master cylinder reservoir (as applicable).

18 Ensure that the brake shoes are correctly located in the cylinder pistons, then carefully refit the brake shoe upper return spring, using a screwdriver to stretch the spring into position.

19 Refit the brake drum as described in Section 7.

20 Bleed the brake hydraulic system as described in Section 2. Providing suitable precautions were taken to minimise loss of fluid, it should only be necessary to bleed the relevant rear brake.

10 Master cylinder –
removal, overhaul and refitting

Note: *New master cylinder retaining nuts will be required when refitting. Before starting work, refer to the warning at the beginning of Section 2 concerning the dangers of hydraulic fluid.*

Removal

1 Remove the master cylinder reservoir cap, and syphon the hydraulic fluid from the reservoir. **Note:** *Do not syphon the fluid by mouth, as it is poisonous; use a syringe or an old poultry baster.* Alternatively, open any convenient bleed screw in the system, and

gently pump the brake pedal to expel the fluid through a plastic tube connected to the screw (see Section 2).

2 Disconnect the battery negative terminal (refer to *Disconnecting the battery* in the Reference Chapter), and the wiring connector from the brake fluid level sender unit **(see illustration)**. Proceed as described under the relevant sub-heading.

Left-hand drive models

3 Wipe clean the area around the brake pipe unions on the side of the master cylinder, and place absorbent rags beneath the pipe unions to catch any surplus fluid. Make a note of the correct fitted positions of the unions, then unscrew the union nuts and carefully withdraw the pipes. Plug or tape over the pipe ends and master cylinder orifices, to minimise the loss of brake fluid and to prevent the entry of dirt into the system. Wash off any spilt fluid immediately with cold water.

4 Slacken and remove the two nuts securing the master cylinder to the vacuum servo unit and discard them; new ones must be used on refitting. Withdraw the master cylinder assembly from the engine compartment, noting that on models with ABS it will be necessary to undo the two retaining nuts securing the fluid reservoir to the engine compartment bulkhead.

10.2 Disconnecting the master cylinder brake fluid level sender wiring connector

10.12a On right-hand drive models, unscrew the retaining bolt and nut . . .

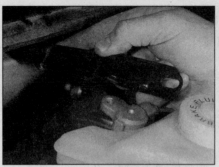

10.12b . . . and remove the support bracket from the master cylinder

10.13a Undo the two retaining nuts (arrowed) . . .

10.13b . . . and remove the master cylinder from the servo unit

10.13c Where necessary, recover the pushrod . . .

10.13d . . . and rubber seal from the servo unit

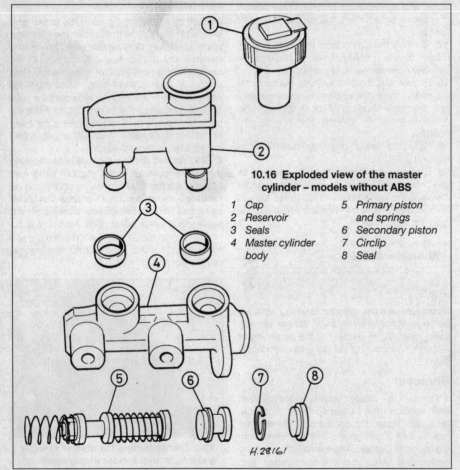

10.16 Exploded view of the master cylinder – models without ABS

1 Cap	5 Primary piston
2 Reservoir	and springs
3 Seals	6 Secondary piston
4 Master cylinder	7 Circlip
body	8 Seal

H.28161

5 Recover the seal which is fitted between the master cylinder and servo. If the servo unit pushrod has come away with the master cylinder, remove it and refit it to the centre of the servo.

Right-hand drive models

6 Remove both windscreen wiper arms as described in Chapter 12.

7 Carefully prise out the wiper spindle sealing grommets from the windscreen cowl panel.

8 Undo the retaining screws, and remove both halves of the windscreen cowl panel from the vehicle.

9 Peel the bonnet seal off the engine compartment bulkhead, and remove it from the vehicle.

10 Unscrew the large plastic nut from each wiper spindle.

11 Prise out the two retaining clips from the centre of the water deflector shield, then release the shield from the engine compartment bulkhead and wiper spindles, and remove it from the vehicle.

12 Unscrew the nut and bolt, and remove the support bracket from the top of the master cylinder fluid reservoir **(see illustrations)**.

13 Remove the master cylinder as described above in paragraphs 3 to 5, ignoring the note concerning models fitted with ABS **(see illustrations)**.

Overhaul

Models with ABS

14 Master cylinder overhaul on models with ABS is not possible, as no spares are available. If the cylinder is thought to be faulty, it must be renewed.

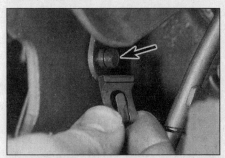

11.2 Slide off the spring clip, and withdraw the clevis pin (arrowed) securing the servo pushrod to the pedal

11.3a Withdraw the locking clip . . .

11.3b . . . then slacken and remove the pivot shaft nut and washer

15 The only parts available individually are the fluid reservoir and its mounting seals. These can be renewed as described below for the non-ABS models.

Models without ABS

16 Unhook the clip (where necessary), and remove the fluid reservoir and reservoir seals from the master cylinder body **(see illustration)**.
17 Carefully prise the seal out of the end of the master cylinder.
18 Using a wooden dowel, press the piston assembly into the master cylinder body, then extract the circlip from the end of the master cylinder bore.
19 Noting the order of removal and the direction of fitting of each component, withdraw the piston assemblies, complete with springs and seals. Tap the body on to a clean wooden surface to dislodge them. If necessary, clamp the master cylinder body in a vice (fitted with soft jaw covers) and use compressed air (applied through the one of the fluid ports) to assist the removal of the piston assemblies. Wear eye protection if compressed air is used.
20 Thoroughly clean all components, using only methylated spirit, isopropyl alcohol or clean hydraulic fluid as a cleaning medium. Never use mineral-based solvents such as petrol or paraffin, which will attack the hydraulic system's rubber components. Dry the components immediately, using compressed air (wear eye protection) or a clean, lint-free cloth.
21 Check all components, and renew any that are worn or damaged. Check particularly the cylinder bores and pistons; the complete assembly should be renewed if these are scratched, worn or corroded. If there is any doubt about the condition of the assembly or of any of its components, renew it. Check that the body's fluid passages are clear.
22 If the assembly is fit for further use, obtain a repair kit from your Vauxhall/Opel dealer. The kit consists of both piston assemblies and springs, as well as a new circlip. Renew all seals disturbed on dismantling, and the piston circlip, as a matter of course; these should never be re-used.
23 On reassembly, soak the piston assemblies in clean hydraulic fluid. Smear clean fluid into the cylinder bore.

24 Insert the pistons into the bore, using a twisting motion to avoid trapping the seal lips. Ensure that all components are refitted in the correct order and the right way round.
25 Press the piston assemblies fully into the bore using a clean wooden dowel, and secure them in position with the new circlip. Ensure that the circlip is correctly located in the groove in the cylinder bore.
26 Fit the new seal to the end of the master cylinder bore.
27 Fit the new mounting seals to the master cylinder body, then refit the reservoir, ensuring it's clipped securely in position.

Refitting

Left-hand drive models

28 Remove all traces of dirt from the master cylinder and servo unit mating surfaces, and check that the pushrod is in position in the servo unit. Inspect the master cylinder seal for signs of wear or damage, and renew if necessary.
29 Fit the seal to the servo and refit the master cylinder, ensuring that the pushrod enters the master cylinder bore centrally. Fit the new master cylinder mounting nuts, and tighten them to the specified torque. On models with ABS, securely tighten the fluid reservoir retaining nuts.
30 Wipe clean the brake pipe unions, refit them to the master cylinder ports, and tighten them to the specified torque.
31 Refill the master cylinder reservoir with new fluid, and bleed the complete hydraulic system as described in Section 2.

11.4a Withdraw the pivot shaft . . .

Right-hand drive models

32 Refit the master cylinder as described in paragraphs 28 to 30, ignoring the note concerning models with ABS.
33 Refit the fluid reservoir support bracket, tightening its retaining nut and bolt to the specified torque setting.
34 Install the components removed for access by reversing the removal procedure.

11 Brake pedal – removal and refitting

Removal

Left-hand drive models

1 Unhook the return spring from the brake pedal.
2 Slide off the spring clip, and withdraw the clevis pin securing the pedal to the servo unit pushrod **(see illustration)**.
3 Remove the locking clip from the brake pedal pivot shaft, then slacken and remove the nut and washer from the shaft **(see illustrations)**.
4 Slide the pivot shaft to the left, and remove the brake pedal and return spring from underneath the facia **(see illustrations)**.
5 Inspect the pedal pivot bush and shaft for signs of wear, and renew if necessary.

Right-hand drive models

6 On models with manual transmission, detach the clutch cable from the pedal as

11.4b . . . and remove the pedal and return spring from the mounting bracket

11.7 On right-hand drive models, it will be necessary to first remove the clutch pedal bracket in order to remove the brake pedal

11.10 Tighten the pivot shaft nut to the specified torque setting, and secure it in position with the locking clip

11.11 Ensure that the servo pushrod clevis pin is securely retained by its spring clip

described in Chapter 6, and unhook the return spring from the pedal.

7 Working in the engine compartment, unscrew the clutch pedal mounting bracket retaining nuts and washers. From inside the vehicle, undo the bracket retaining bolt(s) and remove the bracket assembly from the vehicle **(see illustration)**.

8 Remove the brake pedal as described above in paragraphs 1 to 5.

Refitting

Left-hand drive models

9 Apply a smear of multi-purpose grease to the pedal pivot bush, and fit the return spring to the pedal.

10 Manoeuvre the pedal and spring into position, ensuring it is correctly engaged with the servo pushrod, and insert the pivot shaft bolt from the left-hand side. Fit the washer and nut. Tighten the pivot shaft nut to the specified torque setting, and secure it in position with the locking clip **(see illustration)**.

11 Align the pedal hole with the pushrod end, and insert the clevis pin. Secure the pin in position with the spring clip **(see illustration)**.

12 Hook the return spring over the pedal, and check the operation of the brake pedal.

Right-hand drive models

13 Refit the brake pedal as described above in paragraphs 9 to 12.

14 Refit the clutch pedal mounting bracket, tightening its retaining nuts and bolts securely.

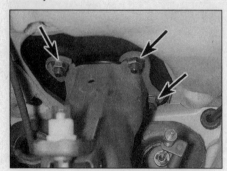

12.16 Servo unit retaining nuts (arrowed, one hidden) – right-hand drive models

15 Where necessary, connect the clutch cable to the clutch pedal, and hook the return spring back into position on the pedal. Adjust the clutch cable as described in Chapter 1.

12 Vacuum servo unit – testing, removal and refitting

Testing

1 To test the operation of the servo unit, with the engine off, depress the footbrake several times to exhaust the vacuum. Now start the engine, keeping the pedal firmly depressed. As the engine starts, there should be a noticeable 'give' in the brake pedal as the vacuum builds up. Allow the engine to run for at least two minutes, then switch it off. The brake pedal should now feel normal, but further applications should result in the pedal feeling firmer, the pedal stroke decreasing with each application.

2 If the servo does not operate as described, first inspect the servo unit check valve as described in Section 13.

3 If the servo unit still fails to operate satisfactorily, the fault lies within the unit itself. Repairs to the unit are not possible; if faulty, the servo unit must be renewed.

Removal

Left-hand drive models

4 On models with ABS, remove the master cylinder as described in Section 10.

5 On models without ABS, undo the two master cylinder retaining nuts, and disengage the unit from the front of the vacuum servo unit. Release the brake pipes from their retaining clips on the bulkhead and body, and position the master cylinder clear of the servo unit, ensuring that no excess strain is placed on the brake pipes. Keep the master cylinder upright, to prevent fluid loss. Discard the retaining nuts; new ones must be used on refitting.

6 Carefully ease the vacuum hose out of the servo unit, taking care not to displace the sealing grommet.

7 Release the cooling system expansion tank

from the bulkhead, and position it clear of the servo.

8 Release the clutch cable from its retainer, and remove the retainer. Also remove the frame.

9 Working from inside the vehicle, slide off the spring clip and withdraw the clevis pin securing the brake pedal to the servo unit pushrod.

10 Slacken and remove the nuts securing the servo unit to the brake pedal mounting bracket, then return to the engine compartment and manoeuvre the servo unit out of position. Recover the gasket from the rear of the servo unit. Discard the gasket and retaining nuts; new ones should be used on refitting.

Right-hand drive models

11 Remove the windscreen wiper motor assembly as described in Chapter 12.

12 Remove the master cylinder as described in Section 10. On some models, it may prove sufficient to unbolt the master cylinder and position it clear of the servo, taking great care not to strain the brake pipes. This removes the need to disconnect the brake pipes and open the hydraulic system.

13 On models with manual transmission, detach the clutch cable from the pedal as described in Chapter 6, and unhook the return spring from the pedal.

14 Working in the engine compartment, unscrew the clutch pedal mounting bracket retaining nuts and washers. From inside the vehicle, undo the bracket retaining bolt(s) and remove the bracket from the vehicle.

15 Unhook the return spring from the brake pedal, then slide off the spring clip and withdraw the clevis pin securing the pedal to the servo unit pushrod.

16 Slacken and remove the nuts securing the servo unit to the pedal mounting bracket, and remove the bracket **(see illustration)**.

17 Return to the engine compartment, and lift the servo unit out of position. Recover the gasket from the rear of the servo unit. Discard the gasket and retaining nuts; new ones should be used on refitting.

Refitting

18 Before refitting the servo, check that the pushrod fork dimension is correct, as follows.

19 Measure the distance from the end face of the servo casing to the centre of the clevis pin hole in the pushrod fork (see illustration). This distance should be 141.5 mm on left-hand drive models and 133.0 mm on right-hand drive models. To make accurate measurement easier, insert a bolt or bar of suitable diameter through the pivot pin hole, and measure to the centre of the bolt or bar.

20 If adjustment is necessary, slacken the locknut, and turn the fork to give the specified dimension. Hold the fork and securely tighten the locknut.

21 Inspect the servo unit check valve sealing grommet for signs of damage or deterioration, and renew if necessary. Proceed as described under the relevant sub-heading.

Left-hand drive models

22 Ensure that the servo and bulkhead mating surfaces are clean and dry.

23 Fit a new gasket to the rear of the servo, and reposition the unit in the engine compartment.

24 From inside the vehicle, ensure that the servo unit pushrod is correctly engaged with the brake pedal, then offer up the pedal mounting bracket and fit the new servo unit mounting nuts. Tighten the nuts to the specified torque setting.

25 Refit the servo unit pushrod-to-brake pedal clevis pin, and secure it in position with the spring clip.

26 Install the frame and clutch cable retainer. Clip the clutch cable back into position.

27 Refit the expansion tank in its original position.

28 Ease the vacuum hose end piece into place in the servo unit, taking great care not to displace or damage the grommet.

29 On models without ABS, refit the master cylinder to the front of the servo unit, ensuring that the servo pushrod enters the master cylinder squarely. Fit the new master cylinder mounting nuts, and tighten them to the specified torque setting. Ensure that the brake pipes are correctly clipped back into position in all the relevant retaining clips.

30 On models with ABS, refit the master cylinder as described in Section 10.

31 On completion, start the engine and check for air leaks at the vacuum hose-to-servo unit connection. Check the operation of the braking system.

Right-hand drive models

32 Install the servo unit as described above in paragraphs 22 to 24.

33 Refit the clutch pedal mounting bracket, tightening its retaining nuts and bolts securely.

34 Where necessary, reconnect the clutch cable to the pedal, and hook the return spring back over the pedal (see Chapter 6). Adjust the clutch cable as described in Chapter 1.

35 Refit the master cylinder as described in Section 10.

36 Refit the windscreen wiper motor as described in Chapter 12.

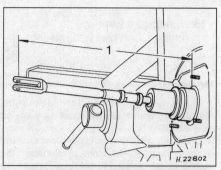

12.19 Prior to refitting the servo unit, ensure that the pushrod length (1) is correctly set – see text

37 On completion, start the engine and check for air leaks at the vacuum hose-to-servo unit connection. Check the operation of the braking system.

13 Vacuum servo unit check valve – removal, testing and refitting

1 The check valve is located in the vacuum hose running from the inlet manifold to the brake servo. Although the valve is available separately from the hoses, in order to remove the valve, the hoses must be cut, and therefore renewed on reassembly. If the valve is to be renewed, it is therefore easier to remove the complete hose/valve assembly, and renew it complete (see illustration).

Removal

2 Carefully ease the vacuum hose out of the servo unit, taking care not to displace the grommet (see illustration).

3 Note the correct routing of the hose, then undo the union nut securing the hose to the inlet manifold and remove the hose assembly from the vehicle.

Testing

4 Examine the check valve and vacuum hose for signs of damage, and renew if necessary.

5 The valve may be tested by blowing through it in both directions. Air should flow through the valve in one direction only: when

blown through from the servo unit end of the valve. Renew the valve if this is not the case.

6 Examine the servo unit rubber sealing grommet for signs of damage or deterioration, and renew as necessary.

Refitting

7 Ensure that the sealing grommet is correctly fitted to the servo unit.

8 Ease the hose union into position in the servo, taking great care not to displace or damage the grommet.

9 Ensure that the hose is correctly routed, and connect it to the inlet manifold, tightening its union nut securely.

10 On completion, start the engine and check for air leaks at the check valve-to-servo unit connection.

14 Handbrake – adjustment

1 To check the handbrake adjustment, fully release the handbrake lever, and apply the footbrake firmly several times. This will establish correct shoe-to-drum clearance, and ensure that the self-adjust mechanism is fully adjusted. Applying normal, moderate pressure, pull the handbrake lever to the fully-applied position, counting the number of clicks emitted from the handbrake ratchet mechanism. If adjustment is correct, there should be 8 clicks before the handbrake is fully applied; if this is not the case, adjust as follows.

2 Chock the front wheels, then jack up the rear of the vehicle, and support securely on axle stands.

3 On Corsa and Corsavan models, the handbrake cable adjuster nut is situated above the rear axle crossmember. On Combo Van models, the handbrake cable adjuster nut is situated directly underneath the handbrake lever; if necessary, unscrew the retaining nuts and remove the exhaust heat shield to improve access to the nut.

4 With the handbrake set on the fourth notch of the ratchet mechanism, rotate the adjusting nut until a reasonable amount of force is

13.1 Vacuum servo unit check valve is integral with the hose, and cannot be renewed separately

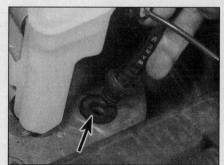

13.2 Ease the vacuum hose out from the servo unit, taking care not to displace the grommet (arrowed)

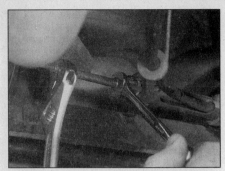

14.4 Adjusting the handbrake cable – Corsa and Corsavan models

required to turn each wheel/hub **(see illustration)**. **Note:** *The force required should be equal for each wheel.* Once this is so, fully release the handbrake lever and check that the wheels/hubs rotate freely. Check the adjustment by applying the handbrake fully whilst counting the clicks emitted from the handbrake ratchet and, if necessary, re-adjust.

5 On completion of adjustment, check the handbrake cables for free movement, and apply a little grease to the adjuster threads and exposed cable ends to prevent corrosion.

6 Refit the exhaust heat shield and/or roadwheels (as applicable) and lower the vehicle to the ground. If the roadwheels have been removed, tighten the roadwheel bolts to the specified torque setting.

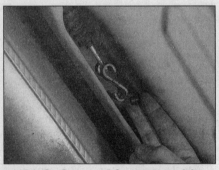

15.3 On Corsa and Corsavan models, remove the grommet and free the cable and connecting link from the handbrake lever

15.7a Unscrew the two retaining bolts . . .

15 Handbrake lever – removal, overhaul and refitting

Removal

1 Chock the front wheels, then jack up the rear of the vehicle, and support securely on axle stands.

2 Undo the retaining nuts, and remove the exhaust heat shield from underneath the vehicle to gain access to the underside of the handbrake lever.

3 On Corsa and Corsavan models, fully slacken the handbrake cable adjuster nut. Remove the grommet from the connecting link joining the front end of the cable to the handbrake lever, and detach the cable **(see illustration)**. Detach the connecting joint from the handbrake lever rod, and remove it from underneath the vehicle.

4 On Combo Van models, slacken and remove the handbrake cable adjuster nut, and detach the cable equaliser plate from the handbrake rod.

5 Remove the left-hand front seat as described in Chapter 11.

6 Peel back the carpet situated at the base of the handbrake lever, to gain access to the handbrake lever mounting bolts via the holes in the vehicle body. If necessary, cut flaps in the carpet using a sharp knife **(see illustration)**.

15.6 Note that it will probably be necessary to cut holes in the carpet to gain access to the handbrake lever retaining bolts

15.7b . . . and remove them through the access holes . . .

7 Unscrew the handbrake lever mounting bolts and withdraw the lever, disconnecting the wiring connector from the handbrake warning light switch as it becomes accessible **(see illustrations)**.

Overhaul

8 A worn ratchet segment can be renewed by driving the securing sleeve from the handbrake lever, using a metal rod or a bolt of suitable diameter.

9 Drive the new sleeve supplied with the new segment into the lever, to permit a little play between the segment and lever.

10 If desired, a new pawl can be fitted after drilling out the original pivot rivet.

11 Rivet the new pawl so that it is still free to move.

12 The handbrake warning light switch can be removed from the lever assembly after unscrewing its retaining bolt.

Refitting

13 Refitting is a reversal of the removal procedure, adjusting the cable as described in Section 14.

16 Handbrake cables – removal and refitting

Corsa and Corsavan

1 The handbrake cable consists of two sections, a long cable (complete with equaliser plate) linking the handbrake lever to the left-hand drum brake, and a short cable linking the right-hand drum brake to the equaliser plate. The equaliser plate links both cables together, and is situated above the rear axle crossmember. Each cable can be renewed individually as follows.

Long cable

2 Undo the retaining nuts, and remove the exhaust heat shield from underneath the vehicle to gain access to the underside of the handbrake lever.

3 Unscrew the handbrake cable adjuster nut, and detach the short cable from the equaliser plate.

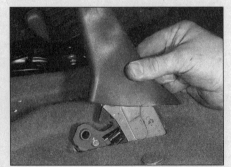

15.7c . . . then lift the handbrake lever out of position

4 Remove the left-hand rear brake drum as described in Section 7.

5 Referring to Section 5, remove the upper and lower return springs, then remove the spring cup, spring and retainer pin, and remove the rear brake shoe. Note that the front shoe and adjuster strut mechanism can be left in position on the backplate.

6 Free the handbrake cable from the retaining clip on the shoe lower pivot, then remove the retaining clip and withdraw the cable from the rear of the backplate **(see illustration)**.

7 Work back along the cable, releasing it from any relevant retaining clips and ties, whilst noting its correct routing **(see illustration)**.

8 Remove the grommet from the connecting link, and detach the front end of the cable from the connecting joint. Remove the cable from underneath the vehicle. Free the connecting link from the handbrake lever rod, and store it with the cable for safe-keeping.

9 On refitting, attach the connecting link to the handbrake lever, then hook the cable into the connecting link. Secure the cables in position with the grommet

10 Work back along the cable, securing it in position with all the relevant clips and ties, and routing it as noted on removal.

11 Insert the cable through the backplate, and secure it in position with the clip. Insert the short cable in the equaliser plate, and screw the adjuster nut onto the cable threads.

12 Ensure that the cable is securely retained by the clip on the shoe lower pivot point, and refit the rear brake shoe as described in Section 5.

13 Ensure that the brake shoes and adjuster strut components are correctly fitted, then refit the brake drum as described in Section 7.

14 Adjust the handbrake cable as described in Section 14.

Short cable

15 Remove the cable as described above in paragraphs 3 to 7, removing the right-hand brake drum instead of the left-hand drum.

16 Refit the cable as described in paragraphs 10 to 14.

Combo Van

17 The handbrake cable consists of two sections of equal length, which run from each rear brake to the equaliser plate. The equaliser plate is secured to the handbrake lever rod by the adjuster nut. The cables cannot be separated from the equaliser plate, and therefore the cable arrangement can only be removed and refitted as an assembly.

Removal

18 Undo the retaining nuts, and remove the exhaust heat shield from underneath the vehicle to gain access to the underside of the handbrake lever.

19 Unscrew the handbrake cable adjuster nut, and detach the equaliser plate from the handbrake lever.

20 Remove the left-hand rear brake drum as described in Section 7.

16.6 Each handbrake cable is secured to the backplate by a retaining clip

21 Referring to Section 5, remove the upper and lower return springs, then remove the spring cup, spring and retainer pin, and remove the rear brake shoe. Note that the front shoe and adjuster strut mechanism can be left in position on the backplate.

22 Free the handbrake cable from the retaining clip on the shoe lower pivot, then remove the retaining clip and withdraw the cable from the rear of the backplate.

23 Repeat the operations in paragraphs 20 to 22 on the right-hand rear brake.

24 Work back along both cables, releasing them from any relevant retaining clips and ties, whilst noting the correct routing. Remove the cable/equaliser plate assembly from underneath the vehicle.

Refitting

25 Connect the equaliser plate to the handbrake lever, and screw on the adjuster nut.

26 Work back along both cables, securing them in position with all the relevant clips and ties, and routing them as noted on removal.

27 Insert the cable through the left-hand backplate, and secure it in position with the clip.

28 Ensure that the cable is securely retained by the clip on the shoe lower pivot point, and refit the rear brake shoe as described in Section 5.

29 Ensure that the brake shoes and adjuster strut components are correctly fitted, then refit the left-hand brake drum as described in Section 7. **Note:** *Do not apply the brake pedal until the right-hand drum has also been installed.*

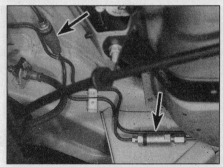

17.1 Rear brake pressure-regulating valve assembly – Corsa and Corsavan models

16.7 Free the cable from any relevant clips or brackets securing it to the vehicle underbody

30 Repeat the operations in paragraphs 27 to 29 on the right-hand brake.

31 Once both drums are in position, with the handbrake fully released, adjust the lining-to-drum clearance by repeatedly depressing the brake pedal 20 to 25 times. Whilst depressing the pedal, have an assistant listen to the rear drums, to check that the adjuster strut is functioning correctly; if so, a clicking sound will be emitted by the strut as the pedal is depressed

32 Adjust the handbrake cable as described in Section 14.

17 Rear brake pressure-regulating valve(s) – removal and refitting

Note: *Before starting work, refer to the warning at the beginning of Section 2 concerning the dangers of hydraulic fluid.*

Removal

1 The pressure-regulating valve is of the load-dependent type, and is mounted underneath the rear of the vehicle. The valve is mounted onto the vehicle underbody, and is connected to the rear axle (Corsa Corsavan) or leaf spring (Combo Van) by a spring **(see illustration)**. As the load being carried by the vehicle is altered, the suspension moves in relation to the vehicle body, altering the tension in the spring. The spring then adjusts the pressure-regulating valve lever so that the correct pressure is applied to the rear brakes to suit the load being carried. The purpose of the valve is to prevent the rear wheels locking up under heavy braking.

2 Minimise fluid loss by first removing the master cylinder reservoir cap and screwing it down onto a piece of polythene.

3 Using pliers, carefully unhook the spring and detach it from the valve.

4 Wipe clean the area around the brake pipe unions on the valve, and place absorbent rags beneath the pipe unions to catch any surplus fluid. Make identification marks on the brake pipes; these marks can then be used on refitting to ensure that each pipe is correctly reconnected.

5 Slacken the union nuts, and disconnect the

17.10 On Corsa and Corsavan models, slacken the pivot bolt . . .

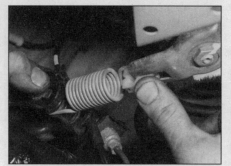

17.11a . . . and adjust the valve as described in the text

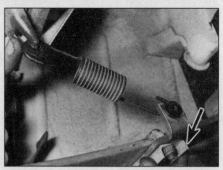

17.11b On Combo van models, adjust the valve as described in the text by repositioning the clamp (arrowed) on the leaf spring

brake pipes from the valve. Plug or tape over the pipe ends and valve orifices, to minimise the loss of brake fluid and to prevent the entry of dirt into the system. Wash off any spilt fluid immediately with cold water.

6 Undo the two bolts, and remove the pressure-regulating valve from underneath the vehicle.

Refitting

7 Refitting is the reverse of the removal procedure, noting the following points:
  a) *Tighten the valve mounting bolts to the specified torque.*
  b) *Ensure that the brake pipes are correctly connected to the valve, and tighten the union nuts to the specified torque settings.*
  c) *Coat the ends of the spring with grease prior to installation.*
  d) *Bleed the complete hydraulic system as described in Section 2.*

8 On completion, adjust the valve as follows.

9 With the vehicle completely unladen, position the car over an inspection pit, or drive it onto ramps so that it is resting on all four wheels.

10 On Corsa and Corsavan models, slacken the front pivot bolt, which secures the valve spring to the axle **(see illustration)**. On Combo Van models, slacken the nuts securing the spring clamp to the right-hand leaf spring.

11 Remove all tension from the spring, then push the pressure-regulating valve lever towards the pivot bolt/clamp (as applicable)

until the lever reaches its stop. Hold it there, then position the pivot bolt/clamp so that all clearance between the spring and valve is removed, without tensioning the spring **(see illustrations)**.

22 On Corsa and Corsavan models, hold the bolt in this position and tighten it to the specified torque setting. On Combo Van models, tighten the spring clamp nuts to the specified torque setting.

18 Stop-light switch – removal, refitting and adjustment

Removal

1 The stop-light switch is located on the pedal bracket behind the facia. To remove the switch, first disconnect the battery negative terminal (refer to *Disconnecting the battery* in the Reference Chapter).

2 Disconnect the wiring plug from the stop-light switch, then unscrew the switch from its mounting bracket **(see illustrations)**.

Refitting and adjustment

3 Refitting is a reversal of removal, adjusting the switch as follows.

4 The switch should be positioned so that the stop-lights are illuminated after the brake pedal has travelled approximately 20 mm. Adjust the position of the switch as required until the stop-lights are functioning correctly.

19 Anti-lock braking system (ABS) – description and system operation

The main ABS component is the modulator assembly, which contains the four solenoid and governor valve assemblies (one for each brake), the electrically-driven return pump, and the fluid reservoir. In addition to the modulator assembly, there is an electronic control unit and four roadwheel sensors; one fitted to each wheel. The purpose of the system is to prevent wheel(s) locking during heavy braking. This is achieved by automatic release of the brake on the relevant wheel if it is on the point of locking, followed by reapplication of the brake.

The solenoid valves are controlled by the electronic control unit, which receives signals from the four wheel sensors (one fitted on each hub), which monitor the speed of rotation of each wheel. By comparing these speed signals from the four wheels, the computer can determine the speed at which the vehicle is travelling. It can then use this information to determine when a wheel is decelerating at an abnormal rate compared to the speed of the vehicle, and thus predict when a wheel is about to lock.

During normal operation, the solenoid valves in the modulator assembly are closed, and the governor valves are in the at-rest position. The system then functions in the same way as a non-ABS braking system does.

If the electronic control unit senses that a wheel is about to lock, the system enters the 'pressure-reduction' phase. The electronic control unit opens the relevant solenoid valve in the modulator assembly. This forces the governor valve against its spring, which then isolates the brake from the master cylinder. The excess fluid in the brake hydraulic line returns from the brake to the modulator reservoir via the restrictor, reducing the hydraulic pressure and releasing the brake. At the same time, the return pump is switched on, to return the fluid to the master cylinder reservoir.

18.2a Disconnect the wiring connector from the stop-light switch . . .

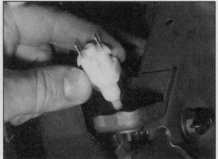

18.2b . . . and unscrew the switch from the pedal bracket

Once the danger of the wheel locking has decreased below the critical point, the system enters the 'pressure-increase' phase, and the electronic control unit closes the solenoid valve. The governor valve then returns under spring pressure, allowing hydraulic pressure from the master cylinder to act on the brake at a reduced pressure, via the restrictor in the modulator. When the pressure in the brake line is equal to the that in the master cylinder, the governor valve returns to the at-rest position, and the braking system returns to normal operation. This cycle can be carried out several times a second.

The action of the solenoid valves and return pump creates pulses in the hydraulic circuit. When the system is functioning, these pulses can be felt through the brake pedal. This is quite normal, and should not be misinterpreted as the brake discs being warped, for example.

The operation of the system is entirely dependent on electrical signals. To prevent the system responding to any inaccurate signals, a built-in safety circuit monitors all signals received by the electronic control unit. The first time the vehicle exceeds 7 km/h after the ignition has been switched on, the electronic control unit tests the readings from each wheel sensor, and the operation of the modulator solenoid valves. If a fault is detected, the system is automatically shut down by the electronic control unit, and the warning light on the instrument panel is illuminated to inform the driver that the system is not operational. Normal braking should still be available, however.

If a fault does develop in the system, the vehicle must be taken to a dealer for fault diagnosis and repair at the earliest possible opportunity. The electronic control unit will store a fault code, which can be read by the dealer using special electronic test equipment.

20 Anti-lock Braking system (ABS) components – removal and refitting

Modulator assembly (early)

Note: *Before starting work, refer to the note at the beginning of Section 2 concerning the dangers of hydraulic fluid.*

Removal

1 Disconnect the battery negative terminal.
2 Unclip the relay cover from the front of the modulator assembly **(see illustration)**.
3 Lift the retaining clip, and disconnect the wiring connector from the modulator assembly **(see illustration)**.
4 Unscrew the master cylinder reservoir filler cap, and top-up the reservoir to the MAX. mark (see *Weekly checks*). Place a piece of polythene over the filler neck, and securely refit the cap. This will minimise brake fluid loss

20.2 Remove the relay cover from the ABS modulator assembly . . .

during subsequent operations. As a precaution, place absorbent rags beneath the modulator brake pipe unions when unscrewing them.
5 Wipe clean the area around the modulator brake pipe unions, then make a note of how the pipes are arranged, to use as a reference on refitting. Unscrew the union nuts, and carefully withdraw the pipes **(see illustration)**.
6 Plug or tape over the pipe ends and modulator orifices, to minimise the loss of brake fluid and to prevent the entry of dirt into the system. Wash off any spilt fluid immediately with cold water.
7 Slacken and remove the mounting nuts, and release the modulator assembly from its mounting bracket. Undo the retaining nut, and disconnect the earth lead from the modulator **(see illustration)**. Remove the assembly from the engine compartment. **Note:** *Do not attempt to dismantle the modulator block hydraulic assembly; overhaul of the unit is not possible.*

Refitting

8 Refitting is the reverse of the removal procedure, noting the following points:
a) *Tighten the modulator block mounting nuts securely.*
b) *Refit the brake pipes to their respective unions, and tighten the union nuts to the specified torque.*
c) *Ensure that the wiring is correctly routed, and that the connector is firmly pressed into position.*
d) *On completion, and prior to refitting the battery, bleed the complete hydraulic*

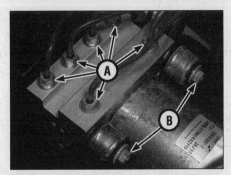

20.5 Modulator brake pipe unions (A) and mounting nuts (B)

20.3 . . . then lift up the retaining clip and disconnect the wiring connector

system as described in Section 2. Ensure that the system is bled in the correct order, to prevent air entering the modulator return pump.

Modulator assembly (late)

Note: *Before starting work, refer to the note at the beginning of Section 2 concerning the dangers of hydraulic fluid.*

Removal

9 Disconnect the battery negative terminal (refer to *Disconnecting the battery* in the Reference Chapter).
10 Pull out the locking bar and disconnect the wiring harness multi-plug connector from the electronic control unit located on the hydraulic modulator.
11 Unscrew the master cylinder reservoir filler cap, and top-up the reservoir to the MAX mark (see *Weekly checks*). Place a piece of polythene over the filler neck, and secure the polythene with the filler cap. This will minimise brake fluid loss during subsequent operations. As a precaution, place absorbent rags beneath the modulator brake pipe unions when unscrewing them.
12 Wipe clean the area around the modulator brake pipe unions, then make a note of how the pipes are arranged, to use as a reference on refitting. Unscrew the union nuts, and carefully withdraw the pipes.
13 Plug or tape over the pipe ends and modulator orifices, to minimise the loss of brake fluid and to prevent the entry of dirt into the system. Wash off any spilt fluid immediately with cold water.

20.7 Modulator earth lead retaining nut (arrowed)

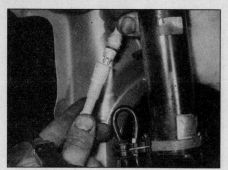

20.33 Disconnect the wiring connector . . .

20.34a . . . then undo the retaining bolt (arrowed) . . .

20.34b . . . and remove the front wheel speed sensor from the vehicle

14 Slacken and remove the mounting nuts, and release the modulator assembly from its mounting bracket. Remove the assembly from the engine compartment.

Refitting

15 Refitting is the reverse of the removal procedure, noting the following points:
a) Tighten the modulator block mounting nuts securely.
b) Refit the brake pipes to their respective unions, and tighten the union nuts to the specified torque.
c) Ensure that the wiring is correctly routed, and that the multi-plug connector is firmly pressed into position and secured with the locking bar.
d) On completion, and prior to refitting the battery, bleed the complete hydraulic system as described in Section 2. Ensure that the system is bled in the correct order, to prevent air entering the modulator return pump.

Electronic control unit (early)

Removal

16 The ABS electronic control unit is mounted beneath the facia, behind the left-hand front footwell side panel. Prior to removing the control unit, disconnect the battery negative lead.
17 On right-hand drive models, remove the storage compartment (where fitted) from underneath the passenger side of the facia. The compartment is secured in position by a retaining screw and clip.
18 Release the retaining clips, and unclip the left-hand front footwell side panel from underneath the facia to gain access to the control unit.
19 Release the control unit from its mounting bracket.
20 Release the retaining clip, disconnect the wiring connector, and remove the control unit from the vehicle.

Refitting

21 Refitting is a reversal of the removal procedure, ensuring that the wiring connector is securely reconnected, and that the control unit is clipped securely into its retaining bracket.

Electronic control unit (late)

Removal

Caution: Separation of the ECU from the hydraulic modulator is not recommended by the manufacturers of the ABS system. Information on this operation is, however, given by Vauxhall/Opel. If difficulties are experienced when refitting the ECU to the modulator, it may be necessary to renew the complete assembly.
Note: *New ECU retaining screws and a new gasket will be required for refitting.*

22 Remove the hydraulic modulator from the car as described previously in this Section.
23 Disconnect the return pump motor wiring plug from the ECU.
24 Undo the six retaining screws and carefully withdraw the ECU upwards and off the hydraulic modulator. Recover the gasket.

Refitting

25 Prior to refitting, clean and then carefully inspect, the condition of the gasket sealing surfaces on the ECU and hydraulic modulator. If the surfaces are in any way deformed, damaged, or rough to the extent that a perfect gasket seal cannot be maintained, the complete modulator and ECU assembly must be renewed.
26 Check to see if there is a spring plate located over the solenoid valves on the hydraulic modulator. If a spring plate is present, it should be removed and discarded.
27 With a new gasket in position, and holding the ECU centrally, carefully lower it over the solenoid valves on the modulator, keeping it square and level.
28 Fit the six new retaining screws, and tighten the four screws around the solenoid area of the modulator, evenly and progressively until they all just make contact with the ECU body. Continue tightening these four screws alternately and progressively until the ECU body just makes contact with the hydraulic modulator. Now tighten the remaining two screws until they also just make contact with the ECU body.
28 Progressively, and working in a diagonal sequence, tighten the four screws in the vicinity of the solenoid area securely. Now tighten the remaining two screws. The ECU must make complete contact with the

hydraulic modulator, with no visible gap around any of the sealing area. If this cannot be achieved, release all the screws and tighten them progressively again. If it is still not possible to obtain correct seating of the unit, the complete assembly must be renewed.
30 Reconnect the return pump motor wiring plug, then refit the hydraulic modulator as described previously in this Section.

Front speed sensor

Removal

31 Disconnect the battery negative terminal (refer to *Disconnecting the battery* in the Reference Chapter).
32 Firmly apply the handbrake, then jack up the front of the car and support it securely on axle stands (see *Jacking and vehicle support*). Remove the appropriate front roadwheel.
33 Trace the wheel speed sensor wiring back to its wiring connector, and release it from its retaining clip. Disconnect the connector **(see illustration)**, and work back along the sensor wiring, freeing it from all the relevant retaining clips and ties.
34 Slacken and remove the bolt securing the sensor to the mounting bracket, and remove the sensor and lead assembly from the vehicle **(see illustrations)**.

Refitting

35 Prior to refitting, apply a thin coat of multi-purpose grease to the sensor mounting bracket.
36 Ensure that the sensor and mounting bracket sealing faces are clean, then fit the sensor to the hub. Refit the retaining bolt, and tighten it securely.
37 Ensure that the sensor wiring is correctly routed, and retained by all the necessary clips. Reconnect it to its wiring connector, and fit the connector into the retaining clip.
38 Refit the roadwheel, aligning the marks made on removal, then lower the vehicle to the ground and tighten the roadwheel bolts to the specified torque.

Rear speed sensor

Removal

39 Chock the front wheels then jack up the rear of the car and support it on axle stands (see *Jacking and vehicle support*).

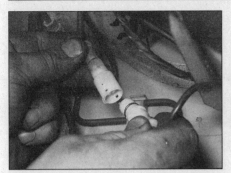

20.40 Disconnecting a rear wheel speed sensor wiring connector

20.42 Removing the sensor from the rear of the backplate

20.44 Turn the sensor in the direction of the arrow, so that the retaining clip (A) is freed from the mounting bracket

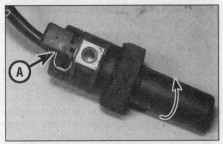

20.45 With the sensor in position and the screw tightened, turn the sensor in the direction of the arrow so that the clip (A) engages with the mounting bracket and the correct air gap is set

20.49 Rear wheel speed sensor toothed ring is an integral part of the brake drum

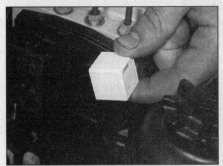

20.52 Relays are a push fit in the modulator assembly

47 Lower the vehicle to the ground.

Front speed sensor rings

48 The front toothed rings are an integral part of the driveshaft outer constant velocity (CV) joints, and cannot be renewed separately. Examine the rings for such damage as chipped or missing teeth. If renewal is necessary, the complete outer constant velocity joint must be renewed, as described in Chapter 8.

Rear speed sensor rings

49 The rear toothed rings are an integral part of the rear brake drum, and cannot be renewed separately **(see illustration)**. Examine the rings for signs of damage such as chipped or missing teeth. If renewal is necessary, the rear brake drum must be renewed as described in Section 7.

Relays (early models)

50 Disconnect the battery negative lead.
51 Both the solenoid relay and return pump relay are located on the front of modulator assembly. To gain access to them, unclip the relay cover from the front of the modulator **(see illustration 20.2)**.
52 Either relay can then be simply pulled out of position **(see illustration)**. The return pump relay is the top relay, and the solenoid valve relay the bottom relay. Refer to Chapter 12 for further information on relays.
53 When refitting, ensure that the relay is securely pushed into position, then refit the cover and connect the battery negative lead.

40 Trace the wiring back from the sensor to its wiring connector, which is situated just near the spare wheel well. Free the connector from its retaining clip, and disconnect the wiring from the main wiring loom **(see illustration)**.
41 Work back along the sensor wiring, and free it from any relevant retaining clips.
42 Slacken and remove the screw securing the sensor unit to the backplate, and withdraw the sensor from the backplate. Remove the sensor and lead assembly from the vehicle **(see illustration)**.

Refitting

43 Prior to refitting, apply a thin coat of multi-purpose grease to the sensor tip. Ensure that the sensor and backplate mating faces are clean.
44 Turn the sensor anti-clockwise to release it from the retaining clip on the mounting bracket. This is vital to ensure that the sensor is correctly positioned on refitting **(see illustration)**.
45 Push the sensor in lightly until it seats, then refit its retaining screw and tighten it securely. With the screw tightened, rotate the sensor clockwise until it engages with the retaining clip **(see illustration)**. As the sensor engages with the clip, it will move out slightly, to leave the correct air gap between the sensor tip and toothed ring on the drum.
46 Ensure that the sensor wiring is correctly routed and retained by all the necessary retaining clips. Reconnect the wiring connector, and fit it back into the retaining clip.

21 Vacuum pump – removal and refitting

Removal

1 The vacuum pump is attached to the rear of the alternator. Access to the pump can be improved by removal of the exhaust pipe heatshield adjacent to it, or alternatively, the alternator may be removed as described in Chapter 5A.
2 Apply the handbrake then jack up the front of the vehicle and support it on axle stands (see *Jacking and vehicle support*).
3 Disconnect the servo vacuum pipe from the pump by counterholding the large union nut and unscrewing the small one.
4 Unscrew the union nut and disconnect the oil feed line from the pump **(see illustration)**.

21.4 Disconnecting the oil feed line from the vacuum pump. Return line arrowed

21.6a Removing the vacuum pump from the alternator

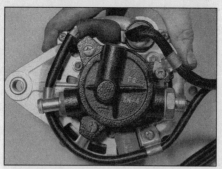

21.6b Ensure that the electrical cables are correctly routed around the vacuum pump

21.7 Renew the O-ring (arrowed) in the alternator casing

5 Release the clip and disconnect the oil return line. Allow any oil to drain into a suitable container and plug or cap all lines.
6 Unscrew the mounting bolts, taking note of any cable clips/supports fitted beneath them, and withdraw the pump from the alternator drive spline **(see illustrations)**.
7 Remove the O-ring from the alternator **(see illustration)**. Discard the O-ring and obtain a new one.

Refitting

8 Refitting is a reversal of removal, noting the following points.
  a) *Before fitting the pump pour approximately 5 cc of clean engine oil into the oil feed aperture.*

  b) *Clean the mating faces of the pump and alternator or cylinder head (as applicable) and fit a new O-ring.*
  c) *With the pump fitted to the alternator ensure that the alternator pulley can be turned easily by hand.*

22 Vacuum pump – testing and overhaul

Note: *A vacuum gauge will be required for this check.*
1 The operation of the braking system vacuum pump can be checked using a vacuum gauge.

2 Disconnect the vacuum pipe from the pump, and connect the gauge to the pump union using a suitable length of hose.
3 Start the engine and allow it to idle, then measure the vacuum created by the pump. As a guide, after one minute, a minimum of approximately 500 mm Hg should be recorded. If the vacuum registered is significantly less than this, it is likely that the pump is faulty. However, seek the advice of a Vauxhall/Opel dealer before condemning the pump.
4 Overhaul of the vacuum pump is not possible, since no components are available separately for it. If faulty, the complete pump assembly must be renewed.

Chapter 10
Suspension and steering

Contents

Degrees of difficulty

Easy, suitable for novice with little experience		Fairly easy, suitable for beginner with some experience		Fairly difficult, suitable for competent DIY mechanic		Difficult, suitable for experienced DIY mechanic		Very difficult, suitable for expert DIY or professional	

Specifications

Front suspension

Type . . . . Independent, with MacPherson struts and forward-facing tie-bars. Anti-roll bar fitted to most models

Rear suspension

Type:
   Corsa and Corsavan . . . . Semi-independent torsion beam, with trailing arms, coil springs and telescopic shock absorbers. Anti-roll bar on some models

   Combo Van models . . . . Tubular axle and leaf springs with telescopic shock absorbers

Steering

Type . . . . Rack-and-pinion. Power assistance standard on certain models, optional on others

Roadwheels

Type . . . . Pressed-steel or aluminium alloy (depending on model)
Size . . . . 5J x 13 and 5.5J x 13

Front wheel alignment and steering angles

	Corsa and Corsavan	Combo Van
Camber angle:		
Up to model year 1996	-35' ± 45'	-45' ± 45'
From model year 1997	-25' ± 45'	-40' ± 45'
Maximum difference between sides	1°	
Castor angle:		
Up to model year 1996	1°50' ± 1°	1°15' ± 1°
From model year 1997	1°50' ± 1°	10' ± 10'
Maximum difference between sides	1°	
Toe setting	-10' ± 10' (1.0 mm toe-out ± 1.0 mm)	

Rear wheel alignment

Camber angle:	
Corsa and Corsavan	-1°30' ± 30'
Combo Van	-25' ± 25'
Maximum difference between sides	30'
Toe setting:	
Corsa and Corsavan	10' +30' -15' (1.0 mm toe-in +3 mm -1.5 mm)
Combo Van	15' ± 10' (1.5 mm toe-in ± 1.0 mm)

Tyres

Pressures	See end of *Weekly Checks* on page 0•17
Corsa and Corsavan	145 R 13, 165/70 R 13 or 165/65 R 13
Combo Van	165/70 R 13

Torque wrench settings

	Nm	lbf ft
Front suspension		
Anti-roll bar clamp nuts*	20	15
Lower arm balljoint clamp bolt nut*	30	22
Lower arm pivot bolt nut:*		
Stage 1	45	33
Stage 2	Angle-tighten a further 45°	
Stage 3	Angle-tighten a further 15°	
Lower arm-to-balljoint/tie-bar bolts:*		
Stage 1	90	66
Stage 2	Angle-tighten a further 30°	
Stage 3	Angle-tighten a further 15°	
Suspension strut-to-swivel hub bolts:*		
Stage 1	50	37
Stage 2	90	66
Stage 3	Angle-tighten a further 45°	
Stage 4	Angle-tighten a further 15°	
Suspension strut upper mounting nuts*	30	22
Tie-bar front nut*	90	66
Tie-bar mounting bush bracket bolts:*		
Stage 1	50	37
Stage 2	Angle-tighten a further 90°	
Stage 3	Angle-tighten a further 15°	
Rear suspension – Corsa and Corsavan models		
Anti-roll bar bolts:*		
Stage 1	60	44
Stage 2	Angle-tighten a further 60°	
Stage 3	Angle-tighten a further 15°	
Hub nut (pre-load)	25	18
Shock absorber:		
Lower bolt	65	48
Upper nut	20	15
Stub axle bolts:*		
Stage 1	50	37
Stage 2	Angle-tighten a further 30°	
Stage 3	Angle-tighten a further 15°	
Trailing arm pivot bolts:*		
Stage 1	50	37
Stage 2	Angle-tighten a further 45°	
Stage 3	Angle-tighten a further 15°	

Torque wrench settings (continued)

	Nm	lbf ft
Rear suspension – Combo Van models		
Bump stop bolt	50	37
Bump stop seat nut	20	15
Hub nut (pre-load)	25	18
Leaf spring pivot bolts	65	48
Shackle nut	35	26
Shock absorber:		
Lower bolt	65	48
Upper bolt	70	52
U-bolt nuts	45	33
Steering		
Intermediate shaft clamp bolt	22	16
Power steering pipe union nuts	28	21
Power steering pump bolts	25	18
Steering column and column clamp bolts	22	16
Steering gear mountings	22	16
Steering wheel nut	20	15
Track rod balljoint locknut	50	37
Track rod balljoint-to-swivel hub nut*	35	26
Roadwheels		
Roadwheel bolts	110	81

Use new nuts/bolts.

1 General information

1 The independent front suspension is of the MacPherson strut type, incorporating coil springs and integral telescopic shock absorbers **(see illustration)**. The MacPherson struts are located by transverse lower suspension arms, which utilise rubber inner mounting bushes, and incorporate a balljoint at the outer ends. The front swivel hubs, which carry the wheel bearings, brake calipers and the hub/disc assemblies, are bolted to the MacPherson struts, and connected to the lower arms via the balljoints. A forward-facing tie-bar connects each lower suspension arm to the vehicle body. On most models, a front anti-roll bar is fitted. The anti-roll bar is rubber-mounted onto the tie-bars by mounting clamps.

2 On Corsa and Corsavan models, the rear suspension is of semi-independent type, consisting of a torsion beam axle and trailing arms, with double-conical coil springs and telescopic shock absorbers **(see illustration)**. The front ends of the trailing arms are attached to the vehicle underbody by horizontal bushes; the rear ends are located by the shock absorbers, which are bolted to

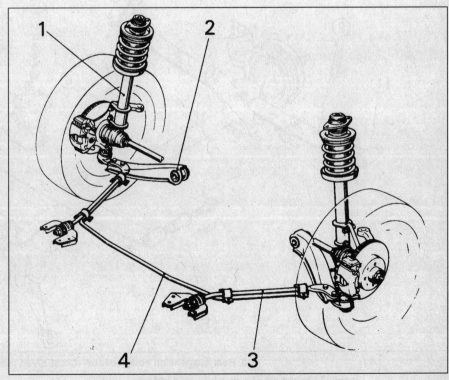

1.1 Front suspension components

1 *MacPherson strut* 2 *Lower arm* 3 *Tie-bar* 4 *Anti-roll bar*

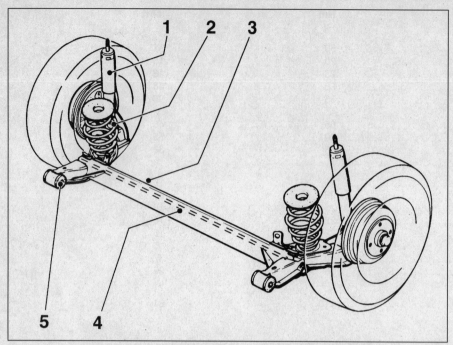

1.2 Rear suspension components – Corsa and Corsavan models

1 Shock absorber   3 Torsion beam axle   5 Trailing arm
2 Coil spring   4 Anti-roll bar (where fitted)

the underbody at their upper ends. The coil springs are mounted independently of the shock absorbers, and act directly between the trailing arms and the underbody. Certain models are fitted with an anti-roll bar, which is bolted onto the underside of each trailing arm.

3 On Combo Van models, the rear suspension consists of a tubular axle and leaf spring arrangement, with telescopic shock absorbers **(see illustration)**. The front end of each leaf spring is bolted directly to the vehicle underbody, and the rear end is attached by a shackle arrangement to allow movement of the spring. The axle is secured to each leaf spring by two U-bolts. The shock absorber upper ends are bolted to the vehicle underbody; the lower ends are bolted to the axle.

4 The steering column is linked to the steering gear by an intermediate shaft. The intermediate shaft has a universal joint fitted to its upper end, and is secured to the column by a clamp bolt. The lower end of the intermediate shaft is attached to the steering gear pinion by means of a clamp bolt.

5 The rack-and-pinion type steering gear is rubber-mounted onto the engine compartment bulkhead, and is connected by two track rods, with balljoints at their outer ends, to the steering arms projecting

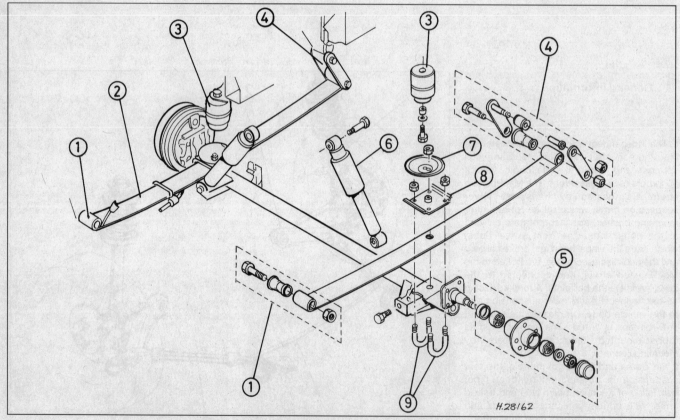

1.3 Rear suspension components – Combo Van models

1 Leaf spring front pivot and bush   4 Shackle   7 Bump stop seat
2 Leaf spring   5 Rear hub assembly   8 Retaining plate
3 Bump stop   6 Shock absorber   9 U-bolts

2.4a Undo the bolts (arrowed) securing the caliper bracket to the swivel hub . . .

2.4b . . . then slide the caliper off the disc, and hook it onto the strut spring using a piece of wire

2.6 Withdraw the clamp bolt, and free the lower arm balljoint from the swivel hub

rearwards from the swivel hubs. The track rod ends are threaded, to facilitate adjustment.

6 Power-assisted steering is fitted as standard or optional equipment, according to model. The power steering is of the conventional hydraulic type, powered by a belt-driven pump, which is driven off the crankshaft pulley.

2 Front swivel hub assembly – removal and refitting

Note: *New retaining nuts and/or bolts will be required for most attachments when refitting (see text).*

Removal

 HAYNES HiNT *If work is being carried out without the aid of an assistant, remove the wheel trim/hub cap (as applicable), then withdraw the split pin and slacken the driveshaft retaining nut prior to jacking up the vehicle.*

1 Firmly apply the handbrake, then jack up the front of the car and support it securely on axle stands (see *Jacking and vehicle support*). Remove the appropriate front roadwheel.
2 Extract the split pin from the driveshaft retaining nut and discard it; a new one must be used on refitting.
3 Refit at least two roadwheel bolts to the front hub, and tighten them securely. Have an assistant firmly depress the brake pedal to prevent the front hub from rotating, then using a socket and extension bar, slacken and remove the driveshaft retaining nut. Alternatively, a tool can be fabricated from two lengths of steel strip (one long, one short) and a nut and bolt; the nut and bolt forming the pivot of a forked tool. Bolt the tool to the hub using two wheel bolts, and hold the tool to prevent the hub from rotating as the driveshaft retaining nut is undone **(see illustration 2.3 in Chapter 8).**
4 Unscrew the two bolts securing the brake caliper mounting bracket to the swivel hub, and slide the caliper assembly off the disc. Using a piece of wire or string, tie the caliper

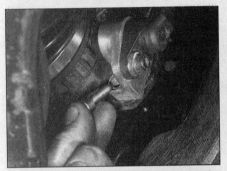

2.7a On models with ABS, slacken and remove the retaining bolt . . .

2.7b . . . and release the wheel speed sensor mounting bracket from the swivel hub

to the front suspension coil spring to avoid placing any strain on the hydraulic brake hose **(see illustrations)**. Discard the caliper mounting bracket bolts – they must be renewed whenever they are disturbed. If the hub bearings are to be disturbed, remove the brake disc as described in Chapter 9.
5 Unscrew the driveshaft retaining nut, and remove the washer. Discard the nut; a new one must be used on refitting.
6 Slacken and remove the lower arm balljoint clamp nut and bolt, and free the lower arm from the swivel hub **(see illustration)**. Discard the clamp bolt nut; a new one must be used on refitting.
7 On models with ABS, undo the bolt securing the wheel speed sensor mounting bracket to the swivel hub, and position the sensor assembly clear of the hub **(see illustrations)**.
8 On all models, slacken and remove the nut

securing the steering gear track rod balljoint to the swivel hub, and release the balljoint tapered shank using a universal balljoint separator. Discard the nut; it should be renewed whenever it is disturbed.
9 Slacken and remove the two nuts and bolts securing the suspension strut to the swivel hub, noting which way around the bolts are inserted **(see illustration)**. Discard the nuts and bolts; they should be renewed whenever they are disturbed.
10 Carefully pull the swivel hub assembly outwards, and withdraw the driveshaft outer constant velocity joint from the hub assembly. If necessary, the shaft can be tapped out of the hub using a soft-faced mallet. Support the driveshaft by suspending it with wire or string, and do not allow it to hang under its own weight. Remove the hub assembly from the vehicle **(see illustration)**.

2.9 Unscrew the nuts and withdraw the bolts securing the suspension strut to the swivel hub

2.10 Free the swivel hub from the end of the driveshaft, and withdraw it from the vehicle

2.11 Engage the swivel hub with the driveshaft constant velocity joint, and fit the washer and new retaining nut

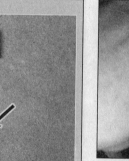

HAYNES HINT

If a suitable tap is not available, cut two slots into the threads of one of the original mounting bolts, and use the bolt to remove the locking compound from the threads.

Refitting

11 Ensure that the driveshaft outer constant velocity joint and hub splines are clean, then slide the hub onto the driveshaft splines. Fit the washer and new driveshaft retaining nut, tightening it by hand only at this stage **(see illustration)**.

12 Engage the swivel hub with the suspension strut, and insert the new bolts from the rear of the strut so that their threads are facing forwards. Fit the new nuts, tightening them by hand only at this stage.

13 Locate the lower arm balljoint in the swivel hub. Insert the clamp bolt from the rear of the swivel hub, so that its threads are facing

3.2 Disc shield retaining screws are accessed through holes in the hub flange

2.13 Fit a new nut to the lower arm balljoint clamp bolt, and tighten it to the specified torque setting

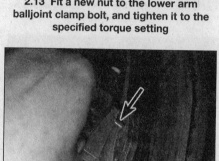

2.19 On models with ABS, ensure that the sensor bracket pin (arrowed) is correctly located in the hub hole when refitting the bracket to the swivel hub

forwards. Fit the new nut to the clamp bolt, and tighten it to the specified torque setting **(see illustration)**.

14 With the hub correctly located, tighten the strut-to-swivel hub bolts through the various stages given in the Specifications at the start of this Chapter.

15 Engage the track rod balljoint in the swivel hub, then fit the new retaining nut and tighten it to the specified torque setting.

16 Refit the brake disc (where removed) to the hub, referring to Chapter 9 for further information.

17 Remove all traces of old thread-locking compound from the brake caliper mounting bracket holes in the swivel hub, ideally by running a tap of the correct size and pitch through them **(see Haynes Hint)**.

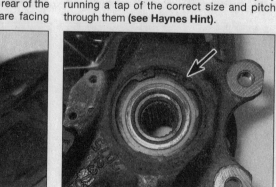

3.4 Hub bearing is retained by a circlip (arrowed)

18 If the threads of the new caliper mounting bracket bolts are not already pre-coated with thread-locking compound, apply a suitable locking compound to them. Slide the caliper assembly into position over the disc, then fit the mounting bolts and tighten them to the specified torque setting (Chapter 9 Specifications).

19 Where necessary, refit the ABS wheel speed sensor bracket to the hub, making sure its locating peg is correctly engaged **(see illustration)**, and tighten the mounting bracket retaining bolt to the specified torque (Chapter 9 Specifications).

20 Using the method employed on removal to prevent rotation, tighten the driveshaft retaining nut through the stages given in the Specifications shown in Chapter 8.

21 With the nut correctly tightened, secure it in position with a new split pin. If the holes in the driveshaft are not aligned with any of the slots in the nut, loosen **(do not tighten)** the nut by the *smallest possible amount* until the split pin can be inserted.

22 Refit the roadwheel, then lower the vehicle to the ground and tighten the roadwheel bolts to the specified torque. Refit the wheel trim/hub cap, where applicable.

| **3** | **Front hub bearings –** renewal | |

Note: *The bearing is sealed, pre-adjusted and pre-lubricated. Never overtighten the drive-shaft nut beyond the specified torque wrench setting in an attempt to 'adjust' the bearing.*

Note: *A press will be required to dismantle and rebuild the assembly; if such a tool is not available, a large bench vice and spacers (such as large sockets) will serve as an adequate substitute. The bearing's inner races are an interference fit on the hub; if the inner race remains on the hub when it is pressed out of the hub carrier, a knife-edged bearing puller will be required to remove it.*

1 Remove the swivel hub assembly as described in Section 2.

2 Undo the screws and remove the brake disc shield from the hub **(see illustration)**. Discard the screws; new ones should be used on refitting.

3 Support the swivel hub securely on blocks or in a vice. Using a tubular spacer which bears only on the inner end of the hub flange, press the hub flange out of the bearing. If the bearing's outboard inner race remains on the hub, remove it using a bearing puller (see note above).

4 Extract the bearing retaining circlips from the swivel hub assembly **(see illustration)**.

5 Where necessary, refit the inner race back in position over the ball cage, and securely support the inner face of the swivel hub. Using a tubular spacer which bears only on the inner race, press the complete bearing assembly out of the swivel hub.

6 Thoroughly clean the hub and swivel hub, removing all traces of dirt and grease. Polish away any burrs or raised edges which might hinder reassembly. Check both assemblies for cracks or any other signs of wear or damage, and renew as necessary. Renew the circlips regardless of their apparent condition.

7 On reassembly, apply a light film of oil to the bearing outer race and hub flange shaft, to aid installation of the bearing. Remove all traces of old thread-locking compound from the disc shield retaining screw holes, ideally by running a tap of the correct size and pitch through them.

8 Install the new outer circlip in the swivel hub. Make sure that the circlip is correctly located in its groove, with its holes situated at the bottom of the hub.

9 Securely support the swivel hub, and locate the bearing in the hub. Press the bearing fully into position, ensuring that it enters the hub squarely, using a tubular spacer which bears only on the bearing outer race.

10 Once the bearing is correctly seated against the outer circlip, secure the bearing in position with the new inner circlip. Make sure that the circlip is correctly located in its groove, with its holes situated at the bottom of the hub.

11 Securely support the outer face of the hub flange, and locate the swivel hub bearing inner race over the end of the hub flange. Press the bearing onto the hub, using a tubular spacer which bears only on the inner race of the hub bearing, until it seats against the hub shoulder. Check that the hub flange rotates freely, and wipe off any excess oil or grease.

12 Fit the disc shield to the hub assembly, and apply a few drops of thread-locking compound to the new screws. Fit the screws, and tighten them securely.

13 Refit the swivel hub assembly as described in Section 2.

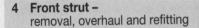

4 Front strut –
removal, overhaul and refitting

Note: *When refitting, new strut-to-swivel hub bolts and nuts, and strut upper mounting nuts, will be required.*

Removal

1 Firmly apply the handbrake, then jack up the front of the car and support it securely on axle stands (see *Jacking and vehicle support*). Remove the appropriate roadwheel.

2 On models with ABS, release the front wheel speed sensor wiring from its clip on the suspension strut (see illustration).

3 Slacken and remove the two nuts and bolts securing the suspension strut to the swivel hub. Discard both nuts and bolts; these must be renewed whenever they are disturbed.

4.2 On models with ABS, free the sensor wiring from its clip on the base of the strut

4.4b . . . and reposition the wiring loom tray to gain access to the strut upper mounting nuts (arrowed)

4 From within the engine compartment, unscrew the two suspension strut upper mounting nuts and discard them; new ones should be used on refitting. On some models, it may be necessary to reposition the wiring loom tray to improve access to the strut upper mounting; the tray is retained by plastic nuts **(see illustrations)**.

5 Release the strut from the swivel hub, and withdraw it from under the wheelarch **(see illustrations)**.

Overhaul

6 Overhaul of the strut should be entrusted to a Vauxhall/Opel dealer or suitably-equipped garage. A spring compressor and numerous other special tools are necessary to ensure correct fitting and torque setting of the upper spring seat and strut piston retaining nut. Any attempt to dismantle the strut without such

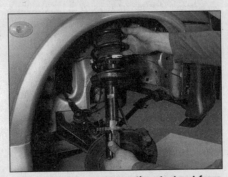

4.5b . . . and manoeuvre the strut out from underneath the wheelarch

4.4a On some models, it may be necessary to undo the nuts (arrowed) . . .

4.5a Release the lower end of the strut from the swivel hub . . .

tools is likely to result in damage or personal injury.

Refitting

7 Manoeuvre the strut assembly into position, ensuring that the top mounting plate is correctly located. Fit the washers and new strut upper mounting nuts, and tighten them to the specified torque setting **(see illustration)**. Refit the wiring loom tray to its original location, where applicable.

8 Engage the lower end of the strut with the swivel hub. Insert the new bolts from the rear of the strut so that their threads are facing forwards. Fit the new nuts to the bolts, and tighten them through the various stages given in the Specifications at the start of this Chapter **(see illustrations)**.

9 On models with ABS, clip the sensor wiring back into its retaining clip.

4.7 Tighten the strut upper mounting nuts to the specified torque setting

4.8a Insert the new bolts from the rear of the strut, so their threads are facing forwards

4.8b Tighten the bolts first to the specified torque settings . . .

4.8c . . . and then through the specified angles

10 Refit the roadwheel, then lower the vehicle to the ground and tighten the roadwheel bolts to the specified torque.

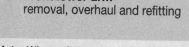

5 Front lower arm – removal, overhaul and refitting

Note: *When refitting, a new pivot bolt nut, and new lower arm-to-balljoint/tie-bar nuts and bolts, will be required.*

Removal

1 Firmly apply the handbrake, then jack up the front of the car and support it securely on axle stands (see *Jacking and vehicle support*). Remove the appropriate front roadwheel.

2 Unscrew the nut and withdraw the pivot bolt securing the lower arm to the vehicle body. Discard the nut; a new one should be used on refitting.

3 Slacken and remove the two nuts and bolts securing the balljoint and tie-bar to the lower arm, and remove the lower arm from the vehicle. Discard the nuts and bolts; new ones should be used on refitting.

Overhaul

4 Thoroughly clean the lower arm and the area around the arm mountings, removing all traces of dirt and underseal if necessary. Check carefully for cracks, distortion, or any other signs of wear or damage, paying particular attention to the pivot bush (**see illustration**). If bush renewal is necessary, the lower arm should be taken to a Vauxhall/Opel dealer or suitably-equipped garage. A hydraulic press and spacers are required to press the bush out of the arm, and to install the new one.

5 Examine the shank of the pivot bolt for signs of wear or scoring, and renew if necessary.

Refitting

6 Offer up the lower arm, aligning it with the tie-bar and balljoint, and install the new bolts and nuts (**see illustration**).

7 Align the inner end of the arm with its mounting, and insert the pivot bolt from the front of the vehicle, so that its threads are facing towards the rear of the vehicle (**see illustration**).

8 Tighten the balljoint/tie-bar-to-lower arm bolt nuts through the various stages given in the Specifications at the start of this Chapter

9 Position a jack underneath the outer end of the lower arm. Raise the jack so that the lower arm is positioned as shown in illustration 5.9a. With the arm correctly positioned, fit the new nut to the pivot bolt, and tighten it through the various stages given in the Specifications at the start of this Chapter (**see illustrations**).

10 Remove the jack from underneath the arm, then refit the roadwheel, aligning the marks made on removal.

11 Lower the vehicle to the ground, and tighten the roadwheel bolts to the specified torque setting.

5.4 Examine the lower arm pivot bush for signs of damage or deterioration, and if necessary renew

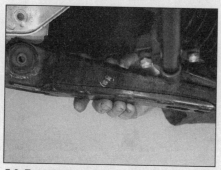

5.6 Engage the outer end of the lower arm with the balljoint and tie-bar, and insert the new bolts . . .

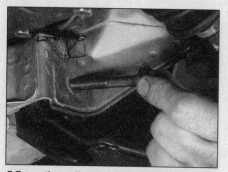

5.7 . . . then align the inner end of the arm, and insert the pivot bolt so its threads are facing towards the rear of the vehicle

5.9a Position a jack beneath the lower arm, and raise it until the angle at the arm is at approximately 80º to the vertical . . .

5.9b . . . then fit a new nut to the pivot bolt, and tighten it through the various stages given in the Specifications

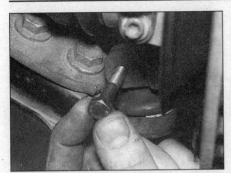

6.2 Slacken and remove the nut and clamp bolt . . .

6.3 . . . then remove the balljoint-to-lower arm/tie-bar bolts (arrowed) . . .

6.4 . . . and withdraw the balljoint from the end of the lower arm

6 Front lower arm balljoint – removal and refitting

Note: *When refitting, a new clamp bolt nut and new balljoint/tie-bar to lower arm nuts and bolts will be required.*

Removal

1 Firmly apply the handbrake, then jack up the front of the car and support it securely on axle stands (see *Jacking and vehicle support*). Remove the appropriate front road-wheel.

2 Slacken and remove the lower arm balljoint clamp nut and bolt, and free the balljoint from the swivel hub **(see illustration)**. Discard the clamp bolt nut; a new one must be used on refitting.

3 Slacken and remove the two nuts and bolts securing the balljoint and tie-bar to the lower arm **(see illustration)**. Discard the nuts and bolts; these should be renewed whenever they are disturbed.

4 Withdraw the balljoint from the lower arm, and remove it from the vehicle **(see illustration)**.

Refitting

5 Align the balljoint with the lower arm and tie-bar, then insert the new bolts **(see illustration)**. Fit the new nuts to the bolts, tightening them by hand only at this stage.

6 Locate the balljoint shank in the swivel hub, and insert the clamp bolt from the rear of the swivel hub, so that its threads are facing forwards.

7 Fit the new nut to the balljoint clamp bolt, and tighten it to the specified torque setting **(see illustration)**. Tighten the balljoint-to-lower arm/tie-bar bolt nuts through the various stages given in the Specifications at the start of this Chapter.

8 Refit the roadwheel, then lower the vehicle to the ground and tighten the roadwheel bolts to the specified torque setting.

9 Check the front wheel alignment and steering angles as described in Section 27.

6.5 Insert the balljoint into the end of the lower arm, and fit the new retaining bolts

7 Front tie-bar – removal, overhaul and refitting

Note: *When refitting, a new tie-bar front mounting nut and anti-roll bar mounting clamp nuts will be required. The balljoint/tie-bar-to-lower arm nuts and bolts must also be renewed, as must the front mounting bracket bolts.*

Removal

1 Firmly apply the handbrake, then jack up the front of the car and support it securely on axle stands (see *Jacking and vehicle support*).

2 Prior to removal, mark the position of the

6.7 Fit a new nut to the balljoint clamp bolt, and tighten it to the specified torque setting

anti-roll bar mounting clamp rubbers on the tie-bar.

3 Unscrew the two nuts from each anti-roll bar clamp, and remove both halves of the clamp. Discard the nuts; new ones must be used on refitting.

4 Slacken the nut securing the front of the tie-bar to its mounting bracket, and remove the nut **(see illustration)**. Discard the nut; a new one should be used on refitting.

5 Slacken and remove the two nuts and bolts securing the tie-bar and balljoint to the lower arm **(see illustration)**. Discard the nuts and bolts; these should be renewed whenever they are disturbed. **Note:** *On some models, it may be necessary to disconnect the lower arm balljoint from the swivel hub to enable the bolts to be withdrawn (see Section 6).*

7.4 Unscrew the retaining nut from the front end of the tie-bar

7.5 Slacken and remove the two bolts (arrowed) securing the tie-bar and balljoint to the lower arm . . .

7.6 . . . then free the front end of the bar from its mounting bush, and recover the washer (arrowed)

6 Free the front end of the tie-bar from its mounting bush, and remove it from the vehicle **(see illustration)**. Slide the washer off the end of the tie-bar.

Overhaul

7 Inspect the tie-bar for signs of damage, paying particular attention to the threads, and renew if necessary. If the anti-roll bar clamp rubbers show any signs of damage or deterioration, they must also be renewed.

8 Examine the front mounting bush and bracket for signs of wear and damage. The bush cannot be renewed separately, and if wear or damage is evident, obtain a new bracket and bush as an assembly. To renew the bracket, undo the three bolts and withdraw the bracket from the crossmember **(see illustration)**. Discard the bracket retaining bolts; they must be renewed whenever they

8.3a Unscrew the anti-roll bar clamp retaining nuts . . .

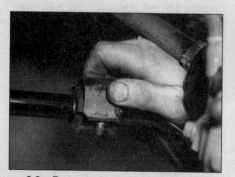

8.3c Recover the upper half of each clamp . . .

7.8 Tie-bar front mounting bush bracket is retained by three bolts (arrowed)

are disturbed. On refitting, remove all traces of old thread-locking compound from the retaining bolt holes in the crossmember, ideally by running a tap of the correct size and pitch through them. Locate the bracket in position and fit the new retaining bolts. Tighten the bolts hand tight only at this stage.

> **HAYNES HiNT**
>
> *If a suitable tap is not available, cut two slots into the threads of one of the original mounting bolts, and use the bolt to remove the locking compound from the threads.*

Refitting

9 Fit the washer to the threaded end of the tie-bar, and insert the tie-bar into its mounting bush.

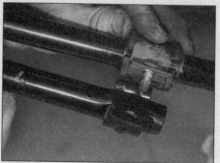

8.3b . . . and free the bar and lower clamp halves from the tie-bar

8.4 . . . and remove the mounting rubber from the tie-bar

10 Align the tie-bar with the lower arm and balljoint, and insert the new retaining bolts. Fit new nuts to the bolts, and tighten the nuts through the various stages given in the Specifications at the start of this Chapter.

11 Fit the new nut to the front of the tie-bar, and tighten it hand tight only at this stage.

12 Install and tighten the anti-roll bar mounting clamps using the information given in Section 8.

13 If not previously done, unscrew the three bolts securing the tie-bar mounting bush bracket to the crossmember. Remove all traces of old thread-locking compound from the retaining bolt holes in the crossmember, ideally by running a tap of the correct size and pitch through them. Fit the new retaining bolts and tighten them hand tight only at this stage.

14 Lower the car to the ground and tighten the three tie-bar mounting bush bracket bolts through the various stages given in the Specifications at the start of this Chapter.

15 Finally, tighten the tie-bar front mounting nut to the specified torque.

8 Front anti-roll bar – removal and refitting

Note: *When refitting, new anti-roll bar mounting clamp nuts will be required.*

Removal

1 Firmly apply the handbrake, then jack up the front of the car and support it securely on axle stands (see *Jacking and vehicle support*).

2 Prior to removal, mark the position of each anti-roll bar mounting clamp rubber on the tie-bars.

3 Unscrew the two nuts from each mounting clamp, and remove both halves of the clamp. As the last clamp is removed, support the anti-roll bar and remove it from underneath the vehicle **(see illustrations)**. Discard all clamp nuts; new ones must be used on refitting.

4 Inspect the mounting clamp rubbers for signs of damage and deterioration, and renew if necessary **(see illustration)**.

Refitting

5 Align all the mounting rubbers with the marks made on the tie-bars prior to removal. Ensure that the flat edge of each rubber is facing downwards.

6 Fit the upper half of each mounting clamp to its relevant rubber.

7 Offer up the anti-roll bar, and fit the lower half of the mounting clamp.

8 Ensure that the clamp half is correctly engaged with the anti-roll bar flats, then couple both halves of each clamp together **(see illustration)**. Fit the new clamp nuts, tightening them by hand only at this stage.

9 With all the clamps loosely installed, check the distance between the right-and left-hand

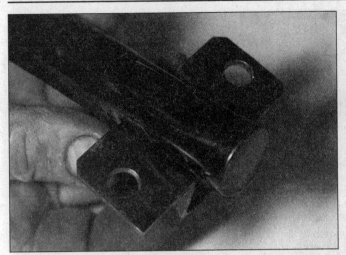

8.8 When refitting, ensure that each lower clamp is correctly engaged with the anti-roll bar flats

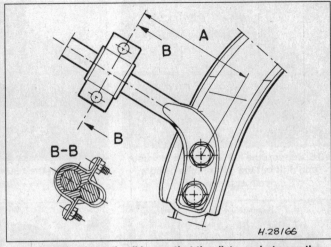

H.28166

8.9 Position the anti-roll bar so that the distance between the left- and right-hand rear clamp and each tie-bar inner bolt (A) is 121 mm. Inset (B) shows cross-sectional view of anti-roll bar and tie-bar

rear clamps and the tie-bar inner bolt **(see illustration)**. Reposition the anti-roll bar as required until both the right- and left-hand clamps are correctly positioned, then go around and tighten all the clamp nuts to the specified torque setting.

10 Lower the vehicle to the ground.

9 Rear hub assembly – removal and refitting

Removal

Corsa and Corsavan models

1 On these models, the rear hub is an integral part of the brake drum. Refer to Chapter 9 for drum removal and refitting details.

2 Check the hub bearing for signs of roughness or damage, and renew if necessary as described in Section 10.

3 With the hub removed, examine the stub axle shaft for signs of wear or damage and, if necessary, renew it as described in Section 11.

Combo Van models

4 Remove the rear brake drum as described in Chapter 9.

5 Prise out the cap from the centre of the hub.

6 Extract the split pin from the hub nut, then slacken and remove the nut.

7 Slide the hub assembly, complete with the toothed washer and outer bearing, off the stub axle.

8 Check the hub bearing for signs of roughness or damage, and renew if necessary as described in Section 10.

9 With the hub removed, examine the stub axle shaft for signs of wear or damage. If renewal is necessary, the complete rear axle must be renewed; it is not possible to separate the stub axles from the axle.

Refitting

Corsa and Corsavan models

10 Refit the brake drum as described in Chapter 9.

Combo Van models

11 Ensure that the stub axle is clean, and apply a smear of grease to the lip of the hub oil seal.

12 Slide the hub, outer bearing and toothed washer onto the stub axle, ensuring that the toothed washer is correctly engaged with the stub axle slot.

13 Refit the hub nut, tightening it to the specified pre-load torque setting whilst rotating the hub to settle the bearings in position. Gradually slacken the hub nut until the position is found where it is just possible to move the toothed washer from side-to-side using a screwdriver. **Note:** *Only a small amount of force should be needed to move the washer; do not use the screwdriver as a lever to move the washer.* When the hub nut is correctly posit-ioned, secure it in position with a new split pin.

14 If the stub axle holes are not aligned with any of the slots in the hub nut, tighten the nut by the *smallest possible amount* until the split pin can be inserted. With the nut in this

10.3 Lever the oil seal out from the hub with a flat-bladed screwdriver

position, check that it is still possible to move the toothed washer. If it is, insert the split pin and secure it in position. If it is not possible to move the washer, slacken the nut slightly until the next hub nut slot/axle hole aligns. Check that it is possible to move the toothed washer, then secure the hub nut in position with the new split pin.

15 Fit the cap to the centre of the hub.

16 Install the brake drum as described in Chapter 9.

10 Rear hub bearings – renewal

1 On Corsa and Corsavan models, remove the rear brake drum as described in Chapter 9. On Combo Van models, remove the hub as described in Section 9.

2 If not already done, remove the toothed washer from the drum/hub, and lift out the outer taper roller bearing.

3 Using a suitable flat-bladed screwdriver, lever the oil seal out of the rear of the drum/hub, noting which way around it is fitted **(see illustration)**.

4 Remove the inner taper roller bearing from the inside of the drum/hub.

5 Support the drum/hub, and tap the outer bearing outer race out of position, using a hammer and metal drift which just passes through the centre of the inner bearing outer race **(see illustration)**.

6 Turn the drum/hub over, and tap the inner bearing outer race out of position.

7 Thoroughly clean the hub, removing all traces of dirt and grease. Polish away any burrs or raised edges which might hinder reassembly. Check the drum/hub surface for cracks or any other signs of wear or damage, and renew it if necessary. The bearings and oil seal must be renewed whenever they are

10.5 Support the hub on blocks of wood, and drift out the outer races using a hammer and punch

10.9a Insert the outer race into the hub . . .

10.9b . . . and drift it into position using a hammer and tubular drift

10.12a Work the grease well into the roller bearings . . .

10.12b . . . and smear the outer race surfaces

10.13 Fit the taper roller bearing to the innermost outer race . . .

disturbed, as removal will almost certainly damage the outer races. Obtain new bearings, an oil seal, and a small quantity of the special bearing grease (90 510 336) from your Vauxhall/Opel dealer. In the absence of the special grease, a good-quality lithium-based grease may be used instead.

8 On reassembly, apply a light film of clean engine oil to each bearing outer race, to aid installation.

9 Securely support the drum/hub, and locate the outer bearing outer race in the hub. Tap the outer race fully into position, using a tubular spacer which bears only on the outer edge of the race, and ensuring that it enters the hub squarely (see illustrations).

10 Turn the drum/hub over, and install the inner bearing outer race in the same way.

11 Ensure that both outer races are correctly seated in the hub, and wipe them clean.

12 Work the grease well into both the taper roller bearings, and apply a smear of grease to the outer races (see illustrations).

13 Fit the taper roller bearing to the innermost outer race (see illustration).

14 Press the oil seal into the rear of the drum/hub, ensuring that its sealing lip is facing inwards (see illustration). Position the seal so that it is flush with the hub face, or until its lip abuts the rear of the drum/hub. If necessary, the seal can be tapped into position using a suitable tubular drift which bears only on the hard outer edge of the seal.

15 Turn the drum/hub over, fit the taper roller bearing to the outer race, and install the toothed washer.

16 Pack the hub bearings with a suitable grease.

17 On Corsa and Corsavan models, install the brake drum as described in Chapter 9.

18 On Combo Van models, refit the hub assembly as described in Section 9.

11 Rear stub axle – removal and refitting

Corsa and Corsavan models

Note: *When refitting, new stub axle retaining bolts must be used.*

Removal

1 Remove the brake drum as described in Chapter 9.

2 Position a jack underneath the relevant trailing arm, and raise the jack until it is just supporting the weight of the arm.

3 Undo the lower shock absorber mounting bolt, and swing the shock absorber away from the trailing arm to gain access to the stub axle retaining bolts.

4 Slacken and remove the retaining bolts,

10.14 . . . then press the oil seal into position

11.4a On Corsa and Corsavan models, undo the four retaining bolts (arrowed) . . .

11.4b . . . and remove the stub axle (shown with brake shoes removed)

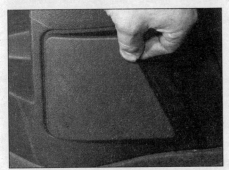

12.3a On Corsa models, unclip the trim cover . . .

12.3b . . . and remove the cap to gain access to the shock absorber upper mounting nut

12.4 Slacken the mounting nut whilst retaining the piston with an open-ended spanner

and remove the stub axle from the trailing arm **(see illustrations)**. Discard the retaining bolts; new ones must be used on refitting.

5 Inspect the stub axle surface for signs of damage such as scoring, and renew if necessary.

Refitting

6 Ensure that the mating surfaces of the stub axle and backplate are clean and dry. Check the backplate for signs of damage, and remove any burrs with a fine file or emery cloth.

7 Offer up the stub axle, and fit the new retaining bolts. Tighten the retaining bolts through the various stages given in the Specifications at the start of this Chapter.

8 Align the shock absorber with the trailing arm, then fit its lower mounting bolt, tightening it to the specified torque.

9 Remove the jack from underneath the

trailing arm, and refit the brake drum as described in Chapter 9.

Combo Van models

10 On Combo Van models, the stub axles are an integral part of the rear axle, and cannot be removed separately. If a stub axle is damaged, the complete axle assembly must be renewed. Refer to Section 15 for axle removal and refitting details.

12 Rear shock absorber – removal, testing and refitting

Removal

Corsa and Corsavan models

1 Chock the front wheels then jack up the

rear of the car and support it on axle stands (see *Jacking and vehicle support*).

2 Position a jack underneath the relevant trailing arm, and raise the jack until it is just supporting the weight of the arm.

3 Working in the luggage compartment, prise out the trim cover and/or remove the trim cap (as applicable) to gain access to the shock absorber upper mounting nut **(see illustrations)**.

4 Slacken and remove the nut, and lift off the plate and rubber mounting damper. If necessary, to prevent the shock absorber piston rotating as the nut is slackened, retain it using an open-ended spanner on the flats on the upper end of the piston **(see illustration)**.

5 Slacken and remove the lower shock absorber mounting bolt, then lower the shock absorber out of position and remove it from underneath the vehicle **(see illustrations)**.

6 Remove the rubber damper, spacer and dust cover from the shock absorber piston.

Combo Van

7 Chock the front wheels then jack up the rear of the car and support it on axle stands (see *Jacking and vehicle support*).

8 Position a jack underneath the axle, and raise the jack until it is just supporting the weight of the axle.

9 Note the orientation of the shock absorber, then slacken and remove the upper and lower shock absorber mounting bolts, and remove the shock absorber from underneath the vehicle **(see illustrations)**.

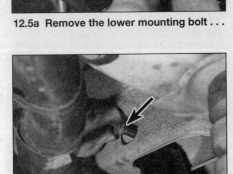

12.5a Remove the lower mounting bolt . . .

12.5b . . . then free the shock absorber from the trailing arm, and manoeuvre it out from underneath the vehicle

12.9a On Combo Van models, slacken and remove the upper (arrowed) . . .

12.9b . . . and lower mounting bolts . . .

12.9c . . . and remove the shock absorber from underneath the vehicle

12.15 Tightening the shock absorber lower mounting bolt – Corsa models

12.21 Tightening the shock absorber lower mounting bolt – Combo Van models

Testing

10 Examine the shock absorber for signs of fluid leakage or damage. Test the operation of the strut, while holding it in an upright position, by moving the piston through a full stroke, and then through short strokes of 50 to 100 mm. In both cases, the resistance felt should be smooth and continuous. If the resistance is jerky, or uneven, or if there is any visible sign of wear or damage to the strut, renewal is necessary. Also check the rubber mounting bush(es) for damage and deterioration. If the bushes are damaged or worn, the complete shock absorber will have to be renewed, as the mounting bushes are not available separately. Inspect the shanks of the mounting bolts for signs of wear or damage, and renew as necessary.

11 On Corsa and Corsavan models, examine the upper mounting rubber dampers for signs

of damage or deterioration, and renew if necessary.

Refitting

Corsa and Corsavan

12 Ensure that the rubber bump stops are in position on the piston, then operate the piston fully through several strokes to prime it.

13 Fully extend the piston, then slide the dust cover, spacer and rubber damper onto the piston.

14 Manoeuvre the shock absorber into position, ensuring that the piston is correctly located in the hole in the vehicle body.

15 Insert the shock absorber lower mounting bolt, and tighten it to the specified torque setting **(see illustration)**.

16 From inside the luggage compartment, refit the rubber mounting damper and plate to the piston.

17 Fit the upper mounting nut, and tighten it to the specified torque setting. If necessary, prevent the piston rotating as described in paragraph 4.

18 Refit the trim cap/cover (as applicable).

19 Remove the jack from underneath the trailing arm, and lower the vehicle to the ground.

Combo Van

20 Operate the shock absorber fully through several strokes to prime it, then manoeuvre it into position underneath the vehicle.

21 Ensure that the shock absorber is positioned the correct way up, and insert both the upper and lower mounting bolts. Tighten both mounting bolts to their specified torque settings **(see illustration)**.

22 Remove the jack from underneath the axle, and lower the vehicle to the ground.

13 Rear coil spring (Corsa and Corsavan) – removal and refitting

Note: *Both coil springs are removed at the same time.*

Removal

1 Chock the front wheels then jack up the rear of the car and support it on axle stands (see *Jacking and vehicle support*). Remove both rear roadwheels.

2 Position a jack underneath the right-hand trailing arm, and raise the jack until it is just supporting the weight of the arm.

3 Undo the shock absorber lower mounting bolt, and disengage the right-hand shock absorber from the trailing arm.

4 Remove the spring connecting the rear brake pressure-regulating valve to the axle (Chapter 9) **(see illustration)**.

5 Detach the rear brake pipes from their clips on the vehicle underbody and axle **(see illustrations)**, then slowly lower the jack until it is no longer supporting the trailing arm. With the trailing arm unsupported, check that no excess strain is being placed on the brake pipes.

6 Position the jack underneath the left-hand trailing arm, and raise the jack until it is supporting the weight of the arm.

7 Undo the lower shock absorber mounting bolt, and disengage the left-hand shock absorber from the trailing arm.

8 Slowly lower the jack, keeping watch on the brake pipes to ensure no excess strain is placed on them, until it is possible to withdraw the right-hand coil spring. Note which way around the spring is installed, and recover the upper and lower spring seats.

9 Remove the left-hand spring, noting which way around it is installed, and recover both the upper and lower spring seats **(see illustrations)**.

10 If the vehicle is to be left for some time with the springs removed, lift up the trailing arms and refit the shock absorber lower

13.4 Unhook the spring from the rear brake pressure-regulating valve

13.5a Slide out the retaining clips . . .

13.5b . . . and free the rear brake pipes from the vehicle underbody brackets

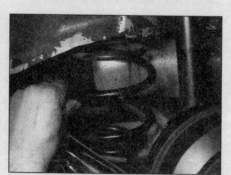

13.9a Lower the rear axle, then remove the coil springs . . .

mounting bolts. **Note:** *Do not allow the rear axle assembly to hang unsupported.*

11 Inspect the springs closely for signs of damage, such as cracking, and check the spring seats for signs of wear or damage. Renew worn components as necessary.

Refitting

12 If the shock absorber lower bolts were refitted in paragraph 10, remove them now, and lower the trailing arms.

13 Install the upper and lower spring seats in position on the underbody and trailing arms.

14 Manoeuvre the left-hand coil spring into position, noting that the smaller-diameter end of the spring must be uppermost (towards the vehicle body). Ensure that the spring is correctly located in both the upper and lower seats.

15 Fit the right-hand spring in the same way.

16 With both springs correctly seated, lift the left-hand trailing arm up on the jack, and align the shock absorber with its mounting bracket. Refit the shock absorber lower mounting bolt, and tighten it to the specified torque setting.

17 Repeat the operation on the right-hand side, and remove the jack.

18 Locate the rear brake pipes back in position, and secure them with the retaining clips.

19 Refit the brake pressure-regulating valve spring, and adjust the valve as described in Chapter 9.

20 Refit the roadwheels, then lower the vehicle to the ground, and tighten the roadwheel bolts to the specified torque.

13.9b . . . and recover the upper . . .

13.9c . . . and lower spring seats

---

14 Rear leaf spring and bump stop (Combo Van) – removal, inspection and refitting

Removal

1 Chock the front wheels then jack up the rear of the car and support it on axle stands (see *Jacking and vehicle support*). Remove the relevant rear roadwheel, then proceed as described under the relevant sub-heading.

Leaf spring

2 Unscrew the two retaining nuts, and release the handbrake cable bracket from the spring **(see illustrations)**.

3 If the right-hand leaf spring is being removed, unscrew the two retaining nuts, and detach the rear brake pressure-regulating

valve spring clamp from the leaf spring **(see illustration)**.

4 Place a jack underneath the rear axle, and raise the jack so that it is supporting the weight of the axle.

5 Slacken and remove the front pivot bolt securing the leaf spring to the vehicle body, and the rear pivot bolt securing the spring to the shackle **(see illustrations)**.

6 Lower the axle slightly, then unscrew the nut and remove the bump stop seat from the top of the leaf spring **(see illustration)**.

7 Unscrew the four U-bolt retaining nuts, then remove both U-bolts and the retaining plate **(see illustrations)**.

8 Remove the leaf spring from underneath the vehicle.

9 Undo the shackle nut, and remove both halves of the shackle from underneath the vehicle **(see illustration)**.

14.2a Undo the two retaining nuts (arrowed) . . .

14.2b . . . and detach the handbrake cable bracket from the leaf spring

14.3 If the right-hand spring is being removed, also remove the brake pressure-regulating valve spring clamp

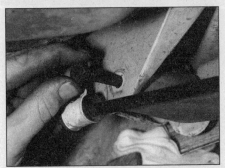

14.5a Slacken and remove the front pivot bolt . . .

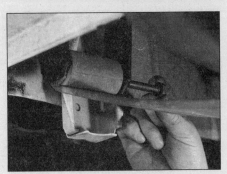

14.5b . . . and the rear bolt securing the spring to the shackle

14.6 Undo the nut (arrowed) and remove the bump stop seat from the spring

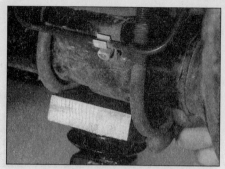

14.7a Undo the retaining nuts, then withdraw both U-bolts . . .

14.7b . . . and remove the retaining plate

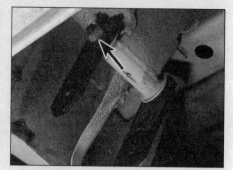

14.9 Undo the nut (arrowed) and remove the shackle

14.10 Unscrew the retaining bolt from the centre of the bump stop, and remove the stop from the vehicle

14.12 Remove the shackle bushes from the vehicle, and inspect them for wear

14.15a Insert the shackle plate from the inboard side . . .

Bump stop

10 Unscrew the bump stop retaining bolt, and remove the stop from the vehicle **(see illustration)**. Withdraw the bolt, and recover the spacer and washer.

Inspection

11 Closely inspect the leaf spring and shackle for signs of damage, such as cracking, especially around the pivot points. Renew components as necessary.

12 Inspect the spring and shackle pivot bushes for signs of wear, and renew if necessary. A hydraulic press and spacers will be required to renew the leaf spring bushes, but the shackle-to-body bush halves can be easily levered out of position and the new ones installed **(see illustration)**.

13 Examine the pivot bolts and shackle stud for signs of scoring, and renew worn components as necessary.

14 Check the rubber bump stop, and renew it if the rubber shows signs of damage or deterioration.

Refitting

Leaf spring

15 Insert the shackle plate with the stud through from the inboard side of the bracket, and fit the plain plate on the outside. Fit the nut, tightening it by hand only at this stage **(see illustrations)**.

16 Engage the leaf spring with the shackle and front mounting bracket. Note that the locating pin on the base of the spring is offset. Make sure that the spring is fitted with the shorter distance between the spring pivot bush and locating pin facing towards the front of the vehicle.

17 Insert the front and rear spring pivot bolts, and tighten the pivot bolts and shackle nut to the specified torque setting **(see illustrations)**.

18 Lift the axle into position, ensuring its hole is correctly engaged with the locating pin on the base of the leaf spring **(see illustration)**.

19 Refit the retaining plate to the top of the

14.15b . . . and fit the plain plate on the outside

14.17a Tighten the rear pivot bolt . . .

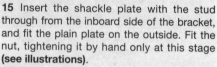
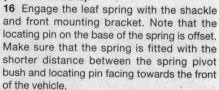
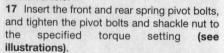

14.17b . . . and the front pivot bolt to the specified torque

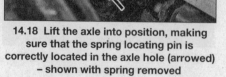

14.18 Lift the axle into position, making sure that the spring locating pin is correctly located in the axle hole (arrowed) – shown with spring removed

spring, and install both the U-bolts and retaining nuts. Tighten the retaining nuts evenly and progressively to the specified torque (see illustration), ensuring that an equal length of thread is visible above each nut. If there is a difference of more than 3 mm between any two, slacken the retaining nuts and repeat the tightening sequence.

20 Fit the bump stop seat to the retaining plate, aligning its locating peg with innermost retaining plate hole, and tighten its retaining nut to the specified torque (see illustration).

21 Refit the handbrake cable clamp to the leaf spring, and securely tighten its retaining nuts.

22 On the right-hand spring, refit the brake pressure-regulating valve clamp to the spring, and adjust the valve as described in Chapter 9.

23 Refit the roadwheel, then lower the vehicle to the ground, and tighten the roadwheel bolts to the specified torque.

Bump stop

24 Insert the washer into the bump stop, and fit the spacer and retaining bolt (see illustrations).

25 Fit the bump stop to the vehicle, and tighten the retaining bolt to the specified torque.

26 Refit the roadwheel, then lower the vehicle to the ground, and tighten the roadwheel bolts to the specified torque.

15 Rear axle – removal and refitting

Removal

1 Chock the front wheels then jack up the rear of the car and support it on axle stands (see *Jacking and vehicle support*). Remove both rear roadwheels.

2 Unscrew the brake master cylinder fluid reservoir cap and screw it down onto a piece of polythene to minimise fluid loss during the following procedure. Proceed as described under the relevant sub-heading.

Corsa and Corsavan models

Note: *New trailing arm pivot bolts and nuts will be required when refitting.*

3 Undo the retaining nuts, and remove the exhaust heat shield from underneath the vehicle to gain access to the underside of the handbrake lever.

4 Referring to Chapter 9, unscrew the handbrake cable adjuster nut, then remove the grommet from the connecting link, and detach the front end of the cable from the connecting joint. Work back along the cable, releasing it from any relevant retaining clips and ties, so that the cable is free to be removed with the axle.

5 On models with ABS, disconnect the rear wheel speed sensors at the wiring connectors. Free the sensor wiring from all its

14.19 Tighten the U-bolt retaining nuts to the specified torque as described in text

14.24a When refitting the bump stop, do not omit the washer from inside the stop . . .

retaining clips, so that it is free to be removed with the axle.

6 Trace the brake pipes back from the backplates to their unions situated directly above the axle. Slacken the union nuts, and disconnect the pipes. Plug the pipe ends, to minimise fluid loss and prevent the entry of dirt into the hydraulic system. Remove the retaining clips, and release the pipes from the axle/vehicle body.

7 Remove the left- and right-hand coil springs as described in Section 13, then place the jack underneath the centre of the axle.

8 Slacken and remove the nut and pivot bolt securing each trailing arm to the vehicle underbody (see illustration). Discard the nuts and bolts; new ones should be used on refitting.

9 Make a final check that all necessary components have been disconnected and positioned so that they will not hinder the

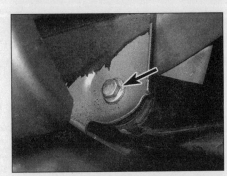

15.8 Trailing arm pivot bolt (arrowed) – Corsa and Corsavan models

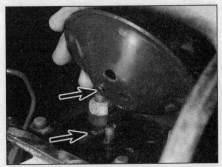

14.20 Fit the bump stop seat, making sure its locating peg is engaged with the inner retaining plate hole (arrowed)

14.24b . . . or the spacer from the top of the bump stop

removal procedure. Carefully lower the axle assembly out of position, and remove it from underneath the vehicle.

10 Inspect the trailing arm bushes for signs of damage or deterioration, and renew if necessary. Bush renewal should be entrusted to a Vauxhall/Opel dealer, or to a suitably-equipped garage with access to a hydraulic press and spacers.

Combo Van

11 Undo the retaining nuts, and remove the exhaust heat shield from underneath the vehicle to gain access to the underside of the handbrake lever and cable.

12 Referring to Chapter 9, unscrew the handbrake cable adjuster nut, then remove the equaliser plate from the handbrake lever. Work back along each cable, releasing it from any relevant retaining clips and ties, so that the cable assembly is free to be removed with the axle.

13 Trace the brake pipes back from the backplates to their unions on the top of the axle. Slacken the union nuts, and disconnect the pipes. Plug the pipe ends, to minimise fluid loss and prevent the entry of dirt into the hydraulic system. Remove the retaining clips, and release the pipes from the axle (see illustration).

14 Unscrew both the left- and right-hand shock absorber lower mounting bolts, and free both shock absorbers from the axle.

15 Position a jack beneath the centre of the axle, and raise the jack until it is supporting the weight of the axle.

15.13 Remove the retaining clips (arrowed), and release the brake pipes from the top of the axle

16 Unscrew the nut, and remove the bump stop seat from the top of the both the left- and right-hand leaf springs.

17 Unscrew the four U-bolt retaining nuts, then remove both U-bolts and the retaining plate from the left-hand leaf spring. Remove the U-bolts and retaining plate from the right-hand leaf spring in the same way.

18 Make a final check that all necessary components have been disconnected and positioned so that they will not hinder the removal procedure. Carefully lower the axle assembly out of position, and remove it from underneath the vehicle.

Refitting

Corsa and Corsavan models

19 Refitting is a reverse of the removal procedure, bearing in mind the following points:

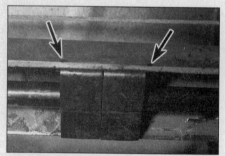

16.2 Prior to removal, mark the positions (arrowed) of the rubber dampers on the axle crossmember

16.4a ... then withdraw the anti-roll bar ...

a) Ensure that the trailing arm and mounting bracket surfaces are clean and dry. Raise the axle assembly into position, and insert the new trailing arm pivot bolts, tightening them by hand only at this stage.
b) Ensure that the brake pipes, handbrake cables and wiring (as applicable) are correctly routed, and retained by all the necessary retaining clips.
c) Tighten all the brake pipe union nuts to the specified torque, and bleed the braking system, with reference to Chapter 9.
d) Adjust the handbrake cable as described in Chapter 9. Also adjust the rear brake pressure-regulating valve once the vehicle is on the ground.
e) On completion, lower the vehicle to the ground, and tighten the roadwheel bolts to the specified torque.
f) With the vehicle resting on its wheels and two assistants seated in the front seats, tighten the trailing arm pivot bolts through the various stages given in the Specifications at the start of this Chapter.

Combo Van models

20 Refitting is a reverse of the removal procedure, bearing in mind the following points:
a) Ensure that the holes in the axle are correctly aligned with the locating pegs on the leaf springs when raising the axle into position.
b) Install the U-bolts, retaining plates and bump stop seats as described in Section 14.
c) Ensure that the brake pipes, handbrake cables and wiring (as applicable) are

16.3 Slacken and remove the nut and bolt securing the anti-roll bar to each trailing arm ...

16.4b ... and recover the rubber dampers

correctly routed and retained by all the necessary retaining clips.
d) Tighten all the brake pipe union nuts to the specified torque, and bleed the braking system, with reference to Chapter 9.
e) Adjust the handbrake cable and rear brake pressure-regulating valve as described in Chapter 9.
f) On completion, lower the vehicle to the ground, and tighten the roadwheel bolts to the specified torque.

16 Rear anti-roll bar (Corsa and Corsavan) – removal and refitting

Note: New retaining bolts will be required on refitting.

Removal

1 Chock the front wheels then jack up the rear of the car and support it on axle stands (see Jacking and vehicle support). Remove one of the rear roadwheels.
2 Prior to removal, mark the position of the rubber dampers on the axle crossmember (see illustration).
3 Slacken and remove the bolts securing the anti-roll bar to the trailing arms (see illustration). Discard the bolts; new ones must be used on refitting.
4 Withdraw the bar from the side on which the roadwheel has been removed. If the bar is tight, remove the opposite roadwheel, and drift the bar out using a hammer and soft metal drift. Recover the dampers from the bar as they are released (see illustrations).
5 Inspect the rubber dampers for signs of damage or deterioration, and renew as necessary.

Refitting

6 To ease installation, coat the anti-roll bar with soapy water.
7 Insert the anti-roll bar in through the trailing arm, and locate the rubber dampers on the bar. Align the rubber dampers with the marks made prior to removal, and seat them in the axle crossmember.
8 Slide the anti-roll bar fully into position, so that it is correctly engaged in the opposite trailing arm.

16.9a Insert the new anti-roll bar retaining bolts ...

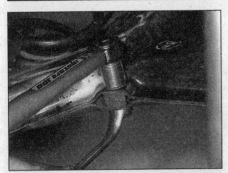

16.9b . . . and tighten them to the specified torque, and then through the specified angles

9 Install the new retaining bolts, then refit the washers and nuts. Tighten both bolts first to the specified torque, and then through the specified angles given in the Specifications at the start of this Chapter **(see illustrations)**.
10 Refit the roadwheel(s), aligning the marks made on removal. Lower the vehicle to the ground, and tighten the roadwheel bolts to the specified torque.

17 Steering wheel – removal and refitting

Note: *A puller will be required to draw the steering wheel off the column splines. A new retaining nut lockwasher will be required when refitting.*

17.3 Ease the horn button out from the steering wheel, and disconnect its wiring

17.7 With the steering wheel removed, lift the spring from the column

Models without an air bag

Removal

1 Disconnect the battery negative terminal (refer to *Disconnecting the battery* in the Reference Chapter).
2 Set the front wheels in the straight-ahead position, and release the steering lock by inserting the ignition key.
3 Carefully ease the horn button out from the steering wheel, and disconnect its wiring **(see illustration)**.
4 Using a screwdriver, prise back the tabs on the retaining nut lockwasher **(see illustration)**.
5 Unscrew the retaining nut, and lift off the lockwasher. Discard the lockwasher; a new one should be used on refitting.
6 Make alignment marks between the steering wheel and steering column shaft.
7 A 2-legged puller will now be required to free the steering wheel from its splines. Locate the legs of the puller in the holes in the centre of the wheel, and draw the steering wheel off the column splines. Lift off the steering wheel, and remove the spring from the column shaft **(see illustration)**.

Refitting

8 Check that the indicator cancelling lug/horn button contact pad fitted to the rear of steering wheel is in good condition, and if necessary renew it. To release the pad, depress the two clips located inside the steering wheel **(see illustration)**.
9 Ensure that the indicator switch stalk is in its central (OFF) position. Failure to do this

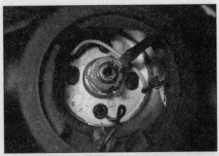

17.4 Using a screwdriver, bend down the tabs of the lockwasher from the steering wheel nut

17.8 Removing the indicator cancelling lug/horn button contact pad from the steering wheel

could lead to the steering wheel lug breaking the switch tab as the steering wheel is refitted.
10 Fit the spring to the column, then locate the wheel on the column splines, aligning the marks made on removal.
11 Fit the new lockwasher, and screw on the retaining nut **(see illustration)**. Tighten the retaining nut to the specified torque, and secure it in position with the lockwasher tabs.
12 Reconnect the wiring connectors to the horn button, and refit the button in the centre of the steering wheel.
13 Reconnect the battery, and check the operation of the horn.

Models with an air bag

 Warning: Make sure that the safety recommendations given in Chapter 12 are followed, to prevent personal injury.

Removal

14 Remove the air bag as described in Chapter 12.
15 Set the front wheels in the straight-ahead position, then lock the column in position after removing the ignition key.
16 Slacken and remove the two screws securing the wiring contact unit to the steering wheel.
17 Release the horn wiring connector from the steering wheel, and disconnect it.
18 Remove the steering wheel as described above in paragraphs 4 to 7, taking great care not to damage the wiring contact unit.
19 Disconnect the contact unit wiring connectors, and slide the contact unit off the steering column, noting its correct fitted position.

Refitting

20 Prior to installation, it is necessary to set the contact unit to its centre position. To do this, hold the outside of the unit, and rotate the centre of the contact unit anti-clockwise until sharp resistance is felt. From this point, turn the centre back through two-and-a-half turns in a clockwise direction, and align the arrow markings on the centre and outer parts of the contact unit **(see illustration)**.
21 With the contact unit correctly centralised, install the unit in the rear of the steering wheel, routing the wiring connectors through the

17.11 Fit the new lockwasher, engaging its tabs with the wheel cut-outs (arrowed)

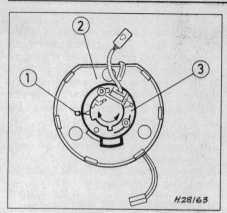

17.20 Air bag wiring contact unit. Centralise the unit as described in text before fitting it to the steering wheel

1 Arrow markings	2 Contact unit
	3 Centre

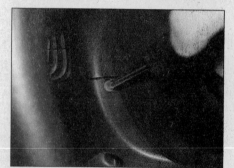

18.2 Removing an upper steering column shroud retaining screw

relevant wheel aperture, and secure it in position with the retaining screws. Reconnect the horn wiring connector and clip it into the steering wheel recess.

22 Ensure that the indicator switch stalk is in its central (OFF) position, then refit the steering wheel to the column, aligning the marks made prior to removal. When locating the steering wheel on the splines, make sure that the contact unit is correctly engaged with both the steering column and indicator switch.

23 Fit the new lockwasher, and screw on the retaining nut. Tighten the retaining nut to the specified torque, and secure it in position with the lockwasher tabs.

24 Reconnect the contact unit wiring connectors, and clip them into position on the steering column.

25 Release the steering lock, and refit the air bag as described in Chapter 12.

18 Ignition switch/ steering column lock – removal and refitting

Removal

1 Disconnect the battery negative terminal (refer to *Disconnecting the battery* in the Reference Chapter).

2 With the steering wheel in the straight-ahead position, turn the wheel 90° to the left, then prise off the trim cap and remove the left upper shroud screw **(see illustration)**. Turn

the wheel 180° to the right and remove the right upper screw. Remove the rubber seal from the ignition switch/lock, then undo the lower retaining screws and remove the lower steering column shroud. Proceed as described under the relevant sub-heading.

Lock cylinder

3 Insert the ignition key into the ignition switch/lock, and turn it to position I.

4 Insert a thin rod into the hole in the lock housing, press the rod to release the detent spring, and pull out the lock cylinder using the key **(see illustrations)**. If the lock cylinder will not come out easily, turn the key to position II and try and withdraw it.

Ignition switch wiring block

5 Disconnect the wiring connector from the ignition switch wiring block **(see illustration)**.

6 Slacken the two grub screws (one at the front and one at the rear), and withdraw the wiring block from the end of the switch housing **(see illustrations)**.

Refitting

Lock cylinder

7 Insert the ignition key into the lock cylinder. There are two different types of lock cylinder; early types have a hook on the inner end of the lock cylinder housing, and later types do not **(see illustration)**. The early-type cylinder must be installed with the key in position II, while the later type is installed with the key in position I.

8 Ensure that the centre of the ignition switch

18.4a Insert the rod (arrowed) into the lock housing hole, then with the ignition key correctly positioned (see text) . . .

18.4b . . . withdraw the lock cylinder

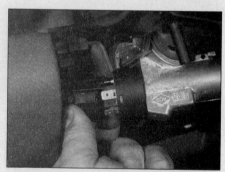

18.5 Disconnect the wiring connector . . .

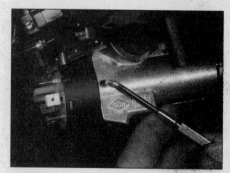

18.6a . . . then undo the grub screws . . .

18.6b . . . and remove the ignition switch wiring block

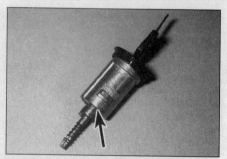

18.7 Later type of lock cylinder. Early types have a hook cast onto the end of the lock cylinder in the position indicated

18.8 Prior to installing the lock cylinder, depress the steering lock mechanism block with a screwdriver

wiring block is correctly aligned with the lock cylinder rod flats. If necessary, rotate the switch centre using a suitable screwdriver. If the steering column lock has been actuated, release the lock by depressing the locking mechanism block in the column housing **(see illustration)**.

9 Insert the cylinder into the housing until the detent spring clicks into position, then check the operation of the lock cylinder and steering lock.

10 Refit the steering column shroud, tightening its retaining screws securely, and fit the rubber to the switch/lock. Reconnect the battery.

Ignition switch wiring block

11 Refit the ignition switch to the housing, ensuring that the switch centre is correctly engaged with lock cylinder rod flats.

12 Insert both grub screws, and tighten them securely.

13 Reconnect the wiring connector to ignition switch.

14 Refit the steering column shroud, tightening its retaining screws securely. Refit the rubber to the switch/lock, and the trim caps to the upper screws.

15 Reconnect the battery negative terminal, and check the operation of the switch.

---

19 Steering column – removal, inspection and refitting

Removal

1 Disconnect the battery negative terminal (refer to *Disconnecting the battery* in the Reference Chapter).

2 Remove the steering wheel as described in Section 17. On models with an air bag, also remove the contact unit from the steering column.

3 On models without an air bag, remove the rubber seal from the ignition switch/lock, then undo the retaining screws and remove the upper and lower steering column shrouds.

4 Where necessary, undo the nut and release the support bar from the column.

5 Depress the retaining clips, and release the left- and right-hand combination switches from the column. Disconnect the wiring connectors, and remove the switches from the vehicle **(see illustration)**.

6 Disconnect the wiring connectors from the ignition switch wiring block and the horn contact, then release the wiring from the steering column **(see illustration)**.

7 Using paint or similar, make alignment marks between the steering column and intermediate shaft, then slacken and remove the clamp bolt securing the intermediate shaft to the steering column **(see illustration)**.

8 Unscrew the lower mounting bolt securing the steering column to the bulkhead **(see illustration)**.

9 Two fasteners must now be extracted from the column upper mounting bracket. A conventional nut is used on one side of the column, and a shear-head type bolt is used on the other side **(see illustration)**.

10 The shear-head bolt must be removed by drilling down the centre of the bolt, and then using a suitable bolt/stud extractor (sometimes called 'easy-outs'). When drilling the bolt, take care not to damage the facia panel or steering column. A new shear-head bolt will obviously be required for refitting.

11 Release the column assembly from its mountings, then detach it from the intermediate shaft and remove it from the vehicle **(see illustration)**. Handle the column carefully, avoiding knocks or impact of any kind, which may damage the collapsible section of the column housing.

Inspection

12 The steering column incorporates a telescopic safety section. In the event of a front-end crash, the shaft housing collapses,

19.5 Depress the retaining clips, and slide the combination switches out from the column . . .

19.6 . . . and disconnect the wiring connector from the horn contact pin (arrowed)

19.7 Steering column-to-intermediate shaft clamp bolt (arrowed)

19.8 Steering column lower mounting bolt

19.9 Steering column upper mounting nut (A) and shear-head bolt (B)

19.11 Removing the steering column

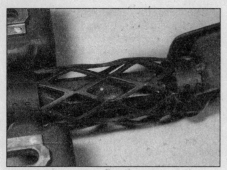

19.12 Inspect the collapsible section of the column for signs of damage, and renew the column assembly if necessary

19.14 Use a new shear-head bolt when refitting the column

and prevents the steering wheel injuring the driver. Before refitting the steering column, examine the column and mountings for signs of damage and deformation, and check the steering shaft for signs of free play in the column bushes **(see illustration)**. If there are signs of damage or play, the column must be renewed. On models not fitted with an air bag, overhaul of the column is possible, but this is a difficult task which should really be entrusted to a Vauxhall/Opel dealer. Consult your dealer for further information.

Refitting

13 Manoeuvre the steering column into position, and engage it with the intermediate shaft universal joint, aligning the marks made on removal.
14 Refit the column upper and lower mounting nut/bolts, and the new shear-head bolt. Tighten all bolts by hand only at this stage **(see illustration)**.
15 Align the intermediate shaft bolt hole with the steering column shaft cut-out so that the clamp bolt can be slid into position. Tighten the bolt by hand only.
16 Tighten the column mounting bolts to the specified torque setting. Tighten the shear-head bolt until its head breaks off.
17 Tighten the clamp bolt to the specified torque setting.
18 Ensure that the wiring is correctly routed, and reconnect it to the ignition switch wiring block and horn contact.
19 Clip the left-and right-hand switches back

into position, and reconnect their wiring connectors.
20 Where necessary, refit the support strut to the column, and securely tighten its retaining nut.
21 On models without an air bag, clip the steering column shrouds into position, and securely tighten the retaining screws. Refit the rubber seal to the ignition switch/lock, then refit the steering wheel as described in Section 17.
22 On models with an air bag, refit the contact unit and steering wheel as described in Section 17.

20 Steering column intermediate shaft – removal, inspection and refitting

Removal

1 Set the front wheels in the straight-ahead position.
2 Using paint or a suitable marker pen, make alignment marks between the intermediate shaft joints and the steering column and steering gear shafts.
3 Slacken and remove the upper clamp bolt and the lower clamp bolt and nut **(see illustrations)**.
4 Disengage the shaft universal joint from the steering column, then slide the shaft from the steering gear pinion and remove it from the vehicle **(see illustration)**.

Inspection

5 Inspect the intermediate shaft universal joint for signs of roughness in its bearings and ease of movement. If either joint is damaged in any way, the complete shaft assembly must be renewed.

Refitting

6 Check that the front wheels are still in the straight-ahead position, and that the steering wheel is correctly positioned.
7 Aligning the marks made on removal, engage the shaft with the steering gear pinion, then locate the universal joint on the steering column end. Install both clamp bolts, tightening them to the specified torque setting.

21 Steering gear assembly – removal, overhaul and refitting

Note: *New track rod balljoint-to-swivel hub nuts will be required when refitting.*

Removal

1 Firmly apply the handbrake, then jack up the front of the car and support it securely on axle stands (see *Jacking and vehicle support*). Remove both front roadwheels.

Manual steering gear

2 Referring to Chapter 2A, support the weight of the engine/transmission unit, and remove the rear engine/transmission mounting rubber and bracket from the vehicle.
3 On models with manual transmission, disconnect the gearchange linkage from the transmission as described in Chapter 7.
4 Slacken and remove the nuts securing the steering gear track rod balljoints to the swivel hubs **(see illustration)**, and release the balljoint tapered shanks using a universal balljoint separator. Discard the nuts; they should be renewed whenever they are disturbed.
5 Remove the intermediate shaft as described in Section 20.
6 Prior to removal, mark the position of the mounting rubbers on the steering gear

20.3a Slacken and remove the steering column-to-intermediate shaft clamp bolt . . .

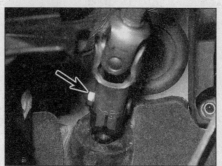

20.3b . . . and the intermediate shaft-to-steering gear clamp bolt and nut (arrowed)

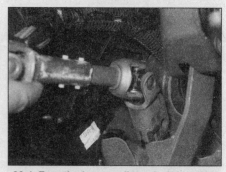

20.4 Free the intermediate shaft from the column and steering gear, and remove it from under the facia

housing. These marks can then be used on refitting to ensure that the steering gear is correctly positioned in the clamps.

7 Slacken and remove the four nuts and washers securing the steering gear to the bulkhead. Note the correct fitted locations of any relevant brackets retained by the nuts, then remove the steering gear mounting clamp(s) **(see illustration)**.

8 Detach the rubber gaiter from the bulkhead, and free the steering gear pinion from the intermediate shaft.

9 Move the steering gear towards the right-hand side of the engine compartment, then lower the left-hand end of the assembly, and manoeuvre the assembly out from underneath the vehicle. Note that it may be necessary to lower the engine slightly to gain the necessary clearance for removal.

Power-assisted steering gear

10 Remove the air cleaner assembly as described in Chapter 4A.

11 On left-hand drive models, to improve access to the steering gear, remove the braking system vacuum servo unit as described in Chapter 9.

12 Remove the intermediate shaft as described in Section 20.

13 On models with manual transmission, disconnect the gearchange linkage from the transmission as described in Chapter 7, and unbolt the clutch cable bracket from the bulkhead. Additionally, on models with electronic power steering, disconnect the end of the clutch cable from the gearbox as described in Chapter 6.

14 Slacken and remove the nuts securing the steering gear track rod balljoints to the swivel hubs, and release the balljoint tapered shanks using a universal balljoint separator. Discard the nuts; they should be renewed whenever they are disturbed.

15 On models with hydraulic power steering, using brake hose clamps, clamp both the supply and return hoses near the power steering fluid reservoir. Mark the unions to ensure that they are correctly positioned on reassembly, then unscrew the feed and return pipe union nuts from the steering gear assembly; be prepared for fluid spillage, and position a suitable container beneath the pipes whilst unscrewing the union nuts **(see illustration)**. Disconnect both pipes, and plug the pipe ends and steering gear orifices, to prevent excessive fluid leakage and the entry of dirt into the hydraulic system.

16 Free the power steering pipes from any relevant retaining clips, and position them clear of the steering gear so that they will not hinder the removal procedure.

17 Referring to Chapter 2A, support the weight of the engine/transmission unit, and remove the rear engine/transmission mounting rubber and bracket from the vehicle.

18 Prior to removal, mark the position of the mounting rubbers on the steering gear

21.4 Unscrew the retaining nuts securing each track rod balljoint to the swivel hubs

housing. These marks can then be used on refitting to ensure that the steering gear is correctly positioned in the clamps.

19 Slacken and remove the four nuts and washers securing the steering gear to the bulkhead. Note the correct fitted locations of any relevant brackets retained by the nuts, then remove the steering gear mounting clamp(s).

20 On models with air conditioning, release the refrigerant pipes from their retaining clips on the bulkhead. **Note:** *Refer to the warning notes in Chapter 3 – do not attempt to disconnect any of the pipes.*

21 Release the rubber gaiter from the bulkhead, then move the steering gear fully towards the right on right-hand drive models, or the left on left-hand drive models. Lower the opposite end of the steering gear, and manoeuvre the assembly out from underneath the vehicle.

Overhaul

22 Examine the steering gear assembly for signs of wear or damage, and check that the rack moves freely throughout the full length of its travel, with no signs of roughness or excessive free play between the steering gear pinion and rack. It is possible to overhaul the steering gear assembly housing components, but this task should be entrusted to a Vauxhall/Opel dealer. The only components which can be renewed easily by the home mechanic are the steering gear gaiters, the track rod balljoints and the track rods (manual steering gear only). Steering gear gaiter, track rod balljoint and track rod renewal procedures are covered in Sections 24, 25 and 26 respectively.

23 On models with hydraulic power-assisted steering, inspect all the steering gear fluid unions for signs of leakage, and check that all union nuts are securely tightened.

24 Inspect the rubber mountings and pinion gear rubber gaiter, and renew them if they show signs of wear or deterioration.

Refitting

Manual steering gear

25 Fit the mounting rubbers to the steering gear, and align them with the marks made

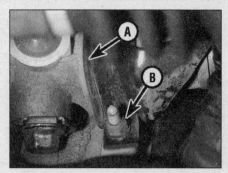

21.7 Steering gear mounting rubber (A) and mounting clamp and nut (B) – viewed from underneath

prior to removal. If a new steering gear assembly is being installed, transfer the marks from the original onto the new assembly.

26 Manoeuvre the steering gear assembly back into position on the bulkhead. With the pinion correctly located in the bulkhead aperture, refit the mounting clamps and retaining nuts, not forgetting to fit the necessary brackets to steering gear mounting studs.

27 Ensure that the rubbers are correctly aligned with the marks made on removal, and tighten the mounting clamp nuts to the specified torque setting.

28 The remainder of refitting is reverse of the removal procedure, noting the following points:

a) *Refit the intermediate shaft as described in Section 20.*

b) *Locate the track rod balljoints in position, fit the new nuts and tighten them to the specified torque.*

c) *Connect the gearchange linkage as described in Chapter 7.*

d) *Refit the engine/transmission mounting as described in Chapter 2A.*

e) *Refit the air cleaner assembly as described in Chapter 4A.*

f) *On completion, check and, if necessary, adjust the front wheel alignment as described in Section 27.*

Power-assisted steering gear

29 Install the steering gear as described above in paragraphs 25 to 27.

21.15 Hydraulic power-assisted steering gear fluid feed and return pipe unions (arrowed) – shown with engine removed for clarity

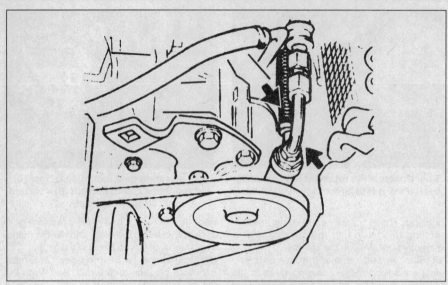
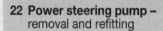

22.5 Power steering pump fluid lines

30 Wipe clean the feed and return pipe unions, and refit them to their respective unions on the steering gear. Tighten the union nuts to the specified torque setting, and ensure that the pipes are securely retained by all the necessary retaining clips.

31 The remainder of the refitting procedure is a direct reversal of the removal sequence, noting the following points:

  a) Refit the intermediate shaft as described in Section 20, and ensure that the rubber gaiter is correctly seated in the bulkhead.

  b) On models with air conditioning, ensure that the refrigerant pipes are securely retained by all the necessary clips.

  c) Locate the track rod balljoints in position, fit the new nuts and tighten them to the specified torque.

  d) Connect the gearchange linkage as described in Chapter 7.

  e) Refit the engine/transmission mounting(s) as described in Chapter 2A.

  f) On completion, remove the clamps from the hoses, and bleed the hydraulic system as described in Section 23.

  g) Check and, if necessary, adjust the front wheel alignment as described in Section 27.

22 Power steering pump –
removed and refitting

Removal

1 Remove the air cleaner assembly as described in Chapter 4A.

2 On models with air conditioning, remove the compressor as described in Chapter 3.

3 Using hose clamps, clamp both the supply and return hoses near the reservoir. Alternatively, unscrew the cap from the power steering hydraulic fluid reservoir, then syphon the fluid into a container. An old poultry baster or hydrometer can be used to draw out the fluid.

4 Remove the auxiliary drivebelt as described in Chapter 1 and remove the tensioning screw. Mark the drivebelt with the direction of travel to ensure correct refitting.

5 Position a container beneath the power steering pump to catch spilled fluid, then unscrew the union bolt and disconnect the pressure line from the pump **(see illustration).**

6 Release the clip and disconnect the return line from the pump. Plug the fluid lines and openings to prevent entry of dust and dirt.

7 Unscrew the mounting bolt and withdraw the power steering pump together with the retaining tie from the bracket on the engine **(see illustrations).** Wrap the pump in cloth rags to prevent fluid being spilt on the vehicle paintwork.

Refitting

8 Locate the power steering pump and retaining tie on the bracket, then insert the bolt and tighten to the specified torque.

9 Reconnect the return line and secure with the clip.

10 Reconnect the pressure line and refit the union bolt. Tighten the union bolt to the specified torque. Remove any hose clamps fitted.

11 Refit the tensioning screw then refit and tension the auxiliary drivebelt as described in Chapter 1.

12 On models with air conditioning, refit the compressor as described in Chapter 3.

13 Refit the air cleaner as described in Chapter 4A.

14 Fill the hydraulic fluid reservoir with fresh fluid and bleed the system as described in Section 23.

23 Power steering system –
bleeding

1 With the engine stopped, fill the fluid reservoir right up to the brim with the specified type of fluid. This is more important if fluid has been lost after work has been carried out, or if the system has been leaking. Otherwise, top the level up to the relevant mark (see paragraph 5).

2 Have an assistant start the engine, while you keep watch on the fluid level. Be prepared to add more fluid as the engine starts, as the fluid level may drop quickly. The fluid level must be kept above the MIN mark at all times, or air will be drawn into the system.

3 With the engine running at idle speed, turn the steering wheel slowly two or three times approximately 45° to the left and right of the centre, then turn the wheel twice from lock-to-lock. Do not hold the wheel on either lock, as this places strain on the hydraulic system. Repeat this procedure until bubbles cease to appear in fluid reservoir, topping-up as necessary.

4 If, when turning the steering, an abnormal noise is heard from the fluid lines, it indicates that there is still air in the system. Check this by turning the wheels to the straight-ahead position and switching off the engine. If the fluid level in the reservoir rises, then air is present in the system, and further bleeding is necessary.

5 Once all air is removed from the system, stop the engine and check the fluid level. With

22.7a Remove the power steering pump mounting bolts . . .

22.7b . . . and remove the pump

the fluid at operating temperature (80°C), the level should be on the MAX mark; with the fluid cold (20°C), the level should be on the MIN mark. Correct the level by topping-up, or by removing fluid using a syringe or similar, as necessary.

24 Steering gear rubber gaiters – renewal

1 Remove the track rod balljoint as described in Section 25.
2 Mark the correct fitted position of the gaiter on the track rod, then release the retaining clips, and slide the gaiter off the steering gear housing and track rod end.
3 Thoroughly clean the track rod and the steering gear housing, using fine abrasive paper to polish off any corrosion, burrs or sharp edges which might damage the new gaiter's sealing lips on installation. Scrape off all grease from the old gaiter, and apply to the track rod inner balljoint.
4 Carefully slide the new gaiter onto the track rod end, and locate it on the steering gear housing. Align the outer edge of the gaiter with the mark made on the track rod prior to removal, then secure it in position with new retaining clips.
5 Refit the track rod balljoint as described in Section 25.

25 Track rod balljoint – removal and refitting

Note: *A new track rod balljoint-to-swivel hub nut will be required when refitting.*

Removal

1 Firmly apply the handbrake, then jack up the front of the car and support it securely on axle stands (see *Jacking and vehicle support*). Remove the appropriate front roadwheel.
2 If the balljoint is to be re-used, use a straight-edge and a scriber, or similar, to mark its relationship to the track rod.
3 Hold the track rod, and unscrew the balljoint locknut by a quarter of a turn.
4 Slacken and remove the nut securing the track rod balljoint to the swivel hub, and release the balljoint tapered shank using a universal balljoint separator **(see illustration)**. Discard the nut; a new one must be used of refitting.
5 Counting the exact number of turns necessary to do so, unscrew the balljoint from the track rod end.
6 Count the number of exposed threads between the end of the track rod and the locknut, and record this figure. If a new gaiter is to be fitted, unscrew the locknut from the track rod.
7 Carefully clean the balljoint and the track rod threads. Renew the balljoint if there is

excessive free play of the balljoint shank, or if the shank is excessively stiff. If the balljoint gaiter is damaged, the complete balljoint assembly must be renewed; it is not possible to obtain the gaiter separately.

Refitting

8 If it was removed, screw the locknut onto the track rod threads, and position it so that the same number of exposed threads are visible as was noted prior to removal.
9 Screw the balljoint into the track rod by the number of turns noted on removal. This should bring the balljoint locknut to within a quarter of a turn from the locknut, with the alignment marks that were made (if applicable) on removal lined up.
10 Refit the balljoint shank to the swivel hub, then fit a new retaining nut and tighten it to the specified torque setting.
11 Refit the roadwheel, then lower the vehicle to the ground and tighten the roadwheel bolts to the specified torque setting.
12 Check and, if necessary, adjust the front wheel toe setting as described in Section 27. Tighten the balljoint locknut to the specified torque setting on completion.

26 Track rod – renewal

Manual steering gear

Note: *When refitting, a new track rod balljoint-to-swivel hub nut, and new gaiter retaining clips, will be required.*
1 Remove the track rod balljoint as described in Section 25.
2 Release the retaining clips, and slide the steering gear gaiter off the end of the track rod as described in Section 24.
3 Extend the steering rack from the housing. Prevent the rack from rotating using an open-ended spanner located on the rack flats, and slacken the track rod inner balljoint from the rack end.
4 Unscrew the track rod assembly, and remove it along with its spacer.
5 Remove the track rod assembly, and

25.4 Release the track rod balljoint from the swivel hub using a universal balljoint separator

examine the track rod inner balljoint for signs of slackness or tight spots. Check that the track rod itself is straight and free from damage. If necessary, renew the track rod; it is also recommended that the steering gear gaiter/dust cover is renewed.
6 Locate the spacer on the end of the steering rack, and screw the balljoint into the steering rack. Tighten the track rod balljoint to the specified torque, whilst retaining the steering rack with an open-ended spanner.
7 Install the steering gaiter and track rod balljoint as described in Sections 24 and 25.

Power-assisted steering gear

8 On models with either hydraulic, or electronic power-assisted steering, the track rods are not available separately. If a track rod is damaged in any way, the complete steering gear assembly must be renewed. Refer to your Vauxhall/Opel dealer for further information on parts availability.

27 Wheel alignment and steering angles – general information

1 Accurate front wheel alignment is essential for precise steering and handling, and for even tyre wear. Before carrying out any checking or adjusting operations, make sure that the tyres are correctly inflated, that all steering and suspension joints and linkages are in sound condition, and that the wheels are not buckled or distorted, particularly around the rims. It will also be necessary to have the vehicle positioned on flat, level ground, with enough space to push the car backwards and forwards through about half its length.
2 Front wheel alignment consists of four factors **(see illustration overleaf)**:
   Camber is the angle at which the roadwheels are set from the vertical, when viewed from the front or rear of the vehicle. Positive camber is the angle (in degrees) that the wheels are tilted outwards at the top from the vertical.
   Castor is the angle between the steering axis and a vertical line when viewed from each side of the vehicle. Positive castor is indicated when the steering axis is inclined towards the rear of the vehicle at its upper end.
   Steering axis inclination is the angle, when viewed from the front or rear of the vehicle, between the vertical and an imaginary line drawn between the upper and lower front suspension strut mountings.
   Toe setting is the amount by which the distance between the front inside edges of the roadwheels differs from that between the rear inside edges, when measured at hub height. If the distance between the front edges is less than at the rear, the wheels are said to 'toe-in'. If it is greater than at the rear, the wheels are said to 'toe-out'.
3 Camber, castor and steering axis inclination

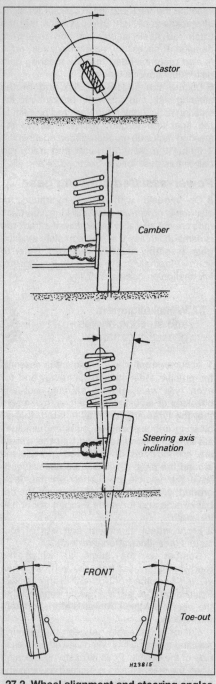

Castor

Camber

Steering axis
inclination

FRONT

Toe-out

H23815

27.2 Wheel alignment and steering angles

are set during manufacture, and are not adjustable. Unless the vehicle has suffered accident damage, or there is gross wear in the suspension mountings or joints, it can be assumed that these settings are correct. If for any reason it is believed that they are not correct, the task of checking them should be left to a Vauxhall/Opel dealer, who will have the necessary special equipment needed to measure the small angles involved.

4 It is, however, within the scope of the home mechanic to check and adjust the front wheel toe setting. To do this, a tracking gauge must first be obtained. Two types of gauge are available, and can be obtained from motor accessory shops. The first type measures the distance between the front and rear inside edges of the roadwheels, as previously described, with the vehicle stationary. The second type, known as a 'scuff plate', measures the actual position of the contact surface of the tyre, in relation to the road surface, with the vehicle in motion. This is achieved by pushing or driving the front tyre over a plate, which then moves slightly according to the scuff of the tyre, and shows this movement on a scale. Both types have their advantages and disadvantages, but either can give satisfactory results if used correctly and carefully.

5 Many tyre specialists will also check toe settings free, or for a nominal charge. Considering the initial cost of obtaining a tracking gauge, and then becoming experienced with its use, it may actually be beneficial to have the whole job done by a tyre specialist or similar company. The actual procedure for using a tracking gauge is, however, outlined in the following paragraphs to show the work involved.

6 Make sure that the steering is in the straight-ahead position when making measurements.

7 If adjustment is necessary, chock the rear wheels, apply the handbrake, then jack up the front of the vehicle and support it securely on axle stands. Turn the steering wheel onto full-left lock, and record the number of exposed threads on the right-hand track rod end. Now turn the steering onto full-right lock, and

record the number of threads on the left-hand side. If there are the same number of threads visible on both sides, then subsequent adjustment should be made equally on both sides. If there are more threads visible on one side than the other, it will be necessary to compensate for this during adjustment. It is most important that, after adjustment, the same number of threads are visible on each track rod end.

8 First clean the track rod threads; if they are corroded, apply penetrating fluid before starting adjustment. Release the rubber gaiter outer clips, then peel back the gaiters and apply a smear of grease, so that the gaiters will not be twisted or strained as their respective track rods are rotated.

9 Use a straight-edge and a scriber, or similar, to mark the relationship of each track rod to its balljoint then, holding each track rod in turn, unscrew its locknut fully.

10 Alter the length of the track rods, bearing in mind the note made in paragraph 7, screwing them into or out of the balljoints by rotating the track rod using an open-ended spanner fitted to the track rod flats provided. Shortening the track rods (screwing them into their balljoints) will reduce toe-in/increase toe-out.

11 When the setting is correct, hold the track rods and securely tighten the balljoint locknuts. Check that the balljoints are seated correctly in their sockets, and count the exposed threads to check the length of both track rods. If they are not the same, then the adjustment has not been made equally, and problems will be encountered with tyre scrubbing in turns; also, the steering wheel spokes will no longer be horizontal when the wheels are in the straight-ahead position.

12 If the track rod lengths are the same, check that the toe setting has been correctly adjusted by lowering the vehicle to the ground and re-checking the toe setting; re-adjust if necessary. If the setting is correct, tighten the track rod balljoint locknuts to the specified torque setting. Ensure that the rubber gaiters are seated correctly and are not twisted or strained, and secure them in position with the retaining clips.

Chapter 11
Bodywork and fittings

Contents

Degrees of difficulty

Easy, suitable for novice with little experience	**Fairly easy,** suitable for beginner with some experience	**Fairly difficult,** suitable for competent DIY mechanic	**Difficult,** suitable for experienced DIY mechanic	**Very difficult,** suitable for expert DIY or professional

Specifications

Torque wrench settings	Nm	lbf ft
Facia fasteners:		
Facia end screws	6	4
Facia-to-bulkhead nuts	22	16
Support bracket screws	6	4
Front seat bolts	20	15
Rear seat:		
Corsa and Corsavan (split rear seat):		
Seat back-to-bracket bolts	30	22
Seat back-to-hinge bolts	20	15
Combo Van:		
Seat back bolts	20	15
Seat belt anchorage bolts	35	26
Seat belt height adjuster ratchet bolts	20	15
Seat belt inertia reel bolt	35	26

1 General information

The bodyshell is made of pressed-steel sections, and is available in three- and five-door Hatchback versions, as well as two different forms of Van. Most components are welded together, but some use is made of structural adhesives; the front wings are bolted on.

The bonnet, doors, and some other vulnerable panels, are made of zinc-coated metal, and are further protected by being coated with an anti-chip primer, prior to being sprayed.

Extensive use is made of plastic materials, mainly on the interior, but also in exterior components. The front and rear bumpers are injection-moulded from a synthetic material which is very strong and yet light. Plastic components such as wheelarch liners are fitted to the underside of the vehicle, to improve the body's resistance to corrosion.

2 Maintenance – bodywork and underframe

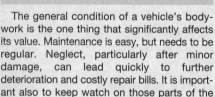

The general condition of a vehicle's bodywork is the one thing that significantly affects its value. Maintenance is easy, but needs to be regular. Neglect, particularly after minor damage, can lead quickly to further deterioration and costly repair bills. It is important also to keep watch on those parts of the vehicle not immediately visible, for instance the underside, inside all the wheelarches, and the lower part of the engine compartment.

The basic maintenance routine for the bodywork is washing – preferably with a lot of water, from a hose. This will remove all the loose solids which may have stuck to the vehicle. It is important to flush these off in such a way as to prevent grit from scratching the finish. The wheelarches and underframe need washing in the same way, to remove any accumulated mud, which will retain moisture and tend to encourage rust. Paradoxically enough, the best time to clean the underframe and wheelarches is in wet weather, when the mud is thoroughly wet and soft. In very wet weather, the underframe is usually cleaned of large accumulations automatically, and this is a good time for inspection.

Periodically, except on vehicles with a wax-based underbody protective coating, it is a good idea to have the whole of the underframe of the vehicle steam-cleaned, engine compartment included, so that a thorough inspection can be carried out to see what minor repairs and renovations are necessary. Steam-cleaning is available at many garages, and is necessary for the removal of the accumulation of oily grime, which sometimes is allowed to become thick in certain areas. If steam-cleaning facilities are not available, there are some excellent grease solvents available which can be brush-applied; the dirt can then be simply hosed off. Note that these methods should not be used on vehicles with wax-based underbody protective coating, or the coating will be removed. Such vehicles should be inspected annually, preferably just prior to Winter, when the underbody should be washed down, and any damage to the wax coating repaired. Ideally, a completely fresh coat should be applied. It would also be worth considering the use of such wax-based protection for injection into door panels, sills, box sections, etc, as an additional safeguard against rust damage, where such protection is not provided by the vehicle manufacturer.

After washing paintwork, wipe off with a chamois leather to give an unspotted clear finish. A coat of clear protective wax polish will give added protection against chemical pollutants in the air. If the paintwork sheen has dulled or oxidised, use a cleaner/polisher combination to restore the brilliance of the shine. This requires a little effort, but such dulling is usually caused because regular washing has been neglected. Care needs to be taken with metallic paintwork, as special non-abrasive cleaner/polisher is required to avoid damage to the finish. Always check that the door and ventilator opening drain holes and pipes are completely clear, so that water can be drained out. Brightwork should be treated in the same way as paintwork. Windscreens and windows can be kept clear of the smeary film which often appears, by the use of proprietary glass cleaner. Never use any form of wax or other body or chromium polish on glass.

3 Maintenance – upholstery and carpets

Mats and carpets should be brushed or vacuum-cleaned regularly, to keep them free of grit. If they are badly stained, remove them from the vehicle for scrubbing or sponging, and make quite sure they are dry before refitting. Seats and interior trim panels can be kept clean by wiping with a damp cloth. If they do become stained (which can be more apparent on light-coloured upholstery), use a little liquid detergent and a soft nail brush to scour the grime out of the grain of the material. Do not forget to keep the headlining clean in the same way as the upholstery. When using liquid cleaners inside the vehicle, do not over-wet the surfaces being cleaned. Excessive damp could get into the seams and padded interior, causing stains, offensive odours or even rot.

> **HAYNES HiNT** *If the inside of the vehicle gets wet accidentally, it is worthwhile taking some trouble to dry it out properly, particularly where carpets are involved. Do not leave oil or electric heaters inside the vehicle for this purpose.*

4 Minor body damage – repair

Repairs of minor scratches

If the scratch is very superficial, and does not penetrate to the metal of the bodywork, repair is very simple. Lightly rub the area of the scratch with a paintwork renovator, or a very fine cutting paste, to remove loose paint from the scratch, and to clear the surrounding bodywork of wax polish. Rinse the area with clean water.

Apply touch-up paint to the scratch using a fine paint brush; continue to apply fine layers of paint until the surface of the paint in the scratch is level with the surrounding paintwork. Allow the new paint at least two weeks to harden, then blend it into the surrounding paintwork by rubbing the scratch area with a paintwork renovator or a very fine cutting paste. Finally, apply wax polish.

Where the scratch has penetrated right through to the metal of the bodywork, causing the metal to rust, a different repair technique is required. Remove any loose rust from the bottom of the scratch with a penknife, then apply rust-inhibiting paint to prevent the formation of rust in the future. Using a rubber or nylon applicator, fill the scratch with bodystopper paste. If required, this paste can be mixed with cellulose thinners to provide a very thin paste which is ideal for filling narrow scratches. Before the stopper-paste in the scratch hardens, wrap a piece of smooth cotton rag around the top of a finger. Dip the finger in cellulose thinners, and quickly sweep it across the surface of the stopper-paste in the scratch; this will ensure that the surface of the stopper-paste is slightly hollowed. The scratch can now be painted over as described earlier in this Section.

Repairs of dents

When deep denting of the vehicle's bodywork has taken place, the first task is to pull the dent out, until the affected bodywork almost attains its original shape. There is little point in trying to restore the original shape completely, as the metal in the damaged area will have stretched on impact, and cannot be reshaped fully to its original contour. It is better to bring the level of the dent up to a point which is about 3 mm below the level of the surrounding bodywork. In cases where the dent is very shallow anyway, it is not worth trying to pull it out at all. If the underside of the dent is accessible, it can be hammered out gently from behind, using a mallet with a wooden or plastic head. Whilst doing this, hold a suitable block of wood firmly against the outside of the panel, to absorb the impact from the hammer blows and thus prevent a large area of the bodywork from being 'belled-out'.

Should the dent be in a section of the bodywork which has a double skin, or some other factor making it inaccessible from behind, a different technique is called for. Drill several small holes through the metal inside the area – particularly in the deeper section. Then screw long self-tapping screws into the holes, just sufficiently for them to gain a good purchase in the metal. Now the dent can be pulled out by pulling on the protruding heads of the screws with a pair of pliers.

The next stage of the repair is the removal of the paint from the damaged area, and from an inch or so of the surrounding 'sound' bodywork. This is accomplished most easily by using a wire brush or abrasive pad on a power drill, although it can be done just as effectively by hand, using sheets of abrasive paper. To complete the preparation for filling, score the surface of the bare metal with a screwdriver or the tang of a file, or alternatively, drill small holes in the affected area. This will provide a really good 'key' for the filler paste.

To complete the repair, see the Section on filling and respraying.

Repairs of rust holes or gashes

Remove all paint from the affected area, and from an inch or so of the surrounding 'sound' bodywork, using an abrasive pad or a wire brush on a power drill. If these are not available, a few sheets of abrasive paper will do the job most effectively. With the paint removed, you will be able to judge the severity of the corrosion, and therefore decide whether to renew the whole panel (if this is possible) or to repair the affected area. New body panels are not as expensive as most people think, and it is often quicker and more satisfactory to fit a new panel than to attempt to repair large areas of corrosion.

Remove all fittings from the affected area, except those which will act as a guide to the original shape of the damaged bodywork (eg headlight shells etc). Then, using tin snips or a hacksaw blade, remove all loose metal and any other metal badly affected by corrosion. Hammer the edges of the hole inwards, in order to create a slight depression for the filler paste.

Wire-brush the affected area to remove the powdery rust from the surface of the remaining metal. Paint the affected area with rust-inhibiting paint, if the back of the rusted area is accessible, treat this also.

Before filling can take place, it will be necessary to block the hole in some way. This can be achieved by the use of aluminium or plastic mesh, or aluminium tape.

Aluminium or plastic mesh, or glass-fibre matting, is probably the best material to use for a large hole. Cut a piece to the approximate size and shape of the hole to be filled, then position it in the hole so that its edges are below the level of the surrounding bodywork. It can be retained in position by several blobs of filler paste around its periphery.

Aluminium tape should be used for small or very narrow holes. Pull a piece off the roll, trim it to the approximate size and shape required, then pull off the backing paper (if used) and stick the tape over the hole; it can be overlapped if the thickness of one piece is insufficient. Burnish down the edges of the tape with the handle of a screwdriver or similar, to ensure that the tape is securely attached to the metal underneath.

Filling and respraying

Before using this Section, see the Sections on dent, deep scratch, rust holes and gash repairs.

Many types of bodyfiller are available, but generally speaking, those proprietary kits which contain a tin of filler paste and a tube of resin hardener are best for this type of repair. A wide, flexible plastic or nylon applicator will be found invaluable for imparting a smooth and well-contoured finish to the surface of the filler.

Mix up a little filler on a clean piece of card or board – measure the hardener carefully (follow the maker's instructions on the pack), otherwise the filler will set too rapidly or too slowly. Using the applicator, apply the filler paste to the prepared area; draw the applicator across the surface of the filler to achieve the correct contour and to level the surface. As soon as a contour that approximates to the correct one is achieved, stop working the paste – if you carry on too long, the paste will become sticky and begin to 'pick-up' on the applicator. Continue to add thin layers of filler paste at 20-minute intervals, until the level of the filler is just proud of the surrounding bodywork.

Once the filler has hardened, the excess can be removed using a metal plane or file. From then on, progressively-finer grades of abrasive paper should be used, starting with a 40-grade production paper, and finishing with a 400-grade wet-and-dry paper. Always wrap the abrasive paper around a flat rubber, cork, or wooden block – otherwise the surface of the filler will not be completely flat. During the smoothing of the filler surface, the wet-and-dry paper should be periodically rinsed in water. This will ensure that a very smooth finish is imparted to the filler at the final stage.

At this stage, the 'dent' should be surrounded by a ring of bare metal, which in turn should be encircled by the finely 'feathered' edge of the good paintwork. Rinse the repair area with clean water, until all of the dust produced by the rubbing-down operation has gone.

Spray the whole area with a light coat of primer – this will show up any imperfections in the surface of the filler. Repair these imperfections with fresh filler paste or bodystopper, and once more smooth the surface with abrasive paper. Repeat this spray-and-repair procedure until you are satisfied that the surface of the filler, and the feathered edge of the paintwork, are perfect. Clean the repair area with clean water, and allow to dry fully.

HAYNES HINT

If bodystopper is used, it can be mixed with cellulose thinners to form a really thin paste which is ideal for filling small holes.

The repair area is now ready for final spraying. Paint spraying must be carried out in a warm, dry, windless and dust-free atmosphere. This condition can be created artificially if you have access to a large indoor working area, but if you are forced to work in the open, you will have to pick your day very carefully. If you are working indoors, dousing the floor in the work area with water will help to settle the dust which would otherwise be in the atmosphere. If the repair area is confined to one body panel, mask off the surrounding panels; this will help to minimise the effects of a slight mis-match in paint colours. Bodywork fittings (eg chrome strips, door handles etc) will also need to be masked off. Use genuine masking tape, and several thicknesses of newspaper, for the masking operations.

Before commencing to spray, agitate the aerosol can thoroughly, then spray a test area (an old tin, or similar) until the technique is mastered. Cover the repair area with a thick coat of primer; the thickness should be built up using several thin layers of paint, rather than one thick one. Using 400-grade wet-and-dry paper, rub down the surface of the primer until it is really smooth. While doing this, the work area should be thoroughly doused with water, and the wet-and-dry paper periodically rinsed in water. Allow to dry before spraying on more paint.

Spray on the top coat, again building up the thickness by using several thin layers of paint. Start spraying at one edge of the repair area, and then, using a side-to-side motion, work until the whole repair area and about 2 inches of the surrounding original paintwork is covered. Remove all masking material 10 to 15 minutes after spraying on the final coat of paint.

Allow the new paint at least two weeks to harden, then, using a paintwork renovator, or a very fine cutting paste, blend the edges of the paint into the existing paintwork. Finally, apply wax polish.

Plastic components

With the use of more and more plastic body components by the vehicle manufacturers (eg bumpers. spoilers, and in some cases major body panels), rectification of more serious damage to such items has become a matter of either entrusting repair work to a specialist in this field, or renewing complete components. Repair of such damage by the DIY owner is not really feasible, owing to the cost of the equipment and materials required for effecting such repairs. The basic technique involves making a groove along the line of the crack in the plastic, using a rotary burr in a power drill. The damaged part is then welded

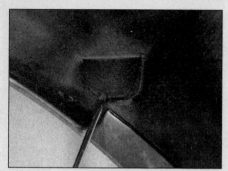

6.2a Unclip the access cover in the wheelarch liner . . .

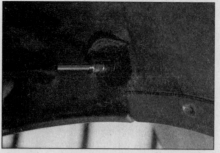

6.2b . . . to gain access to the bumper retaining nut (viewed from underneath the wheelarch liner)

6.3 Unscrew the bolts securing the bumper mounting brackets to the crossmember, one on each side of the radiator grille aperture

back together, using a hot-air gun to heat up and fuse a plastic filler rod into the groove. Any excess plastic is then removed, and the area rubbed down to a smooth finish. It is important that a filler rod of the correct plastic is used, as body components can be made of a variety of different types (eg polycarbonate, ABS, polypropylene).

Damage of a less serious nature (abrasions, minor cracks etc) can be repaired by the DIY owner using a two-part epoxy filler repair material. Once mixed in equal proportions, this is used in similar fashion to the bodywork filler used on metal panels. The filler is usually cured in twenty to thirty minutes, ready for sanding and painting.

If the owner is renewing a complete component himself, or if he has repaired it with epoxy filler, he will be left with the problem of finding a suitable paint for finishing which is compatible with the type of plastic used. At one time, the use of a universal paint was not possible, owing to the complex range of plastics encountered in body component applications. Standard paints, generally speaking, will not bond to plastic or rubber satisfactorily. However, it is now possible to obtain a plastic body parts finishing kit which consists of a pre-primer treatment, a primer and coloured top coat. Full instructions are normally supplied with a kit, but basically, the method of use is to first apply the pre-primer to the component concerned, and allow it to dry for up to 30 minutes. Then the primer is applied, and left to dry for about an hour before finally applying the special-coloured

top coat. The result is a correctly-coloured component, where the paint will flex with the plastic or rubber, a property that standard paint does not normally possess.

5 Major body damage – repair

Where serious damage has occurred, or large areas need renewal due to neglect, it means that complete new panels will need welding-in, and this is best left to professionals. If the damage is due to impact, it will also be necessary to check completely the alignment of the bodyshell, and this can only be carried out accurately by a Vauxhall/Opel dealer, using special jigs. If the body is left misaligned, it is primarily dangerous as the car will not handle properly, and secondly, uneven stresses will be imposed on the steering, suspension and possibly transmission, causing abnormal wear, or complete failure, particularly to such items as the tyres.

6 Front bumper – removal and refitting

Removal

1 Firmly apply the handbrake, then jack up the front of the car and support it securely on axle stands (see *Jacking and vehicle support*).

2 Unclip the access covers, situated at the top of each wheelarch liner, and unscrew the two plastic nuts (one on each side) securing either end of the bumper to the vehicle **(see illustrations)**. Note that the plastic retaining nuts should be discarded, and new ones used on refitting.

3 Remove the radiator grille as described in Section 22, then unscrew the two bolts securing the bumper mounting brackets to the crossmember, one located on each side of the radiator grille aperture **(see illustration)**.

4 Slacken and remove the three bolts securing the bottom of the bumper to the vehicle body **(see illustration)**.

5 On models with front foglights, disconnect the wiring connector from each light unit.

6 Undo the four screws (two on either side) securing the ends of the bumper to the wheelarch liner **(see illustration)**.

7 With the aid of an assistant, release the bumper ends from the wheelarch outer trim covers, and remove the bumper from the front of the vehicle **(see illustration)**. On models with headlight washers, note that it will be necessary to disconnect the supply hose from the T-piece as it becomes accessible.

Refitting

8 Refitting is a reversal of the removal procedure, using new plastic nuts, and ensuring that all bumper fasteners are securely tightened.

6.4 Front bumper-to-body bolts (arrowed)

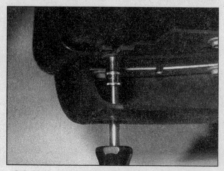

6.6 Unscrewing a bumper-to-wheelarch liner lower screw

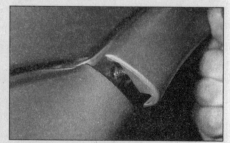

6.7 Carefully ease the wheelarch outer trim covers away from the vehicle, then release the bumper ends and remove the bumper from the vehicle

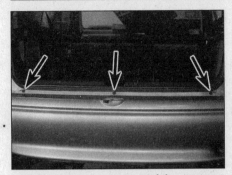

7.2 Rear bumper upper retaining screws (arrowed)

7.3 Unscrew the four screws securing the bottom of the bumper to the vehicle . . .

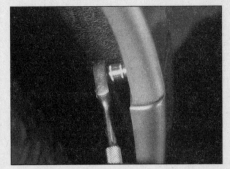

7.4 . . . and the plastic nut securing each end of the bumper to the wheelarch

7.5 Release the bumper ends from the wheelarch outer trim covers, and remove the rear bumper

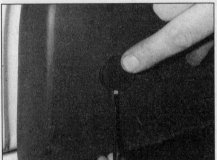

7.7a On Combo Van models, prise out the trim plug from either end of the bumper . . .

7.7b . . . then slacken and remove the bumper end bolts

7 Rear bumper –
removal and refitting

Removal

Corsa and Corsavan

1 Remove the number plate light unit as described in Chapter 12.

2 Open the tailgate, and undo the three screws securing the top of the bumper to the vehicle (see illustration).

3 Slacken and remove the four screws securing the bottom of the bumper to the vehicle body (see illustration).

4 Unscrew the two plastic nuts (one on either side) securing the ends of the bumper to the inside of the wheelarch (see illustration). Note that the plastic nuts should be discarded, and new ones used on refitting.

5 With the aid of an assistant, unclip the bumper ends from the wheelarch outer trim covers, and remove the bumper from the rear of the vehicle (see illustration).

Combo Van

6 Remove both rear number plate light units as described in Chapter 12.

7 Prise out the trim plug from either end of the bumper to gain access to the bumper retaining bolts, then slacken and remove the two mounting bolts (one on either end) (see illustrations).

8 Undo the three screws securing the bottom of the bumper to the vehicle, and the four screws securing the top of the bumper to the vehicle (see illustration).

9 Lift the bumper away from the rear of the vehicle (see illustration).

10 If necessary, slide the foam wedges out from between the bumper mountings, and unbolt the mountings from the vehicle body.

7.8 Unscrew the four upper screws (arrowed) and the lower screws . . .

7.9 . . . and remove the bumper

7.10a Remove the foam wedges . . .

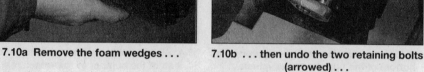
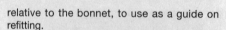

7.10b . . . then undo the two retaining bolts (arrowed) . . .

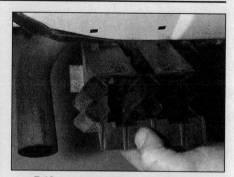

7.10c . . . and unhook the bumper mounting from the vehicle

Each mounting is retained by two bolts (see illustrations).

Refitting

11 Refitting is a reverse of the relevant removal procedure, ensuring that all disturbed fasteners are securely tightened. Before bolting the bumper in position, ensure that the number plate light wiring is fed through the bumper aperture(s).

8 Bonnet –
removal, refitting and adjustment

Removal

1 Open the bonnet, and have an assistant support it. Using a pencil or felt-tip pen, mark the outline position of each bonnet hinge

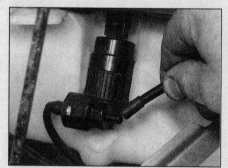

8.2 Disconnect the washer hose from the reservoir pump . . .

8.3b . . . and lift the bonnet away from the vehicle with the aid of an assistant

relative to the bonnet, to use as a guide on refitting.
2 Undo the retaining screws, and lift the left-hand windscreen cowl panel to improve access to the washer reservoir. Undo the reservoir retaining nut, then disconnect the windscreen washer supply pipe from the reservoir pump, and release it from the bonnet hinge (see illustration).
3 Undo the bonnet retaining bolts and, with the help of an assistant, carefully lift the bonnet clear (see illustrations). Store the bonnet out of the way, in a safe place. Inspect the hinge for signs of wear or damage. If hinge renewal is necessary, the vehicle must be taken to a Vauxhall/Opel dealer, as renewal requires the windscreen to be removed (see Section 20).

Refitting and adjustment

4 With the aid of an assistant, offer up the

8.3a . . . then undo the bonnet retaining bolts . . .

9.1 Slackening the bonnet release cable clamp screw

bonnet, and loosely fit the retaining bolts. Align the hinges with the marks made on removal, then tighten the retaining bolts securely. Reconnect the windscreen washer supply pipe.
5 Close the bonnet, and check for alignment with the adjacent panels. If necessary, slacken the bonnet support bolts, and realign the bonnet to suit. Once the bonnet is correctly aligned, securely tighten the bolts.
6 Once the bonnet is correctly aligned, check that the bonnet fastens and releases in a satisfactory manner, and if necessary adjust the lock striker as described in Section 10.

9 Bonnet release cable –
removal and refitting

Removal

1 Open the bonnet, and unscrew the release cable retaining clamp screw from the body crossmember (see illustration).
2 Release the outer cable from the clamp, then detach the inner cable from the lock spring.
3 Work back along the cable, releasing it from all the relevant retaining clips and ties, whilst noting its correct routing. Release the rubber sealing grommet from the engine compartment bulkhead, and tie a piece of string to the cable end, this can then be used to draw the cable back into position.
4 From inside the vehicle, unclip the bonnet release lever from the side of the driver's footwell.
5 Withdraw the lever and cable assembly from inside the vehicle. Once the cable end appears, untie the string and leave it in position in the vehicle; the string can then be used to draw the new cable back into position.

Refitting

6 Tie the string to the end of the cable, and use the string to draw the bonnet release cable through from inside the vehicle into the engine compartment. Once the cable is through, untie the string.
7 Ensure that the cable is correctly routed and retained by all the relevant clips and ties,

then seat the outer cable grommet in the engine compartment bulkhead.

8 Connect the inner cable to the lock spring, and seat the outer cable in its retaining clamp. Position the outer cable so that all free play is removed from the inner cable, then securely tighten its clamp screw.

9 Check the operation of the bonnet release lever before shutting the bonnet.

10 Bonnet lock components – removal and refitting

Bonnet lock hook

1 Drill out the pivot pin, and remove the lock hook and return spring from the bonnet (see illustration).

2 On refitting, locate the hook and spring in the bonnet bracket, and insert a new pivot pin. Secure the pin in position by flattening its end with a suitable pair of pliers.

Lock striker

3 Slacken the striker locknut, then unscrew the striker from the bonnet and recover the washer. If necessary, unscrew the locknut from the end of the striker, and remove the spring and spring seats.

4 Where necessary, fit the spring and spring seats to the striker, and screw on the locknut. Fit the washer to the striker, and screw the striker into position in the bonnet, tightening it only lightly at this stage.

5 Hold the locknut, and adjust the position of the striker so that the distance from the lower spring seat to the inside of the bonnet is 40 to 45 mm (see illustration).

6 When the striker is correctly positioned, securely tighten the locknut.

Lock spring

7 Unhook the spring from the body crossmember, then free it from the release cable and remove it from the vehicle.

8 On refitting, ensure that the spring is correctly engaged with the cable and crossmember. Check the operation of the bonnet release lever before shutting the bonnet.

10.1 Bonnet lock hook is removed by drilling out its pivot pin (arrowed)

11 Door – removal, refitting and adjustment

Removal

All front and Corsa rear doors

1 Open the door to gain access to the wiring connector which is fitted to the front edge of the door.

2 Disconnect the wiring connector from the front edge of the door. To do this, unscrew the connector locking ring, then pull the connector away from the door (see illustration).

3 Using a suitable hammer and punch, tap out the roll pin securing the door check link to the vehicle body (see illustration).

11.2 Release the locking ring, and disconnect the wiring connector from the door

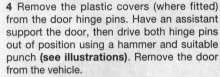

10.5 When refitting, adjust the position of the bonnet lock striker as described in text

4 Remove the plastic covers (where fitted) from the door hinge pins. Have an assistant support the door, then drive both hinge pins out of position using a hammer and suitable punch (see illustrations). Remove the door from the vehicle.

5 Inspect the hinge pins for signs of wear or damage, and renew if necessary. The check link roll pin should be renewed as a matter of course.

Combo Van rear door

6 Open the rear door, and release the check link spring from the door pin (see illustration).

7 Where necessary, trace the wiring back from the door to its wiring connectors in the main vehicle body. Disconnect the wiring connectors, then free the grommet from the

11.3 Tap out the check link roll pin using a suitable hammer and punch

11.4a Remove the upper plastic cover . . .

11.4b . . . and lower plastic cover . . .

11.4c . . . then tap out the hinge pins whilst an assistant supports the weight of the door

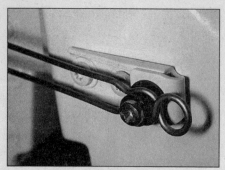

11.6 On the Combo Van rear door, release the check link spring from the door pin

11.7a Unclip the wiring from the vehicle body . . .

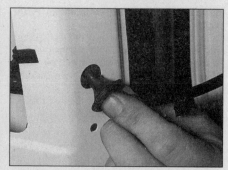

11.7b . . . then release the grommet . . .

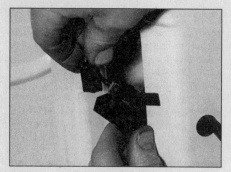

11.7c . . . and disconnect the relevant rear door wiring

11.8 Unscrew the hinge retaining bolts and remove the door

13 Door closure may be adjusted by altering the position of the door lock striker on the body. Slacken the striker retaining bolts, reposition the striker as required, then securely retighten the bolts.

Combo Van rear door

14 Slight adjustment of the doors can be achieved by slackening the hinge retaining bolts and repositioning the hinge/door.

15 Door closure may be adjusted by altering the position of the door lock striker on the door/body (as applicable). Slacken the striker retaining bolts, reposition the striker as required, then securely retighten the bolts (see illustrations).

vehicle body, and withdraw the wiring loom so that it is free to be removed with the door (see illustrations).

8 Have an assistant support the door, then slacken and remove the four hinge retaining bolts and remove the door from the vehicle (see illustration).

9 If necessary, the hinge(s) can then be unbolted and removed.

Refitting

All front and Corsa rear doors

10 Refitting is the reversal of removal, using a new check link roll pin.

Combo Van rear door

11 Refitting is a reversal of the removal procedure, tightening the hinge bolts securely, and ensuring that the wiring is securely reconnected.

Adjustment

All front and Corsa rear doors

12 Adjustment of the door position is not possible; the hinges are welded to the vehicle body and door, and cannot be repositioned. Misalignment of the door can only be caused by accident damage or wear of the hinge pins.

12 Door inner trim panel – removal and refitting

Removal

Front door

1 Unscrew the door pocket retaining screws, and pull the pocket downwards and away from the door to release its retaining clips. On models with electric windows, disconnect the window switch wiring connectors as the pocket is removed (see illustrations).

11.15a Rear door lock striker – Combo Van

11.15b Rear door latch striker – Combo Van

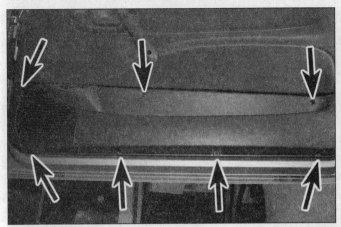

12.1a Undo the retaining screws (arrowed) and remove the door pocket

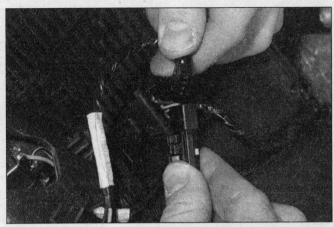

12.1b Where necessary, disconnect the electric window switch wiring connectors as the pocket is removed

2 Lift the inner door lock handle, and carefully prise the handle trim cover out from the door trim panel **(see illustration)**.

3 Where necessary, remove the loudspeaker from the armrest handle as described in Chapter 12, and free the electric exterior mirror or passenger side window switch (as applicable) from the armrest **(see illustration)**.

4 Undo the three retaining screws, and remove the armrest handle from the door **(see illustration)**.

5 Undo the retaining screw (where fitted) and unclip the exterior mirror inner trim panel from the door. On models with manually-operated mirrors, it will be necessary to pull the knob

off the adjusting lever in order to remove the panel **(see illustrations)**.

6 On models with manual windows, release the retaining clip and remove the window regulator handle. To release the clip, fabricate a hook from a piece of welding rod, and use the rod to hook the clip out from between the handle and bezel **(see illustration)**. Slide the handle off the regulator, and remove handle bezel.

7 Carefully prise the window inner sealing strip from the top edge of the door trim panel **(see illustration)**.

8 Slacken and remove the retaining screws on the rear edge of the panel, and at the front

12.2 Lift the handle, and unclip the handle trim cover from the door panel

12.3 Where necessary, carefully prise the exterior mirror switch out of the armrest

12.4 Undo the retaining screws (arrowed) and remove the armrest – three-door model shown

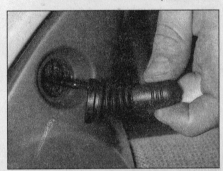

12.5a On models with manually-operated exterior mirrors, it will be necessary to remove the knob from the adjusting lever . . .

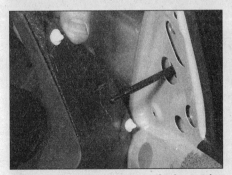

12.5b . . . in order to remove the inner trim panel

12.6 On models with manual windows, unhook the regulator handle retaining clip using a piece of welding rod

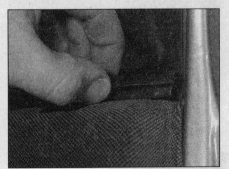

12.7 Carefully prise out the window sealing strip from the top of the inner trim panel

12.8a Undo the front . . .

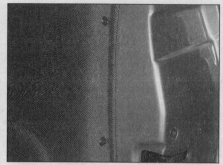

12.8b . . . and rear retaining screws from the trim panel . . .

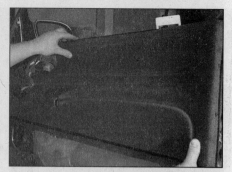

12.8c . . . and remove the trim panel from the door – three-door model shown

12.9 Undo the two screws, and remove the handle from the rear door

12.10 Unclip the trim cover from the door inner handle

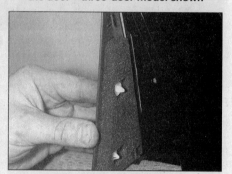

12.12 Unclip the inner trim panel from the rear door . . .

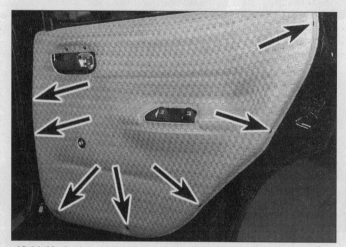

12.13 . . . then prise out the window sealing strip from the top of the door

of the panel, directly below the exterior mirror, and remove the trim panel from the door (see illustrations).

Rear door

9 Undo the retaining screws, and remove the handle from the rear door (see illustration).

10 Lift the inner door lock handle, and carefully prise the handle trim cover out from the door trim panel (see illustration).

11 Remove the window regulator handle as described in paragraph 6.

12 Carefully prise the inner trim panel away from the rear of the door (see illustration).

13 Carefully prise the window inner sealing strip from the top edge of the door trim panel (see illustration). The strip retaining clips should stay in position on the door; if they are loose, remove then and store with the sealing strip.

14 Unscrew the retaining screws from the edge of the door trim panel, and remove the panel from the door (see illustration).

Refitting

15 Refitting is the reverse of the relevant removal procedure. On models with manual windows, fit the retaining clip to the regulator handle before fitting the handle onto the regulator (see illustration).

12.14 Undo the retaining screws (arrowed) and remove the inner trim panel from the rear door

12.15 When refitting, fit the clip (arrowed) to the regulator handle before fitting the handle to the door

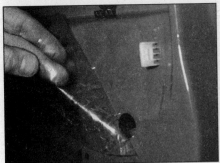

13.2 Carefully peel the weathershield away from the door to gain access to the lock components

13.4 The interior handle simply unclips from the door

13.8a Undo the two nuts . . .

13 Door handle and lock components – removal and refitting

Removal

Interior handle

1 Remove the door inner trim panel as described in Section 12.
2 Peel the polythene weathershield away from the door to gain access to the door lock components **(see illustration)**. Where necessary, cut around the trim panel screw brackets, using a sharp knife, to release the weathershield.
3 Release the retaining clip by pivoting it away from the link rod, and detach the rod from the lock assembly.
4 Unclip the interior handle from the door, and remove it complete with the rod **(see illustration)**.

Front exterior handle

5 Remove the door inner trim panel as described in Section 12, and peel back the weathershield (see paragraph 2).
6 With the window fully raised, undo the retaining bolt(s) from the base of the window guide, and manoeuvre the guide out from the door.
7 Release the retaining clips by pivoting them away from the link rods, and free the link rods from the lock assembly.

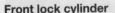

13.8b . . . then free the lock cylinder mounting plate from the rear of the exterior door handle

8 Unscrew the two handle retaining nuts, and detach the lock cylinder mounting plate from the rear of the handle **(see illustrations)**.
9 Lift the retaining clips on the base of the handle, and remove the handle from the outside of the door.

Front lock cylinder

10 Remove the exterior door handle as described above, then manoeuvre the lock cylinder mounting plate out of the door. Where necessary, trace the wiring back from the central locking/alarm microswitch, and disconnect it at the wiring connector to enable the plate to be removed.
11 With the mounting plate removed, insert the key into the lock cylinder, then prise off the C-clip from rear of the mounting plate. Lift

13.11a Remove the C-clip . . .

off the link rod bracket and spring, noting their correct fitted locations, and withdraw the lock cylinder **(see illustrations)**.

Front lock

12 Remove the door inner trim panel as described in Section 12, and peel back the weathershield (see paragraph 2).
13 Remove the window guide as described in paragraph 6.
14 Undo the three retaining screws, and manoeuvre the lock assembly out of the door. On models with central locking, disconnect the wiring connector from the servo unit as it becomes accessible **(see illustrations)**.

Rear exterior handle (Corsa)

15 Remove the door inner trim panel as described in Section 12, and peel back the

13.11b . . . then lift off the link rod bracket and spring, noting its correct fitted position . . .

13.11c . . . and withdraw the lock cylinder

13.14a Undo the three retaining screws . . .

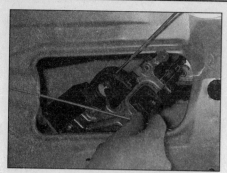

13.14b . . . then remove the lock assembly from the door

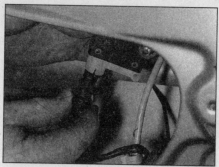

13.14c On models with central locking, disconnect the wiring connector from the servo unit before removing the lock

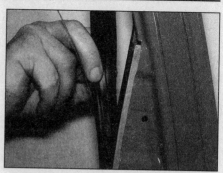

13.16 Free the sealing strip from the rear of the door to gain access to the guide upper retaining bolt

13.17a Slacken and remove the upper window guide retaining bolt . . .

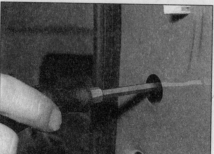

13.17b . . . and lower retaining bolt . . .

weathershield (see paragraph 2). Carefully prise the outer trim panel away from the door.
16 Wind the window fully down, and release the window sealing strip from the rear of the door and guide, to gain access to the retaining bolt **(see illustration)**.
17 Undo the two guide retaining bolts, and manoeuvre the guide upwards and out from the door **(see illustrations)**.
18 Release the retaining clips by pivoting them away from the link rods, and free the link rods from the lock assembly **(see illustration)**.
19 Undo the two nuts, and free the mounting plate assembly from the rear of the handle **(see illustration)**.
20 Lift the retaining clips on the base of the handle, then remove the handle from the outside of the door, freeing its link rod from the lock **(see illustration)**.

Rear lock (Corsa)

21 Remove the exterior handle as described above, and manoeuvre out the mounting plate assembly **(see illustration)**.
22 Undo the three retaining screws, and remove the lock assembly **(see illustrations)**. On models with central locking, disconnect the wiring connector from the servo unit as it becomes accessible.

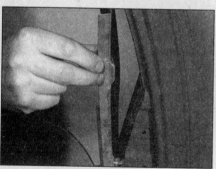

13.17c . . . and manoeuvre the guide upwards and out of the rear door

13.18 Pivot the retaining clip (arrowed) away from each link rod, and disconnect the rods from the lock

13.19 Undo the two nuts, and free the mounting plate from the rear of the exterior handle

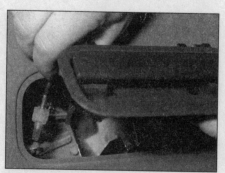

13.20 Remove the exterior handle from the door, freeing its link rod from the lock

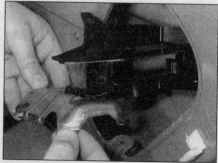

13.21 Remove the lock cylinder mounting plate from the door to improve access to the rear door lock

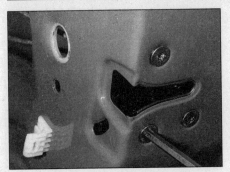

13.22a Undo the three retaining screws . . .

13.22b . . . and remove the lock assembly from the rear door

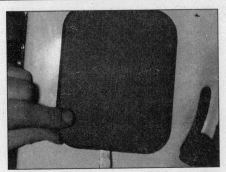

13.23a On Combo Van models, prise out the access cover . . .

Rear lock and lock cylinder (Combo Van)

23 Carefully prise the access cover out from the rear door. To further improve access, prise out the retaining clips and remove the trim panel from the centre of the door **(see illustrations)**.

24 Release the retaining clips by pivoting them away from the link rods, and free the link rods from the lock assembly **(see illustration)**.

25 Undo the two retaining nuts, then free the lock cylinder mounting plate from the rear of the handle. Undo the three lock assembly retaining screws, and manoeuvre the lock and cylinder mounting plate assembly out of the door **(see illustrations)**.

26 Release the retaining clip, and separate the lock and mounting plate **(see illustration)**.

27 If necessary, to remove the lock cylinder, insert the key into the lock cylinder, then prise off the C-clip from rear of the mounting plate. Lift off the link rod bracket and spring, noting their correct fitted locations, and withdraw the lock cylinder **(see illustration)**.

Rear handle (Combo Van)

28 Remove the lock and lock cylinder mounting plate as described above.

13.23b . . . and remove the trim panel to gain access to the lock

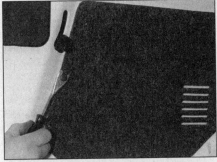

13.25a Free the lock cylinder mounting plate from the handle . . .

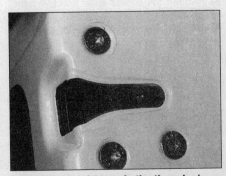

13.24 Link rod pivot clips (arrowed) are released by pivoting them away from the rod

13.25b . . . then undo the three lock retaining screws . . .

13.25c . . . and manoeuvre the lock and cylinder mounting plate assembly out of the door

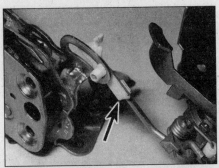

13.26 Release the retaining clip (arrowed), and separate the lock from the lock cylinder mounting plate

13.27 Lock cylinder and associated components are retained by a C-clip

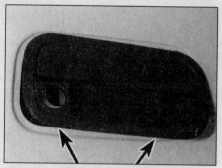

13.29 Door handle is retained by two clips (locations arrowed)

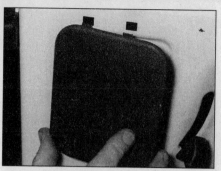

13.30 Remove the access cover to reveal the latch lock

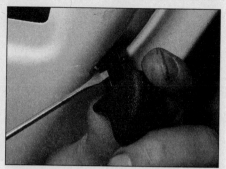

13.31 Release the retaining clip, and slide the knob off the latch lock handle

29 Lift the retaining clips on the base of the handle, and remove the handle from the outside of the door **(see illustration)**.

Rear latch lock (Combo Van)

30 Carefully prise the access cover from the rear door **(see illustration)**. To further improve access, prise out the retaining clips and remove the trim panel from the centre of the door.
31 Release the retaining clip, and pull the knob off the latch handle **(see illustration)**.
32 Release the retaining clips by pivoting them away from the link rods, and free both link rods from the lock **(see illustration)**.
33 Undo the three retaining screws, and manoeuvre the latch lock out from the door **(see illustration)**.

Rear latches (Combo Van)

34 Remove the access cover and trim panel as described in paragraph 30.
35 Release the relevant retaining clip by

pivoting it away from the link rod, and free the link rod from the lock.
36 Undo the screws securing the latch to the door, and guide the latch and link rod out of position **(see illustrations)**.
37 If necessary, remove the second latch in the same way.

Refitting

38 Refitting is the reverse of the removal sequence, noting the following points:

a) *If a lock cylinder has been removed, on refitting ensure that the spring and link rod bracket are correctly positioned and are securely held by the C-clip. Check the operation of the lock cylinder, making sure that the spring returns the cylinder to its central position, before refitting the plate to the door.*
b) *Ensure that all link rods are securely held in position by their retaining clips.*

c) *Apply grease to all lock and link rod pivot points.*
d) *Before installing the relevant trim panel, thoroughly check the operation of all the door lock handles and, where necessary, the central locking system, and ensure that the weathershield is correctly positioned.*
e) *On models with side air bags incorporated in the front seats, it is vitally important that the polythene weathershield fitted behind the trim panel is undamaged and perfectly sealed to the door around its complete contact area. If this is not the case the side air bag impact sensor may not function correctly. If the weathershield was damaged in any way during removal, or if a perfect seal cannot be made, renew the weathershield.*

14 Door window glass and regulator – removal and refitting

Removal

1 Remove the door inner trim panel as described in Section 12.
2 Peel the polythene weathershield away from the door to gain access to the door lock components. Where necessary, cut around the trim panel screw brackets, using a sharp knife, to release the weathershield. Proceed as described under the relevant sub-heading.

Front manual window

3 With the window fully raised, undo the retaining bolt(s) from the base of the window rear guide, and manoeuvre the guide out from the door.
4 Wind the window down, and position it so its guide is in the centre of the door aperture.
5 Mark the position of the regulator guide retaining bolts on the door, then undo the two bolts and release the regulator bracket from the door. The marks can then be used on refitting to make sure the bracket is correctly positioned.
6 Release the regulator rollers from the ends of the window glass guide rail, then lift the glass and manoeuvre it out from the door.

13.32 Detach both link rods (arrowed) from the lock . . .

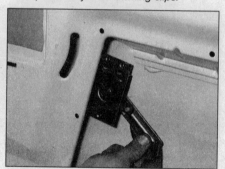

13.33 . . . and manoeuvre the lock out from the door

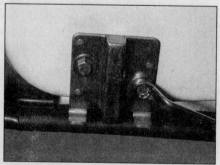

13.36a Undo the two bolts . . .

13.36b . . . and slide the latch and link rod out from the door

14.7 Removing the front door window glass

14.12a Undo the two retaining bolts (arrowed) . . .

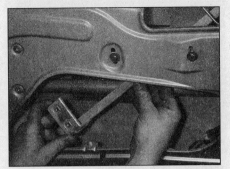

14.12b . . . then manoeuvre the window guide out from the door

Front electric window

7 Remove the regulator assembly as described below. The glass can then be lifted out from the door **(see illustration)**.

Rear

8 Carefully prise the outer trim panel away from the door.

9 Wind the window fully down, then release the window sealing strip from the rear of the door and guide, to gain access to the guide retaining bolt.

10 Undo the two bolts, and remove the window guide from the door **(see illustrations 13.17a, 13.17b and 13.17c)**.

11 Tilt the window glass forwards, and free the window guide from the regulator mechanism. The glass can then be manoeuvred out from the door.

Front regulator

Note: *A pop-rivet gun and suitable rivets will be required when refitting. The rivet heads should be approximately 4.8 mm in diameter and 11 mm in length.*

12 With the window fully raised, undo the retaining bolt(s) from the base of the window guide, and manoeuvre the guide out from the door **(see illustrations)**.

13 Position the window so that its guide rail is in the centre of the door aperture, and wedge it in position with a suitable wooden or rubber wedge.

14 Mark the position of the regulator guide retaining bolts on the door, then undo the two bolts and remove the guide **(see illustrations)**.

14.14a Mark the position of the regulator guide bolts on the door, then undo the bolts . . .

15 Using an 8.5 mm drill bit, drill out the rivets securing the regulator assembly to the door, taking great care not to damage the door panel. With all the rivets removed, free the regulator rollers from the ends of the window

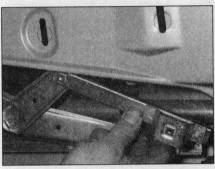

14.14b . . . and remove the guide

glass guide rail, and manoeuvre the regulator assembly out through the door aperture. On models with electric windows, disconnect the wiring connector from the regulator as it becomes accessible **(see illustrations)**.

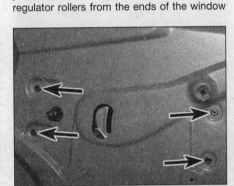

14.15a Front door window regulator retaining rivets (arrowed) – manual window

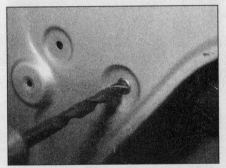

14.15b Carefully drill out the rivets with a suitable drill . . .

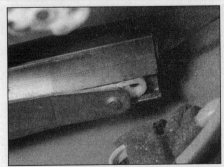

14.15c . . . then free the regulator rollers from the window glass . . .

14.15d . . . and remove the regulator assembly from the door

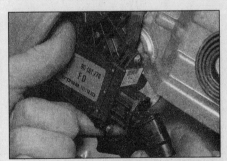

14.15e On models with electric windows, disconnect the wiring connector from the regulator as it is removed

Rear regulator

Note: *A pop-rivet gun and suitable rivets will be required when refitting. The rivet heads should be approximately 4.8 mm in diameter and 11 mm in length.*

16 Position the window so that its guide rail is in the centre of the lower door aperture, and wedge it in position with a suitable wooden or rubber wedge.

17 Using an 8.5 mm drill bit, drill out the rivets securing the regulator assembly to the door, taking great care not to damage the door panel **(see illustration)**.

18 With all the rivets removed, free the regulator from the glass guide rail, and manoeuvre it out through the door aperture.

Refitting

19 Refitting is the reverse of the removal procedure, noting the following points:

a) *Where the regulator has been removed, remove the remains of the old rivets before fitting the regulator to the door. Engage the regulator with the window glass, and secure it in position with new pop-rivets.*

b) *On the front window, align the regulator guide bolts with the marks made on removal, then tighten them securely.*

c) *Check the window moves smoothly and easily up and down, without any sign of tight spots. If the window movement is stiff, trace and rectify the cause. On the front window, movement is adjustable by slackening the regulator guide bolts and*

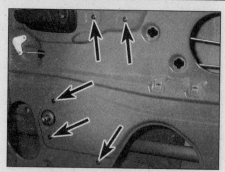

14.17 Rear door window regulator retaining rivets (arrowed) – five-door models

moving the bolts up and down the slotted holes. Find the position where the window movement is the easiest, then securely tighten the bolts.

d) *Refit the weathershield, making sure it is securely stuck to the door, then install the trim panel as described in Section 12.*

15 Tailgate and support struts – removal and refitting

Removal

Tailgate

1 Disconnect the battery negative terminal

(refer to *Disconnecting the battery* in the Reference Chapter).

2 Open the tailgate, and detach the parcel shelf cords. Undo the retaining screws, and remove the lifter hooks from the tailgate **(see illustration)**.

3 Carefully prise out the retaining clips, and remove the inner trim panel from the tailgate **(see illustration)**.

4 Disconnect the wiring connectors from the tailgate wiper motor, central locking components and/or courtesy light switch (as applicable). Undo the relevant tailgate wiper motor bolt, and free the earth lead. Also disconnect the wiring connector from the heated rear window element. Tie a suitable length of string to the end of the wiring loom, then free the grommet from the top of the tailgate and withdraw the wiring loom **(see illustrations)**. When the end of the loom appears, untie the string and leave it in position in the tailgate; it can then be used to draw the wiring back into position when refitting.

5 Where necessary, prise out the washer jet from the tailgate/spoiler (as applicable), and disconnect it from the washer hose **(see illustrations)**. Tie a suitable length of string to the hose end, then withdraw the hose, leaving the string in position in the same way as for the wiring.

6 Have an assistant support the tailgate, then raise the spring clips and pull the support struts off their balljoint mountings on the tailgate. Prise out the hinge pin retaining clips,

15.2 Undo the retaining screws, and remove the parcel shelf lifter hooks from the tailgate . . .

15.3 . . . then prise out the retaining clips and remove the inner trim panel

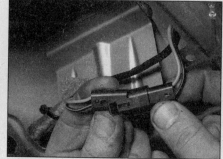

15.4a Disconnect the various wiring connectors situated behind the trim panel . . .

15.4b . . . and the heated rear window wiring connector . . .

15.4c . . . then remove the grommet and withdraw the wiring from the tailgate

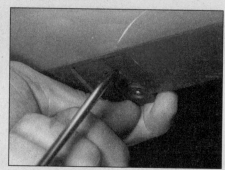

15.5a Prise the washer jet out from the tailgate . . .

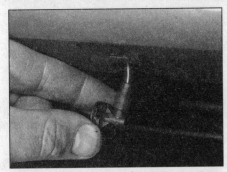

15.5b . . . and disconnect it from the hose

15.6a Remove the retaining clips . . .

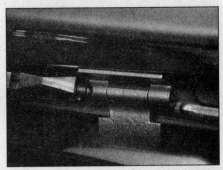

15.6b . . . then withdraw the hinge pin and lift off the tailgate

then tap both hinge pins out of position and remove the tailgate from the vehicle **(see illustrations).**

7 Examine the hinge pins for signs of wear or damage, and renew if necessary.

Support struts

8 Support the tailgate in the open position using a stout piece of wood, or with the help of an assistant.

9 Raise the spring clips, and pull the support strut off its balljoint mountings on the tailgate and vehicle body **(see illustration).**

Refitting

Tailgate

10 Refitting is a reversal of the removal procedure, noting the following points:

a) *Prior to refitting, apply a smear of multi-purpose grease to the hinge pins.*

b) *Ensure that the hinge pins are securely retained by their clips, and that the support struts are securely held in position by their spring clips.*

c) *Use the string to draw the wiring loom and washer hose through into position, and ensure that all wiring connectors are correctly reconnected.*

Support struts

11 Refitting is a reverse of the removal procedure, ensuring that the strut is securely retained by its spring clips.

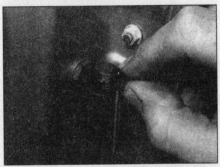

15.9 Lift the retaining clip, and free the support strut from its balljoints

16 Tailgate lock components – removal and refitting

Removal

1 Release the rear parcel shelf lifting cords from the tailgate, then unclip the shelf and remove it from the vehicle.

2 Undo the retaining screws, and remove the parcel shelf lifting cord hooks from the tailgate trim panel.

3 Carefully prise out the retaining clips, and remove the trim panel from the tailgate. Proceed as described under the relevant sub-heading.

16.5 Tailgate lock is retained by three screws (arrowed)

Lock

4 From inside the tailgate, release the retaining clip by pivoting it away from the link rod, and detach the rod from the lock assembly.

5 Slacken and remove the three screws, and remove the lock from the tailgate **(see illustration).**

Lock cylinder

6 From inside the tailgate, release the retaining clip by pivoting it away from the link rod, and detach the rod from the lock cylinder **(see illustration).**

7 Where necessary, release the retaining clip and detach the central locking/alarm micro-switch from the top of the lock cylinder **(see illustration).**

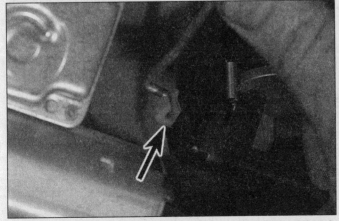

16.6 Release the retaining clip (arrowed) and detach the link rod from the tailgate lock cylinder casting

16.7 Where necessary, release the microswitch from the top of the casting

16.8a Undo the three nuts (arrowed), then remove the lock cylinder casting from inside the tailgate ...

16.8b ... and the exterior handle from the outside

16.9 Lock cylinder roll pin can be tapped out with a suitable punch

8 Undo the three nuts and remove the exterior handle; the lock cylinder casting can then be manoeuvred out of the tailgate (see illustrations).

9 To dismantle the assembly, insert the key into the lock cylinder, then tap out the roll pin from the rear of the cylinder housing using a suitable pin punch, and remove the link rod bracket from the rear of the cylinder (see illustration). Note which way around the bracket is fitted. Discard the roll pin; a new one should be used on refitting.

10 Release the retaining catches, remove the trim cover, and free the lock cylinder housing from the casting. The lock cylinder can then be withdrawn from its housing.

Refitting

Lock

11 Refitting is a reverse of the removal procedure.

Lock cylinder

12 Insert the lock cylinder into its housing, and insert the housing and spring into the main casting. Refit the link rod bracket, making sure it is fitted the correct way around, and secure it in position with a new roll pin. Check the operation of the lock, then refit the trim cover.

13 Refit the lock cylinder casting and exterior handle to the tailgate, then fit the retaining nuts and tighten them to the specified torque.

On models with central locking, make sure that the casting is correctly engaged with the servo unit rod before tightening the retaining nuts.

14 Connect the link rod, and secure it in position with the clip.

15 Where necessary, clip the alarm/central locking switch back onto the lock assembly.

16 Refit the trim panel and parcel shelf.

17 Central locking components – removal and refitting

Electronic control unit

1 The ECU is located behind the right-hand footwell trim panel.

2 Release the retaining clip, then remove the ECU mounting bracket from the side of the footwell and withdraw the insulation panel (see illustrations).

3 Undo the two bolts and remove the central locking ECU from the vehicle, disconnecting the wiring connector as it becomes accessible (see illustration).

4 Refitting is the reverse of removal.

Front door servo

5 Remove the relevant lock assembly as described in Section 13.

6 Undo the two retaining screws, and detach the servo unit from the lock (see illustration).

7 Refitting is the reverse of removal.

Rear door servo

Corsa

8 Remove the relevant lock assembly as described in Section 13.

9 Undo the two retaining screws, and detach the servo unit from the lock.

10 Refitting is the reverse of removal.

Combo Van

11 Carefully prise the access cover out from the rear door. To further improve access, prise out the retaining clips and remove the trim panel from the centre of the door (see illustrations).

17.2a Unclip the ECU mounting bracket ...

17.2b ... and remove the insulation panel ...

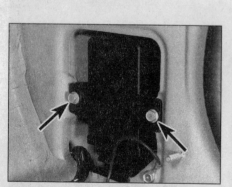

17.3 ... to gain access to the central locking control unit (retaining bolts arrowed)

17.6 Front door lock servo unit is retained by two screws (arrowed)

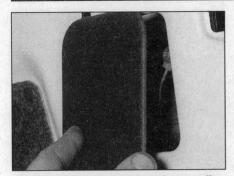

17.11a On Combo Van rear door, unclip the access cover . . .

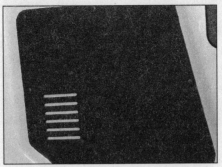

17.11b . . . and remove the trim panel to improve access to the servo unit

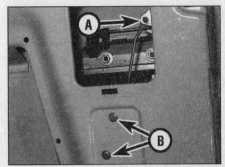

17.13a Detach the link rod (A) and undo the retaining screws (B) . . .

12 Release the retaining clip by pivoting it away from the link rod, and free the servo unit link rod from the lock assembly.

13 Undo the two retaining screws and remove the servo unit from the door, disconnecting its wiring connector as it becomes accessible **(see illustrations)**.

14 Refitting is the reverse of removal. Prior to installing the trim panel, check the operation of the servo unit.

Tailgate servo

15 Remove the tailgate inner trim panel as described in paragraphs 1 to 3 of Section 16.

16 Undo the two bolts and manoeuvre the servo unit out of position, disconnecting the wiring connector as it becomes accessible **(see illustrations)**.

17 Refitting is the reverse of removal, ensuring that the servo rod is correctly engaged with the lock casting **(see illustration)**. Prior to installing the trim panel, check the operation of the servo unit.

Fuel filler cap servo

18 Remove the right-hand rear light unit as described in Chapter 12.

19 Disconnect the servo unit wiring connector, then undo the retaining screws and manoeuvre the servo out through the rear light aperture **(see illustrations)**.

17.13b . . . then remove the servo unit and disconnect its wiring connector

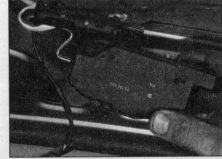

17.16b . . . and remove the servo unit from the tailgate

17.16a Disconnect the wiring connector, then undo the retaining bolts (arrowed) . . .

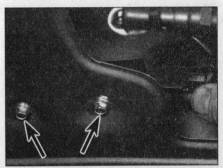

17.17 When refitting, ensure that the servo unit rod (arrowed) is correctly engaged with the lock

17.19a Disconnect the wiring connector . . .

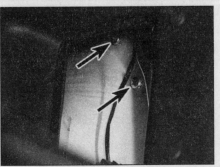

17.19b . . . then undo the two retaining screws (arrowed) . . .

17.19c . . . and remove the fuel filler cap servo unit

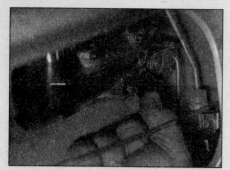

17.24a When refitting, ensure that the microswitch is correctly located on the pins . . .

17.24b . . . and secure it in position with the retaining clip

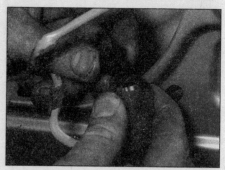

17.24c Make sure that the switch wiring is correctly routed, and reconnect the wiring connector

20 Refitting is the reverse of removal, ensuring that the servo unit rod is correctly engaged with the filler cap hole. Check the operation of the servo unit before refitting the light unit.

Door microswitch

21 Remove the door inner trim panel as described in Section 12.
22 Peel the polythene weathershield away from the door to gain access to the door lock. Where necessary, cut around the trim panel screw brackets, using a sharp knife, to release the weathershield.
23 Using a suitable screwdriver, prise off the switch retaining clip, and disengage the switch from the lock cylinder mounting plate. Trace the wiring back to its connector, then disconnect it and remove the switch from the door.
24 Refitting is the reverse of the removal, making sure that the switch is correctly located on the mounting plate pins. Also ensure that the wiring is routed around the back of the window guide so that it doesn't foul the window movement **(see illustrations)**.

Tailgate lock microswitch

25 Remove the tailgate trim panel as described in paragraphs 1 to 3 of Section 16.
26 Using a suitable screwdriver, prise off the switch retaining clip, and disengage the

switch from the lock cylinder mounting plate **(see illustration)**. Trace the wiring back to its connector, then disconnect it and remove the switch from the tailgate.
27 Refitting is the reverse of the removal, making sure that the switch is correctly located and securely retained by its clip.

18 Electric window components – removal and refitting

Note: *Every time the battery is disconnected, or the electric window motors are disconnected, it will be necessary when reconnecting to reprogramme the motors, to restore the one-touch function of the buttons. To do this, fully close both front windows. With the windows closed, depress the up button of the driver's side window for approximately 5 seconds, then release it and depress the passenger side window up button for approximately 5 seconds.*

Window switches

1 Refer to Chapter 12.

Window winder motors

2 Remove the regulator mechanism as described in Section 14.
3 Prior to removing the motor, it is necessary to secure the regulator arm to the mounting

bracket, to prevent it moving as the motor is removed. The arm is spring-loaded, and if it is not secured in position, it will be forcibly twisted as the motor is removed, and could severely damage your hands.
4 With the regulator arm secured, slacken and remove the three retaining screws, and separate the motor and regulator **(see illustration)**. Do not attempt to dismantle the motor assembly, as it is a sealed unit.
5 Fit the motor assembly to the regulator, and securely tighten its retaining screws.
6 Release the regulator arm, and install the regulator mechanism as described in Section 14.

19 Exterior mirror and associated components – removal and refitting

Note: *There are two different manufacturers of the exterior mirrors fitted to Corsa models, and the individual mirror components are not interchangeable between the two types. This mirror type is indicated by a symbol on the rubber seal located on the inside of the mirror (the mirror must be removed to see this)* **(see illustration)**. *Identify the mirror type before ordering mirror spares.*

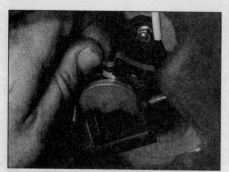

17.26 Release the retaining clip and remove the microswitch from the tailgate lock

18.4 Electric window motor retaining screws (arrowed)

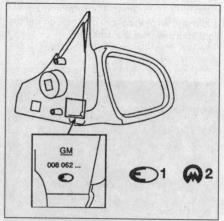

19.0 Exterior mirror manufacturer's identification markings

1 Engelmann   2 Fico

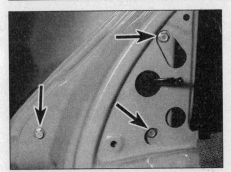

19.3 Exterior mirror retaining bolts
(arrowed) – manually-operated mirror

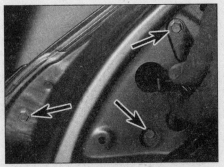

19.5 Disconnect the wiring connector,
then undo the three retaining bolts
(arrowed) . . .

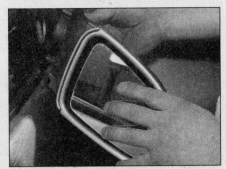

19.6 . . . and remove the mirror from the
door

Manually-operated mirror

1 Pull off the knob from the mirror adjusting lever.
2 Undo the screw (where fitted), and unclip the inner trim panel from the door.
3 Undo the retaining bolts, and remove the mirror assembly from the outside of the door (see illustration).
4 Refitting is the reverse of removal.

Electrically-operated mirror

5 Undo the retaining screw (where fitted), and unclip the exterior mirror inner trim panel from the door. Disconnect the wiring connector from the mirror (see illustration).
6 Undo the three retaining bolts, and remove the mirror assembly from the outside of the door (see illustration).
7 Refitting is a reverse of the removal procedure.

Mirror glass

8 Insert a wide plastic or wooden wedge between the mirror glass and mirror housing, and carefully prise the glass from its balljoints (see illustration). Take great care when removing the glass; do not use excessive force, as the glass is easily broken (wear thick gloves, particularly if removing an already-broken mirror glass).
9 Remove the glass from the mirror. On models with electric mirrors, disconnect the wiring connectors from the mirror heating element as they become accessible (see illustration).
10 When refitting, carefully clip the glass back into position, ensuring that it is correctly located on each of its balljoints (see illustration).

Mirror motor

11 Remove the mirror glass as described above.
12 Undo the three screws and remove the motor assembly, disconnecting its wiring connectors as they become accessible (see illustration).
13 Refitting is the reverse of removal.

Mirror switch

14 Refer to Chapter 12.

20 Windscreen, tailgate and fixed window glass – general information

1 These areas of glass are secured by the tight fit of the weatherstrip in the body aperture, and are bonded in position with a special adhesive. The removal and refitting of these areas of fixed glass is a difficult, messy and time-consuming task, which is considered beyond the scope of the home mechanic. It is difficult, unless one has plenty of practice, to obtain a secure, waterproof fit. Furthermore, the task carries a high risk of breakage; this applies especially to the laminated glass windscreen. In view of this, owners are strongly advised to have this sort

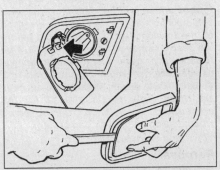

19.8 Using a wooden wedge to prise the
window glass out of position. Inset shows
heating element wiring connections on
electrically-operated mirror

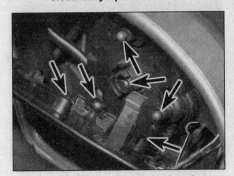

19.10 Align the balljoints and sockets
(arrowed) when refitting the mirror glass

of work carried out by one of the many specialist windscreen fitters, or a Vauxhall/Opel dealer.

21 Sunroof – general information

1 A manual or electric sunroof was offered as an optional extra on most models, and is fitted as standard equipment on some models.
2 Due to the complexity of the sunroof mechanism, considerable expertise is needed to repair, replace or adjust the sunroof components successfully. Removal of the roof first requires the headlining to be removed, which is a complex and tedious operation in

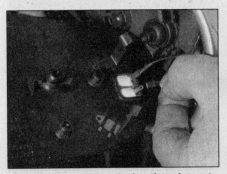

19.9 Disconnecting the heating element
wiring connections – electrically-operated
mirrors

19.12 Motor retaining screws (arrowed) –
electrically-operated mirror

itself, and not a task to be undertaken lightly (See Section 26). Therefore, any problems with the sunroof should be referred to a Vauxhall/Opel dealer.

3 On models with an electric sunroof, if the sunroof motor fails to operate, first check the relevant fuse. If the fault cannot be traced and rectified, the sunroof can be opened and closed manually using a suitable Allen wrench to turn the motor spindle. To gain access to the motor spindle, carefully prise out the trim cover situated at the rear of the sunroof. Insert the Allen key in the motor spindle, and turn to move the sunroof to the required position. A suitable Allen key is supplied with the vehicle, and should be found in the glovebox.

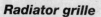

22 Body exterior fittings – removal and refitting

Radiator grille

1 Open the bonnet and unscrew the two bolts securing the radiator grille to the engine compartment front crossmember.

2 Similarly unscrew the two bolts securing the bumper mounting brackets to the crossmember, one located on each side of the radiator grille.

3 Ease the bumper mounting brackets forward slightly and release the radiator grille lower retaining clip strip.

4 Lift the radiator grille upwards from its location.

5 Refitting is a reversal of removal.

Wheelarch liners and body under-panels

6 The various plastic covers fitted to the underside of the vehicle are secured in position by a mixture of screws, nuts and retaining clips, and removal will be fairly obvious on inspection. Work methodically around the liner/panel, removing its retaining screws and releasing its retaining clips until it is free to be removed from the underside of the vehicle. Most clips used on the vehicle, with the exception of the fasteners which are used to secure the wheelarch liners, are simply prised out of position. The wheelarch liner clips are released by tapping their centre pins through the clip, and then removing the outer section of the clip; new clips will be required on refitting if the centre pins are not recovered.

7 When refitting, renew any retaining clips that may have been broken on removal, and ensure that the panel is securely retained by all the relevant clips, nuts and screws. Vauxhall/Opel also recommend that plastic nuts (where used) are renewed, regardless of their apparent condition, whenever they are disturbed.

Body trim strips and badges

8 The various body trim strips and badges are held in position with a special adhesive tape. Removal requires the trim/badge to be heated, to soften the adhesive, and then cut away from the surface. Due to the high risk of damage to the vehicle's paintwork during this operation, it is recommended that this task should be entrusted to a Vauxhall/Opel dealer.

23 Seats – removal and refitting

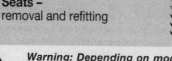

Warning: Depending on model, the front seats may be equipped with mechanical or pyrotechnic seat belt tensioners, and side air bags may be built into the outer sides of the seats. The seat belt tensioners and side air bags may cause injury if triggered accidentally. Before carrying out any work on the front seats, always ensure that the safety fork is inserted into the seat belt tensioner cylinder, to prevent the possibility of the tensioner being accidentally triggered (see paragraphs 2 and 3 below). Seats should always be transported and installed with the safety fork in place. If the tensioner has been triggered due to a sudden impact or accident, the unit must be renewed, as it cannot be reset. A triggered tensioner mechanism can be identified by the yellow tongue which will be visible on the seat belt stalk buckle. If a seat is to be disposed of, the tensioner must be triggered before the seat is removed from the vehicle. Due to safety considerations, tensioner renewal or seat disposal must be entrusted to a Vauxhall/Opel dealer. Where side air bags are fitted, refer to Chapter 12 for the precautions which should be observed when dealing with an air bag system.

Removal

Front seat

1 On models with side air bags or pyrotechnic seat belt tensioners, observe the

following precautions before attempting to remove the seat:
   a) *Remove the ignition key.*
   b) *Disconnect the battery negative terminal (refer to 'Disconnecting the battery' in the Reference Section of this manual), and wait for two minutes before carrying out any further work.*

2 Undo the retaining screws, and remove the trim panel from the outside of the seat to gain access to the outer seat guide rail bolt. Locate the plastic safety fork, which is clipped onto the rear of the tensioner. Insert the safety fork into the slot provided in the tensioner cylinder, ensuring that the fork engages securely **(see illustrations)**.

3 On models with side air bags, pyrotechnic seat belt tensioners or heated seats, disconnect the wiring connector which is situated underneath the seat.

4 Slide the seat fully forwards, then slacken and remove the seat rear retaining bolts.

5 Move the seat forwards to disengage the seat guide rails from the floor brackets, and lift the seat out of the vehicle.

Rear seat cushion – Corsa and Corsavan

6 Prise off the trim covers from the rear seat cushion hinges.

7 Slacken and remove the two retaining bolts, then release the seat cushion clips and remove the cushion from the vehicle.

One-piece rear seat backrest – Corsa and Corsavan

8 Open up the tailgate, and remove the rear parcel shelf.

9 Fold the rear seat backrest forwards, and remove the spring clip from the left- and right-hand seat backrest pivot pins.

10 Using a small flat-bladed screwdriver, release the retaining clips, and remove the left- and right-hand pivot pin guides from the vehicle. The seat backrest can then be manoeuvred out of the vehicle.

Two-piece (split folding) rear seat backrest – Corsa and Corsavan

11 Open up the tailgate, and remove the rear parcel shelf.

12 Unclip the trim covers from the left- and right-hand seat backrest hinges.

23.2a Unclip the safety fork from the rear of the seat belt tensioner . . .

23.2b . . . and insert it into the slot, making sure that it is correctly engaged with the tensioner pin (arrowed)

13 Prise out the retaining clips, and peel back the carpet from the rear of the seats to gain access to the centre pivot of the seat. Undo the four retaining screws, and remove the hinge.

14 Undo the left- and right-hand seat backrest retaining bolts, and remove the seat assembly.

Rear seat cushion – Combo Van

15 Fold back the carpet from front of the seat to gain access to the seat pivot pins.

16 Prise off the C-clip from each pin, then withdraw both pins and remove the seat cushion from the vehicle.

Rear seat backrest – Combo Van

17 Where necessary, undo the retaining bolts and remove the luggage compartment grille from the vehicle.

18 Fold the seat backrest forwards, then undo the retaining bolts from the left- and right-hand seat hinges and remove the backrest from the vehicle.

Refitting

Front seats

19 Refitting is a reverse of the removal procedure, noting the following points:
a) Remove all traces of old thread-locking compound from the threads of the seat retaining bolts, and clean the threaded holes in the vehicle floor, ideally by running a tap of the correct size and pitch down them.
b) Apply a suitable thread-locking compound to the threads of the seat bolts. Refit the bolts, and tighten them to the specified torque setting.
c) Prior to refitting the trim panel, remove the safety fork from the seat belt tensioner, and clip it back into position on the outside of the tensioner.
d) Reconnect the battery negative terminal.

Rear seats – all models

21 Refitting is a reverse of the removal procedure, tightening the seat mounting bolts to the specified torque (where applicable).

24 Front seat belt tensioning mechanism – general information

All models covered in this manual are fitted with a front seat belt tensioner system. On pre-1999 models a mechanical system is used and on 1999 models onward, pyrotechnic tensioners are fitted. Both systems are designed to instantaneously take up any slack in the seat belt in the case of a sudden frontal impact, therefore reducing the possibility of injury to the front seat occupants. Each front seat is fitted with its own system, the components of which are mounted in the seat frame **(see illustration)**.

The seat belt tensioner is triggered by a frontal impact causing a deceleration of six

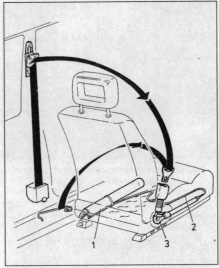

24.1 Seat belt tensioner mechanism components

1 Tensioner unit, containing pre-tensioned spring
2 Cable
3 Pivot

times the force of gravity or greater. Lesser impacts, including impacts from behind, will not trigger the system.

On the mechanical type tensioners, when the system is triggered, a pre-tensioned spring draws back the seat belt via a cable which acts on the seat belt stalk. The cable can move by up to 80.0 mm, which therefore reduces the slack in the seat belt around the shoulders and waist of the occupant by a similar amount.

On the pyrotechnic type seat belt tensioner, the tensioner is actuated by a gas generator cartridge connected to the seat belt stalk.

There is a risk of injury if the system is triggered inadvertently when working on the vehicle, and it is therefore strongly recommended that any work involving the seat belt tensioner system is entrusted to a Vauxhall/Opel dealer. Refer to the warning given at the beginning of Section 23 before contemplating any work on the front seats.

25 Seat belt components – removal and refitting

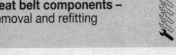

Removal

Front seat belt – three-door models

1 Prise off the trim cover from the upper seat belt mounting. Unscrew the mounting bolt, and recover the washer and spacer from behind the belt anchorage **(see illustration)**.

2 Remove the trim cap, then slacken and remove bolt and washer securing the seat belt mounting rail to the floor. Disengage the rail from the floor and the seat belt, and remove it **(see illustrations)**.

3 Remove the rear seat backrest as described in Section 23.

25.1 On three-door models, unscrew the front seat belt upper mounting bolt, and recover the spacer and washer from behind the belt anchorage

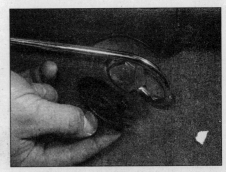

25.2a Remove the trim cap . . .

25.2b . . . then unscrew the retaining bolt and washer . . .

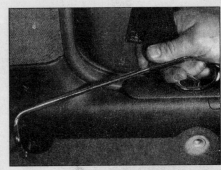

25.2c . . . and disengage the seat belt mounting rail from the floor and seat belt, and remove it from the vehicle

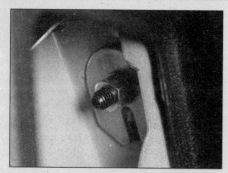

25.5a Unscrew the retaining nut and washer . . .

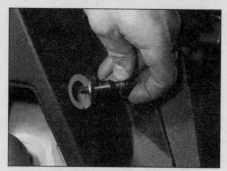

25.5b . . . and remove the seat pin and washer (where fitted)

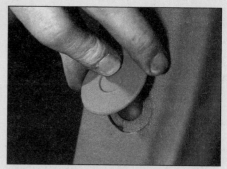

25.6a Prise out the circular plug (where fitted) from the front of the luggage compartment side trim panel

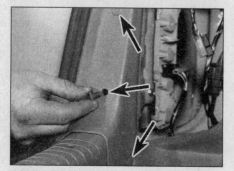

25.6b Prise out the three retaining clips (arrowed) from the rear of the panel . . .

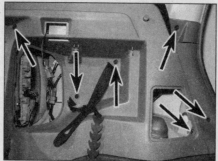

25.6c . . . then undo the retaining screws (arrowed) and remove the panel

pin and washer from the vehicle (see illustrations).

6 Prise out the retaining clips from the rear of the panel, and the circular plug/seat stop buffer (as applicable) from the front of the panel. Slacken and remove all the panel retaining screws, then release the panel from the vehicle body and disconnect the speaker wiring connector (where fitted) (see illustrations).

7 Position the luggage compartment panel clear of the rear seat side trim panel. There is no need to undo the rear seat belt anchorages.

8 Undo the two screws, and release the sill trim panel from the front edge of the rear seat side trim panel (see illustration).

9 Slacken and remove the rear retaining screw from the base of the panel (see illustration).

10 Peel the door sealing strip away from the front edge of the rear seat side panel, then unclip the top of the panel and remove it from the vehicle (see illustrations).

11 Undo the inertia reel retaining bolt, and remove the seat belt assembly from the vehicle. If necessary, the seat belt height adjuster ratchet can be removed as follows.

12 Prise out the hook from the top of the door pillar panel. Undo the upper and lower retaining screws, and remove the trim panel to gain access to the seat belt height adjuster ratchet. Undo the two bolts and remove the ratchet (see illustrations).

4 If the left-hand seat belt is to be removed, remove the interior light unit from the luggage compartment trim panel as described in Chapter 12.

5 Remove the rear shock absorber access panel from the relevant luggage compartment side trim panel. Where necessary, undo the retaining nut and washer, and remove the seat

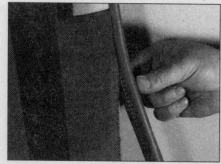

25.8 Undo the two screws, and release the sill trim panel from the rear seat side trim panel

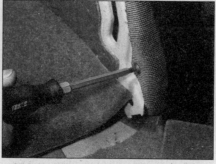

25.9 Undo the rear retaining screw . . .

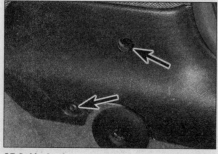

25.10a . . . then peel the door sealing strip away from the front of the panel . . .

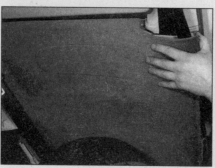

25.10b . . . and unclip the panel from the vehicle

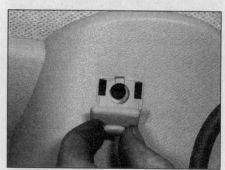

25.12a Remove the hook from the door pillar panel, and unscrew the upper retaining screw . . .

25.12b . . . then undo the lower retaining screw . . .

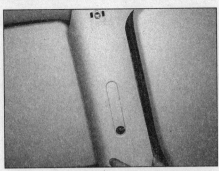

25.12c . . . and remove the door pillar trim panel

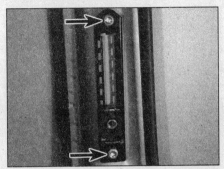

25.12d Seat belt height adjuster ratchet is retained by two bolts (arrowed)

Front seat belt – five-door and Combo Van models

13 Prise off the trim cap from the seat belt upper mounting. Unscrew the mounting bolt, and recover the washer and spacer from behind the belt anchorage **(see illustrations)**.

14 Remove the trim caps from the door pillar trim panel to reveal the retaining screws, then undo both screws and free the panels. Unclip the two panel sections, and remove them from the vehicle **(see illustration)**.

15 Prise off the trim cap from the lower seat belt mounting. Unscrew the mounting bolt, and recover the washer, spacer and trim cover from behind the belt anchorage.

16 Undo the inertia reel retaining bolt, and remove the seat belt assembly from the vehicle **(see illustration)**. If necessary, undo the retaining bolts and remove the seat belt ratchet mechanism from the door pillar.

Rear seat side belt – three-door and five-door models

17 Carry out the operations described above in paragraphs 3 to 6.

18 Prise off the trim cover from the upper seat belt mounting. Unscrew the mounting bolt, and recover the washer and spacer from behind the belt anchorage **(see illustration)**.

19 Unscrew the lower seat belt mounting bolt and washer, then undo the inertia reel retaining bolt. Remove the guide from the luggage compartment trim panel, then free the belt and remove it from the vehicle **(see illustrations)**. If necessary, the seat belt

25.13a Unclip the trim cap . . .

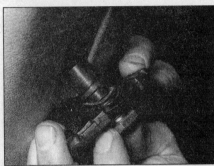

25.13b . . . then unscrew the mounting bolt, and recover the washer and spacer from behind the belt anchorage

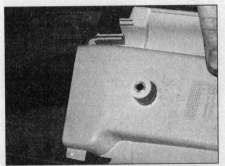

25.14 Unclip the two halves of the door pillar trim panel, and remove them

25.16 Undo the inertia reel retaining bolt (arrowed) and remove the seat belt assembly

25.18 Unscrew the rear seat belt upper mounting bolt, noting the correct fitted position of the washer and spacer

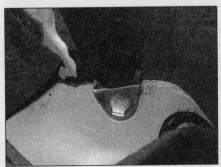

25.19a Unscrew the lower mounting bolt . . .

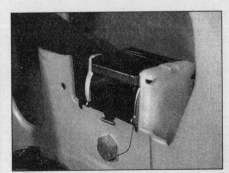

25.19b . . . and the inertia reel retaining bolt . . .

25.19c ... then remove the guide, and feed the belt through the luggage compartment trim panel

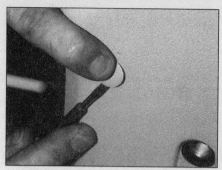

25.20a On three-door models, prise out the trim cap ...

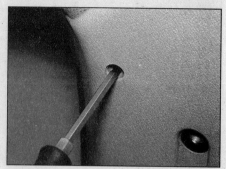

25.20b ... then undo the upper retaining screw ...

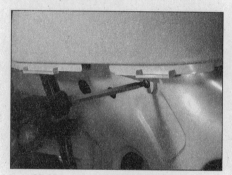

25.20c ... and the lower retaining screw ...

25.20d ... and unclip the trim panel from the vehicle

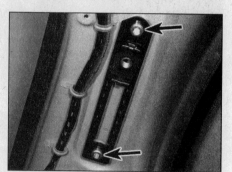

25.21 Rear seat belt height adjuster mechanism is retained by two bolts (arrowed)

height adjuster ratchet can be removed as follows.

20 On three-door models, prise out the trim cap from the top of the rear window trim panel, then undo both the upper and lower panel retaining screws. Unclip the retaining clips, situated along the top edge of the panel, and free it from the door pillar trim panel **(see illustrations)**. **Note:** *It may be necessary to remove the hook and undo the door pillar panel upper screw first (see paragraph 12).* Undo the two retaining bolts and remove the ratchet.

21 On five-door models, prise out the trim caps, then undo the retaining screws and remove the rear quarter window trim panel. Undo the two retaining bolts, and remove the ratchet **(see illustration)**.

Rear seat side belt – Combo Van models

22 Where necessary, undo the retaining bolts and remove the luggage compartment grille from the vehicle.

23 Fold the rear seat cushion forwards, then prise out the retaining clips and remove the trim panel from either side of the seat belt inertia reel.

24 Undo the retaining screws, and remove the cover from the inertia reel.

25 Unclip the trim cover from the upper belt mounting. Undo the bolt, and recover the washer and spacer from behind the belt anchorage.

26 Undo the lower seat belt and inertia reel retaining bolts, and remove the seat belt from the vehicle.

Rear seat centre belt and buckles – all models

27 Fold the rear seat cushion forwards, and unscrew the relevant bolt securing the belt or buckle to the floor **(see illustration)**.

Refitting

28 Refitting is a reversal of the removal procedure, ensuring that all the mounting bolts are tightened to the specified torque, where applicable **(see illustration)**. Make sure that any trim panels disturbed during removal are securely retained by all the relevant retaining clips.

---

26 Interior trim – removal and refitting

Interior trim panels

1 The interior trim panels are secured using either screws or various types of trim fasteners, usually studs or clips.

2 Check that there are no other panels overlapping the one to be removed; usually there is a sequence that has to be followed that will become obvious on close inspection.

3 Remove all obvious fasteners, such as screws. If the panel will not come free, it is held by hidden clips or fasteners. These are usually situated around the edge of the panel,

25.27 Rear seat belt buckle retaining bolt

25.28 When refitting, tighten the seat belt mounting bolts to their specified torque settings

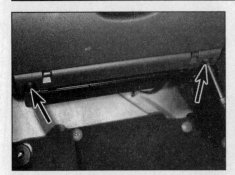

26.6 Unscrew the glovebox lower retaining screws (arrowed) . . .

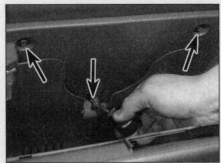

26.7a . . . then undo the three upper retaining screws (arrowed) . . .

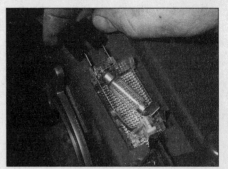

26.7b . . . and withdraw the glovebox, disconnecting the wiring connector from the illumination light as it becomes accessible

and can be prised up to release them; note, however, that they can break quite easily, so replacements should be available. The best way of releasing such clips (in the absence of the correct type of tool) is to use a large flat-bladed screwdriver. Note in many cases that the adjacent sealing strip must be prised back to release a panel.

4 When removing a panel, **never** use excessive force, or the panel may be damaged; always check carefully that all fasteners have been removed or released before attempting to withdraw a panel.

5 Refitting is the reverse of the removal procedure; secure the fasteners by pressing them firmly into place, and ensure that all

disturbed components are secured correctly, to prevent rattles.

Glovebox

6 Slacken and remove the two glovebox lower retaining screws **(see illustration)**.

7 Open up the glovebox lid, and undo the three upper retaining screws situated inside the glovebox (on models with a passenger's air bag, the centre screw is not fitted). Slide the glovebox out of position, disconnecting the wiring connectors from the glovebox illumination light and anti-theft warning system control unit (where fitted) as they becomes accessible **(see illustrations)**.

8 Refitting is the reverse of removal.

Carpets

9 The passenger compartment floor carpet is in one piece, and is secured at its edges by screws or clips, usually the same fasteners used to secure the various adjoining trim panels.

10 Carpet removal and refitting is reasonably straightforward, but very time-consuming. All adjoining trim panels must be removed first, as must components such as the seats, the centre console and seat belt lower anchorages.

Headlining

11 The headlining is clipped to the roof, and can only be withdrawn once all fittings such as the grab handles, sunvisors, sunroof (if fitted), windscreen and rear quarter windows and related trim panels have been removed, and the door, tailgate and sunroof aperture sealing strips have been prised clear.

12 Note that headlining removal requires considerable skill and experience if it is to be carried out without damage, and is therefore best entrusted to an expert.

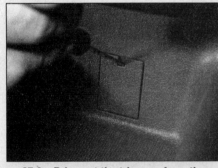

27.2a Prise out the trim cap from the centre console storage compartment . . .

27.2b . . . to gain access to the retaining screw

27 Centre console – removal and refitting

Removal

1 Firmly apply the handbrake, and slide both front seats fully rearwards.

2 Prise out the trim cap from the front of the centre console storage compartment, and unscrew the retaining screw **(see illustrations)**.

3 Unclip the gear lever gaiter from the centre console, and fold it back over the gear lever **(see illustration)**.

4 Slide the console to the rear to disengage it from its retaining clip, and lift it upwards and over the gear lever **(see illustration)**.

27.3 Unclip the gaiter and fold it back over the gear lever

27.4 Move the centre console to the rear to free it from its retaining clips, and lift it over the gear lever

Refitting

5 Refitting is the reverse of removal.

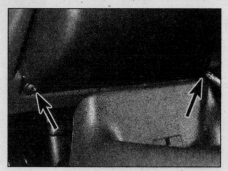

28.6a Undo the two lower retaining screws . . .

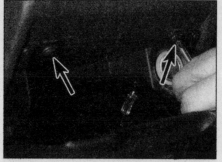

28.6b . . . then open up the ashtray, and undo the two upper retaining screws

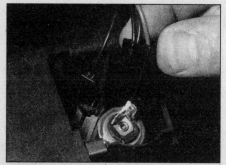

28.6c Withdraw the ashtray from the facia, and disconnect its wiring connectors

28 Facia panel assembly – removal and refitting

HAYNES HINT *Label each wiring connector as it is disconnected from its relevant component. The labels will prove useful when refitting, as a guide to routing the wiring and feeding it through the facia apertures.*

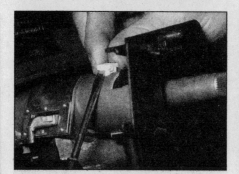

28.10a Prise out the two retaining clips . . .

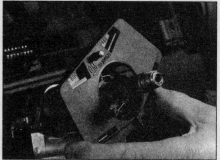

28.10b . . . then turn the combination switch mounting bracket anti-clockwise, and slide it off the steering column

Removal

1 Disconnect the battery negative terminal (refer to *Disconnecting the battery* in the Reference Chapter).
2 Remove the following components as described in Chapter 12:
a) *Instrument panel.*
b) *Windscreen wiper motor.*
c) *Radio/cassette player.*
d) *Clock/multi/function unit display.*
e) *Steering column combination switches.*
3 Remove the following components as described in Chapter 3:
a) *Heater/ventilation control unit.*
b) *Driver's side vent housing.*
c) *Passenger side heater duct.*
4 Remove the glovebox as described in Section 26.
5 Remove the storage compartment (where fitted) from underneath the passenger side of

the facia. The compartment is secured in position by a retaining screw and clip.
6 Undo the two lower ashtray retaining screws, then open up the ashtray and remove the two upper retaining screws. Withdraw the ashtray from the centre of the facia, disconnecting the wiring connectors from the rear of the unit as they become accessible (see illustrations).
7 Remove the centre console as described in Section 27.
8 Undo the retaining screws, and release the fusebox from the driver's side of the facia, and the relay carrier from the top of the glovebox aperture. See Section 3 of Chapter 12 for further information. There is no need to disconnect any of the above components – they can be left in position
9 Remove the steering wheel as described in Chapter 10.

10 Prise out the two retaining clips from the combination switch mounting bracket, then twist the bracket anti-clockwise and slide it off the top of the steering column (see illustrations).
11 Disconnect the wiring connector from the stop-light switch. On models with an air bag, disconnect the control unit wiring connector, then undo the retaining screws and remove the control unit from the vehicle.
12 Undo the retaining screws, and remove the support bracket from the base of the centre of the facia (see illustration).
13 Where necessary, undo the screw securing the radio/cassette mounting bracket in position, then slide out the bracket, freeing it from the aerial lead and wiring connector (see illustrations).
14 Release the retaining clips and, noting its

28.12 Removing the support bracket from the centre of the facia

28.13a Undo the retaining screw (arrowed), then slide out the radio/cassette bracket, freeing the wiring connector . . .

28.13b . . . and aerial lead from the rear of the bracket

correct routing, free the wiring loom from the metal frame of the facia panel. Also slide the instrument panel wiring connector out from its clip on the facia **(see illustrations)**.

15 Undo the two retaining screws from the left-hand end of the facia panel, and the two screws from the facia right-hand end **(see illustration)**.

16 Return to the engine compartment, and undo the three retaining nuts securing the facia to the bulkhead **(see illustration)**.

17 The facia panel is now free to be removed. Pull the panel away from the bulkhead, then remove the facia assembly, noting the correct routing of the wiring harnesses, and feeding the wiring back through the facia apertures.

Refitting

18 Refitting is a reversal of the removal procedure, noting the following points:
a) Manoeuvre the facia into position and, using the labels stuck on during removal, ensure that the wiring is correctly routed and fed through the relevant facia apertures.
b) Clip the facia back into position, then refit all the facia fasteners and tighten them to their specified torque settings.
c) On completion, reconnect the battery and check that all the electrical components and switches function correctly.

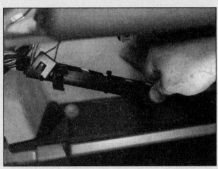

28.14a Release the retaining clips and ties, and free the wiring from the facia metal frame . . .

28.14b . . . and the instrument panel wiring connector from the facia

28.15 Undo the facia side retaining screws . . .

28.16 . . . then undo the nuts securing the facia assembly to the engine compartment bulkhead

Chapter 12
Body electrical systems

Contents

Degrees of difficulty

Easy, suitable for novice with little experience	**Fairly easy,** suitable for beginner with some experience	**Fairly difficult,** suitable for competent DIY mechanic	**Difficult,** suitable for experienced DIY mechanic	**Very difficult,** suitable for expert DIY or professional

Specifications

System type . . . . 12 volt negative earth

Bulbs	**Wattage**
Direction indicator side repeater	5
Direction indicator	21
Front foglight	55
Front sidelight	5
Headlight	60/55
Instrument panel illumination lights	2
Instrument panel warning lights	1.2
Interior lights	10
Number plate light	10
Rear foglight	21
Reversing light	21
Stop/tail light	21/5

Torque wrench settings	**Nm**	**lbf ft**
Air bag unit retaining screws	10	7
Windscreen wiper motor	25	18

1 General information and precautions

Warning: Before carrying out any work on the electrical system, read through the precautions given in 'Safety first!' at the beginning of this manual, and in Chapter 5A.

1 The electrical system is of the 12 volt negative earth type. Power for the lights and all electrical accessories is supplied by a lead-acid type battery, which is charged by the engine-driven alternator.

2 This Chapter covers repair and service procedures for the various electrical components not associated with the engine. Information on the battery, alternator and starter motor can be found in Chapter 5A.

3 It should be noted that, prior to working on any component in the electrical system, the battery negative terminal should first be disconnected, to prevent the possibility of electrical short-circuits and/or fires.

Caution: Before proceeding, refer to 'Disconnecting the battery' in the Reference Chapter for further information.

2 Electrical fault finding – general information

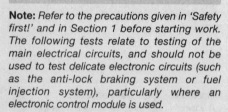

Note: *Refer to the precautions given in 'Safety first!' and in Section 1 before starting work. The following tests relate to testing of the main electrical circuits, and should not be used to test delicate electronic circuits (such as the anti-lock braking system or fuel injection system), particularly where an electronic control module is used.*

General

1 A typical electrical circuit consists of an electrical component, any switches, relays, motors, fuses, fusible links or circuit breakers related to that component, and the wiring and connectors which link the component to both the battery and the vehicle body. To help to pinpoint a problem in an electrical circuit, wiring diagrams are included at the end of this Chapter.

2 Before attempting to diagnose an electrical fault, first study the appropriate wiring diagram to obtain a complete understanding of the components included in the particular circuit concerned. The possible sources of a fault can be narrowed down by noting if other components related to the circuit are operating properly. If several components or circuits fail at one time, the problem is likely to be related to a shared fuse or earth connection.

3 Electrical problems usually stem from simple causes, such as loose or corroded connections, a faulty earth connection, a blown fuse, a melted fusible link, or a faulty relay (refer to Section 3 for details of testing relays). Inspect the condition of all fuses, wires and connections in a problem circuit before testing the components. Use the wiring diagrams to determine which terminal connections will need to be checked in order to pinpoint the trouble-spot.

4 The basic tools required for electrical fault-finding include a circuit tester or voltmeter (a 12 volt bulb with a set of test leads can also be used for certain tests); a self-powered test light (sometimes known as a continuity tester); an ohmmeter (to measure resistance); a battery and set of test leads; and a jumper wire, preferably with a circuit breaker or fuse incorporated, which can be used to bypass suspect wires or electrical components. Before attempting to locate a problem with test instruments, use the wiring diagram to determine where to make the connections.

5 To find the source of an intermittent wiring fault (usually due to a poor or dirty connection, or damaged wiring insulation), a 'wiggle' test can be performed on the wiring. This involves wiggling the wiring by hand to see if the fault occurs as the wiring is moved. It should be possible to narrow down the source of the fault to a particular section of wiring. This method of testing can be used in conjunction with any of the tests described in the following sub-Sections.

6 Apart from problems due to poor connections, two basic types of fault can occur in an electrical circuit – open-circuit, or short-circuit.

7 Open-circuit faults are caused by a break somewhere in the circuit, which prevents current from flowing. An open-circuit fault will prevent a component from working, but will not cause the relevant circuit fuse to blow.

8 Short-circuit faults are caused by a 'short' somewhere in the circuit, which allows the current flowing in the circuit to 'escape' along an alternative route, usually to earth. Short-circuit faults are normally caused by a breakdown in wiring insulation, which allows a feed wire to touch either another wire, or an earthed component such as the bodyshell. A short-circuit fault will normally cause the relevant circuit fuse to blow.

Finding an open-circuit

9 To check for an open-circuit, connect one lead of a circuit tester or voltmeter to either the negative battery terminal or a known good earth.

10 Connect the other lead to a connector in the circuit being tested, preferably nearest to the battery or fuse.

11 Switch on the circuit, bearing in mind that some circuits are live only when the ignition switch is turned to a particular position.

12 If voltage is present (indicated either by the tester bulb lighting or a voltmeter reading, as applicable), this means that the section of the circuit between the relevant connector and the battery is problem-free.

13 Continue to check the remainder of the circuit in the same fashion.

14 When a point is reached at which no voltage is present, the problem must lie between that point and the previous test point with voltage. Most problems can be traced to a broken, corroded or loose connection.

Finding a short-circuit

15 To check for a short-circuit, first disconnect the load(s) from the circuit (loads are the components which draw current from a circuit, such as bulbs, motors, heating elements, etc).

16 Remove the relevant fuse from the circuit, and connect a circuit tester or voltmeter to the fuse connections.

17 Switch on the circuit, bearing in mind that some circuits are live only when the ignition switch is turned to a particular position.

18 If voltage is present (indicated either by the tester bulb lighting or a voltmeter reading, as applicable), this means that there is a short-circuit.

19 If no voltage is present, but the fuse still blows with the load(s) connected, this indicates an internal fault in the load(s).

Finding an earth fault

20 The battery negative terminal is connected to 'earth' – the metal of the engine/transmission unit and the car body – and most systems are wired so that they only receive a positive feed, the current returning via the metal of the car body. This means that the component mounting and the body form part of that circuit. Loose or corroded mountings can therefore cause a range of electrical faults, ranging from total failure of a circuit, to a puzzling partial fault. In particular, lights may shine dimly (especially when another circuit sharing the same earth point is in operation), motors (eg, wiper motors or the radiator cooling fan motor) may run slowly, and the operation of one circuit may have an apparently-unrelated effect on another. Note that on many vehicles, earth straps are used between certain components, such as the engine/transmission and the body, usually where there is no metal-to-metal contact between components, due to flexible rubber mountings, etc.

21 To check whether a component is properly earthed, disconnect the battery, and connect one lead of an ohmmeter to a known good earth point. Connect the other lead to the wire or earth connection being tested. The resistance reading should be zero; if not, check the connection as follows.

22 If an earth connection is thought to be faulty, dismantle the connection, and clean back to bare metal both the bodyshell and the wire terminal or the component earth connection mating surface. Be careful to remove all traces of dirt and corrosion, then use a knife to trim away any paint, so that a clean metal-to-metal joint is made. On reassembly, tighten the joint fasteners securely; if a wire terminal is being refitted,

use serrated washers between the terminal and the bodyshell, to ensure a clean and secure connection. When the connection is remade, prevent the onset of corrosion in the future by applying a coat of petroleum jelly or silicone-based grease. Alternatively, at regular intervals, spray on a proprietary ignition sealer or a water-dispersant lubricant.

3 Fuses and relays – general information

Fuses

1 Most of the fuses are located behind the driver's side lower facia panel, with additional fuses on some models being located in the junction box in the engine compartment **(see illustrations)**. The junction box is located next to the master cylinder brake fluid reservoir.

2 To gain access to fusebox, unclip the access panel from the driver's side of the facia. To gain access to those in the junction box, unclip the junction box lid.

3.1a Unclip the cover from the driver's side of the facia to gain access to most of the fuses

3.1b Additional fuses and relays are located in the junction box in the engine compartment (right-hand drive model)

3 The fuse number is marked on the fusebox next to each fuse. A list of the circuits each fuse protects is given in the Specifications at the start of this Chapter.

4 To remove a fuse, first switch off the circuit concerned (or the ignition), then pull the fuse out of its terminals. The wire within the fuse is clearly visible; if the fuse is blown, it will be broken or melted.

5 Always renew a fuse with one of an identical rating; never use a fuse with a different rating from the original, nor substitute anything else. Never renew a fuse

more than once without tracing the source of the trouble. The fuse rating is stamped on top of the fuse; note that the fuses are also colour-coded for easy recognition.

6 If a new fuse blows immediately, find the cause before renewing it again; a short to earth as a result of faulty insulation is most likely. Where a fuse protects more than one circuit, try to isolate the defect by switching on each circuit in turn (if possible) until the fuse blows again. Always carry a supply of spare fuses of each relevant rating on the vehicle, a spare of each rating should be clipped into the base of the fusebox.

Relays

7 The majority of relays are located in the top of the fusebox behind the driver's side lower facia panel. Additional relays may be located on the relay carriers which are situated behind the facia above the glovebox, behind the right-hand footwell trim panel, or in the engine compartment junction box. Full details of relay locations are given in the Specifications at the start of this Chapter, and in the accompanying illustrations **(see illustrations)**.

8 To gain access to the fusebox relays, unclip the fusebox access panel from the facia, then undo the two retaining screws and lower the fusebox out from the facia **(see illustrations)**.

9 To gain access to the facia relay carrier, remove the glovebox as described in Chapter 11, Section 26. Undo the two retaining screws, and lower the anti-theft alarm control unit (where fitted) out from the top of the glovebox aperture. Undo the two screws, and

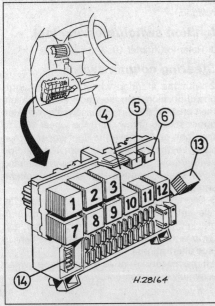

3.7a Fusebox relay locations and identification numbers

1 Exterior mirror heating timer relay (K35)
2 Turn signal relay (K10)
3 Tailgate wiper relay (K30)
4 Not used
5 Front foglight relay (K5)
6 Rear foglight relay (K89)
7 Windscreen wiper relay (K8)
8 Heated rear window relay (K1)
9 'Lights-on' warning buzzer (H19)
10 Anti-theft alarm horn relay (K63)
11 Headlight washer system relay (K97)
12 Anti-theft alarm immobiliser relay (K3)
13 Daytime driving light relay (K59)
14 Diagnostic plug (for use by Vauxhall/Opel dealer)

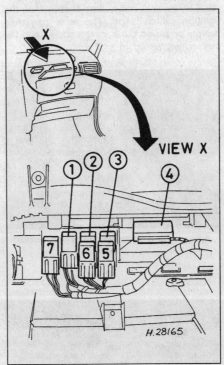

3.7b Relay carrier relay locations and identification numbers

1 Cooling fan relay (K51)
2 Cooling fan relay (K52)
3 Cooling fan relay (K26)
4 Anti-theft alarm control unit
5 Air conditioning relay (K6)
6 Air conditioning cooling fan relay (K7)
7 Cooling fan relay (high-speed) (K67)

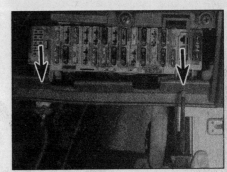

3.8a Undo the two retaining screws (arrowed) . . .

3.8b . . . and lower the fusebox out of position to gain access to the relays

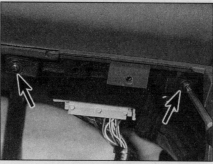

3.9a Undo the two retaining screws (arrowed) . . .

3.9b . . . and lower the anti-theft alarm control unit out of position to gain access to the relay carrier

lower the relay carrier plate out from the top of the glovebox aperture **(see illustrations)**.

10 To gain access to the relay carrier behind the right-hand footwell trim panel, open the front door and where applicable, remove the storage tray from under the facia. Remove the screw securing the front of the sill trim panel and lift up the front edge of the panel. Remove the screw and plastic clip securing the footwell trim panel. Carefully pull back the weatherstrip from the front edge of the door aperture to expose the edge of the footwell trim panel, then withdraw the trim panel from the footwell.

11 If a circuit or system controlled by a relay develops a fault and the relay is suspect,

operate the system; if the relay is functioning, it should be possible to hear it click as it is energised. If this is the case, the fault lies with the components or wiring of the system. If the relay is not being energised, then either the relay is not receiving a main supply or a switching voltage, or the relay itself is faulty. Testing is by the substitution of a known good unit, but be careful; while some relays are identical in appearance and in operation, others look similar but perform different functions.

12 To renew a relay, first ensure that the ignition switch is off. The relay can then simply be pulled out from the socket and the new relay pressed in.

| 4 | Switches |
| | – removal and refitting |

Note: *Disconnect the battery negative terminal (refer to 'Disconnecting the battery' in the Reference Chapter) before removing any switch, and reconnect the terminal after refitting.*

Ignition switch/steering lock

1 Refer to Chapter 10.

Steering column switch

2 With the steering wheel in the straight-ahead position, turn the wheel 90° to the left, then prise off the trim cap and remove the left upper shroud screw. Turn the wheel 180° to the right, and remove the right upper screw. Remove the rubber seal from the ignition switch/lock, then undo the lower retaining screws and remove the steering column shrouds **(see illustrations)**.

3 Depress the retaining clips, and release the relevant switch assembly from the column bracket. Disconnect the wiring connector, and remove the switch assembly from the vehicle **(see illustrations)**.

4 If necessary, remove the opposite switch assembly in the same way.

4.2a Prise out the trim plugs from the top of the steering column shrouds . . .

4.2b . . . and unscrew the upper shroud screws

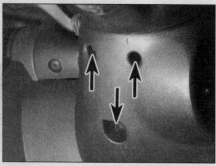

4.2c Unscrew the three lower shroud retaining screws (arrowed) . . .

4.2d . . . then remove the rubber seal from the ignition switch/lock . . .

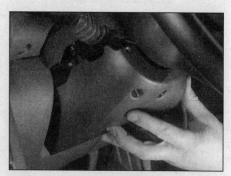

4.2e . . . and remove both shrouds from the column

4.3a Depress the retaining clips, then slide out the switch (shown with steering wheel removed for clarity) . . .

4.3b . . . and disconnect its wiring connector

4.7 Release the retaining clip with a flat-bladed screwdriver, and pull off the lighting switch knob

5 Refitting is a reversal of the removal procedure.

Lighting switch

Note: *Incorporating instruments dimmer and interior lights.*

6 Turn the knob to the headlight 'on' position, and pull the knob out.

7 Insert a small screwdriver or suitable rod through the hole in the bottom of the knob, then depress the switch knob retaining clip and remove the knob **(see illustration)**.

8 Depress the switch retaining clips, pull the switch out from the facia, and disconnect the wiring connector **(see illustration)**.

9 Note that the switch assembly cannot be dismantled; if any of its functions are faulty, the complete assembly must be renewed.

10 Refitting is a reversal of the removal procedure.

Foglight, heated seat and headlight beam adjuster switches

11 To remove the facia pushbutton switches, a suitable hooked tool is needed. A suitable tool can be fabricated from a strip of 2 mm steel which is approximately 5 mm in width (a small hacksaw blade works well). Bend the

end of the strip through 90° so that there is a hook approximately 4 mm in length at a right-angle to the strip.

12 Manoeuvre the strip into position, taking great care not to damage the switch or facia panel. Locate the hook behind the switch, and use it to pull the switch out of position **(see illustration)**.

13 On refitting, push the switch into position until it clicks into position.

Hazard warning switch

14 Depress the switch so that it is set in the 'on' position.

15 Using a small flat-bladed screwdriver, carefully lever the switch out of position,

4.8 Depress the retaining clips, and withdraw the lighting switch from the facia

taking great care not to mark the switch or vent panel **(see illustration)**.

16 On refitting, push the switch in until it clicks into position.

Rear window/fan switch

17 Pull the switch out so that it is set in the 'on' position.

18 Insert a small screwdriver or suitable rod through the hole in the bottom of the knob, then depress the switch knob retaining clip and remove the knob **(see illustration)**.

19 Depress the switch retaining clips, and pull the switch out from the facia **(see illustration)**.

20 Refitting is the reverse of removal.

4.12 Using the hooked tool to withdraw the front foglight switch

4.15 Removing the hazard warning light switch. Note the use of a piece of card to avoid marking the switch surround

4.18 Release the retaining clip with a suitable screwdriver, and pull off the knob

4.19 Depress the retaining clips, and withdraw the heated rear window/blower motor switch from the facia

4.22 Undo the retaining bolt, and remove the handbrake warning light switch from the lever

4.25 Withdraw the courtesy light switch from the door pillar, and disconnect its wiring connector

4.28 Removing the luggage compartment light switch – Combo Van models

Handbrake warning switch

21 Remove the handbrake lever as described in Chapter 9.
22 Undo the bolt, and remove the switch from the lever (see illustration).
23 Install the new switch, securely tightening its retaining bolt, and refit the handbrake lever as described in Chapter 9.

Stop-light switch

24 Refer to Chapter 9.

Courtesy light switch

25 Open the door, then undo the switch retaining screw. Withdraw the switch from the pillar, disconnecting its wiring connector as it becomes accessible (see illustration). Tie a piece of string to the wiring, to prevent it falling back into the door pillar.
26 Refitting is a reverse of the removal procedure.

Luggage area light switch

27 On Corsa and Corsavan models, the switch is fitted to the bottom of the tailgate. On Combo Van models, the switch is fitted to the right-hand side of the vehicle body, on the outside edge of the rear door.
28 Undo the retaining screw, then withdraw the switch and disconnect it from its wiring connector (see illustration). Tie a piece of string to the wiring, to prevent it falling back into the tailgate/vehicle body (as applicable).

29 Refitting is a reverse of the removal procedure.

Driver's door window switch

30 Unscrew the door pocket retaining screws, and pull the pocket downwards and away from the door to release its retaining clips (see illustration). Disconnect the switch wiring connectors.
31 Release the retaining clips, and remove the relevant switch from the panel (see illustration).
32 Refitting is the reverse of removal, ensuring that the wiring is correctly routed inside the door pocket.

Passenger door window switch

33 Remove the door inner trim panel as described in Chapter 11.
34 Disconnect the switch wiring connector, and remove the switch from the vehicle.
35 Refitting is the reverse of removal.

Electric mirror switch

36 Remove the door inner trim panel as described in Chapter 11.
37 Disconnect the switch wiring connector, and remove the switch from the vehicle (see illustration).
38 Refitting is the reverse of removal.

Electric sunroof switch

39 Carefully prise the sunroof switch out of

position, and disconnect it from its wiring connector.
40 When refitting, connect the wiring connector, and clip the switch back into position.

Air conditioning switch

41 The air conditioning system control switch is an integral part of the heating/ventilation control unit, and cannot be removed. Should the switch become faulty, the complete control unit assembly must be renewed (see Chapter 3).

Horn switch

Models without driver's air bag

42 Carefully ease the horn button out from the steering wheel, and disconnect its wiring connector.
43 Reconnect the wiring connector and push the button back into position.

Models with driver's air bag

44 Remove the driver's air bag as described in Section 27.
45 Using a small screwdriver, carefully release the relevant switch from the switch holder in the steering wheel.
46 Disconnect the wiring connector and remove the switch.
47 Refit the wiring connector and switch, then refit the air bag as described in Section 27.

4.30 To remove the driver's door electric window switches, remove the door pocket . . .

4.31 . . . then release the retaining clips, and slide the relevant switch out of the pocket

4.37 Disconnect the wiring connector, and remove the electric mirror switch from the door

5 Bulbs (exterior lights) – renewal

General

1 Whenever a bulb is renewed, note the following points:

a) *Disconnect the battery negative terminal (refer to 'Disconnecting the battery' in the Reference Chapter).*

b) *Remember that if the light has just been in use, the bulb may be extremely hot.*

c) *Always check the bulb contacts and holder, ensuring that there is clean metal-to-metal contact between the bulb and its live(s) and earth. Clean off any corrosion or dirt before fitting a new bulb.*

d) *Wherever bayonet-type bulbs are fitted, ensure that the live contact(s) bear firmly against the bulb contact.*

e) *Always ensure that the new bulb is of the correct rating, and that it is completely clean before fitting it; this applies particularly to headlight/foglight bulbs (see below).*

Headlight

2 Working in the engine compartment, disconnect the wiring connector from the rear of the headlight, then remove the rubber dust cover. Note that if the right-hand bulb is being renewed, it will be necessary to unclip the intake duct from the air cleaner housing to improve access **(see illustrations)**.

3 Unhook and release the ends of the bulb retaining clip, and release it from the rear of the light unit.

4 Withdraw the bulb **(see illustration)**.

5 When handling the new bulb, use a tissue or clean cloth to avoid touching the glass with the fingers; moisture and grease from the skin can cause blackening and rapid failure of this type of bulb. If the glass is accidentally touched, wipe it clean using methylated spirit.

6 Install the new bulb, ensuring that its locating tabs are correctly located in the light cut-outs.

5.2a To improve access to the right-hand headlight unit, release the fastener . . .

5.2b . . . and remove the intake duct from the air cleaner housing

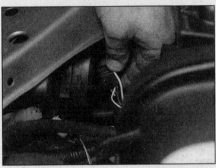

5.2c Disconnect the wiring connector . . .

5.2d . . . and remove the rubber cover from the rear of the headlight

7 Refit the dust cover to the rear of the light unit, and reconnect the wiring connector.

Front sidelight

8 Working in the engine compartment, push the bulbholder inwards, then twist it anti-clockwise to release it from the rear of the headlight unit **(see illustration)**. Note that if the right-hand bulb is being renewed, it will be necessary to unclip the intake duct from the air cleaner housing to improve access.

9 The bulb is of the capless (push-fit) type, and can be removed by simply pulling it out of the bulbholder.

10 Refitting is the reverse of the removal procedure, ensuring that the bulbholder is securely clipped into position.

Front direction indicator

11 Working in the engine compartment, twist the bulbholder anti-clockwise, and remove it from the rear of the headlight unit. Note that if the right-hand bulb is being renewed, it will be necessary to unclip the intake duct from the air cleaner housing to improve access.

12 The bulb is a bayonet fit in the holder, and can be removed by pressing it and twisting in an anti-clockwise direction **(see illustration)**.

13 Refitting is a reverse of the removal procedure.

Direction indicator side repeater

14 Carefully prise the rear edge of the indicator side repeater light out from the wing,

5.4 Release the retaining clip (arrowed) and withdraw the headlight bulb

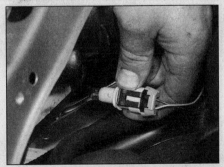

5.8 Removing the sidelight bulbholder from the headlight unit

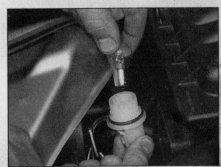

5.12 Front direction turn signal bulb is a bayonet fit in its holder

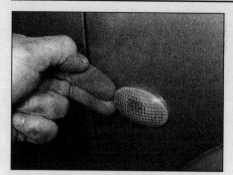

5.14 Lift the rear of the indicator side repeater light to release it from the wing

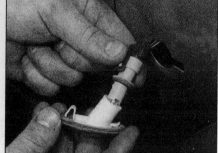

5.15a Release the bulbholder from the rear of the light unit . . .

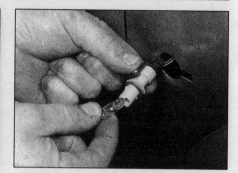

5.15b . . . then pull the bulb out of the holder

if necessary using a suitable plastic wedge, taking great care not damage the painted finish of the wing (see illustration).

15 Withdraw the light unit from the wing, and pull the bulbholder out of the light unit. The bulb is of the capless (push-fit) type, and can be removed by simply pulling it out of the bulbholder (see illustrations).

16 Refitting is a reverse of the removal procedure.

Front foglight

17 If necessary, to improve access to the rear of the foglight, firmly apply the handbrake, then jack up the front of the car and support it securely on axle stands (see *Jacking and vehicle support*).

18 Disconnect the wiring connector from the rear of the foglight unit. Twist the cover anti-clockwise, and free it from the rear of the foglight (see illustration).

19 Disconnect the bulb wire from the cover terminal, then release the spring clip and withdraw the foglight bulb from the rear of the light unit (see illustrations).

20 When handling the new bulb, use a tissue or clean cloth to avoid touching the glass with the fingers; moisture and grease from the skin can cause blackening and rapid failure of this type of bulb. If the glass is accidentally touched, wipe it clean using methylated spirit.

21 Insert the new bulb, making sure it is correctly located, and secure it in position with the spring clip.

22 Connect the bulb wire to the cover terminal, then refit the cover to the rear of the

unit. Connect the wiring connector to the cover, and lower the vehicle to the ground (where applicable).

Rear light cluster

23 From inside the vehicle luggage compartment, depress the retaining catches, and open the trim panel flap to gain access to the rear of the light unit (see illustration).

24 Release the rear light cluster retaining catch(es), and free the bulbholder assembly from the rear of the light unit (see illustration).

25 The relevant bulb can then be renewed; all bulbs have a bayonet fitting (see illustration). Note that the stop/tail light bulb has offset locating pins, to prevent it being installed incorrectly.

26 Refitting is the reverse of the removal

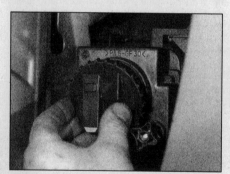

5.18 Twist the cover anti-clockwise to release it from the rear of the foglight

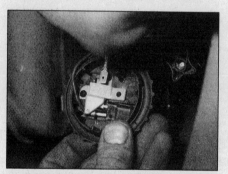

5.19a Disconnect the bulb from the cover . . .

5.19b . . . then release the retaining clip . . .

5.19c . . . and withdraw the foglight bulb from the rear of the unit

5.23 Release the retaining clips, and remove the trim cover to gain access to the rear of the rear light cluster – Combo Van models

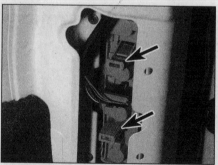

5.24 Depress the retaining catches (arrowed) . . .

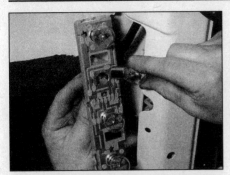

5.25 . . . then withdraw the bulbholder and remove the relevant bulb

5.27 On Corsa and Corsavan models, carefully prise the rear number plate light out from the bumper . . .

5.28a . . . then unclip the lens . . .

5.28b . . . and remove the bulb, which is a bayonet fit in the light unit

5.30 On Combo Van models, release the relevant number plate light from the bumper as described in the text . . .

5.31a . . . then unclip the cover . . .

sequence, ensuring that the bulbholder is securely clipped into position.

Number plate light

Corsa and Corsavan models

27 Using a small flat-bladed screwdriver, carefully prise the light out from the rear bumper **(see illustration)**.
28 Unclip the lens from the light unit, and remove the bulb. The bulb is a bayonet fit in the holder, and can be removed by pressing it and twisting anti-clockwise **(see illustrations)**.
29 Refitting is a reverse of the removal procedure.

Combo Van models

30 On the left-hand side, lift up the light unit, and prise out the base of the unit from the bumper. On the right-hand side, push down on the light unit, and prise out the top of the unit from the bumper **(see illustration)**.
31 Withdraw the light unit, then release the retaining clips and open it up. The bulb is a bayonet fit in the holder, and can be removed by pressing it and twisting anti-clockwise **(see illustrations)**.
32 Refitting is a reverse of the removal procedure.

High-level stop-light

33 The high-level stop-light bulbs are of the LED (light emitting diode) type and cannot be individually renewed.

6 Bulbs (interior lights) – renewal

General

1 Refer to Section 5, paragraph 1.

Front courtesy light

2 Using a suitable screwdriver, carefully prise the light unit out of position, and release the bulb from the light unit contacts **(see illustrations)**.
3 Install the new bulb, ensuring that it is securely held in position by the contacts, and clip the light unit back into position.

5.31b . . . and remove the bulb

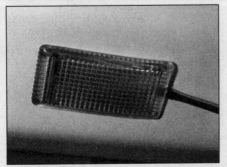

6.2a Carefully prise the courtesy light unit out of position using a small screwdriver . . .

6.2b . . . and release the bulb from its wiring contacts

6.10 Removing an instrument panel illumination/warning light bulb

6.14 Removing the clock/multi-function display illumination bulb

6.17 Withdraw the ashtray unit from the facia . . .

Rear courtesy light

4 Using a small flat-bladed screwdriver, carefully prise the light unit out from its surround. Disconnect the wiring connector, and remove the light.

5 Unclip the heat shield from the light unit, and release the bulb from its contacts.

6 Install the new bulb, ensuring that it is securely held in position by the contacts, and clip the heat shield back into position.

7 Connect the wiring connector, and clip the light back into position in the surround.

Luggage compartment light

8 Refer to the information given above in paragraphs 2 and 3.

Instrument panel lights

9 Remove the instrument panel as described in Section 9.

10 Twist the relevant bulbholder anti-clockwise, and withdraw it from the rear of the panel (see illustration).

11 All bulbs are integral with their holders. Be very careful to ensure that the new bulbs are of the correct rating, the same as those removed; this is especially important in the case of the ignition/no-charge warning light.

12 Refit the bulbholder to the rear of the instrument panel, then refit the instrument panel as described in Section 9.

Clock/multi-function display

13 Remove the clock/multi-function display unit as described in Section 11.

14 Twist the bulbholder anti-clockwise, and withdraw it from the rear of the clock (see illustration). The bulb is integral with its holder.

15 Refit the bulbholder to the rear of the unit, then refit the unit as described in Section 11.

Ashtray/cigarette lighter

16 Open the ashtray, and remove the cigarette lighter insert.

17 Undo the retaining screws, and withdraw the ashtray from the centre of the facia, disconnecting the wiring connectors from the rear of the unit as they become accessible (see illustration).

18 Slide the illumination bulbholder out of the panel, and renew the bulb (see illustration). The bulbs is of the capless (push-fit) type; pull the old bulb out of the holder, and press the new one into position.

19 Slide the illumination bulbholder back into position, and refit the ashtray by reversing the removal procedure.

Heater control illumination

20 Withdraw the heater control panel as described in Chapter 3, so that access to the rear of the panel can be gained. Note there is no need to remove the panel completely; the control cables can be left attached.

21 Unclip the bulbholder from the rear of the control unit (see illustration). The bulbs are of the capless (push-fit) type; pull the relevant bulb out of the holder, and press the new one into position.

22 Refit the bulbholder, and install the control panel as described in Chapter 3.

Glovebox light

23 Open the glovebox. Using a small flat-bladed screwdriver, carefully prise the light unit out of position, then release the bulb from its contacts.

24 Install the new bulb, ensuring it is securely held in position by the contacts, and clip the light unit back into position.

Switch illumination

25 All the switches are fitted with illumination bulbs; some are also fitted with a bulb to show when the circuit concerned is operating. These bulbs are an integral part of the switch assembly, and cannot be obtained separately. Bulb replacement will therefore require the renewal of the complete switch assembly.

7 Exterior light units – removal and refitting

Note: *Disconnect the battery negative terminal (refer to 'Disconnecting the battery' in the Reference Chapter) before removing any light unit, and reconnect the terminal after refitting.*

Headlight

1 Unscrew the two screws securing the relevant end of the front bumper to the wheelarch liner. Unclip the access cover from the top of the liner, and unscrew the plastic nut securing the bumper to the vehicle. Discard the nut; a new one should be used on refitting.

2 Open the bonnet, then slacken and remove the bolts securing the radiator grille section of the bumper to the crossmember, and the two bolts securing the headlight to the crossmember (see illustrations).

3 Release the bumper end from the wheelarch outer trim cover, then hold and push down on the bumper end, and manoeuvre the headlight out of position. Disconnect the wiring connectors from rear of the unit as they become accessible, and remove the headlight unit from the vehicle (see illustrations).

6.18 . . . then disconnect the wiring connectors and remove the illumination bulb from the rear of the unit

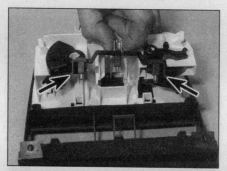

6.21 Release the retaining clips (arrowed), and withdraw the bulbholder from the rear of the heater control panel

7.2a Undo the bolts securing the radiator grille section of the front bumper to the crossmember . . .

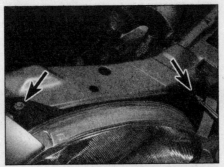

7.2b . . . then undo the two headlight unit retaining bolts (arrowed)

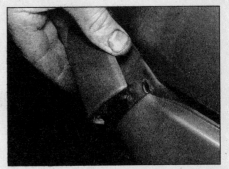

7.3a Release the end of the bumper from the wheelarch outer trim cover . . .

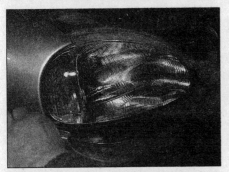

7.3b . . . then push the bumper down and withdraw the headlight unit . . .

7.3c . . . disconnecting the wiring connectors as they become accessible

7.4 Where fitted, remove the headlight beam adjustment motor as described in text

4 On models with a headlight beam adjustment system, if necessary, rotate the adjustment motor clockwise to free the motor from the rear of the headlight unit, and pull the motor squarely away to disconnect its balljoint **(see illustration)**. On refitting, align the motor balljoint with the light unit socket, and clip it into position. Engage the motor assembly with the light, and twist it anti-clockwise to secure it in position.

5 Refitting is a direct reversal of the removal procedure. On completion, check the head-light beam alignment using the information given in Section 8.

Direction indicator light

6 The front direction indicator lights are integral with the headlight units. Removal and refitting is as described above.

Front side repeater light

7 Carefully prise the rear edge of the indicator side repeater light out from the wing, if necessary using a suitable plastic wedge, taking great care not damage the painted finish of the wing.

8 Withdraw the light unit from the wing, and disconnect its wiring connector. Tie a piece of string to the wiring, to prevent it falling back into the wing.

9 On refitting, connect the wiring connector, and clip the light unit back into position.

Front foglight

10 Release the relevant end of the front bumper from the vehicle, as described above in paragraphs 1 to 3, ignoring the references to the headlight. If necessary, jack up the front

of the vehicle and support it on axle stands to improve access to the foglight.

11 Disconnect the wiring connector, then undo the three foglight retaining screws and remove the light unit from the bumper **(see illustrations)**.

12 Refit the light unit to the bumper, and securely tighten its retaining screws.

13 Secure the front bumper in position, and adjust the foglight aim using the adjuster on the rear of the light unit **(see illustration)**.

Rear light cluster

14 From inside the luggage compartment, depress the retaining catches and open up the trim panel flap to gain access to the rear of the light unit.

15 Disconnect the wiring connector from the rear of the bulbholder.

7.11a Disconnect the foglight wiring connector . . .

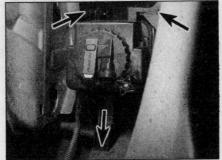

7.11b . . . then undo the three retaining screws (arrowed) . . .

7.11c . . . and remove the light unit from the rear of the bumper

7.13 Foglight aim is adjusted using the adjuster on the rear of the unit

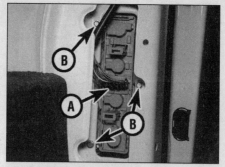

7.16 Rear light unit wiring connector (A) and retaining bolts (B) – Combo Van models

7.18 Removing the rear number plate light unit – Corsa and Corsavan models

16 Slacken and remove the rear light unit retaining bolts, and withdraw the light unit from the rear of the vehicle **(see illustration)**.
17 Refitting is a reverse of the removal procedure, tightening the retaining bolts securely.

Number plate light

Corsa and Corsavan models

18 Using a small flat-bladed screwdriver, carefully prise the light out from the rear bumper, and disconnect it from the wiring connectors **(see illustration)**.
19 When refitting, connect the wiring connector, and clip the light back into the bumper.

Combo Van models

20 On the left-hand side, lift up the light unit, and prise out the base of the unit from the bumper. On the right-hand side, push the light unit down, and prise out the top of the unit from the bumper.
21 Withdraw the light unit, and disconnect the wiring connectors **(see illustration)**.
22 When refitting, connect the wiring connectors, and clip the light back into the bumper.

High-level stop-light

23 Open the tailgate or rear doors as applicable.
24 Undo the screw at each end securing the light body to the mounting brackets and withdraw the light unit from its location.

25 Release the wiring harness, disconnect the wiring connector and remove the light unit.
26 Refitting is a reversal of removal.

---

8   Headlight beam alignment – general information

1 Accurate adjustment of the headlight beam is only possible using optical beam-setting equipment, and this work should therefore be carried out by a Vauxhall/Opel dealer or suitably-equipped workshop.
2 For reference, the headlights can be adjusted using the adjuster assemblies fitted to the top and bottom of each light unit. The top adjuster, accessed through a hole in the crossmember, alters the horizontal position of the beam. The bottom adjuster alters the vertical aim of the beam **(see illustration)**.
3 Some models have an electrically-operated headlight beam adjustment system, controlled via a switch in the facia. The recommended settings are as follows.

Corsa and Corsavan with rear seats

0   Front seat(s) occupied
1   All seats occupied
2   All seats occupied, and load in luggage compartment
3   Driver's seat occupied and load in the luggage compartment

Combo Van and Corsavan without rear seats

0   Seat(s) occupied
1   Seats occupied and load compartment approximately half-loaded
2   Seats occupied and luggage compartment fully loaded
3   Driver's seat only occupied and luggage compartment fully loaded

Note: *When adjusting the headlight aim, ensure that the switch is set to position 0.*

---

9   Instrument panel – removal and refitting

Removal

1 Disconnect the battery negative terminal (refer to *Disconnecting the battery* in the Reference Chapter).
2 With the steering wheel in the straight-ahead position, turn the wheel 90° to the left, then prise off the trim cap and remove the left upper shroud screw. Turn the wheel 180° to the right, and remove the right upper screw. Remove the rubber seal from the ignition switch/lock, then undo the lower retaining screws and remove the steering column shrouds.
3 Undo the three retaining screws, and remove the instrument panel shroud from the facia **(see illustrations)**. Recover the two shroud retaining clips.
4 On early models with a cable-driven mechanical speedometer, unscrew the speedometer cable lower end from the transmission unit. If necessary, remove the battery, then jack up the front of the vehicle and support it on axle stands to improve access to the cable.
5 Unscrew the two retaining screws from the base of the instrument panel **(see illustration)**.
6 Using a small flat-bladed screwdriver, depress the panel upper retaining clip, and withdraw the panel from the facia. The wiring connector disconnects automatically as the panel is removed **(see illustration)**.

7.21 Removing a rear number plate light unit – Combo Van models

8.2 Adjusting the headlight horizontal beam using a suitable screwdriver (vertical beam adjuster arrowed)

7 Depress the retaining clip, disconnect the speedometer cable (where applicable), and remove the instrument panel from the vehicle.

Refitting

8 Where applicable, connect the speedometer cable to the rear of the panel, making sure it is securely retained by the clip, and connect the panel wiring connectors.
9 Clip the panel back into position, aligning it with its wiring connector, and secure it in position with the two retaining screws.
10 Refit the instrument panel shroud, and securely tighten its retaining screws.
11 Install the upper and lower steering column shrouds, and securely tighten all the retaining screws. Fit the rubber seal to the ignition switch/lock and the trim caps to the upper screws.
12 Connect the lower end of the speedometer cable to the transmission, and tighten it securely.
13 Reconnect the battery, and check the operation of the panel warning lights to ensure that they are functioning correctly.

10 Instrument panel components – removal and refitting

General

1 Remove the instrument panel as described in Section 9, then proceed as described under the relevant sub-heading.

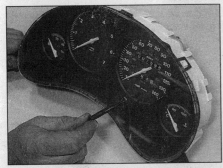

10.2a Pull out the trip odometer reset pin . . .

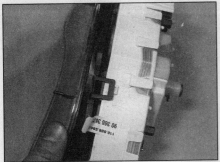

10.2b . . . then release the retaining clips and remove the lens from the front of the instrument panel

9.3a Undo the three instrument panel shroud retaining screws (shown with steering wheel removed for clarity) . . .

9.5 Undo the panel retaining screws (A), then release the clip (B) . . .

Speedometer

2 Remove the reset pin for the trip odometer, then carefully release the retaining clips and remove the lens from the front of the instrument panel **(see illustrations)**.
3 Carefully detach the printed circuit from the speedometer housing **(see illustration)**.
4 Undo the retaining screws, and remove the speedometer from the rear of the instrument panel **(see illustration)**.
5 Refitting is a reverse of the removal procedure. Do not overtighten the instrument panel fasteners, as the plastic is easily cracked.

Tachometer

6 Remove the lens from the panel as described in paragraph 2.

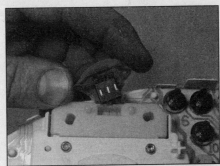

10.3 Carefully detach the printed circuit from the top of the speedometer housing

9.3b . . . and manoeuvre the shroud out of position

9.6 . . . and withdraw the instrument panel from the facia

7 Undo the retaining screws, and lift the tachometer out from the panel assembly.
8 When refitting, ensure that the tachometer pins are correctly aligned with the panel housing, then refit the retaining screws. Do not overtighten the screws, as the plastic is easily cracked. Clip the lens back onto the panel, and refit the trip odometer reset pin.

Temperature gauge

9 Remove the lens from the panel as described in paragraph 2.
10 Undo the retaining nuts securing the wiring to the temperature gauge terminals, and lift the gauge out from the panel **(see illustration 10.4)**.

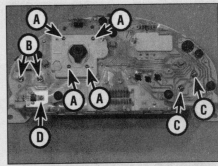

10.4 Instrument panel components (high-specification panel with tachometer)

A Speedometer retaining screws
B Temperature gauge nuts
C Fuel gauge nuts
D Voltage stabiliser

10.15 Undo the retaining screw (arrowed) and disconnect the voltage stabiliser from the rear of the instrument panel

11 Refitting is the reverse of removal. Do not overtighten the retaining nuts, as the plastic is easily cracked.

Fuel gauge

12 Remove the lens from the panel as described in paragraph 2.
13 Undo the retaining nuts securing the wiring to the fuel gauge terminals, and lift the gauge out from the panel (see illustration 10.4).
14 Refitting is the reverse of removal. Do not overtighten the retaining nuts, as the plastic is easily cracked.

Voltage stabiliser

15 Undo the retaining screw, then carefully pull the stabiliser from the instrument panel wiring pins (see illustration).
16 When refitting, ease the stabiliser onto the pins, and secure it in position with the retaining screw.

Printed circuit

17 Remove all the instruments and the voltage stabiliser as described above.
18 Remove all the bulbholders from the rear of the case by twisting them in an anti-clockwise direction. Release the printed circuit from its retaining pins, and remove it from the rear of the case.
19 Refitting is a reversal of the removal procedure, ensuring that the printed circuit is

correctly located on all the necessary retaining pins.

11 Clock/multi-function display components – removal and refitting

1 The clock/multi-function display unit is fitted to the centre of the facia. The display panel shows the time; on higher-specification models, it also shows the outside air temperature and/or the radio station.

Clock/multi-function display unit

Removal

2 Disconnect the battery negative terminal (refer to *Disconnecting the battery* in the Reference Chapter).
3 Remove both the centre heater/ventilation vents from the facia, as described in Chapter 3.
4 Undo the two retaining screws located in the vent apertures, then withdraw the clock/multi-function display from the facia (see illustrations).
5 Disconnect the wiring connector, and remove the unit from the vehicle (see illustration).

Refitting

6 Reconnect the wiring connector, then manoeuvre the unit back into position.
7 Securely tighten the screws, and install the vents as described in Chapter 3.
8 Reconnect the battery negative terminal, then reset the clock and enter the radio security code.

Air temperature sensor

Removal

9 The multi-function unit air temperature sensor is mounted in the front of the vehicle, directly behind the centre of the bumper. The sensor is accessible through the bumper grille.
10 Depress the retaining clips, then free the sensor from the rear of its bracket. Disconnect the sensor from its wiring connector, and remove it from the vehicle.

Refitting

11 Connect the sensor to the wiring connector, and clip it back into position in the bumper.

12 'Lights-on' warning system – general information

1 Most vehicles covered in this manual are equipped with a 'lights-on' warning system. The purpose of the system is to warn the driver that the lights have been left on. Once the ignition switch has been turned off; the buzzer will sound when a door is opened. The system consists of a buzzer unit which is linked to the driver's door courtesy light switch.
2 To gain access to the buzzer unit, unclip the fusebox access panel from the facia, then undo the two retaining screws and lower the fusebox out from the facia. The buzzer is the third unit from the left in the lower row of relays. The unit is a push-fit in the fusebox.
3 Refer to Section 4 for information on courtesy light switch removal.

13 Cigarette lighter – removal and refitting

Removal

1 Open the ashtray, and remove the cigarette lighter insert.
2 Undo the retaining screws, and withdraw the ashtray from the centre of the facia. Disconnect the wiring connectors from the rear of the unit as they become accessible.
3 Release the retaining tangs and push out the metal insert, then remove the plastic outer section of the lighter.

Refitting

4 Refitting is a reversal of the removal procedure.

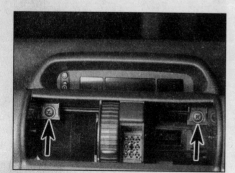

11.4a Undo the two retaining screws (arrowed) . . .

11.4b . . . then lift the multi-function display away from the facia . . .

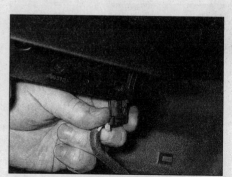

11.5 . . . and disconnect its wiring connector

14.2 Horn unit is retained by a single bolt (arrowed)

16.3 Lift the nut cover, then undo the retaining nut and lift off the wiper arm

HAYNES HINT *Stick a piece of masking tape along the edge of the wiper blade, to use as an alignment aid on refitting.*

14 Horn – removal and refitting

Removal

1 Remove the front bumper as described in Chapter 11.
2 Undo the retaining bolt and remove the horn, disconnecting its wiring connectors as they become accessible **(see illustration)**.

Refitting

3 Refitting is the reverse of removal.

15 Speedometer drive cable – removal and refitting

Removal

Note: *The following procedure is only applicable to early models with a mechanical speedometer. An electric speedometer is fitted to later models and is operated by the vehicle speed sensor on the gearbox/ transmission.*
1 Remove the instrument panel as described in Section 9. Tie a piece string to the upper end of the cable; this can then be used to draw the cable back into position.

2 Free the speedometer cable from any relevant retaining clips and ties, noting its correct routing.
3 Release the cable grommet from the engine compartment bulkhead, and withdraw the cable forwards and out through the bulkhead. Once the cable is free, untie the string and leave it in position in the vehicle; the string can then be used to draw the new cable back into position.

Refitting

4 Tie the string to the end of the cable, then use the string to draw the speedometer cable through from the engine compartment and into position. Once the cable is through, untie the string.
5 Ensure that the cable is correctly routed, and retained by all the relevant clips and ties, then seat the outer cable grommet in the engine compartment bulkhead.
6 Refit the instrument panel as described in Section 9.

16 Wiper arm – removal and refitting

Removal

1 Operate the wiper motor, then switch it off so that the wiper arm returns to the at-rest (parked) position.

2 Lift up the wiper arm spindle nut cover, then slacken and remove the spindle nut.
3 Lift the blade off the glass, and pull the wiper arm off its spindle **(see illustration)**. If necessary, the arm can be levered off the spindle using a suitable flat-bladed screwdriver.
Note: *If both windscreen wiper arms are to be removed at the same time, mark them for identification. The arms are not interchangeable; the passenger-side wiper arm is longer than the driver's-side arm, and its shaft is also cranked slightly.*

Refitting

4 Ensure that the wiper arm and spindle splines are clean and dry, then refit the arm to the spindle, aligning the wiper blade with the tape fitted on removal. Refit the spindle nut, tightening it securely, and clip the nut cover back in position.

17 Windscreen wiper motor and linkage – removal and refitting

Removal

1 Disconnect the battery negative terminal (refer to *Disconnecting the battery* in the Reference Chapter).
2 Remove the wiper arms as described in the previous Section.
3 Undo the retaining screws, and remove both halves of the windscreen cowl panel from the vehicle **(see illustration)**.
4 Peel the bonnet seal off the engine compartment bulkhead, and remove it from the vehicle.
5 Unscrew the large plastic nut from each wiper spindle **(see illustration)**.
6 Prise out the two clips from the centre of the water deflector shield. Release the shield from the engine compartment bulkhead and wiper spindles, and remove it from the vehicle **(see illustrations)**.

17.3 Removing the right-hand windscreen cowl panel

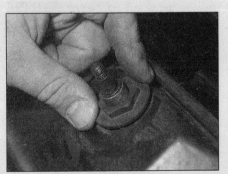

17.5 Unscrew the large plastic nut from each wiper spindle . . .

17.6a . . . then prise out the two clips . . .

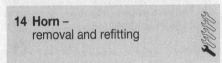

17.6b . . . and remove the water deflector shield from the vehicle

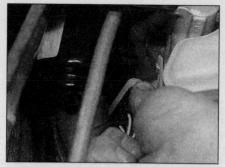

17.7a Disconnect the wiring connector . . .

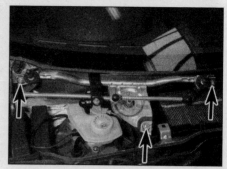

17.7b . . . then undo the three retaining bolts (arrowed) . . .

7 Disconnect the wiring connector from the wiper motor. Undo the three retaining bolts, and remove the wiper motor and linkage assembly out from the vehicle **(see illustrations).**

8 If necessary, mark the relative positions of the motor shaft and linkage arm, then unscrew the retaining nut from the motor spindle. Free the wiper linkage from the spindle, then remove the three motor retaining bolts, and separate the motor and linkage **(see illustration). Note:** *It is not necessary to remove the linkage assembly from the vehicle to remove the motor.*

Refitting

9 Where necessary, assemble the motor and linkage, and securely tighten the motor retaining bolts. Locate the linkage arm on the motor spindle, aligning the marks made prior to removal, and securely tighten its retaining nut.

10 Manoeuvre the motor assembly back into position in the vehicle. Refit the three retaining bolts, and tighten them to the specified torque setting.

11 Reconnect the wiper motor wiring connector.

12 Refit the water deflector, making sure it is correctly located on the bulkhead and wiper spindles, and secure it in position with the two clips and wiper spindle nuts.

13 Install both halves of the windscreen cowl, and securely tighten the retaining screws.

14 Refit the bonnet seal to the engine compartment bulkhead.

15 Install both the wiper arms as described in Section 16, and reconnect the battery negative terminal.

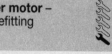

18 Tailgate wiper motor – removal and refitting

Removal

1 Remove the wiper arm as described in Section 16.

2 Remove the plastic cover from the wiper spindle, then unscrew the retaining nut, and lift the washer and outer mounting rubber off the spindle **(see illustrations).**

3 Open the tailgate, and detach the parcel shelf cords. Undo the retaining screws, and remove the lifter hooks from the tailgate **(see illustration).**

4 Carefully prise out the retaining clips, and remove the inner trim panel from the tailgate.

17.7c . . . and remove the wiper motor and linkage assembly from the vehicle (right-hand drive model)

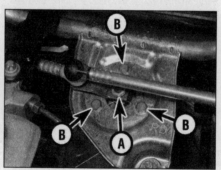

17.8 Windscreen wiper motor spindle nut (A) and retaining bolts (B)

18.2a Remove the plastic cover from the tailgate wiper motor spindle . . .

18.2b . . . then undo the retaining nut . . .

18.2c . . . and lift off the washer and outer mounting rubber (arrowed)

18.3 Undo the retaining screws, and remove the parcel shelf lifter cords from the tailgate

5 Disconnect the wiper motor wiring connector, and release the wiring from any relevant retaining clips.

6 Slacken and remove the wiper motor mounting bolts, noting the correct fitted location of the earth leads, and remove the wiper motor. Recover the collars from either side of each motor mounting rubber, and slide the inner mounting rubber off the motor spindle **(see illustrations)**.

7 Examine the motor mounting rubbers for signs of damage or deterioration, and renew as necessary.

Refitting

8 Slide the inner mounting rubber onto the motor spindle, and ensure that the rubbers are correctly fitted to the motor mountings.

9 Position a collar on each side of the motor mounting rubbers, and refit the motor to the tailgate. Fit the mounting bolts, not forgetting to fit the earth leads to the bolts, and tighten them securely.

10 Reconnect the wiper motor wiring connector.

11 Refit the trim panel to the tailgate, ensuring that it is securely retained by all of its clips. Install the lifter cords.

12 Slide the outer mounting rubber and washer onto the wiper spindle, then fit the retaining nut. Securely tighten the retaining nut, and refit the plastic cover.

13 Refit the wiper arm as described in Section 16.

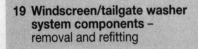

19 Windscreen/tailgate washer system components – removal and refitting

Washer system reservoir

1 Remove the windscreen cowl panels as described in paragraphs 1 to 4 of Section 17.

2 Unscrew the fluid reservoir retaining nut **(see illustration)**, then release the reservoir from its retaining bracket.

3 Disconnect the wiring connector from the washer pump, then disconnect the hose(s) from the base of the pump and remove the reservoir from the vehicle **(see illustrations)**. Wash off any spilt fluid with cold water.

4 Refitting is the reverse of removal, ensuring that the washer hose(s) are securely connected.

Washer pump

5 Remove the washer reservoir as described above.

6 Tip out the contents of the reservoir, then carefully ease the pump out from the reservoir and recover its sealing grommet **(see illustration)**.

7 Refitting is the reverse of removal, using a new sealing grommet if the original one shows signs of damage or deterioration.

Windscreen washer jets

8 Carefully prise the nozzle from the bonnet,

18.6a Undo the wiper motor mounting bolts, noting the correct fitted positions of the earth leads (arrowed)

taking great care not to damage the paintwork.

9 Disconnect the nozzle from its fluid hose, and remove it from the vehicle. Tie a piece of string to the hose, to prevent it falling back into the bonnet.

10 On refitting, securely connect the nozzle to the hose, and clip it into position in the bonnet. Check the operation of the jet. If necessary, adjust the nozzle using a pin, aiming the spray to a point slightly above the centre of the swept area.

Tailgate washer jet

11 Carefully prise the washer jet out of the top of the tailgate/spoiler (as applicable), and disconnect it from its supply pipe. Whilst the jet is removed, tie a piece of string to the

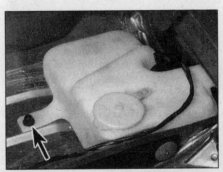

19.2 Undo the retaining nut (arrowed) . . .

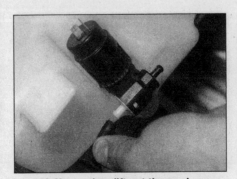

19.3b . . . then lift out the washer reservoir, and disconnect hoses from the pump

18.6b Remove the wiper motor from the tailgate, and slide off the inner mounting rubber

supply pipe, to ensure that it does not fall back into the tailgate.

12 When refitting, ensure that the jet is clipped securely in position. Check the operation of the jet. If necessary, adjust the nozzle using a pin, aiming the spray to a point slightly above the centre of the swept area.

20 Headlight washer system components – removal and refitting

Washer system reservoir

1 Firmly apply the handbrake, then jack up the front of the car and support it securely on axle stands (see *Jacking and vehicle support*).

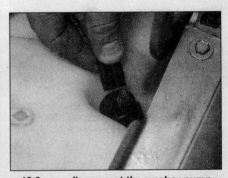

19.3a . . . disconnect the washer pump wiring connector . . .

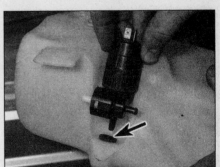

19.6 Ease the pump out of the reservoir, and recover the sealing grommet (arrowed)

21.4 Removing the radio/cassette player using the special DIN tools

22.2a Unclip the small (treble) loudspeaker from the door panel . . .

22.2b . . . and disconnect its wiring connector

Remove the left-hand front roadwheel, making alignment marks between the wheel and hub.

2 Undo the retaining nuts and screws, then release the retaining fasteners and remove the left-hand wheelarch liner (see Chapter 11, Section 22). Discard the nuts and fasteners; new ones should be used on refitting.

3 Remove the front bumper as described in Chapter 11.

4 Slacken and remove the retaining bolts, then lower the reservoir out from underneath the wing to gain access to the washer pump.

5 Slacken the retaining clip, and disconnect the hose from the washer pump. Disconnect the pump wiring connector, and remove the reservoir from the vehicle.

6 Refitting is the reverse of removal.

Washer pump

7 Remove the washer reservoir as described above.

8 Tip out the contents of the reservoir, then carefully ease the pump out from the reservoir and recover its sealing grommet.

9 Refitting is the reverse of removal. Use a new sealing grommet if the original one shows signs of damage or deterioration.

Washer nozzles

10 Remove the front bumper as described in Chapter 11.

11 Undo the two retaining bolts, and remove the nozzle from the bumper.

12 On refitting, securely tighten the retaining bolts and refit the bumper as described in Chapter 11.

21 Radio/cassette player – removal and refitting

Note: *The following removal and refitting procedure is for the range of radio/cassette units which Vauxhall/Opel fit as standard equipment. Removal and refitting procedures of non-standard units may differ slightly.*

Removal

1 All the radio/cassette players fitted by Vauxhall/Opel have DIN standard fixings. Two special tools, obtainable from most car accessory shops, are required for removal. Alternatively, suitable tools can be fabricated from 3 mm diameter wire, such as welding rod.

2 Disconnect the battery negative terminal (refer to *Disconnecting the battery* in the Reference Chapter).

3 Unscrew the four grub screws from the corners of the radio/cassette player, using a suitable Allen key.

4 Insert the tools into the holes exposed by removal of the grub screws, and push them until they snap into place. The radio/cassette player can then be slid out of the facia **(see illustration)**.

Refitting

5 To refit the radio/cassette player, simply push the unit into the facia until the retaining lugs snap into place, then refit the grub screws. On completion, reconnect the battery and enter the radio security code, where applicable.

22 Speakers – removal and refitting

Front small (treble) speaker

1 Lift the front door inner handle, and carefully prise the handle trim cover out from the door trim panel.

2 Unclip the speaker from the handle, disconnecting its wiring connectors as they become accessible **(see illustrations)**.

3 Refitting is the reverse of removal.

Front large (bass) speaker

4 Undo the retaining screws, and free the door pocket from the inner trim panel, disconnecting the window switch wiring connector(s) (where applicable) as they become accessible.

5 Undo the retaining screws, then free the speaker from the door. Disconnect the wiring connectors and remove the speaker **(see illustrations)**.

6 Refitting is the reverse of removal.

Rear speaker

7 Remove the rear parcel shelf. If the left speaker is to be removed, remove the interior light unit from the trim panel as described in Section 6.

8 Remove the rear shock absorber access panel from the trim panel.

9 Prise out the retaining clips from the rear of the panel, and the circular plug/seat stop buffer (as applicable) from the front of the panel. Slacken and remove all the panel retaining screws, and release the panel from the vehicle body. Disconnect the speaker wiring connector, and turn the panel around to gain access to the speaker **(see illustrations)**.

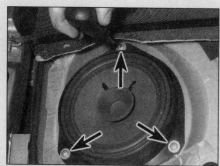

22.5a Undo the three retaining screws (arrowed) . . .

22.5b . . . then withdraw the large (bass) loudspeaker from the door, and disconnect its wiring connector

22.9a Release the luggage compartment trim panel from the vehicle . . .

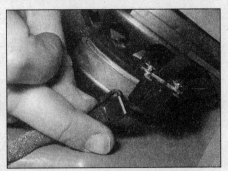

22.9b . . . then turn it around and disconnect the wiring connector from the rear loudspeaker

22.10 Undo the three retaining screws, and remove the speaker from the trim panel

Note that it is not necessary to detach the seat belt unless the trim panel is to be removed.

10 Undo the three retaining screws, and remove the speaker from the trim panel (see illustration).

11 Refitting is a reverse of the removal procedure. Make sure that the trim panel is securely retained by all the relevant clips and screws. If the left trim panel is being installed, do not forget to feed the interior light wiring through the trim panel aperture before fastening the panel in position.

23 Radio aerial – removal and refitting

Corsa and Corsavan

Removal

1 Open the tailgate, then prise out the trim clips and release the rear of the headlining from the roof. Carefully peel the headlining back until access is gained to the aerial retaining nut and wiring connectors.

2 Disconnect both wiring connectors, then undo the retaining nut and remove the aerial from the roof.

Refitting

3 Locate the aerial in roof hole and refit its retaining nut, tightening it securely. Reconnect the wiring connectors, then clip the headlining back into position

Combo Van

Removal

4 Firmly apply the handbrake, then jack up the front of the car and support it securely on axle stands (see Jacking and vehicle support). Remove the left-hand front roadwheel.

5 Undo the retaining nuts and screws, then release the retaining fasteners and remove the left-hand wheelarch liner (refer to Chapter 11, Section 22). Discard the nuts and fasteners; new ones should be used when refitting.

6 From inside the vehicle, release the

retaining clips and remove the trim panel from the left-hand front footwell.

7 Reach up behind the facia, and disconnect the aerial lead from the rear of the radio/cassette player. Work back along the aerial lead, releasing it from the all the relevant retaining clips and ties, noting how the lead is routed. If necessary, to improve access, remove the storage compartment from underneath the facia; the compartment is retained by a single screw and retaining clip.

8 From underneath the wing, release the grommet and withdraw the aerial lead. Unscrew the aerial nut, remove the washer and rubber, then release the aerial from its lower retaining clip. Remove the aerial and lead from underneath the wing.

Refitting

9 Insert the aerial from underneath the wing, and clip it into position. Fit the rubber and washer onto the aerial, and securely tighten the retaining nut.

10 Pass the aerial lead through into the vehicle, and seat the rubber grommet in the vehicle body.

11 From inside the vehicle, ensure that the lead is correctly routed, and secure it in position with all the necessary clips and ties. Reconnect the lead to the rear of the radio/cassette player. Where necessary, refit the storage compartment.

12 Refit the footwell trim panel, making sure that it is securely retained by its clips.

13 Install the wheelarch liner, securing it in position with new nuts and clips.

14 Refit the roadwheel, then lower the vehicle to the ground and tighten the roadwheel bolts to the specified torque.

24 Anti-theft alarm system – general information

Note: This information is applicable only to the anti-theft alarm system fitted by Vauxhall/Opel as standard equipment.

1 Some models in the range are fitted with an anti-theft alarm system as standard

equipment. The alarm is automatically armed and disarmed when the deadlocks are locked and unlocked using the driver's door lock. The alarm has switches on all the doors (including the tailgate), the bonnet, the radio/cassette player and the ignition and starter circuits. If the tailgate, bonnet or any of the doors are opened whilst the alarm is set, the alarm horn will sound and the hazard warning lights will flash. The alarm also has an immobiliser function which makes the ignition and starter circuits inoperable whilst the alarm is triggered.

2 The alarm system performs a self-test every time it is switched on; this test takes approximately 10 seconds. During the self-test, the LED (light emitting diode) in the hazard warning light switch will come on. If the LED flashes, then either the tailgate, bonnet or one of the doors is open, or there is a fault in the circuit. After the initial 10-second period, the LED will flash to indicate that the alarm is switched on. On unlocking the driver's door lock, the LED will illuminate for approximately 1 second, then go out, indicating that the alarm has been switched off.

3 With the alarm set, if the tailgate is unlocked, the tailgate switch sensing will automatically be switched off, but the door and bonnet switches will still be active. Once the tailgate is shut and locked again, the tailgate switch sensing will be switched back on after approximately 10 seconds.

4 Should the alarm system develop a fault, the vehicle should be taken to a Vauxhall/Opel dealer for examination.

25 Heated front seat components – removal and refitting

Heater mats

1 On models with heated front seats, a heater mat is fitted to the both the seat back and seat cushion. Renewal of either heater mat involves peeling back the upholstery, removing the old mat, sticking the new mat in

position and then refitting the upholstery. Note that upholstery removal and refitting requires considerable skill and experience if it is to be carried out successfully, and is therefore best entrusted to your Vauxhall/Opel dealer. In practice, it will be very difficult for the home mechanic to carry out the job without ruining the upholstery.

Heated seat switches

2 Refer to Section 4.

26 Air bag system – general information and precautions

General information

A driver's air bag is fitted as standard equipment on certain models, and is an option on all other models. The air bag is fitted in the steering wheel centre pad. Additionally, a passenger's air bag located in the facia, and side air bags located in the front seats are also optionally available.

The system is armed only when the ignition is switched on, however, a reserve power source maintains a power supply to the system in the event of a break in the main electrical supply. The steering wheel and facia air bags are activated by a 'g' sensor (deceleration sensor), and controlled by an electronic control unit located under the centre console. The side air bags are activated by severe side impact and operate independently of the main system and of each other. A separate electrical supply, control unit and sensor is provided for each side air bag.

The air bags are inflated by a gas generator, which forces the bag out from its location in the steering wheel, facia or seat back frame.

Precautions

 Warning: The following precautions must be observed when working on vehicles equipped with an air bag system, to prevent the possibility of personal injury.

General precautions

The following precautions **must** be observed when carrying out work on a vehicle equipped with an air bag:

a) Do not disconnect the battery with the engine running.
b) Before carrying out any work in the vicinity of the air bag, removal of any of the air bag components, or any welding work on the vehicle, de-activate the system as described in the following sub-Section.
c) Do not attempt to test any of the air bag system circuits using test meters or any other test equipment.
d) If the air bag warning light comes on, or any fault in the system is suspected,

consult a Vauxhall/Opel dealer without delay. **Do not** attempt to carry out fault diagnosis, or any dismantling of the components.

Precautions to be taken when handling an air bag

a) Transport the air bag by itself, bag upward.
b) Do not put your arms around the air bag.
c) Carry the air bag close to the body, bag outward.
d) Do not drop the air bag or expose it to impacts.
e) Do not attempt to dismantle the air bag unit.
f) Do not connect any form of electrical equipment to any part of the air bag circuit.

Precautions to be taken when storing an air bag unit

a) Store the unit in a cupboard with the air bag upward.
b) Do not expose the air bag to temperatures above 80°C.
c) Do not expose the air bag to flames.
d) Do not attempt to dispose of the air bag – consult a Vauxhall/Opel dealer.
e) Never refit an air bag which is known to be faulty or damaged.

De-activation of air bag system

The system must be de-activated before carrying out any work on the air bag components or surrounding area:

a) Switch on the ignition and check the operation of the air bag warning light on the instrument panel. The light should illuminate when the ignition is switched on, then extinguish.
b) Switch off the ignition.
c) Remove the ignition key.
d) Switch off all electrical equipment.
e) Disconnect the battery negative terminal (refer to 'Disconnecting the battery' in the Reference Section of this manual).
f) Insulate the battery negative terminal and the end of the battery negative lead to prevent any possibility of contact.
g) Wait for at least two minutes before carrying out any further work. Wait at least ten minutes if the air bag warning light did not operate correctly.

Activation of air bag system

To activate the system on completion of any work, proceed as follows:

a) Ensure that there are no occupants in the vehicle, and that there are no loose objects around the vicinity of the steering wheel. Close the vehicle doors and windows.
b) Ensure that the ignition is switched off then reconnect the battery negative terminal.
c) Open the driver's door and switch on the ignition, without reaching in front of the steering wheel. Check that the air bag

warning light illuminates briefly then extinguishes.
d) Switch off the ignition.
e) If the air bag warning light does not operate as described in paragraph c), consult a Vauxhall/Opel dealer before driving the vehicle.

27 Air bag system components – removal and refitting

 Warning: Refer to the precautions given in Section 26 before attempting to carry out work on any of the air bag components.

1 De-activate the air bag system as described in the previous Section, then proceed as described under the relevant heading.

Driver's air bag

2 With the steering wheel in the straight-ahead position, turn the wheel 90° to the left, then prise off the trim cap and remove the left upper shroud screw. Turn the wheel 180° to the right, and remove the right upper screw. Remove the rubber seal from the ignition switch/lock, then undo the lower retaining screws and remove the steering column shrouds.
3 With the steering wheel positioned in the straight-ahead position, turn the wheel 90° to the right to gain access to the left-hand air bag retaining bolt. Unscrew the bolt from the rear of the steering wheel, then turn the wheel 180° to the left to gain access to the right-hand air bag retaining bolt. Unscrew the right-hand retaining bolt, then return the steering wheel to the straight-ahead position.
4 Carefully lift the air bag assembly away from the steering wheel, and disconnect the wiring connector from the rear of the unit. Note that the air bag must not be knocked or dropped, and should be stored the correct way up, with its padded surface uppermost.
5 Refitting is a reversal of the removal procedure. Tighten the air bag retaining screws to the specified torque setting.

Passenger's air bag

6 Remove the battery as described in Chapter 5A.
7 Remove the glovebox as described in Chapter 11, Section 26.
8 Remove the heater/ventilation vent and duct on the passenger's side as described in Chapter 3.
9 Remove the windscreen cowl panel and the water deflector shield as described in Section 17 of this Chapter.
10 From the engine compartment side, undo the nuts securing the air bag mounting brackets, and facia panel fastening to the bulkhead.

11 Unscrew the facia panel attachments on the passenger's side.

12 Disconnect the air bag wiring plug from the side of the unit.

13 Undo the nuts securing the air bag to the mounting brackets, Ease the facia away from the bulkhead as necessary and remove the air bag from the mounting brackets. Note that the air bag must not be knocked or dropped, and should be stored the correct way up (as mounted in the vehicle).

14 Refitting is a reversal of the removal procedure. Tighten the air bag retaining nuts to the specified torque setting.

Side air bags

15 The side air bags are located internally within the front seat back and no attempt should be made to remove them. Any suspected problems with the side air bag system should be referred to a Vauxhall/Opel dealer.

Air bag control unit

16 Remove the centre console as described in Chapter 11.

17 Disconnect the control unit wiring connector, then undo the retaining screws and remove the control unit from the vehicle.

18 Refitting is the reverse of removal. If a new control unit is being installed, the vehicle must be taken to a Vauxhall/Opel dealer for the control unit to be reprogrammed at the earliest possible opportunity. **Note:** *The air bag system will not be operational until the new control unit is reprogrammed; this will be indicated by the warning light in the instrument panel being illuminated.*

Air bag wiring contact unit

19 The wiring contact unit is fitted to the underside of the steering wheel, and provides the electrical supply to both the air bag and horn buttons. The unit is removed and refitted with the steering wheel (see Chapter 10).

Vauxhall Corsa 1993 to 1997 wiring diagrams

Diagram 1

Key to symbols

Bulb	
Switch	
Multiple contact switch (ganged)	
Fuse/fusible link and current rating	F5 30A
Resistor	
Variable resistor	
Connecting wires	
Plug and socket contact	
Item no.	2
Pump/motor	M
Earth point and location	E22
Gauge/meter	
Diode	
Wire splice or soldered joint	
Solenoid actuator	
Light emitting diode (LED)	
Wire colour (brown with black tracer)	Br/Sw
Screened cable	

Dashed outline denotes part of a larger item, containing in this case an electronic or solid state device.
6 - unspecified connector pin 6.
T14/9 - 14 pin connector, pin 9.

6 T14/9

Earth locations

E1	Right bulkhead
E2	Left bulkhead
E3	Tunnel
E4	Left engine earth
E5	Right engine earth
E6	Body rear
E7	Steering column

Relays

Relay	Location
Anti-theft alarm horn	Fusebox
Anti-theft alarm immobiliser	Fusebox
Cooling fan	Behind right-hand footwell trim panel
Cooling fan	Relay carrier above glovebox
Cooling fan	Relay carrier above glovebox
Cooling fan high speed	Relay carrier above glovebox
Exterior mirror heating	Fusebox
Front foglight	Fusebox
Headlight washer pump	Fusebox
Heated rear screen	Fusebox
'Lights-on' buzzer	Fusebox
Rear foglight	Fusebox
Tailgate wiper	Fusebox
Turn signal	Fusebox
Windscreen wiper	Fusebox

Fuses

Fuse	Rating	Circuit protected
F1	20A	Direction indicators, diagnostic connector, interior lights, horn, triple info display and radio
F3	30A	Heated rear window
F6	10A	Rear fog lights
F8	10A	LH parking/tail light
F9	20A	Front fog lights
F10	10A	LH high beam headlight
F11	30A	Headlight washer
F12	10A	LH low beam headlight, headlight leveling
F13	20A	Central locking
F15	30A	Heating
F16	30A	Wash/wipe
F17	10A	Electric mirrors, interior lights, electric windows, radio, heated rear window, triple info display, instrument cluster
F18	20A	Central locking, reversing lights, cigarette lighter, seat heating, diesel control module
F19	10A	Triple info display instrument illumination
F20	30A	Engine cooling
F21	15A	Stop lights, hazard warning lights, instrument cluster
F22	10A	ABS
F23	10A	RH parking/tail light
F25	10A	RH high beam headlight
F27	10A	RH low beam headlight
F28	30A	Electric windows
F36	30A	Filter heating
F41	80A	Glow plugs

H32768

Wire colours

Bl	Blue	**Pu**	Purple
Br	Brown	**Ro**	Red
Ge	Yellow	**Sw**	Black
Gr	Grey	**Vi**	Violet
Gn	Green	**Ws**	White
Or	Orange		

Key to items

1	Battery	8	Diagnostic connector
2	Ignition switch	9	Telephone connection
3	Main fuse box	10	LH rear speaker
4	Alternator	11	RH rear speaker
5	Starter motor	12	LH front speaker
6	Aerial amplifier	13	LH front tweeter
7	Radio	14	RH front tweeter

15	RH front speaker
16	Triple info display
17	Outside temperature sensor
18	Passenger's airbag
19	Airbag module
20	Driver's airbag
21	Airbag contact unit

Diagram 2

MTS
H32769

Starting and charging

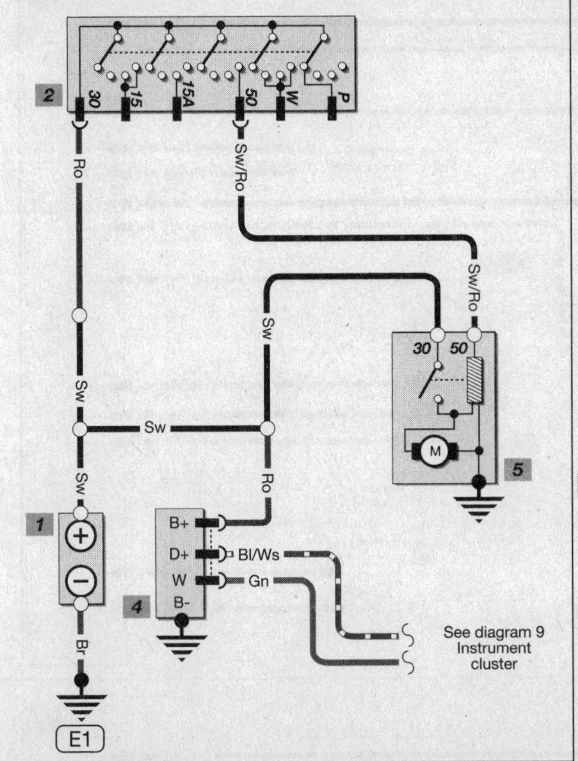

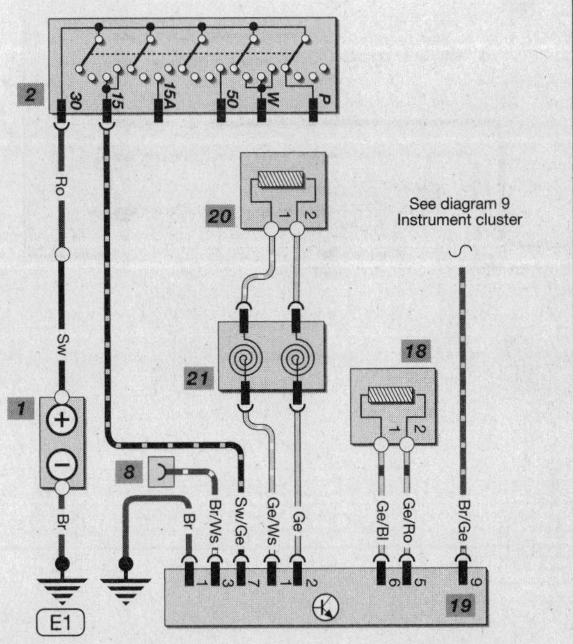

Radio with triple info display

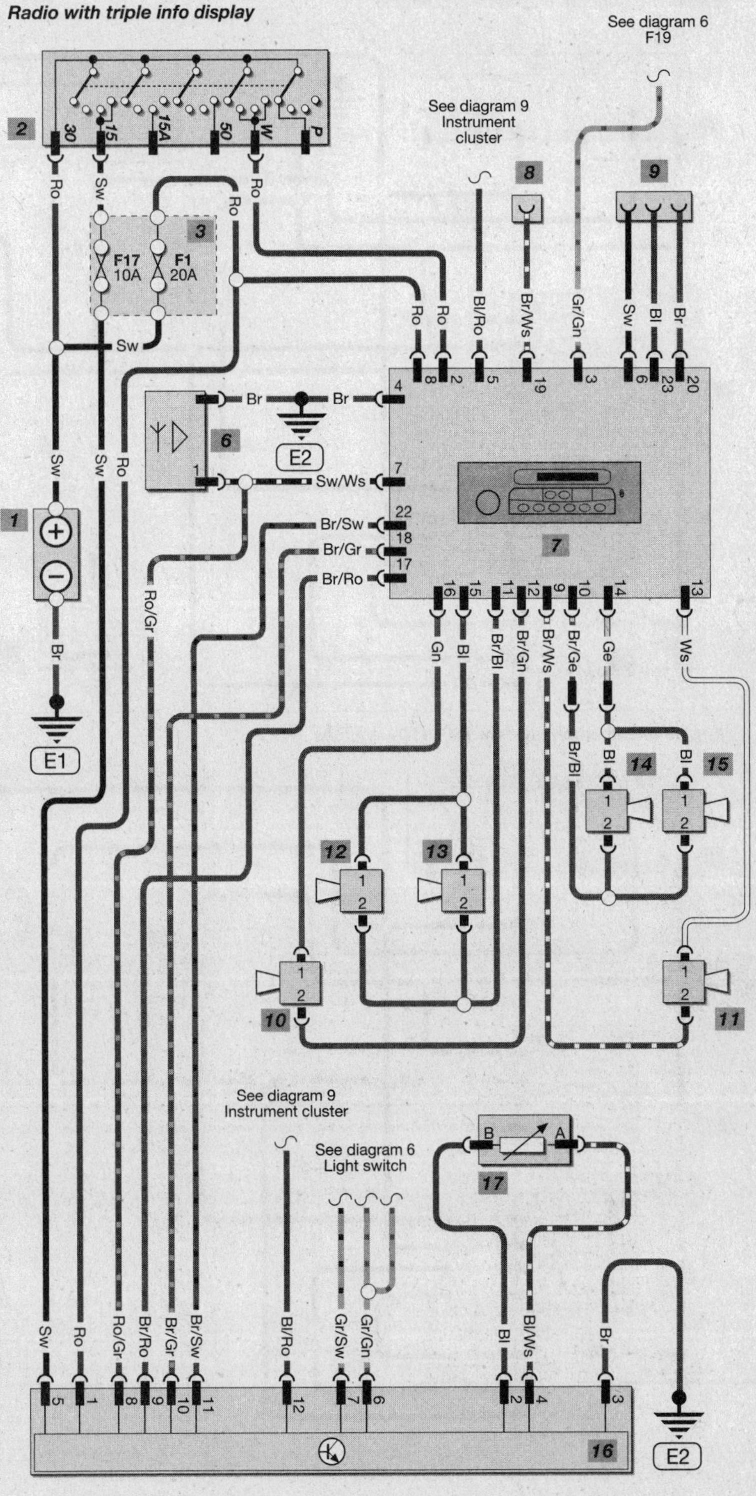

Airbag system

Wire colours

Bl	Blue	**Pu**	Purple
Br	Brown	**Ro**	Red
Ge	Yellow	**Sw**	Black
Gr	Grey	**Vi**	Violet
Gn	Green	**Ws**	White
Or	Orange		

Key to items

1 Battery
2 Ignition switch
3 Main fuse box
22 Diesel control module
23 Glow plug relay
24 Glow plugs
25 Filter heating relay

26 Filter heater
27 Coolant temperature switch
28 Fuel pump, position,
   control lever sensor
29 EGR solenoid valve
30 Engine speed sensor

Diagram 3

MTS
H32770

Engine management system 17D engine

Engine management system 15D, 15DT engines

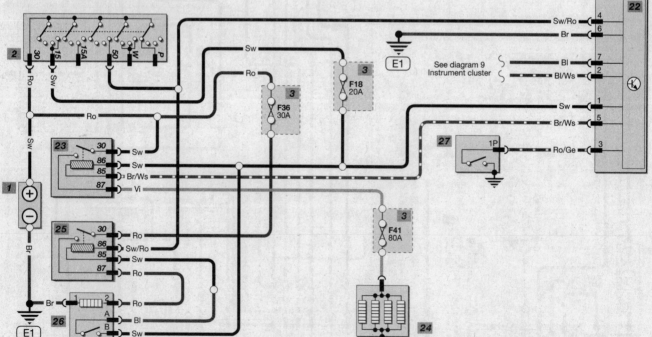

Wire colours

Bl	Blue	**Pu**	Purple
Br	Brown	**Ro**	Red
Ge	Yellow	**Sw**	Black
Gr	Grey	**Vi**	Violet
Gn	Green	**Ws**	White
Or	Orange		

Key to items

1 Battery
2 Ignition switch
3 Main fuse box
8 Diagnostic connector
31 Driver's window switch
32 Passenger's window switch
33 Driver's window motor

34 Passenger's window motor
35 ABS control module
36 Front left wheel sensor
37 Front right wheel sensor
38 Rear left wheel sensor
39 Rear right wheel sensor

40 Speed sensor
41 Fuel solenoid valve
42 Heated power mirror relay
43 Heated power mirror switch
44 Driver's power mirror
45 Passenger's power mirror

Diagram 4

MTS
H32771

Electric windows

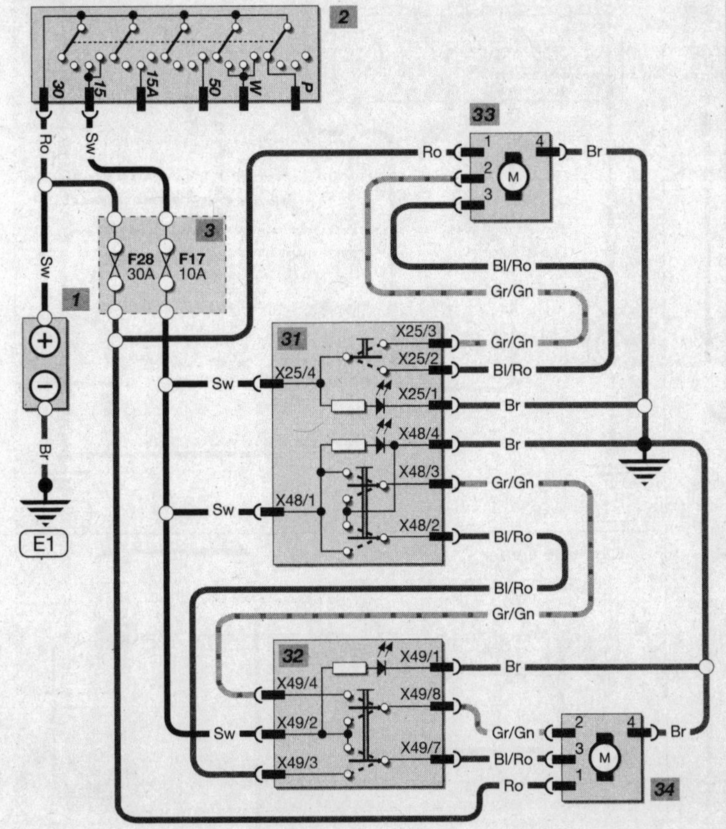

ABS

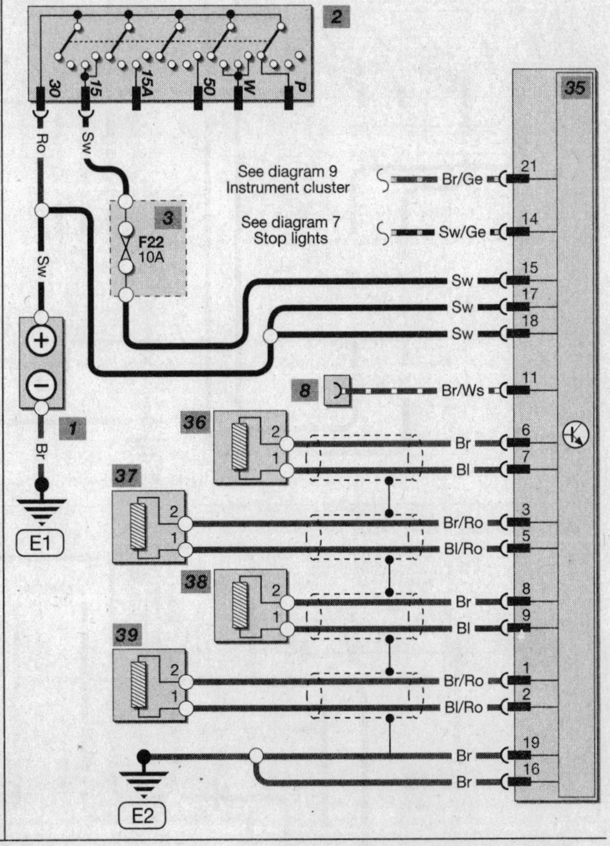

See diagram 9
Instrument cluster

See diagram 7
Stop lights

Vehicle speed sensor

See diagram 9
Instrument cluster

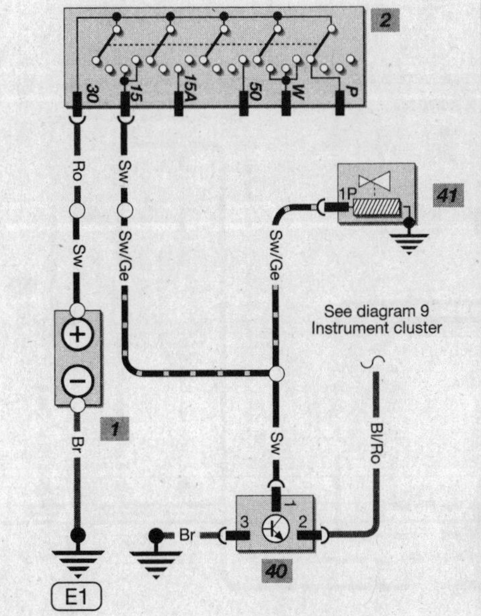

Heated power mirrors

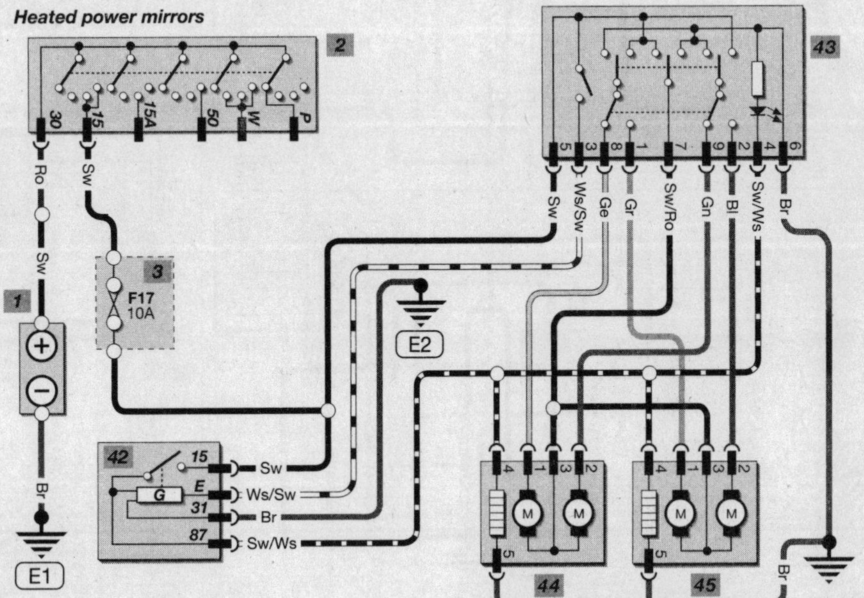

Diagram 5

Wire colours		Key to items			
Bl Blue	**Pu** Purple	1 Battery	47 Blower motor	53 Horn switch	
Br Brown	**Ro** Red	2 Ignition switch	48 Radiator fan	54 Cigarette lighter	
Ge Yellow	**Sw** Black	3 Main fuse box	49 Radiator fan test connector	55 Heated rear window relay	
Gr Grey	**Vi** Violet	21 Airbag contact unit	50 Radiator fan preresistor	56 LH heated rear window	
Gn Green	**Ws** White	27 Coolant temperature switch	51 Horn	57 RH heated rear window	
Or Orange		46 Heater controls	52 Horn relay		

* Airbag only

MTS H32772

Heater Blower

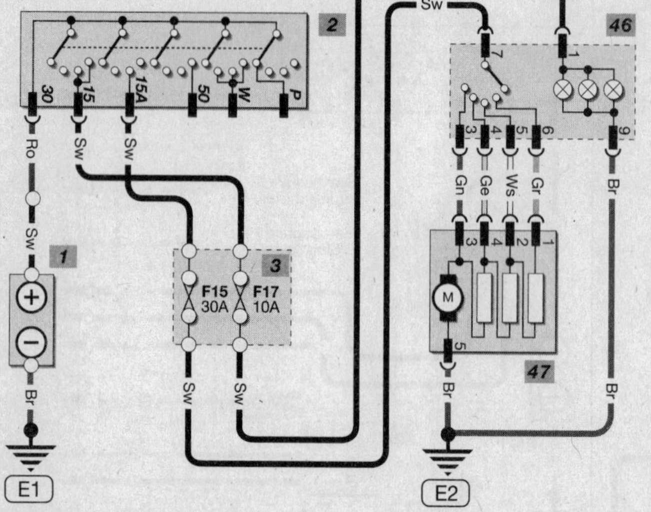

Engine cooling (15DT)

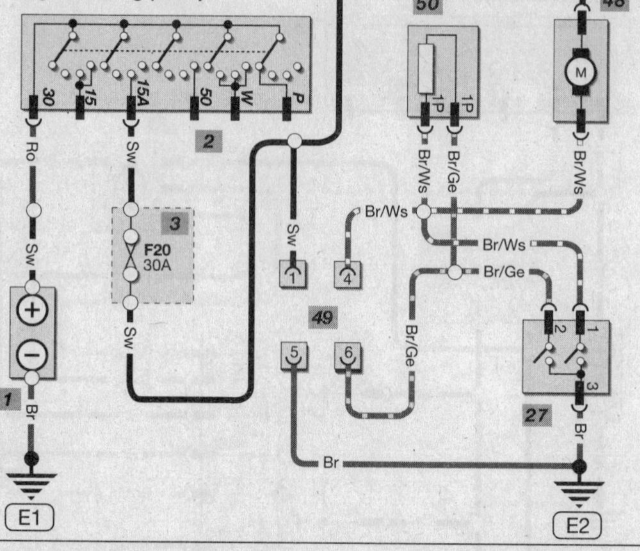

Engine cooling (15D, 17D)

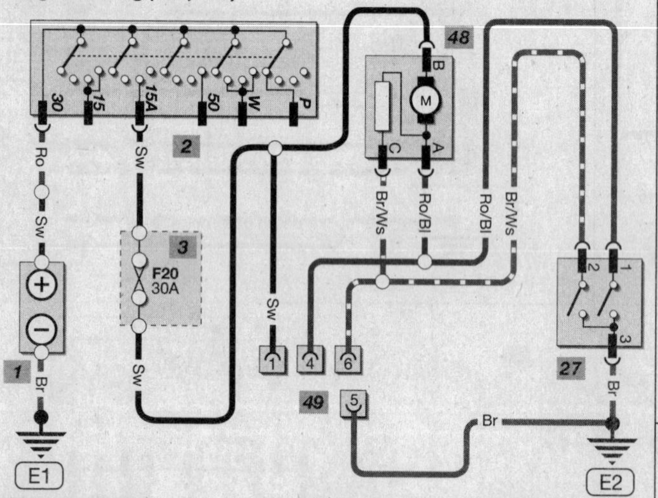

Cigarette lighter

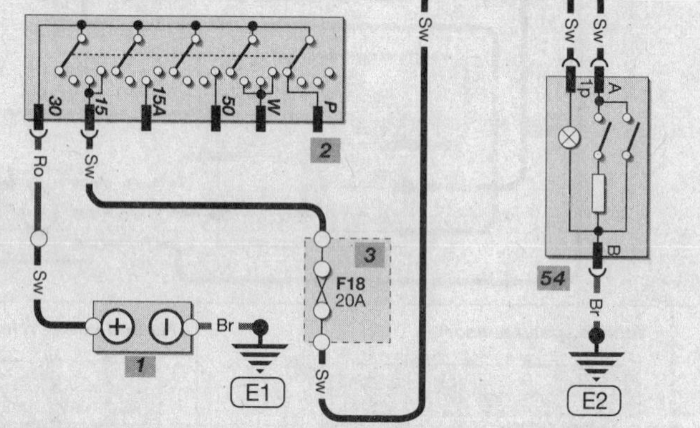

Horn

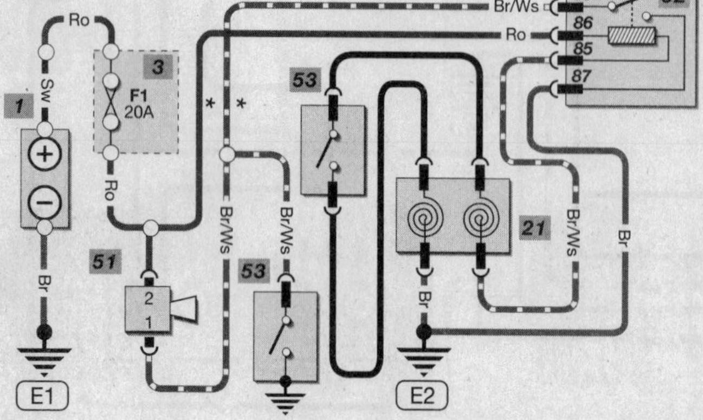

Heated rear window (Combo)

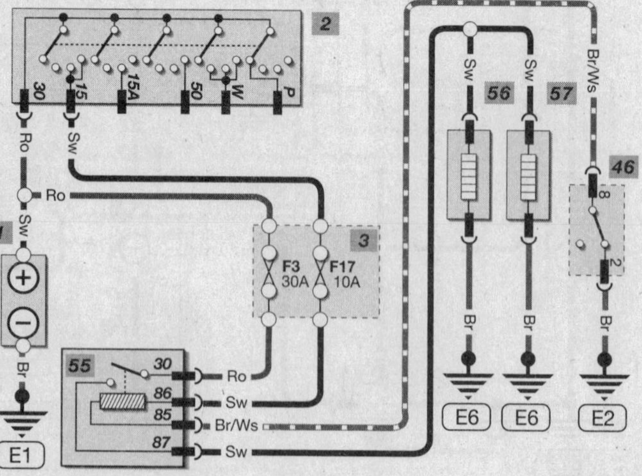

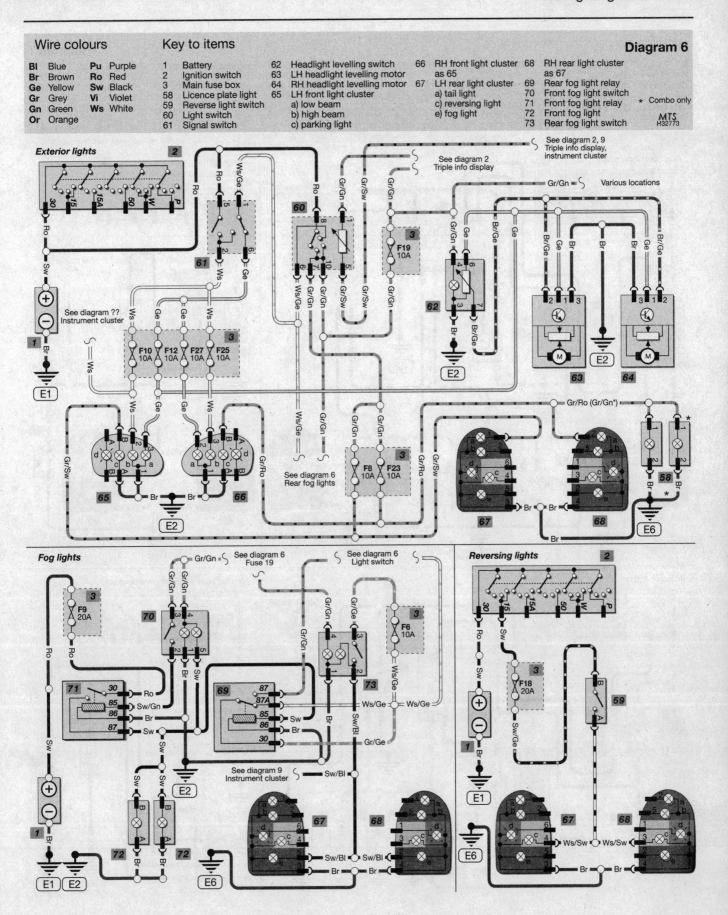

Diagram 6

Wire colours

Bl	Blue	Pu	Purple
Br	Brown	Ro	Red
Ge	Yellow	Sw	Black
Gr	Grey	Vi	Violet
Gn	Green	Ws	White
Or	Orange		

Key to items

1 Battery
2 Ignition switch
3 Main fuse box
58 Licence plate light
59 Reverse light switch
60 Light switch
61 Signal switch
62 Headlight levelling switch
63 LH headlight levelling motor
64 RH headlight levelling motor
65 LH front light cluster
a) low beam
b) high beam
c) parking light
66 RH front light cluster as 65
67 LH rear light cluster
a) tail light
c) reversing light
e) fog light
68 RH rear light cluster as 67
69 Rear fog light relay
70 Front fog light switch
71 Front fog light relay
72 Front fog light
73 Rear fog light switch

* Combo only

MTS
H32773

Exterior lights

Fog lights

Reversing lights

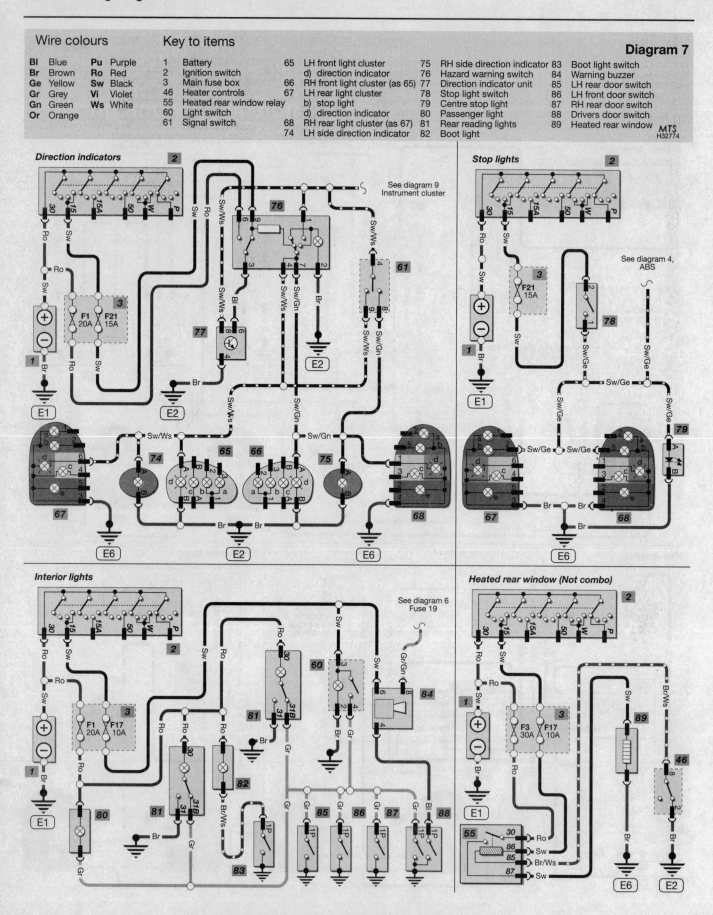

Wire colours

Bl	Blue	Pu	Purple
Br	Brown	Ro	Red
Ge	Yellow	Sw	Black
Gr	Grey	Vi	Violet
Gn	Green	Ws	White
Or	Orange		

Key to items

1 Battery
2 Ignition switch
3 Main fuse box
46 Heater controls
55 Heated rear window relay
60 Light switch
61 Signal switch
65 LH front light cluster
  d) direction indicator
66 RH front light cluster (as 65)
67 LH rear light cluster
  b) stop light
  d) direction indicator
68 RH rear light cluster (as 67)
74 LH side direction indicator
75 RH side direction indicator
76 Hazard warning switch
77 Direction indicator unit
78 Stop light switch
79 Centre stop light
80 Passenger light
81 Rear reading lights
82 Boot light
83 Boot light switch
84 Warning buzzer
85 LH rear door switch
86 LH front door switch
87 RH rear door switch
88 Drivers door switch
89 Heated rear window

Diagram 7

MTS
H32774

Direction indicators

Stop lights

See diagram 9
Instrument cluster

See diagram 4,
ABS

Interior lights

Heated rear window (Not combo)

See diagram 6
Fuse 19

Wire colours

Bl Blue	**Pu** Purple
Br Brown	**Ro** Red
Ge Yellow	**Sw** Black
Gr Grey	**Vi** Violet
Gn Green	**Ws** White
Or Orange	

Key to items

1 Battery
2 Ignition switch
3 Main fuse box
90 Headlight washer relay
91 Headlight washer pump
92 Washer pump
93 Wash/wipe switch

94 Rear window wiper
95 Rear window wiper relay
96 Windscreen wiper
97 Windscreen wiper relay
98 Central locking control unit
99 Front passenger switch
100 Drivers switch

101 Drivers door lock motor
102 Passenger door lock motor
103 RH rear door lock motor
104 LH rear door lock motor
105 Trunk lid lock motor
106 Fuel flap lock motor
107 LH front seat heating switch

108 LH front seat heater
109 RH front seat heating switch
110 RH front seat heater

Diagram 8

★ Without item 97   *MTS*
H32775

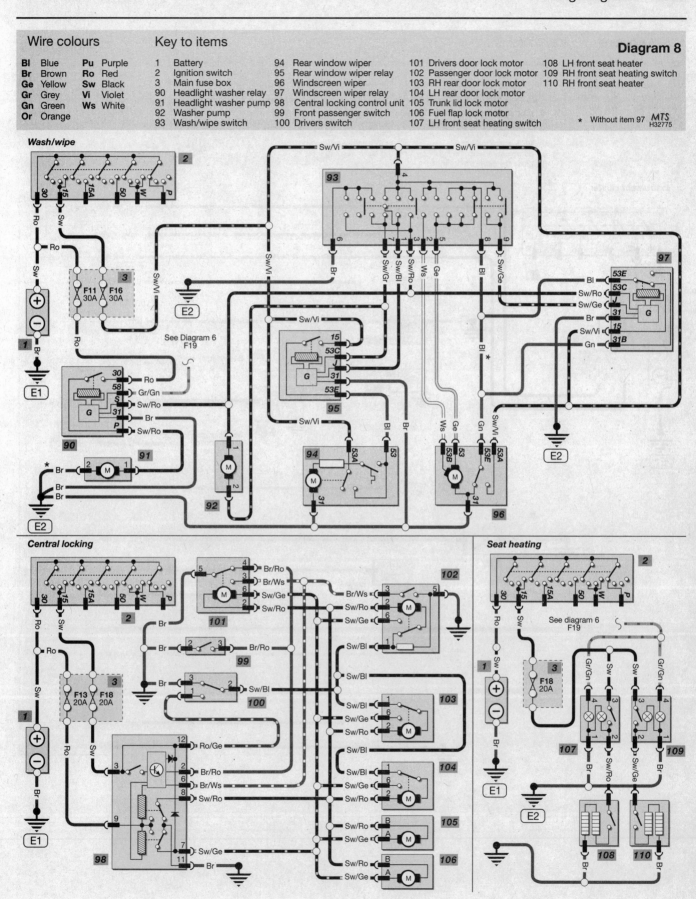

Wire colours

Bl	Blue	Pu	Purple
Br	Brown	Ro	Red
Ge	Yellow	Sw	Black
Gr	Grey	Vi	Violet
Gn	Green	Ws	White
Or	Orange		

Key to items

1 Battery
2 Ignition switch
3 Main fuse box
8 Diagnostic connector
111 Instrument cluster
  a) turn signal light
  b) charge warning light
  c) brake warning light
  d) ABS warning light
  e) oil pressure warning light
  f) glow period warning light

111 Instrument cluster cont.
  g) airbag warning light
  h) low fuel warning light
  i) fuel gauge
  j) coolant temp gauge
  k) speedometer
  l) tachometer
  m) instrument illumination
  n) high beam warning light
  o) fog light warning light

112 Brake fluid switch
113 Handbrake switch
114 Oil pressure switch
115 Fuel level sensor
116 Coolant temp sensor

Diagram 9

MTS
H32776

Instrument cluster

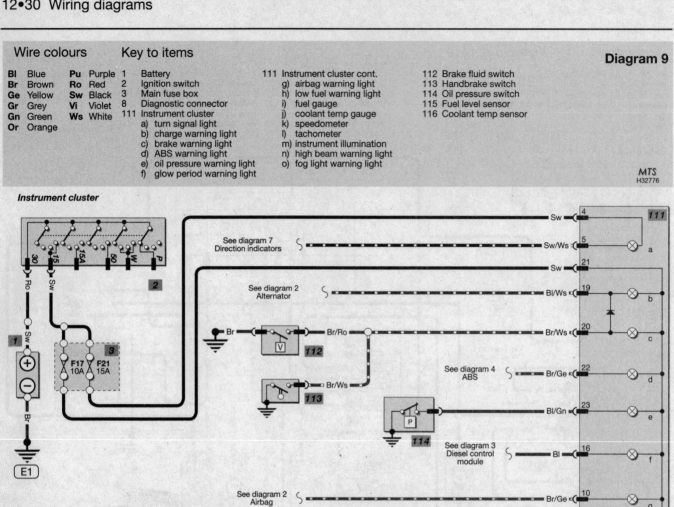

Vauxhall Corsa 1997 to 2000 wiring diagrams

Diagram 1

Key to symbols

Bulb	⊗
Switch	
Multiple contact switch (ganged)	
Fuse/fusible link and current rating	F5 30A
Resistor	
Variable resistor	
Connecting wires	
Plug and socket contact	
Item no.	2
Pump/motor	M
Earth point and location	E22
Gauge/meter	
Diode	
Wire splice or soldered joint	
Solenoid actuator	
Light emitting diode (LED)	
Wire colour (brown with black tracer)	Br/Sw
Screened cable	

Dashed outline denotes part of a larger item, containing in this case an electronic or solid state device.
6 - unspecified connector pin 6.
T14/9 - 14 pin connector, pin 9.

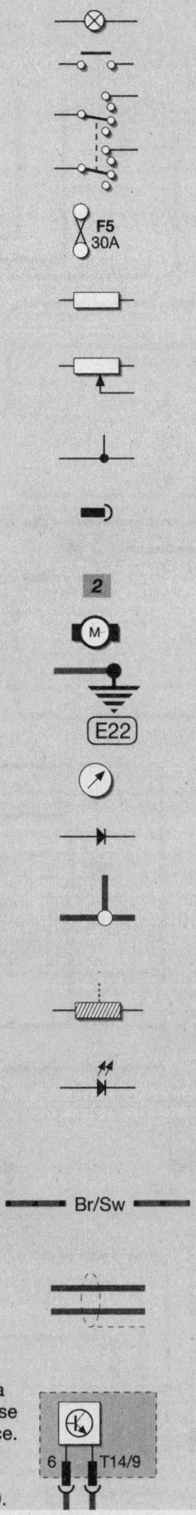

Earth locations

E1	Right bulkhead
E2	Left bulkhead
E3	Tunnel
E4	Left engine earth
E5	Right engine earth
E6	Body rear
E7	Steering column

Relays

Relay	Location
Anti-theft alarm horn	Fusebox
Anti-theft alarm immobiliser	Fusebox
Cooling fan	Behind right-hand footwell trim panel
Cooling fan	Relay carrier above glovebox
Cooling fan	Relay carrier above glovebox
Cooling fan high speed	Relay carrier above glovebox
Exterior mirror heating	Fusebox
Front foglight	Fusebox
Fuel pump	Behind right-hand footwell trim panel
Headlight washer pump	Fusebox
Heated rear screen	Fusebox
'Lights-on' buzzer	Fusebox
Rear foglight	Fusebox
Tailgate wiper	Fusebox
Turn signal	Fusebox
Windscreen wiper	Fusebox

Fuses

Fuse	Rating	Circuit protected
F1	20A	Direction indicators, diagnostic connector, interior lights, horn, triple info display and radio
F3	30A	Heated rear window
F6	10A	Rear fog lights
F8	10A	LH parking/tail light
F9	20A	Front fog lights
F10	10A	LH high beam headlight
F11	30A	Headlight washer
F12	10A	LH low beam headlight
F13	20A	Central locking
F15	30A	Heating
F16	30A	Wash/wipe
F17	10A	Electric mirrors, interior lights, electric windows, triple info display, engine cooling, power steering, instrument cluster
F18	20A	Central locking, reversing lights, heated rear window, cigarette lighter, speed sensor, seat heating, diesel control module
F19	10A	Triple info display, instrument illumination
F20	30A	Engine cooling
F21	15A	Stop lights, hazard warning lights, instrument cluster
F22	10A	ABS
F23	10A	RH parking/tail light
F25	10A	RH high beam headlight
F26	20A	Fuel pump
F27	10A	RH low beam headlight
F28	30A	Electric windows
F36	30A	Filter heating
F41	80A	Glow plugs

Wire colours

Bl	Blue	**Pu**	Purple
Br	Brown	**Ro**	Red
Ge	Yellow	**Sw**	Black
Gr	Grey	**Vi**	Violet
Gn	Green	**Ws**	White
Or	Orange		

Key to items

1 Battery
2 Ignition switch
3 Main fuse box
4 Alternator
5 Starter motor
6 Aerial amplifier
7 Radio
8 Diagnostic connector
9 Telephone connection
10 LH rear speaker
11 RH rear speaker
12 LH front speaker
13 LH front tweeter
14 RH front tweeter
15 RH front speaker
16 Passenger's airbag
17 Passenger's side airbag
18 Driver's side airbag
19 Passenger's side airbag sensor
20 Airbag module
21 LH seatbelt pretensioner
22 RH seatbelt pretensioner
23 Driver's airbag
24 Airbag contact unit
25 Driver's side airbag sensor

★ Combo only

Diagram 2

MTS
H32778

Starting and charging

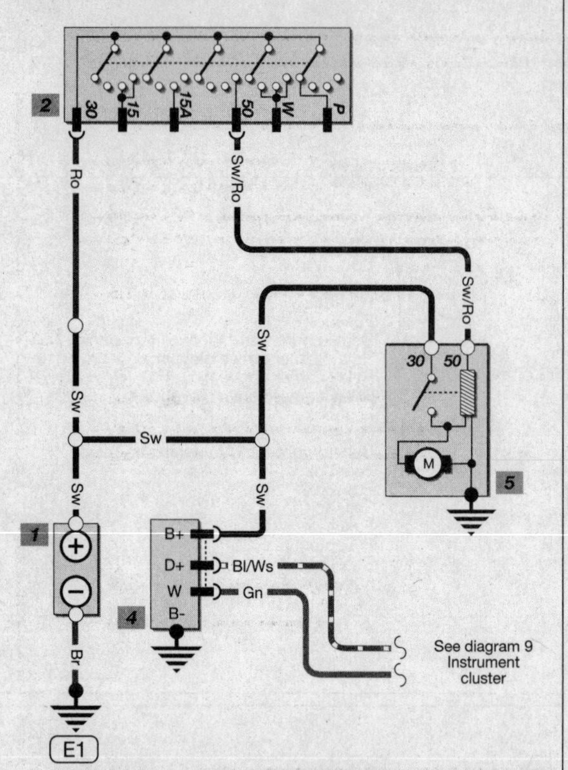

Typical radio

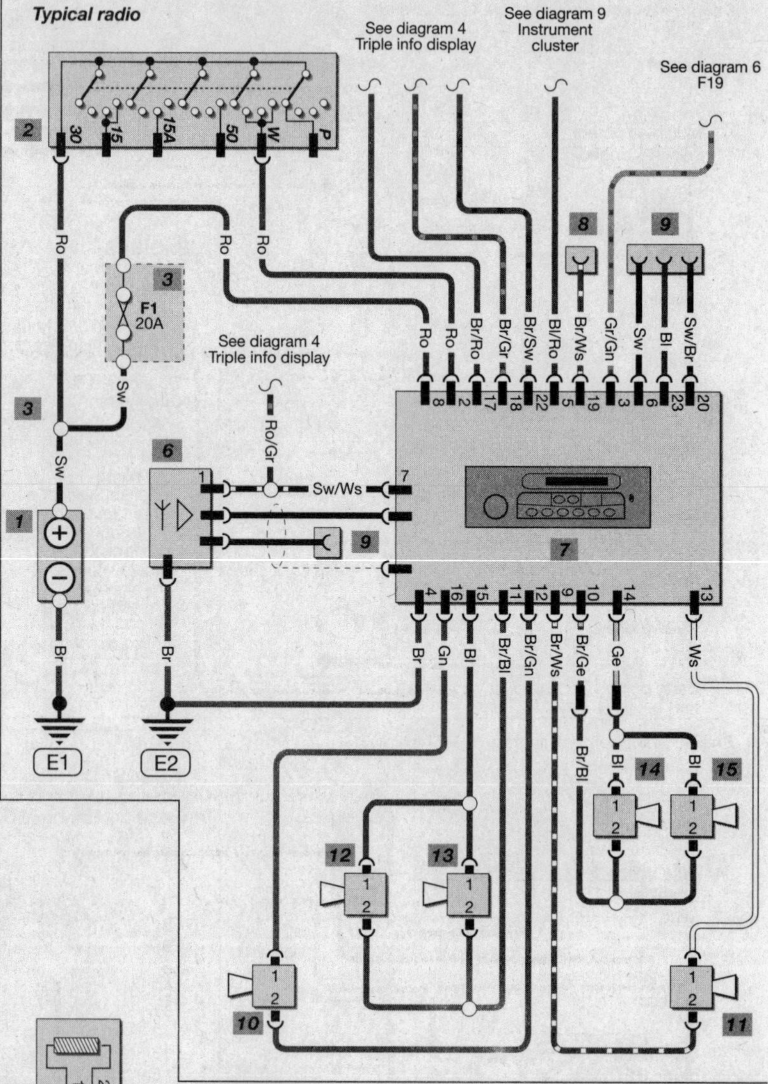

See diagram 4
Triple info display

See diagram 9
Instrument cluster

See diagram 6
F19

See diagram 4
Triple info display

See diagram 9
Instrument cluster

Airbag system

See diagram 9
Instrument cluster

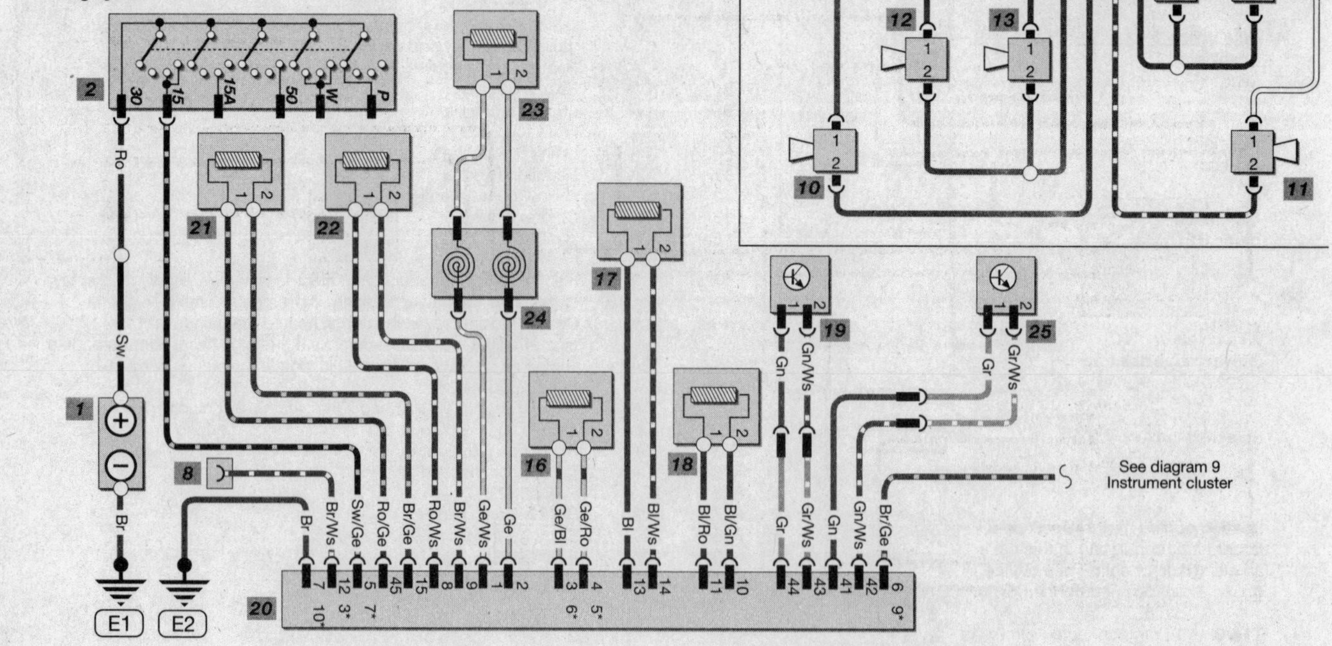

Wire colours

Bl	Blue	**Pu**	Purple
Br	Brown	**Ro**	Red
Ge	Yellow	**Sw**	Black
Gr	Grey	**Vi**	Violet
Gn	Green	**Ws**	White
Or	Orange		

Key to items

1 Battery
2 Ignition switch
3 Main fuse box
26 Diesel control module
27 Glow plug relay
28 Glow plugs
29 Filter heating relay
30 Filter heater
31 Coolant temperature switch
32 Fuel pump, position, control lever sensor
33 EGR solenoid valve
34 Engine speed sensor

Diagram 3

MTS
H32779

Engine management system X17D engine

Engine management system X15DT engine

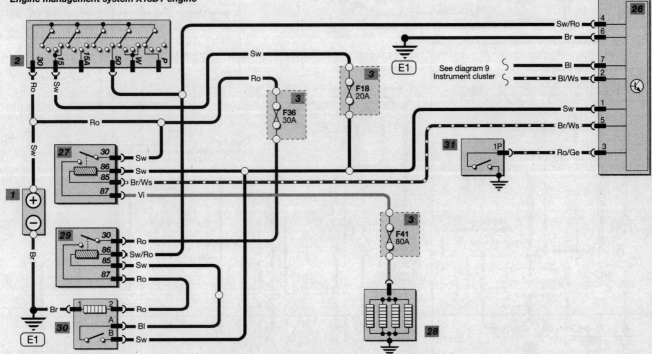

Wire colours

Bl	Blue	**Pu**	Purple
Br	Brown	**Ro**	Red
Ge	Yellow	**Sw**	Black
Gr	Grey	**Vi**	Violet
Gn	Green	**Ws**	White
Or	Orange		

Key to items

1 Battery
2 Ignition switch
3 Main fuse box
8 Diagnostic connector
35 Driver's window switch
36 Passenger's window switch

37 Driver's window motor
38 Passenger's window motor
39 ABS control module
40 Front left wheel sensor
41 Front right wheel sensor
42 Rear left wheel sensor

43 Rear right wheel sensor
44 Speed sensor
45 Fuel solenoid valve
46 Triple info display
47 Outside temperature sensor

Diagram 4

MTS
H32780

Electric windows

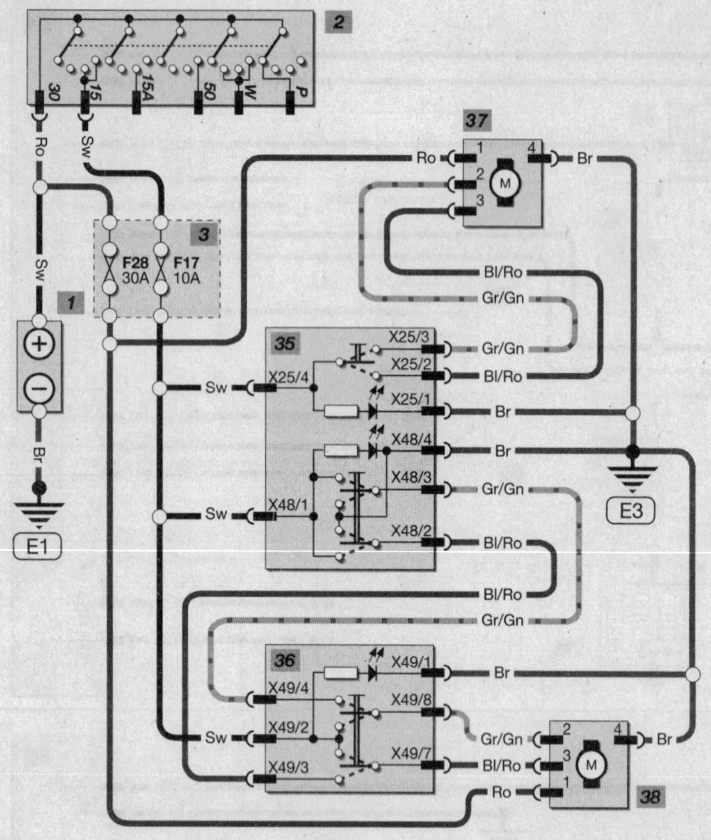

ABS

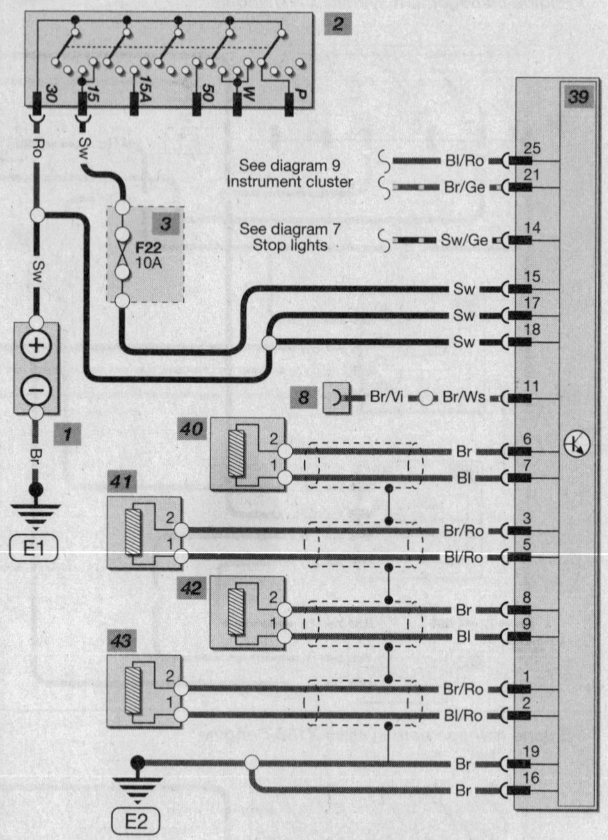

See diagram 9
Instrument cluster

See diagram 7
Stop lights

Vehicle speed sensor

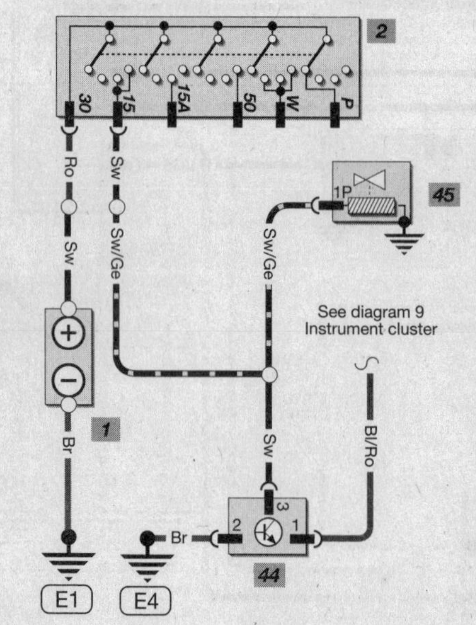

Triple info display

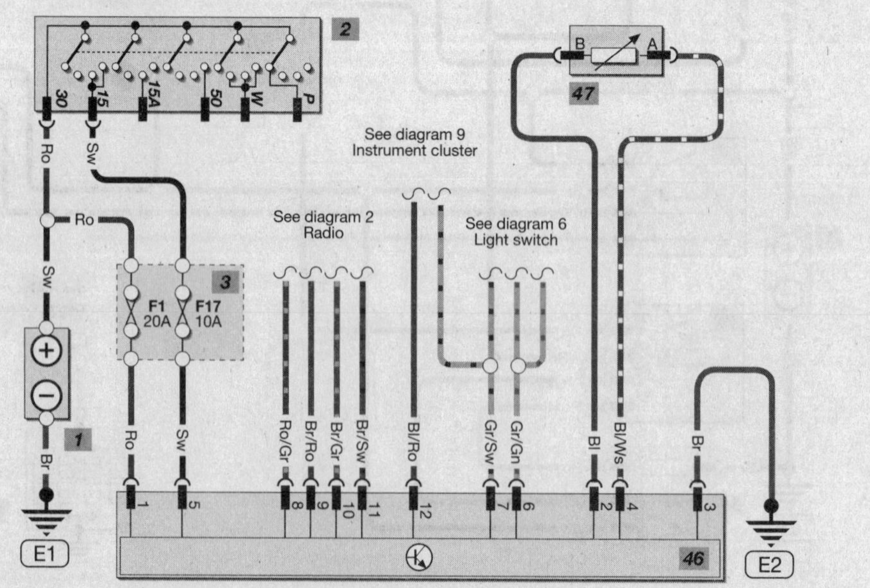

See diagram 9
Instrument cluster

See diagram 2
Radio

See diagram 6
Light switch

See diagram 9
Instrument cluster

Wire colours

Bl	Blue	Pu	Purple
Br	Brown	Ro	Red
Ge	Yellow	Sw	Black
Gr	Grey	Vi	Violet
Gn	Green	Ws	White
Or	Orange		

Key to items

1 Battery
2 Ignition switch
3 Main fuse box
24 Airbag contact unit
31 Coolant temperature switch
48 Heater controls
49 Blower motor
50 Radiator fan
51 Radiator fan test connector
52 Radiator fan preresistor
53 Horn
54 Horn relay
55 Horn switch
56 Cigarette lighter
57 Heated rear window relay
58 LH heated rear window
59 RH heated rear window

★ Airbag only

Diagram 5

MTS
H32781

Heater Blower

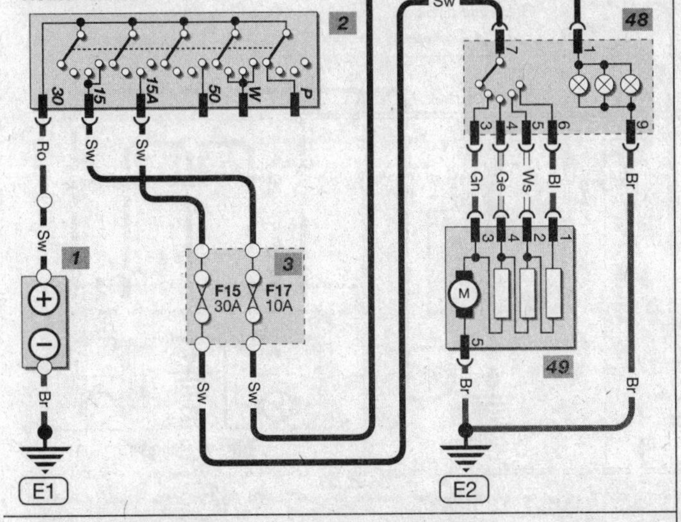

Engine cooling (X15DT)

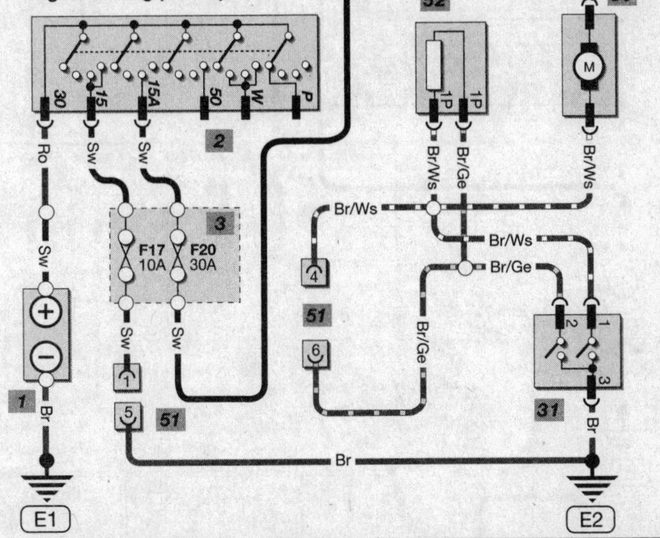

Engine cooling (X17D)

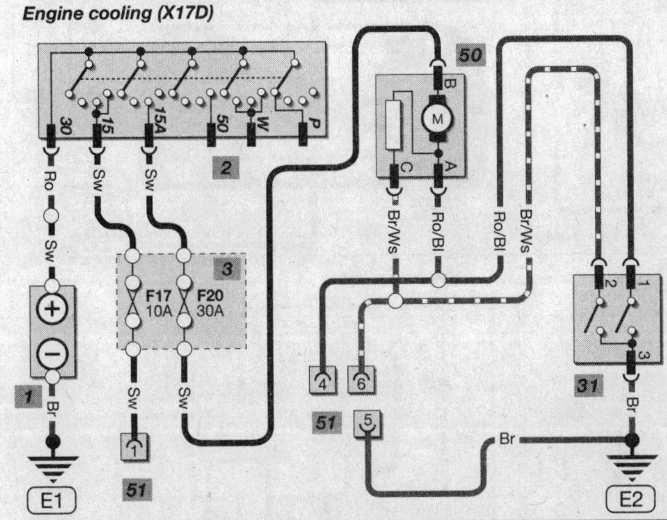

Cigarette lighter

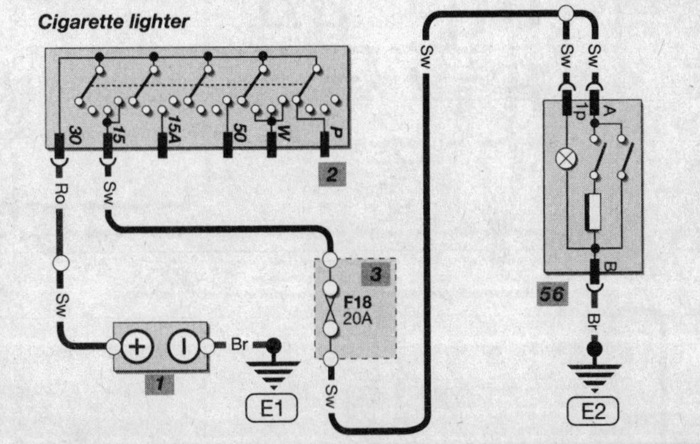

Horn

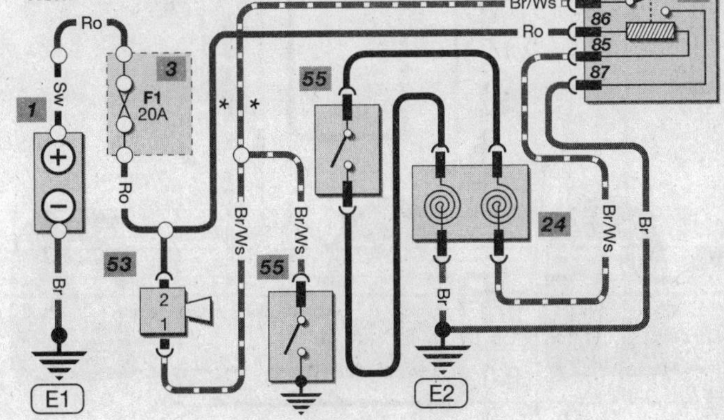

Heated rear window (Combo)

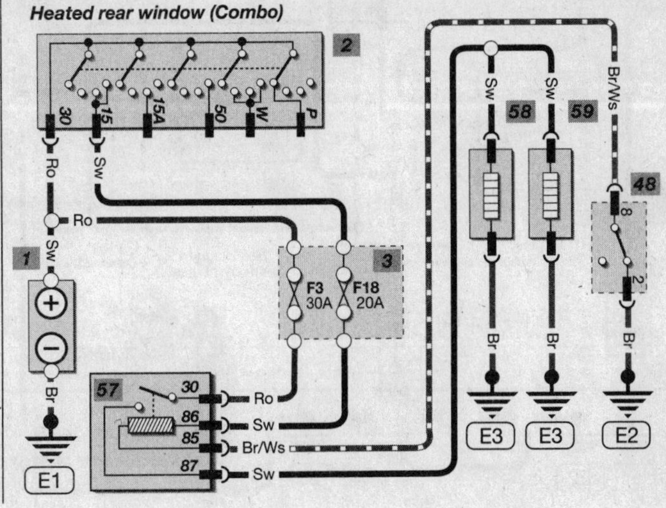

Wire colours

Bl	Blue	**Pu**	Purple
Br	Brown	**Ro**	Red
Ge	Yellow	**Sw**	Black
Gr	Grey	**Vi**	Violet
Gn	Green	**Ws**	White
Or	Orange		

Key to items

1	Battery	64	RH headlight levelling motor
2	Ignition switch	65	LH front light cluster
3	Main fuse box		a) low beam
60	Light switch		b) high beam
61	Signal switch		c) parking light
62	Headlight levelling switch	66	RH front light cluster
63	LH headlight levelling motor		as 65

67	LH rear light cluster
	a) tail light
	c) reversing light
	e) fog light
68	RH rear light cluster
	as 67
69	Licence plate light

70	Front fog light switch
71	Front fog light relay
72	Front fog light
73	Rear fog light switch
74	Rear fog light relay
75	Reverse light switch
★	Combo only

Diagram 6

MTS H32782

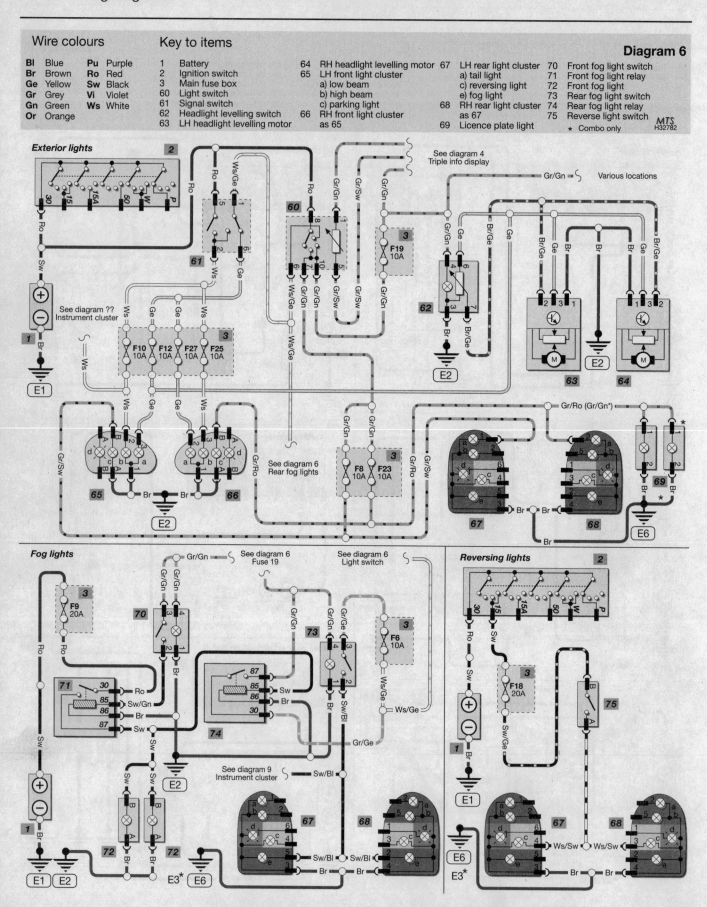

Exterior lights

Fog lights

Reversing lights

Wire colours

Bl	Blue	Pu	Purple
Br	Brown	Ro	Red
Ge	Yellow	Sw	Black
Gr	Grey	Vi	Violet
Gn	Green	Ws	White
Or	Orange		

Key to items

1 Battery
2 Ignition switch
3 Main fuse box
48 Heater controls
57 Heated rear window relay
60 Light switch
61 Signal switch
65 LH front light cluster
 d) direction indicator
66 RH front light cluster (as 65)
67 LH rear light cluster
 b) stop light
 d) direction indicator
68 RH rear light cluster (as 67)
76 LH side direction indicator
77 RH side direction indicator
78 Hazard warning switch
79 Direction indicator unit
80 Stop light switch
81 Centre stop light
82 Passenger light
83 Rear reading lights
84 Boot light
85 Boot light switch
86 Warning buzzer
87 LH rear door switch
88 LH front door switch
89 RH rear door switch
90 Drivers door switch
91 Heated rear window
★ Combo only

Diagram 7

MTS H32783

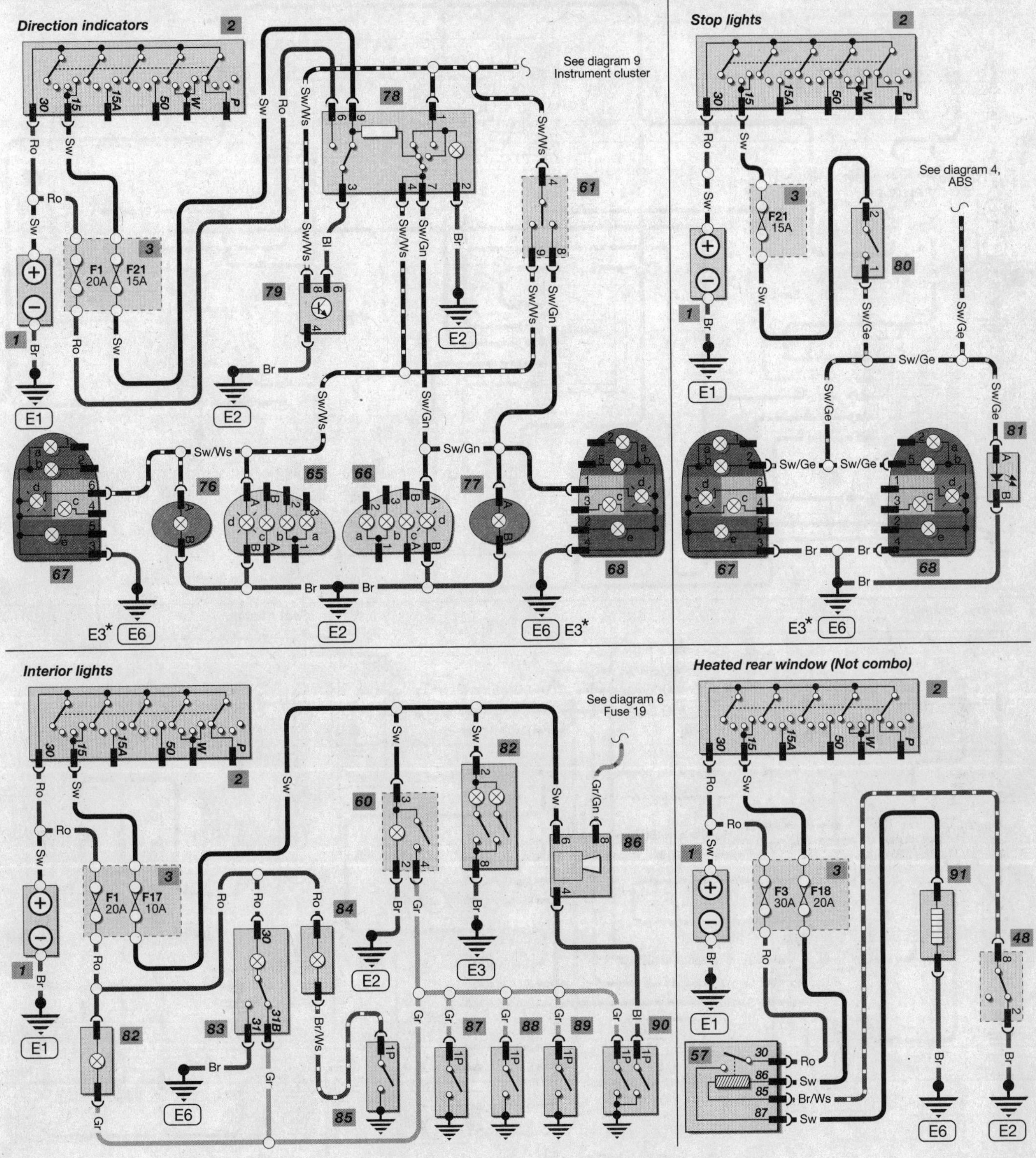

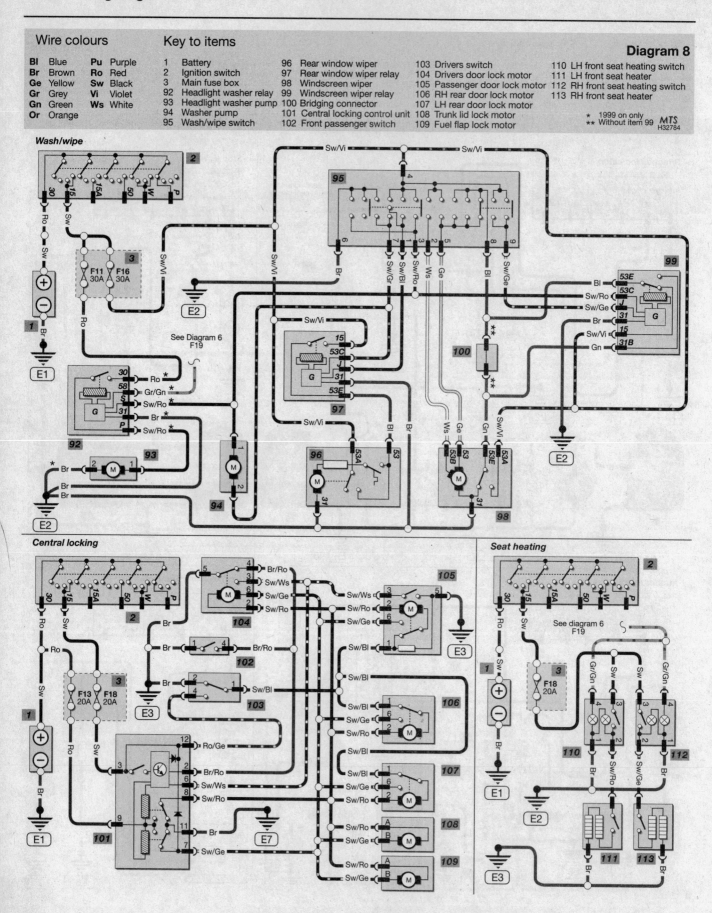

Wire colours

Bl	Blue	Pu	Purple
Br	Brown	Ro	Red
Ge	Yellow	Sw	Black
Gr	Grey	Vi	Violet
Gn	Green	Ws	White
Or	Orange		

Key to items

1 Battery
2 Ignition switch
3 Main fuse box
92 Headlight washer relay
93 Headlight washer pump
94 Washer pump
95 Wash/wipe switch
96 Rear window wiper
97 Rear window wiper relay
98 Windscreen wiper
99 Windscreen wiper relay
100 Bridging connector
101 Central locking control unit
102 Front passenger switch
103 Drivers switch
104 Drivers door lock motor
105 Passenger door lock motor
106 RH rear door lock motor
107 LH rear door lock motor
108 Trunk lid lock motor
109 Fuel flap lock motor
110 LH front seat heating switch
111 LH front seat heater
112 RH front seat heating switch
113 RH front seat heater

Diagram 8

* 1999 on only
** Without item 99

MTS
H32784

Wash/wipe

Central locking

Seat heating

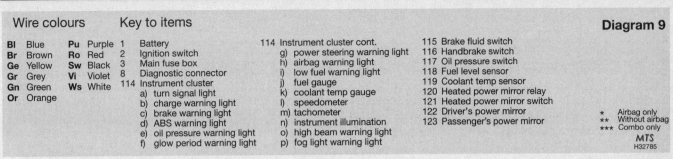

Diagram 9

Wire colours

Bl	Blue	**Pu**	Purple
Br	Brown	**Ro**	Red
Ge	Yellow	**Sw**	Black
Gr	Grey	**Vi**	Violet
Gn	Green	**Ws**	White
Or	Orange		

Key to items

1 Battery
2 Ignition switch
3 Main fuse box
8 Diagnostic connector
114 Instrument cluster
  a) turn signal light
  b) charge warning light
  c) brake warning light
  d) ABS warning light
  e) oil pressure warning light
  f) glow period warning light

114 Instrument cluster cont.
  g) power steering warning light
  h) airbag warning light
  i) low fuel warning light
  j) fuel gauge
  k) coolant temp gauge
  l) speedometer
  m) tachometer
  n) instrument illumination
  o) high beam warning light
  p) fog light warning light

115 Brake fluid switch
116 Handbrake switch
117 Oil pressure switch
118 Fuel level sensor
119 Coolant temp sensor
120 Heated power mirror relay
121 Heated power mirror switch
122 Driver's power mirror
123 Passenger's power mirror

*   Airbag only
**   Without airbag
*** Combo only

MTS
H32785

Instrument cluster

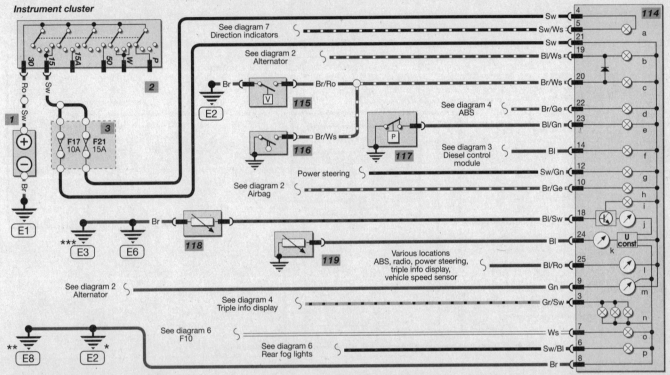

Heated power mirrors

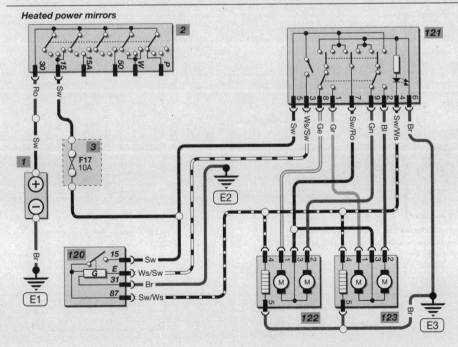

Notes

Dimensions and Weights

Dimensions
Overall length:
    All models except Combo Van .... 3730 mm
    Combo Van models .... 4231 mm
Overall width:
    All models except Combo Van:
        Excluding door mirrors .... 1608 mm
        Including door mirrors .... 1768 mm
    Combo Van models:
        Excluding door mirrors .... 1688 mm
        Including door mirrors .... 2060 mm
Overall height (unladen):
    All models except Combo Van .... 1420 mm
    Combo Van models .... 1805 mm
Wheelbase:
    All models except Combo Van .... 2443 mm
    Combo Van models .... 2480 mm
Front track .... 1387 mm
Rear track:
    All except Combo Van models .... 1388 mm
    Combo Van models .... 1427 mm

Weights
Kerb weight:*
    3-door Hatchback:
        1.5 litre models .... 1015 to 1035 kg
        1.7 litre models .... 1035 to 1055 kg
    5-door Hatchback:
        1.5 litre models .... 1045 to 1065 kg
        1.7 litre models .... 1005 to 1025 kg
    Corsavan models .... 940 to 1025 kg
    Combo Van models .... 995 to 1185 kg
Maximum gross vehicle weight:*
    3-door Hatchback:
        1.5 litre models .... 1435 kg
        1.7 litre models .... 1425 kg
    5-door Hatchback:
        1.5 litre models .... 1465 kg
        1.7 litre models .... 1455 kg
    Corsavan models .... 1425 kg
    Combo Van models .... 1670 kg
Maximum roof rack load:
    All models .... 100 kg
Maximum towing weights:*
    Braked trailer:
        1.5 litre non-turbo models .... 800 kg
        1.5 litre turbo and 1.7 litre models .... 900 kg
    Unbraked traile .... 450 kg
Maximum towing hitch downward load (nose weight) .... 50 kg
*Depending on model and specification. Refer to the VIN plate or a Vauxhall/Opel dealer for exact recommendations.

Length (distance)

Inches (in)	x 25.4	= Millimetres (mm)	x 0.0394	= Inches (in)
Feet (ft)	x 0.305	= Metres (m)	x 3.281	= Feet (ft)
Miles	x 1.609	= Kilometres (km)	x 0.621	= Miles

Volume (capacity)

Cubic inches (cu in; in³)	x 16.387	= Cubic centimetres (cc; cm³)	x 0.061	= Cubic inches (cu in; in³)
Imperial pints (Imp pt)	x 0.568	= Litres (l)	x 1.76	= Imperial pints (Imp pt)
Imperial quarts (Imp qt)	x 1.137	= Litres (l)	x 0.88	= Imperial quarts (Imp qt)
Imperial quarts (Imp qt)	x 1.201	= US quarts (US qt)	x 0.833	= Imperial quarts (Imp qt)
US quarts (US qt)	x 0.946	= Litres (l)	x 1.057	= US quarts (US qt)
Imperial gallons (Imp gal)	x 4.546	= Litres (l)	x 0.22	= Imperial gallons (Imp gal)
Imperial gallons (Imp gal)	x 1.201	= US gallons (US gal)	x 0.833	= Imperial gallons (Imp gal)
US gallons (US gal)	x 3.785	= Litres (l)	x 0.264	= US gallons (US gal)

Mass (weight)

Ounces (oz)	x 28.35	= Grams (g)	x 0.035	= Ounces (oz)
Pounds (lb)	x 0.454	= Kilograms (kg)	x 2.205	= Pounds (lb)

Force

Ounces-force (ozf; oz)	x 0.278	= Newtons (N)	x 3.6	= Ounces-force (ozf; oz)
Pounds-force (lbf; lb)	x 4.448	= Newtons (N)	x 0.225	= Pounds-force (lbf; lb)
Newtons (N)	x 0.1	= Kilograms-force (kgf; kg)	x 9.81	= Newtons (N)

Pressure

Pounds-force per square inch (psi; lbf/in²; lb/in²)	x 0.070	= Kilograms-force per square centimetre (kgf/cm²; kg/cm²)	x 14.223	= Pounds-force per square inch (psi; lbf/in²; lb/in²)
Pounds-force per square inch (psi; lbf/in²; lb/in²)	x 0.068	= Atmospheres (atm)	x 14.696	= Pounds-force per square inch (psi; lbf/in²; lb/in²)
Pounds-force per square inch (psi; lbf/in²; lb/in²)	x 0.069	= Bars	x 14.5	= Pounds-force per square inch (psi; lbf/in²; lb/in²)
Pounds-force per square inch (psi; lbf/in²; lb/in²)	x 6.895	= Kilopascals (kPa)	x 0.145	= Pounds-force per square inch (psi; lbf/in²; lb/in²)
Kilopascals (kPa)	x 0.01	= Kilograms-force per square centimetre (kgf/cm²; kg/cm²)	x 98.1	= Kilopascals (kPa)
Millibar (mbar)	x 100	= Pascals (Pa)	x 0.01	= Millibar (mbar)
Millibar (mbar)	x 0.0145	= Pounds-force per square inch (psi; lbf/in²; lb/in²)	x 68.947	= Millibar (mbar)
Millibar (mbar)	x 0.75	= Millimetres of mercury (mmHg)	x 1.333	= Millibar (mbar)
Millibar (mbar)	x 0.401	= Inches of water (inH$_2$O)	x 2.491	= Millibar (mbar)
Millimetres of mercury (mmHg)	x 0.535	= Inches of water (inH$_2$O)	x 1.868	= Millimetres of mercury (mmHg)
Inches of water (inH$_2$O)	x 0.036	= Pounds-force per square inch (psi; lbf/in²; lb/in²)	x 27.68	= Inches of water (inH$_2$O)

Torque (moment of force)

Pounds-force inches (lbf in; lb in)	x 1.152	= Kilograms-force centimetre (kgf cm; kg cm)	x 0.868	= Pounds-force inches (lbf in; lb in)
Pounds-force inches (lbf in; lb in)	x 0.113	= Newton metres (Nm)	x 8.85	= Pounds-force inches (lbf in; lb in)
Pounds-force inches (lbf in; lb in)	x 0.083	= Pounds-force feet (lbf ft; lb ft)	x 12	= Pounds-force inches (lbf in; lb in)
Pounds-force feet (lbf ft; lb ft)	x 0.138	= Kilograms-force metres (kgf m; kg m)	x 7.233	= Pounds-force feet (lbf ft; lb ft)
Pounds-force feet (lbf ft; lb ft)	x 1.356	= Newton metres (Nm)	x 0.738	= Pounds-force feet (lbf ft; lb ft)
Newton metres (Nm)	x 0.102	= Kilograms-force metres (kgf m; kg m)	x 9.804	= Newton metres (Nm)

Power

Horsepower (hp)	x 745.7	= Watts (W)	x 0.0013	= Horsepower (hp)

Velocity (speed)

Miles per hour (miles/hr; mph)	x 1.609	= Kilometres per hour (km/hr; kph)	x 0.621	= Miles per hour (miles/hr; mph)

Fuel consumption*

Miles per gallon, Imperial (mpg)	x 0.354	= Kilometres per litre (km/l)	x 2.825	= Miles per gallon, Imperial (mpg)
Miles per gallon, US (mpg)	x 0.425	= Kilometres per litre (km/l)	x 2.352	= Miles per gallon, US (mpg)

Temperature

Degrees Fahrenheit = (°C x 1.8) + 32   Degrees Celsius (Degrees Centigrade; °C) = (°F - 32) x 0.56

It is common practice to convert from miles per gallon (mpg) to litres/100 kilometres (l/100km), where mpg x l/100 km = 282

Spare parts are available from many sources, including maker's appointed garages, accessory shops, and motor factors. To be sure of obtaining the correct parts, it will sometimes be necessary to quote the vehicle identification number. If possible, it can also be useful to take the old parts along for positive identification. Items such as starter motors and alternators may be available under a service exchange scheme - any parts returned should be clean.

Our advice regarding spare parts is as follows.

Officially appointed garages

This is the best source of parts which are peculiar to your car, and which are not otherwise generally available (eg, badges, interior trim, certain body panels, etc). It is also the only place at which you should buy parts if the vehicle is still under warranty.

Accessory shops

These are very good places to buy materials and components needed for the maintenance of your car (oil, air and fuel filters, light bulbs, drivebelts, greases, brake pads, tough-up paint, etc). Components of this nature sold by a reputable shop are of the same standard as those used by the car manufacturer.

Besides components, these shops also sell tools and general accessories, usually have convenient opening hours, charge lower prices, and can often be found close to home. Some accessory shops have parts counters where components needed for almost any repair job can be purchased or ordered.

Motor factors

Good factors will stock all the more important components which wear out comparatively quickly, and can sometimes supply individual components needed for the overhaul of a larger assembly (eg, brake seals and hydraulic parts, bearing shells, pistons, valves). They may also handle work such as cylinder block reboring, crankshaft regrinding, etc.

Tyre and exhaust specialists

These outlets may be independent, or members of a local or national chain. They frequently offer competitive prices when compared with a main dealer or local garage, but it will pay to obtain several quotes before making a decision. When researching prices, also ask what 'extras' may be added - for instance fitting a new valve and balancing the wheel are both commonly charged on top of the price of a new tyre.

Other sources

Beware of parts or materials obtained from market stalls, car boot sales or similar outlets. Such items are not invariably sub-standard, but there is little chance of compensation if they do prove unsatisfactory. In the case of safety-critical components such as brake pads, there is the risk not only of financial loss, but also of an accident causing injury or death.

Second-hand components or assemblies obtained from a car breaker can be a good buy in some circumstances, but his sort of purchase is best made by the experienced DIY mechanic.

Vehicle Identification

Modifications are a continuing and unpublished process in vehicle manufacture, quite apart from major model changes. Spare parts manuals and lists are compiled upon a numerical basis, the individual vehicle numbers being essential to correct identification of the component required.

When ordering spare parts, always give as much information as possible. Quote the car model, year of manufacture and vehicle identification and/or engine numbers as appropriate.

The *vehicle identification plate* is riveted on top of the front body panel and includes the Vehicle Identification Number (VIN), vehicle weight information and paint and trim colour codes.

The *Vehicle Identification Number (VIN)* is given on the vehicle identification plate and is also stamped into the body floor panel between the right-hand front seat and the door sill panel; lift the flap in the carpet to see it **(see illustrations)**.

The engine number is stamped on a horizontal flat located on the exhaust manifold side of the cylinder block, at the transmission end. The first part of the engine number gives the engine code **(see illustration)**.

Vauxhall/Opel use a 'Car pass' scheme for vehicle identification. This is a card which is issued to the customer when the car is first purchased. It contains important information, eg, VIN number, key number and radio code. It also includes a special code for diagnostic equipment, therefore it must be kept in a secure place and not in the vehicle.

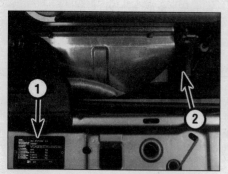

Vehicle Identification Number (VIN) plate (1) and engine number (2) locations

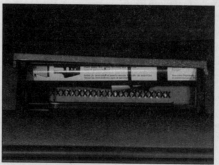

Vehicle Identification Number (VIN) plate on body floor panel

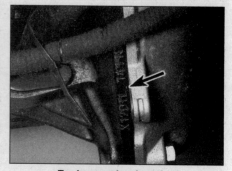

Engine number location

Whenever servicing, repair or overhaul work is carried out on the car or its components, observe the following procedures and instructions. This will assist in carrying out the operation efficiently and to a professional standard of workmanship.

Joint mating faces and gaskets

When separating components at their mating faces, never insert screwdrivers or similar implements into the joint between the faces in order to prise them apart. This can cause severe damage which results in oil leaks, coolant leaks, etc upon reassembly. Separation is usually achieved by tapping along the joint with a soft-faced hammer in order to break the seal. However, note that this method may not be suitable where dowels are used for component location.

Where a gasket is used between the mating faces of two components, a new one must be fitted on reassembly; fit it dry unless otherwise stated in the repair procedure. Make sure that the mating faces are clean and dry, with all traces of old gasket removed. When cleaning a joint face, use a tool which is unlikely to score or damage the face, and remove any burrs or nicks with an oilstone or fine file.

Make sure that tapped holes are cleaned with a pipe cleaner, and keep them free of jointing compound, if this is being used, unless specifically instructed otherwise.

Ensure that all orifices, channels or pipes are clear, and blow through them, preferably using compressed air.

Oil seals

Oil seals can be removed by levering them out with a wide flat-bladed screwdriver or similar implement. Alternatively, a number of self-tapping screws may be screwed into the seal, and these used as a purchase for pliers or some similar device in order to pull the seal free.

Whenever an oil seal is removed from its working location, either individually or as part of an assembly, it should be renewed.

The very fine sealing lip of the seal is easily damaged, and will not seal if the surface it contacts is not completely clean and free from scratches, nicks or grooves. If the original sealing surface of the component cannot be restored, and the manufacturer has not made provision for slight relocation of the seal relative to the sealing surface, the component should be renewed.

Protect the lips of the seal from any surface which may damage them in the course of fitting. Use tape or a conical sleeve where possible. Lubricate the seal lips with oil before fitting and, on dual-lipped seals, fill the space between the lips with grease.

Unless otherwise stated, oil seals must be fitted with their sealing lips toward the lubricant to be sealed.

Use a tubular drift or block of wood of the appropriate size to install the seal and, if the seal housing is shouldered, drive the seal down to the shoulder. If the seal housing is unshouldered, the seal should be fitted with its face flush with the housing top face (unless otherwise instructed).

Screw threads and fastenings

Seized nuts, bolts and screws are quite a common occurrence where corrosion has set in, and the use of penetrating oil or releasing fluid will often overcome this problem if the offending item is soaked for a while before attempting to release it. The use of an impact driver may also provide a means of releasing such stubborn fastening devices, when used in conjunction with the appropriate screwdriver bit or socket. If none of these methods works, it may be necessary to resort to the careful application of heat, or the use of a hacksaw or nut splitter device.

Studs are usually removed by locking two nuts together on the threaded part, and then using a spanner on the lower nut to unscrew the stud. Studs or bolts which have broken off below the surface of the component in which they are mounted can sometimes be removed using a stud extractor. Always ensure that a blind tapped hole is completely free from oil, grease, water or other fluid before installing the bolt or stud. Failure to do this could cause the housing to crack due to the hydraulic action of the bolt or stud as it is screwed in.

When tightening a castellated nut to accept a split pin, tighten the nut to the specified torque, where applicable, and then tighten further to the next split pin hole. Never slacken the nut to align the split pin hole, unless stated in the repair procedure.

When checking or retightening a nut or bolt to a specified torque setting, slacken the nut or bolt by a quarter of a turn, and then retighten to the specified setting. However, this should not be attempted where angular tightening has been used.

For some screw fastenings, notably cylinder head bolts or nuts, torque wrench settings are no longer specified for the latter stages of tightening, "angle-tightening" being called up instead. Typically, a fairly low torque wrench setting will be applied to the bolts/nuts in the correct sequence, followed by one or more stages of tightening through specified angles.

Locknuts, locktabs and washers

Any fastening which will rotate against a component or housing during tightening should always have a washer between it and the relevant component or housing.

Spring or split washers should always be renewed when they are used to lock a critical component such as a big-end bearing retaining bolt or nut. Locktabs which are folded over to retain a nut or bolt should always be renewed.

Self-locking nuts can be re-used in non-critical areas, providing resistance can be felt when the locking portion passes over the bolt or stud thread. However, it should be noted that self-locking stiffnuts tend to lose their effectiveness after long periods of use, and should then be renewed as a matter of course.

Split pins must always be replaced with new ones of the correct size for the hole.

When thread-locking compound is found on the threads of a fastener which is to be re-used, it should be cleaned off with a wire brush and solvent, and fresh compound applied on reassembly.

Special tools

Some repair procedures in this manual entail the use of special tools such as a press, two or three-legged pullers, spring compressors, etc. Wherever possible, suitable readily-available alternatives to the manufacturer's special tools are described, and are shown in use. In some instances, where no alternative is possible, it has been necessary to resort to the use of a manufacturer's tool, and this has been done for reasons of safety as well as the efficient completion of the repair operation. Unless you are highly-skilled and have a thorough understanding of the procedures described, never attempt to bypass the use of any special tool when the procedure described specifies its use. Not only is there a very great risk of personal injury, but expensive damage could be caused to the components involved.

Environmental considerations

When disposing of used engine oil, brake fluid, antifreeze, etc, give due consideration to any detrimental environmental effects. Do not, for instance, pour any of the above liquids down drains into the general sewage system, or onto the ground to soak away. Many local council refuse tips provide a facility for waste oil disposal, as do some garages. If none of these facilities are available, consult your local Environmental Health Department, or the National Rivers Authority, for further advice.

With the universal tightening-up of legislation regarding the emission of environmentally-harmful substances from motor vehicles, most vehicles have tamperproof devices fitted to the main adjustment points of the fuel system. These devices are primarily designed to prevent unqualified persons from adjusting the fuel/air mixture, with the chance of a consequent increase in toxic emissions. If such devices are found during servicing or overhaul, they should, wherever possible, be renewed or refitted in accordance with the manufacturer's requirements or current legislation.

OIL CARE
FOLLOW THE CODE

OIL BANK LINE
0800 66 33 66
www.oilbankline.org.uk

Note: It is antisocial and illegal to dump oil down the drain. To find the location of your local oil recycling bank, call this number free.

The jack supplied with the vehicle tool kit should only be used for changing roadwheels – see *Wheel changing* at the front of this manual. When carrying out any other kind of work, raise the vehicle using a hydraulic jack, and always supplement the jack with axle stands positioned under the vehicle jacking points.

When jacking up the vehicle with a trolley jack, position the jack head under one of the relevant jacking points (note that the jacking points for use with a hydraulic jack are different to those for use with the vehicle jack). **Do not** jack the vehicle under the sump or any of the steering or suspension components. Supplement the jack using axle stands (**see illustrations**).

⚠️ *Warning: Never work under, around, or near a raised vehicle, unless it is adequately supported in at least two places.*

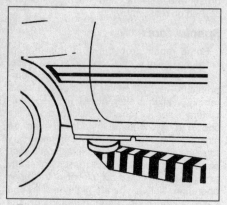

Rear jacking point for hydraulic jack or axle stands

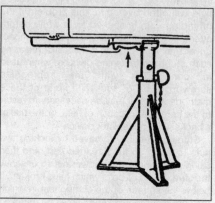

Front jacking point for hydraulic jack or axle stands

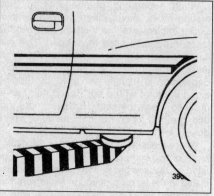

Axle stands should be placed under, or adjacent to the jacking point (arrowed)

Disconnecting the battery

Numerous systems fitted to the vehicle require battery power to be available at all times, either to ensure their continued operation (such as the clock) or to maintain control unit memories which would be erased if the battery were to be disconnected. Whenever the battery is to be disconnected therefore, first note the following, to ensure that there are no unforeseen consequences of this action:

a) First, on any vehicle with central locking, it is a wise precaution to remove the key from the ignition, and to keep it with you, so that it does not get locked in, if the central locking should engage accidentally when the battery is reconnected.

b) Depending on model and specification, the Vauxhall anti-theft alarm system may be of the type which is automatically activated when the vehicle battery is disconnected and/or reconnected. To prevent the alarm sounding on models so equipped, switch the ignition on, then off, and disconnect the battery within 15 seconds. If the alarm is activated when the battery is reconnected, switch the ignition on then off to deactivate the alarm.

c) If a security-coded audio unit is fitted, and the unit and/or the battery is disconnected, the unit will not function again on reconnection until the correct security code is entered. Details of this procedure, which varies according to the unit fitted, are given in the vehicle audio system operating instructions. Ensure you have the correct code before you disconnect the battery. If you do not have the code or details of the correct procedure, but can supply proof of ownership and a legitimate reason for wanting this information, a Vauxhall dealer may be able to help.

Devices known as 'memory-savers' (or 'code-savers') can be used to avoid some of the above problems. Precise details vary according to the device used. Typically, it is plugged into the cigarette lighter, and is connected by its own wires to a spare battery; the vehicle's own battery is then disconnected from the electrical system, leaving the 'memory-saver' to pass sufficient current to maintain audio unit security codes and any other memory values, and also to run permanently-live circuits such as the clock.

⚠️ *Warning: Some of these devices allow a considerable amount of current to pass, which can mean that many of the vehicle's systems are still operational when the main battery is disconnected. If a 'memory saver' is used, ensure that the circuit concerned is actually 'dead' before carrying out any work on it!*

Introduction

A selection of good tools is a fundamental requirement for anyone contemplating the maintenance and repair of a motor vehicle. For the owner who does not possess any, their purchase will prove a considerable expense, offsetting some of the savings made by doing-it-yourself. However, provided that the tools purchased meet the relevant national safety standards and are of good quality, they will last for many years and prove an extremely worthwhile investment.

To help the average owner to decide which tools are needed to carry out the various tasks detailed in this manual, we have compiled three lists of tools under the following headings: *Maintenance and minor repair, Repair and overhaul,* and *Special*. Newcomers to practical mechanics should start off with the *Maintenance and minor repair* tool kit, and confine themselves to the simpler jobs around the vehicle. Then, as confidence and experience grow, more difficult tasks can be undertaken, with extra tools being purchased as, and when, they are needed. In this way, a *Maintenance and minor repair* tool kit can be built up into a *Repair and overhaul* tool kit over a considerable period of time, without any major cash outlays. The experienced do-it-yourselfer will have a tool kit good enough for most repair and overhaul procedures, and will add tools from the *Special* category when it is felt that the expense is justified by the amount of use to which these tools will be put.

Maintenance and minor repair tool kit

The tools given in this list should be considered as a minimum requirement if routine maintenance, servicing and minor repair operations are to be undertaken. We recommend the purchase of combination spanners (ring one end, open-ended the other); although more expensive than open-ended ones, they do give the advantages of both types of spanner.

☐ *Combination spanners:*
 Metric - 8 to 19 mm inclusive
☐ *Adjustable spanner - 35 mm jaw (approx.)*
☐ *Spark plug spanner (with rubber insert) - petrol models*
☐ *Spark plug gap adjustment tool - petrol models*
☐ *Set of feeler gauges*
☐ *Brake bleed nipple spanner*
☐ *Screwdrivers:*
 Flat blade - 100 mm long x 6 mm dia
 Cross blade - 100 mm long x 6 mm dia
 Torx - various sizes (not all vehicles)
☐ *Combination pliers*
☐ *Hacksaw (junior)*
☐ *Tyre pump*
☐ *Tyre pressure gauge*
☐ *Oil can*
☐ *Oil filter removal tool*
☐ *Fine emery cloth*
☐ *Wire brush (small)*
☐ *Funnel (medium size)*
☐ *Sump drain plug key (not all vehicles)*

Repair and overhaul tool kit

These tools are virtually essential for anyone undertaking any major repairs to a motor vehicle, and are additional to those given in the *Maintenance and minor repair* list. Included in this list is a comprehensive set of sockets. Although these are expensive, they will be found invaluable as they are so versatile - particularly if various drives are included in the set. We recommend the half-inch square-drive type, as this can be used with most proprietary torque wrenches.

The tools in this list will sometimes need to be supplemented by tools from the *Special* list:

☐ *Sockets (or box spanners) to cover range in previous list (including Torx sockets)*
☐ *Reversible ratchet drive (for use with sockets)*
☐ *Extension piece, 250 mm (for use with sockets)*
☐ *Universal joint (for use with sockets)*
☐ *Flexible handle or sliding T "breaker bar" (for use with sockets)*
☐ *Torque wrench (for use with sockets)*
☐ *Self-locking grips*
☐ *Ball pein hammer*
☐ *Soft-faced mallet (plastic or rubber)*
☐ *Screwdrivers:*
 Flat blade - long & sturdy, short (chubby), and narrow (electrician's) types
 Cross blade – long & sturdy, and short (chubby) types
☐ *Pliers:*
 Long-nosed
 Side cutters (electrician's)
 Circlip (internal and external)
☐ *Cold chisel - 25 mm*
☐ *Scriber*
☐ *Scraper*
☐ *Centre-punch*
☐ *Pin punch*
☐ *Hacksaw*
☐ *Brake hose clamp*
☐ *Brake/clutch bleeding kit*
☐ *Selection of twist drills*
☐ *Steel rule/straight-edge*
☐ *Allen keys (inc. splined/Torx type)*
☐ *Selection of files*
☐ *Wire brush*
☐ *Axle stands*
☐ *Jack (strong trolley or hydraulic type)*
☐ *Light with extension lead*
☐ *Universal electrical multi-meter*

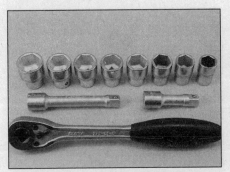

Sockets and reversible ratchet drive

Brake bleeding kit

Torx key, socket and bit

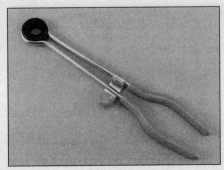

Hose clamp

Angular-tightening gauge

Special tools

The tools in this list are those which are not used regularly, are expensive to buy, or which need to be used in accordance with their manufacturers' instructions. Unless relatively difficult mechanical jobs are undertaken frequently, it will not be economic to buy many of these tools. Where this is the case, you could consider clubbing together with friends (or joining a motorists' club) to make a joint purchase, or borrowing the tools against a deposit from a local garage or tool hire specialist. It is worth noting that many of the larger DIY superstores now carry a large range of special tools for hire at modest rates.

The following list contains only those tools and instruments freely available to the public, and not those special tools produced by the vehicle manufacturer specifically for its dealer network. You will find occasional references to these manufacturers' special tools in the text of this manual. Generally, an alternative method of doing the job without the vehicle manufacturers' special tool is given. However, sometimes there is no alternative to using them. Where this is the case and the relevant tool cannot be bought or borrowed, you will have to entrust the work to a dealer.

☐ Angular-tightening gauge
☐ Valve spring compressor
☐ Valve grinding tool
☐ Piston ring compressor
☐ Piston ring removal/installation tool
☐ Cylinder bore hone
☐ Balljoint separator
☐ Coil spring compressors (where applicable)
☐ Two/three-legged hub and bearing puller
☐ Impact screwdriver
☐ Micrometer and/or vernier calipers
☐ Dial gauge
☐ Stroboscopic timing light
☐ Dwell angle meter/tachometer
☐ Fault code reader
☐ Cylinder compression gauge
☐ Hand-operated vacuum pump and gauge
☐ Clutch plate alignment set
☐ Brake shoe steady spring cup removal tool
☐ Bush and bearing removal/installation set
☐ Stud extractors
☐ Tap and die set
☐ Lifting tackle
☐ Trolley jack

Buying tools

Reputable motor accessory shops and superstores often offer excellent quality tools at discount prices, so it pays to shop around.

Remember, you don't have to buy the most expensive items on the shelf, but it is always advisable to steer clear of the very cheap tools. Beware of 'bargains' offered on market stalls or at car boot sales. There are plenty of good tools around at reasonable prices, but always aim to purchase items which meet the relevant national safety standards. If in doubt, ask the proprietor or manager of the shop for advice before making a purchase.

Care and maintenance of tools

Having purchased a reasonable tool kit, it is necessary to keep the tools in a clean and serviceable condition. After use, always wipe off any dirt, grease and metal particles using a clean, dry cloth, before putting the tools away. Never leave them lying around after they have been used. A simple tool rack on the garage or workshop wall for items such as screwdrivers and pliers is a good idea. Store all normal spanners and sockets in a metal box. Any measuring instruments, gauges, meters, etc, must be carefully stored where they cannot be damaged or become rusty.

Take a little care when tools are used. Hammer heads inevitably become marked, and screwdrivers lose the keen edge on their blades from time to time. A little timely attention with emery cloth or a file will soon restore items like this to a good finish.

Working facilities

Not to be forgotten when discussing tools is the workshop itself. If anything more than routine maintenance is to be carried out, a suitable working area becomes essential.

It is appreciated that many an owner-mechanic is forced by circumstances to remove an engine or similar item without the benefit of a garage or workshop. Having done this, any repairs should always be done under the cover of a roof.

Wherever possible, any dismantling should be done on a clean, flat workbench or table at a suitable working height.

Any workbench needs a vice; one with a jaw opening of 100 mm is suitable for most jobs. As mentioned previously, some clean dry storage space is also required for tools, as well as for any lubricants, cleaning fluids, touch-up paints etc, which become necessary.

Another item which may be required, and which has a much more general usage, is an electric drill with a chuck capacity of at least 8 mm. This, together with a good range of twist drills, is virtually essential for fitting accessories.

Last, but not least, always keep a supply of old newspapers and clean, lint-free rags available, and try to keep any working area as clean as possible.

Micrometers

Dial test indicator ("dial gauge")

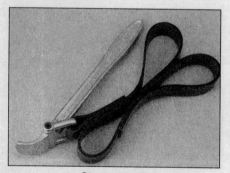

Strap wrench

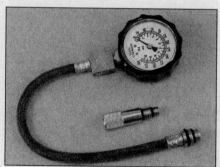

Compression tester

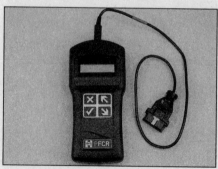

Fault code reader

This is a guide to getting your vehicle through the MOT test. Obviously it will not be possible to examine the vehicle to the same standard as the professional MOT tester. However, working through the following checks will enable you to identify any problem areas before submitting the vehicle for the test.

Where a testable component is in borderline condition, the tester has discretion in deciding whether to pass or fail it. The basis of such discretion is whether the tester would be happy for a close relative or friend to use the vehicle with the component in that condition. If the vehicle presented is clean and evidently well cared for, the tester may be more inclined to pass a borderline component than if the vehicle is scruffy and apparently neglected.

It has only been possible to summarise the test requirements here, based on the regulations in force at the time of printing. Test standards are becoming increasingly stringent, although there are some exemptions for older vehicles.

An assistant will be needed to help carry out some of these checks.

The checks have been sub-divided into four categories, as follows:

1 Checks carried out **FROM THE DRIVER'S SEAT**

2 Checks carried out **WITH THE VEHICLE ON THE GROUND**

3 Checks carried out **WITH THE VEHICLE RAISED AND THE WHEELS FREE TO TURN**

4 Checks carried out on **YOUR VEHICLE'S EXHAUST EMISSION SYSTEM**

1 Checks carried out **FROM THE DRIVER'S SEAT**

Handbrake

☐ Test the operation of the handbrake. Excessive travel (too many clicks) indicates incorrect brake or cable adjustment.

☐ Check that the handbrake cannot be released by tapping the lever sideways. Check the security of the lever mountings.

Footbrake

☐ Depress the brake pedal and check that it does not creep down to the floor, indicating a master cylinder fault. Release the pedal, wait a few seconds, then depress it again. If the pedal travels nearly to the floor before firm resistance is felt, brake adjustment or repair is necessary. If the pedal feels spongy, there is air in the hydraulic system which must be removed by bleeding.

☐ Check that the brake pedal is secure and in good condition. Check also for signs of fluid leaks on the pedal, floor or carpets, which would indicate failed seals in the brake master cylinder.

☐ Check the servo unit (when applicable) by operating the brake pedal several times, then keeping the pedal depressed and starting the engine. As the engine starts, the pedal will move down slightly. If not, the vacuum hose or the servo itself may be faulty.

Steering wheel and column

☐ Examine the steering wheel for fractures or looseness of the hub, spokes or rim.

☐ Move the steering wheel from side to side and then up and down. Check that the steering wheel is not loose on the column, indicating wear or a loose retaining nut. Continue moving the steering wheel as before, but also turn it slightly from left to right.

☐ Check that the steering wheel is not loose on the column, and that there is no abnormal

movement of the steering wheel, indicating wear in the column support bearings or couplings.

Windscreen, mirrors and sunvisor

☐ The windscreen must be free of cracks or other significant damage within the driver's field of view. (Small stone chips are acceptable.) Rear view mirrors must be secure, intact, and capable of being adjusted.

☐ The driver's sunvisor must be capable of being stored in the "up" position.

Seat belts and seats

Note: *The following checks are applicable to all seat belts, front and rear.*

☐ Examine the webbing of all the belts (including rear belts if fitted) for cuts, serious fraying or deterioration. Fasten and unfasten each belt to check the buckles. If applicable, check the retracting mechanism. Check the security of all seat belt mountings accessible from inside the vehicle.

☐ Seat belts with pre-tensioners, once activated, have a "flag" or similar showing on the seat belt stalk. This, in itself, is not a reason for test failure.

☐ The front seats themselves must be securely attached and the backrests must lock in the upright position.

Doors

☐ Both front doors must be able to be opened and closed from outside and inside, and must latch securely when closed.

2 Checks carried out WITH THE VEHICLE ON THE GROUND

Vehicle identification

☐ Number plates must be in good condition, secure and legible, with letters and numbers correctly spaced – spacing at (A) should be at least twice that at (B).

☐ The VIN plate and/or homologation plate must be legible.

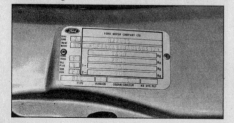

Electrical equipment

☐ Switch on the ignition and check the operation of the horn.

☐ Check the windscreen washers and wipers, examining the wiper blades; renew damaged or perished blades. Also check the operation of the stop-lights.

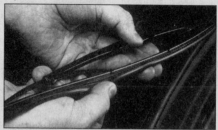

☐ Check the operation of the sidelights and number plate lights. The lenses and reflectors must be secure, clean and undamaged.

☐ Check the operation and alignment of the headlights. The headlight reflectors must not be tarnished and the lenses must be undamaged.

☐ Switch on the ignition and check the operation of the direction indicators (including the instrument panel tell-tale) and the hazard warning lights. Operation of the sidelights and stop-lights must not affect the indicators - if it does, the cause is usually a bad earth at the rear light cluster.

☐ Check the operation of the rear foglight(s), including the warning light on the instrument panel or in the switch.

☐ The ABS warning light must illuminate in accordance with the manufacturers' design. For most vehicles, the ABS warning light should illuminate when the ignition is switched on, and (if the system is operating properly) extinguish after a few seconds. Refer to the owner's handbook.

Footbrake

☐ Examine the master cylinder, brake pipes and servo unit for leaks, loose mountings, corrosion or other damage.

☐ The fluid reservoir must be secure and the fluid level must be between the upper (**A**) and lower (**B**) markings.

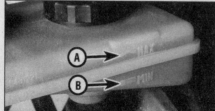

☐ Inspect both front brake flexible hoses for cracks or deterioration of the rubber. Turn the steering from lock to lock, and ensure that the hoses do not contact the wheel, tyre, or any part of the steering or suspension mechanism. With the brake pedal firmly depressed, check the hoses for bulges or leaks under pressure.

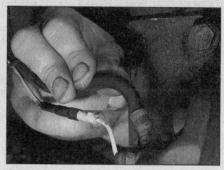

Steering and suspension

☐ Have your assistant turn the steering wheel from side to side slightly, up to the point where the steering gear just begins to transmit this movement to the roadwheels. Check for excessive free play between the steering wheel and the steering gear, indicating wear or insecurity of the steering column joints, the column-to-steering gear coupling, or the steering gear itself.

☐ Have your assistant turn the steering wheel more vigorously in each direction, so that the roadwheels just begin to turn. As this is done, examine all the steering joints, linkages, fittings and attachments. Renew any component that shows signs of wear or damage. On vehicles with power steering, check the security and condition of the steering pump, drivebelt and hoses.

☐ Check that the vehicle is standing level, and at approximately the correct ride height.

Shock absorbers

☐ Depress each corner of the vehicle in turn, then release it. The vehicle should rise and then settle in its normal position. If the vehicle continues to rise and fall, the shock absorber is defective. A shock absorber which has seized will also cause the vehicle to fail.

Exhaust system

☐ Start the engine. With your assistant holding a rag over the tailpipe, check the entire system for leaks. Repair or renew leaking sections.

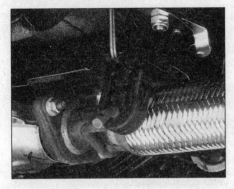

3 Checks carried out **WITH THE VEHICLE RAISED AND THE WHEELS FREE TO TURN**

Jack up the front and rear of the vehicle, and securely support it on axle stands. Position the stands clear of the suspension assemblies. Ensure that the wheels are clear of the ground and that the steering can be turned from lock to lock.

Steering mechanism

☐ Have your assistant turn the steering from lock to lock. Check that the steering turns smoothly, and that no part of the steering mechanism, including a wheel or tyre, fouls any brake hose or pipe or any part of the body structure.
☐ Examine the steering rack rubber gaiters for damage or insecurity of the retaining clips. If power steering is fitted, check for signs of damage or leakage of the fluid hoses, pipes or connections. Also check for excessive stiffness or binding of the steering, a missing split pin or locking device, or severe corrosion of the body structure within 30 cm of any steering component attachment point.

Front and rear suspension and wheel bearings

☐ Starting at the front right-hand side, grasp the roadwheel at the 3 o'clock and 9 o'clock positions and rock gently but firmly. Check for free play or insecurity at the wheel bearings, suspension balljoints, or suspension mountings, pivots and attachments.
☐ Now grasp the wheel at the 12 o'clock and 6 o'clock positions and repeat the previous inspection. Spin the wheel, and check for roughness or tightness of the front wheel bearing.

☐ If excess free play is suspected at a component pivot point, this can be confirmed by using a large screwdriver or similar tool and levering between the mounting and the component attachment. This will confirm whether the wear is in the pivot bush, its retaining bolt, or in the mounting itself (the bolt holes can often become elongated).

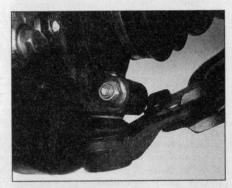

☐ Carry out all the above checks at the other front wheel, and then at both rear wheels.

Springs and shock absorbers

☐ Examine the suspension struts (when applicable) for serious fluid leakage, corrosion, or damage to the casing. Also check the security of the mounting points.
☐ If coil springs are fitted, check that the spring ends locate in their seats, and that the spring is not corroded, cracked or broken.
☐ If leaf springs are fitted, check that all leaves are intact, that the axle is securely attached to each spring, and that there is no deterioration of the spring eye mountings, bushes, and shackles.

☐ The same general checks apply to vehicles fitted with other suspension types, such as torsion bars, hydraulic displacer units, etc. Ensure that all mountings and attachments are secure, that there are no signs of excessive wear, corrosion or damage, and (on hydraulic types) that there are no fluid leaks or damaged pipes.
☐ Inspect the shock absorbers for signs of serious fluid leakage. Check for wear of the mounting bushes or attachments, or damage to the body of the unit.

Driveshafts (fwd vehicles only)

☐ Rotate each front wheel in turn and inspect the constant velocity joint gaiters for splits or damage. Also check that each driveshaft is straight and undamaged.

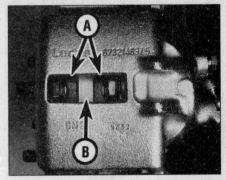

Braking system

☐ If possible without dismantling, check brake pad wear and disc condition. Ensure that the friction lining material has not worn excessively, (A) and that the discs are not fractured, pitted, scored or badly worn (B).

☐ Examine all the rigid brake pipes underneath the vehicle, and the flexible hose(s) at the rear. Look for corrosion, chafing or insecurity of the pipes, and for signs of bulging under pressure, chafing, splits or deterioration of the flexible hoses.
☐ Look for signs of fluid leaks at the brake calipers or on the brake backplates. Repair or renew leaking components.
☐ Slowly spin each wheel, while your assistant depresses and releases the footbrake. Ensure that each brake is operating and does not bind when the pedal is released.

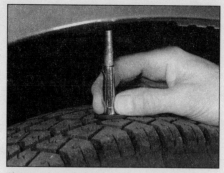

☐ Examine the handbrake mechanism, checking for frayed or broken cables, excessive corrosion, or wear or insecurity of the linkage. Check that the mechanism works on each relevant wheel, and releases fully, without binding.
☐ It is not possible to test brake efficiency without special equipment, but a road test can be carried out later to check that the vehicle pulls up in a straight line.

Fuel and exhaust systems

☐ Inspect the fuel tank (including the filler cap), fuel pipes, hoses and unions. All components must be secure and free from leaks.
☐ Examine the exhaust system over its entire length, checking for any damaged, broken or missing mountings, security of the retaining clamps and rust or corrosion.

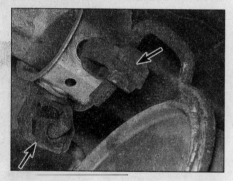

Wheels and tyres

☐ Examine the sidewalls and tread area of each tyre in turn. Check for cuts, tears, lumps, bulges, separation of the tread, and exposure of the ply or cord due to wear or damage. Check that the tyre bead is correctly seated on the wheel rim, that the valve is sound and properly seated, and that the wheel is not distorted or damaged.
☐ Check that the tyres are of the correct size for the vehicle, that they are of the same size and type on each axle, and that the pressures are correct.
☐ Check the tyre tread depth. The legal minimum at the time of writing is 1.6 mm over at least three-quarters of the tread width. Abnormal tread wear may indicate incorrect front wheel alignment.

Body corrosion

☐ Check the condition of the entire vehicle structure for signs of corrosion in load-bearing areas. (These include chassis box sections, side sills, cross-members, pillars, and all suspension, steering, braking system and seat belt mountings and anchorages.) Any corrosion which has seriously reduced the thickness of a load-bearing area is likely to cause the vehicle to fail. In this case professional repairs are likely to be needed.
☐ Damage or corrosion which causes sharp or otherwise dangerous edges to be exposed will also cause the vehicle to fail.

4 Checks carried out on YOUR VEHICLE'S EXHAUST EMISSION SYSTEM

Petrol models

☐ Have the engine at normal operating temperature, and make sure that it is in good tune (ignition system in good order, air filter element clean, etc).
☐ Before any measurements are carried out, raise the engine speed to around 2500 rpm, and hold it at this speed for 20 seconds. Allow the engine speed to return to idle, and watch for smoke emissions from the exhaust tailpipe. If the idle speed is obviously much too high, or if dense blue or clearly-visible black smoke comes from the tailpipe for more than 5 seconds, the vehicle will fail. As a rule of thumb, blue smoke signifies oil being burnt (engine wear) while black smoke signifies unburnt fuel (dirty air cleaner element, or other carburettor or fuel system fault).
☐ An exhaust gas analyser capable of measuring carbon monoxide (CO) and hydrocarbons (HC) is now needed. If such an instrument cannot be hired or borrowed, a local garage may agree to perform the check for a small fee.

CO emissions (mixture)

☐ At the time of writing, for vehicles first used between 1st August 1975 and 31st July 1986 (P to C registration), the CO level must not exceed 4.5% by volume. For vehicles first used between 1st August 1986 and 31st July 1992 (D to J registration), the CO level must not exceed 3.5% by volume. Vehicles first

used after 1st August 1992 (K registration) must conform to the manufacturer's specification. The MOT tester has access to a DOT database or emissions handbook, which lists the CO and HC limits for each make and model of vehicle. The CO level is measured with the engine at idle speed, and at "fast idle". The following limits are given as a general guide:

> *At idle speed -*
> CO level no more than 0.5%
> *At "fast idle" (2500 to 3000 rpm) -*
> CO level no more than 0.3%
> (Minimum oil temperature 60°C)

☐ If the CO level cannot be reduced far enough to pass the test (and the fuel and ignition systems are otherwise in good condition) then the carburettor is badly worn, or there is some problem in the fuel injection system or catalytic converter (as applicable).

HC emissions

☐ With the CO within limits, HC emissions for vehicles first used between 1st August 1975 and 31st July 1992 (P to J registration) must not exceed 1200 ppm. Vehicles first used after 1st August 1992 (K registration) must conform to the manufacturer's specification. The MOT tester has access to a DOT database or emissions handbook, which lists the CO and HC limits for each make and model of vehicle. The HC level is measured with the engine at "fast idle". The following is given as a general guide:

> *At "fast idle" (2500 to 3000 rpm) -*
> HC level no more than 200 ppm
> (Minimum oil temperature 60°C)

☐ Excessive HC emissions are caused by incomplete combustion, the causes of which can include oil being burnt, mechanical wear and ignition/fuel system malfunction.

Diesel models

☐ The only emission test applicable to Diesel engines is the measuring of exhaust smoke density. The test involves accelerating the engine several times to its maximum unloaded speed.

Note: *It is of the utmost importance that the engine timing belt is in good condition before the test is carried out.*

☐ The limits for Diesel engine exhaust smoke, introduced in September 1995 are:
Vehicles first used before 1st August 1979:
Exempt from metered smoke testing, but must not emit "dense blue or clearly visible black smoke for a period of more than 5 seconds at idle" or "dense blue or clearly visible black smoke during acceleration which would obscure the view of other road users".
Non-turbocharged vehicles first used after 1st August 1979: 2.5m-1
Turbocharged vehicles first used after 1st August 1979: 3.0m-1
☐ Excessive smoke can be caused by a dirty air cleaner element. Otherwise, professional advice may be needed to find the cause.

Engine

- [ ] Engine fails to rotate when attempting to start
- [ ] Low cranking speed
- [ ] Engine rotates, but will not start
- [ ] Engine difficult to start
- [ ] Starter motor noisy or excessively-rough in engagement
- [ ] Engine starts but stops again
- [ ] Engine will not stop when switched off
- [ ] Engine runs erratically
- [ ] Engine misfires at idle speed
- [ ] Engine misfires throughout the driving speed range
- [ ] Engine hesitates on acceleration
- [ ] Engine stalls
- [ ] Engine lacks power
- [ ] Engine backfires
- [ ] Oil consumption excessive
- [ ] Low oil pressure
- [ ] High oil pressure
- [ ] Crankcase pressure excessive (oil being blown out)
- [ ] Engine runs-on after switching off
- [ ] Vibration
- [ ] Engine noises

Cooling system

- [ ] Overheating
- [ ] Overcooling
- [ ] External coolant leakage
- [ ] Internal coolant leakage
- [ ] Corrosion

Fuel and exhaust systems

- [ ] Excessive fuel consumption
- [ ] Injector pipe(s) break or split repeatedly
- [ ] Fuel leakage and/or fuel odour
- [ ] Excessive noise or fumes from the exhaust system
- [ ] Black smoke in exhaust
- [ ] Blue or white smoke in exhaust

Clutch

- [ ] Pedal travels to floor - no pressure or very little resistance
- [ ] Clutch fails to disengage (unable to select gears)
- [ ] Clutch slips (engine speed increases, with no increase in vehicle speed)
- [ ] Judder as clutch is engaged
- [ ] Noise when depressing or releasing clutch pedal

Manual transmission

- [ ] Noisy in neutral with engine running
- [ ] Noisy in one particular gear
- [ ] Difficulty engaging gears
- [ ] Jumps out of gear
- [ ] Vibration
- [ ] Lubricant leaks

Driveshafts

- [ ] Vibration when accelerating or decelerating
- [ ] Clicking or knocking noise on turns (at slow speed on full-lock)

Braking system

- [ ] Vehicle pulls to one side under braking
- [ ] Noise (grinding or high-pitched squeal) when brakes applied
- [ ] Excessive brake pedal travel
- [ ] Brake pedal feels spongy when depressed
- [ ] Excessive brake pedal effort required to stop vehicle
- [ ] Judder felt through brake pedal or steering wheel when braking
- [ ] Pedal pulsates when braking hard
- [ ] Brakes binding
- [ ] Rear wheels locking under normal braking
- [ ] Vehicle pulls to one side
- [ ] Wheel wobble and vibration
- [ ] Excessive pitching and/or rolling around corners, or during braking
- [ ] Wandering or general instability
- [ ] Excessively-stiff steering
- [ ] Excessive play in steering
- [ ] Lack of power assistance
- [ ] Tyre wear excessive

Electrical system

- [ ] Battery will not hold a charge for more than a few days
- [ ] Ignition/no-charge warning light remains illuminated with engine running
- [ ] Ignition/no-charge warning light fails to come on
- [ ] Lights inoperative
- [ ] Instrument readings inaccurate or erratic
- [ ] Horn inoperative, or unsatisfactory in operation
- [ ] Windscreen/tailgate wipers inoperative, or unsatisfactory in operation
- [ ] Windscreen/tailgate washers inoperative, or unsatisfactory in operation
- [ ] Electric windows inoperative, or unsatisfactory in operation
- [ ] Central locking system inoperative, or unsatisfactory in operation

Introduction

The vehicle owner who does his or her own maintenance according to the recommended service schedules should not have to use this section of the manual very often. Modern component reliability is such that, provided those items subject to wear or deterioration are inspected or renewed at the specified intervals, sudden failure is comparatively rare. Faults do not usually just happen as a result of sudden failure, but develop over a period of time. Major mechanical failures in particular are usually preceded by characteristic symptoms over hundreds or even thousands of miles. Those components which do occasionally fail without warning are often small and easily carried in the vehicle.

With any fault-finding, the first step is to decide where to begin investigations. Sometimes this is obvious, but on other occasions, a little detective work will be necessary. The owner who makes half a dozen haphazard adjustments or replacements may be successful in curing a fault (or its symptoms), but will be none the wiser if the fault recurs, and ultimately may have spent more time and money than was necessary. A calm and logical approach will be found to be more satisfactory in the long run. Always take into account any warning signs or abnormalities that may have been noticed in the period preceding the fault - power loss, high or low gauge readings, unusual smells, etc - and remember that failure of components such as fuses or spark plugs may only be pointers to some underlying fault.

The pages which follow provide an easy-reference guide to the more common problems which may occur during the operation of the vehicle. These problems and their possible causes are grouped under headings denoting various components or systems, such as Engine, Cooling system, etc. The Chapter and/or Section which deals with the problem is also shown in brackets. Whatever the fault, certain basic principles apply. These are as follows:

Verify the fault. This is simply a matter of

being sure that you know what the symptoms are before starting work. This is particularly important if you are investigating a fault for someone else, who may not have described it very accurately.

Don't overlook the obvious. For example, if the vehicle won't start, is there fuel in the tank? (Don't take anyone else's word on this particular point, and don't trust the fuel gauge either!) If an electrical fault is indicated, look for loose or broken wires before digging out the test gear.

Cure the disease, not the symptom. Substituting a flat battery with a fully-charged one will get you off the hard shoulder, but if the underlying cause is not attended to, the new battery will go the same way. Similarly, changing oil-fouled spark plugs for a new set will get you moving again, but remember that the reason for the fouling (if it wasn't simply an incorrect grade of plug) will have to be established and corrected.

Don't take anything for granted. Particularly, don't forget that a 'new' component may itself be defective (especially if it's been rattling around in the boot for months), and don't leave components out of a fault diagnosis sequence just because they are new or recently-fitted. When you do finally diagnose a difficult fault, you'll probably realise that all the evidence was there from the start.

The majority of starting problems on small diesel engines are electrical in origin. The mechanic who is familiar with petrol engines but less so with diesel may be inclined to view the diesel's injectors and pump in the same light as the spark plugs and distributor, but this is generally a mistake.

When investigating complaints of difficult starting for someone else, make sure that the correct starting procedure is understood and is being followed. Some drivers are unaware of the significance of the preheating warning light - many modern engines are sufficiently forgiving for this not to matter in mild weather, but with the onset of winter problems begin.

As a rule of thumb, if the engine is difficult to start but runs well when it has finally got going, the problem is electrical (battery, starter motor or preheating system). If poor performance is combined with difficult starting, the problem is likely to be in the fuel system. The low pressure (supply) side of the fuel system should be checked before suspecting the injectors and injection pump. Normally the pump is the last item to suspect, since unless it has been tampered with there is no reason for it to be at fault.

Engine

Engine fails to rotate when attempting to start

- [ ] Battery terminal connections loose or corroded (see *Weekly checks*).
- [ ] Battery discharged or faulty (Chapter 5).
- [ ] Broken, loose or disconnected wiring in the starting circuit (Chapter 5).
- [ ] Defective starter solenoid or switch (Chapter 5).
- [ ] Defective starter motor (Chapter 5).
- [ ] Starter pinion or flywheel ring gear teeth loose or broken (Chapters 2 and 5).
- [ ] Engine earth strap broken or disconnected (Chapter 5).

Low cranking speed

- [ ] Inadequate battery capacity.
- [ ] Incorrect grade of oil (Lubricants and fluids).
- [ ] High resistance in starter motor circuit.
- [ ] Starter motor internal fault.

Engine rotates, but will not start

- [ ] Fuel tank empty.
- [ ] Air in fuel system.
- [ ] Fuel waxing (in very cold weather) or contaminated.
- [ ] Fuel feed restriction.
- [ ] Battery discharged (engine rotates slowly) (Chapter 5).
- [ ] Battery terminal connections loose or corroded (see *Weekly checks*).
- [ ] Preheating system faulty (Chapter 5).
- [ ] Stop solenoid faulty (Chapter 4).
- [ ] Overfuelling or cold start advance mechanism defective (Chapter 4).
- [ ] Poor compression (Chapter 2).
- [ ] Injection pump internal fault (Chapter 4).
- [ ] Major mechanical failure (eg camshaft drive) (Chapter 2).

Engine difficult to start

- [ ] Incorrect starting procedure.
- [ ] Battery or starter motor fault.
- [ ] Battery terminal connections loose or corroded (see *Weekly checks*).
- [ ] Preheating system faulty (Chapter 5).
- [ ] Air in fuel system.
- [ ] Fuel feed restriction.
- [ ] Low cylinder compressions (Chapter 2).
- [ ] Air filter element dirty or clogged (Chapter 1).
- [ ] Valve clearances incorrect (Chapter 2).
- [ ] Valves sticking.
- [ ] Blockage in exhaust system.
- [ ] Valve timing incorrect.
- [ ] Injector(s) faulty (Chapter 4).
- [ ] Injection pump timing incorrect (Chapter 4).
- [ ] Injection pump internal fault.

Starter motor noisy or excessively-rough in engagement

- [ ] Starter pinion or flywheel ring gear teeth loose or broken (Chapters 2 and 5).
- [ ] Starter motor mounting bolts loose or missing (Chapter 5).
- [ ] Starter motor internal components worn or damaged (Chapter 5).

Engine starts but stops again

- [ ] Fuel very low in tank.
- [ ] Air in fuel system.
- [ ] Idle adjustment incorrect (Chapter 1).
- [ ] Fuel hose restriction.
- [ ] Air cleaner dirty.
- [ ] Blockage in induction system.
- [ ] Blockage in exhaust system.
- [ ] Injector(s) faulty (Chapter 4).

Engine (continued)

Engine will not stop when switched off

☐ Stop solenoid defective.

Engine runs erratically

☐ Air filter element clogged (Chapter 1).
☐ Uneven or low cylinder compressions (Chapter 2).
☐ Camshaft lobes worn (Chapter 2).
☐ Timing belt incorrectly fitted (Chapter 2).
☐ Faulty injector(s) (Chapter 4).
☐ Operating temperature incorrect.
☐ Accelerator linkage maladjusted or sticking (Chapter 4).
☐ Blockage in induction system.
☐ Air in fuel system.
☐ Injector pipe(s) wrongly connected or wrong type.
☐ Fuel hose restriction.
☐ Valve clearances incorrect (Chapter 2).
☐ Valve(s) sticking.
☐ Valve spring(s) broken or weak.
☐ Valve timing incorrect.
☐ Injection pump mountings loose (Chapter 4).
☐ Injection pump timing incorrect (Chapter 4).
☐ Injection pump faulty (Chapter 4).

Engine misfires at idle speed

☐ Air cleaner dirty.
☐ Blockage in induction system.
☐ Air in fuel system.
☐ Fuel feed restriction.
☐ Valve clearances incorrect (Chapter 2).
☐ Valve(s) sticking.
☐ Valve spring(s) weak or broken.
☐ Poor compression (Chapter 2).
☐ Overheating.
☐ Injector pipe(s) wrongly connected or wrong type.
☐ Valve timing incorrect.
☐ Injector(s) faulty or wrong type (Chapter 4).
☐ Injection pump timing incorrect (Chapter 4).
☐ Injection pump faulty or wrong type (Chapter 4).
☐ Disconnected, leaking, or perished crankcase ventilation hoses (Chapter 4).

Engine misfires throughout the driving speed range

☐ Fuel filter choked (Chapter 1).
☐ Fuel tank vent blocked, or fuel pipes restricted (Chapter 4).
☐ Faulty injector(s) (Chapter 4).
☐ Uneven or low cylinder compressions (Chapter 2).

Engine hesitates on acceleration

☐ Faulty injector(s) (Chapter 4).

Engine stalls

☐ Fuel filter choked (Chapter 1).
☐ Fuel tank vent blocked, or fuel pipes restricted (Chapter 4).
☐ Faulty injector(s) (Chapter 4).

Engine lacks power

☐ Timing belt incorrectly fitted or tensioned (Chapter 2).
☐ Brakes binding (Chapters 1 and 9).
☐ Clutch slipping (Chapter 6).

Engine backfires

☐ Accelerator linkage not moving through full travel (cable slack or pedal obstructed) (Chapter 4).
☐ Injection pump control linkages sticking or maladjusted (Chapter 4).
☐ Air cleaner dirty (Chapter 1).
☐ Blockage in induction system.
☐ Air in fuel system.
☐ Fuel feed restriction.
☐ Valve timing incorrect.
☐ Injection pump timing incorrect (Chapter 4).
☐ Blockage in exhaust system.
☐ Turbo boost pressure inadequate, when applicable.
☐ Valve clearances incorrect (Chapter 2).
☐ Poor compression (Chapter 2).
☐ Injector(s) faulty or wrong type (Chapter 4).
☐ Injection pump faulty (Chapter 4).
☐ Timing belt incorrectly fitted or tensioned (Chapter 2).

Oil consumption excessive

☐ External leakage (standing or running).
☐ New engine not yet run-in.
☐ Engine oil incorrect grade or poor quality (Lubricants and fluids).
☐ Oil level too high (Weekly checks).
☐ Crankcase ventilation system obstructed.
☐ Oil leaking from oil feed pipe into fuel feed pipe.
☐ Oil leakage from ancillary component (vacuum pump, etc).
☐ Oil leaking into coolant.
☐ Oil leaking into injection pump.
☐ Air cleaner dirty (Chapter 1).
☐ Blockage in induction system.
☐ Cylinder bores glazed.
☐ Piston rings broken or worn (Chapter 2).
☐ Pistons and/or bores worn (Chapter 2).
☐ Valve stems or guides worn (Chapter 2).
☐ Valve stem oil seals worn (Chapter 2).

Low oil pressure

☐ Low oil level, or incorrect oil grade (Weekly checks).
☐ Faulty oil pressure sensor (Chapter 5).
☐ Worn engine bearings and/or oil pump (Chapter 2).
☐ High engine operating temperature (Chapter 3).
☐ Oil pressure relief valve defective (Chapter 2).
☐ Oil pick-up strainer clogged (Chapter 2).
☐ Oil filter clogged (Chapter 1).
☐ Overheating.
☐ Oil contaminated.
☐ Gauge or warning light sender inaccurate.
☐ Oil pump suction pipe loose or cracked.
☐ Oil pressure relief valve defective or stuck open.
☐ Oil pump worn (Chapter 2).
☐ Crankshaft bearings worn (Chapter 2).

High oil pressure

☐ Oil grade or quality incorrect (Lubricants and fluids).
☐ Gauge inaccurate.
☐ Oil pressure relief valve stuck shut.

Engine (continued)

Crankcase pressure excessive (oil being blown out)

☐ Blockage in crankcase ventilation system.
☐ Leakage in vacuum pump or exhauster.
☐ Piston rings broken or sticking (Chapter 2).
☐ Pistons or bores worn (Chapter 2).
☐ Head gasket blown (Chapter 2).

Engine runs-on after switching off

☐ Excessive carbon build-up in engine (Chapter 2).
☐ High engine operating temperature (Chapter 3).
☐ Faulty stop solenoid (Chapter 4).

Vibration

☐ Accelerator linkage sticking (Chapter 4).
☐ Engine mountings loose or worn (Chapter 3).
☐ Cooling fan damaged or loose.
☐ Crankshaft pulley/damper damaged or loose (Chapter 3).
☐ Injector pipe(s) wrongly connected or wrong type (Chapter 4).
☐ Valve(s) sticking (Chapter 3).
☐ Flywheel or (when applicable) flywheel housing loose (Chapter 3).
☐ Poor (uneven) compression (Section 3).

Engine noises

Pre-ignition (pinking) or knocking during acceleration or under load

☐ Excessive carbon build-up in engine (Chapter 2).
☐ Air in fuel system (Section 4).
☐ Fuel grade incorrect or quality poor (Lubricants and fluids).
☐ Injector(s) faulty or wrong type (Chapter 4).
☐ Valve spring(s) weak or broken.

☐ Valve(s) sticking.
☐ Valve clearances incorrect (Chapter 2).
☐ Valve timing incorrect.
☐ Injection pump timing incorrect (Chapter 4).
☐ Piston protrusion excessive/head gasket thickness inadequate (after repair) (Chapter 2).
☐ Valve recess incorrect (after repair) (Chapter 2).
☐ Piston rings broken or worn (Chapter 2).
☐ Pistons and/or bores worn (Chapter 2).
☐ Crankshaft bearings worn or damaged (Chapter 2).
☐ Small-end bearings worn (Chapter 2).
☐ Camshaft worn (Chapter 2).

Whistling or wheezing noises

☐ Leaking exhaust manifold gasket or pipe-to-manifold joint (Chapter 4).
☐ Leaking vacuum hose (Chapters 4, 5 and 9).
☐ Blowing cylinder head gasket (Chapter 2).

Tapping or rattling noises

☐ Worn valve gear or camshaft (Chapter 2).
☐ Ancillary component fault (coolant pump, alternator, etc) (Chapters 3, 5, etc).

Knocking or thumping noises

☐ Worn big-end bearings (regular heavy knocking, perhaps less under load) (Chapter 2).
☐ Worn main bearings (rumbling and knocking, perhaps worsening under load) (Chapter 2).
☐ Piston slap (most noticeable when cold) (Chapter 2).
☐ Ancillary component fault (coolant pump, alternator, etc) (Chapters 3, 5, etc).

Cooling system

Overheating

- [ ] Insufficient coolant in system (*Weekly checks*).
- [ ] Thermostat faulty or missing (Chapter 3).
- [ ] Radiator core blocked, or grille restricted (Chapter 3).
- [ ] Electric cooling fan or thermostatic switch faulty (Chapter 3).
- [ ] Inaccurate temperature gauge sender unit (Chapter 3).
- [ ] Airlock in cooling system (Chapter 3).
- [ ] Expansion tank pressure cap faulty (Chapter 3).
- [ ] Engine oil level too high (Chapter 2).
- [ ] Coolant pump defective (Chapter 3).
- [ ] Coolant hoses blocked or collapsed.
- [ ] Air cleaner dirty (Chapter 1).
- [ ] Blockage in induction system.
- [ ] Blockage in exhaust system.
- [ ] Head gasket blown (Chapter 2).
- [ ] Cylinder head cracked or warped (Chapter 2).
- [ ] Valve timing incorrect.
- [ ] Injection pump timing incorrect (over-advanced) (Chapter 4).
- [ ] Injector(s) faulty or wrong type (Chapter 4).
- [ ] Injection pump faulty (Chapter 4).
- [ ] Imminent seizure (piston pick-up).

Overcooling

- [ ] Thermostat faulty (Chapter 3).
- [ ] Inaccurate temperature gauge sender unit (Chapter 3).

External coolant leakage

- [ ] Deteriorated or damaged hoses or hose clips (Chapter 1).
- [ ] Radiator core or heater matrix leaking (Chapter 3).
- [ ] Pressure cap faulty (Chapter 3).
- [ ] Coolant pump internal seal leaking (Chapter 3).
- [ ] Coolant pump-to-block seal leaking (Chapter 3).
- [ ] Boiling due to overheating (Chapter 3).
- [ ] Core plug leaking (Chapter 2).

Internal coolant leakage

- [ ] Leaking cylinder head gasket (Chapter 2).
- [ ] Cracked cylinder head or cylinder block (Chapter 2).

Corrosion

- [ ] Infrequent draining and flushing (Chapter 1).
- [ ] Incorrect coolant mixture or inappropriate coolant type (see *Weekly checks*).

Fuel and exhaust systems

Excessive fuel consumption

- [ ] Air filter element dirty or clogged (Chapter 1).
- [ ] Faulty injector(s) (Chapter 4).
- [ ] Tyres under-inflated (see *Weekly checks*).
- [ ] External leakage.
- [ ] Fuel passing into.
- [ ] Blockage in induction system.
- [ ] Valve clearances incorrect (Chapter 2).
- [ ] Valve(s) sticking.
- [ ] Valve spring(s) weak.
- [ ] Poor compression (Chapter 2).
- [ ] Valve timing incorrect.
- [ ] Injection pump timing incorrect (Chapter 4).
- [ ] Injection pump faulty (Chapter 4).

Injector pipe(s) break or split repeatedly

- [ ] Missing or wrongly located clamps.
- [ ] Wrong type or length of pipe.
- [ ] Faulty injector (Chapter 4).

Fuel leakage and/or fuel odour

- [ ] Damaged or corroded fuel tank, pipes or connections (Chapter 4).

Excessive noise or fumes from the exhaust system

- [ ] Leaking exhaust system or manifold joints (Chapters 1 and 4).
- [ ] Leaking, corroded or damaged silencers or pipe (Chapters 1 and 4).
- [ ] Broken mountings causing body or suspension contact (Chapter 1).

Black smoke in exhaust

- [ ] Air cleaner dirty (Chapter 1).
- [ ] Blockage in induction system.
- [ ] Valve clearances incorrect (Chapter 2).
- [ ] Poor compression (Chapter 2).
- [ ] Turbo boost pressure inadequate, when applicable.
- [ ] Blockage in exhaust system.
- [ ] Valve timing incorrect.
- [ ] Injector(s) faulty or wrong type (Chapter 4).
- [ ] Injection pump timing incorrect (Chapter 4).
- [ ] Injection pump faulty (Chapter 4).

Blue or white smoke in exhaust

- [ ] Engine oil incorrect grade or poor quality (Lubricants and fluids).
- [ ] Glow plug(s) defective, or controller faulty (smoke at start-up only) (Chapter 5).
- [ ] Air cleaner dirty (Chapter 1).
- [ ] Blockage in induction system.
- [ ] Valve timing incorrect.
- [ ] Injection pump timing incorrect (Chapter 4).
- [ ] Injector(s) defective, or heat shields damaged or missing (Chapter 4).
- [ ] Engine running too cool.
- [ ] Oil entering via valve stems.
- [ ] Poor compression (Chapter 2).
- [ ] Head gasket blown (Chapter 2).
- [ ] Piston rings broken or worn (Chapter 2).
- [ ] Pistons and/or bores worn (Chapter 2).

Clutch

Pedal travels to floor - no pressure or very little resistance

☐ Air in hydraulic system/faulty master or slave cylinder (Chapter 6).
☐ Faulty hydraulic release system (Chapter 6).
☐ Broken clutch release bearing or arm (Chapter 6).
☐ Broken diaphragm spring in clutch pressure plate (Chapter 6).

Clutch fails to disengage (unable to select gears)

☐ Air in hydraulic system/faulty master or slave cylinder (Chapter 6).
☐ Faulty hydraulic release system (Chapter 6).
☐ Clutch disc sticking on gearbox input shaft splines (Chapter 6).
☐ Clutch disc sticking to flywheel or pressure plate (Chapter 6).
☐ Faulty pressure plate assembly (Chapter 6).
☐ Clutch release mechanism worn or incorrectly assembled (Chapter 6).

Clutch slips (engine speed increases, with no increase in vehicle speed)

☐ Faulty hydraulic release system (Chapter 6).
☐ Clutch disc linings excessively worn (Chapter 6).
☐ Clutch disc linings contaminated with oil or grease (Chapter 6).
☐ Faulty pressure plate or weak diaphragm spring (Chapter 6).

Judder as clutch is engaged

☐ Clutch disc linings contaminated with oil or grease (Chapter 6).
☐ Clutch disc linings excessively worn (Chapter 6).
☐ Faulty or distorted pressure plate or diaphragm spring (Chapter 6).
☐ Worn or loose engine or gearbox mountings (Chapter 2).
☐ Clutch disc hub or gearbox input shaft splines worn (Chapter 6).

Noise when depressing or releasing clutch pedal

☐ Worn clutch release bearing (Chapter 6).
☐ Worn or dry clutch pedal pivot (Chapter 6).
☐ Faulty pressure plate assembly (Chapter 6).
☐ Pressure plate diaphragm spring broken (Chapter 6).
☐ Broken clutch friction plate cushioning springs (Chapter 6).

Manual transmission

Noisy in neutral with engine running

☐ Input shaft bearings worn (noise apparent with clutch pedal released, but not when depressed) (Chapter 7).*.
☐ Clutch release bearing worn (noise apparent with clutch pedal depressed, possibly less when released) (Chapter 6).

Noisy in one particular gear

☐ Worn, damaged or chipped gear teeth (Chapter 7).*.

Difficulty engaging gears

☐ Clutch faulty (Chapter 6).
☐ Worn or damaged gear linkage (Chapter 7).
☐ Worn synchroniser units (Chapter 7).*.

Jumps out of gear

☐ Worn or damaged gear linkage (Chapter 7).
☐ Worn synchroniser units (Chapter 7).*.
☐ Worn selector forks (Chapter 7).*.

Vibration

☐ Lack of oil (Chapter 1).
☐ Worn bearings (Chapter 7).*.

Lubricant leaks

☐ Leaking oil seal (Chapter 7).
☐ Leaking housing joint (Chapter 7).*.
☐ Leaking input shaft oil seal (Chapter 7).*.

*Although the corrective action necessary to remedy the symptoms described is beyond the scope of the home mechanic, the above information should be helpful in isolating the cause of the condition, so that the owner can communicate clearly with a professional mechanic.

Driveshafts

Vibration when accelerating or decelerating

☐ Worn inner constant velocity joint (Chapter 8).
☐ Bent or distorted driveshaft (Chapter 8).
☐ Worn intermediate bearing - where applicable (Chapter 8).

Clicking or knocking noise on turns (at slow speed on full-lock)

☐ Worn outer constant velocity joint (Chapter 8).
☐ Lack of constant velocity joint lubricant, possibly due to damaged gaiter (Chapter 8).

Braking system

Note: *Before assuming that a brake problem exists, make sure that the tyres are in good condition and correctly inflated, that the front wheel alignment is correct, and that the vehicle is not loaded with weight in an unequal manner. Apart from checking the condition of all pipe and hose connections, any faults occurring on the anti-lock braking system should be referred to a Renault dealer for diagnosis.*

Vehicle pulls to one side under braking

☐ Worn, defective, damaged or contaminated front or rear brake pads/shoes on one side (Chapters 1 and 9).
☐ Seized or partially-seized front or rear brake caliper/wheel cylinder piston (Chapter 9).
☐ A mixture of brake pad/shoe lining materials fitted between sides (Chapter 9).
☐ Brake caliper or rear brake backplate mounting bolts loose (Chapter 9).
☐ Worn or damaged steering or suspension components (Chapters 1 and 10).

Noise (grinding or high-pitched squeal) when brakes applied

☐ Brake pad/shoe friction lining material worn down to metal backing (Chapters 1 and 9).
☐ Excessive corrosion of brake disc or drum - may be apparent after the vehicle has been standing for some time (Chapters 1 and 9).
☐ Foreign object (stone chipping, etc) trapped between brake disc and shield (Chapters 1 and 9).

Excessive brake pedal travel

☐ Faulty rear drum brake self-adjust mechanism (Chapter 9).
☐ Faulty master cylinder (Chapter 9).
☐ Air in hydraulic system (Chapter 9).
☐ Faulty vacuum servo unit (Chapter 9).
☐ Faulty vacuum pump (Chapter 9).

Brake pedal feels spongy when depressed

☐ Air in hydraulic system (Chapter 9).
☐ Deteriorated flexible rubber brake hoses (Chapters 1 and 9).
☐ Master cylinder mountings loose (Chapter 9).
☐ Faulty master cylinder (Chapter 9).

Excessive brake pedal effort required to stop vehicle

☐ Faulty vacuum servo unit (Chapter 9).
☐ Disconnected, damaged or insecure brake servo vacuum hose (Chapters 1 and 9).
☐ Faulty vacuum pump (Chapter 9).
☐ Primary or secondary hydraulic circuit failure (Chapter 9).
☐ Seized brake caliper or wheel cylinder piston(s) (Chapter 9).
☐ Brake pads/shoes incorrectly fitted (Chapter 9).
☐ Incorrect grade of brake pads/shoes fitted (Chapter 9).
☐ Brake pads/shoe linings contaminated (Chapter 9).

Judder felt through brake pedal or steering wheel when braking

☐ Excessive run-out or distortion of brake disc(s) or drum(s) (Chapter 9).
☐ Brake pad/shoe linings worn (Chapters 1 and 9).
☐ Brake caliper or rear brake backplate mounting bolts loose (Chapter 9).
☐ Wear in suspension or steering components or mountings (Chapters 1 and 10).

Pedal pulsates when braking hard

☐ Normal feature of ABS - no fault.

Brakes binding

☐ Seized brake caliper/wheel cylinder piston(s) (Chapter 9).
☐ Incorrectly-adjusted handbrake mechanism (Chapter 9).
☐ Faulty master cylinder (Chapter 9).

Rear wheels locking under normal braking

☐ Rear brake pad/shoe linings contaminated (Chapters 1 and 9).
☐ Rear brake discs/drums warped (Chapters 1 and 9).

Steering and suspension

Note: *Before diagnosing suspension or steering faults, be sure that the trouble is not due to incorrect tyre pressures, mixtures of tyre types, or binding brakes.*

Vehicle pulls to one side

- ☐ Defective tyre (see *Weekly checks*).
- ☐ Excessive wear in suspension or steering components (Chapters 1 and 10).
- ☐ Incorrect front wheel alignment (Chapter 10).
- ☐ Accident damage to steering or suspension components (Chapters 1 and 10).

Wheel wobble and vibration

- ☐ Front roadwheels out of balance (vibration felt mainly through the steering wheel) (Chapter 10).
- ☐ Rear roadwheels out of balance (vibration felt throughout the vehicle) (Chapter 10).
- ☐ Roadwheels damaged or distorted (Chapter 10).
- ☐ Faulty or damaged tyre (*Weekly checks*).
- ☐ Worn steering or suspension joints, bushes or components (Chapters 1 and 10).
- ☐ Wheel bolts loose (Chapter 1 and 10).

Excessive pitching and/or rolling around corners, or during braking

- ☐ Defective shock absorbers (Chapters 1 and 10).
- ☐ Broken or weak coil spring and/or suspension component (Chapters 1 and 10).
- ☐ Worn or damaged anti-roll bar or mountings (Chapter 10).

Wandering or general instability

- ☐ Incorrect front wheel alignment (Chapter 10).
- ☐ Worn steering or suspension joints, bushes or components (Chapters 1 and 10).
- ☐ Roadwheels out of balance (Chapter 10).
- ☐ Faulty or damaged tyre (*Weekly checks*).
- ☐ Wheel bolts loose (Chapter 10).
- ☐ Defective shock absorbers (Chapters 1 and 10).

Excessively-stiff steering

- ☐ Seized track rod end balljoint or suspension balljoint (Chapters 1 and 10).
- ☐ Broken or incorrectly adjusted auxiliary drivebelt (Chapter 1).
- ☐ Incorrect front wheel alignment (Chapter 10).
- ☐ Steering gear damaged (Chapter 10).

Excessive play in steering

- ☐ Worn steering column universal joint(s) (Chapter 10).
- ☐ Worn steering track rod end balljoints (Chapters 1 and 10).
- ☐ Worn steering gear (Chapter 10).
- ☐ Worn steering or suspension joints, bushes or components (Chapters 1 and 10).

Lack of power assistance

- ☐ Broken or incorrectly-adjusted auxiliary drivebelt (Chapter 1).
- ☐ Incorrect power steering fluid level (*Weekly checks*).
- ☐ Restriction in power steering fluid hoses (Chapter 10).
- ☐ Faulty power steering pump (Chapter 10).
- ☐ Faulty steering gear (Chapter 10).

Tyre wear excessive

Tyres worn on inside or outside edges

- ☐ Tyres under-inflated (wear on both edges) (*Weekly checks*).
- ☐ Incorrect camber or castor angles (wear on one edge only) (Chapter 10).
- ☐ Worn steering or suspension joints, bushes or components (Chapters 1 and 10).
- ☐ Excessively-hard cornering.
- ☐ Accident damage.

Tyre treads exhibit feathered edges

- ☐ Incorrect toe setting (Chapter 10).

Tyres worn in centre of tread

- ☐ Tyres over-inflated (*Weekly checks*).

Tyres worn on inside and outside edges

- ☐ Tyres under-inflated (*Weekly checks*).
- ☐ Worn shock absorbers (Chapter 10).

Tyres worn unevenly

- ☐ Tyres/wheels out of balance (*Weekly checks*).
- ☐ Excessive wheel or tyre run-out (Chapter 10).
- ☐ Worn shock absorbers (Chapters 1 and 10).
- ☐ Faulty tyre (*Weekly checks*).

Electrical system

Note: *For problems associated with the starting system, refer to the faults listed under 'Engine' earlier in this Section.*

Battery will not hold a charge for more than a few days

- ☐ Battery defective internally (Chapter 5).
- ☐ Battery electrolyte level low - where applicable (*Weekly checks*).
- ☐ Battery terminal connections loose or corroded (*Weekly checks*).
- ☐ Auxiliary drivebelt worn - or incorrectly adjusted, where applicable (Chapter 1).
- ☐ Alternator not charging at correct output (Chapter 5).
- ☐ Alternator or voltage regulator faulty (Chapter 5).
- ☐ Short-circuit causing continual battery drain (Chapters 5 and 12).

Ignition/no-charge warning light remains illuminated with engine running

- ☐ Auxiliary drivebelt broken, worn, or incorrectly adjusted (Chapter 1).
- ☐ Internal fault in alternator or voltage regulator (Chapter 5).
- ☐ Broken, disconnected, or loose wiring in charging circuit (Chapter 5).

Ignition/no-charge warning light fails to come on

- ☐ Warning light bulb blown (Chapter 12).
- ☐ Broken, disconnected, or loose wiring in warning light circuit (Chapter 12).
- ☐ Alternator faulty (Chapter 5).

Lights inoperative

- ☐ Bulb blown (Chapter 12).
- ☐ Corrosion of bulb or bulbholder contacts (Chapter 12).
- ☐ Blown fuse (Chapter 12).
- ☐ Faulty relay (Chapter 12).
- ☐ Broken, loose, or disconnected wiring (Chapter 12).
- ☐ Faulty switch (Chapter 12).

Instrument readings inaccurate or erratic

Instrument readings increase with engine speed

- ☐ Faulty voltage regulator (Chapter 12).

Fuel or temperature gauges give no reading

- ☐ Faulty gauge sender unit (Chapters 3 and 4).
- ☐ Wiring open-circuit (Chapter 12).
- ☐ Faulty gauge (Chapter 12).

Fuel or temperature gauges give continuous maximum reading

- ☐ Faulty gauge sender unit (Chapters 3 and 4).
- ☐ Wiring short-circuit (Chapter 12).
- ☐ Faulty gauge (Chapter 12).

Horn inoperative, or unsatisfactory in operation

Horn operates all the time

- ☐ Horn contacts permanently bridged or horn push stuck down (Chapter 12).

Horn fails to operate

- ☐ Blown fuse (Chapter 12).
- ☐ Cable or cable connections loose, broken or disconnected (Chapter 12).
- ☐ Faulty horn (Chapter 12).

Horn emits intermittent or unsatisfactory sound

- ☐ Cable connections loose (Chapter 12).
- ☐ Horn mountings loose (Chapter 12).
- ☐ Faulty horn (Chapter 12).

Windscreen/tailgate wipers inoperative, or unsatisfactory in operation

Wipers fail to operate, or operate very slowly

- ☐ Wiper blades stuck to screen, or linkage seized or binding (*Weekly checks* and Chapter 12).
- ☐ Blown fuse (Chapter 12).
- ☐ Cable or cable connections loose, broken or disconnected (Chapter 12).
- ☐ Faulty relay (Chapter 12).
- ☐ Faulty wiper motor (Chapter 12).

Wiper blades sweep over too large or too small an area of the glass

- ☐ Wiper arms incorrectly positioned on spindles (Chapter 12).
- ☐ Excessive wear of wiper linkage (Chapter 12).
- ☐ Wiper motor or linkage mountings loose or insecure (Chapter 12).

Wiper blades fail to clean the glass effectively

- ☐ Wiper blade rubbers worn or perished (*Weekly checks*).
- ☐ Wiper arm tension springs broken, or arm pivots seized (Chapter 12).
- ☐ Insufficient windscreen washer additive to adequately remove road film (*Weekly checks*).

Windscreen/tailgate washers inoperative, or unsatisfactory in operation

One or more washer jets inoperative

- ☐ Blocked washer jet (Chapter 12).
- ☐ Disconnected, kinked or restricted fluid hose (Chapter 12).
- ☐ Insufficient fluid in washer reservoir (*Weekly checks*).

Washer pump fails to operate

- ☐ Broken or disconnected wiring or connections (Chapter 12).
- ☐ Blown fuse (Chapter 12).
- ☐ Faulty washer switch (Chapter 12).
- ☐ Faulty washer pump (Chapter 12).

Washer pump runs for some time before fluid is emitted from jets

- ☐ Faulty one-way valve in fluid supply hose (Chapter 12).

Electric windows inoperative, or unsatisfactory in operation

Window glass will only move in one direction

- ☐ Faulty switch (Chapter 12).

Window glass slow to move

- ☐ Regulator seized or damaged, or in need of lubrication (Chapter 11).
- ☐ Door internal components or trim fouling regulator (Chapter 11).
- ☐ Faulty motor (Chapter 11).

Window glass fails to move

- ☐ Blown fuse (Chapter 12).
- ☐ Faulty relay (Chapter 12).
- ☐ Broken or disconnected wiring or connections (Chapter 12).
- ☐ Faulty motor (Chapter 12).

Electrical system (continued)

Central locking system inoperative, or unsatisfactory in operation

Complete system failure

☐ Blown fuse (Chapter 12).
☐ Faulty relay (Chapter 12).
☐ Broken or disconnected wiring or connections (Chapter 12).
☐ Faulty motor (Chapter 11).

Latch locks but will not unlock, or unlocks but will not lock

☐ Faulty switch (Chapter 12).
☐ Broken or disconnected latch operating rods or levers (Chapter 11).
☐ Faulty relay (Chapter 12).
☐ Faulty motor (Chapter 11).

One solenoid/motor fails to operate

☐ Broken or disconnected wiring or connections (Chapter 12).
☐ Faulty motor (Chapter 11).
☐ Broken, binding or disconnected lock operating rods or levers (Chapter 11).
☐ Fault in door lock (Chapter 11).

A

ABS (Anti-lock brake system) A system, usually electronically controlled, that senses incipient wheel lockup during braking and relieves hydraulic pressure at wheels that are about to skid.

Air bag An inflatable bag hidden in the steering wheel (driver's side) or the dash or glovebox (passenger side). In a head-on collision, the bags inflate, preventing the driver and front passenger from being thrown forward into the steering wheel or windscreen.

Air cleaner A metal or plastic housing, containing a filter element, which removes dust and dirt from the air being drawn into the engine.

Air filter element The actual filter in an air cleaner system, usually manufactured from pleated paper and requiring renewal at regular intervals.

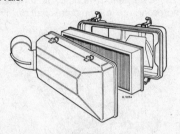

Air filter

Allen key A hexagonal wrench which fits into a recessed hexagonal hole.

Alligator clip A long-nosed spring-loaded metal clip with meshing teeth. Used to make temporary electrical connections.

Alternator A component in the electrical system which converts mechanical energy from a drivebelt into electrical energy to charge the battery and to operate the starting system, ignition system and electrical accessories.

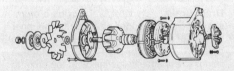

Alternator (exploded view)

Ampere (amp) A unit of measurement for the flow of electric current. One amp is the amount of current produced by one volt acting through a resistance of one ohm.

Anaerobic sealer A substance used to prevent bolts and screws from loosening. Anaerobic means that it does not require oxygen for activation. The Loctite brand is widely used.

Antifreeze A substance (usually ethylene glycol) mixed with water, and added to a vehicle's cooling system, to prevent freezing of the coolant in winter. Antifreeze also contains chemicals to inhibit corrosion and the formation of rust and other deposits that would tend to clog the radiator and coolant passages and reduce cooling efficiency.

Anti-seize compound A coating that reduces the risk of seizing on fasteners that are subjected to high temperatures, such as exhaust manifold bolts and nuts.

Anti-seize compound

Asbestos A natural fibrous mineral with great heat resistance, commonly used in the composition of brake friction materials. Asbestos is a health hazard and the dust created by brake systems should never be inhaled or ingested.

Axle A shaft on which a wheel revolves, or which revolves with a wheel. Also, a solid beam that connects the two wheels at one end of the vehicle. An axle which also transmits power to the wheels is known as a live axle.

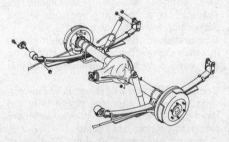

Axle assembly

Axleshaft A single rotating shaft, on either side of the differential, which delivers power from the final drive assembly to the drive wheels. Also called a driveshaft or a halfshaft.

B

Ball bearing An anti-friction bearing consisting of a hardened inner and outer race with hardened steel balls between two races.

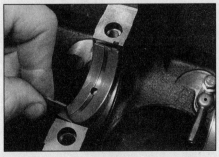

Bearing

Bearing The curved surface on a shaft or in a bore, or the part assembled into either, that permits relative motion between them with minimum wear and friction.

Big-end bearing The bearing in the end of the connecting rod that's attached to the crankshaft.

Bleed nipple A valve on a brake wheel cylinder, caliper or other hydraulic component that is opened to purge the hydraulic system of air. Also called a bleed screw.

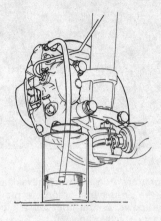

Brake bleeding

Brake bleeding Procedure for removing air from lines of a hydraulic brake system.

Brake disc The component of a disc brake that rotates with the wheels.

Brake drum The component of a drum brake that rotates with the wheels.

Brake linings The friction material which contacts the brake disc or drum to retard the vehicle's speed. The linings are bonded or riveted to the brake pads or shoes.

Brake pads The replaceable friction pads that pinch the brake disc when the brakes are applied. Brake pads consist of a friction material bonded or riveted to a rigid backing plate.

Brake shoe The crescent-shaped carrier to which the brake linings are mounted and which forces the lining against the rotating drum during braking.

Braking systems For more information on braking systems, consult the *Haynes Automotive Brake Manual*.

Breaker bar A long socket wrench handle providing greater leverage.

Bulkhead The insulated partition between the engine and the passenger compartment.

C

Caliper The non-rotating part of a disc-brake assembly that straddles the disc and carries the brake pads. The caliper also contains the hydraulic components that cause the pads to pinch the disc when the brakes are applied. A caliper is also a measuring tool that can be set to measure inside or outside dimensions of an object.

Camshaft A rotating shaft on which a series of cam lobes operate the valve mechanisms. The camshaft may be driven by gears, by sprockets and chain or by sprockets and a belt.

Canister A container in an evaporative emission control system; contains activated charcoal granules to trap vapours from the fuel system.

Canister

Carburettor A device which mixes fuel with air in the proper proportions to provide a desired power output from a spark ignition internal combustion engine.

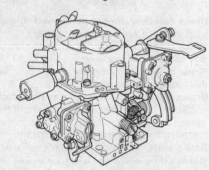

Carburettor

Castellated Resembling the parapets along the top of a castle wall. For example, a castellated balljoint stud nut.

Castellated nut

Castor In wheel alignment, the backward or forward tilt of the steering axis. Castor is positive when the steering axis is inclined rearward at the top.

Catalytic converter A silencer-like device in the exhaust system which converts certain pollutants in the exhaust gases into less harmful substances.

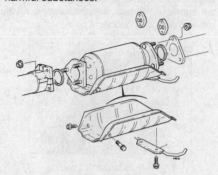

Catalytic converter

Circlip A ring-shaped clip used to prevent endwise movement of cylindrical parts and shafts. An internal circlip is installed in a groove in a housing; an external circlip fits into a groove on the outside of a cylindrical piece such as a shaft.

Clearance The amount of space between two parts. For example, between a piston and a cylinder, between a bearing and a journal, etc.

Coil spring A spiral of elastic steel found in various sizes throughout a vehicle, for example as a springing medium in the suspension and in the valve train.

Compression Reduction in volume, and increase in pressure and temperature, of a gas, caused by squeezing it into a smaller space.

Compression ratio The relationship between cylinder volume when the piston is at top dead centre and cylinder volume when the piston is at bottom dead centre.

Constant velocity (CV) joint A type of universal joint that cancels out vibrations caused by driving power being transmitted through an angle.

Core plug A disc or cup-shaped metal device inserted in a hole in a casting through which core was removed when the casting was formed. Also known as a freeze plug or expansion plug.

Crankcase The lower part of the engine block in which the crankshaft rotates.

Crankshaft The main rotating member, or shaft, running the length of the crankcase, with offset "throws" to which the connecting rods are attached.

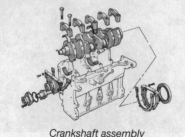

Crankshaft assembly

Crocodile clip See Alligator clip

D

Diagnostic code Code numbers obtained by accessing the diagnostic mode of an engine management computer. This code can be used to determine the area in the system where a malfunction may be located.

Disc brake A brake design incorporating a rotating disc onto which brake pads are squeezed. The resulting friction converts the energy of a moving vehicle into heat.

Double-overhead cam (DOHC) An engine that uses two overhead camshafts, usually one for the intake valves and one for the exhaust valves.

Drivebelt(s) The belt(s) used to drive accessories such as the alternator, water pump, power steering pump, air conditioning compressor, etc. off the crankshaft pulley.

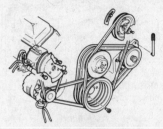

Accessory drivebelts

Driveshaft Any shaft used to transmit motion. Commonly used when referring to the axleshafts on a front wheel drive vehicle.

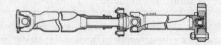

Driveshaft

Drum brake A type of brake using a drum-shaped metal cylinder attached to the inner surface of the wheel. When the brake pedal is pressed, curved brake shoes with friction linings press against the inside of the drum to slow or stop the vehicle.

Drum brake assembly

E

EGR valve A valve used to introduce exhaust gases into the intake air stream.

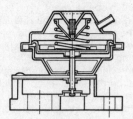

EGR valve

Electronic control unit (ECU) A computer which controls (for instance) ignition and fuel injection systems, or an anti-lock braking system. For more information refer to the *Haynes Automotive Electrical and Electronic Systems Manual*.

Electronic Fuel Injection (EFI) A computer controlled fuel system that distributes fuel through an injector located in each intake port of the engine.

Emergency brake A braking system, independent of the main hydraulic system, that can be used to slow or stop the vehicle if the primary brakes fail, or to hold the vehicle stationary even though the brake pedal isn't depressed. It usually consists of a hand lever that actuates either front or rear brakes mechanically through a series of cables and linkages. Also known as a handbrake or parking brake.

Endfloat The amount of lengthwise movement between two parts. As applied to a crankshaft, the distance that the crankshaft can move forward and back in the cylinder block.

Engine management system (EMS) A computer controlled system which manages the fuel injection and the ignition systems in an integrated fashion.

Exhaust manifold A part with several passages through which exhaust gases leave the engine combustion chambers and enter the exhaust pipe.

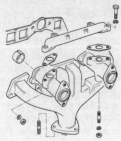

Exhaust manifold

F

Fan clutch A viscous (fluid) drive coupling device which permits variable engine fan speeds in relation to engine speeds.

Feeler blade A thin strip or blade of hardened steel, ground to an exact thickness, used to check or measure clearances between parts.

Feeler blade

Firing order The order in which the engine cylinders fire, or deliver their power strokes, beginning with the number one cylinder.

Flywheel A heavy spinning wheel in which energy is absorbed and stored by means of momentum. On cars, the flywheel is attached to the crankshaft to smooth out firing impulses.

Free play The amount of travel before any action takes place. The "looseness" in a linkage, or an assembly of parts, between the initial application of force and actual movement. For example, the distance the brake pedal moves before the pistons in the master cylinder are actuated.

Fuse An electrical device which protects a circuit against accidental overload. The typical fuse contains a soft piece of metal which is calibrated to melt at a predetermined current flow (expressed as amps) and break the circuit.

Fusible link A circuit protection device consisting of a conductor surrounded by heat-resistant insulation. The conductor is smaller than the wire it protects, so it acts as the weakest link in the circuit. Unlike a blown fuse, a failed fusible link must frequently be cut from the wire for replacement.

G

Gap The distance the spark must travel in jumping from the centre electrode to the side

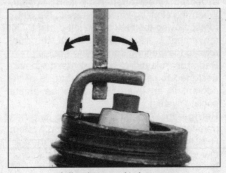

Adjusting spark plug gap

electrode in a spark plug. Also refers to the spacing between the points in a contact breaker assembly in a conventional points-type ignition, or to the distance between the reluctor or rotor and the pickup coil in an electronic ignition.

Gasket Any thin, soft material - usually cork, cardboard, asbestos or soft metal - installed between two metal surfaces to ensure a good seal. For instance, the cylinder head gasket seals the joint between the block and the cylinder head.

Gasket

Gauge An instrument panel display used to monitor engine conditions. A gauge with a movable pointer on a dial or a fixed scale is an analogue gauge. A gauge with a numerical readout is called a digital gauge.

H

Halfshaft A rotating shaft that transmits power from the final drive unit to a drive wheel, usually when referring to a live rear axle.

Harmonic balancer A device designed to reduce torsion or twisting vibration in the crankshaft. May be incorporated in the crankshaft pulley. Also known as a vibration damper.

Hone An abrasive tool for correcting small irregularities or differences in diameter in an engine cylinder, brake cylinder, etc.

Hydraulic tappet A tappet that utilises hydraulic pressure from the engine's lubrication system to maintain zero clearance (constant contact with both camshaft and valve stem). Automatically adjusts to variation in valve stem length. Hydraulic tappets also reduce valve noise.

I

Ignition timing The moment at which the spark plug fires, usually expressed in the number of crankshaft degrees before the piston reaches the top of its stroke.

Inlet manifold A tube or housing with passages through which flows the air-fuel mixture (carburettor vehicles and vehicles with throttle body injection) or air only (port fuel-injected vehicles) to the port openings in the cylinder head.

J

Jump start Starting the engine of a vehicle with a discharged or weak battery by attaching jump leads from the weak battery to a charged or helper battery.

L

Load Sensing Proportioning Valve (LSPV) A brake hydraulic system control valve that works like a proportioning valve, but also takes into consideration the amount of weight carried by the rear axle.

Locknut A nut used to lock an adjustment nut, or other threaded component, in place. For example, a locknut is employed to keep the adjusting nut on the rocker arm in position.

Lockwasher A form of washer designed to prevent an attaching nut from working loose.

M

MacPherson strut A type of front suspension system devised by Earle MacPherson at Ford of England. In its original form, a simple lateral link with the anti-roll bar creates the lower control arm. A long strut - an integral coil spring and shock absorber - is mounted between the body and the steering knuckle. Many modern so-called MacPherson strut systems use a conventional lower A-arm and don't rely on the anti-roll bar for location.

Multimeter An electrical test instrument with the capability to measure voltage, current and resistance.

N

NOx Oxides of Nitrogen. A common toxic pollutant emitted by petrol and diesel engines at higher temperatures.

O

Ohm The unit of electrical resistance. One volt applied to a resistance of one ohm will produce a current of one amp.

Ohmmeter An instrument for measuring electrical resistance.

O-ring A type of sealing ring made of a special rubber-like material; in use, the O-ring is compressed into a groove to provide the sealing action.

O-ring

Overhead cam (ohc) engine An engine with the camshaft(s) located on top of the cylinder head(s).

Overhead valve (ohv) engine An engine with the valves located in the cylinder head, but with the camshaft located in the engine block.

Oxygen sensor A device installed in the engine exhaust manifold, which senses the oxygen content in the exhaust and converts this information into an electric current. Also called a Lambda sensor.

P

Phillips screw A type of screw head having a cross instead of a slot for a corresponding type of screwdriver.

Plastigage A thin strip of plastic thread, available in different sizes, used for measuring clearances. For example, a strip of Plastigage is laid across a bearing journal. The parts are assembled and dismantled; the width of the crushed strip indicates the clearance between journal and bearing.

Plastigage

Propeller shaft The long hollow tube with universal joints at both ends that carries power from the transmission to the differential on front-engined rear wheel drive vehicles.

Proportioning valve A hydraulic control valve which limits the amount of pressure to the rear brakes during panic stops to prevent wheel lock-up.

R

Rack-and-pinion steering A steering system with a pinion gear on the end of the steering shaft that mates with a rack (think of a geared wheel opened up and laid flat). When the steering wheel is turned, the pinion turns, moving the rack to the left or right. This movement is transmitted through the track rods to the steering arms at the wheels.

Radiator A liquid-to-air heat transfer device designed to reduce the temperature of the coolant in an internal combustion engine cooling system.

Refrigerant Any substance used as a heat transfer agent in an air-conditioning system. R-12 has been the principle refrigerant for many years; recently, however, manufacturers have begun using R-134a, a non-CFC substance that is considered less harmful to the ozone in the upper atmosphere.

Rocker arm A lever arm that rocks on a shaft or pivots on a stud. In an overhead valve engine, the rocker arm converts the upward movement of the pushrod into a downward movement to open a valve.

Rotor In a distributor, the rotating device inside the cap that connects the centre electrode and the outer terminals as it turns, distributing the high voltage from the coil secondary winding to the proper spark plug. Also, that part of an alternator which rotates inside the stator. Also, the rotating assembly of a turbocharger, including the compressor wheel, shaft and turbine wheel.

Runout The amount of wobble (in-and-out movement) of a gear or wheel as it's rotated. The amount a shaft rotates "out-of-true." The out-of-round condition of a rotating part.

S

Sealant A liquid or paste used to prevent leakage at a joint. Sometimes used in conjunction with a gasket.

Sealed beam lamp An older headlight design which integrates the reflector, lens and filaments into a hermetically-sealed one-piece unit. When a filament burns out or the lens cracks, the entire unit is simply replaced.

Serpentine drivebelt A single, long, wide accessory drivebelt that's used on some newer vehicles to drive all the accessories, instead of a series of smaller, shorter belts. Serpentine drivebelts are usually tensioned by an automatic tensioner.

Serpentine drivebelt

Shim Thin spacer, commonly used to adjust the clearance or relative positions between two parts. For example, shims inserted into or under bucket tappets control valve clearances. Clearance is adjusted by changing the thickness of the shim.

Slide hammer A special puller that screws into or hooks onto a component such as a shaft or bearing; a heavy sliding handle on the shaft bottoms against the end of the shaft to knock the component free.

Sprocket A tooth or projection on the periphery of a wheel, shaped to engage with a chain or drivebelt. Commonly used to refer to the sprocket wheel itself.

Starter inhibitor switch On vehicles with an automatic transmission, a switch that prevents starting if the vehicle is not in Neutral or Park.

Strut See MacPherson strut.

T

Tappet A cylindrical component which transmits motion from the cam to the valve stem, either directly or via a pushrod and rocker arm. Also called a cam follower.

Thermostat A heat-controlled valve that regulates the flow of coolant between the cylinder block and the radiator, so maintaining optimum engine operating temperature. A thermostat is also used in some air cleaners in which the temperature is regulated.

Thrust bearing The bearing in the clutch assembly that is moved in to the release levers by clutch pedal action to disengage the clutch. Also referred to as a release bearing.

Timing belt A toothed belt which drives the camshaft. Serious engine damage may result if it breaks in service.

Timing chain A chain which drives the camshaft.

Toe-in The amount the front wheels are closer together at the front than at the rear. On rear wheel drive vehicles, a slight amount of toe-in is usually specified to keep the front wheels running parallel on the road by offsetting other forces that tend to spread the wheels apart.

Toe-out The amount the front wheels are closer together at the rear than at the front. On front wheel drive vehicles, a slight amount of toe-out is usually specified.

Tools For full information on choosing and using tools, refer to the *Haynes Automotive Tools Manual*.

Tracer A stripe of a second colour applied to a wire insulator to distinguish that wire from another one with the same colour insulator.

Tune-up A process of accurate and careful adjustments and parts replacement to obtain the best possible engine performance.

Turbocharger A centrifugal device, driven by exhaust gases, that pressurises the intake air. Normally used to increase the power output from a given engine displacement, but can also be used primarily to reduce exhaust emissions (as on VW's "Umwelt" Diesel engine).

U

Universal joint or U-joint A double-pivoted connection for transmitting power from a driving to a driven shaft through an angle. A U-joint consists of two Y-shaped yokes and a cross-shaped member called the spider.

V

Valve A device through which the flow of liquid, gas, vacuum, or loose material in bulk may be started, stopped, or regulated by a movable part that opens, shuts, or partially obstructs one or more ports or passageways. A valve is also the movable part of such a device.

Valve clearance The clearance between the valve tip (the end of the valve stem) and the rocker arm or tappet. The valve clearance is measured when the valve is closed.

Vernier caliper A precision measuring instrument that measures inside and outside dimensions. Not quite as accurate as a micrometer, but more convenient.

Viscosity The thickness of a liquid or its resistance to flow.

Volt A unit for expressing electrical "pressure" in a circuit. One volt that will produce a current of one ampere through a resistance of one ohm.

W

Welding Various processes used to join metal items by heating the areas to be joined to a molten state and fusing them together. For more information refer to the *Haynes Automotive Welding Manual*.

Wiring diagram A drawing portraying the components and wires in a vehicle's electrical system, using standardised symbols. For more information refer to the *Haynes Automotive Electrical and Electronic Systems Manual*.

Note: *References throughout this index are in the form* **"Chapter number"** • **"Page number"**

D

Dents – 11•2
Diesel injection equipment – 0•5
Differential (driveshaft) oil seals – 7•4
Dimensions – REF•2
Direction indicator – 12•7, 12•11
Disconnecting the battery – REF•6
Discs – 1•9, 9•7
Doors – 11•7, 11•8, 11•14, 11•18, 11•20, 12•6, REF•10
Drivebelts – 1•7
Driveshafts – 8•1 et seq, REF•11
  fault finding – REF•18
  gaiters – 1•12, 8•3
  oil seals – 7•4
Drivetrain – 1•10
Drums – 9•8
Ducts – 3•9

E

Earth fault – 12•2
EGR valve – 4B•2
Electric cooling fan – 3•3, 3•4
Electric shock – 0•5
Electric windows – 11•20
  switch – 12•6
Electrical equipment – 1•10, REF•10
Electrical systems – 0•17, 1•9
  fault finding – 12•2, REF•21, REF•22
Electronic control unit
  ABS – 9•20
  central locking – 11•18
Emission control systems – 1•8, 4B•1 et seq, REF•12
Engine in-car repair procedures – 2A•1 et seq
  fault finding – REF•14, REF•15, REF•16
Engine oil – 0•12, 0•17, 1•6
Engine removal and overhaul procedures – 2B•1 et seq
Environmental considerations – REF•5
Exhaust gas recirculation (EGR) – 4B•1, 4B•2
Exhaust manifold – 4A•13
Exhaust specialists – REF•4
Exhaust system – 4A•13, REF•11, REF•12

F

Facia panel – 11•28
Fan – 3•3, 3•4
  switch – 12•5
Fault finding – 0•7, REF•13 et seq
  braking system – REF•19
  clutch – REF•18
  cooling system – REF•17
  driveshafts – REF•18
  electrical system – 12•2
  electrical system – REF•21, REF•22
  engine – REF•14, REF•15, REF•16
  fuel and exhaust systems – REF•17
  manual transmission – REF•18
  steering and suspension – REF•20
Filling – 11•3
Filters
  air – 1•10, 4A•2
  fuel – 1•8, 5B•2

oil – 1•6
  pollen – 1•10
Fire – 0•5
Fixed window glass – 11•21
Fluids – 0•17
  leaks – 1•9
Flywheel – 2A•16
Foglight – 12•8, 12•11
  switch – 12•5
Followers – 2A•10
Fuel and exhaust systems – 4A•1 et seq, REF•12
  fault finding – REF•17
Fuel filler cap lock – 11•19
Fuel filter – 1•8, 1•11
  heater – 5B•2
Fuel gauge – 12•14
  sender unit – 4A•4
Fuel injection pump – 4A•6
Fuel injectors – 4A•8
Fuel tank – 4A•4
Fume or gas intoxication – 0•5
Fuses – 5B•2, 12•3

G

Gaiters
  driveshaft – 1•12, 8•3
  steering gear – 10•25
Gashes – 11•3
Gaskets – REF•5
Gearchange linkage/mechanism – 7•2, 7•3
General repair procedures – REF•5
Glossary of technical terms – REF•23 et seq
Glovebox – 11•27
  light – 12•10
Glow plugs – 5B•1
Grille – 11•22

H

Handbrake – 9•15, 9•16, REF•9
  warning switch – 12•6
Handles – 11•11
Hazard warning switch – 12•5
Headlight – 12•7, 12•10
  beam adjuster switch – 12•5
  beam alignment – 12•12
  washer system – 12•17
Headlining – 11•27
Heat shield(s) – 4A•13
Heated front seats – 12•19
  switch – 12•5
Heater/ventilation system – 3•5
  blower motor – 3•7, 3•8
  control illumination – 12•10
  fan switch – 12•5
  matrix – 3•6
High-level stop-light – 12•9, 12•12
Hinge lubrication – 1•11
Horn – 12•15
  switch – 12•6
Hoses – 1•9, 3•2, 9•3
Hub bearings – 10•6, 10•11
Hydrofluoric acid – 0•5

Haynes Manuals – The Complete List

Title	Book No.
ALFA ROMEO Alfasud/Sprint (74 - 88) up to F *	0292
Alfa Romeo Alfetta (73 - 87) up to E *	0531
AUDI 80, 90 & Coupe Petrol (79 - Nov 88) up to F	0605
Audi 80, 90 & Coupe Petrol (Oct 86 - 90) D to H	1491
Audi 100 & 200 Petrol (Oct 82 - 90) up to H	0907
Audi 100 & A6 Petrol & Diesel (May 91 - May 97) H to P	3504
Audi A3 Petrol & Diesel (96 - May 03) P to 03	4253
Audi A4 Petrol & Diesel (95 - Feb 00) M to V	3575
AUSTIN A35 & A40 (56 - 67) up to F *	0118
Austin/MG/Rover Maestro 1.3 & 1.6 Petrol (83 - 95) up to M	0922
Austin/MG Metro (80 - May 90) up to G	0718
Austin/Rover Montego 1.3 & 1.6 Petrol (84 - 94) A to L	1066
Austin/MG/Rover Montego 2.0 Petrol (84 - 95) A to M	1067
Mini (59 - 69) up to H *	0527
Mini (69 - 01) up to X	0646
Austin/Rover 2.0 litre Diesel Engine (86 - 93) C to L	1857
Austin Healey 100/6 & 3000 (56 - 68) up to G *	0049
BEDFORD CF Petrol (69 - 87) up to E	0163
Bedford/Vauxhall Rascal & Suzuki Supercarry (86 - Oct 94) C to M	3015
BMW 316, 320 & 320i (4-cyl) (75 - Feb 83) up to Y*	0276
BMW 320, 320i, 323i & 325i (6-cyl) (Oct 77 - Sept 87) up to E	0815
BMW 3- & 5-Series Petrol (81 - 91) up to J	1948
BMW 3-Series Petrol (Apr 91 - 96) H to N	3210
BMW 3-Series Petrol (Sept 98 - 03) S to 53	4067
BMW 520i & 525e (Oct 81 - June 88) up to E	1560
BMW 525, 528 & 528i (73 - Sept 81) up to X *	0632
BMW 5-Series 6-cyl Petrol (April 96 - Aug 03) N to 03	4151
BMW 1500, 1502, 1600, 1602, 2000 & 2002 (59 - 77) up to S *	0240
CHRYSLER PT Cruiser Petrol (00 - 03) W to 53	4058
CITROËN 2CV, Ami & Dyane (67 - 90) up to H	0196
Citroën AX Petrol & Diesel (87 - 97) D to P	3014
Citroën Berlingo & Peugeot Partner Petrol & Diesel (96 - 05) P to 55	4281
Citroën BX Petrol (83 - 94) A to L	0908
Citroën C15 Van Petrol & Diesel (89 - Oct 98) F to S	3509
Citroën C3 Petrol & Diesel (02 - 05) 51 to 05	4197
Citroën CX Petrol (75 - 88) up to F	0528
Citroën Saxo Petrol & Diesel (96 - 04) N to 54	3506
Citroën Visa Petrol (79 - 88) up to F	0620
Citroën Xantia Petrol & Diesel (93 - 01) K to Y	3082
Citroën XM Petrol & Diesel (89 - 00) G to X	3451
Citroën Xsara Petrol & Diesel (97 - Sept 00) R to W	3751
Citroën Xsara Picasso Petrol & Diesel (00 - 02) W to 52	3944
Citroën ZX Diesel (91 - 98) J to S	1922
Citroën ZX Petrol (91 - 98) H to S	1881
Citroën 1.7 & 1.9 litre Diesel Engine (84 - 96) A to N	1379
FIAT 126 (73 - 87) up to E *	0305
Fiat 500 (57 - 73) up to M *	0090
Fiat Bravo & Brava Petrol (95 - 00) N to W	3572
Fiat Cinquecento (93 - 98) K to R	3501
Fiat Panda (81 - 95) up to M	0793
Fiat Punto Petrol & Diesel (94 - Oct 99) L to V	3251
Fiat Punto Petrol (Oct 99 - July 03) V to 03	4066
Fiat Regata Petrol (84 - 88) A to F	1167
Fiat Tipo Petrol (88 - 91) E to J	1625
Fiat Uno Petrol (83 - 95) up to M	0923
Fiat X1/9 (74 - 89) up to G *	0273
FORD Anglia (59 - 68) up to G *	0001
Ford Capri II (& III) 1.6 & 2.0 (74 - 87) up to E *	0283
Ford Capri II (& III) 2.8 & 3.0 V6 (74 - 87) up to E	1309
Ford Cortina Mk III 1300 & 1600 (70 - 76) up to P *	0070
Ford Escort Mk I 1100 & 1300 (68 - 74) up to N *	0171
Ford Escort Mk I Mexico, RS 1600 & RS 2000 (70 - 74) up to N *	0139
Ford Escort Mk II Mexico, RS 1800 & RS 2000 (75 - 80) up to W *	0735
Ford Escort (75 - Aug 80) up to V *	0280
Ford Escort Petrol (Sept 80 - Sept 90) up to H	0686
Ford Escort & Orion Petrol (Sept 90 - 00) H to X	1737
Ford Escort & Orion Diesel (Sept 90 - 00) H to X	4081
Ford Fiesta (76 - Aug 83) up to Y	0334
Ford Fiesta Petrol (Aug 83 - Feb 89) A to F	1030
Ford Fiesta Petrol (Feb 89 - Oct 95) F to N	1595
Ford Fiesta Petrol & Diesel (Oct 95 - Mar 02) N to 02	3397
Ford Fiesta Petrol & Diesel (Apr 02 - 05) 02 to 54	4170
Ford Focus Petrol & Diesel (98 - 01) S to Y	3759
Ford Focus Petrol & Diesel (Oct 01 - 04) 51 to 54	4167
Ford Galaxy Petrol & Diesel (95 - Aug 00) M to W	3984
Ford Granada Petrol (Sept 77 - Feb 85) up to B *	0481
Ford Granada & Scorpio Petrol (Mar 85 - 94) B to M	1245
Ford Ka (96 - 02) P to 52	3570
Ford Mondeo Petrol (93 - Sept 00) K to X	1923
Ford Mondeo Petrol & Diesel (Oct 00 - Jul 03) X to 03	3990
Ford Mondeo Diesel (93 - 96) L to N	3465
Ford Orion Petrol (83 - Sept 90) up to H	1009
Ford Sierra 4-cyl Petrol (82 - 93) up to K	0903
Ford Sierra V6 Petrol (82 - 91) up to J	0904
Ford Transit Petrol (Mk 2) (78 - Jan 86) up to C	0719
Ford Transit Petrol (Mk 3) (Feb 86 - 89) C to G	1468
Ford Transit Diesel (Feb 86 - 99) C to T	3019
Ford 1.6 & 1.8 litre Diesel Engine (84 - 96) A to N	1172
Ford 2.1, 2.3 & 2.5 litre Diesel Engine (77 - 90) up to H	1606
FREIGHT ROVER Sherpa Petrol (74 - 87) up to E	0463
HILLMAN Avenger (70 - 82) up to Y	0037
Hillman Imp (63 - 76) up to R *	0022
HONDA Civic (Feb 84 - Oct 87) A to E	1226
Honda Civic (Nov 91 - 96) J to N	3199
Honda Civic (Mar 95 - 00) M to X	4050
HYUNDAI Pony (85 - 94) C to M	3398
JAGUAR E Type (61 - 72) up to L *	0140
Jaguar MkI & II, 240 & 340 (55 - 69) up to H *	0098
Jaguar XJ6, XJ & Sovereign; Daimler Sovereign (68 - Oct 86) up to D	0242
Jaguar XJ6 & Sovereign (Oct 86 - Sept 94) D to M	3261
Jaguar XJ12, XJS & Sovereign; Daimler Double Six (72 - 88) up to F	0478
JEEP Cherokee Petrol (93 - 96) K to N	1943
LADA 1200, 1300, 1500 & 1600 (74 - 91) up to J	0413
Lada Samara (87 - 91) D to J	1610
LAND ROVER 90, 110 & Defender Diesel (83 - 95) up to N	3017
Land Rover Discovery Petrol & Diesel (89 - 98) G to S	3016
Land Rover Freelander Petrol & Diesel (97 - 02) R to 52	3929
Land Rover Series IIA & III Diesel (58 - 85) up to C	0529
Land Rover Series II, IIA & III 4-cyl Petrol (58 - 85) up to C	0314
MAZDA 323 (Mar 81 - Oct 89) up to G	1608
Mazda 323 (Oct 89 - 98) G to R	3455
Mazda 626 (May 83 - Sept 87) up to E	0929
Mazda B1600, B1800 & B2000 Pick-up Petrol (72 - 88) up to F	0267
Mazda RX-7 (79 - 85) up to C *	0460
MERCEDES-BENZ 190, 190E & 190D Petrol & Diesel (83 - 93) A to L	3450
Mercedes-Benz 200D, 240D, 240TD, 300D & 300TD 123 Series Diesel (Oct 76 - 85) up	1114
Mercedes-Benz 250 & 280 (68 - 72) up to L *	0346
Mercedes-Benz 250 & 280 123 Series Petrol (Oct 76 - 84) up to B *	0677
Mercedes-Benz 124 Series Petrol & Diesel (85 - Aug 93) C to K	3253
Mercedes-Benz C-Class Petrol & Diesel (93 - Aug 00) L to W	3511
MGA (55 - 62) *	0475
MGB (62 - 80) up to W	0111
MG Midget & Austin-Healey Sprite (58 - 80) up to W *	0265
MINI Petrol (July 01 - 05) Y to 05	4273
MITSUBISHI Shogun & L200 Pick-Ups Petrol (83 - 94) up to M	1944
MORRIS Ital 1.3 (80 - 84) up to B	0705
Morris Minor 1000 (56 - 71) up to K	0024
NISSAN Almera Petrol (95 - Feb 00) N to V	4053
Nissan Bluebird (May 84 - Mar 86) A to C	1223
Nissan Bluebird Petrol (Mar 86 - 90) C to H	1473
Nissan Cherry (Sept 82 - 86) up to D	1031
Nissan Micra (83 - Jan 93) up to K	0931
Nissan Micra (93 - 02) K to 52	3254
Nissan Primera Petrol (90 - Aug 99) H to T	1851
Nissan Stanza (82 - 86) up to D	0824
Nissan Sunny Petrol (May 82 - Oct 86) up to D	0895
Nissan Sunny Petrol (Oct 86 - Mar 91) D to H	1378
Nissan Sunny Petrol (Apr 91 - 95) H to N	3219
OPEL Ascona & Manta (B Series) (Sept 75 - 88) up to F *	0316
Opel Ascona Petrol (81 - 88)	3215
Opel Astra Petrol (Oct 91 - Feb 98)	3156
Opel Corsa Petrol (83 - Mar 93)	3160
Opel Corsa Petrol (Mar 93 - 97)	3159
Opel Kadett Petrol (Nov 79 - Oct 84) up to B	0634
Opel Kadett Petrol (Oct 84 - Oct 91)	3196
Opel Omega & Senator Petrol (Nov 86 - 94)	3157
Opel Rekord Petrol (Feb 78 - Oct 86) up to D	0543
Opel Vectra Petrol (Oct 88 - Oct 95)	3158
PEUGEOT 106 Petrol & Diesel (91 - 04) J to 53	1882
Peugeot 205 Petrol (83 - 97) A to P	0932
Peugeot 206 Petrol & Diesel (98 - 01) S to X	3757
Peugeot 306 Petrol & Diesel (93 - 02) K to 02	3073
Peugeot 307 Petrol & Diesel (01 - 04) Y to 54	4147
Peugeot 309 Petrol (86 - 93) C to K	1266
Peugeot 405 Petrol (88 - 97) E to P	1559
Peugeot 405 Diesel (88 - 97) E to P	3198
Peugeot 406 Petrol & Diesel (96 - Mar 99) N to T	3394
Peugeot 406 Petrol & Diesel (Mar 99 - 02) T to 52	3982
Peugeot 505 Petrol (79 - 89) up to G	0762
Peugeot 1.7/1.8 & 1.9 litre Diesel Engine (82 - 96) up to N	0950
Peugeot 2.0, 2.1, 2.3 & 2.5 litre Diesel Engines (74 - 90) up to H	1607
PORSCHE 911 (65 - 85) up to C	0264
Porsche 924 & 924 Turbo (76 - 85) up to C	0397
PROTON (89 - 97) F to P	3255
RANGE ROVER V8 Petrol (70 - Oct 92) up to K	0606
RELIANT Robin & Kitten (73 - 83) up to A *	0436
RENAULT 4 (61 - 86) up to D *	0072

* Classic reprint

Preserving Our Motoring Heritage

< The Model J Duesenberg Derham Tourster. Only eight of these magnificent cars were ever built – this is the only example to be found outside the United States of America

Almost every car you've ever loved, loathed or desired is gathered under one roof at the Haynes Motor Museum. Over 300 immaculately presented cars and motorbikes represent every aspect of our motoring heritage, from elegant reminders of bygone days, such as the superb Model J Duesenberg to curiosities like the bug-eyed BMW Isetta. There are also many old friends and flames. Perhaps you remember the 1959 Ford Popular that you did your courting in? The magnificent 'Red Collection' is a spectacle of classic sports cars including AC, Alfa Romeo, Austin Healey, Ferrari, Lamborghini, Maserati, MG, Riley, Porsche and Triumph.

A Perfect Day Out

Each and every vehicle at the Haynes Motor Museum has played its part in the history and culture of Motoring. Today, they make a wonderful spectacle and a great day out for all the family. Bring the kids, bring Mum and Dad, but above all bring your camera to capture those golden memories for ever. You will also find an impressive array of motoring memorabilia, a comfortable 70 seat video cinema and one of the most extensive transport book shops in Britain. The Pit Stop Cafe serves everything from a cup of tea to wholesome, home-made meals or, if you prefer, you can enjoy the large picnic area nestled in the beautiful rural surroundings of Somerset.

> John Haynes O.B.E., Founder and Chairman of the museum at the wheel of a Haynes Light 12.

< Graham Hill's Lola Cosworth Formula 1 car next to a 1934 Riley Sports.

The Museum is situated on the A359 Yeovil to Frome road at Sparkford, just off the A303 in Somerset. It is about 40 miles south of Bristol, and 25 minutes drive from the M5 intersection at Taunton.

Open 9.30am - 5.30pm (10.00am - 4.00pm Winter) 7 days a week, *except Christmas Day, Boxing Day and New Years Day*
Special rates available for schools, coach parties and outings Charitable Trust No. 292048